Essentials of
TREASURY MANAGEMENT

CTP *Body of Knowledge*

THE GLOBAL STANDARD OF EXCELLENCE IN CORPORATE TREASURY

Fifth Edition, Second Printing

Jim Washam, PhD, CTP, FP&A

Matthew D. Hill, PhD, CTP, FP&A

ASSOCIATION FOR FINANCIAL PROFESSIONALS

4520 East-West Highway, Suite 800, Bethesda, Maryland 20814, USA
TEL: +1 301.907.2862   **FAX:** +1 301.907.2864

www.AFPonline.org

ASSOCIATION FOR FINANCIAL PROFESSIONALS

ESSENTIALS OF TREASURY MANAGEMENT, *FIFTH EDITION*

Copyright 2017 by the Association for Financial Professionals (AFP).

All inquiries should be addressed to:

Association for Financial Professionals

4520 East-West Highway, Suite 800

Bethesda, MD 20814, USA

TEL: +1 301.907.2862   **FAX:** +1 301.907.2864   **E-MAIL:** AFP@AFPonline.org

www.AFPonline.org

ISBN 978-0-9829481-1-8

Copy Editor: Angie Woodward, The Caviart Group (awoodward@thecaviartgroup.com)

Graphic Design and Layout: Rob Myers (jerseymyers@gmail.com)

EDITORS' ACKNOWLEDGMENTS

The development of *Essentials of Treasury Management, Fifth Edition*, could not be accomplished without the support and funding of the Association for Financial Professionals (AFP), headed by Jim Kaitz (President and CEO). Donna Berzellini, CTP (Managing Director, Certification), Caitlin Hennessey (Certification Specialist), and Stacy Saul (Director of Examinations) contributed an enormous amount of time and effort in completing this revision. Donna provided excellent leadership, resource suggestions, and technical insights throughout the process.

We would like to thank the CTP Body of Knowledge (BOK) Committee for the many hours spent reviewing drafts and suggesting improvements. Their work was crucial in determining the proper amount of coverage dedicated to each topic, the necessary level of detail, and the best organizational structure for the material. Further, the BOK Committee provided valuable insight into new developments in treasury and how those topics should appear in the book. Tim Hesler, CTP, served as the committee chair and provided numerous helpful comments on each chapter.

We thank the Arkansas State University Center for Treasury and Financial Analytics for providing support throughout the project.

Jim would like to thank his family for their patience during this process. Jana, Alex, and Rachel have been the best support group he could ever ask for. Jim is especially grateful for Jana, who has been his wife, partner, and best friend for many years.

Matt is deeply appreciative of the support received from his wife, Katie. Throughout the revision process, she was a continual source of energy and optimism.

Jim Washam, PhD, CTP, FP&A

McAdams Frierson Professor of Bank Management & Associate Dean

Arkansas State University

Matthew D. Hill, PhD, CTP, FP&A

Director of the Center for Treasury and Financial Analytics

Arkansas State University

III

ABOUT THE EDITORS

Jim Washam, PhD, CTP, FP&A

Jim Washam has been a member of the finance faculty at Arkansas State University for 28 years. He holds the McAdams Frierson Professorship in Bank Management and currently serves as the Associate Dean for the College of Business. Jim's primary teaching and research areas are treasury management and financial risk management. His work in the areas of liquidity management, financial risk management, and derivative securities has been published in a number of journals, including the *International Journal of Finance, AFP Exchange,* and *Review of Quantitative Finance and Accounting.*

In addition to his duties at Arkansas State, Jim has 20 years of experience in the design and delivery of treasury management training programs. His clients have included multinational corporations, community banks, municipal governments, global financial institutions, universities, and nongovernmental organizations. These projects have focused primarily on cash, liquidity, and risk management.

Jim is a member of the Association for Financial Professionals (AFP), Kansas City AFP, Mid-South AFP, and the Financial Management Association International. He has been on the faculty of AFP since 1996, and is a frequent speaker at regional, national, and international conferences. He is a Certified Treasury Professional (CTP) and Certified Corporate Financial Planning and Analysis Professional (FP&A). Jim holds a PhD in Finance, with minors in Quantitative Methods and Financial Institutions, from the University of Mississippi.

Matthew D. Hill, PhD, CTP, FP&A

Matt serves as the Director of Arkansas State University's Center for Treasury and Financial Analytics. He is a coauthor of *Short-Term Financial Management, Fifth Edition,* a textbook covering the principles and practice of short-term financial decision making. Matt has received research awards for his academic studies on liquidity analysis and short-term financial management.

Matt has partnered with the Association for Financial Professionals (AFP) in developing and delivering courses that prepare participants for the Certified Treasury Professional (CTP) and Certified Corporate Financial Planning and Analysis Professional (FP&A) examinations. He has also provided corporate training on cash flow forecasting and short-term valuation using statistical approaches and Monte Carlo simulation methods.

Matt is a frequent presenter at regional and national AFP meetings, and he has written for the *AFP Exchange.* He holds a PhD in Finance from Mississippi State University.

MEMBERS OF THE 2017-2019

CERTIFIED TREASURY PROFESSIONAL (CTP) BODY OF KNOWLEDGE (BOK) COMMITTEE

Timothy T. Hesler, CTP
Chair, BOK Committee
Assistant Treasurer, Global Banking,
Cash Management and Treasury
Operations
New York University
New York, NY

Saba Ahmed, CTP
Principal
Softbank Group
San Carlos, CA

Rodolfo Espinosa, CTP
Treasury Director
Bridgestone Americas
Nashville, TN

James Gilligan, CTP, FP&A
Assistant Treasurer
Great Plains Energy Inc.
Kansas City, MO

Ernest Humphrey, CTP
CEO and Founder
360 Thought Leadership
Greenwood, IN

Nichole Krause, CTP
Treasurer
Zendesk
San Francisco, CA

Danielle Massey, CTP
Finance Manager
King & Spalding LLP
Atlanta, GA

Kristy McKay, CTP
Manager, Treasury
MAPFRE Insurance
Webster, MA

Teresa Mimms, CTP, FP&A
Past Chair, BOK Committee
Chair, Certification Committee
Assistant Director of Treasury
Operations
Purdue University
West Lafayette, IN

Greg Moore, CTP
Director, Treasury
AutoNation, Inc.
Fort Lauderdale, FL

Salina Morrow, CTP
Treasury Manager
Children's Medical Center of Dallas
Dallas, TX

Min Hee Ok, CTP
Director of Treasury
TEGNA Inc.
Chantilly, VA

Michelle Palombo, AAP, CTP
Managing Director,
Global Client Access
BNY Mellon
Pittsburgh, PA

Russell Paquette, CTP
Treasurer
Vulcan Inc.
Seattle, WA

Steve Phillips, CTP, FP&A
Director/Assistant Treasurer
Cash America International, Inc.
Ft. Worth, TX

Joseph Riepl, CTP
Director, Treasury
MSG Networks
New York, NY

Hugo Rios, CTP
Policy Advisor, Banking Unit
Ontario Financing Authority
Toronto, ON
CANADA

Ernest Smith, CTP, FP&A
Senior Vice President, Regional Sales
Manager, North Texas Treasury
Management Sales
BBVA Compass
Dallas, TX

Brian Strope, CTP
Assistant Vice President of Treasury &
Risk Management
Rockefeller Group International, Inc.
New York, NY

Len Thompson, CTP
Assistant Controller
Riverside Transport, Inc.
Parkville, MO

Timothy Todd, CTP
Corporate Controller
Archdiocese of Denver
Denver, CO

OTHER SUBJECT-MATTER EXPERT CONTRIBUTORS

Fred Butterfield, CTP
Denver, CO

Thomas Hunt, CTP
Director, Treasury Services
Association for Financial Professionals
Bethesda, MD

TABLE OF CONTENTS

PART II: THE TREASURY MANAGEMENT ENVIRONMENT

PART III: FINANCIAL REPORTING AND ANALYSIS

PART IV: WORKING CAPITAL MANAGEMENT

CHAPTER 10: INTRODUCTION TO WORKING CAPITAL 243

PART V: RISK MANAGEMENT

PART VI: FINANCIAL MANAGEMENT

CHAPTER 19: LONG-TERM INVESTMENTS 513

LIST OF EXHIBITS

CHAPTER 7

CHAPTER 8

CHAPTER 9

CHAPTER 10

CHAPTER 11

CHAPTER 12

CHAPTER 13

CHAPTER 14

CHAPTER 15

CHAPTER 16

CHAPTER 17

CHAPTER 19

CHAPTER 20

PART I
Introduction to Treasury Management

INTRODUCTION
Introduction to the Study of Treasury Management

CHAPTER 1
Role of Treasury Management

INTRODUCTION
Introduction to the Study of Treasury Management

I. INTRODUCTION

II. THE EVOLVING ROLE OF THE TREASURY PROFESSIONAL

III. ORGANIZATION OF *ESSENTIALS OF TREASURY MANAGEMENT*

IV. SUMMARY

I. INTRODUCTION

Treasury management covers the various tools, techniques, and skills needed to manage an enterprise's overall financial holdings. The field, and as a result this book, covers a wide variety of topics.

The terms *treasury management* and *cash management* are often used synonymously but are actually quite different. Treasury management covers all aspects involved in managing an entity's financial assets (the treasury), while cash management is a subset of treasury management that focuses primarily on the day-to-day management of the entity's cash flow and liquidity. Cash management typically includes collections, disbursements, banking, and short-term borrowing and investment. Treasury management is the broader topic that goes beyond simple cash management to deal with longer-term borrowing and investing, capital management, and operational, financial, and reputational risk. The ultimate objective of both treasury management and cash management is to maximize the enterprise's liquidity while minimizing cost and risk within the overall framework of the firm's strategic plan.

II. THE EVOLVING ROLE OF THE TREASURY PROFESSIONAL

This book presents and discusses all of the various aspects of treasury management. It covers the generally accepted principles and practices used to manage a firm's liquidity, capital, and risk management functions. As such, it also represents the body of knowledge that needs to be mastered to earn the Certified Treasury Professional (CTP) credential. The CTP certification, which is sponsored by the Association for Financial Professionals (AFP), serves as a benchmark of competency and is recognized as the leading credential in corporate treasury worldwide.

Because the management of treasury functions takes place in a dynamic, ever-evolving environment, the related body of knowledge changes over time. The evolution of the profession is apparent not only in the rapid expansion of the day-to-day methodologies and tools treasury professionals use, but also in the types of responsibilities boards of directors and chief executive officers place on treasury professionals. This ongoing change creates a need to periodically update any book or text that discusses the profession.

AFP facilitates an update of the CTP body of knowledge every three years based on an in-depth job analysis study conducted with a wide variety of treasury professionals and industry experts. The job analysis process provides a systematic procedure of identifying and validating the performance domains of the treasury professional and the knowledge and skills that are necessary to execute job responsibilities. The analysis includes:

- Field interviews with practitioners to create an inventory of critical responsibilities and knowledge domains
- Development and execution of a comprehensive survey sent to a diverse cross-section of practitioners from various industries, geographic regions, and professional roles
- Analysis of the results

Survey respondents (nearly 1,000 for the most recent survey) validate the job tasks and responsibilities, and rank the importance of each. Treasury practitioners with experience in the various subject areas then work with the content editors, who are also subject-matter experts, to update the actual body of knowledge.

As reflected in the title, this is the fifth edition of *Essentials of Treasury Management*. Each edition of this book is updated to reflect the changes that have occurred in the profession since the previous edition. As in previous editions, one of the goals of this book is to explain how and why particular methods and analytical tools are used, including when it is appropriate to use them and how the results should be interpreted. The objective of all business decisions should be to increase the economic value of the business, either immediately or over the long term. This goal applies no less to treasury responsibilities and decisions than it does to other areas of a firm's operations.

Economic value in the marketplace is tied directly to financial performance. Financial markets weigh a firm's performance relative to market participants' expectations for that firm. A treasury professional has to weigh considerations of cost, efficiency, risk, and expected return on investment when choosing among treasury management tools and investment and borrowing alternatives, as well as when making decisions that affect the timing of cash flows. The treasury professional must make choices with an understanding of their impact on firm value, while simultaneously ensuring an adequate level of safety represented by appropriate liquidity and risk mitigation practices.

It should also be noted that while this book focuses primarily on the typical for-profit corporation, many of the principles and practices in the treasury area also apply in the not-for-profit and government sectors. The organizational goals may be slightly different, but the concept of providing best-practice treasury operations in the most efficient manner is consistent.

III. ORGANIZATION OF *ESSENTIALS OF TREASURY MANAGEMENT*

This book is organized into six major parts. Part I, Introduction to Treasury Management, which includes this introduction, presents an overview of the role of treasury management and discusses how the treasury function fits within an entity's overall management structure.

Part II, The Treasury Management Environment, discusses the external environment in which treasury operates. This includes an overview of the legal and regulatory environment, as well as a discussion of the major players and markets with which treasury has to interact.

Part III, Financial Reporting and Analysis, covers financial statements and tools for analysis of business decisions and financial performance. Understanding the impact of financial decisions on a firm's financial position and performance is essential as treasury professionals take a more strategic role within organizations.

Part IV, Working Capital Management, discusses the tools and techniques used to manage an entity's short-term financial assets, including but not limited to cash and other liquid assets. As it has evolved, the treasury management profession has gone beyond traditional cash and liquidity management to broader working capital activities. This includes the various activities that correspond to what is traditionally referred to as the *cash management function* of treasury management.

Part V, Risk Management, focuses on the various areas of risk that face treasury operations. Risk management has always been a key concern of treasury professionals, and developments over the last few years in both the financial markets and the economy have made risk management even more important than in the past. There are, in fact, risk management implications to virtually all treasury decisions. This section discusses traditional financial risk management and issues related to operational and enterprise risk management that are now typically part of the treasury mandate. Given the importance of internal controls, treasury policies and procedures are also covered here.

Finally, Part VI, Financial Management, goes beyond the day-to-day operations of corporate cash management and looks at the overall issues of financial management in an organization. This material is important for two primary reasons. First, the tasks and responsibilities of treasury management have a significant impact on an entity's overall financial management, and an entity's financial management goals and objectives have a corresponding impact on the overall operations and objectives of treasury. Second, as treasury management continues to evolve, many of the tasks that historically were considered solely the purview of finance are becoming part of the treasury mandate. As such, the traditional tools of financial management have become an important part of the knowledge base of any treasury professional.

Each chapter in this book discusses a particular facet of treasury management. Each starts with a high-level overview of the material to be presented and ends with a summary of the key issues discussed. Diagrams and charts are included where appropriate. In addition, the book includes a glossary of key terminology used in the profession.

IV. SUMMARY

The topic of treasury management covers the various tools, techniques, and skills needed to manage an enterprise's overall financial holdings. This book presents the current body of knowledge required by an effective treasury professional in fulfilling that function, based on a survey of working treasury professionals. The body of knowledge is constantly growing and evolving as the role of treasury management grows and evolves to meet the needs of a changing business environment.

CHAPTER 1
Role of Treasury Management

I. INTRODUCTION

II. THE ROLE AND ORGANIZATION OF TREASURY MANAGEMENT
   A. Overall Goal and Objectives
   B. Treasury Operations/Cash Management
   C. Bank Relationship Management
   D. Reporting and Information Sharing

III. FINANCE AND TREASURY ORGANIZATION
   A. Financial Professionals in an Organization
   B. Treasury Organizational Structure

IV. CORPORATE GOVERNANCE
   A. The Challenges of Corporate Governance
   B. Role of Board of Directors Related to Treasury
   C. Role of Independent Directors

V. SUMMARY

I. INTRODUCTION

Treasury management refers to the area of finance that oversees the effective and efficient use of a company's financial assets. Specifically, treasury management involves daily liquidity management tasks that ensure the availability of adequate cash resources needed to sustain ongoing operations. By ensuring the availability of funds, treasury management enables the implementation of initiatives designed to achieve the firm's overall financial objectives.

This chapter discusses the basic role and objectives of treasury management, the potential organizational structures for treasury, and the relationship between treasury management and corporate financial management. The chapter closes with a discussion of corporate governance and its impact on treasury.

II. THE ROLE AND ORGANIZATION OF TREASURY MANAGEMENT

A. Overall Goal and Objectives

The primary goal of treasury management is to effectively and efficiently manage an organization's cash and related financial assets to provide the financial flexibility needed to achieve the organization's objectives in a manner consistent with the overall strategic plan. This goal is critical because all firms, no matter how successful, have a finite and variable amount of liquid assets on hand during a given period of time.

The major objectives of treasury management include:

- **Maintain Liquidity:**[1] Ensure the ability to meet current and future financial obligations in a timely and cost-effective manner.

- **Optimize Cash Resources:** Establish policies and procedures, and implement strategies to manage low-yielding cash balances while providing adequate liquidity. Invest excess cash balances to generate interest income, or pay down debt to reduce interest expense.

- **Maintain Access to Short-Term Financing:** Establish and maintain access to short-term credit facilities while minimizing borrowing costs. Short-term credit facilities are commonly used to finance investments in operating working capital (e.g., accounts receivable or inventory) and to provide temporary financing for capital investments. With the latter, the short-term borrowing is generally replaced with longer-term financing.

- **Manage Investments:** Invest excess funds in a prudent manner for both short- and long-term needs. Preservation of principal is the primary investment objective, followed by ensuring liquidity and maximizing overall return. Investment activities should be conducted in accordance with a board-approved investment policy.

- **Maintain Access to Medium- and Long-Term Financing:** Maintain access to medium- and long-term debt and equity financing to support planned asset expansion and the existing asset base. Provide the financial flexibility necessary to make strategic investments as opportunities arise.

- **Manage Risk:** Identify, measure, analyze, and mitigate exposure to organizational risks such as financial risks (e.g., interest rate, foreign exchange, and commodity risks), regulatory risks (e.g., compliance risks), and operational risks (e.g., supplier and fraud risks).

---

1. *Liquidity* can refer to asset liquidity or firm liquidity. *Asset liquidity* refers to the ability to quickly convert an asset into cash without a significant loss of value. Thus, assets that can easily be bought or sold are referred to as *liquid assets*. By definition, cash is the most liquid asset. *Firm liquidity* refers to a firm's ability to meet its financial obligations on a timely basis as well as its ability to take advantage of investments as they arise.

- **Manage Information and Technology:** Select, implement, and manage technology solutions to gather and analyze financial information. Proper information management strategies may be used to improve cash visibility, achieve straight-through processing, and increase operational efficiencies.

- **Collaborate with Other Departments and Share Financial Information:** Coordinate functions and communicate effectively with other departments to help ensure that cash is efficiently utilized.

- **Manage External Parties:** Manage relationships with external stakeholders, including banks/financial institutions, customers, and suppliers, among others, to effectively use financial assets while minimizing risk and expense.

The first four objectives represent core cash management activities performed by treasury professionals. Cash management activities ensure that the firm can meet its short-term obligations. Poor cash management can cause even profitable companies to experience financial distress.

Managing the firm's operating cash flows is a key aspect of cash management. The cash conversion cycle (illustrated in Exhibit 1.1) outlines the sequence of operating cash flows typically experienced by a firm. The exhibit indicates that the firm in question will require internal financing (e.g., cash holdings) or external financing (e.g., short-term credit facilities) to fund the working capital gap created by the operating cycle.

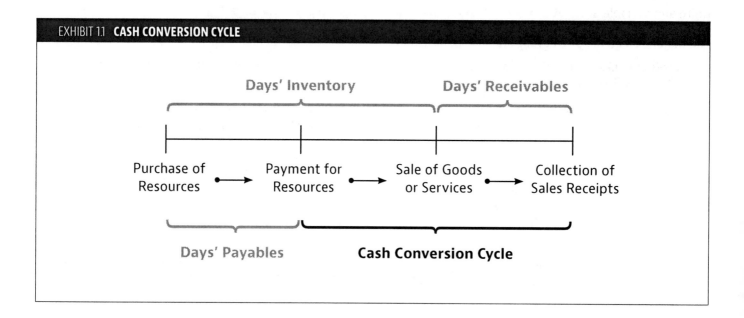

EXHIBIT 1.1 CASH CONVERSION CYCLE

B. Treasury Operations/Cash Management

Daily treasury operations (e.g., cash management) activities may include:

- Calculating the cash position
- Monitoring cash balances on deposit at financial institutions
- Collecting, concentrating, and disbursing cash

- Investing and borrowing funds on a short-term basis when needed
- Developing cash flow forecasts
- Researching and reconciling exception items, such as unexpected charges on bank accounts, missing deposits, and outstanding checks
- Coordinating efforts with other finance areas, such as accounts receivable, accounts payable, tax, and accounting
- Managing bank and investment administration and relationships, including the procurement of related services

C. Bank Relationship Management

The treasury department is often responsible for managing a number of external vendor relationships, the most important of which involves bank relationships. Most companies have multiple banking relationships to limit counterparty risk and to enhance the competitive process. The board of directors typically delegates to treasury the ability to open, maintain, and close bank accounts.

D. Reporting and Information Sharing

Treasury professionals must gather and share information with other internal departments/functions. Examples include procurement, human resources/payroll, legal, accounting and reporting, and information technology, among others (as shown in Exhibit 1.2).

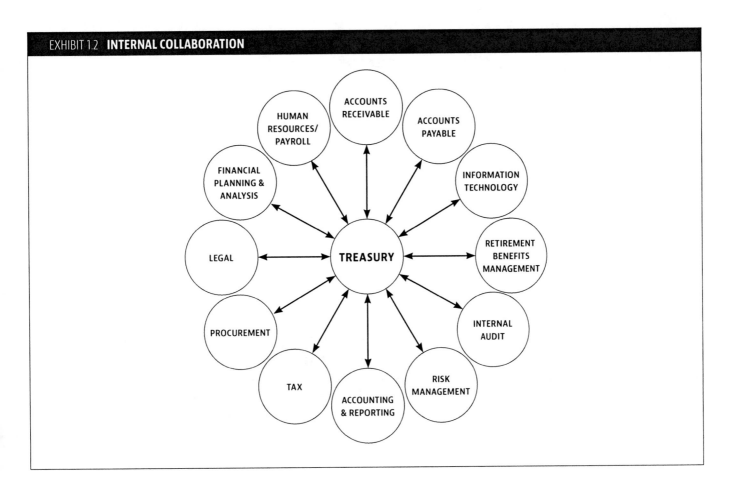

EXHIBIT 1.2 **INTERNAL COLLABORATION**

The activities of these departments directly impact treasury management. Since most of these departments report to managers outside of treasury (e.g., the controller or chief financial officer), treasury employees interact often with these departments to ensure that the objectives of treasury management are met.

While treasury must collect information from other departments, it is equally important for treasury to share information. This is often done using the organization's intranet or enterprise resource planning systems.

Successful treasury management also depends on collaboration with a variety of external entities, such as financial institutions, financial markets, rating agencies, and third-party providers (as illustrated in Exhibit 1.3). These collaborations provide information and/or services that enable treasury to perform its daily functions.

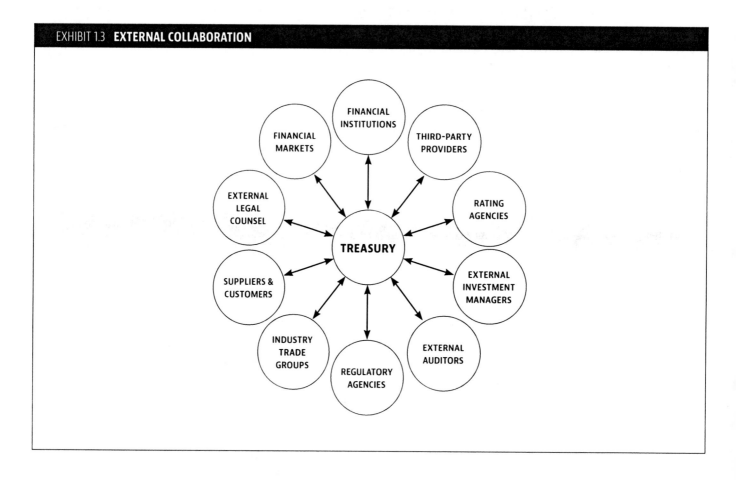

EXHIBIT 1.3 EXTERNAL COLLABORATION

III. FINANCE AND TREASURY ORGANIZATION

Treasury is a component of the financial management function. Along with treasury, the financial management function is comprised of accounting, tax, investor relations, and financial planning and analysis. Responsibilities of these areas include financial reporting, tax management, budgeting, and analysis of capital expenditures. The organization of the treasury and finance functions should be structured to facilitate the achievement of the firm's overall objectives. The organizational structures of these functions vary among industries and companies.

A. Financial Professionals in an Organization

In most large organizations, the senior finance officer is the chief financial officer (CFO). Other possible titles for this role include *director of finance* or *vice president of finance*. The treasurer and the controller normally report directly to the CFO. Some companies have a flatter organizational structure in which functions such as treasury, accounting, information systems, strategic planning, investor relations, and financial planning and analysis report directly to the CFO.

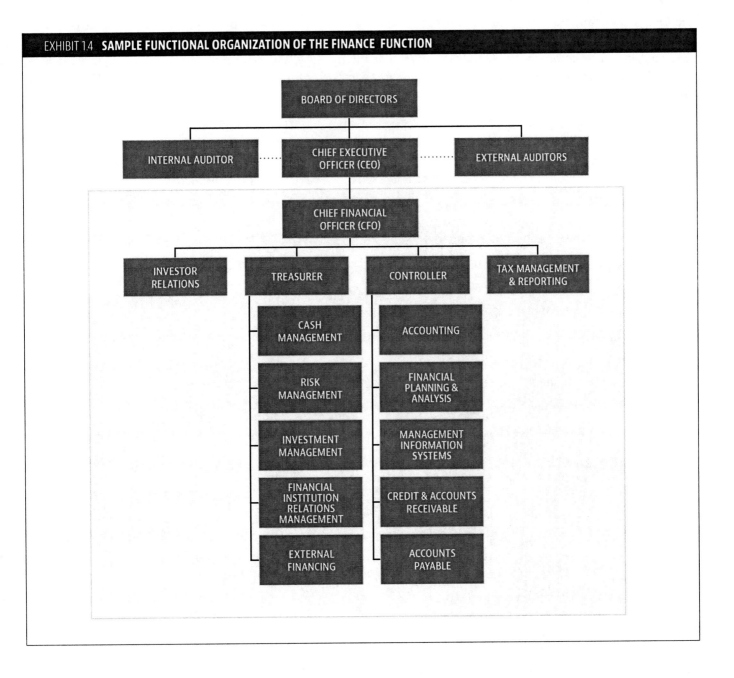

EXHIBIT 1.4 **SAMPLE FUNCTIONAL ORGANIZATION OF THE FINANCE FUNCTION**

Exhibit 1.4 illustrates a typical reporting structure for a large organization. This exhibit is intended to be illustrative and is not necessarily representative of any specific company. Note that the exhibit focuses on function and not title. Titles can be confusing in that one organization may refer to its senior financial officer as the CFO while another organization may use another title. In smaller companies, the structure may be considerably flatter. It is not uncommon for some of these functions to be combined, with each position carrying a greater number of responsibilities.

1. CHIEF FINANCIAL OFFICER (CFO)

The CFO is generally a member of the executive management team that reports to the chief executive officer (CEO). The CFO is responsible for the financial management of the firm, which includes the accounting and treasury functions. In a large company, the CFO usually oversees the treasury, risk, tax, investor relations, financial planning and analysis, and accounting functions. The CFO plays an important role in strategic planning and is pivotal to the capital budgeting and financial planning process.

Additionally, the CFO is responsible for accurate financial reporting. The United States (US) Sarbanes-Oxley Act of 2002 (SOX) makes the CFO of publicly traded companies listed on US stock exchanges personally responsible for the accuracy and completeness of financial statements, and for the development and implementation of adequate internal financial controls. Many other countries and exchanges have similar requirements.

2. TREASURER

The treasurer is primarily responsible for:

- Developing strategy and implementing treasury policies and procedures
- Overseeing daily liquidity and cash management
- Short- and long-term investing
- Arranging both short- and long-term external financing
- Managing financial risks
- Managing relationships with banks/financial institutions and other service providers
- Managing domestic and international payments
- Overseeing financial reporting and compliance

In some companies, the treasurer may also be responsible for insurance, pension or retirement fund assets, or enterprise risk management. The treasurer may delegate these responsibilities.

3. ASSISTANT TREASURER OR MANAGER OF TREASURY OPERATIONS

Larger organizations may have a separate position designated as *assistant treasurer* or *manager of treasury operations*. This position is generally responsible for treasury's daily operations, enabling the treasurer to focus on strategic issues. Some organizations may have more than one assistant treasurer—in some cases, with separate roles for international and domestic treasury operations.

4. CASH MANAGER

The cash manager directs daily cash management operations. Examples of these operations include cash administration, management of bank accounts, and bank relations. Depending upon the size of the company, the cash manager may report to the treasurer or assistant treasurer.

5. CONTROLLER

The controller's primary function is financial reporting, but the function is often also responsible for accounts payable, accounting, budgeting, and coordinating with external auditors. In some companies, accounts receivable, financial planning and analysis, and financial information systems may also report to the controller. In other companies, these functions report directly to the CFO.

6. RISK MANAGER

Overall financial risk management is treasury's responsibility, but other specific risk areas may be assigned to separate risk managers that report to the treasurer or CFO. The risk managers may evaluate and negotiate insurance policies and coverage levels, as well as oversee disaster recovery and business continuity planning. Some organizations have enterprise risk management programs, usually headed by a chief risk officer.

7. INTERNAL AUDITOR

The internal auditor manages the internal audit function to ensure that controls and operating procedures are established to protect the company from losses caused by inefficiency, inaccuracy, or fraud. The internal auditor reports directly to the board of directors to assure the auditor's independence and objectivity. In addition to an internal audit function, companies commonly have board audit committees that follow and monitor internal auditing functions.

8. CREDIT MANAGER

The credit manager preserves and collects accounts receivable, sets corporate credit policies, approves the extension of credit terms and exposure limits to customers, and establishes information systems to monitor accounts receivable. The credit manager may report to the controller, treasurer, or sales manager.

9. ACCOUNTS RECEIVABLE MANAGER

The accounts receivable manager monitors and collects accounts receivable created through credit sales. This role is responsible for the accurate posting of all payments made on accounts and the reconcilement of the payments to the invoices, commonly referred to as the *application of payments*. Treasury must often interact with the accounts receivable manager in order to pass along remittance data that accompany payments received.

10. ACCOUNTS PAYABLE MANAGER

The accounts payable manager ensures that payments are made to vendors and suppliers in a manner that is consistent with credit terms. This process involves maintaining lists of authorized vendors and suppliers, reviewing incoming invoices, matching invoices to approved purchase orders, reviewing invoices for proper approval, and scheduling payments. The accounts payable manager usually reports to the controller.

11. INVESTOR RELATIONS MANAGER/OFFICER

The investor relations manager ensures that both shareholders and bondholders receive up-to-date information on the company, especially on financial reporting that is required by regulatory authorities. In addition, the investor relations manager provides access to annual reports, manages regular investor briefings, and answers questions that current or potential investors may have regarding the company. This position typically reports to the CFO.

B. Treasury Organizational Structure

The treasury department can be organized in a variety of ways. Examples covered below include:

· Cost center versus profit center

· Centralized versus decentralized

· Shared services centers

1. COST CENTER VERSUS PROFIT CENTER

Treasury operations can be organized as a cost or profit center. Organizing treasury as a cost center is a common approach because treasury is usually regarded as a support function and is not expected to directly earn a profit for the firm. A downside to this organizational structure is that management may focus on the cost of treasury operations and not the value provided by the function, leading to difficulties in obtaining an adequate budget and staff.

Alternatively, the treasury function may be organized as a profit center. This would be most appropriate for companies heavily involved in global finance, trade, or risk management. The rationale for establishing treasury as a profit center is that it should generate income from either its trading operations or from hedging/speculative activities. The potential downside to this approach is the risk associated with the pressure to produce profits from these activities.

2. CENTRALIZED VERSUS DECENTRALIZED

A company that has geographically dispersed sales offices (e.g., a multinational company) and has limited personnel may centralize its treasury functions at the company's headquarters. A centralized treasury offers the advantages of stronger control, economies of scale, and lower operating costs. The advantages can be even greater for multinationals as there may be significant tax advantages based on the location of treasury. A disadvantage of a centralized treasury is that field office personnel have reduced autonomy.

A decentralized treasury structure may be used by companies with autonomous subsidiaries and/or multiple operational entities (e.g., manufacturing, distribution, marketing, sales, and finance). An advantage of a decentralized structure is that local subsidiary personnel possess familiarity with local business and banking practices, as well as intimate knowledge of languages, customs, and cultures. In a decentralized structure, field personnel are responsible for some daily treasury functions, but there is often a duplication of effort—and resources—across units. Decentralized or foreign offices may also have a heavier burden in regards to compliance efforts, due to span-of-control issues and the increased need for coordination.

For the purposes of both information and control, local treasury operations generally submit periodic financial management reports to the home office. Typically, these reports summarize bank balances and transaction activities, as well as providing information on key treasury functions, such as cash forecasting, borrowing, investment, and foreign exchange (FX) activities. Best practice is for the home office to review local offices periodically to ensure conformance with policies, procedures, and controls. The internal audit function in large corporations generally serves this purpose.

Some large multinational corporations operate regional treasury centers that combine aspects of centralized and decentralized systems (i.e., while each region is centralized, overall treasury operations are decentralized to the regional centers). These regional centers provide treasury services to specific subsidiaries within a designated geographic area (e.g., North America, Europe, Asia-Pacific, Latin America, the Middle East, or Africa).

The advent of enterprise-wide accounting and information systems combined with automated treasury management systems has resulted in the introduction of hybrid centralized treasury systems (i.e., a combination of both the centralized and decentralized organizational structures). For example, local personnel might be responsible for entering local information, including payment and funds transfer requests, into a common treasury management or accounting system, while a centralized treasury staff manages and is responsible for overall treasury operations.

3. SHARED SERVICES CENTER (SSC)

An SSC is is a department or operation within a multiunit organization that supplies multiple business units with specialized services. Examples include information technology (IT), human resources (HR), or accounts payable (A/P). In some companies the daily treasury operations may be operated as an SSC.

Shared services involve more than just centralized processing or operations. These types of services are often duplicated within multiple operating units, and when they can be consolidated in an SSC, the funding and management can be shared across the enterprise. The resulting SSC becomes an internal service provider and is, in effect, another vendor or supplier to the various operating units that use its services.

An SSC is typically used to:

- Reduce the costs of multiple or duplicate operations
- Standardize processes
- Improve the quality and timeliness of services
- Increase strategic flexibility
- Strengthen internal controls

SSC costs are usually charged back to operating units based on some form of transfer pricing, and overall service is managed based on specific service level agreements that specify how and when the service involved will be provided. In many cases the SSC is outsourced to an external third party.

IV. CORPORATE GOVERNANCE

Corporate governance, the principles and processes that govern firms, impacts treasury management as well as the overall finance function. In general, corporate governance guides managerial decision making to achieve the desired strategic objectives. Subsequently, shareholder wealth is maximized and beneficial outcomes are provided for all stakeholders (e.g., the board of directors, management, customers, employees, suppliers, and society in general). Management assumes the role of trustee or fiduciary for all of the other stakeholders.

A. The Challenges of Corporate Governance

One of the key challenges in corporate governance relates to the separation of ownership and control; shareholders own the company, but executive officers control the firm's operations. This separation of ownership and control is a potential challenge because management may be able to make decisions with little oversight by the shareholders. Governance is also a challenge for not-for-profit entities. These organizations seek to serve the public good, with their boards generally serving as oversight for the public. The same kinds of conflicts that exist in the for-profit sector can exist here between the public and internal management.

It may be more appropriate to think of shareholders as investors rather than owners. This is a somewhat subtle, but important, difference. An investor orientation focuses on asset returns and the composition of investment portfolios. This orientation tends to make most investors passive shareholders, which may induce managers to take actions that benefit themselves at shareholders' expense (e.g., managing short-term profits to maximize employee bonuses in a manner that reduces the long-term value of the organization, or ignoring a very profitable merger offer that would eliminate current management jobs). This issue is referred to as the *agency problem*, where managers are the legal agents acting on behalf of ownership.

To protect shareholders, corporate governance procedures establish a set of checks and balances to place limits on executive prerogatives and to monitor management performance. Examples include the board of directors (especially independent directors), shareholder meetings, independent external auditors, and regulatory agencies. Failures in corporate governance can generally be traced back to a failure on the part of one or more of these components. Therefore, an organization should have a chief audit executive accountable for internal auditing who reports directly to the board of directors' audit committee. The board should provide sufficient funding and other resources for the audit process, including periodic private sessions to discuss risks and controls with the chief auditor.

The board of directors also has the responsibility to act in the best interests of shareholders. In the United States, this is generally interpreted as maximizing shareholder wealth or maximizing the company's stock price over the long term. In other countries, the objectives and responsibilities of the board may be more broad-based.

In many countries, the other stakeholders in the company (e.g., employees/unions, bondholders, bankers, local community, and governments) may also be considered in the company's decision process regarding such issues as salaries and benefits, capital expansion, or product offerings. In planned or socialist economies, the government may be the primary decision maker for companies in that country.

B. Role of Board of Directors Related to Treasury

In larger organizations the board of directors serves as the general authority for all operations, including treasury. It is ultimately the board's responsibility to approve business policies, major initiatives, and contracts. In order to facilitate daily operations, the board will delegate authority for specific functions to treasury, generally via a board resolution. In such a resolution, the board typically grants the treasury function the authority to:

- Open, close, and modify bank accounts
- Establish credit facilities
- Oversee investments
- Issue debt and equity securities
- Devise, implement, and execute risk management strategies

This delegation is usually not open ended, but subject to specific limitations and regular review by the board, which should be clearly spelled out in board-approved policy statements. Overall responsibility and related oversight is still the responsibility of the board, but even its authority may be limited by the company's original articles of incorporation and corporate charter.

C. Role of Independent Directors

Independent directors represent a key component of good corporate governance. In many countries, independent directors (also referred to as *external* or *nonexecutive directors*) are a regulatory requirement. In the United States, any company listed and traded on the New York Stock Exchange (NYSE) is required to comply with the NYSE basic standards regarding independent directors. The United Kingdom (UK) Corporate Governance Code has similar requirements for British corporations. While the specific rules and regulations regarding independent directors may vary by country and stock exchange, many global companies look to NYSE regulations for guidance if they have any thought of ever potentially trading on the NYSE.

As part of the requirements for listing, many exchanges have established basic standards for the role of independent directors. Failure to adhere to these standards could cause significant public embarrassment for the company, as well as a significant loss of investor capital. CEOs must certify to the listing exchange(s) that their companies comply with these standards. Compliant companies are better positioned to attract and retain shareholders because adherence to the standards lowers investors' assessment of ownership risk.

For a director to be considered independent under the NYSE standards, the board must determine that the director has no material relationship with the listed company, either directly or as a partner, shareholder, or officer of the organization. Independent directors must meet in regular executive sessions without management present. A director cannot be considered independent unless he or she has not been an employee or an independent auditor of the company for a continuous five-year period, referred to as a *cooling-off period.*

For NYSE listed companies, independent directors must constitute the majority of the board. Companies must have a nominating committee and a compensation committee (or committees of the company's own determination with the same responsibilities), as well as an audit committee—each comprised solely of independent directors possessing meaningful finance and/or accounting experience.

V. SUMMARY

The primary goal of treasury management is to effectively and efficiently manage cash and related financial assets to provide the financial flexibility needed to achieve the organization's objectives in a manner consistent with the overall strategic plan. Treasury management includes cash management—the subset of treasury management that deals with day-to-day liquidity—as well as broader treasury roles, such as long-term borrowing and investment, and financial risk management.

This chapter discussed the role of treasury management within an organization. It also presented an overview of the typical roles and functions of both treasury management and finance, and reviewed the relationship between the two.

The chapter closed by discussing corporate governance. Exhibit 1.5 depicts the relationship between cash management, treasury management, financial management, and corporate governance. The board of directors has overall authority for setting the direction of a company, approving business policy and initiatives, and authorizing contractual relationships. The portion of that authority related to control of financial assets and bank accounts is typically delegated to finance and treasury within approved limits and guidelines.

EXHIBIT 1.5 **RELATIONSHIP OF CASH MANAGEMENT, TREASURY MANAGEMENT, FINANCIAL MANAGEMENT, AND CORPORATE GOVERNANCE**

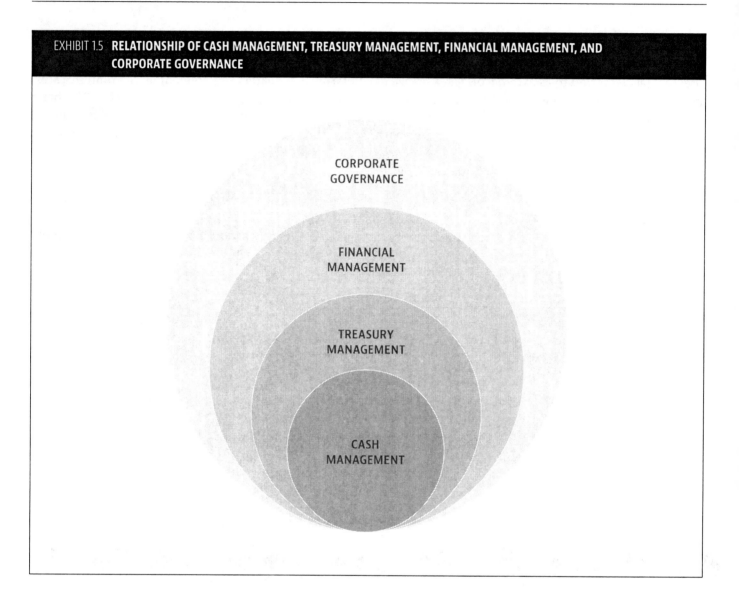

PART II
The Treasury Management Environment

CHAPTER 2
Legal and Regulatory Environment

I. INTRODUCTION

II. GENERAL REGULATORY ENVIRONMENT
A. Specific Areas of Financial Regulation
B. Issues Affecting Financial Regulation

III. PRIMARY REGULATORS AND STANDARD SETTERS IN INTERNATIONAL FINANCIAL MARKETS
A. Central Banks
B. Financial Stability Board (FSB)
C. Bank for International Settlements (BIS)
D. European Payments Council (EPC) and Single Euro Payments Area (SEPA)
E. European Securities and Markets Authority (ESMA)
F. International Association of Deposit Insurers (IADI)
G. International Organization of Securities Commissions (IOSCO)
H. Financial Action Task Force (FATF)
I. International Association of Insurance Supervisors (IAIS)
J. International Swaps and Derivatives Association (ISDA)

IV. US REGULATORY AND LEGAL ENVIRONMENT
A. Regulatory Agencies
B. US Legal Environment

V. TAX CONSIDERATIONS
A. Unitary Taxes and Foreign Tax Credits
B. Capital Tax
C. Asset Tax and Turnover Tax
D. Withholding Tax
E. Sales and Use Taxes
F. Other Taxes

VI. BANKRUPTCY LAWS

    A. Critical Issues in a Business Bankruptcy Decision

    B. Bondholders' Rights

    C. Shareholders' Rights

    D. Types of Bankruptcy in the United States

    E. Formal versus Informal Bankruptcy Procedures

VII. SUMMARY

APPENDIX 2.1: SEPA MEMBER STATES

I. INTRODUCTION

This chapter provides an overview of the legal and regulatory issues that impact financial institutions (FIs) and corporations on a daily basis. These topics are pertinent to treasury management since treasury professionals rely on the products and services provided by FIs. Historically, the financial services industry and its relationships with corporate customers have been very highly regulated. Because this regulation has a significant impact on how FIs operate, it is important that treasury professionals understand the regulatory environment faced by financial service providers.

This chapter begins with a general overview of financial services regulation. The next section provides a high-level overview of the various types of regulators and discusses their connections to the macroeconomy. The chapter also provides an in-depth review of the key areas of the US financial regulatory environment. This coverage of US regulation is motivated by the global impact of the US market and the fact that US financial services regulations are often used as models for regulations adopted in other countries. The final sections of the chapter provide overviews of the Uniform Commercial Code, corporate tax considerations, and bankruptcy laws and regulations.

II. GENERAL REGULATORY ENVIRONMENT

FIs serve a critical role in the economy. Their primary role is in the intermediation of funds, in which FIs provide a mechanism for savers of capital to transfer that capital to those parties with a need for capital. In one instance, a consumer's savings may be used to help another consumer purchase a house or car. In another instance, a worker's pension savings may be used to provide the equity capital for a company to expand its production facilities. Because this vital role of capital transfer is fundamental to the efficient functioning of the economy, FIs generally are regulated closely by monetary and other government authorities.

The most common type of FI is the commercial bank. In the most general case, a bank accepts deposits from both consumers and businesses, and then lends some portion of those deposits to other entities. The acceptance of deposits and provision of loans are the primary criteria used to define a *bank*, sometimes referred to as a *depository institution*. In some cases, a bank may be limited to servicing certain sectors or customer bases, but the deposit and loan criteria are still present. For the purpose of this chapter, the term *bank* will refer to any FI that provides both deposit and loan functions.

One of the primary sources of earnings for banks is the *net interest margin*, which is defined as the difference between the interest rate at which the bank lends to borrowers and the interest rate that the bank pays to depositors for funds held on deposit. This intermediary function results in default/credit risk (i.e., if the borrower does not repay the loan) and liquidity risk (i.e., if depositors withdraw their deposits with little notice). From a bank's point of view, these risks could result in the possible failure of the bank. From the perspective of the economy in general, the risks from bank failures include depositors losing their money and potentially a collapse of the entire banking system.

The primary job of bank regulators is to monitor the credit and liquidity risks relating to potential bank failures and to implement safeguards that can reduce the overall risk of systemic failure (i.e., the collapse of the entire banking system). There are several approaches regulators can take to address these risks, and most countries impose regulatory oversight of some type on the traditional banking functions. Such oversight results in restrictions on the banks' actions in order to manage the overall riskiness of the financial system and reduce the impact of potential bank failures.

A. Specific Areas of Financial Regulation[1]

There are five general areas in which financial regulation is usually concentrated. These include:

1. Monitoring and managing the overall safety and soundness of the banking system
2. Setting and implementing monetary policy
3. Determining guidelines for the chartering of banks and other depository institutions
4. Allocating credit toward certain economic segments and protecting consumers
5. Protecting investors purchasing securities through FIs

These areas are outlined in more detail below. It is important to understand that regulations relating to these areas may vary significantly across countries. While there are ongoing efforts to coordinate the international regulatory environments, as a sovereign nation, each country has the right to enact any regulations it deems necessary for the banks operating in that country. Consequently, a multinational bank may be forced to abide by many sets of regulations.

Much of the following discussion relates primarily to the regulation of banks, which are the primary type of FIs. Other FIs will be discussed where applicable.

1. MONITORING AND MANAGING THE OVERALL SAFETY AND SOUNDNESS OF THE BANKING SYSTEM

The purpose of regulations that monitor and manage the safety and soundness of the banking system is to protect both depositors and borrowers against the risk of failure by banks in the system. The key approaches used to provide this protection include requiring that FIs maintain minimum capital levels, ensuring that FIs have proper investment policies, providing deposit insurance, and performing bank monitoring. Each aspect is discussed in detail below.

One of the primary regulatory approaches is the setting of minimum capital levels required of banks operating within the country. Capital requirements determine how much capital (usually defined as equity funds) the owners of a bank must contribute to the business. This is typically in the form of a ratio of the bank's capital to at-risk assets, where the latter includes loans and other investments. The higher the ratio of capital to assets, the lower the bank's risk. Many regulators use the concept of tiered capital, in which common equity is the first tier (i.e., most stable) while preferred stock and long-term debt form a second tier (i.e., less stable). The concept of tiered capital allows regulators to differentiate the risks of banks with identical ratios of capital to assets.

A second regulatory approach related to the safety and soundness of the banking system is to ensure proper investment policies and diversification on the part of each bank. An example of this would be regulations to ensure that banks make loans that are properly priced for default risk. In most countries, the regulatory authorities will monitor the quality of the loan and investment portfolios of the banks closely, and will generally place restrictions on how much can be loaned or invested in a particular company or industry sector. These are referred to as *impairment of capital rules*. The basic idea is to limit the chances that the failure of one large company, and the resulting defaults on its loans, could lead to a bank's failure.

The failure of a number of large FIs during the global financial crisis of 2007–2009 triggered a discussion on the part of global regulatory authorities of increasing the restrictions on certain types of bank investment activities—specifically, proprietary trading (i.e., the trading of securities on the bank's own account), hedge funds, and private equity businesses—that were thought to have contributed to the recession. One of the earliest proponents of these

---

1. This section is derived partly from: Anthony Saunders and Marcia Cornett, *Financial Institutions Management: A Risk Management Approach*, 6th ed. (New York: McGraw-Hill/Irwin, 2008).

types of restrictions was Paul Volcker, who served as chairman of the US central bank from 1979 to 1987. The US implementation of these restrictions, called the *Volcker rule*, is discussed in the context of US banking regulations later in this chapter.

The third layer of protection with respect to safety and soundness of the banking system arises from deposit insurance. Deposit insurance, which is referred to as a *deposit guarantee* in some countries, is intended to protect the assets of smaller deposit customers (typically consumers, although corporate accounts are also typically covered up to a certain amount) who would be most harmed by a bank failure. To this end, most of these regulations do place some limit on the amount of funds that will be guaranteed. A trade-off associated with the protection afforded by deposit insurance is the concept of *moral hazard*. If the depositors know that their money is insured regardless of which bank they use, then the depositor has a reduced incentive to investigate the bank's creditworthiness. From the banker's perspective, the moral hazard issue is that the bank may undertake a higher level of risk (e.g., make riskier loans or investments), knowing that if the bank fails, the government will protect depositors.

Ultimately, the key benefit of deposit insurance or a guarantee is that it increases the overall confidence in the banking system, especially on the part of smaller depositors. Depositor confidence in any bank is critical to that bank's survival. A lack of consumer confidence can lead to "bank runs," in which a large number of depositors demand the return of their deposits all at once. Since banks are in the business of lending deposits out to other customers, they rarely have enough currency on hand to simultaneously pay off a large group of depositors and can be forced out of business. During the Great Depression in the United States, many banks were forced to close due to bank runs, rather than actual insolvency. During times of financial crisis, some regulators have increased the levels of deposit insurance in order to bolster consumer confidence and prevent a panicked withdrawal of funds by depositors.

A fourth layer of protections stems from regulators imposing bank monitoring and surveillance. This is usually in the form of on-site examinations, as well as requirements that the bank produce accounting statements and other operational and financial reports on a regular basis to be evaluated off-site. The degree of monitoring can vary significantly across countries.

2. SETTING AND IMPLEMENTING MONETARY POLICY

FIs play a key role in the implementation of the monetary policy set by a country's central bank. Monetary policy includes the actions taken by the central bank to control the money supply and interest rates in that country. The issue that arises for the monetary authorities is that the money supply of a country is usually much greater than just the amount of currency (i.e., notes and coin) in circulation. This is a result of the ability of the commercial banking system to effectively multiply the deposits that it holds. This multiplication is done by lending deposits out to companies and individuals, who in turn redeposit those funds back into the system so that they can be lent out a second time, and so on. This multiplication of deposits allows banks to create money and increase the overall money supply. The more loans that are made, the larger the money supply. A certain amount of deposit growth is critical to economic growth, but too much growth can lead to inflation and other economic problems. Determining the optimal size of the money supply is a key element of monetary policy.

In order to manage this multiplication of deposits, most central banks impose reserve restrictions on the commercial banks operating within their systems. For each unit of deposits, some percentage must be maintained as reserves (i.e., not loaned out or invested). These reserves may either be held at the bank, or in many countries, at the central bank. This requirement increases the safety of the overall monetary system and allows the central bank to better control the money supply by changing the reserve requirement, either raising the percentage to contract the supply of money in circulation, or lowering it to encourage lending.

3. DETERMINING GUIDELINES FOR THE CHARTERING OF BANKS AND OTHER DEPOSITORY INSTITUTIONS

The *chartering process* generally refers to the establishment or opening of banks and other depository institutions (e.g., credit unions or savings banks) and the guidelines as to the types of financial services they are allowed to offer. Some countries have very clear distinctions between different types of depository institutions and their services, while other countries allow single institutions to offer a broader range of services. Chartering regulations also typically specify the amount of capital needed to open a bank and may also limit the ownership of banks in a country by foreign entities.

4. ALLOCATING CREDIT TOWARD CERTAIN ECONOMIC SEGMENTS AND PROTECTING CONSUMERS

Many countries have, as part of their financial regulations, a mandate to support certain sectors of the economy, such as housing or farming. Regulations relating to allocation of credit may require that a certain percentage of loans be made to specific sectors, or there may be limits on interest rates, prices, or fees in that sector. Ultimately, these types of regulations may have significant impacts on the lending policies of banks operating within the country.

Consumer protection regulations are designed to protect consumers, who are frequently assumed to lack bargaining power, and are therefore considered "vulnerable" when entering into financial transactions. In many cases, consumer protection regulations are linked to those related to credit allocation. The goal is to provide acceptable access for consumers to financial services, credit, and financial information. These regulations may also be used to prevent financial discrimination against certain sectors of the population.

5. PROTECTING INVESTORS PURCHASING SECURITIES THROUGH FIs

Regulations relating to investor protection are generally aimed at those FIs that provide investment banking or brokerage services. Depending on the country, banks may have restrictions on offering some of these services to depositors, and some FIs only provide investment services. The investor protection regulations are designed to protect investors who purchase securities through various types of FIs. In addition to banks, the FIs in this case include investment banks, brokerages, mutual funds, or pension funds. The most common types of investor protection regulations shield investors against abuses such as insider trading, lack of disclosure, outright malfeasance, and breach of fiduciary responsibilities.[2]

B. Issues Affecting Financial Regulation

As discussed in the previous section, each country has its own set of laws and regulations relating to the chartering and operation of banks within its borders. While there is some level of international cooperation between the various regulatory authorities, there is no true central regulatory authority, which can lead to inconsistencies in various jurisdictions and duplication of regulatory efforts. Ongoing developments and crises in the global financial community have made the problem even more complex.

In the past, a large amount of global business flowed through banks or insurance companies, and there was a limited range of investment vehicles trading in regulated markets. The development of private equity funds, hedge funds, sovereign funds, and other, often unregulated, investment opportunities, has produced a much greater challenge in the regulation of financial markets. In addition, instruments such as derivatives make it much easier for an FI to manage risk on a far greater scale and in more complex ways.

---

2. In some countries, additional protection may be provided against the failure or bankruptcy of brokerages. The protection is generally limited to cash accounts and lost securities, and does not normally include protection from loss of investment security value due to market fluctuations.

Some of the other features of the current global financial environment are:

- A growing dominance of a few, very large FIs that operate in more than one country

- Technology that allows an FI to conduct business virtually anywhere in the world

- Cross-border ownership[3] of most securities exchanges

These changes, coupled with the integration of the global economy, suggest increased future challenges for regulators. The impact in the global economy and financial markets caused by the United Kingdom's vote to leave the European Union (referred to as *Brexit* in the popular press), and the 2010 debt crisis in Greece, Portugal, and Spain, are prime examples of the fact that global financial money and capital markets are highly integrated.

III. PRIMARY REGULATORS AND STANDARD SETTERS IN INTERNATIONAL FINANCIAL MARKETS

While each country maintains its own regulatory structure, there are a number of entities that work cooperatively to try to better manage FIs internationally. This section introduces some of the primary regulators, organizations, and standard-setting groups in the area of global financial markets.

A. Central Banks

A central bank is an entity that is responsible for implementing and managing a country's monetary policy, including the money supply and interest rates. In many countries, the central bank is also responsible for overseeing the commercial banking and payment systems. Examples of central banks include the European Central Bank (ECB), the Bank of England, the Federal Reserve Bank (Fed) in the United States, and the People's Bank of China.

Central banks typically bear responsibility for one or more of the following functions:

- **Monetary Policy:** Many central banks are responsible for implementing monetary policy. This is typically done using tools such as (1) the reserve requirement ratio, which stipulates the minimum percentage of deposits that the bank must keep on hand; (2) open market operations, which include the purchase and/or sale of government securities; and (3) the setting of an official interest rate used for lending to financial institutions (e.g., this rate is referred to as the *discount rate* in the United States).

- **Currency Issuance:** Many central banks are responsible for issuing currency, which they provide to FIs and other investors in exchange for government bonds. The income derived from this activity is called *seigniorage* and is used to fund the central bank's operations or is remitted to the local government.

- **Supervision and Regulation:** Central banks may be directly responsible for supervising and regulating the country's commercial banks. An example of this is the US Federal Reserve.

- **Government Services:** Some central banks provide financial services to their own government, taking the place of commercial banks. They are in effect the government's bank. This can include providing basic deposit and safekeeping services, as well as the sale and redemption of government securities.

- **Depository Institution Services:** Central banks may provide various services to FIs. These services can include the operation of clearing and settlement systems, the provision of coin and currency, and the holding of reserve balances.

---

3. Historically, securities exchanges existed in individual countries and were locally owned, either by investors, financial institutions, and/or regulators. The trend toward global trading has resulted in the consolidation of many of the existing exchanges across national borders, resulting in cross-border ownership.

B. Financial Stability Board (FSB)[4]

The Financial Stability Board is based in Basel, Switzerland, and was established to provide international coordination of national financial authorities and international standard-setting bodies. The FSB works to develop and promote the implementation of effective regulatory, supervisory, and other financial sector policies. The FSB has members from the financial authorities of the G-20[5] nations, as well as from international organizations such as the World Bank, International Monetary Fund (IMF), the Bank for International Settlements (BIS), the Organisation for Economic Co-operation and Development (OECD), and others.

The primary goals of the FSB are to (1) maintain financial stability, (2) promote the openness and transparency of the financial sector, (3) implement international financial standards, and (4) conduct periodic peer reviews. The FSB provides an agenda for strengthening financial systems and the stability of international financial markets, but actual changes to regulations must be enacted by the relevant national financial authorities.

C. Bank for International Settlements (BIS)[6]

The Bank for International Settlements was established in 1930 to deal with international financial issues resulting from the First World War. The BIS is the world's oldest international financial institution and remains the principal center for international central bank cooperation.

Currently, the BIS's activities focus on fostering cooperation among central banks and, increasingly, other agencies in pursuit of monetary and financial stability. Since 1930, central bank cooperation at the BIS has taken place through the regular meetings in Basel of central bank governors and experts from central banks and other agencies. In support of this cooperation, the BIS has developed its own research in financial and monetary economics and makes an important contribution to the collection, compilation, and dissemination of economic and financial statistics.

In the monetary policy field, cooperation at the BIS in the immediate aftermath of the Second World War and until the early 1970s focused on implementing and defending the Bretton Woods Agreement.[7] In the 1970s and 1980s, the focus was on managing cross-border capital flows following the oil crisis and the international debt crisis. The 1970s crises also brought the issue of regulatory supervision of internationally active banks to the fore, resulting in the 1988 Basel Capital Accord and the Basel II revision of 2001–06. More recently, the issue of financial stability in the wake of economic integration and globalization has led to the third round of Basel Accords.

Apart from fostering monetary policy cooperation, the BIS has always performed traditional banking functions for the central bank community (e.g., gold and foreign exchange transactions), as well as trustee and agency functions. The BIS was the agent for the European Payments Union (EPU, 1950–58), helping the European currencies restore convertibility after the Second World War. Similarly, the BIS has acted as the agent for various European exchange rate arrangements, including the European Monetary System (EMS, 1979–94), which preceded the move to a single currency. The BIS has also provided or organized emergency financing to support the international monetary system when needed.

In addition to its operational role, BIS sponsors several committees that support its overall mandate. Some of the principal committees are listed below.

---

4. Information on the FSB was obtained from the FSB website (http://www.financialstabilityboard.org, accessed July 2016).
5. The Group of Twenty, or G-20, is a group of finance ministers and central bank governors from 20 major global economies that have met periodically since 2008 to discuss global economic issues.
6. Information on the BIS was obtained from the BIS website (http://www.bis.org, accessed July 2016).
7. The Bretton Woods Agreement established the rules used to govern monetary relations among the world's major financial powers following the Second World War. The International Monetary Fund (IMF) and the International Bank for Reconstruction and Development (IBRD), both now part of the World Bank, were established as part of the Bretton Woods Agreement.

1. GROUP OF GOVERNORS AND HEADS OF SUPERVISION (GHOS)

The Group of Governors and Heads of Supervision is the governing body of the Basel Committee and is comprised of central bank governors and (non-central-bank) heads of supervision from member countries. The GHOS's secretariat is based at the BIS in Basel.

2. COMMITTEE ON THE GLOBAL FINANCIAL SYSTEM (CGFS)

The Committee on the Global Financial System is a central bank forum for the monitoring and examination of broad issues relating to financial markets and systems. The CGFS helps to elaborate appropriate policy recommendations to support central banks in the fulfillment of their responsibilities for monetary and financial stability. In carrying out this task, the committee places particular emphasis on assisting central bank governors in recognizing, analyzing, and responding to threats to the stability of financial markets and the global financial system.

3. COMMITTEE ON PAYMENT AND SETTLEMENT SYSTEMS (CPSS)

The Committee on Payment and Settlement Systems is a BIS-hosted standard-setting body for payment and securities settlement systems. The CPSS also serves as a forum for central banks to monitor and analyze developments in domestic payment, settlement, and clearing systems, as well as in cross-border and multicurrency settlement schemes.

4. BASEL COMMITTEE ON BANKING SUPERVISION (BCBS)[8]

The Basel Committee on Banking Supervision was established in 1974 in response to the liquidation of the Herstatt Bank in Cologne, Germany. The failure of the Herstatt Bank highlighted the potential systemic risk that could be caused by the failure of one large international bank between the time terms of a financial contract (e.g., a foreign exchange trade) were agreed and the time of actual settlement. The term *Herstatt risk* is now used to refer to foreign exchange settlement risk, especially between bank counterparties. In response to that situation, the G-10[9] banded together and formed a standing committee, the BCBS, under the sponsorship of the BIS.

The BCBS operates as a standard-setting body under the BIS and provides a forum for regular cooperation on banking supervisory matters. Its objective is to reduce systemic risk, enhance the understanding of key supervisory issues, and improve the quality of banking supervision worldwide. It does so by exchanging information on national supervisory issues, approaches, and techniques, as well as developing guidelines and supervisory standards, primarily in the area of capital adequacy.

In 1988 the BCBS published an initial set of minimum capital requirements for banks. This was originally known as the *1988 Basel Capital Accord,* and eventually *Basel I.* Basel I established minimum capital ratios for large banks based upon the credit risk of the various assets of each bank. These initial capital standards were put into effect by the G-10 countries in 1992.

In 2004, the BCBS published the second set of Basel Accords, typically referred to as *Basel II.* Basel II expanded the risk ratings implemented by Basel I and added an assessment of operational risk to the existing credit risk evaluation in establishing core capital requirements for major banks. Basel II was based upon three so-called *pillars:*

- Minimum capital requirements to address credit and operational risk
- Supervisory review, which provided a framework for dealing with and evaluating risk
- Market discipline, which focused on disclosure requirements regarding risk metrics and capital adequacy

8. Information on the BCBS was obtained from the BIS website (http://www.bis.org/bcbs/index.htm, accessed July 2016).
9. The Group of Ten, or G-10, is a group of nations that joined together in 1962 and agreed to make financial resources available to the IMF for borrowing to help stabilize the global economy.

The third Basel Accords (Basel III) were developed in 2011 in response to the global financial crisis of 2007–2009. Basel III extended Basel II to address stress testing and market liquidity risk, as well as capital adequacy. Basel III is scheduled to be implemented through 2018 to strengthen the regulation, supervision, and risk management of the banking sector. As part of Basel III, core capital requirements were increased by approximately 2%, and minimum leverage and liquidity requirements were introduced.

Basel III's stated goals are to:

- Improve the banking sector's ability to absorb shocks arising from financial and economic stress, whatever the source
- Improve risk management and governance
- Strengthen banks' transparency and disclosures

The reforms target:

- Bank-level regulation, which will helps raise the resilience of individual banking institutions to periods of stress
- System-wide risks that can build up across the banking sector, as well as the procyclical amplification of these risks over time

These two approaches to supervision are complementary, as greater resilience at the individual bank level reduces the risk of system-wide shocks.

D. European Payments Council (EPC) and Single Euro Payments Area (SEPA)[10]

The European Payments Council is the coordination and decision-making body of the European banking industry in relation to payments. The purpose of the EPC is to support and promote the Single Euro Payments Area. The EPC develops payment schemes and frameworks that help to realize the integrated euro payments market. In particular, the EPC defines common positions for the cooperative space of payment services.

SEPA is the name of the European Union (EU) payments integration initiative. The SEPA vision was set out by EU governments in the Lisbon agenda in March 2000, which aimed to make Europe more dynamic and competitive. The legislative framework of SEPA is contained in the European Payment Services Directive (PSD).

Following the introduction of euro notes and coins in 2002, the political drivers of the SEPA initiative—EU governments, the European Commission (EC), and the European Central Bank (ECB)—have focused on the integration of the euro payments market. Since then, the political drivers have called upon the payments industry to bolster the common currency by developing a set of harmonized payment systems and frameworks for electronic euro payments, in line with the following overall vision for SEPA:

- Integrating the multitude of existing national euro credit transfer and euro direct debit schemes into a single set of European payment schemes is a natural step toward making the euro a single and fully operational currency.
- Creating a single standard for payment cards across national borders aims at ensuring a consistent customer experience when making or accepting payments with cards throughout the euro area.
- The SEPA program seeks to incentivize increased use of electronic payment instruments by standardizing practices while reducing the cost of wholesale cash distribution.

---

10. Background information in this section was obtained from the EPC website (http://www.europeanpaymentscouncil.eu, accessed July 2016).

SEPA focuses on the technical, legal, and commercial barriers to paying and/or receiving euros cross-border within SEPA boundaries. SEPA establishes minimum standards and common pricing for payments processing within the EU, and consists of two primary concepts:

- Creation of standard credit and debit payment schemes (both high- and low-value)
- Creation of a common payment card framework (both debit and credit)

While SEPA only applies within the EU, any organization that does business within that area is potentially impacted. SEPA currently consists of the 28 EU countries plus three European Economic Area countries. A complete listing of SEPA member states is provided in Appendix 2.1.

E. European Securities and Markets Authority (ESMA)[11]

The European Securities and Markets Authority is an independent EU authority that contributes to safeguarding the stability of the EU's financial system by ensuring the integrity, transparency, efficiency, and orderly functioning of securities markets, as well as enhancing investor protection. In particular, the ESMA fosters supervisory convergence, both amongst securities regulators and across financial sectors, by working closely with the other European supervisory authorities competent in the field of banking (e.g., the European Banking Authority, or EBA), and insurance and occupational pensions (e.g., the European Insurance and Occupational Pensions Authority, or EIOPA).

ESMA's work on securities legislation contributes to the development of a single rule book in Europe. This serves two purposes. First, it ensures the consistent treatment of investors across the EU, enabling an adequate level of protection of investors through effective regulation and supervision. Second, it promotes equal conditions of competition for financial service providers, as well as ensuring the effectiveness and cost efficiency of supervision for supervised companies. As part of its role in standard setting and reducing the scope of regulatory arbitrage, ESMA strengthens international supervisory cooperation. Where requested in European law, ESMA undertakes the supervision of certain entities with pan-European reach.

Finally, ESMA also contributes to the financial stability of the EU, in the short, medium, and long term, through its contribution to the work of the European Systemic Risk Board (ESRB), which identifies potential risks to the financial system and provides advice to diminish possible threats to the financial stability of the EU. ESMA is also responsible for coordinating actions of securities supervisors or adopting emergency measures when a crisis situation arises.

ESMA is partially responsible for the implementation and administration of the European Market Infrastructure Regulation (EMIR), which was adopted by the European Parliament and Council in 2012. EMIR is intended to increase the stability of the over-the-counter (OTC) derivatives market throughout Europe, and implements reporting and clearing obligations for OTC derivatives analogous to the requirements of the Dodd-Frank Act in the United States, as discussed later in this chapter.

F. International Association of Deposit Insurers (IADI)[12]

The International Association of Deposit Insurers was formed in May 2002 to enhance the effectiveness of deposit insurance systems by promoting guidance and international cooperation. Members of IADI conduct research and produce guidance for the benefit of those jurisdictions seeking to establish or improve a deposit insurance system. Members also share their knowledge and expertise through participation in international conferences and other forums.

---

11. Information on ESMA was obtained from the ESMA website (http://www.esma.europa.eu, accessed July 2016).
12. Information on IADI was obtained from the IADI website (http://www.iadi.org, accessed July 2016).

Deposit insurance is a tool implemented by many countries to protect their depositors against loss from the failure of a bank or other financial institution. The amount of protection and the specific details of what is covered vary by country. Deposit insurance is generally only provided on deposit accounts and does not typically cover mutual funds or other types of investments. The main purpose of deposit insurance is to increase depositor confidence and reduce the risk of a potential run on a given bank, thus helping to insure overall financial stability.

G. International Organization of Securities Commissions (IOSCO)[13]

The International Organization of Securities Commissions is recognized as the international standard setter for securities markets. Its membership regulates the vast majority of the world's securities markets, and it is the primary international cooperative forum for securities market regulatory agencies. IOSCO provides comprehensive technical assistance to its members, in particular those that regulate emerging securities markets. Through members' efforts, IOSCO strives to establish and apply rigorous standards of regulation, effectively monitor international securities transactions, and strengthen enforcement against offenses.

H. Financial Action Task Force (FATF)[14]

The Financial Action Task Force is an international organization composed of members from more than 30 countries. The primary purpose of this intergovernmental group is the development and promotion of policies, at both national and international levels, to combat money laundering and terrorist financing.

Since its creation, the FATF has spearheaded the effort to adopt and implement measures designed to counter the use of the financial system by criminals, primarily through anti-money laundering efforts. It monitors members' progress in implementing necessary measures, reviews money laundering and terrorist-financing techniques and countermeasures, and promotes the adoption and implementation of appropriate measures globally. In performing these activities, the FATF collaborates with other international bodies involved in combating both money laundering and the financing of terrorism.

In US regulations, *money laundering* is defined as "any financial transaction which generates an asset or a value as the result of an illegal act, which may involve actions such as tax evasion or false accounting."[15] In some countries (e.g., England), money laundering does not even need to involve money, but can include any economic good. Courts in several major countries have ruled that money laundering has been committed by private individuals, drug dealers, businesses, corrupt officials, members of criminal organizations, and even states. Essentially, any enterprise through which money laundering could occur would come under possible regulation.

Money laundering is a diverse and complex process involving three stages:

- **Placement:** The physical deposit of cash proceeds from illegal activities into an FI
- **Layering:** A series of financial transactions designed to separate cash proceeds from their criminal or terrorist origins
- **Integration:** Creating what appears to be a legitimate explanation for the source of funds (e.g., showing that funds were donated for a charitable purpose)

---

13. Information on IOSCO was obtained from the IOSCO website (http://www.iosco.org/about/, accessed July 2016).
14. Information on FATF was obtained from the FATF website (http://www.fatf-gafi.org, accessed July 2016).
15. From "Money Laundering: A Banker's Guide to Avoiding Problems," published by the Office of the Comptroller of the Currency (OCC), December 2002 (http://www.occ.gov/topics/bank-operations/financial-crime/money-laundering/money-laundering-2002.pdf).

I. International Association of Insurance Supervisors (IAIS)[16]

The International Association of Insurance Supervisors is a standard-setting group that represents insurance regulators and supervisory entities of some 190 jurisdictions in nearly 140 countries, constituting the great majority of the world's insurance premiums. The primary objective of the IAIS is to encourage cooperation among the members on both the international and domestic levels. This cooperation helps to ensure the maintenance of efficient, fair, safe, and stable insurance markets, ultimately benefiting and protecting policyholders.

J. International Swaps and Derivatives Association (ISDA)[17]

The purpose of the International Swaps and Derivatives Association is to improve the safety and efficiency of the world's swaps and derivatives markets. Created in 1985, ISDA's work has led to improved documentation procedures and enforceability of netting and collateral provisions, in an effort to reduce counterparty, credit, and legal risks. ISDA has over 850 member institutions (e.g., corporations, investment managers, government entities), spanning 67 countries.

IV. US REGULATORY AND LEGAL ENVIRONMENT

This section of the chapter focuses on the US regulatory and legal environment. This focus is necessitated by the overall size of the US market and by the fact that US financial regulations are often used as models by other countries.

Historically, the US Congress and federal regulatory agencies have imposed restrictions on FIs to help align and enforce the regulatory objectives presented at the beginning of this chapter. In addition to those basic objectives, financial regulations in the United States have also sought to prevent concentration of economic and political power, as well as encourage institutional specialization. Essentially, the Congress enacts legislation, and the regulatory agencies develop regulations based on that legislation. From the Glass-Steagall Act of 1933 until the Gramm-Leach-Bliley Act of 1999 (GLB), US FIs served very distinct functions. During that time period, the functions of commercial lending and deposit taking, securities underwriting, mortgage origination, and insurance underwriting were legally required to be carried out by separate FIs. This changed in 1999 when GLB removed the barriers among the functions of commercial banking, investment banking, and insurance, allowing FIs a broader range of products and more direct competition.

The landscape of financial regulation in the United States was impacted further by the passage of the Dodd-Frank Wall Street Reform and Consumer Protection Act of 2010 (Dodd-Frank Act). This wide-ranging legislation, passed in the wake of the global financial crisis of 2007–2009, affected almost all types of FIs and significantly changed the regulatory framework for financial activities in the United States.

A. Regulatory Agencies

The United States has a dual banking system. *Dual* refers to the fact that banks are either federally or state chartered. At the federal level, bank supervision is shared primarily by three agencies: the Office of the Comptroller of the Currency (OCC), the Board of Governors of the Federal Reserve System, and the Federal Deposit Insurance Corporation (FDIC). As promulgated by the Dodd-Frank Act, the Financial Stability Oversight Council (FSOC) was created to help oversee the aforementioned primary bank regulators. Furthermore, the FSOC is charged with monitoring systemic risk in financial systems and making recommendations to other regulatory entities.

---

16. Information on the IAIS was obtained from the IAIS website (http://www.iaisweb.org/, accessed July 2016).
17. Information on the ISDA was obtained from the ISDA website (http://www.isda.org/, accessed July 2016).

In addition to the primary regulators mentioned previously, there are a number of agencies and regulatory bodies that are responsible for monitoring specific depository institutions or certain financial services. These include the Consumer Financial Protection Bureau, the Office of Foreign Assets Control, the Financial Crimes Enforcement Network, the National Credit Union Administration, state banking boards and commissions, and the Department of Justice.

There are a large number of other regulators focused on specific segments of the financial environment. These include such agencies/organizations as the Securities and Exchange Commission, the Commodity Futures Trading Commission, and the Financial Industry Regulatory Authority.

1. COMMODITY FUTURES TRADING COMMISSION (CFTC)

The Commodity Futures Trading Commission was created by Congress in 1974 as an independent agency with the mandate to regulate commodity futures and options markets in the United States. As part of the Dodd-Frank Act, the CFTC is required to work with the Securities and Exchange Commission to regulate over-the-counter derivatives so that irresponsible practices and excessive risk taking can no longer escape regulatory oversight.

2. CONSUMER FINANCIAL PROTECTION BUREAU (CFPB)

The Consumer Financial Protection Bureau is an independent consumer protection entity within the Fed that was created in 2010 by the Dodd-Frank Act. The primary reason behind the CFPB's creation was to consolidate and strengthen consumer protection responsibilities and oversee the enforcement of federal laws intended to ensure the fair and equitable access to credit for individuals and communities. To achieve this objective, the CFPB has the authority to examine and enforce regulations for banks and credit unions with assets exceeding $10 billion and all mortgage-related businesses (e.g., lenders, servicers, and mortgage brokers), payday lenders, and student loan providers, among others.

3. DEPARTMENT OF JUSTICE (DOJ)

The Department of Justice, as well as the Fed, reviews and approves proposed bank mergers and holding company acquisitions to determine their impact on competition as part of antitrust legislation. The Federal Bureau of Investigation (FBI), a bureau of the DOJ, plays a central role in investigating FI fraud and theft, as well as in enforcing key money laundering legislation.

4. FEDERAL DEPOSIT INSURANCE CORPORATION (FDIC)

The Federal Deposit Insurance Corporation, which was established in 1933 as part of the Glass-Steagall Act, is an independent agency of the federal government whose primary role is to protect depositors from losses caused by bank insolvency. The FDIC's responsibilities include:

- Providing deposit insurance for all insured FIs
- Supervising selected depository institutions[18]
- Acting as a trustee in the event of bank failures

The FDIC administers the Deposit Insurance Fund (DIF). Insured institutions pay a premium into the fund that is based on their level of deposits and risk profile, as determined by the type and mix of assets and liabilities the institution holds. The fund is backed by the full faith and credit of the US government and covers deposits in checking and savings accounts up to a maximum of $250,000 per depositor.

---

18. The FDIC has direct supervisory authority over state-chartered banks that are not members of the Fed, and backup authority over national and Fed member banks.

5. FINANCIAL CRIMES ENFORCEMENT NETWORK (FinCEN)

The Financial Crimes Enforcement Network serves as the US financial intelligence unit (FIU)[19] and is the primary agency (operating as a bureau of the Treasury) that oversees and implements policies to prevent and detect money laundering by criminal or terrorist organizations. It does this by enforcing counter-money laundering legislation (e.g., the Bank Secrecy Act), which requires reporting large and/or suspicious monetary transfers conducted at banks. FinCEN also provides intelligence and analytical support to law enforcement agencies in the form of reports that are used to build investigations and plan new strategies that combat money laundering.

6. FINANCIAL INDUSTRY REGULATORY AUTHORITY (FINRA)[20]

The Financial Industry Regulatory Authority is the largest independent regulator for all securities firms and registered securities representatives doing business in the United States. It was created in 2007 through the consolidation of the National Association of Securities Dealers (NASD) and the member regulation, enforcement, and arbitration functions of the New York Stock Exchange (NYSE). FINRA's mission is to provide investor protection and market integrity through effective and efficient regulation, as well as through compliance and technology-based services.

FINRA is involved in most aspects of the securities business, including:

- Registering and educating industry participants (e.g., brokers, registered investment advisors)
- Examining brokerage firms
- Writing and enforcing rules related to federal securities laws
- Informing and educating the investing public
- Providing trade reporting and other industry utilities
- Administering the primary dispute resolution forum for investors and registered firms

FINRA also performs market regulation under contract for the NASDAQ Stock Market, the NYSE MKT (formerly known as the *American Stock Exchange*), the International Securities Exchange, and the Chicago Climate Exchange.

7. FINANCIAL STABILITY OVERSIGHT COUNCIL (FSOC)

The primary responsibility of the Financial Stability Oversight Council is to prevent systemic risk from threatening the financial system by identifying threats to financial stability and gaps in regulations, and facilitating coordination across federal and state agencies. It does not directly regulate institutions; instead, this is the primary role of the Fed, FDIC, OCC, and others. While the FSOC has a strong systemic oversight role, it has limited enforcement power and can only make recommendations to the primary regulators.

8. NATIONAL CREDIT UNION ADMINISTRATION (NCUA)

The National Credit Union Administration is an independent federal agency that charters and supervises federal credit unions. The NCUA is backed by the full faith and credit of the US government. It also operates the National Credit Union Share Insurance Fund (NCUSIF), which insures the savings of account holders in all federal credit unions and many state-chartered credit unions.

19. An FIU is a specialized government agency established in many countries to deal with the problems of money laundering and similar financial crimes.
20. Information on FINRA comes from the FINRA website (http://www.finra.org, accessed July 2016).

9. OFFICE OF FOREIGN ASSETS CONTROL (OFAC)

The Office of Foreign Assets Control is an office of the US Treasury Department that administers and enforces economic and trade sanctions against targeted foreign countries, terrorist-sponsoring organizations, and international narcotics traffickers. Based on US foreign policy and national security goals, OFAC can impose controls on financial transactions and freeze foreign assets under US jurisdiction. The role of OFAC was expanded under the USA PATRIOT Act, which is covered later in this chapter.

10. THE SECRET SERVICE

The Secret Service was created in 1865 to suppress counterfeit currency. Now part of the US Department of Homeland Security, its mission statement includes the charge to "safeguard the nation's financial infrastructure and payment systems to preserve the integrity of the economy." In addition to dealing with counterfeit currency, the Secret Service also deals with credit card fraud, check fraud, and identity theft.

11. SECURITIES AND EXCHANGE COMMISSION (SEC)

The Securities and Exchange Commission, which is governed by the securities laws of 1933, 1934, and 1940, is a federal agency designed to maintain a fair and orderly market for investors by regulating and supervising securities sales. The SEC's responsibilities include:

- Registering public offerings of debt or equity securities by banks, bank holding companies, and other corporations
- Setting financial disclosure standards for corporations that sell securities to the public
- Requiring companies with publicly owned securities to file quarterly and annual financial statements
- Regulating mutual funds and investment advisors
- Monitoring insider trading to enforce related regulations

While the role of most agencies that oversee the financial services industry relate to protecting depositors, the SEC focuses on protecting people who invest in stocks, bonds, and derivative instruments. In general, the SEC requires publicly traded firms to disclose all relevant financial information to investors.

B. US Legal Environment

A wide range of regulations affect FIs and their customers. This section provides an outline of significant US federal legislation relating to the financial services industry. The discussion covers seven key areas:

1. Legislation regarding regulation and supervision of FIs and financial services
2. Legislation governing payment systems and instruments
3. Legislation relating to financial crimes, money laundering, and financial disclosure
4. Federal Reserve regulations
5. Regulations relating to investments and securities
6. The Uniform Commercial Code
7. Unclaimed property (escheatment) legislation

1. LEGISLATION REGARDING REGULATION AND SUPERVISION OF FIs AND FINANCIAL SERVICES

a. Federal Reserve Act (1913)

The Federal Reserve Act established the Federal Reserve System and provided the foundation for the current banking system. It requires all banks with a national charter granted by the Office of the Comptroller of the Currency (OCC) to become Reserve banks, and thus become subject to Fed regulation, supervision, and reserve requirements. The act also empowered the Fed to create a national check collection and settlement system through member banks.

b. Glass-Steagall Act (also known as the Banking Act of 1933)

The Glass-Steagall Act was passed to address major issues and problems with the financial services industry stemming from the Great Depression. As initially written, the act:

- Prohibited commercial banks from underwriting securities except for government issues
- Prohibited securities firms from engaging in bank-like activities, such as deposit gathering
- Required the Fed to establish interest rate ceilings on all types of accounts and prohibited the payment of interest on demand deposits (provisions of this act were incorporated in Federal Reserve Regulation Q)
- Created the FDIC to guarantee deposits up to a stipulated maximum amount in order to restore faith in the banking system after numerous Depression-era bank failures

The Gramm-Leach-Bliley Act of 1999, discussed below, repealed almost all of Glass-Steagall with the exception of deposit insurance under the FDIC.

c. Anti-tying Amendments to the Bank Holding Company Act (1970)

The term *tying* refers to the act of requiring an organization or individual to purchase a product or service in order to be allowed to obtain a separate product or service. Under the 1970 amendments to the Bank Holding Company Act of 1956, the federal government prohibits tying in financial services, in an effort to increase competition and remove unfair banking practices. In general, the regulations provide that an FI may not condition the extension of credit on the requirement that the borrower obtain other services from the FI. There are some broad exclusions to the general rule as a result of what is called the *traditional bank product exception*. Under this exception, banks may condition the terms, including price, of an offer based on the requirement that the customer purchase or use other products from the bank, as long as all of the products are available separately to the same customer.

d. Gramm-Leach-Bliley Act (1999)

The Gramm-Leach-Bliley Act eliminates many of the provisions of the Glass-Steagall Act, especially those that created barriers among the functions of commercial banking, investment banking, and insurance. Specifically, this regulation:

- Permits the creation of financial holding companies (FHCs) that can engage in any activity that the Fed considers financial in nature or incidental to it
- Establishes the Fed as the primary regulator of FHCs, which are subject to consolidated capital requirements at the parent company level and bank-style risk management at all levels
- Allows easier entry by foreign banks into the US financial services market
- Includes key provisions relating to consumer protection, including specific regulations regarding the protection of nonpublic personal information

e. Dodd-Frank Wall Street Reform and Consumer Protection Act (2010)

This sweeping legislation was enacted in response to concerns related to the financial services industry in the wake of the global financial crisis of 2007–2009. The act had a major impact on the regulation of banks and other FIs, and brought financial consumer protection under a single authority.

One of the primary objectives of the Dodd-Frank Act was to bring more transparency and accountability to the derivatives market. Specifically, with respect to derivatives, the act:

- **Closes Regulatory Gaps:** It provides the Securities and Exchange Commission (SEC) and the Commodity Futures Trading Commission (CFTC) with authority to regulate over-the-counter (OTC) derivatives, so that irresponsible practices and excessive risk taking can no longer escape regulatory oversight.

- **Requires Central Clearing and Exchange Trading:** It requires central clearing and exchange trading for derivatives that are cleared or settled through exchanges. It also provides a role for both regulators and clearinghouses to determine which contracts should be cleared. In recognition of the fact that many companies enter into OTC derivatives for important economic reasons, including but not limited to risk management, the act provides an exception to the central clearing requirement for some end users. To qualify for the exception, the end user must not be a financial entity, the derivatives must be used only for hedging purposes, and the user must satisfy reporting requirements established by the CFTC.

- **Requires Market Transparency:** It requires data collection and publication through clearinghouses or swap repositories to improve market transparency, and provides regulators with important tools for monitoring and responding to risks.

- **Adds Financial Safeguards:** It increases the safety of the system by ensuring that dealers and major swap participants have adequate financial resources to meet responsibilities. The act also provides regulators with the authority to impose capital and margin requirements on swap dealers and major swap participants, but not on end users.

- **Sets Higher Standards of Conduct:** It establishes a code of conduct for all registered swap dealers and major swap participants when advising a swap entity. When acting as counterparties to a pension fund, endowment fund, or state or local government, dealers are to have a reasonable basis to believe that the fund or governmental entity has an independent representative advising it.

Specific effects of various provisions of this act are discussed throughout this book. As part of the broader act, the Durbin Amendment to Dodd-Frank is a provision intended to limit debit card interchange fees and increase competition in payment processing. Another specific piece of the act, known as the *Volcker rule* after Paul Volcker, the former Fed chairman who first suggested the rule, limits an FI's ability to engage in proprietary trading for its own portfolio. With some exceptions, the Volcker rule also prohibits FIs from owning or sponsoring hedge funds or private equity funds.

2. LEGISLATION GOVERNING PAYMENT SYSTEMS AND INSTRUMENTS

a. Electronic Fund Transfer Act (EFTA) (1978)

The Electronic Fund Transfer Act defines the rights and responsibilities of customers using all electronic funds transfer (EFT) services except wire transfers. Further, it limits customer liability for unauthorized banking transactions involving automated teller machines (ATMs) and point-of-sale (POS) terminals, provided the customer promptly notifies the bank or other institution that issued the card. Provisions of this act are incorporated in Federal Reserve Regulation E.

b. Depository Institutions Deregulation and Monetary Control Act (DIDMCA) (1980)

The Depository Institutions Deregulation and Monetary Control Act impacts both FIs and firms. For the financial services industry, this legislation:

- Requires all deposit-taking institutions to maintain reserves at the Fed
- Makes Fed services such as the discount window and check clearing available to all deposit-taking institutions
- Mandates the Fed to reduce and/or price payment system float and price previously free Fed services according to the standards of a tax-paying vendor

c. Electronic Signatures in Global and National Commerce Act (E-Sign Act) (2000)

The purpose of the Electronic Signatures in Global and National Commerce Act is to grant digital signatures the same legal status as handwritten ink signatures. It establishes the legal certainty of e-commerce transactions and provides a measure of confidence around the enforceability of electronic transactions. Digital signatures are not facsimile signatures, but electronic files used to sign electronic documents.

d. Check Clearing for the 21st Century Act (Check 21) (2003)

The Check Clearing for the 21st Century Act provided the basis for electronic clearing of checks by allowing the substitution of a copy or image of a check for the original document in the clearing process. The act was intended to speed and facilitate the clearing of checks by eliminating the need to exchange physical paper, and improve the overall efficiency of the payment system.

3. LEGISLATION RELATING TO FINANCIAL CRIMES, MONEY LAUNDERING, AND FINANCIAL DISCLOSURE

a. Bank Secrecy Act (BSA) (1970) and Money Laundering Control Act (MLCA) (1986)

The purpose of the Bank Secrecy Act and the Money Laundering Control Act is to control the flow of illegal money, essentially occurring when money is laundered to conceal criminal activities, usually related to drug trafficking, tax evasion, or terrorist activities. While the initial money laundering regulations were directed toward FIs, their impact has broadened over time.

The primary intent of the BSA is to deter money laundering and the use of secret foreign bank accounts. By requiring all FIs to report any suspicious financial transactions, a paper trail is created to assist in detecting and monitoring illegal activities. It is important to note that the term *FI* is very broadly defined, and as a result, the act covers many businesses not normally thought of as FIs. The act requires any trade or business organization that receives $10,000 or more in cash to file Internal Revenue Service (IRS) Form 8300, identifying from whom that cash was received and on whose behalf the transaction was conducted, as well as providing a description of the transaction and the method of payment.

The MLCA enhanced the BSA by making it a crime to structure transactions in such a way as to avoid the reporting requirements of that act. In effect, this defines money laundering and makes it a federal crime. FIs are liable for substantial civil and criminal penalties if they fail to comply with the reporting provisions of anti-money laundering regulations. The MLCA also requires FIs to establish effective "know your customer" (KYC) guidelines, be aware of parties to large-value funds transfers, and file currency transaction reports and criminal referrals. As noted below, the USA PATRIOT Act extended many of the provisions of the MLCA to nonfinancial businesses potentially handling large-value transactions, such as car, boat, plane, and jewelry dealers. Specifically, FIs and other covered organizations must monitor and report the following:

- Activity that is inconsistent with a customer's business

- Attempts by customers to avoid reporting or record-keeping requirements

- Unusual or multiple funds transfer activities

- Customers who provide insufficient or suspicious information

b. USA PATRIOT Act (2001)

In response to the September 11, 2001, attacks on the United States, Congress passed wide-ranging legislation designed to improve overall security, and granted the FBI and the DOJ increased latitude in intelligence-gathering activities. This legislation is named the *Uniting and Strengthening America by Providing Appropriate Tools Required to Intercept and Obstruct Terrorism Act (USA PATRIOT Act)*. The primary impact for FIs is the substantial number of amendments added to the provisions of existing money laundering legislation, such as the BSA. These amendments are intended to make it easier to prevent, detect, and prosecute international money laundering and the financing of terrorism. The PATRIOT Act is subject to periodic renewal by Congress.

Some provisions of the PATRIOT Act are that it:

- Imposes significant obligations upon nonbank FIs, including broker-dealers, credit card companies, and check-cashing services (nonbank FIs were not covered previously by the BSA). It also includes nonfinancial entities potentially handling large-value transactions, such as car, boat, plane, and jewelry dealers.

- Makes all foreign banks with accounts in the United States subject to US jurisdiction, including the power to obtain records and information regarding customers.

- Prohibits US banks from maintaining, either directly or indirectly, correspondent accounts for any *foreign shell banks*, which are defined as foreign banks without a physical presence in any country.

- Prevents US credit card system operators from authorizing foreign banks to issue or accept US credit cards without taking steps to prevent usage by terrorists.

- Requires banks to know their customers, resulting in increased due diligence before taking on new business.

c. Sarbanes-Oxley Act (SOX) (2002)

The primary purpose of the Sarbanes-Oxley Act is to improve disclosure and financial reporting in the wake of a series of dramatic financial scandals during the early 2000s. SOX brought about numerous changes to SEC rules and regulations and created the Public Company Accounting Oversight Board (PCAOB). Specifically, publicly traded firms must:

- Disclose in annual reports the code of ethics applicable to senior financial officers. Companies that change or waive the code must disclose the event by filing a Form 8-K with the SEC or posting a notice on the company's website.

- Disclose in annual reports whether the audit committee has a financial expert.

- Establish and maintain adequate internal controls for financial reporting.

- Require audit committees to preapprove all audit and non-audit services provided by the auditor, and be briefed by auditors on the company's accounting, including alternative approaches that might be preferable to the company's current methods.

SEC Regulation G, which implements much of SOX, requires public companies to reconcile pro forma financial information to financial statements. Companies that issue earnings releases must file them on Form 8-K. Finally, all off-balance-sheet arrangements that may have a material current or future effect on the financial statements or liquidity must be included in the management's discussion and analysis (MD&A) section of the financial statements. While SOX is a US regulation, it has had a significant international impact because it applies to any company traded on a US stock exchange.

d. The Red Flags Rule[21]

The Red Flags Rule refers to regulations that require FIs and creditors to develop and implement written identity theft prevention programs as part of the Fair and Accurate Credit Transactions Act of 2003 (FACT). These programs must provide for the identification of, detection of, and response to patterns, practices, or specific activities (i.e., red flags) that could indicate identity theft.

The Red Flags Rule applies to FIs and creditors with consumer accounts designed to permit multiple payments or transactions—or any other account for which there is a reasonably foreseeable risk of identity theft. Under the rule, an *FI* is defined as a state or national bank, a state or federal savings and loan association, a mutual savings bank, a state or federal credit union, or any other entity that holds a transaction account belonging to a consumer. Most of these institutions are regulated by the federal bank regulatory agencies and NCUA.

e. Foreign Account Tax Compliance Act (FATCA) (2010) and the Report of Foreign Bank and Financial Accounts (FBAR)

The Foreign Account Tax Compliance Act was implemented to address tax noncompliance by US taxpayers with foreign bank accounts. The act requires US taxpayers to file an annual report of all foreign financial accounts and offshore assets. The act also requires foreign financial institutions to report financial accounts held by US taxpayers or foreign entities that are substantially owned by US taxpayers. US persons (including businesses) must file a Report of Foreign Bank and Financial Accounts if the person had a financial interest in or signature authority over at least one account located outside of the United States and the aggregate value of all financial accounts exceeded $10,000 at any time during the year. There is a general exception for corporate signers who are included in a consolidated FBAR filed by their organization.

4. FEDERAL RESERVE REGULATIONS

The Fed defines and enforces several key banking regulations that impact treasury professionals. Some of the major regulations[22] include:

a. Regulation D

Regulation D implements the reserve requirement provision of the Federal Reserve Act of 1913, and imposes uniform reserve requirements on all depository institutions, with different levels of reserves for different types of deposits. The Fed uses this regulation to control the money supply.

---

21. Information on the Red Flags Rule was obtained from the Federal Trade Commission (FTC) website (http://www.ftc.gov, accessed July 2016).
22. Details on all Federal Reserve regulations may be found at http://www.frbservices.org.

b. Regulation E

Regulation E implements provisions of the Electronic Fund Transfer Act of 1978, which establishes the rights, responsibilities, and liabilities of parties engaging in consumer-related EFTs, and also protects consumers using systems such as ATMs, automated clearinghouse (ACH), and credit cards. Regulation E also establishes the guidelines for the documentation of electronic transfers.

c. Regulation J

Regulation J implements the check collection and settlement provision of the Federal Reserve Act of 1913, and establishes procedures, duties, and responsibilities for check collection and settlement through the Fed.

d. Regulation Q

Regulation Q implemented the interest-bearing account restriction of the Glass-Steagall Act of 1933 and barred the paying of interest on any corporate demand deposit accounts. Interest rate ceilings initially set by this regulation on all commercial bank deposit accounts were partially phased out in 1986 by the DIDMCA, and the final restrictions on corporate demand deposits were removed by the Dodd-Frank Act in 2010.

e. Regulation Y

Regulation Y implements various provisions of the Bank Holding Company Act of 1956, the Change in Bank Control Act of 1978, and subsequent revisions covering the acquisition of control of banks and bank holding companies. It defines and regulates the nonbanking activities in which bank holding companies and foreign banking organizations in the United States may engage, including anti-tying restrictions.

f. Regulation Z

Regulation Z applies to the Truth in Lending Act of 1968 (TILA), which is concerned with promoting informed use of credit by consumers. This regulation covers various types of consumer lending (e.g., credit cards, home mortgages, student loans, and installment loans). For treasury professionals, the primary impact of this regulation relates to credit cards offered to their customers; for educational institutions, the impact relates to the use of student loans.

Regulation Z was updated in February of 2010 in order to implement the Credit Card Accountability Responsibility and Disclosure Act of 2009 (Credit CARD Act). As a result, Regulation Z also:

- Protects consumers from unexpected increases in credit card interest rates by generally prohibiting increases in a rate during the first year after an account is opened, as well as any increases in a rate that applies to an existing credit card balance
- Prohibits creditors from issuing a credit card to a consumer who is under the age of 21 unless the consumer can make the required payments or obtains the signature of a parent or other cosigner who is able to do so
- Requires creditors to obtain a consumer's consent before charging fees for transactions that exceed the credit limit
- Limits the high fees associated with subprime credit cards
- Bans creditors from using the two-cycle billing method to impose interest charges[23]
- Prohibits creditors from allocating payments in ways that maximize interest charges

---

23. Two-cycle billing, also known as *double-cycle billing*, is a process used by some creditors to calculate interest charges based on the average balance of the account over two billing periods (the current and prior period), instead of using only the current period. Two-cycle billing effectively wipes out any grace period for account balances and tends to increase the amount of interest charged on credit accounts.

g. Regulation BB

Regulation BB implements the provisions of the Community Reinvestment Act of 1977 as revised in 1995, and requires banks to help meet the credit needs of the entire community in which they do business.

h. Regulation CC

Regulation CC implements the provisions of the Expedited Funds Availability Act of 1987, which establishes rules designed to speed the collection and return of checks, and mandates banks to return unpaid checks expeditiously. This regulation also imposes the same return procedures to payable through drafts that apply to checks, and establishes endorsement standards for banks and companies to follow when depositing and clearing checks.

5. REGULATIONS RELATING TO INVESTMENTS AND SECURITIES

a. Fair Disclosure, Regulation FD[24]

On August 15, 2000, the SEC adopted Regulation FD to address the selective disclosure of information by publicly traded companies and other issuers. Regulation FD provides that when an issuer discloses material nonpublic information to certain individuals or entities—generally, securities market professionals, such as stock analysts, or holders of the issuer's securities who may well trade on the basis of the information—the issuer must make public disclosure of that information.

b. SEC Rule 2a-7[25]

Money market funds (MMFs), which represent portfolios of various money market securities, are governed by SEC Rule 2a-7. This ruling placed stipulations on the securities held by an MMF with the goal of ensuring adequate diversification. By investing excess cash in MMFs, many treasury professionals believed that their firm's liquidity was virtually riskless.

The contraction of credit triggered by the global financial crisis of 2007–2009 caused the Reserve Primary Fund, one of the world's largest MMFs, to "break the buck," which is slang for the fund's net asset value (NAV) dropping below $1.00 per share. This occurred because the fund's various underlying securities dropped in value and the fund ran short on cash due to excess investor redemption requests.

Consequently, the SEC reviewed Rule 2a-7 in hopes of strengthening the health of MMFs. The new rules, instituted in 2016, include a floating NAV for MMFs, redemption fees if a fund's weekly liquid assets fall below a threshold, and the ability to suspend redemptions (using restrictions known as *redemption gates*) for a period of up to 10 business days.[26]

6. THE UNIFORM COMMERCIAL CODE (UCC)

The Uniform Commercial Code is a uniform set of laws governing commercial transactions in the United States. The UCC defines the rights and duties of all parties in a commercial transaction and provides a statutory definition of commonly accepted business practices. Because of the size of the US economy, the UCC has significant impact globally, and various portions of it have been used as a model in developing global trade agreements.

24. Information in this section was taken from the SEC's website (http://www.sec.gov, accessed on July 2016).
25. SEC Rule 2a-7 is also discussed in Chapter 5, Money Markets.
26. Government MMFs are not subject to these rules.

a. Article 3: Negotiable Instruments

The primary provisions of Article 3 involve negotiable instruments, accord and satisfaction, and how banks handle unauthorized signatures. Article 3 is especially relevant for companies receiving paper-based payments.

Initially, checks were permitted to constitute payment made in full (i.e., accord and satisfaction) when a message to that effect was written on the face of the check and the check was deposited. However, this provision allowed for the possibility of inadvertent accord and satisfaction when the customer wrote "paid in full" on a check for a disputed claim, especially for checks collected through a lockbox. The revised section of Article 3 prevents inadvertent accord and satisfaction if the payee discovers the error and returns the payment to the payor within 90 days.

Article 3 also clarifies that a bank's failure to examine a forged drawer's signature is not a failure to exercise ordinary care if it does not violate the bank's procedures and if the procedures do not vary from general banking practices unreasonably. A bank can charge a customer's account only for properly payable checks. Therefore, items with unauthorized signatures do not pass this test. However, a bank customer may be held liable if the customer does not exercise ordinary care related to check issuance and does not notify the bank of any potential discrepancies in a timely manner.

b. Article 4: Bank Deposits and Collections

The provisions of Article 4 include the rights, responsibilities, and definitions of the parties involved in the deposit and collection process. Specifically, Article 4 addresses the relationship between a bank and its customers. Article 4 defines:

- When a bank may charge a customer's account
- The bank's liability to a customer for failing to honor a good check
- The customer's right to stop payment
- The bank's option not to pay an item more than six months old (i.e., stale-dated)
- A customer's duty to report an unauthorized signature or alteration

A bank customer has the duty to examine bank statements within a reasonable time, not to exceed 30 days after the statement becomes available, and to report any unauthorized signatures or alterations. This makes it imperative that companies accurately reconcile bank accounts on a timely basis.

c. Article 4A: Funds Transfers

Article 4A provides a legal framework that outlines the risks, rights, and obligations of parties in connection with electronic funds transfers. Two primary provisions of Article 4A impact:

- **Security Procedures:** A bank must make such procedures available to the customer. Further, the bank and the customer must agree that the procedures are commercially reasonable for verifying payment. Some common security measures include the use of personal identification numbers (PINs), callbacks, encryption, and message authentication.

- **Consequential Damages:** Banks generally are not responsible for consequential damages, which are losses resulting from an action or error made by the bank beyond the actual loss. However, a bank incorrectly executing a payment order remains liable for interest losses or incidental expenses. A bank is liable for consequential damages only when it agrees to assume this liability in a written agreement with the customer.

d. Article 5: Letters of Credit

Article 5 covers US commercial letters of credit (L/Cs) requiring documentary drafts and defines an L/C, documentary draft, and documentary demand for payment. It also defines the various roles of an L/C issuer, the applicant for whom the credit is issued, the beneficiary of the credit, and the advising and confirming banks. Article 5 does not cover standby L/Cs.

e. Article 9: Secured Transactions

Article 9 covers secured transactions, which occur when a lender or creditor requires some type of security or collateral for money it lends or goods it sells. Under this article, any business that requires such a security interest must file a UCC-1 financing statement with its state's office of assessments and taxation. The UCC-1 financing statement form lists collateral specifically assigned to secure the loan. It is a legal document signed by the borrower and lender that helps determine who has a right to the assets in the event of default.

7. UNCLAIMED PROPERTY (ESCHEATMENT) LEGISLATION

In the business world, escheat statutes primarily impact banks or companies that hold unclaimed assets of customers or employees. The most general occurrence of escheat is when an entity such as a bank holds money or property and the property goes unclaimed for some specified period of time (generally referred to as a *dormant account*). If the owner cannot be located, then in many jurisdictions such property can be escheated to the government. Many states maintain websites and databases that allow individuals and companies to search for funds that have been escheated.

For nonbank organizations, escheat is the process of turning over to a state authority (in the United States) unclaimed or abandoned payroll checks, stocks and shares whose owners cannot be traced, or unclaimed/unused rebates, customer purchase deposits or down payments, and gift cards/certificates. Firms are required to file unclaimed property reports annually with each appropriate state and to make a good faith effort to find the owners of dormant accounts. The escheating criteria are driven by individual state regulations and, in many cases, the penalties and interest assessed by the state for failure to comply are often more than the actual amount of unclaimed property. In addition, it should be noted that the appropriate response to escheatment may be complicated by the property owner having addresses in multiple states.

V. TAX CONSIDERATIONS

Multinational companies must deal with tax codes in all the countries where they have sales, employees, and/or operations. This section introduces some of the critical tax issues that should be considered.

A. Unitary Taxes and Foreign Tax Credits

A unitary tax is a tax on a corporation's global income. Some countries levy unitary taxes on corporations operating in their borders in order to prevent them from avoiding taxes by transferring income to another country with a low or no corporate tax. A unitary tax can, however, result in multiple taxation of the same income. To help deal with this problem, some countries with unitary taxes also provide a tax credit for local taxes paid on income earned by foreign operations.

A US company's income derived from its non-US operations typically is included in its tax return to determine the amount of US income tax due. If income from foreign sources has already been subjected to foreign income taxes, the same income is taxed twice. To relieve the effect of double taxation, US tax law grants a US company a tax credit against its total US income tax liability for foreign income taxes paid by the parent and its subsidiaries. This credit is called the *foreign tax credit*. It is allowed only for foreign income taxes that do not exceed US tax rates.

To attract multinational businesses and thereby obtain employment opportunities for their citizens, a number of countries offer tax incentives for subsidiaries that perform certain administrative and financial functions within the host country. The laws governing the taxation of nondomestic income are extremely complex. Treasury professionals are advised to consult with tax experts.

B. Capital Tax

In some foreign countries, particularly those experiencing an increase in economic growth, companies are assessed a capital tax on the initial capital used to establish the new venture, and on subsequent incoming capital or repatriated capital. A capital tax is used as a fiscal tool by some countries to augment tax collections. The tax can also be used by a government to slow foreign direct investment in a country.

C. Asset Tax and Turnover Tax

Despite the fact that a company may not show a profit or owe income tax on an international project, many foreign countries still impose an asset tax. Even though a company may not produce operating profits, it may still owe taxes on the value of accumulated real property or business equipment, or on the value of a financial portfolio. There also may be a turnover tax, which is essentially a sales tax on goods and services.

D. Withholding Tax

Companies may be required to pay taxes when moving funds outside a foreign country. Some countries refer to these taxes as *lifting fees*. They are charged whenever funds are transferred from a resident (domestic) account to a nonresident (foreign) account. Depending on the company's overall foreign tax credit position, some offset may be available on the withholding tax.

E. Sales and Use Taxes

Sales taxes are charged at the point of purchase for certain goods and services, and the tax amount is typically calculated by applying a percentage rate to the taxable price of a sale. In most cases, sales taxes are collected from the buyer by the seller, who then remits the tax to the appropriate government agency/agencies. Sales taxes are commonly charged on sales of goods, but may be charged on sales of services as well.

A use tax is imposed directly on the consumer of goods that were purchased without paying sales tax (generally items purchased from a vendor in another state or over the Internet and delivered to the purchaser by mail or common carrier). Corporations operating in many locations may have to comply with sales and use tax regulations for all the locations in which they operate.

F. Other Taxes

Another tax commonly used by many countries is a value-added tax (VAT), which is a type of sales tax. A separate tax is charged at each discrete stage of production and/or distribution based on the increased value (i.e., value added) occurring at that stage. Other taxes that a company might incur include a transfer tax (in the event of the sale of a company) and perhaps, in the future, an Internet transaction tax on sales.

VI. BANKRUPTCY LAWS

Bankruptcy, or insolvency, affects many organizations each year.[27] A company becomes insolvent if it does not have enough assets to pay its debts or if it cannot pay its debts on their contractual due dates. The terms *bankruptcy* and *insolvency* are often used interchangeably, but in some jurisdictions, such as the United Kingdom, *bankruptcy* refers only to personal insolvency while the general term *insolvency* applies to both corporate and personal insolvency. In addition to the typical financial problems that may force a firm into bankruptcy, management teams may be able to use the bankruptcy laws to protect either the firm's stakeholders or its management.

Insolvency laws vary from country to country but generally insolvency begins when a firm has not been able to meet scheduled payments on its debt. Insolvency may also occur when a firm's projections of cash flows indicate that it will not be able to meet debt payments at some time in the near future. The management and the board of directors are the key decision makers in this process. The major creditors may be involved in the decision concerning insolvency in many cases, and the creditors will force the firm into insolvency in some cases.

Creditors are typically divided into classes based on the seniority or priority of their claims on the distressed company's assets. Secured creditors have a legal security interest in specific assets (i.e., specified in a mortgage or lien) and can take possession of those assets in the event of default of the debt related to those assets. Unsecured creditors do not have an interest in any specific assets, but rather a general claim on any remaining assets after the secured assets are removed. Senior debt is paid before junior debt, and subordinated debt is generally the last to get paid. A listing of the priority of claims in the event of a company's liquidation is provided later in this section.

A. Critical Issues in a Business Bankruptcy Decision

Some of the critical issues that management, the board of directors, and creditors need to address in a bankruptcy include:

- Is the firm's inability to meet scheduled debt payments a temporary cash flow problem, or is it a permanent problem caused by long-term economic and business trends?
- If the problem is temporary, a short-term restructuring arrangement may work, but the impact on the long-term value of the firm must be considered.
- The company may be worth more if liquidated; thus, selling off its pieces may maximize its value to both the bondholders and shareholders.
- Which is the proper procedure for bankruptcy filing if it is required—formal or informal?
- Who will be in charge of the firm during the reorganization—existing management, a special bankruptcy trustee, or special restructuring management?
- What type of bankruptcy is most appropriate for the organization in question?

27. Bankruptcy legislation covers organizations of all kinds, as well as individuals. For the purposes of this book, the primary focus will be on business bankruptcy. This discussion uses US bankruptcy as a model for the overall discussion. Specific issues regarding insolvency or bankruptcy should be researched in the country involved.

B. Bondholders' Rights

The bondholders' rights in bankruptcy are normally senior to those of the equity holders, especially if the bondholders have liens or mortgages on assets owned by the distressed firm. The creditors of a firm generally have the right to force a firm into bankruptcy if scheduled debt payments are not made or if the condition of the firm is such that debt payments may be in default in the near future. This is known as an *involuntary bankruptcy* and is initiated when three or more creditors of the firm petition the federal bankruptcy court to begin proceedings against the firm. This process is actually quite rare in the United States, as creditors that initiate unjustified involuntary bankruptcy proceedings may be held liable for damages to the firm. Voluntary bankruptcy, where the management of the firm petitions the courts for bankruptcy protection, is generally the norm.

C. Shareholders' Rights

Shareholders generally have limited rights in the event of a firm's financial distress. They have the lowest-priority claim on both the earnings stream and the assets of the firm. Preferred stockholders have a higher claim on the firm's assets in liquidation, relative to common shareholders. There are cases where firms under reorganization have been turned over to the creditors and all, or virtually all, of the claims of the shareholders were voided in the process.

D. Types of Bankruptcy in the United States

In the United States, there are several types of bankruptcy available for corporations, municipalities, and individuals. The following are the most common:

- **Chapter 7:** Liquidation of a firm
- **Chapter 9:** Financially distressed municipalities (e.g., city, county, and state government bankruptcies)
- **Chapter 11:** Business reorganization
- **Chapter 13:** Adjustment of debts for individuals with regular income (e.g., personal bankruptcy)
- **Chapter 15:** Establishment of bankruptcy trustees for bankruptcies that involve companies, assets, or individuals in more than one country

Firms filing for bankruptcy have a choice between liquidation under Chapter 7 of the US Bankruptcy Code and reorganization under Chapter 11 of the code. The firm's management makes the initial choice of the type of bankruptcy to file. The reorganization procedure in bankruptcy is designed to allow failing firms that are in temporary financial difficulty, but are worth saving, to continue operating while the claims of the creditors are settled using a collective procedure.

1. CHAPTER 11 BANKRUPTCY (REORGANIZATION)

When a firm files to reorganize under Chapter 11, the existing management typically remains in control. Creditors may petition the bankruptcy court to appoint a trustee, but they must show grounds for suspecting that management is stealing the firm's assets or making preferential transfers to favored creditors. Incompetence of the existing management in running the business is not considered a sufficient reason for appointing a trustee.

Firms that file under Chapter 11 must adopt a reorganization plan. There are two separate procedures for formulating such a plan: the unanimous consent procedure and the cram-down procedure.

a. Unanimous Consent Procedure

Under the unanimous consent procedure, all classes of creditors and equity holders must consent to the reorganization plan, with a two-thirds vote of all members in each class required for consent. The assumption under this plan is that the firm's assets will have a higher value if it reorganizes and continues operating than if it liquidates.

Management is in a strong bargaining position in the negotiations over the reorganization plan because only management can propose a plan during the first four months of the filing, and extensions of this time frame are often granted in this process. Only after all parties have voted on management's initial plan, which may take another two months, can other parties propose alternative plans.

Management can threaten to transfer the firm's bankruptcy filing from Chapter 11 to Chapter 7 if creditors do not agree to the plan. This threat is often most effective in prodding unsecured creditors to agree since they may receive little or nothing in liquidation due to their position in the liquidation hierarchy. Finally, management usually remains in control of the firm during this entire process. Secured creditors may fear that the market value of their lien assets will decline below the market value of their liabilities if the process drags on.

b. Cram-Down Procedure

The cram-down procedure is generally executed by secured creditors and comes into play when a reorganization plan fails to meet the standard for approval by all classes under the unanimous consent procedure, or when the firm is insolvent and the old equity must be eliminated. In a cram-down case, if at least one class of creditors has voted in favor of a plan, then the court may confirm the plan (or a modified version of it) as long as each dissenting class is treated fairly and equitably. The fair and equitable standard closely reflects the absolute priority rule, covered later in this chapter, in that it requires that all unsecured creditors either receive full payment on the face value of their claims, or that all lower rankings receive nothing. It also requires that secured creditors retain their pre-bankruptcy liens on assets or that they receive periodic cash payments equal to the value of their claims.

Cram-down plans usually involve higher transaction costs than unanimous consent plans because the bankruptcy court is likely to require appraisals by outside experts and more court hearings before approving them.

2. CHAPTER 7 BANKRUPTCY (LIQUIDATION)

As opposed to a Chapter 11 reorganization, which strives to preserve the firm as a going entity, Chapter 7 liquidation is a total shutdown of the firm and the orderly liquidation of its assets.

Chapter 7 of the US Bankruptcy Code is designed to accomplish three objectives:

· Provide safeguards against the withdrawal of assets by the owners of the bankrupt firm.

· Provide for an equitable distribution of the assets among creditors.

· Allow insolvent debtors to discharge all of their obligations and start over unhampered by a burden of prior debt.

The distribution of assets in liquidation under Chapter 7 of the code is governed by the following priority of claims (also known as the *absolute priority rule*):

1. Secured creditors are entitled to the proceeds of the sale of specific property pledged for a lien or a mortgage. If the proceeds do not fully satisfy the secured creditors' claims, then the remaining balance of such claims is treated as a general creditor claim, under item #9 below.

2. Trustee's costs to administer and operate the bankrupt firm are reimbursed next.

3. Next are expenses incurred after an involuntary liquidation has begun but before a trustee is appointed.

4. Wages are paid to workers if earned within three months prior to the filing of the bankruptcy petition (subject to current limits).

5. Claims for unpaid contributions to employee benefit plans that should have been paid within six months prior to filing are upheld. These claims, plus wages in item #4, may not exceed current per-wage-earner limits.

6. Unsecured claims for customer deposits, not to exceed current maximum limits, are honored next.

7. Taxes due to federal, state, county, and any other government agencies are paid.

8. Unfunded pension plan liabilities have a claim priority over that of the general creditors for an amount up to 30% of the book value of the common and preferred equity. Any remaining, unfunded pension claims are ranked with the general creditors.

9. Next are general, or unsecured, creditors, which include holders of trade credit, unsecured loans, the unsatisfied portion of secured loans, unfunded pension liabilities, and debenture bonds. This is the final category before equity holders. Holders of subordinated debt also fall into this category, but their claims may be junior to certain holders of senior debt.

10. Preferred stockholders can receive an amount up to the par value of the preferred stock.

11. Common stockholders receive the remaining funds, if any.

E. Formal versus Informal Bankruptcy Procedures

Bankruptcy procedures can be either formal or informal.

1. FORMAL BANKRUPTCY

In a formal bankruptcy procedure, the case is filed and taken before a bankruptcy court for adjudication. The assets are distributed in accordance with the absolute priority rule as outlined in Chapter 7 of the US Bankruptcy Code. The priorities of claims are outlined in the preceding section. There are several types of formal procedures:

- **Free-Fall:** In this case, a firm files or is forced into bankruptcy and has no structured plan for coming out of bankruptcy.

- **Prearranged:** In this case, management has arranged a tentative deal with some of the creditors or parties, but not with all of them. Generally, these deals are done on an informal basis and are not legally binding.

- **Prepackaged:** In this case, management files with the SEC a formal plan that all classes of creditors have voted on and accepted. Essentially, the firm goes to court with all of the details worked out and with everyone agreeing to the plan.

2. INFORMAL BANKRUPTCY

It is possible to perform a reorganization or a liquidation informally. An informal reorganization typically involves a firm that is fundamentally sound, but is undergoing temporary financial difficulties. This is often done outside of bankruptcy in an agreed-upon write-off of some portion of the firm's debts by its creditors.

The firm's creditors work directly with management to establish a plan for returning the firm to a sound financial basis. These plans usually involve some restructuring of the firm's debt, with creditors agreeing either to reduce or reschedule debt payments in order to ensure the firm's continuing operation.

Informal liquidation or assignment is an alternative to Chapter 7 liquidation procedures. In this case, title to the distressed firm's assets is transferred to a third party (called an *assignee* or *trustee*) who liquidates the assets through a sale or public auction. The assignee/trustee then distributes the proceeds to creditors on a pro rata basis, according to the seniority of the claims. The informal liquidation is usually only appropriate for smaller firms and does not automatically result in a full and legal discharge of all the debtor's liabilities.

VII. SUMMARY

Financial regulations impact the products and services available to treasury professionals. Subsequently, treasury professionals should strive to have a working knowledge of the key areas of financial regulation. The evolving nature of the regulatory environment, as precipitated by changes in financial markets, along with cross-border variation in regulations implies that treasury professionals will need to continually update their knowledge.

This chapter provided an overview of the legal and regulatory issues that impact FIs and their treasury management customers on a daily basis. This included a discussion of financial services regulators both globally and within the United States. The chapter closed with an overview of corporate tax issues and a discussion of insolvency.

APPENDIX 2.1: SEPA MEMBER STATES[28]

COUNTRY/TERRITORY	BIC[29]	IBAN	CURRENCY CODE
Åland Islands	FI	FI	EUR
Austria	AT	AT	EUR
Azores	PT	PT	EUR
Belgium	BE	BE	EUR
Bulgaria	BG	BG	BGN
Canary Islands	ES	ES	EUR
Croatia	HR	HR	HRK
Cyprus	CY	CY	EUR
Czech Republic	CZ	CZ	CZK
Denmark	DK	DK	DKK
Estonia	EE	EE	EUR
Finland	FI	FI	EUR
France	FR	FR	EUR
French Guiana	GF	FR	EUR
Germany	DE	DE	EUR
Gibraltar	GI	GI	GIP
Greece	GR	GR	EUR
Guadeloupe	GP	FR	EUR
Hungary	HU	HU	HUF
Iceland	IS	IS	ISK
Ireland	IE	IE	EUR
Isle of Man	IM	GB	GBP
Italy	IT	IT	EUR

28. This information was retrieved in July 2016 from the website for the European Payments Council (www.europeanpaymentscouncil.edu). In July 2016, the United Kingdom had recently voted to leave the EU (i.e., Brexit). Despite this vote, the timeline for the United Kingdom's official eventual exit from the EU remains unclear at the time of this writing.

29. The BIC and IBAN columns include the country code used in the Bank Identification Code (BIC) and International Bank Account Number (IBAN) for each country/territory. BIC and IBAN are discussed in Chapter 3, Banks and Financial Institutions. The currency code identifies the base currency of each country/territory.

COUNTRY/TERRITORY	BIC	IBAN	CURRENCY CODE
Jersey	JE	GB	GBP
Latvia	LV	LV	LVL
Liechtenstein	LI	LI	CHF
Lithuania	LT	LT	LTL
Luxembourg	LU	LU	EUR
Madeira	PT	PT	EUR
Malta	MT	MT	EUR
Martinique	MQ	FR	EUR
Mayotte	YT	FR	EUR
Monaco	MC	MC	EUR
Netherlands	NL	NL	EUR
Norway	NO	NO	NOK
Poland	PL	PL	PLN
Portugal	PT	PT	EUR
Réunion	RE	FR	EUR
Romania	RO	RO	RON
Saint Barthélemy	BL	FR	EUR
Saint Martin (French part)	MF	FR	EUR
Saint Pierre and Miquelon	PM	FR	EUR
San Marino	SM	SM	EUR
Slovakia	SK	SK	EUR
Slovenia	SI	SI	EUR
Spain	ES	ES	EUR
Sweden	SE	SE	SEK
Switzerland	CH	CH	CHF
United Kingdom	GB	GB	GBP

CHAPTER 3
Banks and Financial Institutions

I. INTRODUCTION

II. FINANCIAL INSTITUTIONS: FUNCTIONS AND SERVICES

    A. Global Financial Institutions (FIs)

    B. Commercial Banks

    C. Credit Unions

    D. Investment Banks and Brokerage Firms

    E. Special-Purpose Financial Institutions

III. SUMMARY

I. INTRODUCTION

This chapter discusses the roles and services provided by financial institutions (FIs). In short, FIs help firms obtain capital, invest funds, and manage treasury operations via various products and services. Specific types of FIs described in this chapter include commercial banks, investment banks, credit unions, insurance companies, and finance companies. The terms *FI* and *bank* are used interchangeably to refer to an organization offering financial services to the public. Explicit names like *insurance company, broker-dealer,* or *investment company* refer to a particular type of FI.

II. FINANCIAL INSTITUTIONS: FUNCTIONS AND SERVICES

This section begins with a discussion of global FIs. The remaining sections describe the functions, services, and organizational types of FIs. Changes in financial regulations have blurred the lines that once differentiated the various types of FIs.

A. Global Financial Institutions (FIs)

A global FI operates in multiple countries in more than one region, providing services to both domestic and multinational corporations. Differences in banking structures and financial regulations may impact the way in which global FIs offer services in certain countries. This is because a global FI is required to follow the guidelines of the country in which it is operating, no matter where the global FI is headquartered. Banking systems in most countries have a few large FIs operating on a national basis. Although the requirements for opening bank accounts may vary by country, the general practice is to follow the KYC (or "know your customer") guidelines based on standards established by the Financial Action Task Force (FATF). The FATF makes recommendations on customer due diligence, and each country determines how those obligations will be imposed. Under the FATF recommendations, FIs are prohibited from holding anonymous accounts and are required to conduct due diligence on customers when opening accounts, when carrying out transactions above certain limits, or when there is suspicion of illegal activity. The FATF recommends that FIs perform the following due diligence measures:[1]

- Identify a customer's identity, using independent source documents, data, or information for verification.
- Identify the beneficial account owner and understand the ownership and control structure of the customer for legal persons and arrangements.
- Understand and obtain information on the purpose and nature of the intended business relationship.
- Conduct ongoing due diligence on the business relationship and transactions undertaken.

The relationship between global FIs and their customers can also vary by country. For example, global FIs operating in certain countries (e.g., Austria, Germany, and Switzerland) are permitted to own a minor or even a controlling ownership position in corporations. Also, many countries allow global FIs to lend a large percentage of their capital base to a single customer (generally referred to as a *legal lending limit*). Though these guidelines vary, global FIs often are allowed to lend up to 25% of their capital base to any one nonrelated company. In contrast, the legal lending limit is 15% in the United States.

---

1. From FATF (2012), *International Standards on Combating Money Laundering and the Financing of Terrorism & Proliferation,* published by FATF, updated June 2016 (www.fatf-gafi.org/recommendations.html).

Country-level differences in banking practices can also lead to differences in the way that accounts are handled. For example, in certain countries deposit account holders are allowed to earn interest on positive account balances, and accounts may have automatic overdraft provisions for negative balances.

Certain branches of global FIs may also offer:

- **Foreign currency accounts,** where deposit balances may be held in a currency other than that of the country of location
- **Multicurrency accounts,** in which a customer can use one account to make and receive payments in several currencies
- **Nonresident accounts,** which are owned by people or institutions from outside the country in which the global FI is chartered

Multinational firms must often manage a variety of currencies. Such a firm may be able to manage these currency needs in its home country if foreign currency accounts are offered by its banks. Alternatively, the firm may choose to maintain an account in a foreign currency in the country of that currency, or some combination of the two approaches may be used. A multinational firm's banking structure (i.e., the number and location of FIs it uses to provide operating services) will depend upon the types of collections and disbursements undertaken by the firm, the locations and currencies of the financing and investments utilized by the firm, and the legal and tax regulations of the specific countries involved.

B. Commercial Banks

A commercial bank is an FI that accepts deposits and makes commercial loans. Commercial banks include small, single-site community banks with several million dollars in assets and large, global FIs with trillions in assets. The rules and charters governing commercial banks vary across countries. In the United States, commercial banks must possess a federal or state charter.

The primary services offered by commercial banks include depository accounts and credit services. Additional service areas may include transaction processing, information reporting, trade services, foreign exchange (FX), financial risk management, and fiduciary services. And this is not an exhaustive list—the services offered by FIs will likely continue to grow to meet clients' needs.

1. DEPOSIT ACCOUNTS

Commercial banks commonly offer two basic types of depository accounts:

- Demand deposit accounts or current accounts (referred to as *checking accounts* in the United States)
- Time deposit accounts or noncurrent accounts

a. Demand Deposit Accounts (DDAs) or Current Accounts

A DDA provides a store of value when receiving deposits and a vehicle to facilitate intercompany funds transfers or payments made to vendors. Methods of payment include cash, check, debit card, internal book transfer, or electronic transfer.

DDAs are interest-bearing in many countries, including the United States. For many decades, however, this was not the case as Regulation Q (Reg Q) prohibited FIs operating in the United States from paying interest on DDAs held by for-profit companies. In lieu of interest, corporate account holders received earnings credits, which were used to offset bank service charges. The passage of the Dodd-Frank Act in 2010 has since repealed Reg Q. Still, most US-based firms continue to be compensated for funds held in DDAs with earnings credits.

Another major difference in US and non-US DDAs is the way in which overdrafts are handled. An overdraft occurs when items are presented against a DDA in excess of the balance in that account. In most countries, the general practice is to incorporate both an investment rate and a credit agreement with the DDA so that any positive balances are paid interest, while negative DDA balances result in an automatic loan and an interest charge. Such an arrangement is generally unavailable in the United States for corporate DDAs, unless specific lending arrangements have been previously agreed upon.

b. Time Deposit Accounts (TDAs) or Noncurrent Accounts

TDAs are deposits maintained at an FI for a specified period of time. Early withdrawal is allowed only with prior notification. Further, an early withdrawal may result in a penalty.

A certificate of deposit (CD) is an example of a TDA. Given a deposited amount, a CD holder earns a fixed or variable interest rate over a specified period of time. For CDs under $100,000, the interest rate is usually fixed and nonnegotiable. Interest rates and maturities on CDs valued at more than $100,000 are frequently negotiable, and the interest rate may be fixed or variable.

Other types of TDAs include savings accounts and money market deposit accounts (MMDAs). MMDAs allow firms to earn a competitive market rate of interest on cash balances. While MMDA balances are liquid and covered by deposit insurance, account holders are limited to six transfers or pre-authorized withdrawals (debits) per month. If the transaction limit is exceeded, the FI may impose fees or convert the account to a DDA. Although transfers and pre-authorized debits are limited, in-person teller transactions are unlimited.

c. Nonresident Accounts

A nonresident account may be either a current or noncurrent account. Common uses for nonresident accounts include currency hedging and commercial collections/payments. Nonresident accounts are held at an FI in a given country by an entity whose legal headquarters, residence, or tax status is outside of the country where the account is maintained. For example, a firm incorporated in the United Kingdom might keep a nonresident account with a Chinese bank. Rules regarding nonresident bank accounts vary by country, currency, and account purpose.

d. Account Identification

Account identification is another key aspect that is related to the deposit account services provided by FIs. Since most financial transactions involve transferring value from one bank account to another, it is important to be able to uniquely identify specific banks and the related accounts. This is typically done through a bank identification code and individual account numbers within each bank. Bank identification codes vary not only from country to country but also from bank to bank, which can lead to difficulties in uniquely identifying specific accounts. A number of generally accepted standards have developed in various parts of the world to help deal with this issue:

- The Bank Identification Code, or BIC, is a unique identifier that specifies the FIs involved—in some cases down to the branch level—in a financial transaction. The most commonly used BIC is known as the *SWIFT code* because the system is administered by the Society for Worldwide Interbank Financial Telecommunication (SWIFT).

  A SWIFT code consists of eight or eleven characters, as follows:

    o First four characters—bank code (alphabetic only)

    o Next two characters—ISO 3166-1 alpha-2 country code (alphabetic only)

    o Next two characters—location code (alphanumeric)

    o Last three characters—branch code, optional ("XXX" for primary office) (alphanumeric)

  When an eight-character code is used, it refers to the primary or head office of a given bank.

- A routing transit number (RTN)[2] is a nine-digit bank code used in the United States to route checks and electronic transactions to the proper FI. US banks often have an RTN and a SWIFT BIC. Canadian banks use an eight-digit system managed by Payments Canada in a similar fashion.

- The International Bank Account Number (IBAN) is a way to identify bank accounts across national borders. It was originally adopted by the European Committee for Banking Standards, and later adopted as an international standard by the International Organization for Standardization (ISO). As with the BIC, the current standard is managed by SWIFT. The IBAN was initially developed to simplify payments within the European Union under SEPA. It has since also been implemented by most of Europe and many other countries, especially in the Middle East and in the Caribbean.

  The IBAN consists of up to 34 alphanumeric characters: first, the two-letter ISO 3166-1 alpha-2 country code, then two check digits, and finally, a country-specific Basic Bank Account Number (BBAN). The BBAN format is decided by each national banking community under the restriction that it must be of a fixed length of case-insensitive alphanumeric characters. It includes the domestic bank account number, branch identifier, and potential routing information.

2. CREDIT SERVICES

A primary function provided by commercial banks is financial intermediation, in which a bank lends funds deposited by savers to entities needing capital. Commercial banks offer a wide range of business loans that vary with:

- Borrower type
- Use of proceeds
- Loan maturity

For example, commercial bank loans may have a medium- or longer-term maturity and may be secured with collateral. Loan repayment may be made with the borrower's general operating cash flow, but in some cases repayment may be restricted to cash flows generated by the asset being financed. Loans are usually collateralized by the company's property, plant, or equipment, but the collateral may be limited to the specific asset being financed (e.g., equipment loans or property loans). Leasing divisions of banks provide an alternative to medium- and long-term loans for financing capital equipment.

---

2. RTNs are also often referred to as *ABA numbers* because the system was originally developed and managed by the American Bankers Association. The system is now managed by Accuity.

Short-term business loans (usually with a term of less than a year) may be made to finance investments in operating working capital (e.g., accounts receivable and inventory). Such loans may take a couple of different forms:

- With a term loan or term note, a business borrows a specific amount to be repaid by a specific date.

- With a revolving line of credit (i.e., a revolver), a business can borrow up to a specified amount, repay all or part of the outstanding balance, and borrow again in the future. The revolver may have a clean-up period provision in which the borrower must pay down the balance on the credit line for a relatively short period of time.

Another way that FIs can facilitate the acquisition of credit for corporate customers is through the issuance of commercial paper (CP) and municipal securities (commonly called *munis*). CP consists of unsecured, discounted, short-term promissory notes issued by companies or commercial bank holding companies. FIs typically act as agents to place CP with investors. CP is rated for default risk by credit rating agencies, and the rating has a significant effect on the interest rate. Munis (i.e., sub-sovereign securities) are bonds or notes issued by city, county, or state government entities and generally have some type of income tax exemption for any interest paid on them. Municipals are also rated for default risk.

FIs also offer loan sales and private placements. Loan sales involve the structuring of lending facilities so that short-term loans can be sold to other banks and investors. Private placements are the direct sales of long-term notes to institutional investors (i.e., insurance companies and hedge funds).

3. TRANSACTION-PROCESSING SERVICES

Many FIs provide transaction-processing services related to check, card, and electronic payments. In most countries, FIs control access to the various payment systems, and any payment other than a cash transaction must go through an FI at some point in the process.

4. INFORMATION REPORTING

Financial information is critical for efficient management of a firm's treasury operations. FIs provide a variety of information reporting services that may include both bank-specific and external information. Information reporting services include account balances, transaction details, loans and lines of credit, foreign exchange rates, and investment rates. Balance reporting may be limited to account balances at a single bank, or can include balances from multiple domestic and international banks. FI information reporting solutions are also used to initiate payments and make decisions on exception items.

5. TRADE SERVICES

Large FIs often provide a wide range of services to facilitate the payment and collection of trade obligations. These are often used for international business, but sometimes they are also used domestically. Exhibit 3.1 outlines a few of these services.

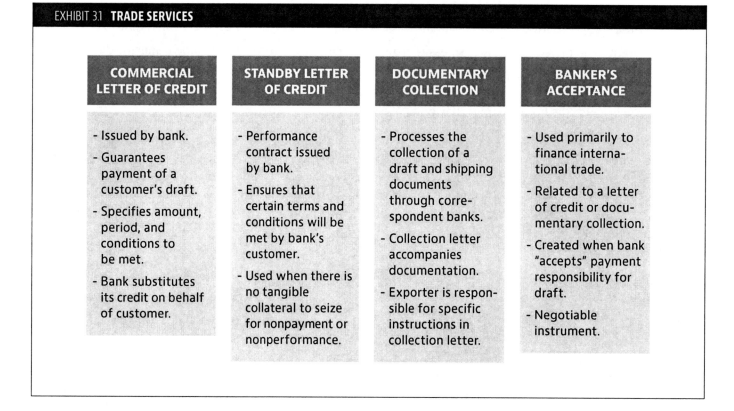

COMMERCIAL LETTER OF CREDIT	STANDBY LETTER OF CREDIT	DOCUMENTARY COLLECTION	BANKER'S ACCEPTANCE
- Issued by bank. - Guarantees payment of a customer's draft. - Specifies amount, period, and conditions to be met. - Bank substitutes its credit on behalf of customer.	- Performance contract issued by bank. - Ensures that certain terms and conditions will be met by bank's customer. - Used when there is no tangible collateral to seize for nonpayment or nonperformance.	- Processes the collection of a draft and shipping documents through correspondent banks. - Collection letter accompanies documentation. - Exporter is responsible for specific instructions in collection letter.	- Used primarily to finance international trade. - Related to a letter of credit or documentary collection. - Created when bank "accepts" payment responsibility for draft. - Negotiable instrument.

EXHIBIT 3.1 TRADE SERVICES

6. FOREIGN EXCHANGE (FX) SERVICES

Large FIs with global networks are major participants in the FX markets, as they offer FX services to customers to facilitate international business and trade. These FX services allow companies to buy or sell internationally traded currencies for either immediate (spot market) or future (forward market) use.

7. FINANCIAL RISK MANAGEMENT SERVICES

Financial risk management services help mitigate the effects of adverse changes in interest rates, FX rates, and commodity prices. Such services include instruction on potential risk mitigation techniques, which might involve the use of financial derivatives. Financial derivatives include forwards, futures, swaps, and options. These instruments are known as *derivatives* because their market value is derived from an underlying asset (e.g., a currency, a commodity, or a security).

8. FIDUCIARY SERVICES

A fiduciary is an individual or institution to which certain property is given to hold in trust according to a trust agreement. Not all fiduciaries are FIs, but FIs often provide fiduciary services (or trust services). A fiduciary has duties and responsibilities that are legally enforceable and that must be executed in a prudent and timely manner.

Fiduciary services provided to corporate customers include:

- Establishing and managing employee pension plans or qualified employee benefit plans
- Acting as a corporate trustee for corporate bond or preferred stock issues
- Monitoring compliance with bond indenture agreements, which are the contractual arrangements between bond issuers and bondholders
- Acting as a transfer agent by keeping records of each purchase and sale of stocks and bonds, including maintaining records of a corporation's shareholders by name, address, and number of shares
- Acting as a registrar by compiling and maintaining lists of current stockholders and bondholders for the purpose of remitting dividend and interest payments
- Acting as a paying agent, whereby an FI receives funds from an issuer of stocks or bonds to pay dividends to stockholders and to pay principal and interest to bondholders
- Offering custody services (such as providing safekeeping for securities), and buying, selling, receiving, and delivering securities based on terms outlined in a custody agreement

C. Credit Unions

Credit unions are member-owned, not-for-profit financial cooperatives that can provide financial services similar to those offered by other types of FIs. Credit unions can also provide access to various payment networks to affiliated clients.

Membership in a credit union was originally restricted to individuals with a common affiliation, such as an employer, association, community organization, or geographic location, but membership was later expanded to include businesses. Members/owners often enjoy higher savings and lower lending rates compared to banks.

Credit unions operate in over 100 countries[3] and are chartered by either federal or state agencies. In the United States, the National Credit Union Administration (NCUA) charters and supervises federal credit unions (about 60% of the total), while the remaining 40% are chartered at the state level. Additionally, NCUA insures the deposits for all federally chartered credit unions and almost all of the state-chartered corporations through the National Credit Union Share Insurance Fund.

D. Investment Banks and Brokerage Firms

Investment banks and brokerage firms provide a wide range of financial services related to the issuance and trading of securities. Both types of FIs are discussed below.

1. INVESTMENT BANKS

The functions offered by investment banks are generally much broader than the narrow range of investment banking services typically offered by commercial banks. Investment banking services provided include (1) securities underwriting; (2) facilitating mergers, acquisitions, divestitures, and other corporate reorganizations; and (3) acting as a broker/financial advisor for institutional clients. Investment banking services may be offered through the investment banking arm of a commercial bank's holding company.

3. From "International Credit Union System" on the website for the World Council of Credit Unions (http://www.woccu.org/about/intlcusystem, accessed August 15, 2016).

The investment banking process relating to the issuance of stocks and bonds generally has three distinct components: origination, underwriting, and distribution. A discussion of each follows.

a. Origination

During the origination phase of security issuance, the investment bank consults with the issuer regarding the characteristics of the issue and any underlying documents. The investment bank also monitors market conditions and advises the issuer about the best time to bring the issue to market in order to maximize issuance price and funds raised.

b. Underwriting

Underwriting is the act of purchasing all or part of a block of securities issued by a company. In effect, the investment bank is an intermediary between the issuer and the investing public. In many cases the original investment bank will seek to reduce its risk by inviting other investment banks to join the underwriting process. This forms an investment banking syndicate.

The two main types of underwriting include full underwriting and best-efforts underwriting. Under a full-underwriting arrangement, the investment bank or syndicate owns the entire issue. The issuer then receives its funds. At that point, the investment bank or syndicate assumes the price and marketability risks associated with the issue. *Price risk* means it may not be possible to sell the entire security issue at the anticipated market price. *Marketing risk* refers to the probability that not all shares will be sold. Both types of risk jeopardize profitability.

In lieu of assuming price and marketing risks, the investment bank or syndicate may assist the issuer on a best-efforts basis. In this case, the issuer pays a fee directly to the investment bank as compensation for advising the firm and marketing the issue. The investment bank does not underwrite the issue; rather, it simply helps place shares through a group of brokerage firms.

c. Distribution

Distribution involves the sale of securities by an investment bank or a syndicate. When a syndicate is formed, one of the investment banks serves as the lead bank (also called the *lead underwriter*). The lead bank assumes most of the management functions and receives most of the fees. Once the underwriting syndicate owns the new securities, each member of the syndicate uses its distribution system to sell the issue.

For full-service investment banks that offer both the underwriting/distribution function (referred to as the *sell* side of the house) and the investment advisory or management function (referred to as the *buy* side), there is a potential for conflict of interest; the sell side may influence the recommendations made by the buy side in order to enhance profitability.

Ideally, research or recommendations provided by the buy side should be independent from the sell side. Both sides should be separated by internal controls and procedures (sometimes referred to as a "wall") that prevent each party from acquiring material nonpublic information (MNPI) from the other side of the transaction and acting upon it.

Insider trading is the illegal trading of securities based on MNPI. Enforcement of insider trading varies by country. In the United States, the SEC monitors and disciplines those engaging in insider trading and enforces related regulations. In the United Kingdom, enforcement is handled by the Financial Conduct Authority (FCA).

It is important to understand that merely possessing MNPI is not a crime. The crime resides in the act of using the information. There is no violation of the law unless an analyst or trader acts on MNPI. Having MNPI but not using it sometimes occurs when a research analyst is "brought over" to work for the underwriting department in order to focus on a particular company. This is known as "bringing someone over the wall" since the individual is being moved from one side of the internal control process (the "wall") to the other. The purpose of such a transfer is to add a knowledgeable opinion to the underwriting process, thereby adding value to it. Once the underwriting process is complete, the research employee who has been brought "over the wall" is not allowed to comment on any information learned in the underwriting process until it has become public knowledge.

2. INSTITUTIONAL AND RETAIL BROKERAGE FIRMS

Brokerage firms specialize in the sale of securities by executing the distribution of an investment bank's intermediation function. The distribution function applies to the initial public offering (IPO) of securities by privately owned firms becoming publicly owned companies, and to existing public companies issuing new securities and debt offerings.

Brokerage firms can be institutional or retail brokers. Institutional brokers' clients are mostly large institutions (e.g., hedge funds or large corporations). Institutional brokers generally transact in large blocks of securities. Retail brokers typically handle smaller investment accounts and transactions for individuals, and may have offices in multiple locations, as well as research services to assist retail clients. Retail commissions (as a percentage of the transaction) are relatively high compared to those charged by institutional brokers because of the increased number of individual retail transactions to process and since the average dollar size per transaction is smaller. The rate charged by institutional brokers may be lower, but the actual commissions received will be higher, due to the larger dollar volumes of the institutional transactions.

Brokerage firms can be further categorized into either discount or full-service firms. Discount brokerages let investors make trades at reduced prices, but provide little or no investment advice. Full-service brokerages have research analysts that provide investment advice to institutions and individual investors. As noted in the previous section, research is for sale and has some guarantee of independence; there should be no linkages between the part of the firm that offers investment advice and the part that is involved in the distribution of new securities. Some full-service brokerages also manage investment portfolios for institutions and individuals.

E. Special-Purpose Financial Institutions

Other miscellaneous FIs focus on specific markets. Examples of these special-purpose FIs include industrial banks, captive finance companies, factors, insurance companies, and asset-based lenders.

1. INDUSTRIAL BANKS

An industrial bank (or an industrial loan company) is an FI with a limited scope of services. Industrial banks sell certificates called *investment shares* and can also accept customer deposits. They then lend the deposits out via installment loans to consumers and small businesses. Industrial banks accept deposits but they do not offer checking accounts. Because of their limited services, industrial banks do not fall under general banking regulatory authority, are locally chartered, and may be owned by nonbank holding companies.

2. CAPTIVE FINANCE COMPANIES

A captive finance company is a type of industrial bank that is a subsidiary of a large industrial corporation and that finances purchases solely of the corporation's products. These FIs typically raise funds in the CP market and lend to other companies and individuals that purchase products from the parent corporation. Having a captive finance company allows the parent firm to extend credit to customers without putting itself directly at risk. Many automobile producers operate captive finance companies.

3. FACTORS

A factor is another type of nonbank financial intermediary. Factors are entities that provide short-term financing to companies by purchasing accounts receivable at a discount.

4. INSURANCE COMPANIES

Insurance companies are also considered nonbank FIs as they are significant investors in the commercial real estate and bond markets. Insurance companies now compete with banks for short- and medium-term loans. They provide mortgage funding, leasing services, guaranteed investment contracts (similar to bank CDs, generally paying interest for one to five years), and universal life insurance policies with long-term savings features.

5. ASSET-BASED LENDERS

FIs, including banks and nonbank lenders, participate in asset-based lending (ABL). With ABL, loans are secured by collateral that is pledged by the borrower. The amount of credit available to the firm is based on the quality of the collateral, which is usually in the form of accounts receivable or inventory. A borrowing base is determined by multiplying the value of eligible collateral by a percentage rate, known as an *advance rate.* Due to the emphasis on collateral, asset-based lenders monitor the collateral closely and consequently make frequent adjustments to the available credit.

III. SUMMARY

FIs play a critical role in the treasury management environment. This chapter presented an overview of the major types of FIs and the services they provide to treasury professionals. The discussion included a review of commercial banks, credit unions, investment banks and brokerages, and special-purpose financial institutions. Historically, commercial banks have been the predominant FI used by treasury professionals because they provide transaction services as well as credit services, but as regulations have changed, other FIs have gained market share in the treasury services arena.

CHAPTER 4
Payment Systems

I. INTRODUCTION

II. PAYMENT SYSTEMS OVERVIEW
- A. Basic Payments
- B. The Payment Process
- C. Settlement versus Finality
- D. Types of Payments

III. CASH PAYMENTS

IV. CHECK-BASED PAYMENT SYSTEMS
- A. On-Us Check Clearing
- B. Transit Check Clearing
- C. Foreign Checks
- D. Endpoints
- E. Deadlines and Deposit Timing
- F. Availability Schedules
- G. Balances and Float
- H. Other Check-Processing Factors That Influence Availability
- I. Additional Paper-Based Instruments

V. LARGE-VALUE ELECTRONIC FUNDS TRANSFER (EFT) OR WIRE TRANSFER SYSTEMS
- A. Real-Time Gross Settlement (RTGS) Systems
- B. Clearing House Interbank Payments System (CHIPS)
- C. TARGET2 and the Single Euro Payments Area (SEPA)
- D. Continuous Linked Settlement (CLS)
- E. Society for Worldwide Interbank Financial Telecommunication (SWIFT)

I. INTRODUCTION

It is important for treasury professionals to understand payment systems because the movement of funds is a fundamental part of the treasury function. This chapter begins with an overview of the basic aspects of payment systems. Next, the chapter provides a detailed review of the common payment systems, including paper, electronic, and card-based payments. The use of cash as a payment mechanism is also discussed. Although cash is technically not a payment system,[1] cash is an important payment method for many firms. Many retailers have implemented significant handling processes to ensure the safety of cash receipts.

II. Payment Systems Overview

A payment system is a series of processes and technologies that transfers monetary value, using cash substitutes, from one party to another.

For noncash payments, the value being transferred is typically stored in depository accounts at a bank.[2] The bank, in turn, is connected to the various payment systems, and processes payments on behalf of its customers or depositors. As an example, most banks are connected to various electronic and paper-based payment systems, such as Fedwire, ACH, TARGET2, Visa, MasterCard, and many others.

A. Basic Payments

In the simplest case, payments involve four participants:

- The **payor** sends a payment and the payor's account is debited (decreased) for the value of the transaction.
- The **payor's bank** (often referred to as the *paying bank*) processes the value transfer on the payor's behalf.
- The **payee or beneficiary** is the receiver of the payment whose account is credited (increased) for the value of the transaction.
- The **payee's bank** (often referred to as the *depository bank*) processes the transaction on behalf of the payee and generally holds the value in an account.

This simple case is illustrated in the four-corner payment system model shown in Exhibit 4.1.

---

1. The exchange of cash is not a payment system because it does not require the use of any outside agency.
2. The term *bank* is used throughout this chapter, even though the financial institution (FI) involved may not be a bank.

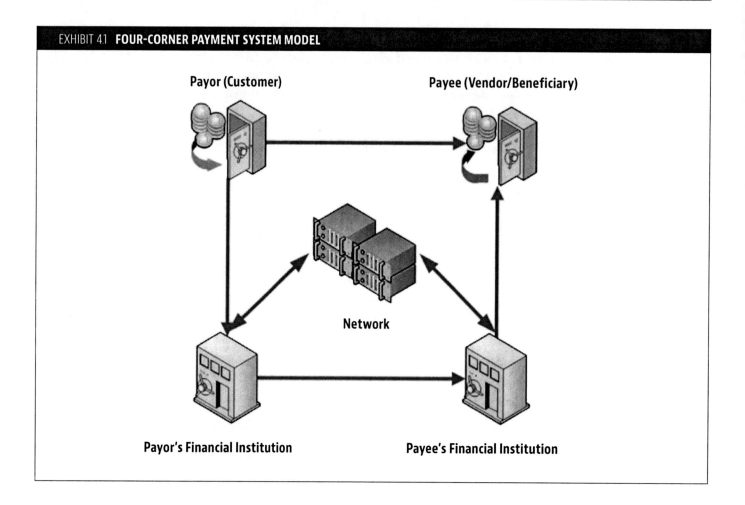

EXHIBIT 4.1 FOUR-CORNER PAYMENT SYSTEM MODEL

Payor (Customer)

Payee (Vendor/Beneficiary)

Network

Payor's Financial Institution

Payee's Financial Institution

While the banks may choose to transfer payment instructions and funds directly with each other, there can be additional parties and intermediaries that help facilitate the transaction. Exhibit 4.1 refers to these intermediaries as the *network*. The network includes central banks (e.g., the US Federal Reserve [the Fed], the European Central Bank [ECB], or the Bank of England) and commercial entities such as the Clearing House Interbank Payments System (CHIPS), Faster Payments, or Visa. The network can also include transaction facilitators (e.g., SWIFT), which transmit information but do not provide funds settlement, and payment systems (e.g., Fedwire in the United States and BOJ-NET in Japan), which include information transmission capabilities and settlement. There may also be entities outside of the four-corner model that participate in the payment process, such as payroll processors, check printers, and systems providers.

B. The Payment Process

From a systems standpoint, there are four elements in the payment process:

- **Payment instructions** consist of the information contained in an electronic transfer (e.g., a wire or automated clearinghouse [ACH] transaction), payment card transaction, or a check. These instructions are from the payor and tell the paying bank to transfer value to the payee through the receiving bank.

- **Payment generation** occurs when the payment instructions are entered into the payment system.
- **Clearing** is the process in which banks use the payment information to transfer money between themselves on behalf of the payor and the beneficiary, either directly or through some external network.
- **Settlement** is the final step in the process and occurs when the beneficiary's bank account is credited and the payor's bank account is charged.

C. Settlement versus Finality

It is important to understand the difference between settlement and finality of payment. *Settlement* refers to the movement of funds from the payor's account to the payee's account. In other words, the payee can use the money involved at settlement. For this reason, the term *availability* can also refer to settlement. *Finality* refers to the point in time at which the funds cannot be taken back or retracted by the payor or the payor's bank. Settlement transitions to finality when a payment is unconditional and irrevocable.

Finality varies depending on the payment system and the parties involved in the transaction. Payment systems that offer immediate and irrevocable value are called *real-time gross settlement (RTGS) systems*. A common example of an RTGS system is a wire transfer system. Others, such as check- or card-based systems, typically provide immediate information, with value following at a later time. But the value is contingent on the payor or the payor's bank not attempting to retract the payment, a right which can exist for several months or more, depending upon the specific payment system.

The actual transfer of funds, or settlement, can be handled in several ways. With domestic transfers (i.e., the parties involved are in the same country), settlement is often handled between the banks using common accounts held at their central bank.

Alternatively, banks can use correspondent accounts to settle their customers' funds transfers. In a correspondent banking relationship, two banks have accounts with each other for the purpose of clearing and settling payments. Generally, smaller banks with limited access to other clearing methods will maintain a correspondent relationship with a larger bank to enable more efficient clearing. In most international funds transfers, correspondent banks play a key role in the settlement process. These correspondent relationships may be reciprocal (i.e., both banks move value both ways and have accounts with each other) or one-way (i.e., a small bank may have an account with a larger bank for clearing purposes).

D. Types of Payments

Payments can be differentiated based on the type of payment system and the parties involved. Both methods of differentiation are discussed in turn.

The various noncash payment systems generally have unique operating characteristics, risks, rules, and settlement mechanisms. The noncash payment types include the following:

- **Checks** are paper-based payments initiated when one party writes a check to pay another. Although they are one of the oldest forms of noncash payment systems, checks are still used throughout the world and are most widely used in the United States.
- **RTGS (real-time gross settlement) or large-value electronic payments** generally refer to wire transfers. Wires are processed individually and in real time (i.e., immediately). Wires have existed since the late 1800s with the invention of the telegraph, but did not become widely used until the early 1900s.

- **Small-value electronic payments,** often referred to as *automated clearinghouse (ACH) payments*, were introduced in the early 1970s as a means to replace checks. ACH payments are value-dated and processed in batches, and typically take one to two days to settle. Same-day ACH is available in the United States for domestic payments of $25,000 or less. Originally ACH payments were intended for "small" payments, such as payroll and consumer transactions. Today, however, the lower cost of ACH transactions has motivated many companies to replace wires and other payment types with ACH transactions.

- **Card-based payments** are payments that settle through one of the large card-processing networks including Visa, MasterCard, China UnionPay, or American Express. Card-based payments may also settle through one of the ATM (automated teller machine) or POS (point-of-sale) systems such as STAR, NYCE, or PULSE in the United States, Interac in Canada, or Telstra in Australia. Originally, card transactions were all credit card payments and were initiated through the presentment of a plastic credit card. Today, card payment methods come in a variety of alternatives, including debit cards, prepaid cards, purchasing cards, virtual cards, ghost cards, and payroll cards—some of which, despite the name, no longer use a physical card.

- **Emerging payments** include mobile wallets, mobile (phone) payments, person-to-person payments, and virtual currencies. Mobile wallets (e.g., Alipay, Google Wallet, Apple Pay) use smartphones and tablets equipped with near field communication (NFC) chips or a bar code. The mobile wallet allows the customer to choose a payment method then tap the phone to a contactless payment device or scan a bar code. Mobile payments allow a user to set up an account with a cell phone provider and transfer money via text message. A personal identification number (PIN) is used for security. Mobile payments do not require a smartphone or a bank account, making the system popular in developing and underbanked countries. Person-to-person payments may be initiated by the payer through a bank (e.g., Quickpay, Popmoney), a nonbank intermediary (e.g., Paypal), or a credit card network (e.g., Visa money transfer). Virtual currencies (e.g., Bitcoin) are in the early stages of development and have gained limited acceptance.

Payments can also be differentiated based upon the identities of the parties involved in the payment transactions:

- **Business-to-business (B2B)** payments move funds from one business to another, typically for vendor payments. While this payment category represents the smallest portion of payment volume, it typically represents the largest segment of payment value. Increasingly, B2B payments are made with electronic payments or via cards.

- **Business-to-consumer (B2C)** payments move funds from businesses to consumers or individuals. An example of a B2C payment is payroll.

- **Consumer-to-business (C2B)** payments move funds from consumers to businesses, typically for purchases and bill payments. Historically, these were largely cash and check payments in the United States, or cash and giro payments[3] in Europe. Now, small-dollar transactions at the point of sale are still often cash, but the majority of the other C2B payments are either card payments at the point of sale or electronic payments made through a bank.

- **Consumer-to-consumer (C2C), or person-to-person (P2P),** payments move funds from one individual to another. Examples include income payments (e.g., babysitting or lawn mowing) and various personal payments (e.g., gifts).

- **Consumer-to-government (C2G)** payments include taxes and other government fees.

- **Business-to-government (B2G)** payments include taxes, fines, and other government fees.

- **Government-to-business (G2B)** payments are usually for vendor payments.

---

3. Giro (or postal giro, since many giro systems are run by the postal system within a country) is a method of transferring money by instructing a bank to directly transfer funds from one bank account to another without the use of checks. Giro payments are initiated by the payor and can be one-time payments or can be recurring standing instructions for a series of payments.

· **Government-to-consumer (G2C)** payments include various government-issued payments such as retirement, social security, and welfare payments. The majority of G2C payments are electronic or card-based.

III. CASH PAYMENTS

In general, cash payments (i.e., those involving currency and coin) are used by consumers to settle small transactions. Cash payments are typically *self-settling*, meaning that the physical transfer of cash provides the clearing network that leads to final settlement (i.e., no banking network is used). Thus, no additional settlement infrastructure is needed for cash transactions. For this reason, cash is generally not considered a separate payment system. Irrespective of cash constituting a specific payment system, cash payments are significant as many types of companies (e.g., retailers, grocers, and restaurants) continue to receive a portion of their payments in the form of cash. In some countries cash represents the prominent payment method for purchasing transactions and for payroll.

A popular misconception is that cash payments are less expensive than other types of payments. Cash represents a security risk. Cash receipts must be safeguarded at the collection point until they can be transported to a bank and deposited into the company's bank account. The cost of this process, which includes items such as locked cash drawers, dual-control procedures, specialized safes, and armored cars, can actually be quite high. Additionally, banks typically charge their corporate customers a fee to receive, count, and verify cash deposits. As a result, cash is a high-cost payment method for most companies.

IV. CHECK-BASED PAYMENT SYSTEMS

Checks (or cheques) are the traditional method that payors, also referred to as *makers* (because they "make" the check), have used to access their bank accounts. While overall check volume is declining, checks are still the primary payment method used for B2B payments in the United States. Checks are also used in many other countries around the world, but the overall volume of checks is much lower in those countries than in the United States.

Depending upon the country, funds from check payments are usually available to depositors in one or two days, but finality can take several weeks or longer, due to stop payment orders and overdraft returns by the paying bank. (See Appendix 4.1 for a more complete list of potential return reasons.)

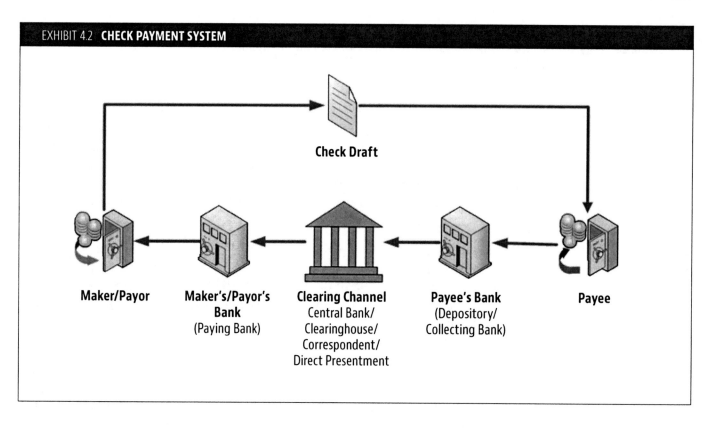

EXHIBIT 4.2 **CHECK PAYMENT SYSTEM**

As illustrated in Exhibit 4.2, the check payment system begins with the deposit or "paying in" of a check—drawn on a domestic bank in local currency—into a payee's account at the payee's bank, referred to as the *bank of first deposit* (also known as the *depository* or *collecting bank*). The check may be deposited either as a physical check or (in the United States) as a check image, using a process referred to as *remote deposit capture (RDC)*.

If the payee has not already scanned the check and deposited it as an electronic image, the check is either scanned at the teller counter, or batched and sent through a reader/sorter at the bank of first deposit, which captures the magnetic ink character recognition (MICR) line information and captures an image of the check. During this scanning process, the amount of the check is captured and added to the information contained in the MICR line on the bottom of each check.

The MICR line is a specially formatted line of machine-readable information on the bottom of a check that contains all the information necessary to process the check through the check-clearing system. It is called the *MICR line* because it is printed with a special magnetic ink used for magnetic ink character recognition, or MICR. Today, many check readers actually use optical character recognition (OCR) to capture the information in a MICR line. Magnetic ink is still used to print the MICR line, however, because of the large number of MICR readers still in use. Check images can only be read via OCR, since the image does not contain any magnetic ink. Exhibit 4.3 illustrates a sample US business check and the elements of the MICR line.[4] Comparable MICR lines are used in other countries.

---

4. US consumer checks differ from business checks in that they are slightly smaller (6 inches versus 8.5 inches) and lack the initial, or auxiliary on-us, field in the MICR line.

EXHIBIT 4.3 SAMPLE US BUSINESS CHECK

```
                                                                                   101
   ANYCOMPANY
   1430 ANY STREET
   ANYTOWN CA 90000                         DATE _____

PAY TO THE                                                    $ [        ]
ORDER OF: _____

_____ DOLLARS

   ANYTOWN BANK
   1000 BANKING WAY
   ANYTOWN CA 90000

MEMO _____                    _____

  ⑈000001010⑈  8 ⑆000024578⑆  1245780 2⑈        ⑈0000000000⑈
```

AUXILIARY ON-US	EPC	ROUTING/ TRANSIT	ON-US / ACCOUNT # / CHECK SERIAL #	AMOUNT
65-46	44	43-32	31-13	POSITION 12-1

FIELDS ARE MADE UP OF POSITIONS

AUXILIARY ON-US FIELD
- This is an eight-digit field used on business checks.
- This number is frequently the check number.
- It assists the drawee bank in providing a variety of account reconciliation services.
- It is a key in providing stop payment and positive pay services.
- It is necessary to prevent check conversion.

EXTERNAL PROCESSING CODE (EPC)
This is a single-digit optional field for special purposes, such as image processing codes, located to the immediate left of the routing number.

ROUTING NUMBER
Also known as the *American Bankers Association (ABA) number* or *routing transit number (RTN)*, the routing number is a nine-digit code that identifies which financial institution the check is drawn upon. The format of the ABA is as follows:

The first two digits of the nine-digit ABA number must be in the ranges 00 through 12, 21 through 32, 61 through 72, or 80.

The digits are assigned as follows:
- 00 is used by the United States government.
- 01 through 12 identify the drawee bank's Federal Reserve district.
- 21 through 32 were assigned only to thrift institutions.
- 61 through 72 are used for electronic transactions.
- 80 is used for traveler's checks.

The third digit represents the particular office of a Federal Reserve Bank serving the drawee bank. The fourth digit historically referred to whether items were given immediate or deferred availability by the Fed.

The following four digits, or digits 5 through 8 of the nine-digit number, designate the specific bank location, served by the designated Federal Reserve office, to which the item must be delivered for payment. Banks can have more than one RTN if they have multiple check-processing locations.

The last digit is known as the *check digit*. This is a mathematical calculation used to verify the accuracy of the routing number.

ON-US/ACCOUNT NUMBER
This field contains the customer account number as assigned to the payor by the drawee bank.

ENCODED AMOUNT OF CHECK
This number should agree with the amount written on the check by the payor. The amount is typically encoded on the check by the depository bank and appears in the lower right-hand corner of the processed check.

After initial capture via scanning or reader/sorter, the checks and/or images are then sorted by the collecting or payee's bank according to the rules of the country's checking system and the clearing channel used to collect the payments, and are sent through the clearing channel as cash letters. This processing is typically done at the bank of first deposit. A cash letter is made up of physical bundles of checks and related control documents. A cash letter form accompanies the bundled checks. The cash letter form includes information such as the depositing institution's routing number, the total dollar amount of items deposited, and the number of items deposited. Although paper checks have historically been submitted to the clearing channel, most items are now sent into the clearing channel via image cash letter. An image cash letter is an electronic file that includes images of the checks being deposited for clearing and the related control documents.

Historically, for settlement to occur, the original check had to be presented to, and be accepted by, the bank on which the check was drawn, referred to as the *paying bank*. Thus, the key event in the check-clearing process was presentment—the physical delivery of a check to the paying bank. This resulted in the creation of a logistical system to physically transport a large number of checks from one bank to another, every night. The term *cash letter* refers to the bundles of physical checks that are sent to a paying bank in exchange for "cash" or some form of bank credit.

This situation has changed in many countries with the introduction of image check processing,[5] which has largely replaced the exchange of physical checks with the exchange of check images. Another result of image check processing has been the development of ancillary services, such as remote deposit capture (RDC). RDC is a service (available primarily in the United States) that allows a payee to scan a check received as payment and transmit the scanned images to a bank for posting and clearing, instead of having to deposit physical checks. Originally designed for larger commercial deposits, RDC is now often available for consumer and small-business depositors as well. Consumers and businesses are now able to deposit checks via images captured on a smartphone.

Regardless of whether the check is paper or an image, value is subtracted from the paying bank's account at the time of presentment through a central bank, a correspondent bank, or some other clearing channel. Following presentment, the paying bank posts the check to the payor's account. Most check processing is automated, and banks rely on account holders to report fraudulent checks, forged endorsements, and alterations.

The paying bank has a limited period of time to conduct a review of the paid check/image and either authorize final payment, or refuse payment and return the check to the bank of first deposit. Returned checks (referred to as *return items*) may be redeposited or charged back to the depositor's account, depending on the return reason. In the United States, banks have until midnight of the business day following the day of receipt of a check (either as an image or a physical document) to complete their review and return any checks, roughly 36 hours.[6] In the United Kingdom, the return deadline is six days from the date the check was deposited at the payee's bank. While other countries have similar rules governing check processing, there are often local variations on such issues as processing time and return requirements. As a result, it is important that treasury professionals know and understand the rules and regulations that apply to checks written or received in the normal course of business. Local banks are usually one of the best sources of this information.

---

5. In the United States, this change occurred in 2004 with the enactment of the Check Clearing for the 21st Century Act (referred to as *Check 21*). While Check 21 did not specifically authorize image presentment of checks, it did create a new negotiable instrument called an *image replacement document (IRD)*. An IRD is a paper reproduction of the original check that contains an image of the front and back of the original check and is the legal equivalent of the original check. As a result, US banks can legally exchange images electronically instead of shipping paper checks, and can use the images to print an IRD when or if someone in the clearing process needs a physical document.
6. The guidelines for returned check items are based on the Federal Reserve's Regulation CC (Reg CC).

A. On-Us Check Clearing

On-us check clearing involves a payee depositing a check in an account at the same bank on which it is drawn. The payee's bank simultaneously debits (decreases) the payor's account and credits (increases) the payee's account. The payee typically receives same-day or immediate availability, if funds are available, and processing fees are often lower than for other checks that require additional processing.

On-we check clearing is similar to on-us but involves a group of banks that use a common third-party vendor for check processing. Since all of the banks' checks are processed at the same time and place, the checks can be treated as if they were on-us items, typically resulting in same-day or immediate availability for the depositor.

B. Transit Check Clearing

Deposited checks drawn on other banks are referred to as *transit checks* and require more processing than on-us or on-we checks. As discussed above, the bank of first deposit must sort these checks into cash letters, which must then be transmitted to the paying bank either directly or via intermediary processors, such as a central bank, a clearing facility, or a correspondent bank (collectively referred to as *clearing channels*) for final settlement.

Four major clearing channels are available in the United States for processing transit checks:

- **Clearinghouse:** Clearinghouses are either formal or informal associations formed by banks in a geographic area to permit the exchange of items drawn on the member participants. Member banks make daily, or sometimes more frequent, presentments to the clearinghouse. The net value (i.e., face amount of items submitted less items received, as calculated on a bank-by-bank basis) is transferred between the banks by debiting and crediting correspondent accounts or through reserve accounts that each bank maintains with the local Federal Reserve Bank.

- **Correspondent Bank:** In this type of clearing, the collecting bank maintains a depository account with another bank, called a *correspondent bank*. The collecting bank sends cash letters to the correspondent bank, which presents the items to the paying bank through a local clearinghouse or the Fed. The collecting bank's depository account at the correspondent bank is then credited with the proceeds of the checks.

- **Direct Send or Direct Exchange:** As an alternative to using the clearing channels just discussed, collecting banks may arrange to send cash letters directly to a paying bank or to a nonlocal Federal Reserve Bank. This process, also referred to as *direct presentment*, enables banks to meet various deposit deadlines and achieve faster clearing times. The collecting bank maintains a depository account with the paying bank or nonlocal Federal Reserve Bank, which is credited with the proceeds of the checks. If the cash letter arrives early enough in the day, the paying bank must settle the same day.

- **Federal Reserve System (Fed):** The Fed also acts as a check-clearing agent. Depository banks can send cash letters to the Fed, which will then clear the checks and transfer values from paying banks to depository banks.

As a result of image processing and electronic presentment of checks in the United States, many checks now clear the same day, with the remainder settling in one day. Finality, however, can still take several weeks due to various types of returned items. Similar options are typically available in most countries, with that country's central bank (or an equivalent processor) substituting for the Fed.

C. Foreign Checks

Foreign checks are checks deposited at a bank in one country that are drawn on a bank in another country. Foreign checks may also be drawn in a foreign currency (e.g., a check in British pounds deposited with a US bank for credit to a US dollar bank account). These checks are normally treated as collection items[7] and processed outside of the normal check-clearing systems. This implies that the depository bank will send the foreign check to a correspondent bank (or a foreign branch of the depository bank, if it has one) in the country in which the foreign check is payable. The correspondent bank will, in turn, process the foreign check locally and eventually remit the proceeds to the depository bank. Because these checks are subject to both foreign exchange (FX) transaction costs and extra processing fees, the bank of first deposit typically will not credit the payee's account until it receives and converts the proceeds of the check to its base currency. As a result, foreign checks can take days or weeks to clear and normally clear for significantly less than the face amount of the check. Due to the complicated nature of clearing these items, some banks do not accept foreign checks for deposit.

One exception to this process is US dollar checks that are drawn on a Canadian bank but have a US MICR line[8] and are deposited into a US bank. Such checks are processed through standard check-processing channels.

D. Endpoints

An endpoint is the location of the paying bank where final settlement occurs. The endpoint is displayed in the routing information, such as the RTN or sort code[9] on the check.

E. Deadlines and Deposit Timing

There are two check deposit-related deadlines established by banks that determine when funds become available: the ledger cutoff time and the deposit deadline. All of the times and deadlines discussed in this section are assumed to be local times at the point of deposit and apply to deposits of checks, either as images or physical documents. The term *deposit* typically refers to deposits of checks and/or cash. Electronic payments are normally "received" rather than deposited, and while they may be subject to processing deadlines, they are not usually subject to deposit deadlines and/or availability schedules. Each bank sets deadlines based on competitive and operational considerations. A particular banking day may start at some time other than midnight, but banking days always consist of 24-hour days—never fractional days. It is important to know when a banking day begins and ends because a deposit made to an interest-bearing account during that time period will earn interest for that day irrespective of when the deposit was made during the banking day.

A bank's ledger cutoff is the time of day when a deposit must be received in order to be posted to the ledger balance of the depositor's account. This time can vary within a bank depending on where and how the items are received. Items deposited after the ledger cutoff time are considered to be received by the bank on the following banking day. For example, if a bank has a published ledger cutoff time of 3:00 p.m., then a deposit made at 2:00 p.m. Friday will be credited to the ledger balance on Friday. However, a deposit made to the same bank account on Friday at 3:30 p.m. would not be credited to the ledger balance until Monday, which is the next banking business day. Ledger balances are granted provisional credit based on the anticipated settlement and finality of the item. The deposit deadline is the time within the banking day when an item must be ready for transit at the depository bank's processing center to qualify for the availability stated in the availability schedule.

---

7. A collection item (also called a *noncash item*) is any item presented to a bank for deposit that the bank will not provisionally credit to the depositor's account. Payment must be received from the payor's bank before the item is credited to the payee's account.
8. Several Canadian banks have requested and been assigned US RTNs.
9. A *sort code* is the name given by banks in the United Kingdom to the bank codes used to route money transfers and payments between banks. It is similar to an RTN in US banks.

F. Availability Schedules

Availability schedules specify, for each drawee endpoint, when a bank grants available credit or collected balances for deposited items. Each bank sets its availability schedule based on its processing schedules, capabilities, and pricing decisions. In order to receive the availability stated on the schedule, the deposited item must be received by the assigned deposit deadline. If the deposit deadline is missed, then availability is delayed. Checks are generally assigned somewhere between zero- and one-day availability for businesses, although in rare cases items may be assigned two-day availability.

Most banks assign availability using the proof-of-deposit (POD) method, in which availability is assigned to each check as it is processed. Availability is determined based on the time and day of deposit and the check's drawee endpoint. Some banks may negotiate special availability for selected, high-volume customers.

The Fed has availability schedules for US banks, correspondent banks have availability schedules for other banks, and banks have availability schedules for customers. Many banks have multiple availability schedules depending on the customer and the volume of business. Because the availability schedule impacts float balances,[10] the schedule a bank offers to a particular customer is part of the pricing decision.

G. Balances and Float

Balance measurements and float calculations are determined by the relationship of the time that a check is deposited to the deadlines set by the depository institution (in contrast, electronic payments are typically available when posted):

- **Ledger balances** are bank balances that reflect all entries to a bank account, regardless of whether the deposited items have been collected and are available for withdrawal. Ledger balances are important for accounting purposes, but not for funds availability or bank compensation purposes. A negative ledger balance results in a ledger overdraft, for which charges can be assessed.

- **Available balances** reflect the amount of funds available for withdrawal from an account, based on the bank's availability schedule and/or local regulations that require specific availability for certain funds (e.g., Reg CC in the United States; other countries may have similar regulations). Available balances may also include overdraft lines of credit.

- **Collected balances** refer to the average ledger balance minus the deposit float. Neither collected balances nor deposit float are regulatory terms. Rather, they are items used by US banks to determine earnings credits on account analysis statements.

- **Daylight overdrafts** occur when financial institutions permit corporations to make payments that exceed the available balance. These overdraft positions are usually eliminated by funds that arrive later in the day. Financial institutions should carefully examine the creditworthiness of a customer before allowing a daylight overdraft.

H. Other Check-Processing Factors That Influence Availability

Several other factors may impact funds availability associated with check-based payments:

- **RDC/Image Capture:** A depositor may elect to use RDC or some other form of image capture for deposited items. Items that are preprocessed using RDC—or some other method of capturing the MICR and payment information—may receive faster availability, a later cutoff time, a later deposit deadline, and/or lower service charges because the customer is, in effect, performing a labor-intensive task for the bank.

---

10. *Float* is defined as the time interval between when a transaction is initially processed and when the value of that transaction is available for use or charged to an account.

- **Reject Items:** Checks that are rejected by a bank's automated check-processing equipment are likely to miss critical deposit deadlines, resulting in delays in availability and additional processing fees. The reason for this is that reject items must be repaired and reprocessed. Most reject items arise either because of physical defects in the MICR line or because the MICR line does not meet banking industry specifications.

- **As-Of Adjustments:** When a check takes longer to clear than the initial availability that was granted, a bank may add the additional time as part of the collected-balance calculation. This practice is referred to as making an *as-of adjustment*. If a bank originally granted one-day availability, but actually cleared the check in two days, then one more day of float is added when calculating collected balances. As-of adjustments are important because they can impact the funds available for use by a depositor. Since as-of adjustments normally reduce available balances, they can also increase bank fees and in extreme cases even result in overdrafts.

- **Value Dating:** Value dating is the practice of debiting or crediting a particular transaction on some date other than the processing date. For example, in Canada it is standard practice to charge a payor's account for the value of a check as of the date the check was written, rather than the date it was actually processed by the bank.

I. Additional Paper-Based Instruments

A number of other less common payment instruments have check-like attributes (e.g., a MICR line and RTNs) and typically clear through the same channels as checks. These include:

- **Cashier's Check/Certified Check:** A cashier's check, also known as an *official bank check*, is a check drawn on a bank's funds. A certified check is drawn on a depositor's checking account, and funds are withdrawn from the depositor's account at the time of certification, to assure payment with a certification or guarantee by the bank. Both carry the signature of a bank officer certifying the check to be genuine and guaranteeing payment. Due to the higher processing costs of certified checks, most banks have replaced them with cashier's checks.

- **Government Warrants:** In government finance, a warrant is an order to pay that instructs a treasurer to pay the warrant holder on demand or after a maturity date. Warrants deposited in a bank are routed (based on the MICR line information) to a collecting bank that processes them as collection items. The collecting bank presents the warrants to the government entity's treasury department for payment each business day. In the United States, warrants are commonly issued by state treasurers for payroll purposes, for accounts payable to vendors, for tax refund payments to taxpayers, and for payments to owners of unclaimed monies.

- **Money Order:** A money order is a prepaid instrument issued by various third parties such as banks, postal services, or consumer outlets (e.g., convenience stores and check-cashing agencies). The purchaser is the instrument's payor, and the money order is the obligation of the issuer.

- **Payable through Draft (PTD):** A PTD is a payment instrument resembling a check that is drawn against the payor rather than the bank. It is handled like a check through the clearing process, but the responsibility for paying the draft lies with the payor, referred to as the *drawee* in the case of drafts. The primary reason companies use drafts is to preserve the right to review the items prior to final payment. Insurance companies often use this type of instrument for claims reimbursement because drafts provide insurers with an opportunity to verify signatures and endorsements before honoring the items.

- **Remotely Created Check (RCC):** RCCs, also known as *pre-authorized drafts*, are used to draw or draft against a payor's account. The check is unsigned, and the payee, rather than the payor, initiates the transaction. RCCs are typically created for a one-time payment, such as a late bill payment or debt settlement. Because they do not bear a signature and can be created without the knowledge of the payor, RCCs are vulnerable to fraud.

As a result, many banks refuse to accept them for deposit. According to Reg CC and most clearinghouse agreements, any bank that transfers or presents an RCC warrants that the check is authorized by the person on whose account the check is drawn.

- **Sight Draft/Time Draft:** A sight draft is usually presented in combination with other documents that verify the terms of a transaction have been met. If all the documentation is in order, then the draft is payable upon presentment (i.e., at sight). A time draft is the same as a sight draft except it is not payable until a specified future date. Time drafts are used for transactions that call for delayed payment. Sight and time drafts are used primarily to support international trade.

- **Traveler's Check:** Traveler's checks are prepaid instruments similar to money orders. Two signatures are usually required by the purchaser: one at issuance and one at the time the check is used to pay for goods or services. Some issuers of traveler's check are replacing them with stored-value cards to improve processing times and reduce fraud.

V. LARGE-VALUE ELECTRONIC FUNDS TRANSFER (EFT) OR WIRE TRANSFER SYSTEMS

Processing large-value electronic funds transfers involves two key elements: clearing and settlement. Clearing is the transfer and confirmation of information between the payor's bank (sending FI) and the payee's bank (receiving FI). Settlement is the actual transfer of funds between the banks, which discharges the payor's obligation to the payee.

Final settlement is irrevocable and unconditional. The finality of the payment is determined by the transfer system's rules and applicable law. The illustration shown in Exhibit 4.4 assumes that the funds transfer takes place within one country. In this case the transaction information and ultimate settlement are all handled through the country's central bank or equivalent. For cross-border payments, the transaction information is sent via an external system,[11] and settlement is handled through correspondent bank accounts.

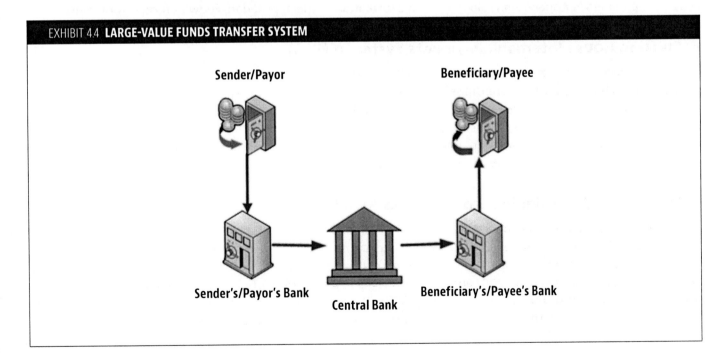

EXHIBIT 4.4 **LARGE-VALUE FUNDS TRANSFER SYSTEM**

Sender/Payor

Beneficiary/Payee

Sender's/Payor's Bank

Central Bank

Beneficiary's/Payee's Bank

11. Systems used to send the transaction information include SWIFT or CLS.

Large-value funds transfer systems consist of either RTGS systems or net settlement systems.

Gross settlement occurs when each transaction results in a separate value transfer between the payor and payee. In most gross settlement systems, the settlement occurs immediately through an RTGS system. Such payments are considered final when processed.

Net settlement occurs when many transactions are combined and then sorted by sending and receiving banks. At day's end (or at another agreed-upon point in time), the net amount either owed by or owed to each bank is determined and only the net amount of value is actually transferred. At this point, electronic credit transactions are considered to be final. Electronic debits may be reversible under certain, specified circumstances. All of the individual transactions are, of course, accounted for on a bookkeeping basis, with each bank making the necessary debits and credits to individual accounts.

A. Real-Time Gross Settlement (RTGS) Systems

RTGS means that the clearing and settlement of each transaction occur continuously during the processing day. Payment to the receiving participant (payee) is final and irrevocable when the RTGS processor (central bank or equivalent) either credits the amount of the payment order to the receiving bank's account or sends notice to the receiving bank, whichever is earlier.

Examples of RTGS systems used for large-value transfers throughout the world include Fedwire (US), CHAPS (United Kingdom), LVTS (Canada), TARGET2 (Europe), and CNAPS (China).[12]

Large-value RTGS payment systems are used by companies to facilitate major transactions that are time sensitive and where the irrevocable receipt of value is required. Because a payment made through these systems is final and irrevocable once made—and because the dollar amounts can be significant—special care and diligence is required in the issuance and processing of wire transfers. An example of an RTGS payment transaction message via the US Fedwire is provided in Appendix 4.2, along with an explanation of the appropriate Fedwire format for the message.

B. Clearing House Interbank Payments System (CHIPS)

CHIPS is a US-based privately owned wire transfer system that settles its transactions through the Fed. Like Fedwire, CHIPS handles both the transmission of funds transfer instruction messages among banks, as well as the settlement of the payment between the banks, and is an RTGS system that provides finality. CHIPS is one of the main electronic funds transfer systems for processing international US dollar funds transfers made among international banks in the United States. To access CHIPS, a bank must have a US presence. As of 2015, CHIPS had 49 participating banks, representing 19 countries, as members.

C. TARGET2 and the Single Euro Payments Area (SEPA)

TARGET2 is based on a common operating platform developed and operated by Banca d'Italia, Banque de France, and Deutsche Bundesbank on behalf of the Eurosystem. The Eurosystem is comprised of the European Central Bank and the central banks of countries using the euro. It is the monetary authority for the euro area. TARGET2 became operational in November 2007 and is Europe's RTGS system. TARGET2, along with its predecessor TARGET, was developed as part of the implementation of SEPA, the Single Euro Payments Area. SEPA, an initiative of the European Union, ensures that electronic payments within the Eurozone are handled in a standardized and

---

12. *CHAPS* refers to the UK's Clearing House Automated Payment System, *LVTS* refers to Canada's Large Value Transfer System, *TARGET2* refers to the second generation of the Trans-European Automated Real-time Gross settlement Express Transfer (TARGET) system, and *CNAPS* refers to the China National Advanced Payment System.

inexpensive manner across all countries of the Eurozone. In effect, cross-border payments within the SEPA boundaries are treated as if they were in-country rather than cross-border payments.

D. Continuous Linked Settlement (CLS)

Continuous linked settlement (CLS) was developed to reduce the risks of working with counterparties. Beginning in the mid-1990s, central banks became increasingly concerned that the high level of settlement risk in existing practices, coupled with an unexpected event or failure, could trigger a serious disruption of the global FX markets and financial system liquidity. In an FX transaction, settlement risk is the risk that one party to the transaction provides the currency it agreed to sell but does not receive the currency it agreed to buy. Thus, the transaction is not settled. The exposure to a single counterparty, even if for a limited time, can have substantial negative consequences for the parties involved.

The solution to eliminate settlement risk was the development of CLS. CLS is a multicurrency FX settlement service that allows a simultaneous exchange of the payments for both sides of the underlying financial transactions (e.g., FX contracts, non-deliverable forward [NDF] contracts, and over-the-counter [OTC] derivative contracts).

The CLS process is managed by CLS Group Holdings AG and includes the CLS Bank International (CLS Bank). It is regulated by the central banks in the countries in which it operates. The group was formed in 1997, and the system has been operating since 2002. As of 2015, CLS membership included 62 member banks and settled payment instructions for FX transactions in 17 currencies.

E. Society for Worldwide Interbank Financial Telecommunication (SWIFT)

SWIFT is not a payment system. SWIFT is a communication system used by most of the banks in the world to transmit payment instructions, among other things, and is therefore often thought of, incorrectly, as an international wire transfer or funds transfer system. SWIFT is an industry-owned, cooperative, interbank telecommunication network that enables banks to send authenticated electronic messages in standard formats. The information that moves through SWIFT ultimately results in value being transferred from one party to another, generally through correspondent banks.

SWIFT was created in Brussels in 1973 with the support of more than 200 large banks in 15 countries. As of 2015, SWIFT included more than 10,000 banking organizations, security institutions, and corporate customers in more than 200 countries. SWIFT communications contain payment-related information, but do not actually transfer value. Communications that are initiated and received by member banks are known as *SWIFT messages*. These messages cover a wide range of international banking services, and include balance reporting, letters of credit (L/Cs), documentary collections, and FX transactions. Through the SWIFT network, a company can request a bank to initiate a balance transfer or foreign payment.

For corporate customers, SWIFT provides a limited membership that allows a corporation to utilize SWIFT's multibank platform to exchange financial information with its banks through one standardized platform. This may allow the corporation to reduce or eliminate transaction costs while increasing the speed of payment and minimizing the necessity of maintaining multiple bank connections in order to send/receive information and initiate payments.

VI. SMALL-VALUE TRANSFER SYSTEMS

Small-value transfer systems are electronic networks for the exchange of smaller payment instructions among FIs, typically on behalf of consumers. Many countries have small-value transfer systems— ACH in the US, Bacs in the United Kingdom, and Electronic Clearing (ECG) in Hong Kong. Small-value transfer payments are payment instructions to either debit or credit a deposit account. They are typically batch-processed, value-dated electronic funds transfers between originating and receiving FIs. An additional feature is that an electronic small-value transaction can transfer more payment-related information than can normally be transmitted via paper-based instruments or wire transfers. Companies use small-value electronic payments for a wide range of transactions.

Small-value transactions can either be credits, such as payroll payments, that are originated by the account holder who is sending funds (the payor), or they can be debits, such as mortgage or loan payments, that are originated by the account holder who is receiving funds (payee). SEPA debit and credit schemes fall into the category of small-value transactions. All small-value transfer systems allow for the processing of credit transactions, but not all systems allow for pre-authorized debits.

A giro payment, available in some countries, is the functional equivalent of an ACH credit. The payor, typically a consumer, authorizes his/her bank to pay the payee, typically a business, through a direct transfer. Although the original authorization from the customer may be received through either paper or electronic bill payment systems, the payment itself is electronic and is usually sent through the country's ACH system. Although the term *giro* is still widely used in many countries, separate giro-processing systems have largely been replaced by electronic small-value transfer systems.

Since small-value transactions can be originated as either credits or debits, the terms *payor* and *payee* are not used to identify the parties to the transaction. Instead, the terms *originator* and *receiver* are used, as shown in the ACH credit transaction in Exhibit 4.5. In a similar manner, the FIs involved in an ACH transaction are not referred to as the *depository* and *paying banks*. Rather, they are called the *originating depository financial institution (ODFI)* and the *receiving depository financial institution (RDFI)*. Unlike checks, which are always created by the payor and move money to the payee, ACH transactions can be either created by the payor to send money to the payee (called *ACH credits* or *credit mandates*), or created by the payee to take money from the payor (called *ACH debits* or *debit mandates*).

EXHIBIT 4.5 CREDIT TRANSACTION IN AN ACH PAYMENT SYSTEM

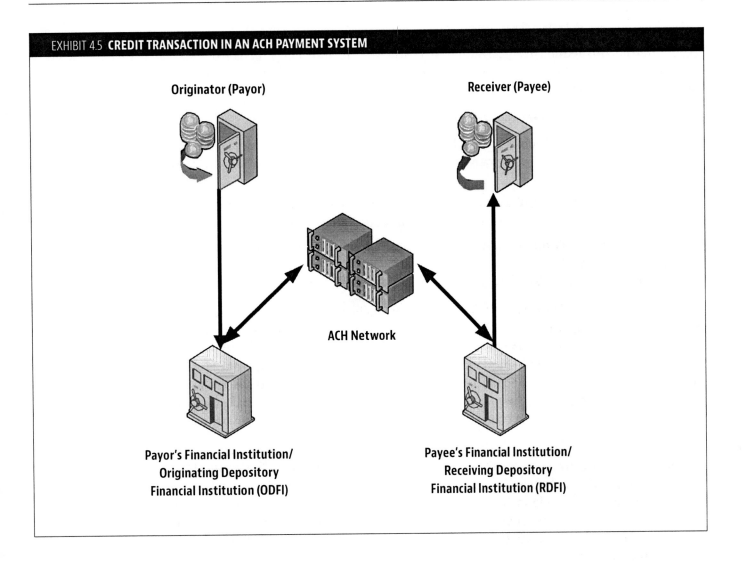

Small-value transactions are typically sent in batches by FIs and third-party service providers to operators for processing one or two business days before settlement dates. The operators then deliver the transactions to the receiving institutions at defined times.

To combat fraud, a considerable range of controls and balances are associated with small-value payments. Examples include debit filters and blocks, which restrict a perpetrator's ability to use a stolen routing transit number and account number to withdraw money from the account using an ACH transaction.

Although these systems typically operate within a specific country, it is possible to send ACH transactions between countries in what are referred to as *cross-border ACH transactions*. This is accomplished through the use of a "gateway" bank or service provider who will receive transactions in one country and then forward them to the ACH system of another country. The US Federal Reserve Bank provides this service, called *FedGlobal ACH Payments*, to over 35 countries as of 2015 (see Appendix 4.3 for the list of countries), and many global banks provide a similar service for their customers.

The standard option for distributing cross-border payments between deposit accounts is known as an *account-to-account transfer*. An account-to-receiver option is also offered and allows funds from accounts at a US depository financial institution to be retrieved by any receiver either at a participating bank location or at a trusted, third-party provider in certain receiving countries.

The FedGlobal service also provides a range of transaction currency options:

· **Fixed-to-Variable:** US dollars are converted to a variable amount of a destination currency based on a competitive exchange rate. Settlement occurs in US dollars between participating US financial institutions and Fed banks.

· **Fixed-to-Fixed—US Dollar to US Dollar:** Payments are both transferred and received in US dollars. Settlement occurs in US dollars and is between participating US financial institutions and Fed banks.

· **Fixed-to-Fixed—Foreign Currency to Foreign Currency:** Payments are both transferred and received in foreign currency. The FX rate and settlement are managed and processed by participating US financial institutions and the respective foreign gateway operators via their foreign correspondent banks.

The growth in acceptance of Internet services and online banking has created a demand for small-value systems that settle more quickly than the traditional ACH systems. In response to this demand, many countries are looking at various options to provide some form of same-day or near real-time transaction. An example of this is the Faster Payments service in the United Kingdom. Faster Payments is a joint development of CHAPS, the UK ACH system, and VocaLink, a large British telecom company, and uses an Internet-based system to provide immediate online payments to customers. Faster Payments was developed by British banks in response to a government demand to reduce the clearing time for ACH transactions. Other countries are looking at similar changes.

There are two ACH operators in the US ACH system: the Fed processes most of the ACH transactions, while a private operator, the Electronic Payments Network (EPN), processes the remainder. NACHA, the Electronic Payments Association (formerly the National Automated Clearing House Association), is a trade organization that is responsible for managing the development, administration, and governance of the ACH system. NACHA is a membership organization of financial institutions and other stakeholders in the ACH system. In addition to administering the rules, standards, and procedures that enable the system to work on a daily basis, NACHA also is responsible for enforcing the rules and various risk management processes.

VII. CARD-BASED PAYMENT SYSTEMS

Credit and debit cards are payment cards issued to individuals and businesses for the purchase of goods, payment for services, and/or access to cash advances and withdrawals. A credit card is issued against a line of credit that the institution or merchant has extended, whereas a debit card is issued against a deposit account belonging to the cardholder. Charge cards are a special type of credit card in which the outstanding balance must be paid off each month.

A. Credit Cards

1. ISSUERS AND TYPES OF CREDIT CARDS

Banks and financial service companies are the primary issuers of credit cards, although some major retailers and oil and fuel service companies issue them as well. The two primary bank-issued cards used in the United States are Visa and MasterCard. The main nonbank card is American Express (Amex), which is issued primarily by Amex itself, though some of its specialty cards may be associated with bank lines of credit. These three cards are offered and accepted on a global basis. China UnionPay is the principal bank card agency in China and, although relatively new, has become one of the largest card issuers and processors in the world, with cards also accepted on a global basis. The JCB (originally Japan Credit Bureau) card is bank-issued and used in about 20 countries, including the United States. Finally, the Discover card is issued primarily by Discover Financial Services and is US-based.

In general, bank-issued cards, Amex, and Discover are known as *open-loop cards* because they are accepted anywhere the card logo is displayed. Cards issued by gas companies, department stores, and other retailers are considered *closed-loop cards*,[13] as the card is accepted only by the issuing company. While several major retailers offer their own card programs, many retailers have moved to issuing private-label or co-branded cards through programs run by large banks and other financial service providers. Many of the large oil companies issue their own credit cards for fuel purchases, and there are several fuel service companies that provide card services to corporate and government entities.

Chip cards (or smart cards) include a computer chip with related circuitry that can be used to store information for security or transaction processing. In the early 1990s, Europay, MasterCard, and Visa agreed to develop common specifications for smart cards as either debit or credit cards. This system, called *EMV* (for Europay, Mastercard, and Visa), was initially released in 1994 and has been upgraded several times since then. With the exception of a few countries, EMV-compliant cards and equipment are widespread. Since not all countries or even all merchants in a country are capable of reading the chip on chip cards, these cards also typically have a magnetic stripe on them in addition to the chip.

EMV chip transactions are more secure than transactions using a magnetic stripe. When a payment is initiated with a magnetic stripe card, the terminal reads data that are stored on the magnetic stripe and routes the information through the payment networks for authorization. A criminal can copy the magnetic stripe data and produce counterfeit cards. An EMV chip, on the other hand, can process information and determine the rules of the transaction through communication with the terminal. This dynamic authentication reduces the possibility of fraud. Chip card transactions may be authenticated by a signature or a PIN. The more secure PIN authentication has been adopted in Europe, Australia, and Canada, while most chip card transactions in the United States are authenticated through signatures. To encourage the use of EMV chip cards in the United States, Visa, Mastercard, Discover, and American Express set October 2015 as the deadline for merchants to support EMV payments. After that date, liability for the cost of counterfeit fraud shifted to merchants if they did not support chip technology, or issuers if a chip card has not been issued to the user.

2. CREDIT CARD TRANSACTIONS

There are several participants in a credit card transaction. Exhibit 4.6 describes these participants and their roles in the credit process.

---

13. Although they are open-loop cards because they are accepted by many merchants, Amex and Discover are sometimes called *closed-loop cards* in reference to the fact that Amex and Discover are both the issuer and the processor for their cards. The now-standard definition of *closed-loop cards* refers to cards that are only accepted by the company that issued them.

EXHIBIT 4.6 **PARTICIPANTS IN A CREDIT CARD TRANSACTION**

CARDHOLDER	A CARDHOLDER RECEIVES A CARD FROM THE ISSUING BANK.
CARD ISSUER	ISSUING BANKS UNDERWRITE AND ISSUE CARDS TO INDIVIDUAL AND BUSINESS CARDHOLDERS WHO MEET CREDIT STANDARDS, OR IN THE CASE OF DEBIT CARDS, HOLD BANK ACCOUNTS WITH THAT FINANCIAL INSTITUTION. THE ISSUING BANK MAINTAINS THE INDIVIDUAL CARD ACCOUNTS, BILLS AND COLLECTS PAYMENTS FROM CARDHOLDERS, AND MONITORS THE PERFORMANCE OF CREDIT CARD RECEIVABLE PORTFOLIOS.
MERCHANT	MERCHANTS ARE BUSINESSES THAT ACCEPT CARDS AS A METHOD OF PAYMENT. MERCHANTS CAN INCLUDE "BRICK AND MORTAR" MERCHANTS (THOSE WITH A PHYSICAL STOREFRONT PRESENCE), E-COMMERCE MERCHANTS (THOSE CONDUCTING TRANSACTIONS ON THE INTERNET), OR MOTO MERCHANTS (THOSE WHO PROCESS ORDERS BY MAIL ORDER OR TELEPHONE ORDER).
MERCHANT ACQUIRER	IN ADDITION TO ISSUING CARDS, BANKS CAN ALSO ACT AS ACQUIRING BANKS FOR BUSINESSES THAT ACCEPT CREDIT CARD PAYMENTS. THE MERCHANT ACQUIRING BANK QUALIFIES BUSINESSES (REFERRED TO AS *MERCHANTS*) THAT ACCEPT CREDIT CARD PAYMENTS. THE MERCHANT ACQUIRING BANK PROVIDES MERCHANTS WITH CREDIT CARD TERMINALS, WHICH MAY BE PURCHASED OR LEASED, AND MAINTAINS DEPOSIT ACCOUNTS THROUGH WHICH THE CREDIT CARD PAYMENTS SETTLE.
ACQUIRING PROCESSOR	MANY MERCHANTS AND MERCHANT ACQUIRING BANKS USE THIRD-PARTY PROCESSORS TO MANAGE THE DAILY SETTLEMENT, AS WELL AS THE INFORMATION FLOWS, RELATED TO CREDIT CARD ACTIVITIES.
ISSUER PROCESSOR	THE ISSUER PROCESSOR PROVIDES A SYSTEM FOR CARD ISSUERS TO BOARD ACCOUNTS, PROVIDES AUTHORIZATIONS, AND OFFERS RISK MANAGEMENT TOOLS TO ISSUERS TO MANAGE THEIR CARD PORTFOLIOS EFFECTIVELY.
NETWORK OPERATOR	NETWORK OPERATORS MAINTAIN COMMUNICATION NETWORKS TO SUPPORT CARD TRANSACTION ACTIVITIES, SUCH AS AUTHORIZATION, CLEARING, AND SETTLEMENT. NETWORK OPERATORS INCLUDE VISA, MASTERCARD, DISCOVER, STAR, NYCE, PULSE, ACCEL, INTERLINK, AND OTHERS.

In addition to the clearing and settlement processes common to all payments, credit card transactions add a third major process: authorization. Credit card transaction processes are illustrated in Exhibit 4.7.

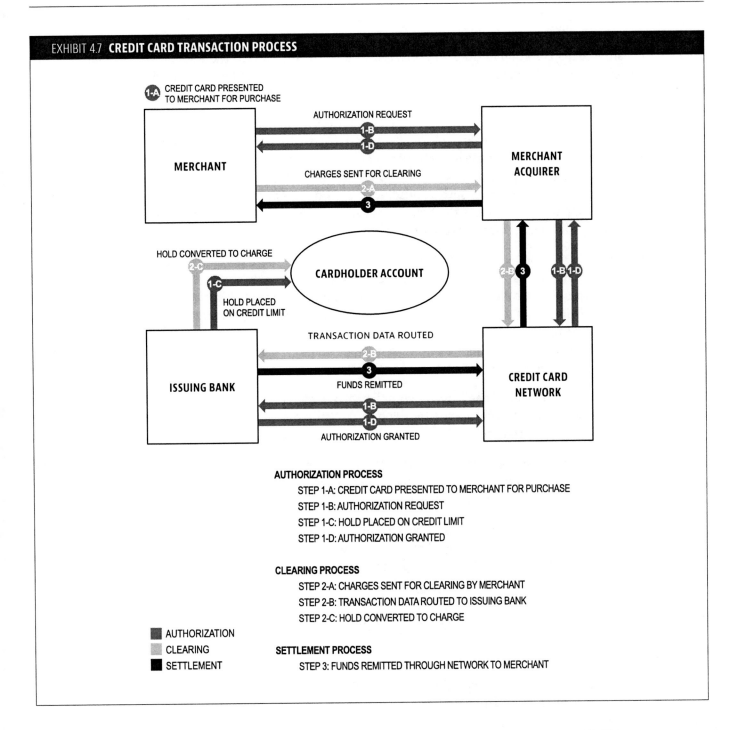

EXHIBIT 4.7 CREDIT CARD TRANSACTION PROCESS

AUTHORIZATION PROCESS
STEP 1-A: CREDIT CARD PRESENTED TO MERCHANT FOR PURCHASE
STEP 1-B: AUTHORIZATION REQUEST
STEP 1-C: HOLD PLACED ON CREDIT LIMIT
STEP 1-D: AUTHORIZATION GRANTED

CLEARING PROCESS
STEP 2-A: CHARGES SENT FOR CLEARING BY MERCHANT
STEP 2-B: TRANSACTION DATA ROUTED TO ISSUING BANK
STEP 2-C: HOLD CONVERTED TO CHARGE

SETTLEMENT PROCESS
STEP 3: FUNDS REMITTED THROUGH NETWORK TO MERCHANT

- AUTHORIZATION
- CLEARING
- SETTLEMENT

The authorization process starts when a customer pays for a purchase using a card (Step 1-A). This process is essentially the equivalent of the payment instruction and generation process outlined for payments in the earlier discussion of the payment process. The merchant submits an online authorization request for the charge amount to its merchant acquiring bank, which is also known as the *merchant acquirer* (Step 1-B). The request usually is transmitted through a point-of-sale (POS) terminal or other electronic communication system. That authorization request is routed through the appropriate card network and subsequently to the issuing bank. The issuing bank reviews the cardholder's account and approves or declines the transaction. If approved, the issuing bank places a hold on the cardholder's credit limit (Step 1-C, referred to as *open-to-buy*) for the amount of the charge. If the purchase is made with a debit card, the issuing bank places a hold on the cardholder's available funds. Then, an authorization response is routed back through the network to the merchant (Step 1-D).

The second major step in a card transaction is the clearing process—the communication of payment information through a card-processing network or channel. Card transaction data are submitted electronically by the merchant to the merchant acquirer, typically at the end of the business day (Step 2-A). The merchant acquirer then forwards the data through the network operator to the issuing bank (Step 2-B). Depending upon the type of card used, the acquirer uses one of several networks, such as Visa, MasterCard, or American Express. When the issuing bank receives the transaction data, it converts the hold on the customer's account to a charge that will appear on the cardholder's monthly billing statement (Step 2-C).

The final step in a card transaction is the settlement process, in which the funds are transferred from the issuing bank to the merchant via the merchant acquirer. The network operator establishes net positions of all settlement participants (issuers/acquirers), collects funds from the issuing bank, and makes transfers to the merchant acquirer through the ACH, Fedwire, or other similar system. Settlement usually occurs the next day following submission of the clearing transaction to the network operator (Step 3). If the card transaction involves more than one currency (i.e., it is a cross-border transaction where a card issued in one country is used for purchases in another country), any foreign currency exchange is handled as part of the settlement process.

The merchant receives settlement either gross or net of any allocated fees. These fees, which are discussed in more detail later in this chapter, include interchange fees due to the issuing bank, any network assessment fees due to the network operator, and any transaction fees due to the merchant acquirer.

If the amount that the merchant receives is the net settlement, then the transaction value is less the fees. If the terms are gross settlement, then the merchant receives full transaction value, and a periodic invoice is received for the amount of the fees due to the respective parties.

Cardholders can dispute a charge assessed to their accounts, which may result in a charge-back to the merchant. Generally, cardholders have a window of anywhere from 60 to 120 days to dispute a transaction. A merchant has an established time period to respond to this charge-back and provide evidence to the validity of the charge, as well as have the charge re-presented by the merchant acquirer. Certain card networks permit up to two charge-back cycles. Then, the process of pre-arbitration and arbitration may occur. However, if a chip card was used but not processed via EMV, the merchant receives the charge-back and is unable to dispute the charge.

B. Debit Cards/EFTPOS[14]

Debit and credit cards have similar features, but debit cards, often referred to as *EFTPOS* in many parts of the world, access funds directly from a cardholder's checking or savings deposit account. Debit cards may be signature-based and/or PIN-based.

- **Signature-Based**: Signature debit cards bear the logos of Visa, MasterCard, or Discover, and are processed in the same manner as credit card transactions using those network operators. The customer signs a receipt at checkout.
- **PIN-Based:** A PIN debit transaction facilitates consumer authorization and authentication through the entry of a PIN at the POS terminal. Authorization and clearing are generally immediate and are facilitated by network operators, such as Maestro (owned by MasterCard), Interlink (owned by Visa), NYCE, STAR, and ACCEL.

14. *EFTPOS* refers to electronic funds transfer (EFT) at the point of sale (POS).

C. Other Varieties of Payment Cards

Some variants of payment cards include purchasing, single-use cards, and stored-value cards (e.g., payroll cards, health reimbursement account cards, and gift cards). The types of payment cards discussed below streamline the purchasing process and offer rebates for the companies that use them:

- **Purchasing Cards:** Purchasing cards (also known as *procurement cards* or *p-cards*) are credit cards used by businesses for the purchase of supplies, inventory, equipment, and service contracts. P-cards are typically used for various types of purchases (high- or low-value) with spending limits established on an individual card basis. Purchases can be limited to approved vendors and suppliers, as determined by the merchant category code (MCC) of the vendor or supplier. From the issuing company's perspective, the principal benefit of a p-card is the replacement of the traditional time-consuming, labor-intensive, paper-based requisition process. Additionally, companies may negotiate a rebate based on charge volume and average transaction size, and they may be able to effectively delay payment since purchased items will not be paid for until the end of the billing cycle. The principal benefit for an employee is that goods and services can be obtained quickly and conveniently without a complicated purchase order process.

- **Travel and Entertainment (T&E) Cards:** These credit cards are used by businesses for employee travel purposes. Travel cards may be incorporated into a company's p-card program (typically referred to as *one-card programs*), or they may be issued as a separate card. These cards work very similarly to p-cards. Card issuers may send companies a regularly scheduled data file of transactions that have been charged by employees for automatic loading, as well as send reconciliation details directly into the company's employee expense system. In addition to rebates, travel card programs may allow the firm to earn travel points. T&E cards, as with p-cards, often can have restrictions on use based on company policy.

- **Fleet Cards:** Fleet cards are similar to T&E cards but are designed to be used for expenditures related to trucks and cars, such as fuel and repairs, and in some cases, other driver expenses, such as food and lodging. Fleet card systems often entitle users to fuel discounts and capture added information, such as vehicle mileage and location.

- **Ghost Cards or Virtual Cards:** These are variations on the p-card that do not involve the use of an actual card. With a ghost card system, a card number is given to a specific vendor and is then used for electronic purchasing and billing purposes.

- **Departmental (Unnamed) Cards:** This is another variation of a p-card in which each department has its own p-card for general use by that department. The card is linked to the department rather than to an individual, and, unlike most cards, there is no individual's name on the card.

- **Single-Use Cards:** Most credit card companies provide additional purchasing security by offering their account holders the ability to generate a single-use or disposable card number. These card numbers look like regular credit card numbers, including embedded expiration dates and security codes, but they will only work for a single use. Single-use cards are often used for travel and entertainment, and by accounts payable departments to pay vendors. Since the number is only good for a set amount and a set period of time, it is a mechanism for fraud control.

- **Stored-Value Cards (SVCs):** These debit cards may be offered by financial institutions, retailers, and other service providers, and they can be branded, open-loop cards (e.g., Visa or MasterCard), or private-label, closed-loop cards (e.g., Starbucks or other merchant gift cards). Generally, open-loop cards can be used almost anywhere while closed-loop cards can only be used at one selected merchant or group of merchants. Gift cards are one of the most commonly used types of stored-value card. The payroll card (or pay card), another stored-value card type, is offered as an alternative payment method to employees who do not have bank accounts and therefore cannot accept direct deposit of funds for their paychecks. The key benefits to employers of moving employees to payroll cards versus checks include reduced payroll costs and lower levels of payroll-related fraud. Another use for stored-value cards is for employee benefit programs, such as flexible spending accounts and health care expense reimbursements. Depending upon the specific card and issuer, SVCs can be either reloadable (i.e., the holder of the card can add more value) or non-reloadable (i.e., the value of the card is limited to the amount originally placed on it).

D. Payment Card Industry Data Security Standard (PCI DSS)

As a result of several system breaches and compromises of data in card networks, the card industry created a governing body to establish and administer a series of strict requirements for the security of card data. Merchants are required to go through an audit of their systems and applications to confirm they are compliant with the Payment Card Industry Data Security Standard (PCI DSS).

The PCI DSS is a worldwide information security standard defined by the Payment Card Industry Security Standards Council. The standard was created to help organizations that process card payments prevent payment card fraud through increased controls of the data they hold and exchange. The standard applies to all organizations that store, process, or transmit cardholder information from any card branded with the logo of one of the major card brands.

Failure to comply with standards or a breach of security can result in substantial fines and possible termination of the acceptance of payment cards.

E. Merchant Card Fees

Merchant card fees are a complex subject and are affected by a large number of variables, including items such as the type of card accepted, the amount of the transaction, the way the card is processed, and the merchant's contract with its bank and/or acquiring processor (sometimes referred to as a *merchant processor*).

The major components of merchant card fees are:

- Interchange fees (referred to simply as *interchange*)
- Assessments
- Processor fees or markups

Interchange typically accounts for the largest portion of overall card fees and represents a fee that is paid to the issuing bank for each transaction. These fees are established by the card brands and go directly to the issuing bank to cover its costs in issuing cards and in processing card transactions.

Interchange fees vary depending upon the method of acquisition and card type. The lowest fees are generally set for cards that the merchant is able to swipe at the point of sale (referred to as *"card present" transactions*.) This allows for accurate transmittal of the data and reduced security concerns (i.e., the actual card is present at the time and point of the transaction, and the cardholder authorizes the transaction). Card transactions accepted over the phone or via the Internet, referred to as *"card not present" transactions* or *mail order or telephone order (MOTO) transactions*, may be assessed higher fees due to the increased risk (e.g., fraud and data errors) from the transaction. In determining interchange fees, *card type* refers to whether the card is a standard card versus a reward card (i.e., cards that offer rewards or points back to the user), as there are typically higher fees on reward cards than on standard (i.e., non-reward) cards, but it also includes whether the card is a debit or credit card. Recent US regulations have impacted interchange fees for debit cards, and as a result, debit card interchange fees are limited to roughly $0.24 per transaction.[15] Credit card fees are typically higher, and while there may be a fixed fee involved, interchange is usually a percentage of the card transaction itself. For example, as of 2016, the Visa interchange fee for a standard, retail consumer credit card in the United States was 1.51% + $0.10. Interchange fees vary by type of transaction, rewards tied to the card, and type of merchant. A full list of interchange fees can typically be found on the card network's website.

Assessment fees are typically calculated as a percentage of the transaction amount and are set by the network operators (e.g., MasterCard, Visa, STAR, or Interlink). These fees can vary based on the type of industry, the method of acceptance, and other factors. The assessment fees are intended to reimburse the network operators for their services and for brand management. Like interchange, assessments do not vary by card processor or acquirer, since they are set by the network operator.

Processor fees or markups, also referred to as *transaction fees,* are set by the individual card processor or merchant acquirer and are the fees charged to process the transaction on the merchant's behalf. These fees are usually based on the expected transaction volume of a given merchant. This is the only portion of merchant card fees that is negotiable. Transaction fees vary significantly from processor to processor.

Merchant fees are typically charged as either bundled pricing or "interchange-plus" pricing. In bundled fees, the merchant is charged one fee by its card processor that covers all of the cost components of the transaction. This type of fee is also referred to as the *merchant discount,* as it is typically subtracted directly from any card settlement. Obviously, merchant discount will be greater than card interchange, in some cases much greater. Smaller merchants or companies with small card volumes tend to pay higher fees. In many cases, the merchant discount is quoted as a flat percentage even though the underlying interchange can vary by transaction. As a result, bundled fees are often quoted high to cover any potential changes in interchange. In interchange-plus pricing, the merchant pays the actual amount of any interchange and assessment fees, plus a stated fee to the card processor. This fee can be either a fixed amount per transaction or a percentage of the value of the transactions.

In addition to the fees already discussed, merchants are also subject to a number of miscellaneous fees for such things as returns, charge-backs, and disputes, as well as for supplies and equipment costs for terminals and card scanners. In some cases these may be included in bundled pricing.

VIII. SUMMARY

This chapter began with a discussion of the basics of how payment systems work, including a discussion of settlement versus finality. A payment system is a series of processes that transfers monetary value from one party to another. *Settlement* is defined as the point at which funds are transferred between the two parties to a transaction and are available for use by the receiving party. This is distinctly different from finality, which is the point at which funds belong to the receiving party and cannot be recalled for such things as non-sufficient funds or fraud.

The remainder of the chapter provided an overview of cash payments as well as each of the major types of payment systems: paper-based (e.g., checks), large-value transfer systems (e.g., wire transfers), small-value transfer systems (e.g., ACH), and card-based systems. Specific issues relevant to each type of payment, including but not limited to timing, settlement, and finality, were also covered.

---

15. From "Average Debit Card Fee by Payment Card Network (2015)," published by the Federal Reserve Board (https://www.federalreserve.gov/paymentsystems/ regii-average-interchange-fee.htm).

Appendix 4.4 provides an overview of the payment systems used in several major countries. The appendix suggests substantial variation across these systems. Within each payment system there are often multiple channels for processing and settling transactions, such as direct presentment versus central bank clearing for checks, or Fedwire versus CHIPS for US wire transfers.

APPENDIX 4.1: CHECK RETURN REASONS

Not Sufficient Funds/Non-sufficient Funds (NSF): At the time the check was presented to the account holder's bank, there were not enough funds in the account to pay the check or draft. NSF checks can be redeposited unless the front of the item is stamped "Do Not Redeposit."

Uncollected Funds (UCF or UF)/Uncollected Funds Hold (UFH): Items are returned because funds in the account are not yet collected and available. UCF checks can be redeposited.

Stop Payment/Stop Pay: The person who originally wrote the check or authorized the draft has revoked his/her authorization. Stop pay checks cannot be redeposited.

Closed Account/Account Closed: The account holder's bank account that was associated with the check is closed. Closed-account items cannot be redeposited.

Unable to Locate Account/Unable to Locate (UTL): The bank cannot find any account with that account number in its records. UTL checks cannot be redeposited.

Frozen Account/Blocked Account: The account is blocked or frozen due to legal action. A bank can be required to freeze an account due to a divorce judgment, tax lien, wage garnishment, court order, or other legal reason. Checks stamped "Frozen Account" cannot be redeposited.

Stale-Dated Check/Stale Check/Expired Check: The check is past the expiration date as set by the check issuer. Some checks are valid only if cashed or deposited within 7 days, 30 days, 90 days, or 180 days. Checks with this time limit may be returned as stale-dated or expired checks, and cannot be redeposited.

Post-Dated/Post-Dated Check: The date on the check is for a future date. Future-dated checks can be returned as post-dated checks. Checks that are returned and stamped "Post-Dated" or "Post-Dated Check" can be redeposited on or after, but not before, the date of the check.

Endorsement Missing/Missing Endorsement: The depositor did not endorse the check. Checks stamped "Endorsement Missing" may be redeposited after adding an appropriate endorsement.

Endorsement Irregular/Irregular Endorsement: There is a problem with the endorsement, such as the endorsement is illegible, the signature does not match the payee name on the check, or the endorsement is not in the correct location. Checks with irregular endorsement may be redeposited after the endorsement issue has been resolved.

Signature(s) Missing: The required signature or signatures on a check are not present. Some checks can be returned for signature missing when two signatures are required to write a check on a particular account and only one signature appears on the check. A check with signature(s) missing cannot be redeposited until the proper signature or signatures are collected.

Signature(s) Irregular: A signature does not match the account holder's, or the signature appears damaged, altered, or otherwise obscured. "Signature(s) Irregular" checks cannot be redeposited. A new item must be obtained from the maker of the check.

Noncash Item/Not Cash Item (NCI): An invalid check, such as a rebate coupon, promotional check, or gift certificate, is deposited in error as a real check. NCI items cannot be redeposited.

Altered Item/Fictitious Item: The check does not match the account holder's records or the bank's records as far as the amount, date, or terms of the check, and is being returned in dispute of its validity. Any alteration can void the check at the discretion of the paying bank. A cross-out, alteration, or change should be initialed by the account holder, but does not always stop returns, especially with high-dollar items. Altered/fictitious items may not be redeposited.

Not Authorized/Unauthorized: The account holder disputed the item during the payment presentment process, or the account has a block such as "No Drafts" or "No Debits." Items returned as not authorized or unauthorized cannot be redeposited.

Refer to Maker (RTM): The account holder must contact the maker of the check to determine why the check was returned. Checks returned as "Refer to Maker" cannot be redeposited.

APPENDIX 4.2: FEDWIRE FORMAT EXAMPLE

The sample shown is a relatively simple US domestic wire going directly from one bank to another. Additional tags and data elements are available and used for more complex payments. In the event that the business function code (tag {3600}) is CTP (Customer Transfer Plus), an additional field with a tag of *{8200}* is used, with the ability to transmit up to 8,994 characters of formatted remittance data. For further information on the Fedwire format, refer to the latest Fedwire Funds Service Format Reference Guide from the Federal Reserve Bank, available at www.frbservices.org.

Definition of Fed Tag Values	Fed Tag[16]	Sample Value
Transaction Dollar Amount: Total wire value with no decimal and no commas (12 positions) (Example: $250.00 = 000000025000)	**{2000}**	**000000025000**
Sending Bank's ABA Number (9 positions), and **Sending Bank's Name**	{3100}	000123790 ABC BANK
Receiving Bank's ABA Number (9 positions), and **Receiving Bank's Name**	**{3400}**	**129999999** **XYZ BANK**
Business Function Code (Transaction Type) (Example: CTR = Customer Transfer, nonbank beneficiary)	**{3600}**	**CTR**
Beneficiary Information (BNF): Beneficiary's account number at receiving bank, including: **ID Code** (If ID code is present, identifier is mandatory, and vice versa.) **Identifier** (34 characters) **Name** (35 characters) **Address** (3 lines of 35 characters each)	**{4200}**	**123456789** Company X
Reference to Beneficiary (RFB): Remittance or other reference information (up to 16 characters)	**{4320}**	ABC123456789
Originator Information (ORG): Originating customer account number from sending bank; name of originating company; and originator's address, city, state, and zip code	{5000}	12345 ABC COMPANY 123 ABC PLAZA NEW YORK NY 10258
Originator to Beneficiary Information (OBI): Additional beneficiary (remittance) information (up to 4 lines of 35 characters each)	**{6000}**	XYZ9999998

16. In "Fed Tag" and "Value" columns, bold font indicates a mandatory field.

APPENDIX 4.3: FEDGLOBAL ACH PAYMENTS COUNTRIES

Austria

Belgium

Canada

Cyprus

Czech Republic

Denmark

Finland

France

Germany

Greece

Ireland

Italy

Luxembourg

Malta

Mexico

Netherlands

Panama

Poland

Portugal

Slovakia

Slovenia

Spain

Sweden

Switzerland

United Kingdom

APPENDIX 4.4: BANKING AND PAYMENT SYSTEMS INFORMATION FOR SELECTED COUNTRIES[17]

A. China

1. BANKING

The Chinese central bank is the People's Bank of China (PBC). Bank supervision is performed by the China Banking Regulatory Commission (CBRC). China applies central bank reporting requirements. These are managed by the State Administration for Foreign Exchange (SAFE), according to the rules set out in the Regulations on Foreign Exchange System of the People's Republic of China (2008) and relevant regulations. Resident entities are permitted to hold foreign currency bank accounts domestically and outside of China, but residents must first gain approval from SAFE for foreign currency bank accounts held abroad. Nonresident entities are permitted to hold foreign currency bank accounts within China. Nonresidents can hold fully convertible renminbi (RMB) trade settlement accounts inside and outside of China but these accounts are subject to restrictions and PBC approval.

China has five major commercial banking institutions, which control over 37% of the country's banking assets. There are also three government-controlled policy banks, established in 1994. There are 12 joint-stock commercial banks, 83 rural commercial banks, 223 rural cooperative banks, 349 village and township banks, and 2,646 rural credit cooperatives, as well as 91 city commercial banks that specialize in retail and corporate commerce. The government indirectly controls the country's commercial banks by maintaining a majority share in each bank. There is an increasing foreign banking presence in China—412 foreign institutions have established operations in China and 41 foreign banks have become locally incorporated, operating 275 branches. Foreign banks, if incorporated locally, are able to offer RMB retail products to Chinese residents and are subject to national treatment.

2. PAYMENTS

China's three main interbank payment clearing systems are CNAPS-LVPS, CNAPS-BEPS,[18] and the Local Clearing House system (LCHs). The RTGS-based China Domestic Foreign Currency Payment System (CDFCPS) was introduced in July 2008 for eight international currencies. In addition, a "Super e-banking" online interbank clearing system for real-time Internet payments and account enquiries was introduced in August 2010. The system linked up the individual online payment systems of approximately 161 financial institutions during 2015.

The most important cashless payment instruments in China are debit cards among individuals, checks between local institutions, and electronic credit transfers for intercity payments. Economic expansion in China's large cities has led to a growth in the use of electronic payments, such as Internet, telephone, and mobile payments.

B. India

1. BANKING

The Reserve Bank of India (RBI) is fully owned by the Indian government and is charged with maintaining monetary stability by directing lending and deposit rates. In addition, the RBI is responsible for FX management, currency issuance, and regulation of the financial system via the Board for Financial Supervision. The RBI compiles

---

17. Information in this appendix was obtained from the executive summaries of the selected countries' *Cash and Treasury Management Country Reports* as provided by AFP for its members through its AFP Country Profiles (http://www.afponline.org/pub/country/profiles.html). The executive summaries used were dated (last updated) August 2016, except for India, which was dated July 2016.
18. LVPS (Large-Value Payment System) and BEPS (Bulk Electronic Payment System) are the application systems of the China National Advanced Payment System (CNAPS).

balance-of-payments data as required by the Foreign Exchange Management Act. Banks that undertake FX trans-actions must submit returns and supporting documents.

Residents and certain nonresidents may hold accounts denominated in Indian rupees (INR) or in a foreign currency both in India and abroad. However, there are a number of restrictions on the different types of accounts permitted. India's banking system is dominated by state-owned commercial and development banks, which provide the majority of financing for domestic and foreign companies. Around 44 foreign banks have established operations in India, but there are restrictions on acquisitions and the expansion of branch networks.

2. PAYMENTS

India operates an RTGS system for high-value electronic payments, as well as a number of payment systems for processing paper-based and retail electronic instruments. India's vast geography requires a network of more than 10,000 access points to its various payment systems. Debit cards are the most commonly used cashless payment instrument in terms of volume, and credit transfers are the mostly widely used in terms of value. Checks and drafts are also commonly used instruments for commercial transactions in India, but cash is the dominant payment method for medium- and small-value transactions.

C. Japan

1. BANKING

The Japanese central bank is the Bank of Japan (BOJ). Bank supervision is performed by the Financial Services Agency. Japan does apply some central bank reporting requirements. These are managed by the Ministry of Finance (MOF) through the BOJ, according to the rules set out in the Foreign Exchange and Foreign Trade Act, and relevant regulations.

Resident entities may hold fully convertible foreign currency bank accounts both domestically and outside Japan. Nonresident entities may hold fully convertible domestic and foreign currency bank accounts within Japan. Japan has four large city banks and a decreasing number of regional banks (64), which are divided into first and second tiers generally according to size and assets. There is a significant foreign banking presence in Japan—53 foreign banks have established branches in Japan.

2. PAYMENTS

Japan's four main interbank payment clearing systems are the BOJ Financial Network System (BOJ-NET), the Foreign Exchange Yen Clearing System (FXYCS), Zengin, and the BCCSs (bill and cheque clearing systems). In addition, there are seven Japanese banks that are settlement members of CLS Bank.

The most important cashless payment instruments in Japan are electronic credit transfers in terms of value and, in terms of volume, payment cards. Checks are primarily used for business-to-business transactions, while direct debits are widely used among individuals and businesses to make regular payments. Though the Japanese have been slower to adopt credit and debit cards, their usage, particularly of credit cards, is increasing rapidly.

D. United Kingdom (UK)

1. BANKING

The United Kingdom's central bank is the Bank of England. Prudential regulation and supervision of the banking sector is performed by the Prudential Regulation Authority (PRA), a part of the Bank of England. The United Kingdom does not impose central bank reporting requirements.

Resident entities are permitted to hold fully convertible domestic currency (pounds, or GBP) and foreign currency bank accounts within and outside the United Kingdom. Nonresident entities are permitted to hold fully convertible domestic and foreign currency bank accounts within the United Kingdom.

The United Kingdom has 157 banks (of both domestic and foreign origin) and 44 building societies. There is a significant foreign banking presence in the United Kingdom and 155 foreign banks have established branches.

2. PAYMENTS

The United Kingdom's four main payment systems are CHAPS, Bacs, the Faster Payments service, and the Cheque and Credit Clearing Company (C&CC) system. The most important cashless payment instruments in the United Kingdom are electronic credit transfers in terms of value and card payments in terms of volume. Checks and direct debits are also popular payment instruments in the United Kingdom. The increased use of electronic and Internet banking by consumers and businesses has led to significant growth in the use of electronic payments.

CHAPTER 5
Money Markets

I. INTRODUCTION

II. GLOBAL MONEY MARKETS
 A. Money Market Participants
 B. Investment Risk Considerations
 C. Types of Money Market Instruments

III. MONEY MARKETS IN THE UNITED STATES
 A. Processing and Clearing of Money Market Instruments in the United States
 B. US Money Market Participants
 C. US Federal Agency and Government-Sponsored Enterprise (GSE) Securities
 D. Municipal Notes, Variable-Rate Demand Obligations (VRDOs), and Tax-Exempt Commercial Paper (CP)

IV. SUMMARY

I. INTRODUCTION

The term *money markets* refers to a global marketplace for short-term financial investments that are easily converted to cash (i.e., highly liquid). Money market securities have a maturity of one year or less and are generally debt instruments. Examples of money market securities include negotiable certificates of deposit, banker's acceptances, government securities (e.g., US Treasury bills, municipal securities), commercial paper, municipal notes, federal funds, and repurchase agreements. This market is used by treasury professionals for investing excess cash or raising short-term funds.

This chapter describes the aspects associated with money markets that are pertinent to treasury professionals. Yield calculations for money market securities are discussed in Chapter 13, Short-Term Investing and Borrowing.

II. GLOBAL MONEY MARKETS

This section describes participants in the money market, investment risk considerations, and types of money market securities.

A. Money Market Participants

Issuers of money market securities include governments, securities dealers, commercial banks, and other corporations (including not-for-profits). In money markets, investors are lenders and issuers are borrowers. That is, investors purchasing money market securities are making short-term loans to issuers. In many cases, money market participants are simultaneously issuers and investors, depending on their liquidity needs at a specific point in time.

A broker-dealer is an entity that trades securities for its own account or on behalf of its customers. When executing trade orders on behalf of a customer, the institution acts as a broker. When executing trades for its own account, the institution acts as a dealer. Securities bought from clients or other firms in the capacity of a dealer may be sold to clients or to other firms, acting again in the capacity of a dealer, or they may become a part of the broker-dealer's own holdings.

Broker-dealers can hold securities in their name, in the customer's name, or in a "street name." In the latter case, the securities are held in the broker's name on behalf of the broker's customer. Holding securities in the street name does not affect the rights of the actual owner of the securities, but does eliminate the need to reregister or reissue securities in the name of the actual owner. This was originally done to simplify trading, as reregistration of securities once took several days. Although this is no longer an issue due to electronic trading systems and the ability to change ownership names immediately, money market securities are still frequently held in the street name. This practice also permits investors to keep their investment activities anonymous, absent any legal requirements for public disclosure.

Although many broker-dealers are independent firms solely involved in broker-dealer services, others are business units or subsidiaries of commercial banks, investment banks, or investment companies.

Broker-dealers are compensated through fees and/or commissions. Broker-dealers play key roles in money markets by placing the majority of new issues in the primary market and by providing secondary markets with the liquidity necessary for outstanding issues. Primary market transactions offer newly issued debt and equity securities to investors, while secondary market transactions involve previously issued securities.

When acting as dealers, these parties also take positions in securities so they can act as the counterparty[1] in the purchase and sale of transactions. The price or yield at which the dealer will sell a security is known as the *ask price*, while the price or yield at which the dealer will purchase a security is known as the *bid price*. The difference between the ask and bid price is called the *spread*, and represents the dealer's profit on a specific transaction. Dealers also enter into repurchase agreements, which are money market transactions used to finance a dealer's securities inventories. Money markets and related securities fall under the jurisdiction of a variety of regulators, depending on the parties to a transaction, the securities involved, and the markets or exchanges on which the instruments are traded.

Central securities depositories (CSDs) are companies that hold securities to enable book-entry transfer of securities. In addition, CSDs may provide trade matching as well as clearing and settlement, thereby increasing the liquidity of the money market. Nearly all short-term securities are issued in noncertificated or book-entry form.

A US-based example of a CSD is the Depository Trust Company (DTC). Other examples include Euroclear (Belgium) and the Singapore Exchange, or SGX (Singapore). Many central securities depositories settle trades in both domestic and international securities through links to local CSDs. The DTC holds over $2 trillion in non-US securities and in American depositary receipts from over 100 nations, due to the large number of trades executed in the United States.

B. Investment Risk Considerations

Although money market instruments are primarily low-risk/low-yield investments, it is critical for treasury professionals to understand the risks associated with this asset class. Specific risk considerations covered here include default/credit risk, liquidity risk, interest rate risk, and foreign exchange risk.

1. DEFAULT/CREDIT RISK

Default or *credit risk* refers to the likelihood that the payments owed to creditors will not be made under the original loan terms. Subsequently, issuers of money market instruments are examined to assess the probability of default risk. Issuers with higher default risk must offer investors a higher yield to compensate for the increased risk. This increased yield represents a risk premium (i.e., the incremental yield above an otherwise comparable security). For the period beginning in 1972 through the first half of 2013, a total of 60 issuers defaulted on approximately $11 billion of commercial paper. Twenty of these defaults were US issuers and 21 were related to European issues. The number of commercial paper defaults peaked in 1990, but was also relatively high in 1994–1995, 2001, and 2008.[2]

The default risk of money market instrument issuers is usually assessed by credit rating agencies, such as Moody's, Standard & Poor's (S&P), Fitch, or DBRS (formerly Dominion Bond Rating Service).[3]

Most issuers of money market instruments have an acceptable credit rating. Some short-term investments may be unrated, which means additional research effort for potential investors. Initially, the investment must be evaluated for credit risk, which could be an involved process. Another concern is that if the security must be resold, then the new purchaser would most likely need to perform a credit risk evaluation on the security. This process could make it difficult to find a buyer—or at a minimum, delay the sale—leading to increased liquidity risk on the investment.

---

1. A counterparty, as the name implies, is the person on the other side of a financial transaction (e.g., to a buyer of securities, the counterparty is the entity selling the security).
2. From "Default and Recovery Rates of Corporate Commercial Paper Issuers, 1972–H1," published by Moody's Investors Service, October 2013 (https://www.moodys .com/Pages/GuideToDefaultResearch.aspx).
3. These are more generally known as *nationally recognized statistical rating organizations (NRSROs)*.

2. LIQUIDITY RISK

A liquid security is an instrument that can be converted quickly and easily into cash with very little exposure to market price risk and for a small transaction cost. Subsequently, *liquidity risk* refers to the likelihood that a security cannot be sold quickly without incurring a substantial loss in value.

The primary determinants of liquidity are marketability and maturity. The existence of an active secondary market ensures that the short-term securities suitable for liquidity management purposes are readily marketable. In terms of maturity, most financial instruments other than money market funds have a maturity date on which the obligation is redeemed. In general, money market instruments with shorter maturities are more liquid.

3. INTEREST RATE RISK

Interest rate risk involves the uncertainty associated with future interest rate levels. Interest rate risk has two components: reinvestment risk and price risk. The potential for lower interest rates results in reinvestment risk. After market interest rates drop, the proceeds from maturing investments will be reinvested at a lower rate. *Price risk* refers to changes in interest rates having an adverse impact on the value of a security. Securities with longer maturities have increased price risk as their market values are more responsive to changes in interest rates. As interest rates increase, the investor demand will be lower for previously issued securities with lower coupon rates. In general, *price risk* refers to the potential for an increase in interest rates. The relationship between the price of the market interest rate and the price of a debt security is illustrated in Exhibit 5.1.

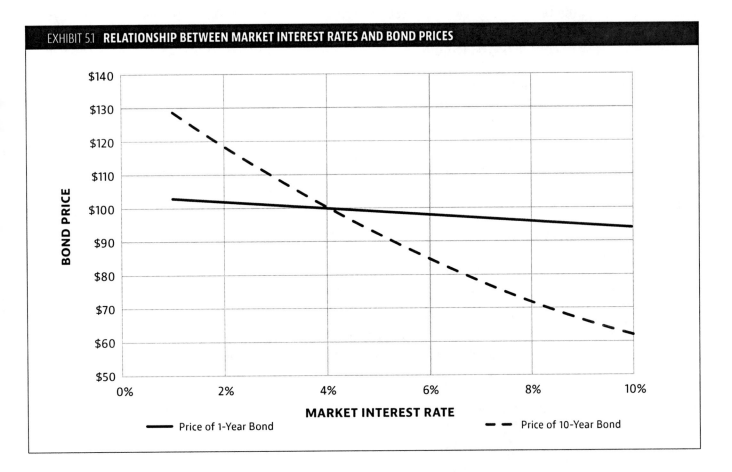

EXHIBIT 5.1 **RELATIONSHIP BETWEEN MARKET INTEREST RATES AND BOND PRICES**

4. FOREIGN EXCHANGE (FX) RISK

FX risk arises when investors purchase securities denominated in foreign currencies. An adverse change in the FX rate can result in a lower rate of return when the proceeds from the investment are converted to the firm's home currency. If the foreign currency depreciates relative to the investor's local currency, then the value of the investment declines. For example, a European investor may purchase US Treasuries. The European investor's FX risk is conditional on the volatility of the exchange rate between the euro and the US dollar. During the holding period, a depreciation in the US dollar relative to the euro will reduce the European investor's return. This occurs because the European investor will exchange the US dollar proceeds (earned on the Treasuries) for fewer euros.

FX risk is present whether the investment is sold prior to maturity or is redeemed at maturity. To limit FX risk, the investment policies for many firms will only permit investment in foreign securities if the security is (1) issued in an economically and politically stable country, and/or (2) suitable as part of an overall currency hedging strategy.

C. Types of Money Market Instruments

This section describes the characteristics of various money market instruments.

1. COMMERCIAL PAPER (CP)

CP refers to tradable promissory notes that represent an unsecured obligation or debt of the issuer (i.e., the CP is not backed or "secured" by any collateral of the issuer). Maturity can range from overnight to 270 days for publicly traded CP (issued in the United States under the SEC Securities Act of 1933 Section 3(a)(3)) and up to 397 days for private-placement CP (issued under Section 4(a)(2) of the same act), but most CP matures in less than 45 days. CP does not usually pay interest during its term; instead, it is issued at a discounted price and the face value is paid at maturity. Therefore, the yield on CP is primarily influenced by the difference between the purchase price and the face value. The dollar discount and yield on CP are influenced by the credit rating of the issuer and by the rating for the specific issue of CP. Most CP is purchased for a specific maturity and is held for the full term. However, CP can be traded on the secondary market prior to maturity.

CP offers investors various advantages. The broad range of available maturities allows investors to choose CP issues with the desired maturity. Also, investment-grade CP is highly liquid. Investors can diversify the risk of their CP holdings by investing in CP across different industries and sectors of the economy. Both Europe and the United States have highly developed CP markets, offering opportunities for geographic diversification.

A disadvantage of investing in CP is that it is not secured against a particular asset. Consequently, CP is commonly issued with credit enhancement. For example, the issuer may acquire either a backup line of credit or standby letter of credit from a financial institution, thereby mitigating the potential for default. Consequently, most investors will want to invest in highly rated individual CP issues and set strict counterparty limits.

Asset-backed commercial paper (ABCP) has most of the features of standard CP listed above, but it is secured against specific assets—usually short-term trade receivables from a single company or a range of companies. ABCP is issued through a sponsoring financial institution, referred to as a *conduit* (which is a separate subsidiary), rather than directly by an issuing company. ABCP may be classified as either *single seller,* if it is backed by assets from a single institution, or *multi-seller,* if it is backed by assets purchased from a number of issuers. As of March 2015, ABCP accounted for approximately 26% of the commercial paper outstanding in the United States.[4]

---

4. This statistic is derived from commercial paper data provided on the website for the Board of Governors of the Federal Reserve System (http://www.federal reserve.gov/releases/cp/outstanding.htm, accessed 11/11/2015).

The primary advantage of ABCP is that it offers more security than standard CP. Investors' interests are protected by some form of asset. In addition, credit enhancement from the sponsoring bank will facilitate timely repayment at maturity.

In terms of disadvantages, the complex structure of ABCP makes it harder to appraise the overall risk of the security and may therefore require the use of third-party credit monitoring. Another disadvantage is that the ABCP market is smaller than the standard CP market. These disadvantages increase the liquidity risk for ABCP. However, investors tend to be rewarded for this extra complexity with a moderately higher rate of return than on standard CP.

2. BANK OBLIGATIONS

Banks raise funds in the money markets through time deposits, banker's acceptances, and repurchase agreements (covered later in this chapter). These are sometimes collectively referred to as *bank paper* or *bank obligations*.

Examples of time deposits include savings accounts, certificates of deposit (CDs), and negotiable CDs. Negotiable CDs are large-value time deposits issued by banks and other financial institutions that are bought and sold on the open market. Negotiable CDs are usually traded in multiples of 100,000 or more (US dollars [USD] or foreign currency equivalent). While all CDs have a fixed maturity, there is an active secondary market for negotiable CDs. Nonnegotiable or retail CDs are issued in many different denominations to consumers and businesses. Drawbacks associated with nonnegotiable CDs include the lack of a secondary market and an inability to redeem them prior to maturity without a penalty.

Investments in CDs are protected by deposit insurance in the United States. Typically, however, deposit insurance limits are too low to provide significant protection against credit risk for most business investors. One solution to this problem in the United States is the Certificate of Deposit Account Registry Service (CDARS). CDARS is a private service that makes it possible to receive full FDIC insurance coverage on amounts up to $50 million by distributing the funds among CDs issued by a network of banks. The investor receives the quoted rate offered by the bank receiving the initial deposit, and CDARS provides the investor with one periodic statement detailing the locations and amounts of its deposits.

Non-US banks and foreign branches of US banks raise funds in global money markets through Eurodollar deposits (commonly referred to as *Eurodollars*). Eurodollars are USD-denominated deposits held in financial institutions outside the United States. Eurodollars may be issued as negotiable Eurodollar CDs or as nonnegotiable Eurodollar time deposits, both of which are interest-bearing. Many multinational businesses invest in these foreign bank issues because they provide the ability to invest in USD-based securities that historically have had a higher rate of interest than comparable US bank securities, due to fewer regulations and a lack of US reserve requirements.

Yankee CDs are USD-denominated CDs sold by US branches of non-US banks. They are typically sold through the New York branches of foreign banks and carry minimum investments of $100,000. As with Eurodollar CDs, Yankees historically had a higher rate of interest than comparable US bank securities, due to regulatory differences and a lack of reserve requirements. Although that difference has largely disappeared as regulations have changed, investors may still use Yankee CDs to provide geographic diversification in their portfolio.

A banker's acceptance (BA) arises from commercial trade. It represents a time draft that is issued by a purchaser of goods to pay a supplier and that has been accepted by the bank on which the draft is drawn. The BA constitutes the bank's unconditional promise to pay the draft at maturity. The holder (i.e., beneficiary) of the BA can either wait until maturity to receive payment in full or sell the BA prior to maturity at a discount.

3. GOVERNMENT PAPER

National, state, and local government agencies raise funds in the money market by issuing short-term promissory notes, referred to as *government paper.*

The market for most countries' government paper is liquid and highly active, due to the government's backing. The yields on government paper tend to be lower than other instruments of comparable maturity because of the lower default risk. In most cases government paper is issued on a discount basis. A variety of maturities are generally available, depending on the government's borrowing requirements, allowing investors to closely match their liquidity requirements.

UK gilts, US Treasuries, German bunds, Japanese government bonds (JGBs), and Mexican government bonds are all examples of sovereign government bonds. The United States, Japan, and Europe have historically been the biggest issuers in the government bond market.[5] While US Treasury issues include Treasury bills (also known as *T-bills*), notes, and bonds, only those maturing within one year are classified as *money market instruments*. Due to a perception of low liquidity and low default risk, US treasuries are generally considered risk-free and serve as the benchmark against which interest rates on other debt securities are compared.

T-bills are money market instruments that are sold at a discount to their par value at maturity and are issued with original maturities of less than one year. At the time of this writing, bills are issued with maturities of 4, 13, 26, and 52 weeks. Newly issued T-bills are sold through a multiple-price, sealed-bid auction. T-bills can be purchased on either a competitive or a noncompetitive basis. For investors submitting competitive bids, the bids are accepted starting with the highest price (i.e., lowest yield) offered, down to the lowest price necessary to sell the entire issue. Noncompetitive bids may also be submitted. In this case, the bidder is guaranteed to receive the desired amount of T-bills at the average price from the competitive bid process.

Eligible banks, broker-dealers, and other private and governmental entities tender bids for specific amounts of the offered securities. Dealer bid and ask yield quotes for T-bills are published daily. In general, the bid discount will exceed the ask discount. This is because the dealer's bid discount represents the discount at which the dealer is willing to buy a given security, while the dealer's ask discount represents the discount at which the dealer is willing to sell a given security.

The secondary market for US treasuries is one of the largest in the world. The liquidity in the US Treasury market coupled with low transaction costs makes T-bills highly marketable. T-bills can be bought and sold in significant volumes with negligible, if any, impact on market prices and yields.

4. FLOATING-RATE NOTES (FRNS)

Firms, banks, sovereigns, and government agencies raise short-term funds via FRNs. In terms of maturity, FRNs sit at the longer end of the money market maturity spectrum, with maturities typically of one year or longer. FRNs pay a regular coupon,[6] as well as the promise of a return of their face value at maturity. The actual return, or margin, on an FRN is a combination of the coupon interest rate and the capital gain or loss that results from an FRN transaction, since FRNs are traded on the secondary market at a discount. If an FRN is trading at par value, then the return is identical to the coupon rate.

---

5. From "Everything You Need to Know About Bonds," published by PIMCO, July 2015 (http://www.pimco.com/resources/education/everything-you-need-to-know-about-bonds).

6. A coupon payment is a regular payment of interest on the face value of the investment. Coupons are typically used in instruments with maturities of greater than one year. The name comes from the fact that securities were historically issued in paper form with coupons that represented each interest payment attached to the bond. Bondholders had to "clip" the coupon from the bond and return it to the issuer to receive the interest payment.

The name *floating-rate note* derives from the fact that the rate of interest resets periodically, based on a reference rate such as the London Interbank Offered Rate (LIBOR) or the Euro Interbank Offered Rate (Euribor). As a result, FRNs are sold at a quoted spread over the stated reference rate. The spread is a rate that remains constant while the reference rate can vary. FRNs can have a variety of special features, such as minimum or maximum coupon rates. Perpetual FRNs are a type of FRN that is issued with no maturity date, and investors can only recapture their capital by selling them on the secondary market.

The variable-rate nature of FRNs makes them very appealing in uncertain interest rate environments and when investors do not want to lock themselves into a fixed rate. FRNs tend to offer relatively attractive yields. Moreover, the regular resetting of the coupon means investors experience less capital volatility than with fixed-interest securities. The creditworthiness of FRNs is generally straightforward to ascertain because they tend to have a published credit rating. However, independent analysis is always recommended, especially when the possibility of a downgrade exists. As with CP, some FRNs are issued with credit enhancements to improve their marketability. In addition, FRNs may be secured by collateral pledged by borrowers.

Similar to fixed-rate bonds, a disadvantage of an FRN investment is that an FRN's capital value can fluctuate in the time between interest rate resets that bring the security's yield in line with the rest of the market.[7] The bid-offer spread of an FRN tends to be wider than the other instruments detailed above, and so regular trading can erode any yield advantage relatively quickly.[8] Like CDs, FRNs tend to be issued with fairly large minimum denominations. Smaller investors may be unable to achieve sufficient counterparty diversification by buying FRNs individually. In this case, it may be more appropriate to access them via a money market fund.

5. REPURCHASE AGREEMENTS (REPOs)

In a typical repo, a bank or securities dealer sells government securities it owns to an investor and agrees to repurchase them at a later date and at a slightly higher price. In most cases, this type of agreement is referred to as a *repo agreement* from the perspective of the entity selling the securities and agreeing to repurchase them at a later date. From the perspective of the entity that buys the securities with a promise to sell them back at a later date, it is generally known as a *reverse repo*. Thus, the repo side of the transaction is actually a short-term borrowing arrangement while the reverse repo side is a short-term investment arrangement.

Repos usually involve the sale and repurchase of government debt. However, repos can be based on any security. Repos are classified as *overnight, term* (two days or longer), and *open* (no maturity date). Term repos may have any maturity agreeable to both parties, but they are rarely for periods of more than a year. An open repo has no maturity date, but rather either party can terminate the agreement on a day-by-day basis.

Since each repo is negotiated individually between two parties, the maturity and yield on the repo can be tailored to each party's requirements (although the yield will generally be determined by market repo rates). Taking legal possession of the underlying security (usually through a broker or dealer) also gives the investor a high degree of comfort, as repos can be sold if the selling counterparty defaults on the agreement, which is referred to as *settlement risk*. To further guard against settlement risk, repo transactions are generally overcollateralized, with the value of the securities exceeding the amount of the repo. When the collateral is held by a broker-dealer and the funds are exchanged through that party, the arrangement is called a *tri-party repo*. This is considered to be the safest method for securing the repo. While repos can be set up simply with standard contracts, the investor needs to perform due diligence to accurately price the exchanged security.

---

7. Fixed-rate bonds pay a fixed rate of interest (usually as a coupon payment) over their life. For example, a 6% bond would pay a coupon equal to 6% of its face value each year it was outstanding. Over the bond's life, only interest is paid. Then, the principal (i.e., face value) is paid at maturity.
8. *Bid-offer spread* refers to the difference in pricing for a security bought or sold through a dealer (i.e., the dealer will buy [bid] a security at one price, but sell [offer] at a higher price).

Exhibit 5.2 provides a comparative listing of the primary money market instruments for treasury professionals.

EXHIBIT 5.2 **COMPARISON OF SHORT-TERM INSTRUMENTS**						
	COMMERCIAL PAPER (CP)	**ASSET-BACKED COMMERCIAL PAPER (ABCP)**	**BANK OBLIGATIONS**	**GOVERNMENT PAPER**	**FLOATING-RATE NOTES (FRNs)**	**REPURCHASE AGREEMENTS (REPOS)**
MATURITY	Overnight– 270 days (average = 30 days)*	Overnight– 270 days (typically <45 days)*	1 day–2 years	4–52 weeks	Variable	Wholly negotiable
ISSUED BY	Companies and financial institutions	Companies and financial institutions	Banks	Governments and municipalities	Companies and financial institutions	Companies and financial institutions
INTEREST RATE	Fixed	Fixed	Fixed***	Fixed	Variable, with periodic reset dates	Negotiable
INTEREST PAID	On maturity**	On maturity**	During term or on maturity**	On maturity**	During term or on maturity	On maturity**
HOW ISSUED	Discount	Discount	Interest-bearing	Discount	Interest-bearing	Specified sales and repurchase price
SECURED	No	Yes	No	No	Yes/No	Yes
ACCESS TO CAPITAL BEFORE MATURITY	Sell on secondary market	Sell on secondary market	Sell on secondary market (for negotiable certificates of deposit and BAs)	Sell on secondary market	Sell on secondary market	Negotiable
INVESTMENT RISKS**	· Credit · Price	· Credit · Liquidity · Price	· Credit · Liquidity	· Credit · Liquidity · Price	· Credit · Liquidity	· Credit · Liquidity

* Although not common, private-placement CP can have a term of up to 397 days.

** Interest is paid via the security being issued at a discount to face value. (Calculation of investment yield of discount securities is discussed in Chapter 13, Short-Term Investing and Borrowing.)

*** Variable rates may be available on issues with maturities of one year or more.

**** Foreign exchange risk will be an issue for any investment denominated in a currency other than the currency of the investor.

6. OTHER TYPES OF MONEY MARKET INVESTMENTS

This section describes additional money market securities, including money market funds and short-duration mutual funds.

a. Money Market Funds (MMFs)

MMFs, known as *unit trusts* in the United Kingdom and Europe, are commingled pools of money market securities. In fact, many of the investments discussed earlier form the basis for these funds. MMFs are typically held by financial institutions, and investors purchase an ownership interest in the fund. MMFs may be offered in the local currency or, where allowed by local regulators, in a foreign currency. In the United States, there are five common types of money market funds:

- **US Treasury Funds:** Assets are invested only in US Treasury securities.
- **Government Funds:** 99.5% of total assets must be invested in cash, government securities, and repurchase agreements collateralized by government securities.
- **Institutional Prime Funds:** Assets are invested in commercial paper, certificates of deposit, government securities, repurchase agreements, and other short-term instruments.
- **Institutional Municipal/Tax-Exempt Funds:** Assets are invested in tax-exempt securities issued by state and local governments.
- **Retail Funds:** Funds are offered to individuals. Institutional investors are restricted from investing in retail money market funds as of October 2016.

Key characteristics of MMFs include diversification and price stability. MMFs usually maintain a dollar-weighted average portfolio maturity of 60 days or less. Consequently, MMFs do not hold securities with maturities exceeding 397 days. In the United States, MMFs are regulated by the SEC, which under Rule 2a-7 restricts investments in MMFs by quality, maturity, and diversity. The 2010 version of this rule imposes minimum liquidity requirements, implements daily and weekly liquidity requirements, and restricts the ability of funds to purchase illiquid and lower-quality securities. The US MMF market is significantly larger than comparable markets in other countries, due to the extensive US regulatory provisions governing MMFs.

Money market funds generally have a net asset value (NAV) set at one unit of the currency of offering (e.g., dollars, pounds, or euros). The primary goal of MMFs is stability and security. As long as the NAV of a fund does not fall below one unit (e.g., $1), referred to as "breaking the buck," the investor's initial principal is secure. Historically, MMFs have been secure investments, and many treasury professionals regard them as the equivalent of cash in the bank.

It should be emphasized that MMFs are not risk-free assets and funds can differ substantially in terms of risk, maturity, and return. In September 2008, the Reserve Primary Fund became the second US MMF to "break the buck." The fund held a considerable amount of commercial paper issued by Lehman Brothers, which was considered worthless after the investment bank failed. This event created a run on the Reserve Primary Fund, which then spread to other MMFs. The funds began to sell securities and hoard cash in order to meet redemption demands. Since MMFs held approximately 40% of outstanding commercial paper at that time, corporations had difficulty finding buyers for new short-term debt. The SEC implemented several rule changes to prevent future runs on MMFs. Initial reforms adopted in 2010 reduced risk by mandating liquidity requirements to allow funds to more easily meet demand for redemptions.

Additional reforms by the SEC are scheduled for implementation in October 2016 (as outlined in Exhibit 5.3). These measures apply to institutional money market funds that do not qualify as government funds. The new rules include a floating NAV, redemption fees if a fund's weekly liquid assets fall below a threshold, and the ability to suspend redemptions (using restrictions known as *redemption gates*) for a period of up to 10 business days. Government MMFs are not subject to these rules.

EXHIBIT 5.3 OCTOBER 2016 MONEY MARKET FUND CHANGES

TYPE OF FUND	NET ASSET VALUE (NAV)	REDEMPTION FEES	REDEMPTION GATES
US Treasury	Stable	No	No
Government	Stable	No	No
Institutional Prime	Floating	Yes	Yes
Institutional Municipal/Tax-Exempt	Floating	Yes	Yes
Retail	Stable	Yes	Yes

Despite the aforementioned risks, MMFs offer numerous benefits. For example, MMFs offer daily liquidity and pay dividends (usually monthly) based on the fund's average yield for the dividend period. Since minimum investments in many MMFs tend to be substantially smaller than those required for direct investments in money market securities, organizations can tailor their short-term portfolios to meet diversification and maturity requirements.

Another benefit of MMFs is that they are more stable than other money market securities during periods of interest rate volatility. For example, when interest rates are falling, MMF managers may extend the maturities of new securities purchases in the fund's underlying portfolio (within regulatory guidelines and limits) to lock in yields. Thus, investors in the fund receive the greater return of longer-term instruments while enjoying the liquidity and stability of principal that can be associated with investments with shorter maturities. The opposite holds true in rising interest rate environments.

The economies of scale of large MMFs imply competitive trading terms and low transaction costs. This helps to ensure that yield is not eroded by active management of the underlying portfolio. Most MMFs offer same-day settlement, making them just as liquid as overnight deposits. Moreover, MMFs are rated by the leading credit rating agencies, which helps investors to assess the funds' default risk.

Overall, MMFs can provide an organization with a low-cost, professionally managed, and marketable securities portfolio. MMFs are also administratively easy to use, helping to free up valuable treasury resources for other tasks. Even though MMFs charge management fees or service charges (based on the investor's balance or level of activity, or on the services provided to the investor), MMFs are more cost effective for many firms than managing a short-term investment portfolio.

b. Short-Duration Mutual Funds

Short-duration mutual funds invest in securities with maturities that exceed the maturities of most money market instruments. While this longer investment maturity offers the prospect of higher returns, it also exposes the investor to increased price volatility. Short-duration mutual funds do not typically have a fixed unit currency value.

The average maturity of securities held in a short-duration mutual fund portfolio is between one and three years. These funds place the majority of their holdings in specific types of instruments, such as government issues, CDs, or CP. Certain mutual fund companies offer various short-duration mutual funds based on maturity. Short-duration mutual funds may be used by investors to implement a strategy that matches investments with forecasted cash flow needs. For example, a treasury professional may place some investable cash in MMFs, other cash in a short-duration mutual fund with an average maturity of 15 months, and still other cash in a fund with an average maturity of 24 months.

III. MONEY MARKETS IN THE UNITED STATES

The US money market is extremely efficient and has substantial economies of scale. Other than the Federal Reserve System (Fed), no single participant is large enough to impact prices. The US money market is routinely accessed by treasury professionals around the world, due to the market's size and perceived safety.[9]

This section of the chapter describes issues that apply to the US money market.

A. Processing and Clearing of Money Market Instruments in the United States

There are two primary entities that provide for the processing and clearing of most money market instruments in the United States. One is the Fed's Commercial Book-Entry System (CBES) (also known as the Treasury/Reserve Automated Debt Entry System, or TRADES), which processes Treasury securities. The second is the Depository Trust & Clearing Corporation (DTCC), the parent company of DTC (the US CSD), which processes all forms of book-entry securities.

1. COMMERCIAL BOOK-ENTRY SYSTEM (CBES)[10]

Operated by the US Treasury, the CBES is a multi-tiered, automated system for purchasing, holding, and transferring marketable treasury securities. CBES exists as a delivery system that provides for the simultaneous transfer of securities against the settlement of funds. Securities owners (or their brokers on their behalf) receive interest and redemption payments wired directly to their linked accounts.

At the top tier of the CBES is the National Book-Entry System (NBES), which is operated by the Fed. For Treasury securities, the Fed operates the NBES in its capacity as the fiscal agent of the US Treasury. The Federal Reserve Banks maintain book-entry accounts for depository institutions, the US Treasury, foreign central banks, and most government-sponsored enterprises (GSEs).

At the middle tier of the CBES, depository institutions hold book-entry accounts for their customers (e.g., brokers, dealers, institutional investors, and trusts). At the lower tier, each broker, dealer, and financial institution maintains book-entry accounts for individual customers, corporations, and other entities.

When an investor purchases securities through a broker, dealer, or financial institution, the securities are held on the book-entry system of that firm. Holding Treasury securities in this manner is known as *indirect holding* since there are one or more entities between the investor and the issuer (US Treasury). The CBES has succeeded in replacing paper securities with electronic records, eliminating the potential for theft, loss, or counterfeiting.

---

9. The Federal Reserve estimated that approximately 34% of all US Treasury debt was held by foreign investors as of July 2015. Source: Federal Reserve Statistical Release Z.1, "Financial Accounts of the United States: Flow of Funds, Balance Sheets, and Integrated Macroeconomic Accounts (Coded Tables)," published by the Board of Governors of the Federal Reserve System, June 9, 2016 (http://www.federalreserve.gov/Releases/Z1/preview/Coded/coded.pdf).
10. Information on the CBES comes from the website for TreasuryDirect, an operation of the US Treasury Department (http://www.treasurydirect.gov/instit /auctfund/held/cbes/cbes.htm, last modified March 6, 2015).

2. DEPOSITORY TRUST & CLEARING CORPORATION (DTCC)[11]

Owned by member financial institutions (e.g., international broker-dealers, correspondent and clearing banks, mutual fund companies, and investment banks), the DTCC is a corporation that works through its subsidiaries to provide clearing, settlement, and information services for equities, corporate and municipal bonds, government and mortgage-backed securities, money market instruments, and over-the-counter derivatives. The DTCC was established in 1999 as a holding company to combine the Depository Trust Company (DTC) and the National Securities Clearing Corporation (NSCC). The DTCC brings significant efficiency to the market clearing process by acting as a legal depository (i.e., holding place) for most stock and bond certificates and by netting transactions among brokers, dealers, mutual funds, insurance companies, and other large institutional investors. The DTCC's depository primarily provides custody and asset servicing for millions of securities issues from the United States, but it also provides servicing for some foreign items.

The DTCC and its subsidiaries operate on an at-cost basis, charging transaction fees for services and then returning excess revenue to its members. All services provided through the clearing corporations and depository are registered with, and regulated by, the US SEC.

B. US Money Market Participants

Participants in the US money market include the same parties discussed earlier in this chapter in Section II, Global Money Markets. US issuers include the US Treasury, federal agencies, government-sponsored enterprises, securities dealers, commercial banks, thrifts, and municipalities, as well as corporations.

In addition, the Fed plays a significant role in the US money market. First, the Fed is responsible for managing the initial sale and subsequent settlement of most book-entry Treasury security sales/purchases. Secondly, the Fed implements US monetary policy through the FOMC (Federal Open Market Committee). The FOMC implements monetary policy through the purchase and sale of Treasury securities in the secondary markets, often using repos, as discussed above. Finally, the Fed buys, sells, and redeems Treasury securities in its role as fiscal agent for the US Treasury.

C. US Federal Agency and Government-Sponsored Enterprise (GSE) Securities

In addition to traditional government paper, such as T-bills, the US federal government has many agencies and GSEs that issue various securities. GSEs are private companies that act as financial intermediaries to provide funds for loans made in the housing, education, and agriculture sectors. Key GSEs include the following:

- Federal National Mortgage Association (FNMA, or Fannie Mae)
- Federal Home Loan Mortgage Corporation (FHLMC, or Freddie Mac)
- Department of Veterans Affairs (VA)
- Government National Mortgage Association (GNMA, or Ginnie Mae)
- Federal Farm Credit Banks Funding Corporation

Although GSEs do not generally have the credit backing of the US government, the importance of GSEs to public welfare has motivated the federal government to intervene in past crises (e.g., Fannie Mae and Freddie Mac during the global financial crisis of 2007–2009).

---

11. Information on the DTCC was obtained from the DTCC website (http://www.dtcc.com/about.aspx, accessed September 12, 2015).

D. Municipal Notes, Variable-Rate Demand Obligations (VRDOs), and Tax-Exempt Commercial Paper (CP)

In addition to paper issued by the federal, state, and local governments, their agencies, authorities, and subdivisions raise funds in the money market through municipal notes, VRDOs, and tax-exempt CP. Many municipal and not-for-profit entity issues are exempt from federal income taxes and/or state income taxes in the state of issuance, making these attractive for investors seeking tax-free income. Dealers provide an active secondary market for these short-term municipal obligations.

Maturities of three months to one year are typical for municipal notes and range up to 270 days for CP. Most of these short-term municipal issues are used by local governments to provide interim financing for general obligation bond projects (e.g., bond anticipation notes, or BANs) or short-term working capital in anticipation of future tax revenues (e.g., tax anticipation notes and revenue bonds).

VRDOs are issued as long-term bonds that carry a short-term liquidity feature, or put. Generally, this put option, which is an investor's option to sell (or put) the instrument back to the issuer at par, allows for liquidation either weekly or monthly and is typically supported by a credit facility, such as a bank letter of credit. While interest from VRDOs is often tax-exempt, VRDOs exist as both taxable and nontaxable instruments.

IV. SUMMARY

Money markets represent a key resource for treasury professionals. These markets provide short-term financing and a repository for short-term investing.

This chapter introduced the concept of global money markets by providing an overview of the participants and the various types of investments available in the global money markets. In addition to direct investments, money market mutual funds and unit trusts offer treasury professionals access to a broad range of diversified securities with minimal financial restrictions.

The chapter also discussed the risks associated with money market securities. Despite these risks, there is a strong secondary market for money market securities. Subsequently, these securities are usually highly liquid and provide ready access to funds when needed.

The chapter concluded with a discussion of short-term money markets in the United States. The US money market is routinely accessed by treasury professionals around the world because of its relative size and the perceived safety of US Treasury securities.

CHAPTER 6
Capital Markets

I. INTRODUCTION

Capital markets comprise the component of financial markets in which firms issue debt and equity securities (in the forms of bonds and stocks, respectively). Accordingly, capital markets provide a major source of funding for investments for many types of organizations in various countries.[1] Treasury professionals must consider the conditions prevailing in capital markets when determining the optimal mix of debt and equity financing that maximizes firm value (i.e., the target capital structure).

The next section of this chapter provides an overview of the operations and participants in the capital markets. The remaining sections cover the basic characteristics of debt and equity securities.

II. OVERVIEW OF CAPITAL MARKETS

A. The Basics of Capital Markets

Financial markets are typically divided into two markets:

- **Money markets**, which include issues with maturities of one year or less
- **Capital markets**, which include issues with maturities extending beyond one year

Capital markets are further subdivided into two markets:

- **Debt market**, which includes fixed-income capital, such as bonds and term loans
- **Equity market**, which includes shares of common and preferred stock

Capital market debt instruments essentially represent a lending arrangement in which the issuer borrows funds from the investor (i.e., lender). Such debt instruments are commonly referred to as *fixed-income securities* because the periodic payment of interest and the repayment of principal are fixed at predetermined values. Investors purchasing debt instruments do not receive ownership in the issuing firm. Capital market debt typically has an original maturity ranging from just over one year to thirty years. Borrowers with a wide range of credit ratings issue debt in the capital markets. In general, the liquidity of debt instruments is inversely related to maturity.

With an equity instrument, the issuing firm exchanges an ownership interest in the firm for capital. This ownership interest may result in the investor earning dividends and capital gains. Unlike a debt instrument, an equity security does not have a fixed maturity date. An equity security's value may fall to $0 if the firm ceases to exist due to bankruptcy, merger, acquisition, or liquidation.

B. Key Participants in Capital Markets

Key participants in capital markets include the issuers of securities, investors purchasing securities, broker-dealers that help capital markets function, and regulators that ensure regulatory compliance. This section provides an overview of these participants and their roles.

1. ISSUERS OF SECURITIES

The issuers of securities represent the supply side of capital markets. The different types of issuers are outlined below. Issuers of debt securities are borrowers, while the issuers of equity securities are selling ownership in their enterprise. In general, governmental and not-for-profit (G/NFP) entities only issue debt securities. The purpose of

---

1. While many countries have globalized their financial markets to attract foreign business, not all developing economies have capital markets. Where capital markets do not exist, banks, international financial organizations, and governmental agencies are the primary providers of capital.

this section is to introduce these market supply participants and discuss the general types of securities they issue. The characteristics and details of the securities issued by these entities are covered in later sections of this chapter.

a. Governments (Ministries of Finance) and Central Banks: Debt Securities

Various governments and central banks raise funds through their respective capital markets by issuing debt securities with varying maturities. These issues are usually (1) backed by the full faith and credit of the issuing government, (2) used to finance fiscal deficits, and (3) issued through the ministry of finance or treasury department. For example, the US Treasury Department raises funds through the sale of Treasury securities (i.e., Treasury bills and interest-bearing notes and bonds).

In many countries, central banks also issue their own securities to finance the acquisition of assets, particularly foreign exchange reserves. They also often conduct open market operations, which involve the purchase and sale of government debt. As a result, both the government and the central bank directly influence the mix of short- and long-term securities held by the public. Some central banks issue bonds as a monetary policy instrument only. In some countries, however, central banks are banned from issuing debt to finance the government.

b. Corporations: Debt and Equity Securities

Corporate entities, including financial institutions, raise capital through the sale of stocks and bonds. Corporations are major issuers of long-term debt in a variety of formats and maturities. Most corporate debt is in the form of three- to ten-year bond issues, although longer terms have historically been available. Corporate borrowers may shift to longer-term bond issues during periods of low interest rates. Term loans greater than one year are also part of this market. On the equity side, corporations are the primary issuers of both preferred and common stock, which represent ownership in those corporations. These issues can take many forms, including hybrid securities (e.g., convertible bonds), which combine both debt and equity features into a single instrument.

c. State-Owned Enterprises: Debt Securities

A state-owned enterprise (SOE) is a firm that is created by a national government in order to participate in or help support various commercial activities on the government's behalf. SOEs can be either wholly or partially owned by a government and are common in many countries. SOEs are known as *crown corporations* in Canada and the United Kingdom and *government-sponsored enterprises (GSEs)* in the United States. Examples include Freddie Mac and Fannie Mae[2] in the United States, Canada Post or VIA Rail Canada in Canada, or Sinosteel Corporation in China.

d. Sub-sovereign Entities: Debt Securities

Sub-sovereign entities are governmental units within a country (e.g., states, counties, cities, and municipalities in the United States). Sub-sovereign entities borrow extensively in the debt markets in many, but not all, countries. In the United States, interest paid to investors on such instruments is generally exempt from federal income taxation, which may make them more attractive to certain types of investors. Tax laws vary significantly from country to country, so investors should be sure to verify the associated tax implications.

e. Mutual Fund Companies: Debt and Equity Securities

Mutual fund companies sell shares in many different types of funds that may acquire money market, bond, or stock instruments. In general, mutual fund securities do not represent a direct issuance of stocks and bonds held

---

2. *Freddie Mac* refers to the Federal Home Loan Mortgage Corporation (FHLMC), and *Fannie Mae* refers to the Federal National Mortgage Association (FNMA).

by the mutual fund sponsor. Rather, they are shares sold by the fund itself, which holds aggregated securities, allowing smaller investors to easily diversify their investments.

2. INVESTORS

Investors represent the demand side of capital markets, and they purchase and hold the securities sold by issuers. Investors generally are categorized as either *retail* or *institutional investors*.

Retail investors include individuals buying small amounts of stocks or bonds for their investment portfolios. In aggregate, retail investors comprise an important component of demand for capital market securities. On the other hand, institutional investors are generally large-scale investors, such as mutual fund companies, insurance companies, money managers, pension funds, firms, and banks. Institutional investors purchase large blocks of securities on behalf of others, as well as for their own portfolios.

3. BROKER-DEALERS (INVESTMENT BANKING AND BROKERAGE FIRMS)[3]

Broker-dealers serve as intermediaries in the purchase and sale of capital market securities. Broker-dealers provide several key roles:

- **Investment bankers** assist issuers in the design and placement of securities issuances. This typically includes underwriting the initial offering.
- **Originators** (i.e., origination desks) are a subset of trading professionals tasked with evaluating, pricing, and managing the placement of new security issues.
- **Securities traders** maintain active, orderly secondary markets for equity and debt instruments.

In addition to the various individual brokerage firms, there are also brokerage firm syndicates, which are selling groups that combine their securities distribution networks in order to more effectively place new securities issues.

4. REGULATORS

The role of regulators is critical to the maintenance of fair and open markets. The regulators that monitor capital markets are generally different from those that monitor the banking markets, and may even be different from those monitoring the money markets, depending on the country. Key capital market regulators in the United States include the Securities and Exchange Commission (SEC), the Financial Industry Regulatory Authority (FINRA), and the Municipal Securities Rulemaking Board (MSRB). In most cases, the role of capital market regulators is to require issuers to provide consistent and transparent disclosure of financial information related to the securities traded and to ensure a fair and level playing field for all market participants. While global capital markets are increasingly integrated, there is no global regulator, which means that each country is responsible for regulating the markets that operate within its borders. It is important to acknowledge that funds invested in capital markets are not insured by the government. Consequently, investors should exercise due diligence when purchasing capital market securities.

5. OTHER PARTICIPANTS

There are other parties involved in the securities markets that should be mentioned because of the important services they provide in the functioning and efficiency of those markets. Examples include:

- **Rating Agencies:** For debt securities, rating agencies (e.g., S&P, Moody's, & Fitch) play a key role in determining the credit risk and the return offered by those securities.

---

3. Many investment banking and brokerage firms also serve as investment advisors, a totally separate function from their role as market intermediaries.

- **Transaction Processors:** Transaction processors are critically involved in the flow of payments from issuers to investors (e.g., payments of interest, principal, and dividends), as well as the record keeping involved in processing transactions.

- **External Auditors:** Accounting firms audit financial statements and check mark-to-market valuations to increase the reliability of financial information used by investors and creditors.

- **Other:** Other parties also play a role in the efficient operation of capital markets. Examples include attorneys, bond trustees, printing companies (e.g., for the printing of securities, official statements, or bond transcripts), proxy solicitors, and data service providers (e.g., news services or market quote services).

C. Division of the Capital Markets

Capital markets are typically distinguished by the channels used to facilitate the purchasing and selling of securities. The major channels for capital market securities are outlined below.

1. PRIMARY MARKETS

Primary markets offer newly issued debt and equity securities to investors when firms or government units sell securities to raise funds. An investment bank or a syndicate of investment banks underwrites a securities issue and then sells the shares to the investing public.

New issues increase the issuer's level of outstanding stock or outstanding debt. If new stock shares are sold by a company with shares already trading on an exchange or the over-the-counter (OTC) market, then the new shares are referred to as a *seasoned equity offering (SEO)* or *follow-on issue*. The market price of existing shares guides the price for new shares.

If a firm issues equity shares to the investing public for the first time, the issue is termed an *initial public offering (IPO)*. In this case, there is no direct market guidance as to the value of a share of stock. Instead, the issuer consults with its investment bankers to select an issue price that represents the highest price per share that can be obtained while simultaneously resulting in selling all the shares in the issue.

When an investment bank or a syndicate of investment banks underwrites a securities issue, the issuing firm receives the funds directly from the bank on the issue date and may then use the funds for their intended purpose. The investment banks market the issue to the investing public through a network of brokerage firms, termed the *syndicate* or *selling group*. The issue is divided among the brokerage firms based on the initial syndication agreement, and the firms, in turn, allocate the securities to individual offices and their registered representatives. Both retail and institutional investors may purchase the securities.

2. SECONDARY MARKETS

After the initial offering is sold to investors, the securities can be bought and sold on the secondary market.[4] Since the securities are bought and sold among investors, the issuing firm experiences neither a change in cash flow nor a change in the number of securities outstanding. These transactions may occur through organized exchanges or through OTC markets, both of which are described below.

Organized stock exchanges facilitate the buying and selling of equity securities. A listing of the 10 top securities exchanges in the world is provided in Appendix 6.1.

---

4. Insiders, such as company founders, owners, managers, employees, and venture capitalists, who are holding a company's stock when it goes public are typically prohibited from reselling their stock during what is referred to as a *lockup period*. The lockup is a contractual restriction that prevents insiders from selling the stock for a period usually lasting 90 to 180 days after the company goes public.

Organized exchanges function in various ways to provide four principal benefits:

- A competitive marketplace where supply and demand determine prices
- Frequent trading to minimize price volatility between individual trades
- Increased depth of capital markets to enable issuers to raise large amounts of capital through securities offerings
- A fair market for exchange participants

Members of OTC markets are securities firms that may choose to maintain an inventory of equity or debt securities, and stand ready to buy those same securities from investors or other dealers wishing to buy or sell them. OTC markets are more decentralized than formal exchanges. They also rely upon electronic communication to conduct trading activity in an auction-style market between participating brokers and dealers. Government, municipal, and corporate debt, and some equity issuances that are not traded on exchanges, are sometimes traded in the OTC markets. Financial markets in developing countries or emerging markets are often run on an OTC basis.

3. PRIVATE MARKETS

In a private or direct placement, securities are not underwritten but are sold to a limited group of institutional investors. While the specific regulations regarding private placement vary from country to country, they generally require that private-placement securities only be sold to a limited number of high net worth investors or to qualified institutional investors (QIIs), referred to in the United States as *qualified institutional buyers (QIBs)*. The investment banking firm, acting as a broker to bring the issuer and investors together, meets with prospective buyers and confirms the details of the offering. Provisions of a private issue may be tailored to meet the needs of the issuing company and the investor(s).

Regulations regarding QIIs vary by country. According to guidelines set forth by the US SEC in Rule 144A, a QIB is an institution that manages at least $100 million in securities, and can be a bank, thrift institution, pension fund, corporation, insurance company, investment company, or employee benefit plan, or an entity owned entirely by qualified investors. A QIB can also be a registered broker-dealer that owns and invests, on a discretionary basis, at least $10 million in the securities of issuers that are not affiliated with the broker-dealer. Private placements often require that an investor attest to its status as a QIB because such private placements may not be marketed to non-QIBs.

A private issue will typically not require the preparation of a detailed prospectus and may be exempt from registration with various local authorities, such as the SEC in the United States or the Financial Conduct Authority (FCA) in the United Kingdom, and can therefore be completed more rapidly than a public offering. Further, a private debt issue typically may have:

- Lower issuance costs, since it is usually exempt from most regulatory registration
- Limited disclosure of proprietary information
- Less restrictive covenants
- A higher interest rate for the investor, to offset the diminished liquidity of the private placement

III. DEBT MARKET

Organizations and governmental entities can raise debt capital in both the short-term money market and long-term capital market. In either case, debt capital typically imposes a fixed payment requirement on the issuer. For firms, the interest portion of these payments is usually tax deductible and must be paid before any payments to equity holders. In addition, debt holders have priority claims on the firm's assets in the event of financial distress.[5] Given the fixed nature and deductibility of interest payments, debt can be an advantageous source of financing.

A. Medium- and Long-Term Borrowing

There are a number of medium- and long-term borrowing instruments. Primary sources are term loans, intermediate-term notes and bonds, and long-term bonds. It is important to understand the seniority of claims (i.e., the order in which debt will be paid in the event of liquidation) when selecting a particular form of debt. Since senior loans are paid before subordinated loans, seniority affects the risk of a given loan, which impacts the interest rate and covenants related to the debt issue. In addition, seniority is used to demarcate the different classes of debt in the event of bankruptcy. In some cases, such as secured or collateralized debt, designated assets are used to satisfy the debt. For unsecured debt, the indenture agreement and covenants related to each debt issue generally determine the priority of claims.

1. TERM LOANS

A term loan has a fixed maturity (usually longer than one year) that can be repaid either in installments or in a single payment. Term loans are typically:

- Issued with an amortized payment structure, which means that the periodic payments represent both interest and principal

- Negotiated with a financial institution and are not normally bought and sold in the secondary market

- Issued for a specific financing need, such as the purchase of a new plant or new equipment, or for general expansion

- Secured by the asset being financed, and the maturity is related to the asset's useful life

For many organizations, lease financing is an alternative to term loans.

2. MEDIUM- OR INTERMEDIATE-TERM NOTES

Companies or government entities issue medium- or intermediate-term notes with maturities ranging from two to ten years. In most cases, these notes pay interest at periodic intervals (e.g., semiannually) and are similar to long-term bonds except for the shorter maturity. Because such securities may be traded actively or because securities dealers may stand ready to make a market in them, medium- or intermediate-term notes are deemed *marketable*, or *liquid*, securities.

3. LONG-TERM BONDS

Long-term bonds are typically issued with original maturities of 10 to 30 years.[6] Unlike loans, which are negotiated with one or more specific lenders, bonds are issued like stock, and are bought and sold on the secondary market. Also unlike loans, bonds are typically not secured against any specific assets of the issuer but are considered unsecured debt. Bond terms (or *tenors*) vary widely, making it possible for an organization to issue long-term debt with characteristics and provisions that suit it best. Most long-term bonds pay coupons, which means that the issuer

---

5. In general, senior debt has a higher priority than junior or subordinated debt. *Subordinated debt* refers to debt that is paid after other creditors have been paid. If there are not enough resources to pay all creditors, the subordinated debt may not be paid, since the senior debt has first claim on any assets.

6. In 1993 Walt Disney and Coca-Cola issued so-called *century bonds* with a term of 100 years. There is ongoing debate as to whether these bonds serve as debt or equity since while they are structured as debt, their long term provides an equity-like feature. A number of other entities, primarily universities, have also offered century bonds since then. Given their long term, a key question is whether the issuer will still be in existence after 100 years.

must make semiannual interest payments at a fixed coupon rate over the life of the bond. The principal (i.e., face or par value) is repaid in full to the bondholder on the bond's maturity date.

In most countries, the bond market is an enormous component of the capital market. The bond market in the United States is the largest in the world. At the time of this writing, the US bond market accounts for about 45% of the global bond market volume.[7] The European Union likewise has a substantial bond market.

Bonds represent a contract between the issuing entity and the bondholders. This contract is known as a *bond indenture*. This contract:

- Describes the bond issue
- Lists collateral, when applicable
- Makes representations and warranties
- Specifies covenants
- States the terms by which the company will provide funds for redemption
- Sets forth the schedule of interest payment dates and amounts, the scheduled maturity date, and any early redemption or call provisions

In the event of bankruptcy, bond issues have differing claim priorities depending on the seniority of the bonds and liens, or pledges, on any assets. The restrictions that are included in indentures can place limits on the use and disposition of assets, on the level and type of working capital, on the payment of dividends, and on the ability to acquire additional financing. Thus, bond values may fall if changing economic or competitive conditions heighten the risk that the indenture requirements will be violated.

Bonds may be issued with a call provision that allows the issuer to retire, or call, the bonds prior to maturity. For example, callable bonds permit the issuer to retire bonds when the opportunity arises to raise new debt at a lower interest rate. Some bonds are also issued with a put provision that allows the buyer to redeem the bond prior to maturity by forcing the issuer to buy the bonds back.

The primary types of bonds are described below.

a. Mortgage Bonds

Mortgage bonds are used to finance specific assets, such as real estate. The pledged assets serve as security against the issue. Mortgage bonds usually include substantial financial covenants or indenture agreements.

b. Debentures

Debentures are unsecured bonds that represent general claims against the issuer's assets and/or cash flows, and may have a higher interest rate than secured bonds. Large, financially secure organizations issue debentures based on their credit rating in the marketplace. Organizations that do not have easily securitized assets must use unsecured borrowing through debentures. Debentures may be issued on a subordinated basis, indicating that the claim on assets is subordinate to designated notes payable, bank loans, or other specified debt. Unsecured bonds may include sovereign, corporate, and municipal bonds.

---

7. This statistic is derived from data provided on the website for the Bank for International Settlements (www.bis.org, accessed September 21, 2015).

c. Convertible Bonds

Convertible bonds are corporate debt securities that can be converted by the holder, or sometimes the issuer, into shares of common or preferred stock at a fixed ratio of shares per bond. Convertible bonds provide the investor with a potential for capital growth. For this reason, investors may accept a somewhat lower interest rate on these bonds compared to bonds that are not convertible.

d. Sovereign Bonds

Bonds issued by a national government are referred to as *sovereign bonds* or *sovereign debt*, and are typically denominated in the currency of the issuing government. This category would include all types of government debt ranging from US government bonds to bonds issued by developing countries. In addition to the credit risk associated with any bond, sovereign debt also carries political risk, and potentially foreign exchange risk if issued in a currency other than the home currency of the investor.

e. Sub-sovereign Bonds (Municipal Bonds)

Sub-sovereign bonds are issued by any level of government below the national or central government, which includes regions, provinces, states, municipalities, etc. In the United States, these bonds are typically referred to as *municipal bonds* (or *munis*). Historically, the market for sub-sovereign bonds has been primarily in the United States, but an international market for these bonds is rapidly expanding due to local governments needing to finance day-to-day operations of public services and capital investments in roads and other infrastructure that cannot be financed by the sovereign government, due to debt ceiling limits or other restrictions.

Bonds issued by government entities are usually in the form of general obligation or revenue bonds. General obligation bonds are paid from the proceeds of general tax revenues. Meanwhile, revenue bonds are repaid from the revenues generated from specific public projects or services (e.g., stadiums, toll roads and bridges, or public utilities).

Sub-sovereign bonds are subject to various national and regional provisions in their country of origin and may have tax implications. For example, most US municipal bonds are exempt from federal and, in some cases, state and local income taxes. Local regulations, and especially tax considerations, should always be considered before investing in sub-sovereign debt.

f. Eurobonds

Despite their name, Eurobonds have nothing to do with the euro or the European Union. A Eurobond (sometimes called an *external bond*) is an international bond that is denominated in a currency other than that of the country in which it is issued. Eurobonds are named based on their face currency (e.g., Euroyen or Eurodollar). An example of this would be a Eurodollar bond that is dominated in US dollars and issued in India by a UK-based company. In this example, the UK company could issue the bond in any country other than the United States because it is denominated in US dollars.

Eurobonds are typically sold simultaneously in many countries outside the country of the borrower. Eurobonds can be an effective financing tool because they give issuers the flexibility to choose the currency and country in which to offer their bond, based on the country's regulatory constraints, their own foreign exchange needs, and their preferred currency. This flexibility provides multinational organizations an ability to create natural hedges.

g. Zero-Coupon Bonds

Zero-coupon bonds do not pay interest and are subsequently issued at a substantial discount below par value. The sole cash outflow for the issuer is the repayment of par value at maturity. There are two advantages for the corporate issuer: (1) there is no cash outflow until maturity, and (2) the issuing company receives an annual tax deduction until maturity.[8]

The disadvantages of zero-coupon bonds are that they generally are not callable or refundable, and investors are required to pay taxes on imputed interest earnings each year, even though no actual payment is received until maturity. Thus, when held in a portfolio that is not tax exempt, there is a negative cash flow stream (i.e., tax outflows) during the bond's life.

h. Floating- or Adjustable-Rate Debt

Floating-rate securities, or floaters, carry interest payments that reset periodically based on movement in a representative interest rate index, such as the London Interbank Offered Rate (LIBOR) or the US T-bill. The rate on these securities is usually stated as a spread above the base index rate (e.g., LIBOR + 3%). The interest rate on floating-rate debt may be reset daily, weekly, monthly, quarterly, semiannually, or annually. The reset frequency is typically based on the index that is used for the security.

This type of debt is attractive to an investor during periods of rising interest rates because the floating-rate debt provides a stable market value and matches current interest rates. Borrowers, on the other hand, may prefer floating-rate debt if they believe that interest rates will drop in the future.

i. High-Yield Bonds

Also referred to as *junk bonds* or *below-investment-grade bonds* (e.g., an investment quality rating of BB+ or lower from S&P, or Ba1 or lower from Moody's), high-yield bonds are issued by less creditworthy entities. Consequently, these bonds offer a higher yield to compensate for increased default risk. Investment-grade bonds may also become high-yield or junk bonds if the issuer's credit rating deteriorates.

j. Other Bonds

Many other types of bonds are used for special purposes or are related to specific types of assets:

- **Income bonds** pay interest only if a company has profits, thus reducing the issuer's risk of issuing debt.
- **Collateral trust bonds** are backed by securities of other companies that are owned by the firm issuing the bond.
- **Equipment trust certificates** are bonds that are secured by movable equipment (e.g., a fleet of trucks or railroad equipment). Each certificate is backed by a specific asset or group of assets (i.e., there is no blanket lien securing the issue).
- **Index bonds** have interest rates tied to an economic index and are often used when a high level of price inflation is present or anticipated.
- **Economic development bonds** typically are issued by developing countries or sponsoring organizations, such as the World Bank or the International Monetary Fund (IMF), to foster development of infrastructure and related projects.
- **Tax increment financing (TIF) bonds** are used primarily for local financing in which a municipality may use all or a portion of new property taxes or sales taxes within a designated district to assist in the project's financing.

---

8. For US tax purposes, the Internal Revenue Service determines an estimated interest payment for each year of the zero-coupon bond. For the issuer, this results in a tax deduction; for the holder, it results in a tax liability.

- **Tender option bonds**, or put bonds, allow the investor to redeem the bond either once during its life or on specified dates. These bonds are usually redeemed at par value.

- **Foreign bonds** are sold in a particular country by a foreign borrower, but they are usually denominated in the domestic currency of the country where issued. These bonds are primarily regulated by the authorities in the country of issue.

- **Multicurrency bonds** are issued as (1) currency option bonds that allow investors to choose among several predetermined currencies, or (2) currency cocktail bonds that are denominated in a standard basket of several currencies (e.g., special drawing rights [SDRs][9]).

- **Green bonds** are used by federally qualified organizations to raise funds to promote sustainability by developing underutilized or abandoned properties (e.g., brownfield sites). Corporate bonds that designate proceeds for environmental projects, renewable energy projects, or making buildings more energy efficient are also known as *green bonds*.

4. OTHER FORMS OF DEBT CAPITAL

Other debt instruments are outlined below.

a. Project Financing

Project financing applies to large projects, often in the energy area (e.g., energy exploration, refineries, and utility power plants). This form of financing is also commonly used for private infrastructure projects, such as stadiums, shopping centers, toll roads, and commercial or residential developments. The typical project financing arrangement is complex, involving several companies or sponsors forming a separate legal entity to operate the project. Lenders are paid from the project's cash flows and generally do not have recourse to the project's individual sponsors or owners.

b. Securitization

Debt instruments are commonly securitized to increase liquidity and to lower the yield paid by issuers. Common corporate assets used in securitization include accounts receivable and inventory. These assets can be bundled to collateralize securities, making them more liquid and attractive to investors. Securitization of debt instruments has occurred because certain financial institutions have been willing to make a market in these instruments, in particular for commercial paper and high-yield bonds.

The resulting securities in a securitized structure are known as *asset-backed securities (ABS)*. An example of this type of security is the credit card market. A financial institution that has outstanding credit card receivables can use them as collateral for ABS that they sell to investors. The resulting cash can then be used for additional lending. This arrangement provides significant liquidity to the card issuers, which benefits both borrowers and lenders. ABS are marketed in many countries around the world, typically by financial institutions that have the ability to put together packages of debt instruments and market the resulting ABS.

c. Off-Balance-Sheet Financing

Off-balance-sheet financing is designed to provide financing that does not appear on the balance sheet. This arrangement may be used by firms with high debt levels or that have restrictive covenants on the use of additional debt. Past examples of off-balance-sheet financing include joint ventures, research and development partnerships, sales of receivables (i.e., factoring), and operating leases.

---

9. The IMF created SDRs, an artificial currency whose asset value is based on a basket of currencies consisting of the euro, Japanese yen, British pound sterling, and US dollar.

Despite the historical popularity of operating leases as a form of off-balance-sheet financing, changes are on the horizon. In February 2016, the US-based Financial Accounting Standards Board (FASB) issued an Accounting Standards Update (ASU) that requires operating leases with terms of more than 12 months to be capitalized on the balance sheet.[10] For publicly traded US firms (or firms in other countries that follow FASB guidance), this change will take effect after December 15, 2018.

5. DEBT CONTRACT PROVISIONS

The use of debt imposes certain restrictions on management. The only way debt holders can protect their interests effectively is to perform due diligence at the time of the initial debt contract and establish certain provisions (e.g., representations, warranties, and covenants) designed to make it difficult for management or shareholders to engage in actions that reduce the debt's value. These provisions also give debt holders additional rights under certain deteriorating conditions (e.g., material adverse changes) or in events of default. This applies to all commercial debt, not just bonds.

In addition, a debt issue may have provisions for early debt retirement, principal repayment, or refinancing of the issue. The debt contract also includes a promissory note that outlines the amount of funds borrowed and the financial terms. Several examples follow.

a. Debt Indentures and Covenants

An indenture is a legal document that outlines the rights and obligations of the borrower and the creditor. This contract includes various restrictive covenants that impose constraints on the actions of management. Covenants may be negative (i.e., actions the company cannot take, such as the double pledging of collateral) or affirmative (i.e., actions the company must take, such as providing regular financial statements or maintaining certain financial ratios). Covenants may also include change-of-control and most-favored-nation clauses[11] that provide the buyer/lender relief in certain circumstances.

The purpose of the indenture is to protect lenders from actions by management that would heighten the risk to lenders or increase the value for equity holders or other stakeholders at the expense of the lenders. Violation of an indenture agreement is usually sufficient grounds for lenders to make the debt immediately due and payable, which may force a company into bankruptcy. In the United States, the SEC must approve indenture agreements in public offerings and ensure that all indenture provisions are met before allowing a company to sell new securities to the general public.

Typical covenants outline:

- The assets involved
- The right of an organization to issue additional debt
- The use of second or junior mortgages
- Sinking fund requirements[12]
- Reporting requirements

---

10. From "FASB Issues New Guidance on Lease Accounting," published by FASB, February 25, 2016 (http://www.fasb.org/jsp/FASB/FASBContent_C/NewsPage&cid=1176167901466).

11. A most-favored-nation (MFN) covenant typically states that the bond issuer cannot offer another buyer better terms before offering those terms or better terms to the first buyer. For example, a bond covenant may have an MFN clause that says that the interest rate on the existing bond will be increased so that it is not less than 25 basis points lower than the interest rate on any new bonds that may be issued.

12. Sinking funds are arrangements for the orderly repayment of debt principal.

- Restrictions involving key financial ratios and liquidity
- Prepayment terms
- Restrictions on dividend policy

b. Representations and Warranties

Representations and warranties are the existing conditions at the time when the loan agreement is executed, as attested to by the borrower. Such conditions generally include:

- Affirmation of the valid, legal existence of the borrowing company
- A resolution by the borrower's board of directors authorizing the borrowing
- The authority of the corporate officers signing the documents
- The borrower's confirmation of compliance with all applicable regulations
- An indemnity protecting the lender from environmental liabilities
- Representation that the execution of the loan agreement does not violate or conflict with the charter or bylaws of the borrower, or any other loan agreements to which the borrower is a party

c. Events of Default

An event of default may occur if a borrower breaches or violates any term or condition under a debt agreement. Examples include:

- Nonpayment of interest or principal when due
- A material adverse change (MAC) clause, which allows the lender to refuse funding or declare a borrower to be in default, even if all agreements are in full compliance[13]
- Violation of a specified covenant
- Incorrect or misrepresented regulations or warranties

The characteristics of events of default include cure periods, remedies, and waivers of default:

- **Cure periods**, often specified in the agreement, provide a period of time in which an event of default may be corrected before the lender may pursue default remedies.
- **Remedies** available to a lender normally include an acceleration of all principal and interest on the debt when a default occurs.
- **Waivers of default** may be given at the lender's discretion, typically for a fee or change in terms.

d. Call and Put Provisions

Call provisions give the issuer the right to call a bond or other security for redemption prior to the original maturity. As compensation to investors for early redemption, a call premium is generally paid when a bond is called. The call premium usually is set on a sliding scale, with larger premiums above par required the earlier an issue is called.

The call privilege is valuable to an issuer because it allows redemption of a bond if interest rates fall and refinancing becomes an attractive option, or if the issuer wishes to retire the debt before maturity for other reasons. As a result, bonds with call provisions typically require a higher coupon rate than noncallable comparable bonds in order to

---

13. Examples of material adverse changes include (1) changes in laws or regulations that have a significant negative impact on the borrower or (2) the loss of a borrower's primary customer.

attract investors. The primary downside to the investor is that if interest rates fall and the bond is called, then the investor is forced to reinvest the call proceeds at a lower rate.

Meanwhile, a put provision allows the investor to force the issuer to repurchase the debt at specified dates. The put provision generally provides that the debt will be redeemed at par, creating a floor price for the debt and providing greater security for the holder. Bonds with put provisions typically trade at a higher price on the secondary market, relative to bonds without a put provision.

e. Sinking Funds

Sinking fund provisions in the indenture agreement require issuers to call, or repurchase on the open market, a portion of the outstanding bond issue each year. In essence, this amortizes the bond's issue over its life. Other provisions require a company to make payments into a trust account, which either repurchases bonds on the open market or amasses a lump sum of cash for retirement of the bonds at maturity.

The usual format for bond issues is for the borrower to pay only the coupon or interest payment until maturity, at which time the issuer repays the bond's face value (i.e., principal). In other words, most bonds are not amortized. Consequently, the existence of a sinking fund arrangement generally increases the safety of the bonds and lowers the required interest rate.

f. Refinancing

Refinancing of bonds is often done following periods of high interest rates. During high interest rate periods, many issuers attach call provisions that allow the bonds to be redeemed prior to maturity. When interest rates fall, companies issue new bonds at a lower interest rate and use the proceeds to retire the older, higher-interest bonds. The primary purpose of this is to take advantage of falling interest rates. Loan agreements sometimes include what is known as a "make whole" provision, which requires the borrower to make an additional payment based on the net present value of the future debt payments to protect the lender's anticipated profit on the original deal.

g. Defeasance of Debt

Defeasance removes debt from the borrower's balance sheet without retiring the debt issue. In this arrangement, the borrower places sufficient funds in escrow, usually in government securities, to pay for interest and principal on the debt issue. Because control of both the debt and escrow funds is relinquished, and payment and retirement of the debt issue is now guaranteed, this debt and the related securities can be removed from the balance sheet. This may allow the issuer to meet the debt levels stipulated in the debt covenants.

h. Promissory Notes

The legal portion of the debt contract is typically referred to as the *promissory note*, which is an unconditional promise to pay a specified amount plus interest at a defined rate either on demand or on a certain date. A promissory note can be issued for each individual borrowing or for a total line amount against which multiple borrowings exist. A master note is a type of promissory note used to simplify the paperwork connected with loans that have multiple advanced features, such as lines of credit and revolvers (i.e., revolving credit agreements). A borrower signs one comprehensive promissory note for the total amount of the line of credit. Any loans or repayments under the note are covered by the terms of the master note.

i. Collateral

Assets used as security for the loan or bond issue are called *collateral*. They may include physical assets (e.g., plant, equipment, and inventory) or financial assets (e.g., receivables and marketable securities). The condition of the assets must be monitored, their value must be appraised, and physical assets may require insurance.

j. Liens

With many secured loans, the lender has a lien or legal claim on the assets used as collateral in the event it cannot take physical possession of the assets. This may be in the form of a mortgage for larger assets or a blanket lien against inventory and receivables. If the borrower defaults on the loan or bond issue, the lender can seize the assets in lieu of repayment. To ensure these claims are valid and enforceable, the lender must generally follow a legal process to establish the claim by filing notice with the appropriate governmental agency, which makes the lien legally enforceable. Lenders often perform a lien search on a potential borrower to determine whether the assets being offered as collateral are already pledged to another creditor.

B. Other Factors Associated with Using Debt Financing

This section discusses miscellaneous factors that often accompany debt financing.

1. CREDIT ENHANCEMENTS

With credit enhancement, the lender is provided with reassurance that the borrower will honor the obligation, through additional collateral, insurance, or a third-party guarantee. Credit enhancement reduces credit/default risk of a debt, thereby increasing the overall credit rating and lowering interest rates. While the most common form of credit enhancement is a guarantee (discussed below), the enhancement may also be in the form of a standby letter of credit or backup line of credit issued by a financial institution (typically used for commercial paper issues).

2. GUARANTEES

When a subsidiary of a larger company borrows funds or issues bonds, lenders may require that another party guarantee the loan (i.e., the guaranteeing party).[14] This requirement allows lenders recourse to the guaranteeing party to obtain payment in the event the subsidiary is in default. There are several levels of guarantees that the guaranteeing party can make regarding the degree of protection offered to a lender:

- **Full Guarantee:** The guaranteeing party fully guarantees any borrowing arrangement by the subsidiary and agrees to take over the loan if the subsidiary fails to make timely payments.
- **Specific-Project Guarantee:** The guaranteeing party guarantees only loans relating to specific projects of the subsidiary, rather than all loans.
- **Guarantee of Payment or Collection:** The guaranteeing party guarantees to make payment on the loan or collect payment from the subsidiary, but only if the subsidiary formally defaults on the loan. This agreement usually requires the lender to initiate default proceedings on the subsidiary and initiate collection efforts before the guaranteeing party becomes involved.
- **Performance Guarantees:** In some cases, the lender may ask for specific performance guarantees relative to the assets being financed. Under a full guarantee, the parent (or other entity) fully guarantees performance by the subsidiary. Under a best-efforts guarantee, the parent agrees to use its best efforts to persuade the subsidiary to perform, but it does not guarantee subsidiary performance.

14. The guaranteeing party may be the parent corporation, sister subsidiary, supplier, customer, or other entity. Further, in some cases a subsidiary may provide a guarantee for the parent.

- **Personal Guarantee:** In some cases, especially for smaller, privately held companies, the lender may require a personal guarantee on the part of the owner or other principals in the business before granting a loan.
- **Comfort Letter:** While not technically a guarantee, this is a letter from another party stating actions that it will or will not take on behalf of the borrower. This type of agreement is not legally enforceable.

3. BOND/CREDIT RATINGS

Bond issues and other long-term debt are assigned quality ratings that reflect the default probability associated with the issuer. Each issue is rated independently by one or more accredited rating agencies. Three aspects of ratings should be considered by corporate issuers.

The first consideration is the rating criteria used by the agency. Ratings are based on both qualitative and quantitative factors. Given the complexity of most large firms, there is no precise mathematical formula that analysts can use to determine the rating; instead, many factors must be taken into account. These factors will vary by industry but include measures such as diversification of product lines, market share, profitability, leverage, and financial policy.

The second consideration is the importance of the ratings to both the firm's investors and management. Many charters restrict institutional investors to only buying investment-grade bonds or better, and these investors make up the bulk of the bond market. Also, a firm's bond rating is considered a direct measure of the risk of the related securities and impacts the overall cost of capital. That is, the rating sets the pricing such that a higher rating reduces the cost of borrowing.

The third consideration relates to changes in ratings. Rating agencies periodically review outstanding debt and may upgrade or downgrade an issue based on changes in either the issuer or the general economic environment. Companies or government entities with downgraded ratings have a more difficult time raising additional capital in the market and will pay a higher interest rate on future bonds issued.

4. MATURITY MATCHING

Maturity matching involves matching the life of a debt issue to the life of the specific assets financed. When possible, managers prefer to match the maturities of debt issues and assets to reduce overall firm risk. The primary risk from a maturity mismatch results from long-term assets being funded with short-term sources. Under this scenario, the short-term debt must continually be rolled over to provide an ongoing funding source. This leads to an adverse exposure to higher interest rates and/or to an inability to raise short-term debt in the future. Also, the maturity dates of securities may be staggered (i.e., laddering) so that the issuing company is not faced with an inordinate amount of debt coming due at one time.

5. EFFECTS OF INTEREST RATE LEVELS AND FORECASTS

The general level of interest rates and economic activity impacts both the use and cost of debt. Also, the forecast of future interest rates impacts both the type of capital raised and the provisions that may be attached to capital issues. Debt issuers must consider the "flight to quality" concept whenever financial market conditions decline. In these times, investors move toward safe or quality investments; hence, the yield spread between high- and low-risk investments increases significantly.[15]

---

15. The movement away from riskier securities during periods of economic uncertainty is often referred to as a "flight to quality" or a "flight to liquidity."

6. AVAILABILITY OF COLLATERAL

Firms with large, unencumbered asset bases can typically borrow at lower rates than companies of the same credit quality and rating that do not have assets to use as collateral. Further, firms with lower operating and financial risk will have a greater ability to borrow on an unsecured basis and obtain funds at lower rates than otherwise comparable firms.

IV. EQUITY SECURITIES

The equity market represents the ownership of publicly owned corporations, consisting of both primary and secondary markets. The market for equity securities spans the globe. Many stocks are cross-listed on multiple exchanges, increasing both the availability of stock for investors and access to the markets for corporations raising funds. A large number of equity markets have consolidated and integrated due to the formation of the European Union and other market alliances.

Another trend in global equity markets is that of privatization, where government-owned assets are sold to private investors or groups. The primary rationale behind this trend is to develop capital markets, widen share ownership, raise money for the government, and change corporate governance.

A. Common Stock

The purchase of common stock or common equity provides an investor with ownership in a firm. Equity financing represents a significant portion of capital for most publicly traded firms. Institutional investors own the majority of all common stock.

1. BALANCE SHEET ACCOUNTS AND DEFINITIONS

Treasury professionals must be aware of three key accounting terms relating to common stock: *par value, retained earnings*, and *additional paid-in capital*. The total amount of stockholders' equity is the sum of these accounts. It is important to realize that these accounts represent only the historical accounting value of the equity and not the current market value.

The three accounting terms are defined as follows:

- **Par or face value** is an arbitrary amount usually stated in the corporate charter that indicates the minimum amount stockholders have put up (or must put up) in the event of bankruptcy. For many publicly traded companies, this is $1 per share or $0. The latter indicates no par value.

- **Retained earnings** represent the earnings, net of dividends paid to shareholders, accumulated since a firm's inception. This balance sheet account is part of stockholders' equity and is an accounting of the money reinvested in the firm in lieu of dividends paid out. It is important to understand that retained earnings are recorded as an accounting entry in the equity section of the balance sheet to reflect profits that have been reinvested in the firm. However, retained earnings do not represent an available pool of funds.

- **Additional paid-in capital (APIC)** is an account that reflects the difference at the time of issue between the par value and the issuance price (less underwriting costs) of newly issued stock. For example, if new stock is issued with a par value of $1 and the firm nets $25 per share, then a $1 per-share increase would be shown in the par value account and a $24 per-share increase would be shown in the APIC account.

In addition to the previous items, three other terms are relevant to the stockholders' equity account:

- **Book value per share** is defined as the total book value of common equity divided by the number of common shares outstanding.

- **Market value per share** is defined as the current price at which a share of stock is traded. Though this is not technically part of the accounting statements, it is often included in reports issued by a company and financial reporting services.

- **Treasury stock** represents shares of common equity that have been reacquired by the issuer. It may be held in the firm's treasury indefinitely, reissued to the public, or retired. Treasury stock receives no dividends and does not carry voting power. It is considered issued, but not outstanding; therefore, it is deducted from any capital calculations. Some jurisdictions do not permit issuers to hold treasury stock—such jurisdictions require that any stock reacquired by the issuer be automatically considered retired.

2. TYPES OF COMMON STOCK

Firms typically have only one class of common stock, but in some cases multiple classes are issued to meet the preferences of different types of investors. Classified stock is typically referred to as *Class A* or *Class B*, but these terms have no standard meaning; rather, these classes are specific to each issuer. Generally, the different classes of stock may limit voting privileges, dividends, and/or resales.

Different classes of stock may be issued to differentiate returns for various divisions of a large, diversified firm. Large, multinational firms often issue stock in this manner to offer nondiversified investments to certain classes of stockholders.

Tracking stock is a separate stock created by a parent company to track the financial progress of a particular line of business. Despite being part of a publicly traded entity, tracking stocks trade under unique ticker symbols. These stocks are meant to create opportunities for investors to buy into a fast-growing unit without investing in the whole firm. The revenues and expenses of the segment being tracked are extracted from the firm's financial statements and are linked to the tracking stock for valuation purposes. However, tracking stocks do not provide stockholders with ownership in the parent company, nor do they include voting rights.

Tracking stocks are also used to create a security that mirrors some key index in the market. A popular example of this type of stock is the SPDR,[16] or Spider (SPY), which is an exchange-traded fund (ETF) that mirrors the returns of the S&P 500 index. Another example is the FXI (iShares China Large-Cap ETF), which mirrors the equity market in China (FTSE China 25).

B. Preferred Stock

Preferred stock is equity that differs from common stock in terms of investor rights and dividend payments. Preferred stock normally does not provide voting rights. The general purpose of preferred stock is to raise capital while still maintaining control of the company. Preferred dividends often occur at fixed levels in perpetuity. In terms of cash flows, preferred stock is more like debt than equity because of the fixed dividend payments. Unlike with debt, where missing interest payments can trigger loan covenants and even bankruptcy, a firm does not risk bankruptcy by missing a preferred stock dividend. Another difference is that preferred dividends are not tax deductible, unlike the interest expense from debt.

---

16. *SPDR is an acronym for S&P's depositary receipt.*

1. MAJOR PROVISIONS OF PREFERRED STOCK ISSUES

Preferred stockholders have priority claim on both earnings and assets before the common stockholders but after debt holders. They are paid the preferred stock dividend in full before any dividend may be paid to common stockholders. The dividend is calculated as a fixed percentage of the par value of a preferred share, and this dividend must be paid if the company has sufficient earnings. For example, if a $100 par value preferred stock certificate states that the dividend is 6% of par, then the annual dividend equals $6.

Most preferred stock accumulates dividends in arrears. This means that any missed preferred dividends must be repaid before dividends are received by common shareholders. Many preferred stock issues have a provision that grants voting rights, and/or the right to elect a representative to the board of directors, if a specified sequence of dividends is missed. The intent is to give preferred stockholders a voice in board deliberations.

Some preferred stock issues may be convertible into either common stock or debt under certain conditions. Either of these features offers more flexibility to the issuer of the preferred stock, as well as a unique investment opportunity to purchasers. In recent years, many new provisions have been offered to help make preferred stock more attractive to investors. These include:

- Voting rights under certain conditions
- Participation in earnings if they exceed a certain level
- Sinking funds to redeem preferred stock
- Maturity dates
- Exchange or call provisions

2. EVALUATION OF PREFERRED STOCK

From the issuer's viewpoint, the main advantage of issuing preferred stock is to lock in financing costs and potentially leverage the return to common shareholders due to the fixed nature of preferred dividends. With preferred stock, a company accomplishes this without increasing default risk. Also, large portions of preferred stock issues are private issues to institutional investors. This usually means substantially lower issuance costs and less stringent disclosure requirements.

From the investor's perspective, preferred stock provides a more predictable income stream relative to common stock. Still, the pricing of preferred stock may be sensitive to interest rate movements, due to the fixed income associated with the dividend. Also, for most US corporate holders of preferred stock, 70 percent of the dividend income may be excluded from federal income tax. This makes preferred stock especially attractive to institutional investors.

3. SOME PARTICULAR USES OF PREFERRED STOCK

Many firms have found the unique features of preferred stock to be an advantageous way to raise capital. Financial institutions have been heavy issuers of preferred stock due to the fact that most regulatory authorities count preferred stock as regulatory capital. In addition, most rating agencies look favorably on the use of preferred stock. Other heavy users of preferred stock financing are firms that are either young/high growth or in financial distress. In both cases, the tax advantages to debt financing are minimal to nonexistent. Thus, the cost differential between debt and preferred stock is very small. When the equity nature of preferred stock is taken into account, this form of financing can be very attractive to such issuers.

C. Hybrid Securities

Hybrid securities are created by combining the elements of two or more different types of securities into one. A hybrid security typically has both debt and equity characteristics. The most common hybrid securities are convertibles and warrants.

1. CONVERTIBLES

Convertible securities are usually bonds or preferred stock that may be exchangeable for common stock at the holder's or issuer's option under certain terms and conditions, and at a pre-stated price. The conversion does not provide any new capital for the issuer. Rather, it simply converts existing debt or preferred stock into common equity. The conversion ratio states the number of stock shares that one bond may be converted to if the owner chooses. The maturity value of the bond and the conversion ratio determine the issue's conversion price. For example, a $1,000 par value bond with a conversion ratio of 20 implies a stock conversion price of $50 (i.e., $1,000 divided by 20 shares).

Most convertibles contain clauses that protect against dilution of value due to stock splits, stock dividends, or reduced stock prices. The typical provision states that if new common stock is sold at a price below the conversion price, then the conversion ratio must be raised, or the conversion price lowered, to the issue price of the new stock.

In the example above, if there was a split, then the conversion ratio has to increase to keep the value of the holdings equal. Before the split, the value was $1,000. Due to the split, the conversion ratio has to be raised to 40 shares per bond so that the value remains $1,000 (i.e., the conversion price is now $25).

Convertibles are advantageous for the issuer in that they offer the ability to sell debt with lower interest rates and fewer restrictive covenants in exchange for allowing the investor to participate in potential capital gains as firm value increases.

Convertibles also may have significant disadvantages for the issuer:

- If the stock price increases significantly during the convertible's life, then the company may have been better off issuing regular debt than refunding the debt with a new stock issue.
- If the convertible issue has a low coupon rate, then that rate is lost if the holders convert the bonds into stock.
- If the stock price does not rise, then a company may be locked into the debt issue, although it is typically at a lower coupon rate than regular debt.

2. WARRANTS (BONDS WITH AN EQUITY PURCHASE OPTION)

Warrants are company-issued options that give the warrant's owner the right to buy a stated number of shares of stock at a specified price for a specified period of time. Warrants often are listed on major exchanges and trade like options.

Unlike convertibles, warrants issued with bonds represent potential additional equity capital for the issuing company. Most warrants are *detachable*, meaning they can be traded separately from the bond. If these warrants are exercised, then the low-coupon bond issue remains outstanding. Therefore, the warrants bring additional funds into a company while keeping debt costs low. Warrants are used extensively by small, rapidly growing companies as "sweeteners" when selling either debt or preferred stock. A bond with warrants has some characteristics of debt and equity, thus creating a hybrid security (i.e., a bond with an equity kicker) that gives a company the ability to expand its mix of securities and appeal to a broader group of investors.

Warrants may dilute the value of the current stockholders' equity and the earnings per share (EPS). Some companies report a fully diluted EPS figure, which assumes that all outstanding warrants were exercised. In the United States, the SEC requires that the disclosure of EPS include:

- Information on the capital structure

- Explanation of the EPS computation

- Identification of common-stock equivalents (including convertibles, rights, and warrants)

- Number of shares converted

- Assumptions made

D. Depositary Receipts

In order to expand the holdings of stock on a global basis, many stock exchanges offer different types of depositary receipts. Typically equity securities, depositary receipts are negotiable financial instruments that trade on a local exchange but actually represent stock ownership in a foreign, publicly listed company. One of the most common depositary receipts is the American depositary receipt (ADR), which allows US investors to effectively own stocks traded on foreign exchanges. These securities are known as global depositary receipts (GDRs) outside the United States.

Regardless of where the original company is located, the issuing company must meet all of the requirements of the exchanges and regulatory authorities of the country where the depositary receipt is traded. It is also possible for a previously unlisted company to conduct an IPO via the depositary receipt markets, either through an exchange listing or on an over-the-counter basis.

The depositary receipt markets offer some significant benefits, especially for issuers in countries with limited financial markets:

- They help increase global trade, including transaction volumes on both local and foreign markets.

- They offer greater exposure and the opportunity to raise capital on a global basis to companies in smaller countries.

- They help reduce market inefficiencies, especially in emerging markets, by allowing for easier global investment in those emerging markets.

V. SUMMARY

While much of the emphasis in treasury management tends to be on short-term debt and investments, capital markets are an important part of the financial infrastructure. Subsequently, capital markets have direct and indirect impacts on many of the decisions made by treasury professionals.

This chapter discussed the major participants in capital markets, including issuers, investors, broker-dealers, and regulators. Capital markets are typically subdivided into debt and equity markets. The major characteristics of each of these types of securities were also introduced.

APPENDIX 6.1: LISTING OF THE WORLD'S TOP 10 STOCK EXCHANGES

(Ranked by Domestic Market Capitalization as of November 30, 2015)[17]

RANK	EXCHANGE NAME	COUNTRY	DOMESTIC MARKET CAP (IN $ BILLIONS)
1	NYSE	United States	18,486
2	NASDAQ	United States	7,499
3	Japan Exchange Group	Japan	4,910
4	Shanghai Stock Exchange	China	4,460
5	LSE Group	United Kingdom	3,975
6	Shenzhen Stock Exchange	China	3,424
7	Euronext	Belgium, France, The Netherlands, and Portugal	3,380
8	Hong Kong Exchanges	Hong Kong	3,165
9	Deutsche Börse	Germany	1,738
10	TMX Group	Canada	1,698

17. From "November 2015 Monthly Statistics," published by World Federation of Exchanges, accessed August 18, 2016 (http://www.world-exchanges.org/home/index.php /statistics/monthly-reports).

CHAPTER 7
Relationship Management and Financial Service Provider (FSP) Selection

---

I. INTRODUCTION

II. RELATIONSHIP MANAGEMENT
    A. Number of Bank Relationships
    B. Documentation
    C. Performance Measurement and Evaluation

III. FSP SELECTION AND THE REQUEST FOR PROPOSAL (RFP) PROCESS
    A. Basics of an RFP
    B. RFP Design
    C. RFP Administration

IV. BANK COMPENSATION PRACTICES
    A. Billing for Bank Services
    B. Value Dating
    C. Account Analysis in the US Commercial Banking System
    D. Comparing and Monitoring Costs among FSPs

V. ASSESSING THE RISK OF FSPs
    A. Assessing Operational Risk of FSPs
    B. Assessing Financial Risk of Global Banks—Basel Accords
    C. Assessing Financial Risk of US Banks
    D. Counterparty Risk
    E. Sovereign and Political Risk
    F. Managing Confidential Information and Conflicts of Interest
    G. Legal and Ethical Issues

VI. SUMMARY

APPENDIX 7.1: SAMPLE BANK SCORECARD

APPENDIX 7.2: RFP ACTIVITY INFORMATION

APPENDIX 7.3: SAMPLE UNIFORM BANK PERFORMANCE REPORT (UBPR)

I. INTRODUCTION

The treasury department relies heavily on the products and services offered by various financial service providers (FSPs). Consequently, treasury is often the focal point for managing relationships with these entities. This chapter begins by discussing the general nature of these relationships. The next part of the chapter outlines a typical selection process (including the request for proposal) used to choose among providers. The selection process is an important topic for treasury personnel to understand given the critical nature of the associated products and services provided. The remainder of the chapter describes the pricing of financial products and services and provides a discussion on assessing the risk of providers.

II. RELATIONSHIP MANAGEMENT

The treasury department must interact with a number of FSPs, including commercial banks, insurers, investment managers, and custody services providers. In some organizations, an employee within treasury is primarily responsible for relationship management. In others, this oversight rests directly with the treasurer. In either case, relationship management entails many responsibilities ranging from day-to-day communication regarding transaction inquiries and problem resolution to quarterly, semiannual, and/or annual performance evaluations and relationship reviews based on agreed-upon metrics and objectives.

Acceptable performance requires the FSP to have in-depth knowledge of the client's operations and needs. Changing providers consumes time, effort, and financial resources. Consequently, treasury professionals are motivated to devote time and effort to managing existing relationships.

Success in every long-term relationship involves mutual accommodation. Factors that increase the mutual benefit and profitability of long-term FSP relationships may include:

· Open and frequent two-way communications

· Regular and timely feedback

· Documentation of expectations of both parties in agreements and legal contracts

· Fairly priced, efficient, and effective financial services/products

· Complete, candid, and timely disclosure of information by both parties

· Compliance with a current legal contract

· Use of service level agreements

A. Number of Bank Relationships

Of the financial institutions that collectively comprise FSPs, treasury must most often work with banks. Banking relationships involve a number of unique considerations due to the types of documentation required, the methods of monitoring risk, and the methods of compensation, all of which are discussed later in this chapter.

A critical concern for treasury management is maintaining the optimal number of banking relationships. The treasurer generally determines the appropriate number of banking relationships that are required given the firm's unique operating and financial characteristics. Specific determinants include the organization's credit needs, existence of multi-country operations, costs of maintaining multiple relationships, concentration risk (e.g., the risk of having a single point of failure), and the relative strengths and capabilities of each bank. Multinational companies may have multiple banking relationships to provide product and service coverage in all countries where the company has a presence. Firms with a complex, over-the-counter/field bank collection and concentration system involving multiple countries may have to deal with a large number of small banks to obtain appropriate geographic coverage.

The types, sophistication, and geographic location of services needed by a firm often dictate multiple banking relationships. Maintaining secondary banking relationships lets the treasury professional shift accounts and services if a significant problem develops with the primary bank.

Allocating business to specific banks is a key part of relationship management. Banks and FSPs in general are fairly sophisticated in understanding the percentage of a client's business they have (i.e., "share of wallet") and will often ask for more business if they feel they are not being given an appropriate share. Treasury personnel should also consider asking specific banks which services they would like to provide, as certain banks may have preferences in the products/services they provide.

Firms with multiple banking relationships often designate one bank as the primary, or lead, institution. While this is more common with credit relationships, some firms follow the same practice with operating services. There may be different lead institutions for credit and other services. While many firms establish multiple relationships to ensure that they have adequate credit facilities, a firm's primary credit bank often serves in the lead role by selling excess credit exposure to other institutions or by acting as an agent for loan syndication.

There are internal and external costs associated with each banking relationship. These costs create the incentive for a firm to optimize the number of banking relationships maintained. In addition, banks have developed more sophisticated methods for measuring relationship profitability, resulting in lower costs for a firm purchasing multiple services.

For example, the pricing of bank loans is often based on interdependent factors such as:

- Cost of funds
- Credit rating
- Total loans committed and outstanding
- Service fees
- Deposit balances maintained
- Range of other services used (e.g., foreign currency or derivatives trading)
- Loan maturity
- Revenue size and importance of the overall relationship to the lending institution
- Competition

Likewise, the pricing of depository and cash management services is based on factors such as:

- Transaction volumes
- Customization
- Exception-handling requirements
- Cost of providing the service
- Operational overhead
- Deposit balances maintained
- Value of other services used (e.g., global trade services, letters of credit, and custody services)
- Credit relationship
- Revenue size and importance of the overall relationship to the bank

B. Documentation

Important documents that are integral to relationship management include service agreements, account resolutions, signature cards, articles of incorporation from the customer, and contracts for depository accounts. The complexity and number of documents required typically increases with the number of countries involved. For example, service providers in many European countries will require a statement of beneficial interest.[1] The complexity of and the need to frequently update documentation has led to the development of electronic bank account management (eBAM).

The remainder of this section describes operational documentation needed for current accounts. Specific topics include account resolutions, signature cards and service agreements, service level agreements, "know your customer" requirements, and statements of beneficial ownership.

1. ACCOUNT RESOLUTIONS

An account resolution (passed by the board) is the basic account or service authorization empowering a representative of the firm to enter into agreements for financial services. The resolution specifies the functions that can be performed by specific individuals or job titles, the people authorized to open and close accounts, and the entire scope and limitations of the relationship.

The account resolution may be general or specific with regard to actions that the FSP may take on behalf of the firm. It can be a standard form used by the provider to serve all customers or it can be customized for a given firm. Some firms have developed their own standard resolutions. The acceptance of such a resolution is subject to negotiation.

In an effort to simplify and reduce the documentation needed to manage an operating relationship, many FSPs now use a master agreement that spells out overall operating requirements and authorizes the provider to operate on behalf of the firm signing the agreement. Once the master agreement is in place, additional accounts or services are covered by separate operating agreements that are addenda to the existing master agreement.

---

1. *Beneficial interest* or *ownership* refers to control over funds or accounts and is separate from signature authority or legal title. It recognizes that the entity in whose name an account is opened with a bank is not necessarily the person who ultimately controls the funds or who is ultimately entitled to the funds. Many countries require a statement of beneficial interest whenever a bank account is opened.

2. SIGNATURE CARDS AND SERVICE AGREEMENTS

FSPs require firms to furnish signatures of authorized signers (or specimens of both facsimile and computerized signatures) for all accounts. In conjunction with any signature card, providers typically provide a standardized set of service agreements to companies when relationships are established and accounts are opened. Service agreements are contracts—legal documents that describe the requirements and expectations of both the purchaser and provider of a specific service or services. There may be a master service agreement relating to the overall relationship and then separate service agreements for each specific service area (e.g., deposit accounts, card services, and lockboxes). These documents provide the terms and conditions of the account—many of which can be negotiated as with any other contract, as well as the responsibilities of the FSP and the account holders in the maintenance of accounts. The elements of a service agreement often include:

- Contract length and adjustments
- Information on funds availability
- Time frames during which errors must be reported
- The right of offset against accounts resulting from fees owed
- Liability clauses defining responsibilities for specified risks
- Other terms and conditions of the relationship

Agreement terms are periodically amended, and notice may be distributed via the account statements and/or postings to the FSP's website. Depending upon the countries in which the accounts are domiciled, the provider may also require incumbency certificates, which are documents used to confirm the identity of the signing officers of a corporation.

3. SERVICE LEVEL AGREEMENTS (SLAs)

An SLA may be a separate document or part of the service agreement. The SLA is primarily concerned with the definition of the specific services provided and the operating metrics used to measure the level of service provided. SLAs also typically include a description of any penalties for failure to comply with the requirements of the agreement. The elements of an SLA often include:

- Operational policies and procedures (including the detailed processing requirements for each service; a list of required information and related reports; a list of individuals authorized to make changes; and a description of the issue escalation and resolution process)
- Performance standards and calculations that define agreed-upon levels of service performance and quality

4. "KNOW YOUR CUSTOMER" (KYC) AND STATEMENTS OF BENEFICIAL OWNERSHIP

To prevent money laundering and other financial crimes, many countries have significantly strengthened their requirements regarding corporate relationships with financial institutions and, in particular, the opening of accounts. These activities go under the general title of KYC, which requires the FSP to perform varying amounts of due diligence to determine the legitimacy of any new customers, as well as the identities of the individuals who have access or control over the funds in those accounts. Collectively, these due diligence efforts are usually referred to as *customer identification programs (CIPs)*. The nature and extent of customer identification programs may vary by country but will typically require a firm to provide copies of its articles of incorporation and identification of all signers on any accounts—through provision of copies (often certified) of driver's licenses or passports, as well as formal statements of beneficial ownership.

C. Performance Measurement and Evaluation

Service quality is crucial to the corporate-financial institution relationship. A company must determine its performance expectations clearly with regard to quality standards. These expectations should be based on the service levels stipulated in its agreements with the FSP as discussed above and documented in SLAs. These expectations should also be detailed in the original request for proposal (RFP) that was used to select the FSP.

Two of the most common types of performance measurement techniques are scorecards (i.e., report cards) and relationship reviews.

1. SCORECARD

A scorecard is a management tool used to qualitatively and quantitatively measure the FSP's performance. The primary purpose of a scorecard is to provide feedback on the service provided and the benefit received. The scorecard also allows the provider to better understand how the customer perceives the combination of the quality and cost of the services provided. In addition, the scorecard provides a tool to measure the relative value of current service relationships and evaluate FSPs on the issues that the firm deems to be important. Finally, the scorecard can be used in support of continuous improvement and communication between both parties, and as a way to clarify how well the services are delivered. Although treasury is typically the focal point of the scorecard process, it is important to get input and feedback from other areas of the firm that may be affected by the relationship (e.g., accounting, accounts payable, or accounts receivable).

A sample scorecard is provided in Appendix 7.1.

2. RELATIONSHIP REVIEW

A relationship review is another procedure firms use to assess service levels and responsiveness, both quantitatively and qualitatively. Reviews may be formal or informal. Formal reviews typically involve a quarterly, semiannual, or annual meeting of the senior management representatives from both parties. Informal reviews typically involve weekly or monthly contacts by individuals responsible for day-to-day relationship management. FSPs also often initiate relationship reviews by preparing summaries of services, fees, error rates, and other relationship information, as well as an introduction to new products and services. Relationship reviews enable discussion of future needs and strategies in a true two-way dialogue. The key elements of these discussions include the presentation of new ideas and suggestions for process improvements, as well as both plans for growth and change. These meetings are an excellent time to discuss current and planned allocation of services, as well as share of wallet.

III. FSP SELECTION AND THE REQUEST FOR PROPOSAL (RFP) PROCESS

When paired with good strategic thinking and design, the RFP process is an effective tool for acquiring treasury products and services. Alternatively, an ad hoc approach can lead to an unwieldy network of providers, resulting in inefficiencies and unnecessary costs. The RFP process will be strengthened by receiving input from non-treasury departments, including operations, tax, legal, accounting, information technology, compliance/audit, and procurement.

Before submitting an RFP, it is helpful to determine whether an RFP is required. Alternatives to an RFP include:

- **Request for Information (RFI):** With an RFI, the firm provides a formal description of its needs and asks selected providers to provide general information as to how they could meet the firm's needs.

- **Request for Quotation (RFQ):** An RFQ is used by a firm to invite providers to bid on specific products or services. It is similar to an RFP, but is best suited to products and services that are essentially standardized, which makes each supplier's quote easily comparable to others.

When selection involves a product or service that is essential to treasury management, the formal RFP process is usually worth the time and effort. (See Exhibit 7.1 for a comparison of selection methods.) Many firms require a formal RFP for contracts or purchases over a certain amount. A well-designed RFP will ensure that the firm has included the proper set of providers and given them the information required to recommend the appropriate products and services. The benefit of the RFP process goes even further by ensuring that these products and services are offered at the best price and that the relationships with all FSPs are managed well.

EXHIBIT 7.1 COMPARISON OF VENDOR SELECTION METHODS

	INFORMAL REVIEW	REQUEST FOR INFORMATION (RFI)	REQUEST FOR QUOTATION (RFQ)	REQUEST FOR PROPOSAL (RFP)
PURPOSE	Solicit vendors for potential solutions to existing problems	Identify vendors that are willing and able to provide products and services; typically used as a prelude to an RFP or RFQ	Solicit binding price quotes from vendors on comparable products and services	Solicit proposed solutions and proposed pricing from selected vendors
PROJECT TYPE	Small	Small to large	Commodity purchases of all sizes	Large-scale purchase of products or services
FORMAT	Informal	Structured, with information regarding problem to be addressed	Detailed product/service specifications	Detailed description of company and product/service needs
EXPECTED RESULT	Suggested solutions	List of potential vendors and their qualifications	Price quote	Vendors' recommended solution(s), capabilities, and proposed pricing
FINAL OUTCOME	Change to existing services	Typically, RFP or RFQ; occasionally, contract negotiations	Purchase order	Contract negotiations and implementation

This section of the chapter describes the:

- Basics of an RFP
- RFP design
- RFP administration

The discussion that follows assumes that the treasurer has decided to use an RFP to solicit providers for a new treasury service or product.

A. Basics of an RFP

Before designing and administering the RFP, the treasury department should:

- **Define the Objective:** This involves developing and articulating a clear understanding of the factors driving the required products or services. Such factors may be strategic or operational. Clearly defining the objective and identifying the key drivers will allow for an improved selection process.

- **Determine the Business Requirements:** Business requirements spell out what the firm hopes to accomplish, including the needs of the various stakeholders. Business requirements are sometimes prioritized as *must have, nice to have,* and *neutral.* In the case of a treasury management system, the information technology department might require that the system be installed on company servers, while treasury might insist that it accommodate a certain number of users globally, and legal might demand that only domestic providers be considered, for security reasons.

- **Develop the Project Plan**: Project plans identify the tasks that comprise the project and define completion dates, assigned resources, and task dependencies. Exhibit 7.2 provides an outline of the major steps and approximate timing for a complex global RFP.

EXHIBIT 7.2 RFP PROJECT STEPS

ELEMENT	TIME REQUIRED
Define objectives and develop project plan	1 week
Assemble project team	2 weeks
Develop business requirements	2 weeks
Obtain relevant transaction/use data	4 weeks
Develop account/systems architecture	2 weeks
Perform vendor scan	2 weeks
Create vendor long list	1 week
Determine RFP format	1 week
Develop RFP questions	1 week
Issue and administer RFP	4–6 weeks
Review and score proposals and pricing	2 weeks
Host vendor presentations	1 week
Select vendor	1 week
Implement project	3–12 months

B. RFP Design

There are two basic elements in any RFP design: the substance of the required products or services, and the form in which the RFP is delivered. Both are described below.

The substance of an RFP describes the firm's basic operating structure, lists the RFP's objectives, describes the expected activity information associated with the product/service required, states the desired outcome delivered by the product/service, and specifies administrative requirements. In short, the substance of the RFP provides the potential providers with a road map of the firm's desired deliverables. Appendix 7.2 provides a discussion of activity information specific to banking RFPs.

The form of the RFP determines (1) how the RFP will be received by the potential providers and (2) the way in which responses will be compared by the issuing firm. It is relatively easy to prepare and distribute the RFP. There are a number of options when it comes to form. For simple RFPs, a word-processing document inviting a structured response by e-mail may be sufficient. As the scale and complexity of the desired product/service increases, other possibilities may include workbooks with multiple spreadsheets, PDF files, or RFP templates hosted through the firm's secured website.

No matter the approach taken, the design objective should be simplicity and understandability for the respondent and clear and comparable responses for subsequent analysis by the issuer.

C. RFP Administration

RFP administration is divided into six major tasks, with activity occurring at various points throughout the process, as described below:

1. **Development of a Long List:** This step involves treasury managers determining the potential FSPs that are capable of providing the desired products/services. If the initial list is too long, then additional criteria can be added to refine the list to a manageable length. When the long list is complete, it is advisable to make the potential providers aware of the impending RFP.

2. **Issuance of the RFP:** Once the RFP is issued to the providers on the long list, the issuing firm and the providers are on a shared timeline. The firm should let all the participants know the rules and timeline that will be followed in the RFP process. It is highly probable that the providers will ask for clarification on points within the RFP. These questions should come to a single point of contact. It is recommended that all questions and answers be shared with the entire bidder pool.

3. **Evaluation of Responses and Creation of a Short List:** In this step, the review team should determine the appropriate areas of evaluation (i.e., the basic categories of the RFP) and create a scoring and weighting methodology. The scoring can be used to select a short list and to identify potential strengths or weaknesses to be explored in the final meetings. After determining the short list, it is appropriate to perform any needed due diligence reviews regarding financial capacity and stability, as well as any legal issues.

4. **Meetings and Demonstrations:** This step provides an opportunity to ask detailed questions regarding the treasury solutions proposed by the FSP as well as to assess how the implementation will be handled.

5. **Selection and Contract Negotiation:** After the meetings and demonstrations are complete, the evaluation committee should review the updated scoring and identify the preferred provider. Depending upon company requirements, this may require further review and ratification by senior management. Once an FSP has been selected, the final details of the contracts and service requirements must be worked out with the finalist.

The process is not complete until the final contracts are negotiated, which is why many firms do not notify the other providers until contracting is complete.

6. **Implementation and Post-Project Review:** The RFP process concludes with the implementation and review. In terms of time and effort, implementation is often the largest component of the RFP. Depending upon the size of the project, it may be advisable to break the implementation into sections. This allows the opportunity to test new practices and procedures in one area before they are rolled out company-wide. For example, with a global banking RFP, it may be advisable to take a regional approach to implementation and solve problems that occur in one region. The purpose of the post-project review is to determine the steps and procedures that went well and why. It is a learning experience for both the company and the chosen FSP that can be used going forward while managing the relationship.

IV. BANK COMPENSATION PRACTICES

Bank compensation refers to the way in which a bank is compensated for the entire set of products and services (i.e., the complete "book of business") provided to a particular firm. This includes credit or lending services, operating services, and trust or investment management services. Some banks look at compensation for each type of service separately, but the vast majority look at the profitability of the total relationship. In many cases, banks are willing to reduce the price of one product or service and use it as a loss leader with a given client in hopes of making up that loss on other more profitable areas of business. As a result, it is important that treasury professionals look at the total cost of each banking relationship and manage the relationships accordingly. Compensation can come in the form of fees, balances, or some combination of the two. The mix can vary depending upon the desires of both the bank and the firm.

A. Billing for Bank Services

Banks are typically compensated by fees, which are typically netted against any actual or imputed interest earned on funds held in accounts. Banking services are often bundled[2] and paid for with a combination of required balances in deposit accounts and value dating (discussed below). As larger banks expanded outside of their home country and began competing for services globally, many banks began to unbundle their services and charge specific fees for specific services. In an effort to help companies manage these unbundled services, TWIST[3] has developed standards for electronic billing of bank services. Various groups, including AFP, are working to standardize international banking service descriptions and provide a standardized service code structure that can be used for billing. Designed specifically to work with the TWIST BSB format,[4] the AFP Global Service Codes™ include over 800 codes for banking services that are widely adopted across Europe, the Middle East, Africa, and the Pacific Rim.

In contrast to the corporate banking practices in most other countries, where banks charge explicit fees and pay interest on deposits, most banks in the United States provide corporations with earnings credits, which are essentially imputed interest. Earnings credits can be used to offset service charges. Earnings credits are attributable to US federal regulations that barred banks from paying interest on commercial accounts.[5] Earnings credits allow depositors to be compensated for the value of the balances they have at the bank, in lieu of actual interest. An example of the computation of the amount of the earnings credit is shown later in this chapter.

---

2. Bundling of services is the practice of either charging a single fee for a group of services or charging different fees for specific services depending upon which services are used. For example, a bank might charge a very low price on a product or service that is normally closely scrutinized. The bank may then charge a higher fee for other products/services that are not as closely scrutinized.

3. The Transaction Workflow Innovation Standards Team (TWIST) is a not-for-profit industry group formed to rationalize financial industry standards by creating user-driven, nonproprietary, and internally consistent XML-based standards for the financial supply chain.

4. The TWIST BSB (bank services billing) format is incorporated into the ISO 20022 standard.

5. This practice was prompted by the Reg Q prohibition against paying interest on DDA accounts. This regulation was repealed in 2010, as part of the Dodd-Frank Act.

B. Value Dating

Outside the United States, banks often use value dating as compensation for services provided to corporate customers. Under a value-dating system, a bank sets a forward value date when determining the date on which the value of funds is credited to an account and establishes a back value date when determining the date on which the value of funds is debited from an account. For example, when a deposit is forward valued, the date of the credit to the customer's account is later than the actual date on which the item is added to the ledger balance. Similarly, when a withdrawal is back valued, the date of the debit to the account is earlier than the actual date on which the item is deducted from the ledger balance at the bank. This reduces available balances, which in turn reduces interest earned on the account. In effect, the bank is compensated during the value-dating period either by not having to pay interest on positive balances or by earning interest charged on negative balances. In some countries, value dating is standardized among the major clearing banks, while in other countries, it is negotiated on a customer-by-customer or item-by-item basis.

EXHIBIT 7.3 **BANK STATEMENT SHOWING VALUE DATING**

The Globe Bank
21 New Globe Walk Bankside
London SE1 9DT

Account Type: Current Account—Commercial
Account Name: ABC Ltd
Account Number: 9999888889999
Sort Code: 22-15-44
BIC: GLBKGB2XXXX

Date	Description	Paid Out	Paid In	Value Date	Account Balance
01.09.2016	Opening Balance				255,918.25
01.09.2016	Cheque	1,455.00		30.08.2016	254,463.25
01.09.2016	Cheque	2,155.00		29.08.2016	252,308.25
01.09.2016	Wire	25,000.00		01.09.2016	227,308.25
02.09.2016	Wire	35,000.00		02.09.2016	192,308.25
02.09.2016	Cheque	5,615.25		01.09.2016	186,693.00
02.09.2016	Faster Payment		500.00	02.09.2016	187,193.00
02.09.2016	Deposit		24,515.25	03.09.2016	211,708.25
03.09.2016	Cheque	1,000.00		01.09.2016	210,708.25
03.09.2016	Wire	50,000.00		03.09.2016	160,708.25
03.09.2016	Faster Payment		255.00	03.09.2016	160,963.25
03.09.2016	Deposit		55,125.00	04.09.2016	216,088.25
03.09.2016	Cheque	155.00		02.09.2016	215,933.25
04.09.2016	Wire	75,000.00		04.09.2016	140,933.25
04.09.2016	Service Charge	145.00		04.09.2016	140,788.25

Exhibit 7.3 provides an example of how value dating may appear on a bank statement. In this example, the account balance shown at the end of 02.09.2016 (or September 2) is 211,708.25, yet the amount that is available for earning interest would only be 186,038.00. This is because the deposit of 24,515.25 has a value date of September 3, and the two cheques posted after September 2 (for 1,000.00 and 155.00) were back valued to September 2 or earlier.

While US banks do not typically value-date transactions, they achieve similar results through the use of availability of funds and as-of adjustments.

C. Account Analysis in the US Commercial Banking System

As previously noted, US banks typically provide their corporate customers with imputed interest on demand deposit account (DDA) balances using earnings credit analysis (ECA) systems. The rate used to calculate this imputed interest is called the *earnings credit rate (ECR)* and is typically negotiable as part of the initial selection process. Banks can, and often do, change the ECR without notifying their customers, resulting in unexpected fees or unused balances at the end of a billing period.

An account analysis statement serves as the bank's bill for services rendered and shows the process used to determine the fees charged and the earnings accrued during the period in question. This practice is typically not seen outside of the United States where invoices for services are more common. The account analysis statement typically provides the following information to a bank's commercial customers:

- Services provided
- Balances maintained
- Transaction/item volumes processed
- Charges assessed
- Earnings credit allowances

It is important to note that banks may not use the same terminology when describing products/services. Some services and fees may be combined into a single line item or flat fee, and these combinations may vary from bank to bank. Fee structures are as varied and complex as the account analysis formats. Any fees owed, after deducting the earnings credits, are typically debited directly from the account. In some cases, however, the bank may be willing to invoice the firm's accounts payable department for the fees. Exhibit 7.4 provides an example of an account analysis statement.

EXHIBIT 7.4 ACCOUNT ANALYSIS STATEMENT

ABC BANK—CORPORATE BANKING ANALYSIS

Global Manufacturing Company
1234 Main Street, Anytown, Arkansas
Date: 7/1/2016
ECR: 1.00%

Relationship Manager:	J. Sellsmore
Company Contact:	M. Cash
Days in Month:	30
Month Ending:	6/30/2016

BALANCE SUMMARY	
AVERAGE LEDGER BALANCE	$658,987.50
LESS: AVERAGE FLOAT	-55,934.89
AVERAGE COLLECTED BALANCE	$603,052.61
LESS: RESERVE REQUIREMENT (10%)	-60,305.26
AVERAGE AVAILABLE BALANCE	$542,747.35
LESS: BALANCE REQUIRED	-6,796,360.83
NET AVAILABLE BALANCE	-$6,253,613.48

EARNINGS CREDIT SUMMARY	
AVAILABLE BALANCE FOR EARNINGS CREDIT	$542,747.35
EARNINGS CREDIT ALLOWANCE	$446.09
LESS: CHARGE FOR SERVICES	-5,586.05
NET SERVICE CREDIT	-$5,139.96
SERVICE CHARGE AMOUNT	$5,139.96

ACTIVITY	VOLUME	UNIT PRICE	FEES REQUIRED	BALANCE REQUIRED
GENERAL ACCOUNT SERVICE				
ACCOUNT MAINTENANCE FLAT FEE	4	20.00	$80.00	$97,333.33
DEPOSITORY SERVICES				
CREDITS	94	0.25	23.50	$28,591.67
DEPOSITED ITEMS	1,745	0.08	139.60	$169,846.67
RETURN ITEMS	15	2.00	30.00	$36,500.00
DEBITS	1,598	0.10	159.80	$194,423.33
STOP PAYMENTS	5	18.00	90.00	$109,500.00
LOCKBOX SERVICES				
WHOLESALE LOCKBOX MAINTENANCE FEE	3	105.00	315.00	$383,250.00
ITEM PROCESSING FEE	486	0.40	194.40	$236,520.00
ZBA CONTROLLED DISBURSEMENT SERVICES				
ZBA MAINTENANCE	1	40.00	40.00	$48,666.67
CONTROLLED DISBURSEMENT NOTIFICATION	1	45.00	45.00	$54,750.00
FUNDS TRANSFER SERVICES				
ACH MAINTENANCE	1	55.00	55.00	$66,916.67
ACH ITEMS	145	0.12	17.40	$21,170.00
INCOMING WIRE TRANSFERS	24	7.00	168.00	$204,400.00
OUTGOING WIRE TRANSFERS	8	12.00	96.00	$116,800.00
INTERNATIONAL SERVICES				
INTERNATIONAL WIRES: OUTBOUND	26	25.00	650.00	$790,833.33
INTERNATIONAL COLLECTION ITEMS	125	20.00	2,500.00	$3,041,666.67
FOREIGN EXCHANGE TRANSACTIONS	87	10.00	870.00	$1,058,500.00
ACCOUNT RECONCILIATION SERVICES				
RECONCILIATION MAINTENANCE - PARTIAL	1	50.00	50.00	$60,833.33
CHECKS RECONCILIATION	1,247	0.05	62.35	$75,859.17
TOTALS			$5,586.05	$6,796,360.83

1. ACCOUNT ANALYSIS STANDARDS

Since 1986, AFP Service Codes™ have been recognized as the standard for identifying balances and charges that appear on account analysis statements and in responding to RFPs.[6] AFP Service Codes are six-character, alphanumeric codes used by banks to provide standard, uniform references and terms for identifying, describing, and reporting bank services, as well as the associated charges. By simplifying and organizing the often varied and complex terminology used to identify bank services, the codes also help to resolve volume and pricing errors.

The Accredited Standards Committee (ASC) X12 of the American National Standards Institute (ANSI) has developed a standardized format (Account Analysis Transaction Set 822) for financial institutions to use when sending account analysis statements to account holders electronically. The ASC X12 822 transaction set accommodates the AFP standard account analysis format and AFP Service Codes.

It is important for firms to review their account analysis statements in a timely manner to ensure accuracy. Commercial software packages, databases, and spreadsheets can be used for this purpose.

2. ACCOUNT ANALYSIS TERMINOLOGY

The following are common terms used in account analysis statements:

- **Average Ledger Balance:** This is the sum of the daily ending ledger balances (both positive and negative) divided by the number of days in the analysis period. Balances used in the calculation are net of any current-period adjustments.

- **Average Deposit Float:** This is the sum of the daily dollar amount of items (primarily checks) in the process of collection divided by the number of calendar or business days in the analysis period.

- **Average Collected Balance:** This is the sum of the daily ending collected balances (both positive and negative) divided by the number of days in the analysis period. In many account analysis statements, this item is calculated as the average ledger balance minus the average deposit float.

- **Reserve Requirement:** In the context of an earnings credit computation, the reserve requirement represents the amount that the bank must maintain with the Federal Reserve.[7] Historically, reserve balances that were needed in order to satisfy the reserve requirement were nonearning, hence the practice of deducting this reserve from balances that received an earnings credit. Just as commercial banks are now allowed to pay interest on commercial accounts, US reserve banks can now pay interest on reserve balances. Many banks, however, still deduct the reserve from available balances in calculating earnings credits. As with most things related to analysis statements, the amount of funds deducted for reserve requirements is usually negotiable.

- **FDIC Fees:** As with the reserve requirement, banks sometimes charge customers fees to cover the cost of federally mandated deposit insurance. While the FDIC does not object to these fees, in 2012 the FDIC ordered banks to stop labeling these fees as *FDIC fees* (or using other government agency names), as this could mislead customers into thinking the fees go to the government instead of to the banks.

- **Service Charges:** These are the explicit fees or prices charged for services provided by a bank. Service charges are either expressed as a flat monthly fee or as a per-item or per-unit price. In the case of the latter, the unit price is multiplied by the volume to arrive at the analysis period total.

- **Available or Investable Balance:** The available balance, sometimes referred to as the *investable balance*, represents the balance in the customer's account that the bank was able to invest in income-producing assets

---

6. It should be noted that these standards are not necessarily used in all account analysis statements.
7. As of the date of this writing, the reserve requirement was 10% of collected balances.

during the account analysis period. Some banks calculate the investable balance as the average collected balance minus the reserve requirement balance. The investable balance can be a surplus or deficit.

· **Earnings Credit Allowance and the ECR:** The earnings credit allowance is the total dollar value of credit that can be used to offset the service charges incurred during the analysis period. It is calculated by multiplying the investable balance by the ECR for the period in question. The methods used for determining the ECR vary. A commonly used basis for the ECR is the 90-day T-bill rate, but banks can base ECRs on their own internal requirements and rates. For example, some banks reduce the ECR by the applied reserve requirement (a reserve-adjusted ECR), and calculate the earnings credit using the average collected balance instead of the investable balance.

3. ACCOUNT ANALYSIS CALCULATIONS

The following formula is generally used to measure the earnings credit:[8]

$$EC = CB \times (1 - RR) \times ECR \times \left(\frac{D}{365} \right)$$

Where:

EC = Earnings credit

CB = Average collected balances

RR = Reserve requirement

ECR = Earnings credit rate

D = Number of days in the month (Note: Some banks use the ECR divided by 12 to determine this monthly calculation instead of using the actual number of days.)

An example of this calculation appears in Exhibit 7.5.

---

8. These equations are generally representative of those used for account analysis statements, though the actual calculation format may vary from bank to bank.

EXHIBIT 7.5 EARNINGS CREDIT CALCULATION

ASSUMPTIONS:

AVERAGE LEDGER BALANCE	$250,000
DEPOSIT FLOAT	$30,000
RESERVE REQUIREMENT	10%
EARNINGS CREDIT RATE	1%
SERVICE CHARGES FOR THE MONTH	$1,000
DAYS IN MONTH	30

AVERAGE COLLECTED BALANCE CALCULATION

AVERAGE LEDGER BALANCE	$250,000
LESS: DEPOSIT FLOAT	(30,000)
EQUALS: AVERAGE COLLECTED BALANCE	$220,000

$$\text{EARNINGS CREDIT} = \text{COLLECTED BALANCE} \times (1 - \text{RESERVE REQUIREMENT}) \times \left(\text{EARNINGS CREDIT RATE} \times \frac{\text{DAYS IN MONTH}}{365}\right)$$

$$EC = CB \times (1 - RR) \times ECR \times \left(\frac{D}{365}\right)$$

$$= \$220,000 \times (1 - 0.10) \times \left(0.01 \times \frac{30}{365}\right)$$

$$= \$220,000 \times 0.9 \times (0.01 \times 0.0822) = \$162.76$$

The calculations indicate that the firm's monthly earnings credit equaled $162.76. Since the monthly charges equal $1,000, the bank will debit $837.24 from the firm's account.

Overall, the firm's monthly $220,000 average collected balance results in an earnings credit that is insufficient to cover the service provider's $1,000 charges for the month. It would be of interest to know the average collected balance that would be required so that the earnings credit exactly offsets the bank's charges. This is determined by rearranging the previous formula to solve for the collected balances required. The revised formula is:

$$CB = \frac{SC}{ECR \times \left(\frac{D}{365}\right) \times (1 - RR)}$$

Where:

CB = Average collected balances required to pay service charges

SC = Monthly service charges

ECR = Earnings credit rate

RR = Reserve requirement

D = Number of days in the month (Note: Some banks use the ECR divided by 12 to determine this monthly calculation instead of using the actual number of days.)

An example of this calculation is presented in Exhibit 7.6.

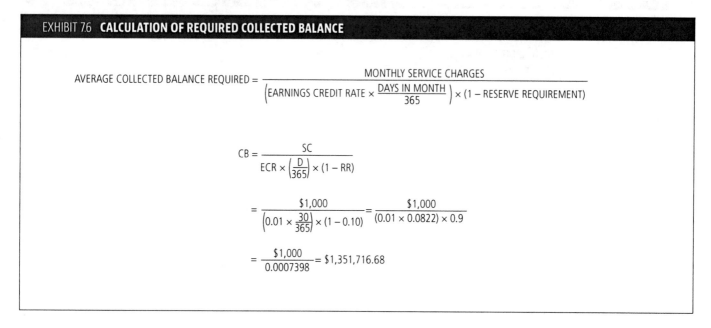

EXHIBIT 7.6   CALCULATION OF REQUIRED COLLECTED BALANCE

$$\text{AVERAGE COLLECTED BALANCE REQUIRED} = \frac{\text{MONTHLY SERVICE CHARGES}}{\left(\text{EARNINGS CREDIT RATE} \times \frac{\text{DAYS IN MONTH}}{365}\right) \times (1 - \text{RESERVE REQUIREMENT})}$$

$$CB = \frac{SC}{ECR \times \left(\frac{D}{365}\right) \times (1 - RR)}$$

$$= \frac{\$1,000}{\left(0.01 \times \frac{30}{365}\right) \times (1 - 0.10)} = \frac{\$1,000}{(0.01 \times 0.0822) \times 0.9}$$

$$= \frac{\$1,000}{0.0007398} = \$1,351,716.68$$

An average collected balance of $1,351,716.68 is required to produce an earnings credit that offsets the $1,000 service charges. Thus, the average collected balance must be increased by $1,131,716.68 (i.e., the $1,351,716.68 in Exhibit 7.6 minus the $220,000.00 in Exhibit 7.5) to offset the charges.

4. FEE VERSUS BALANCE COMPENSATION

The treasury department must choose between compensating banks with fees or balances. An analysis of the company's bank fees, earnings credit rate, and short-term interest rates, combined with company policy, will determine whether it is better to hold excess balances and reduce bank service charges or to maintain lower balances and increase short-term investments.

Fee compensation (e.g., lower account balances) may be preferred when short-term investments offer a higher yield than that provided by the ECR. The use of fees for compensation is even more compelling when the firm can use excess balances to pay down short-term debt, which is typically at a rate much higher than the ECR. Another benefit of fee-based compensation is that fees can be budgeted and compared with other costs, while balances are not as directly comparable.

Alternatively, certain firms may prefer to cover service charges with excess balances. Motives for balance compensation include the following:

- Balance compensation lets the firm take advantage of excess collected balances that arise from unanticipated deposits or precautionary transaction balances.
- The potential exists for more favorable pricing for loans and other services if collected balances are maintained.
- Earnings credits are not taxable, whereas the return earned on many short-term investments is taxable.
- ECRs may exceed available short-term investment rates.

Some of the disadvantages of balance compensation include the following:

- ECRs are not always known until after the applicable billing period.
- Earnings in excess of analysis fees are unusable and are typically not carried forward to future years.
- Balances in excess of the FDIC insurance limit may be at risk of loss in the event the bank is closed.

Some banks prefer fee compensation because deposit balances increase the liabilities on their balance sheet. This may lead to a need for additional capital to meet regulatory requirements. A second reason why banks often prefer fee compensation is that fees from deposit services are viewed as a low-risk source of earnings.

The principal reason why a bank may prefer balance compensation is that deposits may be used to fund loans and investments at rates exceeding the ECR provided to an account holder.

D. Comparing and Monitoring Costs among FSPs

Firms usually compare FSP service charges during their selection process and then during periodic relationship reviews. This process is important not only to validate the reasonableness of pricing over time, but also to confirm that the service provider is actually abiding by any negotiated pricing. One source for comparable bank service charge data is Phoenix-Hecht's *The Blue Book of Bank Prices*. *The Blue Book* is published annually and provides a comparison of various key service charges.

Developing a precise comparison of pricing, whether during the RFP selection process or during relationship reviews, can be a difficult exercise, but it can be simplified with a carefully prepared template or spreadsheet for bank fee analysis, prepared ahead of time by the treasury professional. It is often helpful to share this template with the various FSPs so that they understand how they are being evaluated. Banks have varying approaches to bundling products and services—the charging basis can be quite different (e.g., per user or per location), and terminology and descriptions for services are not standardized (e.g., *pooling, sweeping,* and *concentration* can be used interchangeably at one bank and refer to separate services and price points at another).

A well-designed comparison template also requires that prices be specified in a common currency, such as US dollars or euro. For example, a bank might suggest that since all bank services provided in Singapore are billed in Singapore dollars, these prices should also be quoted in the same currency. A good counter to that request is that the primary purpose of the analysis template is comparability.

The comparison template should include comparisons for each of the primary service charges. In general, the broad categories of service charges are:

- Implementation
- Maintenance
- Account services
- Transaction processing
- Information delivery
- Technology

The only valid method of comparing costs is to calculate the bottom-line cost of a specific set of services based on the processing volumes and balances that a firm expects to have.

Adding to the difficulty of comparing and monitoring ongoing costs is the fact that while many FSPs provide monthly analysis statements, others may calculate their account analysis quarterly, semiannually, or annually. If an account holder's balances fluctuate from month to month, then quarterly, semiannual, or annual analysis periods allow excess balances in one month to offset charges in other months. Consultants can help firms compare service charges from an FSP or multiple FSPs.

There are a number of automated tools available to help with the review and validation of bank pricing, but many firms use spreadsheets. There are also a number of third-party services that provide comparable information on service charges that can be used as benchmarks.

V. ASSESSING THE RISK OF FSPs

The viability of FSPs is of paramount importance because an operations breakdown, information compromise, or financial failure could significantly disrupt the firm's ability to perform basic liquidity management activities. Accordingly, the operating practices and creditworthiness of FSPs must be assessed periodically.

Assessing the risk of FSPs is necessary as these entities control a firm's information flows, related records, and liquid assets. The FSP must have adequate backup systems and disaster recovery procedures. These procedures should be evaluated at the outset of a relationship and periodically thereafter. SLAs and contract provisions should indicate specific rights and responsibilities of the parties in the event of a service interruption.

A. Assessing Operational Risk of FSPs

An FSP's operational risk can be monitored via the provider's SOC 1 Report[9]. The Statement on Standards for Attestation Engagements (SSAE) No. 18, *Attestation Standards: Clarification and Recodification,* was finalized by the Auditing Standards Board of the American Institute of Certified Public Accountants (AICPA) in 2016 and is the authoritative guidance for reporting on service organizations. Performance and reporting requirements for SOC 1 Reports are covered in SSAE 18, AT-C section 320, *Reporting on an Examination of Controls at a Service Organization Relevant to User Entities' Internal Control Over Financial Reporting.*

SSAE 18 complies with the International Standard on Assurance Engagements (ISAE) No. 3402, *Assurance Reports on Controls at a Service Organization*, which was issued in December 2009 by the International Auditing and Assurance Standards Board (IAASB), part of the International Federation of Accountants (IFAC). ISAE 3402 was developed to provide an international assurance standard for allowing public accountants to issue a report for use by user organizations and their auditors (i.e., user auditors) on the controls at a service organization that are likely to be a part of the user organization's system of internal controls over financial reporting.

FSPs receive significant value from having an SOC 1 or ISAE 3402 engagement performed and report issued. An FSP's audit report with an unqualified opinion that is issued by an independent accounting firm differentiates the FSP from its peers by demonstrating the establishment of effectively designed control objectives and activities. A service auditor's report also helps an FSP build trust with its customers.

---

9. An SOC 1 Report is the first of a set of Service Organization Controls (SOC) Reports introduced by the AICPA. SOC 1 is designed for engagements performed under SSAE 18.

Without a current service auditor's report, an FSP may have to entertain multiple audit requests from its customers and their respective auditors. Multiple visits from user auditors can strain the organization's resources. A service auditor's report ensures that all user organizations and their auditors have access to the same information. This will satisfy the user auditor's requirements in many cases.

The service auditor's reports provides valuable information on the FSP's controls and the effectiveness of those controls. The customer receives a detailed description of the FSP's controls and the suitability of the design of the controls (i.e., a Type 1 report) and an independent assessment of whether the controls were placed in operation, suitably designed, and operating effectively (i.e., a Type 2 report).

The firm should provide the service auditor's report to its auditors. Without a service auditor's report, the firm would likely have to incur additional costs in sending its auditors to the FSP to perform additional audit procedures.

B. Assessing Financial Risk of Global Banks—Basel Accords

The Basel Accords are the result of a round of meetings and discussions by central bankers from around the world who originally met in Basel, Switzerland, in 1988 to discuss the need to modify capital requirements for banks, based upon perceived credit risk. These meetings and deliberations produced a set of minimal capital requirements for banks and came to be known as the *1988 Basel Capital Accord*. There have subsequently been two more rounds of Basel discussions, and the Basel Accords now include specific requirements around assessment of and provision for operational risk in addition to credit risk. And more discussions are planned.

C. Assessing Financial Risk of US Banks

One of the primary publicly available tools for assessing the general financial risk of a US bank is the Uniform Bank Performance Report (UBPR), published by the Federal Financial Institutions Examination Council (FFIEC). The UBPR is an analytical tool created for supervisory, examination, and management purposes. In a concise format, it shows the impact of management decisions and economic conditions on a bank's performance and balance sheet composition. The performance and composition data contained in the report can be used to help evaluate the adequacy of earnings, liquidity, capital, asset/liability management, and growth management. Bankers and examiners alike can use this report to further their understanding of a bank's financial condition and, through such understanding, perform their duties more effectively.[10]

By analyzing the data contained in the UBPR, the user can obtain an overall picture of the bank's financial health and discover conditions that might require further analysis and investigation. The UBPR presents three types of data for use in the financial analysis of a bank:

- Data for the specific bank
- Data for a peer group of banks similar in size and economic environment
- Percentile rankings

A thorough understanding of these data groups and their interrelationships and limitations is essential in order to use the UBPR effectively. As a general rule, any analysis should compare the bank to its peer group, consider the bank's trends over time, and recognize trends and changes in peer group averages.[11] A sample UBPR is provided in Appendix 7.3.

---

10. From "UBPR" on FFIEC's website (http://www.ffiec.gov/UBPR.htm, last modified August 3, 2016).
11. From "A User's Guide for the Uniform Bank Performance Report," published by FFIEC, December 2008 (http://www.ffiec.gov/PDF/UBPR/UBPR_12-08.pdf).

D. Counterparty Risk

Counterparty risk refers to the risk that a counterparty in a contract will not meet its contractual obligations. This applies as much or more to contracts with FSPs, who may be acting as custodians of company funds and information, as it does to any investment decision. This is a very real risk and should be considered when evaluating a contract for services of any kind with a bank or FSP.

E. Sovereign and Political Risk

Global account management requires an understanding of sovereign and political risks. *Sovereign risk* refers to the risk that a government may default on its debt.

Political risk is the term applied to the variety of actions that a government may take that negatively impact a firm's operations and/or value. It includes the risk that a firm's operations in a foreign country may be nationalized or expropriated by the government of that country. *Nationalization* refers to a government takeover of all firms in a specific industry, often involving ore extraction, petroleum, transportation, or power generation and distribution businesses. *Expropriation* refers to a government takeover of a single firm, with or without compensation. Experience suggests that when compensation is made, it is significantly less than the market value of the expro- priated firm. Political risk may also take the form of regulatory or policy changes. For example, a central bank could alter its monetary policy significantly or impose currency regulations that would reduce the value of FX contracts or currency trades. Other types of political risk include:

- **Blocked Currencies:** Profits cannot be converted from the local currency into a major trading currency.
- **Forced Reinvestment:** Funds cannot be transferred out of the country in any form, or the amount that can be transferred is limited.
- **Required Majority Ownership:** Firms must be owned by resident nationals.

Multinational firms are exposed to varying degrees of political risk depending upon attitudes and policies of the host country and the nature of the business. A firm with operations in foreign countries must be knowledgeable about the laws, regulations, taxes, and customs that govern business activities, as well as the overall political and social dynamics of the countries where capital is invested.

F. Managing Confidential Information and Conflicts of Interest

FSPs often have access to confidential information about a firm's customer base. A treasurer must know if, and under what conditions, this information may be shared with affiliates of the FSP or other parties, to prevent the loss of confidentiality. Some firms document this with a nondisclosure agreement.

A conflict of interest may arise when a particular FSP serves in multiple capacities. For example, an FSP with a lending relationship with a specific firm may also serve as the firm's bond trustee. If the borrower becomes distressed, there is a risk that the FSP might protect its own interests at the expense of the bondholders and other investors. Traditionally, FSPs have established a notional barrier (sometimes referred to as a "wall") against information flows between functional divisions to prevent such abuses. Employees are typically not permitted to work on both sides of the "wall," and there are internal controls about what information may be passed "over the wall."

FSPs may form business alliances that provide complementary areas of expertise or superior cost efficiencies. These alliances often result in the FSP outsourcing services to another party or corporate entity. For example, many FSPs outsource their credit card merchant processing operations to third parties. In these cases, information is shared with outside parties and disclosure to the customer is generally required.

G. Legal and Ethical Issues

In many countries, commissions or fees that would be considered bribes in the United States are deeply ingrained in the commercial culture. However, the Foreign Corrupt Practices Act (FCPA) forbids US firms from engaging in these practices. Many other countries have similar laws and regulations. US firms also must consider whether their foreign activities may come under the jurisdiction of the Office of Foreign Assets Control (OFAC), which is an office of the US Treasury Department that administers and enforces economic and trade sanctions against targeted foreign countries, terrorist-sponsoring organizations, and international narcotics traffickers, as required by legislation, foreign policy, and national security goals. OFAC has the authority to impose controls on financial transactions and freeze foreign assets under US jurisdiction.

VI. SUMMARY

The detailed information provided in this chapter assists treasury professionals in managing relationships with FSPs, and banks in particular. This chapter also discussed the RFP and selection process, as applied to the selection of FSPs. This process requires hard work and diligent planning across various departments. Using a formalized process helps to insure buy-in from both management and other operational units. It does take time, however, and treasury should be realistic about the required level of commitment as well as expectations.

Once an FSP is selected, relationship management is an important part of the treasury professional's job. Relationship management goes beyond assessing the quality of the products or services provided; it includes assessment of compensation and ongoing assessment of FSP risk. These and other key elements of relationship management were discussed in this chapter. Good relationship management takes time and effort. But given the work needed to change FSPs, investing in relationship management provides substantial dividends.

Key Equations

Earnings Credit =

$$\text{Collected Balance} \times (1 - \text{Reserve Requirement}) \times \text{Earnings Credit Rate} \times \left(\frac{\text{Days in Month}}{365} \right)$$

Average Collected Balance Required =

$$\frac{\text{Monthly Service Charges}}{\text{Earnings Credit Rate} \times \left(\frac{\text{Days in Month}}{365} \right) \times (1 - \text{Reserve Requirement})}$$

APPENDIX 7.1: SAMPLE BANK SCORECARD[12]

SAMPLE BANK SCORECARD

COMPANY NAME

Bank Name: Any Bank Name

Acct Officer: Any Relationship Manager

Time Period: Any Time Period

BANKING SERVICES EVALUATION

SECTION 1	N/A	Excellent	Satisfactory	Poor	Unacceptable	Rating
			GENERAL CUSTOMER SERVICE			
1. Level of Competence	○ Not Applicable	○ Rating of 4	○ Rating of 3	○ Rating of 2	○ Rating of 1	
2. Courteous Professional Behavior	○ Not Applicable	○ Rating of 4	○ Rating of 3	○ Rating of 2	○ Rating of 1	
3. Telephone Availability	○ Not Applicable	○ Rating of 4	○ Rating of 3	○ Rating of 2	○ Rating of 1	
4. Backup Coverage	○ Not Applicable	○ Rating of 4	○ Rating of 3	○ Rating of 2	○ Rating of 1	
5. Response Correctness	○ Not Applicable	○ Rating of 4	○ Rating of 3	○ Rating of 2	○ Rating of 1	
6. Timeliness of Response	○ Not Applicable	○ Rating of 4	○ Rating of 3	○ Rating of 2	○ Rating of 1	
7. Follow Through on Commitments	○ Not Applicable	○ Rating of 4	○ Rating of 3	○ Rating of 2	○ Rating of 1	
8. Overall Problem Solving	○ Not Applicable	○ Rating of 4	○ Rating of 3	○ Rating of 2	○ Rating of 1	
9. Knowledge of Bank's Policies/Procedures	○ Not Applicable	○ Rating of 4	○ Rating of 3	○ Rating of 2	○ Rating of 1	
10. Knowledge of Bank's Cash Mgmt Products	○ Not Applicable	○ Rating of 4	○ Rating of 3	○ Rating of 2	○ Rating of 1	
Custom Field	○ Not Applicable	○ Rating of 4	○ Rating of 3	○ Rating of 2	○ Rating of 1	
Custom Field	○ Not Applicable	○ Rating of 4	○ Rating of 3	○ Rating of 2	○ Rating of 1	
Custom Field	○ Not Applicable	○ Rating of 4	○ Rating of 3	○ Rating of 2	○ Rating of 1	
Custom Field	○ Not Applicable	○ Rating of 4	○ Rating of 3	○ Rating of 2	○ Rating of 1	

Average =   Total =

Comments: _____

_____

_____

12. The sample bank scorecard is taken from the "AFP Bank Scorecard" published in April 2009 and available through AFP's website (http://www.afponline.org/mbr/res/topics/Bank_Scorecard.html?terms=bank_scorecard).

SAMPLE BANK SCORECARD (CONTINUED)

SECTION 2	RELATIONSHIP MANAGER					
	N/A	Excellent	Satisfactory	Poor	Unacceptable	Rating
1. Knowledge of Bank's Cash Mgmt Products	○ Not Applicable	○ Rating of 4	○ Rating of 3	○ Rating of 2	○ Rating of 1	
2. Ability to Match Services to our Needs	○ Not Applicable	○ Rating of 4	○ Rating of 3	○ Rating of 2	○ Rating of 1	
3. Follow-up on Requests	○ Not Applicable	○ Rating of 4	○ Rating of 3	○ Rating of 2	○ Rating of 1	
4. Company and Industry Knowledge	○ Not Applicable	○ Rating of 4	○ Rating of 3	○ Rating of 2	○ Rating of 1	
5. Calling Frequency [Excellent = ___ visits / yr]	○ Not Applicable	○ Rating of 4	○ Rating of 3	○ Rating of 2	○ Rating of 1	
6. Ease of Access—General	○ Not Applicable	○ Rating of 4	○ Rating of 3	○ Rating of 2	○ Rating of 1	
7. Ease of Access—Emergency	○ Not Applicable	○ Rating of 4	○ Rating of 3	○ Rating of 2	○ Rating of 1	
Custom Field	○ Not Applicable	○ Rating of 4	○ Rating of 3	○ Rating of 2	○ Rating of 1	
Custom Field	○ Not Applicable	○ Rating of 4	○ Rating of 3	○ Rating of 2	○ Rating of 1	
Custom Field	○ Not Applicable	○ Rating of 4	○ Rating of 3	○ Rating of 2	○ Rating of 1	
Custom Field	○ Not Applicable	○ Rating of 4	○ Rating of 3	○ Rating of 2	○ Rating of 1	

Average =   Total =

Comments: _____

_____

_____

SAMPLE BANK SCORECARD (CONTINUED)

SECTION 3	TECHNICAL RELIABILITY					
	N/A	Excellent	Satisfactory	Poor	Unacceptable	Rating
1. Service Level Agreement (SLA) Compliance	O Not Applicable	O Rating of 4	O Rating of 3	O Rating of 2	O Rating of 1	
2. System Response Time to Inquiry	O Not Applicable	O Rating of 4	O Rating of 3	O Rating of 2	O Rating of 1	
3. Security / Ease of Application & Practical	O Not Applicable	O Rating of 4	O Rating of 3	O Rating of 2	O Rating of 1	
4. Problem Resolution	O Not Applicable	O Rating of 4	O Rating of 3	O Rating of 2	O Rating of 1	
5. Timeliness of Data Availability	O Not Applicable	O Rating of 4	O Rating of 3	O Rating of 2	O Rating of 1	
6. Communication of System Status	O Not Applicable	O Rating of 4	O Rating of 3	O Rating of 2	O Rating of 1	
7. System Outages	O Not Applicable	O Rating of 4	O Rating of 3	O Rating of 2	O Rating of 1	
Custom Field	O Not Applicable	O Rating of 4	O Rating of 3	O Rating of 2	O Rating of 1	
Custom Field	O Not Applicable	O Rating of 4	O Rating of 3	O Rating of 2	O Rating of 1	
Custom Field	O Not Applicable	O Rating of 4	O Rating of 3	O Rating of 2	O Rating of 1	
Custom Field	O Not Applicable	O Rating of 4	O Rating of 3	O Rating of 2	O Rating of 1	

Average =   **Total =**

Comments: _____

_____

_____

Direct Transmission	N/A	Excellent	Satisfactory	Poor	Unacceptable	Rating
1. FTP Access	O Not Applicable	O Rating of 4	O Rating of 3	O Rating of 2	O Rating of 1	
2. Timeliness of Transactions	O Not Applicable	O Rating of 4	O Rating of 3	O Rating of 2	O Rating of 1	
3. Security / Ease of Application & Practical	O Not Applicable	O Rating of 4	O Rating of 3	O Rating of 2	O Rating of 1	
4. Problem Resolution	O Not Applicable	O Rating of 4	O Rating of 3	O Rating of 2	O Rating of 1	
5. Overall Benefit to Customer	O Not Applicable	O Rating of 4	O Rating of 3	O Rating of 2	O Rating of 1	
Custom Field	O Not Applicable	O Rating of 4	O Rating of 3	O Rating of 2	O Rating of 1	
Custom Field	O Not Applicable	O Rating of 4	O Rating of 3	O Rating of 2	O Rating of 1	
Custom Field	O Not Applicable	O Rating of 4	O Rating of 3	O Rating of 2	O Rating of 1	
Custom Field	O Not Applicable	O Rating of 4	O Rating of 3	O Rating of 2	O Rating of 1	

Average =   **Total =**

Comments: _____

_____

_____

SECTION TOTAL   **Average =**   **Total =**

SAMPLE BANK SCORECARD (CONTINUED)

COMPANY NAME
Bank Name: Any Bank Name
Acct Officer: Any Relationship Manager
Time Period: Any Time Period

BANKING SERVICES EVALUATION

SCORING SUMMARY	QUALITATIVE	
	Average	Total
1. GENERAL CUSTOMER SERVICE	0.0	0
2. RELATIONSHIP MANAGER	0.0	0
3. TECHNICAL RELIABILITY	0.0	0
SECTION AVERAGE / TOTAL	0.0	0

SCORING SUMMARY	QUANTITATIVE	
	Average	Total
1. ACCOUNT ANALYSIS	0.0	0
2. BANK SAFETY AND SOUNDNESS (DR, FIN STABILITY)	0.0	0
SECTION AVERAGE / TOTAL	0.0	0

SCORING SUMMARY	PAYMENTS	
	Average	Total
1. DISBURSEMENT SERVICES	0.0	0
2. REMOTE DEPOSIT SERVICES	0.0	0
3. DEPOSIT SERVICES	0.0	0
SECTION AVERAGE / TOTAL	0.0	0

SAMPLE BANK SCORECARD (CONTINUED)

SCORING SUMMARY	INFORMATION REPORTING	
	Average	Total
1. INFORMATION REPORTING (include any type of balance reporting)	0.0	0
2. ACCOUNT RECONCILEMENT	0.0	0
3. WEB / OTHER SERVICE	0.0	0
4. POSITIVE PAY	0.0	0
SECTION AVERAGE / TOTAL	0.0	0

SCORING SUMMARY	MISCELLANEOUS	
	Average	Total
1. INTERNATIONAL SERVICES	0.0	0
2. INVESTMENT / BROKERAGE SERVICES	0.0	0
3. THIRD-PARTY VENDORS	0.0	0
4. CARDS COMMERCIAL	0.0	0
SECTION AVERAGE / TOTAL	0.0	0

SCORING SUMMARY	LOCKBOX	
	Average	Total
1. ITEM PROCESSING	0.0	0
2. INFORMATION REPORTING	0.0	0
SECTION AVERAGE / TOTAL	0.0	0

SCORING SUMMARY	TOTAL SCORES
WEIGHTED AVERAGE TOTAL	0.0
SECTION AVERAGE / TOTAL	0.0

APPENDIX 7.2: RFP ACTIVITY INFORMATION[13]

A company may be a household name in Europe and the United States, but a relative unknown in Asia-Pacific or Latin America. If prospective vendors do not realize the size and scope of the potential business, they will not devote the right resources to develop a proper response to an RFP. The RFP process addresses this in two ways: (1) through the development of business requirements—discussed in the body of Chapter 7—and (2) through the relevant transaction and use data, which demonstrate the scale and are the subject of this appendix.

Company Overview

Detailed and accurate information allows vendors to clearly assess whether they are capable of—and interested in—handling the types of transactions required. This will lead to a thorough and well-thought-out proposal that is a direct result of the RFP.

RFP activity information should develop a clear picture of the company's business footprint that may include detailed information on:

1. **Legal Entity Structure:** This portion of the activity information provides the legal names and ownership structure for the company on a global and/or regional basis, depending on the scope of the RFP. This should be outlined in a chart showing the ownership, business/product lines covered, tax/legal status (e.g., branch, subsidiary, check-the-box), functional currency, and nature of business conducted (e.g., sales, manufacturing, or distribution). Most companies have current legal entity diagrams, and treasury can add value to these by including business details on the activities performed at each entity and how the entities relate to one another—including regional financial oversight, intercompany flows, and commissionaire arrangements.

2. **Organization:** This overview shows the hierarchy of job functions, including who has responsibility for banking relationships, the management of cash at the local and regional level, and investment and borrowing decisions.

3. **Current Bank Account or Systems Architecture:** For a banking RFP, this should show all bank accounts, including the name of the bank, the branch where the account is domiciled, the currency of the account, and the average monthly cash balances. Where possible, the account hierarchies (such as zero-balancing and sweeping) should be indicated so that there is a clear picture of how the company currently manages its cash flows. For a TMS or other type of RFP, it should show the systems deployed and their interconnection.

4. **Planned Bank Account or Systems Architecture:** For a banking RFP, this can be a description or a series of diagrams of what bank structure is planned. The description should fully describe techniques that will be used, such as European pooling, local currency pooling in select countries, US dollar (USD) pooling in Asia-Pacific, entrust loan arrangements in China, cash concentration in Mexico, or zero balance accounts (ZBAs) in the United States. For a systems project, this should show what is desired in terms of the number of systems and how they will relate to one another.

5. **Transaction Values, Volumes, and Types:** Information provided should include the average monthly value of cash flows and the volume of transactions, along with the type of payment instruments (e.g., wire payments, ACH, and check). This information must be provided by currency (e.g., US dollars, euros, and Japanese yen), and it is advisable to list all amounts in the local currency, rather than converting them all to the company's functional currency. The required information can easily be obtained from account analyses for accounts in the United States but is more difficult to obtain for accounts in other countries. It is usually necessary to create a spreadsheet or other data request to collect the required information from international sources.

---

13. Much of this material is provided courtesy of Treasury Alliance Group LLC and is taken from its white paper, "The Request for Proposal Process: A Treasurer's Guide," published in 2012 (http://www.treasuryalliance.com/assets/publications/cash/Treasury_Alliance_Group_RFP_Guide.pdf).

This can be a somewhat frustrating exercise, and it can be tempting to rely on information from the company's enterprise resource planning (ERP) system. Unfortunately, what is important for a treasurer may not be important to an accountant. There is really very little choice but to go through the detailed work to gather the correct information. The information should be as specific as possible. For example, it should specify whether electronic payments are local bulk payments (ACH) or cross-border transfers, delineate which transactions are intercompany or third-party, and segregate payroll volumes and amounts.

6. **Banking Services:** The services used by the business in the relevant geographies should be outlined. In addition to traditional services such as bank accounts, wire transfers, and web-based balance reporting/ transaction initiation, most global companies require services such as payroll, rent guarantees, export guarantees, import letters of credit, VAT (value-added tax) reimbursements, tax payments, and specialized software. As with the transaction values and volumes, it is a good idea to structure a data request to all of the company's related operations to make sure that the inventory of services is as complete as possible. It is best to understand the full array of services needed before working with the banks.

APPENDIX 7.3: SAMPLE UNIFORM BANK PERFORMANCE REPORT (UBPR)[14]

FDIC Certificate #
OCC Charter # 0
Public Report

FRB District/ID_RSSD
County:

FIRST STATE BANK, THE
Summary Ratios--Page 1

Summary Ratios 2/18/2013 7:51:50 PM

	12/31/2012 BANK	PG 15	PCT	12/31/2011 BANK	PG 15	PCT	12/31/2010 BANK	PG 15	PCT	12/31/2009 BANK	PG 15	PCT	12/31/2008 BANK	PG 15	PCT
Earnings and Profitability															
Percent of Average Assets:															
Interest Income (TE)	4.07	3.92	57	5.38	4.29	90	6.04	4.68	93	6.49	5.09	95	6.99	5.79	93
- Interest Expense	0.72	0.53	77	1.38	0.74	96	1.67	1.02	94	2.03	1.34	92	2.90	1.97	95
Net Interest Income (TE)	3.35	3.38	48	4.00	3.53	75	4.38	3.65	83	4.46	3.73	84	4.10	3.81	68
+ Noninterest Income	0.33	0.44	38	0.26	0.48	23	0.32	0.50	31	0.52	0.51	60	0.43	0.55	43
- Noninterest Expense	3.40	2.88	73	2.61	2.96	37	2.42	3.09	19	2.68	3.17	28	2.39	3.09	19
- Provision: Loan & Lease Losses	0.00	0.08	46	0.00	0.12	36	8.48	0.19	99	1.02	0.28	87	1.01	0.16	93
Pretax Operating Income (TE)	0.27	0.89	18	1.65	0.93	83	-6.20	0.86	0	1.27	0.84	67	1.13	1.11	47
+ Realized Gains/Losses Sec	0.00	0.03	71	0.00	0.02	71	0.00	0.02	75	0.00	0.02	73	0.00	0.01	75
Pretax Net Operating Income (TE)	0.27	0.94	16	1.65	0.97	82	-6.20	0.89	0	1.27	0.86	65	1.13	1.10	47
Net Operating Income	0.21	0.75	15	1.66	0.77	91	-5.01	0.72	0	0.78	0.68	51	0.71	0.89	38
Adjusted Net Operating Income	0.21	0.76	16	1.44	0.78	82	-1.72	0.73	2	0.97	0.72	59	0.57	0.89	30
Net Inc Attrib to Min Ints	0.00	0.00	99	0.00	0.00	99	0.00	0.00	99	0.00	0.00	99	N/A	0.00	N/A
Net Income Adjusted Sub S	0.21	0.63	15	1.66	0.65	97	-5.01	0.60	0	0.78	0.56	61	0.71	0.74	44
Net Income	0.21	0.75	15	1.66	0.77	91	-5.01	0.72	0	0.78	0.68	51	0.71	0.89	38
Margin Analysis:															
Avg Earning Assets to Avg Assets	93.55	91.39	61	99.57	91.34	99	94.97	91.09	78	96.21	91.82	86	96.38	93.35	83
Avg Int-Bearing Funds to Avg Assets	76.56	69.44	80	85.01	70.76	97	82.62	71.69	93	82.39	71.42	93	80.46	71.34	88
Int Inc (TE) to Avg Earn Assets	4.35	4.33	51	5.40	4.72	78	6.36	5.17	89	6.74	5.57	91	7.26	6.21	91
Int Expense to Avg Earn Assets	0.77	0.59	75	1.39	0.81	94	1.76	1.12	93	2.11	1.47	91	3.01	2.11	93
Net Int Inc-TE to Avg Earn Assets	3.58	3.73	43	4.01	3.89	57	4.61	4.03	77	4.63	4.08	78	4.25	4.09	60
Loan & Lease Analysis:															
Net Loss to Average Total LN&LS	0.00	0.15	39	0.28	0.23	71	6.78	0.35	99	1.10	0.45	81	1.56	0.28	91
Earnings Coverage of Net Losses (X)	N/A	25.90	N/A	7.54	23.57	47	0.44	14.90	11	2.70	16.28	34	1.84	24.81	20
LN&LS Allowance to LN&LS Not HFS	0.00	1.69	0	6.20	1.69	98	5.36	1.65	97	0.90	1.67	14	0.75	1.56	7
LN&LS Allowance to Net Losses (X)	N/A	21.16	N/A	19.22	16.75	72	0.77	11.87	8	0.87	11.37	13	0.48	16.47	4
LN&LS Allowance to Total LN&LS	0.00	1.68	0	6.20	1.68	98	5.36	1.64	97	0.90	1.67	14	0.75	1.56	7
Total LN&LS-90+ Days Past Due	2.34	0.21	95	0.69	0.22	83	0.32	0.18	77	3.08	0.30	96	0.49	0.27	75
-Nonaccrual	6.02	0.88	96	7.25	0.85	96	1.84	0.88	78	1.47	0.95	72	0.38	0.75	56
-Total	8.36	1.22	97	7.94	1.20	96	2.17	1.19	75	4.55	1.41	87	0.87	1.16	54
Liquidity															
Net Non Core Fund Dep New $250M	-57.52	-21.59	12	-24.57	-15.74	27	-21.08	-13.78	28	21.95	1.80	83	13.18	3.07	66
Net Loans & Leases to Assets	58.64	47.90	74	73.25	50.51	89	72.13	52.81	87	78.51	54.22	94	74.40	55.39	89
Capitalization															
Tier One Leverage Capital	10.59	11.13	51	6.64	11.35	1	4.14	11.42	0	9.35	11.73	27	9.43	12.05	26
Cash Dividends to Net Income	0.00	38.52	28	18.33	38.04	37	-3.10	39.88	2	47.20	43.12	53	26.40	56.26	29

14. The sample report is from FFIEC's website (https://cdr.ffiec.gov/public/Reports/UbprReportPrint.aspx, accessed February 18, 2013).

PART III
Financial Reporting and Analysis

CHAPTER 8
Financial Accounting and Reporting

I. INTRODUCTION

II. ACCOUNTING CONCEPTS AND STANDARDS
A. Global Accounting Standards

B. US Accounting Standards

C. US Generally Accepted Accounting Principles (US GAAP) versus International Financial Reporting Standards (IFRS)

III. FINANCIAL REPORTING STATEMENTS
A. Auditing and Financial Statement Reliability

B. Types of Financial Statements

IV. ACCOUNTING FOR DERIVATIVES, HEDGES, AND FOREIGN EXCHANGE (FX) TRANSLATION
A. Derivatives and Hedge Accounting

B. FX Translation Accounting

V. ACCOUNTING FOR GOVERNMENTAL AND NOT-FOR-PROFIT (G/NFP) ORGANIZATIONS

VI. SUMMARY

I. INTRODUCTION

This chapter describes the accounting principles that govern the creation of financial statements. Treasury professionals use financial statements to determine the firm's:

- Overall liquidity level
- Ability to generate revenues from assets and control costs
- Capital structure

Financial statements provide a historical record that can form the basis for future expectations of performance. Subsequently, it is important that the financial reporting process promote consistency and comparability across firms in the development of financial statements.

This chapter opens by distinguishing between US accounting standards (which are rules-based) and global accounting standards (which are principles-based). Next, the chapter describes the auditing process and the primary types of financial statements. A brief discussion of accounting for derivatives, hedges, and foreign exchange (FX) translation is provided, due to its impact on daily treasury operations. The chapter concludes by discussing accounting issues that are unique to governmental units and not-for-profit organizations.

II. ACCOUNTING CONCEPTS AND STANDARDS

This section covers the basics of accounting concepts and standards for firms throughout the world, as well as for US firms specifically. The primary objective of the section is to provide treasury professionals with a better understanding of the International Financial Reporting Standards (IFRS) and the US Generally Accepted Accounting Principles (US GAAP) followed in the United States.

A. Global Accounting Standards

One of the primary goals of accounting standards is to facilitate accurate, consistent, and meaningful comparisons across firms. The International Accounting Standards Board (IASB) determines accounting standards at the global level through a set of pronouncements called the *International Financial Reporting Standards (IFRS)*, as laid out in the Conceptual Framework published by the IASB. IFRS stipulates a number of qualitative characteristics or general principles that accountants (and other financial professionals) are expected to follow in selecting and applying appropriate accounting policies for their organization. These characteristics include:

- **Relevance:** Information provided must be of value to decision makers and have predictive value, confirmatory value, or both.
- **Materiality:** Information presented must be material, or in other words, must have a significant impact on the financial position of the firm. Materiality of specific information should be judged in regards to the circumstances of the firm and the transaction.
- **Faithful Representation:** Financial information should faithfully represent the reported transactions. To the extent possible, it should be complete, neutral, and free from error.
- **Comparability:** Information must be presented in a form that allows it to be compared with prior periods and with other firms in a similar line of business. Financial statements should be appropriately restated to reflect changes in accounting policy that may impact comparability.

- **Verifiability:** Information presented must be neutral and unbiased, and must fairly represent the business transactions being reported.

- **Timeliness:** Information should be presented to decision makers in time to be capable of influencing their decisions within the limits of reliability and completeness.

- **Understandability:** Information must be presented in a manner that will make it as understandable as possible for non-accountants with a reasonable knowledge of business. Relevant information, however, should not be omitted just because it is complex and hard to understand.

- **Completeness (The Cost Constraint):** Within the limits of reasonable cost, information must be complete enough to make it usable and reliable.

In addition to these qualitative characteristics, IFRS lays out key elements (e.g., assets, liabilities, equity, income, expenses, and cash flows) that must be reported in financial statements. These basic elements should be reported if they are likely to create future economic impacts and can be reliably measured.

As of May 2016, 119 countries or jurisdictions required the use of IFRS for all or most domestic reporting, and another 12 permitted the use of IFRS for most or all companies. In two jurisdictions, IFRS is required only for financial institutions. Some jurisdictions have adopted a modified version of IFRS, carving out certain standards or delaying implementation times.[1]

B. US Accounting Standards

US accounting standards are governed by a detailed set of rules referred to as *US Generally Accepted Accounting Principles*, or US GAAP. This set of accounting standards is developed by the Financial Accounting Standards Board (FASB), an independent, self-regulating organization formed in 1973. US GAAP is published in the form of Accounting Standards Codification (ASC) Topics.[2]

The Securities and Exchange Commission (SEC) enforces US GAAP, and all US firms with publicly traded securities must file audited financial statements with the SEC, using Form 10-K annually and Form 10-Q quarterly. SEC filings for specific companies may be obtained through the SEC's EDGAR database or through the respective firm's website.[3]

In addition, the SEC has authority over the Public Company Accounting Oversight Board (PCAOB). The PCAOB was created by the Sarbanes-Oxley Act of 2002 with the goal of protecting investors by promoting accurate independent audit reports through oversight of public company audits.

The SEC enjoys broad powers with respect to prescribing accounting practices for financial statement filings. It issues specific reporting guidance within its Financial Reporting Releases (FRRs). SEC Regulation S-X outlines reporting requirements, and additional guidance can be gleaned from decisions the SEC renders on various cases.

Despite this broad power, the SEC's philosophy is that the private sector retains the initiative for establishing and improving accounting standards. Therefore, the SEC relies on the FASB for this purpose. Financial Reporting Release No. 1 (FRR 1) recognizes accounting standards issued by the FASB as the authoritative standards for financial reporting. Accordingly, financial statements conforming to US GAAP presumably satisfy the SEC's requirements.

---

1. From: Paul Pacter, *Pocket Guide to IFRS® Standards: the global financial reporting language*, published by the IFRS Foundation, 2016 (http://www.ifrs.org/Use-around-the-world/Documents/2016-pocket-guide.pdf).

2. ASC Topics were formerly known as *Financial Accounting Standards (FASs)*.

3. *EDGAR* is an acronym for Electronic Data Gathering, Analysis, and Retrieval. The EDGAR database can be accessed via the SEC's website at http://www.sec.gov/edgar.shtml.

Adherence to US GAAP is crucial since investors, lenders, and trade creditors must have confidence that accounting information is created across companies consistently.

Four basic principles underlying US GAAP include the:

- **Measurement Principle:** Most assets and liabilities are reported at historical cost (i.e., there must be an evidentiary basis such as an invoice, receipt, or record of payment made or funds received). An important exception to this principle is the reporting for certain marketable securities, which must be reported at current market value (also known as *fair value*).

- **Revenue Recognition Principle:** Revenue is reported when (1) cash or a claim for cash is received in exchange for goods or services, and (2) the earnings process is substantially complete. A typical *claim for cash* refers to accounts receivable—the assets that represent revenues from sales that have been recognized, but not yet collected. When funds are collected, the accounts receivable balance decreases and the cash balance increases, without any impact on income. This is because the revenue was recognized when the receivable was generated.

- **Expense Recognition Principle:** Expenses must be reported when the revenues with which they are associated are recognized. This is referred to as the *matching principle*. Long-lived or fixed assets are capitalized (i.e., recorded as assets on the balance sheet) and depreciated over time because they usually produce revenues during multiple accounting periods. This practice matches an asset's cost to the revenues it produces. Under the revenue recognition and matching principles, sales are reported even though cash has not been received. Similarly, expenses are reported even though cash has not been paid out. This forms the basis for accrual accounting.

- **Full-Disclosure Principle:** Any information that may influence the judgment and decisions of a user of financial information should be disclosed.

Accrual accounting conforms to US GAAP. Accrual accounting requires the extensive use of supportable estimates and judgments, providing flexibility in the timing and the amounts reported in the financial statements. Accrual-based income is more useful to external decision makers because it provides a better basis for assessing historical activity and possibly for making predictions about a company's future earnings and cash flows. For these reasons most firms use accrual accounting.

FASB's guidelines also give a permissible range of latitude for making estimates and judgments required in accrual accounting. Managers can take advantage of the latitudes allowed in timing revenues and expenses in order to report the highest level of accounting income. This practice is referred to as *earnings management*. Although managers have latitude for making estimates, they are expected to use a consistent methodology in order to avoid providing misleading estimates and to promote transparency. Companies should always strive to report the most appropriate revenue or expense recognition timing based on US GAAP. Earnings manipulation occurs if an accountant intentionally distorts the timing of revenues or expenses, or creates distortions in other ways to alter reported accounting income (e.g., possibly to earn a bonus, enhance a career, reduce the appearance of earnings volatility, please a superior, meet the expectations of shareholders, or beat previously reported earnings guidance). Earnings manipulation will result in serious legal consequences for the company.

As an alternative to accrual accounting, accounting methods that do not comply with US GAAP (e.g., cash basis accounting and modified cash basis accounting) may be used by certain nonpublic businesses. With cash basis accounting, revenues and expenses are reported only when cash is received or disbursed. Cash basis accounting is primarily used by smaller nonpublic companies due to simplified record keeping. Modified cash basis accounting adopts some elements of accrual accounting, such as reporting accounts receivable as revenues, and capitalizing and depreciating fixed assets. Professional service firms use modified cash basis accounting extensively.[4]

C. US Generally Accepted Accounting Principles (US GAAP) versus International Financial Reporting Standards (IFRS)

While there is substantial overlap between IFRS and US GAAP, there are also some key differences. The primary difference is that IFRS is principles-based while US GAAP is rules-based. An advantage of a principles-based system is that it provides reasonable guidance for finding the "correct" solution to specific accounting transactions that are not spelled out in a rules-based system. A disadvantage of a principles-based system is that it might result in different interpretations of specific situations.

Other selected differences between IFRS and US GAAP include (but are not limited to) the following:[5]

- IFRS does not permit last-in, first-out (LIFO) inventory costing methods.

- IFRS uses a single-step method for impairment write-downs rather than the two-step method used in US GAAP. This increases the probability of write-downs with IFRS.

- IFRS requires capitalization of development costs once certain qualifying criteria are met. US GAAP generally requires development costs to be expensed as incurred, except for costs related to the development of software, for which capitalization is required once certain criteria are met.

While both the IASB and FASB continue to discuss and work toward the convergence of US GAAP and IFRS, it appears that there are no current plans to require US-based firms to change from US GAAP to IFRS. As a result, multinational firms that are registered in the United States and report to the SEC are required to follow US GAAP for their consolidated global financial statements. Such firms may also still need to produce IFRS statements for individual foreign subsidiaries for statutory reporting purposes.

In 2012, the Staff of the SEC's Office of the Chief Accountant published its report (referred to as the *Final Staff Report*) on its IFRS Work Plan. The report concluded that adopting IFRS as authoritative guidance in the United States is not supported by the vast majority of participants in the US capital markets, and would not be consistent with the methods of incorporation followed by other major capital markets (e.g., the endorsement process followed by the European Commission). The report also stated that while IFRS is typically perceived to be of high quality, there are areas where differences remain and inconsistencies exist in the application of IFRS globally.

III. FINANCIAL REPORTING STATEMENTS

The form and content of financial statements are determined by the end user's requirements. For example, the reporting requirements for internal financial statements are dramatically different from those for external (or published) financial statements. The distinction warrants attention:

- **Internal financial statements** are used by corporate insiders (e.g., owner-operators and senior management) to manage daily operations. Examples include month-end income statements and balance sheets as well as management dashboards and other internal metrics. These statements are used to quickly analyze performance, which may lead to corrective actions. They are a part of management accounting and are not required to comply with US GAAP or IFRS.

---

4. Restrictions on the use of cash accounting methods or other accounting methods that do not comply with US GAAP are effectively set by the Internal Revenue Service (IRS). While cash accounting is frequently used by small businesses, the IRS allows its use in businesses (including corporations) with up to $5 million in annual revenues and in farm businesses of any size. One noteworthy area in which conformity with US GAAP is required involves inventory; firms with inventory are required to use accrual accounting for at least the inventory accounting.

5. From "IFRS FAQs" on the IFRS Resources website maintained by the American Institute of Certified Public Accountants (AICPA) (http://www.ifrs.com/ifrs_faqs.html, accessed December 21, 2015).

· **External financial statements** are used by existing and potential shareholders, analysts, and creditors (among other stakeholders) to gather information about the financial status of an entity. External financial statements are used for investment and credit decisions. Due to their intended use, external financial statements are required to comply with US GAAP or IFRS.

This chapter focuses on external financial statements. Publicly traded companies incorporated in the United States must conform to the SEC reporting requirements outlined in Regulation S-X, mentioned earlier in this chapter, in order to be considered *audited financial statements*. A company may produce its own financial reporting statements, or it may employ an accountant or an accounting firm to produce them. Companies large enough to employ professional accountants typically produce the statements themselves. Internal statements, even when prepared by a certified public accountant, must include the term *unaudited* in the title to differentiate them from financial statements that are audited.

A. Auditing and Financial Statement Reliability

The importance of financial statement reliability has led to the development of various accounting certifications. In the United States, the primary accounting certification is the Certified Public Accountant (CPA), while in the United Kingdom, India, and many other former British colonies, it is the Chartered Accountant (CA). The primary accounting certification in Canada is the Chartered Professional Accountant (CPA). Regulatory requirements in many jurisdictions, including the United States, often require that in addition to being certified, public accountants and external auditors must also be licensed by the appropriate regulatory body. Although most countries have their own national accounting and auditing certifications, there are a number of internationally recognized certifications. These certifications are especially valuable in transitional and developing economies where the quality of the national certification is low. The most popular international accounting certification is offered by the Association of Chartered Certified Accountants (ACCA).

Independent audits have historically been relied upon to certify whether a set of financial statements accurately represents a firm's activities. However, several prominent accounting scandals eroded confidence in the audit process.[6] To restore confidence in the integrity of financial statements, the US Congress passed the Sarbanes-Oxley Act (SOX). SOX established a set of controls over audit procedures and disclosure requirements, and provided an administrative vehicle to implement and oversee them. Key aspects of the audit process are discussed below.

1. AUDIT PROCESS

An audit is an examination of a company's financial statements by an accounting firm independent of the reporting company, in accordance with generally accepted auditing standards.[7] The purpose of an independent audit report is to render an opinion regarding the relevance, completeness, and accuracy of the various financial statements (along with other supporting materials). In addition, the auditor examines the strengths of the company's internal controls and processes. The auditor's opinion does not comment on financial fitness, but rather on whether the financial statements fairly reflect the company's financial position and are comparable to prior periods. Readers of financial statements will know the identity of the audit firm and the accounting standards applied during the audit.

An independent audit firm, often a division of a public accounting firm, begins an audit by studying the business. The first step involves examining the internal control procedures for reliability. Based on that information, the

6. Some of the more notable examples were Bernie Madoff, Enron, Lehman Brothers, Tyco International, WorldCom (now MCI), Parmalat, HealthSouth Corporation, Anglo Irish Bank, and Satyam Computer Services.
7. The International Auditing and Assurance Standards Board (IAASB) is a global organization that coordinates auditing standards. In the United States, audits are typically performed in accordance with the generally accepted auditing standards (GAAS) promulgated by the Auditing Standards Board (ASB) of the American Institute of Certified Public Accountants (AICPA).

auditor establishes procedures for reconciling the information in the financial statements against the evidence in support of them (e.g., invoices, bank statements, or customer orders). This is done on a sample basis, with the sample size based on the strengths of the internal controls. Weak internal controls require a larger sample, while stronger internal controls require a smaller sample.

It is important to understand the concept of materiality as it relates to the audit process. In most accounting applications, there is usually a significant degree of judgment involved in the preparation of the accounts (e.g., the judgment required in determining bad debt estimates). Where decisions are required about the appropriateness of a particular accounting judgment, the materiality convention suggests that this should only be an issue if the judgment is significant, or material, to the presentation of the accounts. The concept of materiality is therefore an important issue for auditors.

Next, the independent auditor determines whether the financial statements comply with the appropriate accounting rules (e.g., IFRS or US GAAP). The auditor must then confirm that all information contained in the financial statements is proper and that all matters material to an assessment of the financial position are included, as well as any accompanying explanatory notes and tables. Finally, the auditor issues a report to the board of directors that discusses items of interest that arise from the audit. The auditor will issue an opinion about the relevance, completeness, and accuracy of the financial statements and supporting notes. In addition to the report to the board, the auditor will provide a letter to company management that discusses significant policies and estimates used, as well as any specific difficulties encountered during the review.

2. AUDIT OPINIONS

There are five types of audit opinions rendered by the independent auditor. The highest is the standard unqualified opinion. If a standard unqualified opinion cannot be rendered, then the appropriate opinion depends on the nature and materiality (i.e., degree) of the exceptions identified by the auditor. Each type of opinion is described below:

- **Standard Unqualified Opinion:** The auditor concludes that the financial statements fairly represent the company's activities and that the following conditions were met:

    o All required financial statements were provided.

    o Generally accepted auditing standards (GAAS) were followed in conducting the audit.

    o The statements were presented in accordance with the appropriate accounting standards (e.g., US GAAP or IFRS).

    o The statements are consistent and comparable to the prior year's statements.

- **Unqualified Opinion with Explanatory Paragraph, or Modified Unqualified Opinion:** When immaterial deviations from appropriate standards occur, an unqualified opinion with explanatory paragraph, or modified unqualified opinion, is appropriate. This happens when:

    o Some information requires special emphasis.

    o There is a change in who performs the audit.

    o The auditor questions the company's ability to continue.

- **Qualified Opinion:** If exceptions are material but do not overshadow the usefulness of the information, then a qualified opinion is given. Exceptions are noted in the written opinion.

- **Adverse Opinion:** An adverse opinion is required when exceptions are so material that the auditor determines the financial statements may be misleading.

- **Disclaimer of Opinion:** A disclaimer is a statement that the auditor cannot render an opinion. A disclaimer is required if the auditor is not independent of the company being audited or if the scope of the audit is so limited that no basis for forming an opinion exists.

Generally, end users give more credence to audited financial statements than to unaudited financial statements, and in turn give more credence to audited financials with an unqualified opinion versus those that are qualified. Even so, since the opinion is not a comment on financial fitness, an end user must still carefully analyze the information contained in financial statements when making decisions.

It should be noted that only publicly traded companies are required to have their financial statements audited. While some nonpublic companies may have audited financial statements, they are not typically required to do so, unless there are regulatory or debt requirements that mandate an audit. Unaudited financial statements prepared by an external accountant are referred to as *compilations* and do not include an auditor's opinion. While companies that do not require an audit may have external accounting firms assist in the preparation of financial statements, these statements are not considered audited financial statements because they do not involve the level of review or verification required for an audit.

B. Types of Financial Statements

Regulatory authorities in most countries require publicly traded firms to file quarterly and annual financial statements that consist of a(n):

- Balance sheet
- Income statement
- Statement of retained earnings
- Statement of cash flows

In addition, the financial statements commonly include a management's discussion and analysis (MD&A) section and accompanying notes.

The following sections describe the balance sheet, income statement, and statement of cash flows. The statement formats presented follow Regulation S-X, which establishes the SEC's requirements for publicly traded firms incorporated in the United States.

1. BALANCE SHEET

A balance sheet, or statement of financial position, reports a firm's financial condition at a specific point in time. The primary accounts included on the balance sheet include assets, liabilities, and shareholders' equity. The value for a specific account represents the book value at that point in time. This is why a specific date typically appears on the heading of balance sheets (e.g., December 31, 2016). In terms of the accounts, assets represent the resources that the firm can use to produce economic benefits, while liabilities and equity represent the means by which assets are financed. By construction, the following balance sheet equation must hold:

$$\text{Assets} = \text{Liabilities} + \text{Shareholders' Equity}$$

Exhibit 8.1 presents an example of a balance sheet.

EXHIBIT 8.1 **SAMPLE BALANCE SHEET**			
AS OF DECEMBER 31			
ASSETS	**2016**	**2015**	**CHANGE**
CASH	$ 1,500,000	$ 1,000,000	$ 500,000
SHORT-TERM INVESTMENTS	1,300,000	1,500,000	(200,000)
ACCOUNTS RECEIVABLE	1,700,000	1,300,000	400,000
INVENTORY	2,600,000	2,100,000	500,000
PREPAID EXPENSES	900,000	900,000	-
TOTAL CURRENT ASSETS	$ 8,000,000	$ 6,800,000	$ 1,200,000
GROSS PROPERTY, PLANT & EQUIPMENT	9,000,000	8,100,000	900,000
LESS: ACCUMULATED DEPRECIATION	1,500,000	1,300,000	200,000
NET PROPERTY, PLANT & EQUIPMENT	7,500,000	6,800,000	700,000
INTANGIBLE ASSETS	500,000	500,000	-
TOTAL ASSETS	$ 16,000,000	$ 14,100,000	$ 1,900,000
LIABILITIES AND SHAREHOLDERS' EQUITY	**2016**	**2015**	**CHANGE**
ACCOUNTS PAYABLE	$ 1,600,000	1,200,000	$ 400,000
SHORT-TERM NOTES PAYABLE	1,800,000	1,300,000	500,000
TOTAL CURRENT LIABILITIES	$ 3,400,000	$ 2,500,000	$ 900,000
LONG-TERM DEBT	3,900,000	3,500,000	400,000
TOTAL LIABILITIES	$ 7,300,000	$ 6,000,000	$ 1,300,000
COMMON STOCK AT PAR VALUE	200,000	200,000	-
PAID-IN CAPITAL	3,600,000	3,600,000	-
RETAINED EARNINGS	4,900,000	4,300,000	600,000
TOTAL EQUITY	$ 8,700,000	$ 8,100,000	$ 600,000
TOTAL LIABILITIES AND EQUITY	$ 16,000,000	$ 14,100,000	$ 1,900,000

a. Assets

Assets are expected to provide future economic benefits for a company. To be reported as an asset on the balance sheet, the resource must be objectively quantifiable with a reasonable degree of accuracy. The valuation of most nonfinancial assets is based on historical cost, while financial assets may be listed at historical cost or market value, depending on their classification. Assets are listed on the balance sheet in order of decreasing liquidity. The primary categories of assets include the following:

- **Current assets** are defined as cash or assets that are expected to be converted into cash within one year of the balance sheet date or the company's operating cycle, whichever is longer. Examples of current assets include cash, marketable securities, accounts receivable, inventories, and prepaid expenses (e.g., insurance premiums).

- **Fixed assets** include investments in property, buildings, machinery, and equipment. Fixed assets are commonly listed as "Property, Plant and Equipment" on the balance sheet and are also referred to as *capital assets*. Fixed assets are generally not as liquid as current assets and are recorded at cost when acquired. Beginning in December 2018, public companies in the United States will be required to recognize assets for all leases with lease terms of 12 months or more. Nonpublic companies will be required to recognize these assets beginning in December 2019. Fixed assets that are used up or decline in value over time are depreciated (i.e., expensed) over their useful lives. The book value of a depreciable asset is its acquisition cost minus the accumulated depreciation.[8] An example of a fixed asset that is not depreciated is land.

- **Noncurrent assets** include assets that are not fixed assets or current assets. Examples include investments in bonds and stocks of other firms, and intangible assets. Intangible assets include long-term assets that lack physical substance. Examples include goodwill, trademarks, and patents. There is often a high degree of uncertainty concerning the future value of intangible assets. If an intangible asset has a finite useful life, then it may be amortized over its legal or useful life. But if the intangible asset has an indefinite useful life, it is not amortized. In this case the intangible asset must be evaluated annually for any decline in value, which would then be charged against income.

b. Liabilities

Liabilities represent financial obligations that are expected to be repaid with the future economic benefits generated by assets. The liabilities section of the balance sheet provides insight on the financing of assets. The primary liability categories include current liabilities and long-term liabilities, as described below:

- **Current liabilities** are typically defined as obligations that are expected to be repaid within one year. Common types of current liabilities include accounts payable (e.g., trade payables), operating accruals, short-term notes payable, and the current portion of long-term debt. Accounts payable are amounts due to vendors for purchases of items or services. Accounts payable and operating accruals (e.g., wages payable and taxes payable) comprise the operating liability accounts. Short-term notes payable typically stem from short-term bank loans or commercial paper. Another type of current liability is deferred revenue. Deferred revenue is accounts receivable booked or cash received in advance of the revenue being recognized on the income statement because the product or service has not been provided or earned.

- **Long-term liabilities** are not expected to be repaid within the next year. Examples of long-term liabilities include term loans, lease obligations, mortgages, and bonds that are due beyond one year.

Before concluding this section on liabilities, a note on terminology is warranted. The term *liability* refers to an amount that is owed, regardless of the form. *Debt*, however, refers to obligations that require interest payments.

---

8. Note that accumulated depreciation on the balance sheet is considered a *contra account* (more specifically, a *contra asset*), because it is subtracted from gross fixed assets to arrive at net fixed assets.

Due to this, debt is a subset of liabilities. For example, an accounts payable is a liability but is not a debt, whereas a notes payable is both a liability and a debt.

c. Shareholders' Equity

Shareholders' equity is the difference between assets and liabilities, and thus represents what would remain if all assets were sold and all liabilities were repaid. In effect, equity is the financing generated by ongoing operations and that is contributed by the owners of the firm. The shareholders' equity section of the balance sheet consists of two major categories:

- **Contributed capital** is the cash invested by shareholders. This section is further subdivided as needed to show various classes of stock (if multiple classes exist), such as common and preferred stock. In general, preferred stock is listed first.

- **Retained earnings** represents the accumulation of earnings that are retained from operations. When the firm earns net income, the income may be distributed to the shareholders as dividends and/or reinvested in the firm. The amount that is reinvested in the firm at the end of any given accounting period represents an addition to retained earnings. For example, suppose that a firm has net income of $100 million. If dividends of $60 million are paid out to shareholders, the remaining $40 million represents an addition to retained earnings. The retained earnings account on the balance sheet records the accumulated retained earnings at a point in time. If the firm's retained earnings at the beginning of the period totaled $500 million, the year-end value of retained earnings on the balance sheet will be $540 million. Retained earnings increase from the retention of profits. Distributions to shareholders via dividends reduce retained earnings.

The statement of changes in shareholders' equity summarizes transactions that affect this account. Specifically, this statement reconciles the ending balance of shareholders' equity to the beginning balance.

2. INCOME STATEMENT

The income statement is commonly referred to as the *statement of earnings*, the *statement of operations*, or the *profit and loss statement*. The income statement summarizes:

- Revenues earned

- Expenses incurred, including cost of goods sold, fixed operating costs, interest, and taxes

- Other income and expenses, including FX gains and losses, interest income, and other nonoperating income and expenses over an accounting period

Consequently, the income statement summarizes the profit/loss incurred during the period in question. The order of items on the income statement progresses from those activities most closely associated with the primary revenue-generating activities to those with a less direct relationship. Accounts on the income statement are measured over a specific span of time. If, for example, a revenue number is quoted, it would not have meaning if one did not know whether it represented monthly, quarterly, or annual revenue. For this reason the span of time that the income statement covers is noted at the top of the income statement (e.g., "January 1–December 31, 2016," or "For the Year Ending December 31, 2016").

Exhibit 8.2 presents an example of an income statement. While categories of expenses appearing on the income statement vary across firms, a brief description of the major line items portrayed in Exhibit 8.2 follows the exhibit.

EXHIBIT 8.2 SAMPLE INCOME STATEMENT

FOR THE YEAR ENDING DECEMBER 31

	2016	2015	CHANGE
REVENUES	$ 15,000,000	$ 12,500,000	$ 2,500,000
COST OF GOODS SOLD	9,200,000	7,400,000	1,800,000
GROSS PROFIT	$ 5,800,000	$ 5,100,000	$ 700,000
OPERATING EXPENSES	4,000,000	3,500,000	500,000
DEPRECIATION	200,000	150,000	50,000
OPERATING INCOME/EBIT	$ 1,600,000	$ 1,450,000	$ 150,000
INTEREST EXPENSE	300,000	245,000	55,000
NET PROFIT BEFORE TAXES	$ 1,300,000	$ 1,205,000	$ 95,000
PROVISION FOR INCOME TAXES	450,000	370,000	80,000
NET INCOME	$ 850,000	$ 835,000	$ 15,000
SHARES OUTSTANDING	100,000	100,000	-
EARNINGS PER SHARE (EPS)	$8.50	$8.35	$0.15

STATEMENT OF RETAINED EARNINGS	2016	2015	CHANGE
BEGINNING RETAINED EARNINGS	$ 4,300,000	$ 3,715,000	$ 585,000
EARNINGS AVAILABLE FOR COMMON SHAREHOLDERS	850,000	835,000	15,000
COMMON STOCK DIVIDENDS PAID	250,000	250,000	-
ADDITION TO RETAINED EARNINGS	$ 600,000	$ 585,000	$ 15,000
ENDING RETAINED EARNINGS	$ 4,900,000	$ 4,300,000	$ 600,000

Revenues represent the sum of recognized or earned sales. The cost of goods sold (COGS) is the expense associated with providing the goods or services sold. COGS includes labor and material directly used in manufacturing the product sold, as well as any indirect or allocated manufacturing expenses. These costs are called *product costs*. The term *gross profit* is usually used for revenues less COGS.

Operating expenses (e.g., selling or administrative expenses) represent general expenses incurred in the course of operations but that are not directly associated with the production of goods and services. Most operating expenses are considered period expenses because they occur over a period of time and cannot be attributed to specific units of goods or services sold. Examples of period expenses include marketing and administrative salaries.

The income statement also accounts for income and expenses that stem from nonoperating activities. Examples include interest income/expense and realized currency gains/losses. Collectively, these nonoperating items are listed as *other income and expenses*. Income before taxes is calculated as operating income adjusted for other income and expenses. Net income is income before taxes minus income tax expenses.

A common measure of operating profitability is earnings before interest, taxes, depreciation, and amortization (EBITDA). Though widely used, EBITDA is not a US GAAP measure. After depreciation and amortization are subtracted, the remaining amount is referred to as *earnings before interest and taxes (EBIT)*. The term *operating income* refers to EBIT. EBIT is traditionally used to evaluate a firm's ability to generate operating profits and to meet its financial and tax obligations. EBITDA adds noncash expenses (depreciation and amortization) back to EBIT to produce a measure that more accurately reflects the cash operating profit, and it is commonly used as a proxy for cash flow. EBITDA first came into common use with leveraged buyouts in the 1980s, when it was used to indicate the ability to service debt. As time passed, EBITDA became a popular profitability measure for firms in industries with expensive assets that had to be written down over long periods.

In addition to net income, US GAAP requires the reporting of *comprehensive income*, which is defined as net income adjusted for various gains and losses not reported on the income statement. Adjustments include:

· Unrealized gains and losses on investments

· Minimum pension liability adjustments

· Foreign currency translation adjustments

· Changes in the market values of financial instruments qualifying as hedges

Comprehensive income is reported in the statement of changes in shareholders' equity or in a separate statement of comprehensive income.

As noted earlier, the balance sheet presents the accounting value of asset, liability, and equity accounts at a point in time. In contrast, all elements of income, including comprehensive income, capture economic activities that occur over a specific time period. These economic flows explain the differences between the beginning-of-period and end-of-period balance sheet account levels. The statement of cash flows details transactions that explain changes in the cash balance from the beginning to the end of the accounting period.

3. STATEMENT OF CASH FLOWS

The statement of cash flows provides a detailed breakdown of the sources and uses of cash throughout a certain time period. The statement of cash flows categorizes cash flows on the basis of whether the cash flow resulted from (1) operating activities, (2) investing activities, or (3) financing activities. This financial statement is made necessary by the use of accrual accounting, in which revenues and expenses may be recognized in a reporting period other than when the corresponding cash transaction occurs. Consequently, net income may not indicate the cash flow earned during the period. For example, an accounts receivable balance represents a revenue that shows up in net income but that is not yet an inflow of cash. Importantly, the statement of cash flows indicates a firm's ability to generate cash flow to repay financial obligations, as well as dividends to shareholders.

To develop a statement of cash flows, the balance sheet and income statement are needed. In terms of the balance sheet, the various changes in balance sheet accounts (from one period to the next) show the sources and uses of funds, as described below:

Sources of Funds:

- **Decrease in an Asset:** The reduction of noncash assets produces funds via an increase in cash flow. For example, as accounts receivable are collected, cash flow increases while the accounts receivable balance is lowered.

- **Increase in a Liability:** Liabilities represent financing, so an increase in a liability increases available funds. Examples include the purchase of inventory using trade credit or a bank loan.

Uses of Funds:

- **Increase in an Asset:** A cash outflow occurs when investments in noncash assets occur. For example, a purchase of raw materials increases inventory but uses funds, assuming that the purchase is not made on trade credit.

- **Decrease in a Liability:** Funds are used to repay liabilities. Examples include the use of cash to pay off a loan, redeem a long-term bond, or to repay an accounts payable balance.

The statement of cash flows may be prepared using either the direct or the indirect method:

- The **indirect method** starts with net income and adjusts it to reflect the impact of noncash transactions during the reporting period. Net income is adjusted by changes in balance sheet accounts from the prior period. Specific adjustments include depreciation, amortization, accounts receivable, inventory, accounts payable, accrued wages payable, prepaid insurance, and income taxes payable, among others. One difference between US GAAP rules and IFRS principles is that under US GAAP, dividends received from a company's investing activities are reported as an operating activity, not an investing activity.

- The **direct method** reports the gross cash receipts and disbursements without examining any adjustments needed to calculate accrued net income. Operating activities are examined, and the total cash flow attributable to each activity is computed. The direct method starts by converting accrual accounts to a cash amount. The direct method generally provides users more information about actual uses of cash.

The indirect method is more commonly used because it is easier to prepare. Under US GAAP, public firms must still provide a supplementary report very similar to the indirect cash flow report even if they use the direct method.

Exhibits 8.3A and 8.3B show a statement of cash flows based on information from the balance sheet in Exhibit 8.1 and the income statement in Exhibit 8.2. The statement of cash flows in Exhibit 8.3A is prepared using the indirect method.

EXHIBIT 8.3A SAMPLE STATEMENT OF CASH FLOWS—INDIRECT METHOD		
FOR THE YEAR ENDING DECEMBER 31, 2016		
CASH FLOWS FROM OPERATING ACTIVITIES		
NET INCOME	$ 850,000	
ADJUSTMENTS TO RECONCILE NET INCOME TO OPERATING CASH		
DEPRECIATION	200,000	
DECREASE (INCREASE) IN ACCOUNTS RECEIVABLE	(400,000)	
DECREASE (INCREASE) IN INVENTORY	(500,000)	
INCREASE (DECREASE) IN ACCOUNTS PAYABLE	400,000	
NET CASH PROVIDED BY (USED FOR) OPERATING ACTIVITIES		$ 550,000
CASH FLOWS FROM INVESTING ACTIVITIES		
CAPITAL EXPENDITURES	$ (900,000)	
DECREASE (INCREASE) IN SHORT-TERM INVESTMENTS	200,000	
NET CASH PROVIDED BY (USED FOR) INVESTING ACTIVITIES		$ (700,000)
CASH FLOWS FROM FINANCING ACTIVITIES		
INCREASE (DECREASE) IN SHORT-TERM BORROWING	$ 500,000	
INCREASE (DECREASE) IN LONG-TERM DEBT	400,000	
DIVIDENDS PAID	(250,000)	
NET CASH PROVIDED BY (USED FOR) FINANCING ACTIVITIES		$ 650,000
NET CASH INCREASE (DECREASE)		$ 500,000
CASH AT BEGINNING OF YEAR		$ 1,000,000
CASH AT END OF YEAR		$ 1,500,000

The statement of cash flows begins with the operating activities section. As a first step, net income is adjusted for depreciation expense. Depreciation expense is added to net income since it is a noncash expense. Next, any changes in accounts receivable, inventory, accounts payable, or operating accruals are accounted for. These items represent the cash inflows and outflows related to daily operations. In sum, the firm generated $550,000 in operating cash flow. The collective increase in accounts receivable and inventory had a considerable impact on operating cash flow.

The investing activities section pertains to nonoperating assets. Over the year in question, $900,000 was used to purchase capital assets. Also, the liquidation or maturity of short-term investments produced $200,000 in investment cash flow. The net effect resulted in a $700,000 cash outflow from investing activities.

The financing activities section pertains to strategic financing decisions. Common cash inflows from financing activities include borrowings and equity issuances. Meanwhile, common cash outflows from this section include the repayment of debt, dividends, and stock repurchases. Over the course of the year, notes payable increased by $500,000, an additional $400,000 in long-term debt was issued, and $250,000 in dividends were distributed to shareholders. Consequently, financing activities produced a $650,000 cash inflow.

Summing the inflows and outflows of cash from the three sections shows a $500,000 net increase in cash. The balance sheet in Exhibit 8.1 similarly shows a $500,000 increase in the cash account during the last year. Importantly, the statement of cash flows shows the factors that caused this change.

The indirect method is more common, but a statement of cash flows may also be prepared using the direct method. Exhibit 8.3B is the statement of cash flows prepared using the direct method.

EXHIBIT 8.3B SAMPLE STATEMENT OF CASH FLOWS—DIRECT METHOD

FOR THE YEAR ENDING DECEMBER 31, 2016

CASH FLOWS FROM OPERATING ACTIVITIES

CASH RECEIPTS FROM CUSTOMERS	$ 14,600,000	
CASH PAYMENTS		
TO SUPPLIERS	(9,300,000)	
FOR OPERATING EXPENSES	(4,000,000)	
FOR INTEREST	(300,000)	
FOR INCOME TAXES	(450,000)	
NET CASH PROVIDED BY (USED FOR) OPERATING ACTIVITIES		$ 550,000

CASH FLOWS FROM INVESTING ACTIVITIES

EQUIPMENT PURCHASE	$ (900,000)	
SALE OF SHORT-TERM INVESTMENTS	200,000	
NET CASH PROVIDED BY (USED FOR) INVESTING ACTIVITIES		$ (700,000)

CASH FLOWS FROM FINANCING ACTIVITIES

SHORT-TERM LOAN	$ 500,000	
ISSUANCE OF LONG-TERM DEBT	400,000	
PAYMENT OF CASH DIVIDENDS	(250,000)	
NET CASH PROVIDED BY (USED FOR) FINANCING ACTIVITIES		$ 650,000

NET CASH INCREASE (DECREASE)		$ 500,000
CASH AT BEGINNING OF YEAR		$ 1,000,000
CASH AT END OF YEAR		$ 1,500,000

Overall, the statement of cash flows provides an indication of a firm's ability to remain a going concern. To remain viable, positive cash flow must be earned from operating activities. In the short term, managers can mitigate the effects of negative operating cash flows by selling assets or by raising new financing. However, a reduced asset base may make it even more difficult to produce future operating cash flows. Also, firms that consistently have negative operating cash flows will find it difficult to raise new financing cash flows.

IV. ACCOUNTING FOR DERIVATIVES, HEDGES, AND FOREIGN EXCHANGE (FX) TRANSLATION

As markets for derivatives and hedging products have expanded, so have the accounting guidelines for reporting their use. This section reviews the major reporting issues associated with derivatives and hedge accounting and with FX translation accounting.

A. Derivatives and Hedge Accounting

A derivative is a financial instrument whose value is derived from some underlying financial asset. Derivatives can be forward, futures, option, and swap contracts. For firms that follow IASB regulations, the applicable guideline is International Accounting Standard (IAS) 39: *Financial Instruments: Recognition and Measurement.*[9] This statement covers accounting for both derivatives and hedging. Under US GAAP, the applicable guidelines are found in ASC Topic 815: *Derivatives and Hedging.* ASC Topic 820: *Fair Value Measurements* and ASC Topic 825: *Financial Instruments* cover the valuation of derivative instruments.

Under either IAS or ASC Topic guidelines, the accounting for the gains and losses arising from changes in a derivative's fair value generally depends on the instrument's designation. Gains and losses arising from any revaluation of derivatives are reported in current-period income, provided the derivatives are not designated as hedge instruments.

If a derivative is designated as a hedge against fluctuations in the value of a specific asset or liability on the balance sheet, then gains and losses of the revaluation are recognized as income or expense together with the offsetting gains and losses of the hedged item. This type of hedge is a *fair value hedge*.

Hedges designed to minimize fluctuations in the cash flow values of forecasted transactions include cash flow hedges and foreign currency transaction hedges. Gains and losses on such hedges are reported in comprehensive income and are not reported in current income until the related transactions impact current income. Rules for classifying derivative transactions are complex and detailed. ASC Topic 815 in its current form was developed from several FAS statements and amendments as the area of derivative instruments evolved over the last 25 years.

Hedges may also be designated as *net investment hedges*. Net investment hedges are designed to hedge currency risk associated with the translation of subsidiary (or other foreign operations) financial statements into the parent firm's functional currency.

ASC Topic 820 provides the guidelines for the application of fair value measurement. Prior to this guideline, multiple definitions and applications of *fair value measurement* could be applied to assets and liabilities. Under Topic 820, *fair value* of an asset or liability is defined by determining the price that would be received in an asset sale or the price paid to transfer a liability. The valuation price must be market-based and take into consideration all observable valuation inputs, such as competition and risk. ASC Topic 825 later expanded this application by stating that fair value should be applied to all financial assets and liabilities except for certain specified types of assets.[10]

IFRS handles hedge accounting similarly to US GAAP. Assets and liabilities must be carried on the balance sheet at fair market value. Effective hedges are booked within comprehensive income on the income statement, while the gain or loss on the noneffective portion of a hedge is booked within net income. Hedge effectiveness is the degree to which changes in fair value or cash flows of the hedged item that are attributable to a hedged risk are offset by changes in the fair value or cash flows of the hedging instrument.

---

9. IFRS 9: *Financial Instruments* will replace IAS 39 for reporting periods beginning on or after January 1, 2018. IFRS 9 includes a new approach to classification for the measurement of financial assets and liabilities, and a new expected loss impairment model related to credit losses. IFRS 9 revises the model for hedge accounting with improved disclosures related to risk management activity.

10. Topic 825 was codified from FAS 159. More information on the specifics of these guidelines can be found on the FASB website (http://www.fasb.org/st/summary/stsum159.shtml).

B. FX Translation Accounting

Firms that consolidate the results of foreign operations or subsidiaries denominated in the currency of the foreign country must generally translate the foreign financial statements into their reporting or base currency (sometimes referred to as their *home currency*). IAS 21: *The Effects of Changes in Foreign Exchange Rates* provides the basis for doing this. IAS 21 is substantially similar to accounting treatment under US GAAP (ASC Topic 830: *Foreign Currency Matters*).

The task of foreign currency translation is essentially determining the correct exchange rate to be used in converting each financial statement line item from the foreign currency to the parent company's functional currency. The translation adjustment is an inherent result of this process, in which balance sheet and income statement items are translated at different rates. Under IAS 21, the basic steps in this process are:[11]

- **Determine the functional currency of the subsidiary:** The *functional currency* is defined as the currency of the primary economic environment in which the entity operates. Normally, the majority of the subsidiary's business activities are transacted in that currency. This task can be more difficult than it seems and may require significant judgment. The subsidiary's functional currency is not necessarily its home currency (i.e., the currency of the country in which the subsidiary's headquarters are located) or the currency in which the subsidiary keeps its books.

- **Translate the foreign currency financial statements into the functional currency of the subsidiary:**

  o Foreign currency monetary items (i.e., cash or items readily convertible into cash) are translated at the closing exchange rate.

  o Nonmonetary items that are reported at historical cost are translated using the exchange rate on the transaction date.

  o Nonmonetary items that are reported at fair value in the foreign currency are translated using the exchange rate as of the date of the fair value measurement.

  o Resulting exchange differences are reported in comprehensive income.

- **Translate the functional currency financial statements of the subsidiary into the reporting currency of the parent company:** Multinational corporations operating in a number of currencies need to report the consolidated financial statements in a common currency (referred to as the *reporting currency*). If the firm wishes to present the financial statements in a currency other than the functional currency (i.e., the home currency), the financial statements will be translated from the functional currency to the reporting currency using the following procedure:

  o Assets and liabilities are translated at the closing exchange rate as of the statement date

  o Income and expenses are translated into the reporting currency at the exchange rate on the transaction date

  o All resulting exchange differences are reported in comprehensive income

Foreign currency translation is more than a simple mechanical exercise. A thorough understanding of IAS 21 is required, and many aspects of this process require significant management judgment (and footnoting in the financial statements), especially as it relates to determining the functional currency of the subsidiary.

---

11. From "Technical Summary, IAS 21: *The Effects of Changes in Foreign Exchange Rates*," published by IFRS, January 2012 (http://www.ifrs.org/documents/ias21.pdf).

V. ACCOUNTING FOR GOVERNMENTAL AND NOT-FOR-PROFIT (G/NFP) ORGANIZATIONS

Governmental and not-for-profit (G/NFP) organizations are organized to serve a collective group (i.e., no shareholders/owners). Governmental agencies provide goods, services, or information to benefit the public as a whole or its particular segments. Cash is raised primarily through taxes and fees paid by members of the community. Not-for-profit organizations also provide goods, services, and information to benefit particular segments of society. Not-for-profits raise cash through donations and grants. In most cases, the accounting concepts covered earlier in this chapter are applicable to G/NFP organizations. Some of the unique characteristics of G/NFPs include the following:

- The term *equity* is replaced with *fund balance* or *net worth* in the accounting statements. Consequently, financial accounting processes for G/NFPs differ from those of for-profit firms.

- The focus of reporting is on compliance and accountability, as opposed to profitability. In the United States, NFPs typically must comply with US GAAP, while governments follow the rules and procedures developed by the Governmental Accounting Standards Board (GASB). The GASB is the authoritative standard-setting body for state and local governments, as well as for public schools, state universities, and other government-affiliated agencies.

VI. SUMMARY

The financial reporting process is essential to the development of quality financial statements, whether for internal or external use. This chapter introduced the basic concepts underlying international and US accounting principles. The differences were also described. The structure of external financial statements was presented, along with a discussion of how those statements are audited for external validation. Lastly, some treasury-specific topics regarding hedge accounting and FX reporting were presented.

CHAPTER 9
Financial Planning and Analysis

I. INTRODUCTION

II. TIME VALUE OF MONEY
    A. Future Value
    B. Present Value

III. CAPITAL BUDGETING
    A. Identifying Relevant Cash Flows
    B. Determining the Cost of Capital
    C. Using Capital Budgeting Metrics

IV. BUDGETING
    A. Budgets and Financial Plans
    B. The Budgeting Process
    C. Uses of Budgets

V. COST BEHAVIOR
    A. Types of Costs
    B. Break-Even Analysis
    C. Leverage

VI. FINANCIAL STATEMENT ANALYSIS
    A. Liquidity or Working Capital Ratios
    B. Efficiency or Asset Management Ratios
    C. Debt Management Ratios
    D. Profitability Ratios
    E. Integrated Ratio Analysis

I. INTRODUCTION

Treasury plays an important role in financial planning and decision-making processes. For example, treasury professionals not only develop and implement financial and operating plans for the treasury area, but they also incorporate the financial and operating plans of all other departments in order to forecast the liquidity requirements for the overall enterprise. As part of this role, treasury professionals must identify and arrange financing sources, and analyze potential investment opportunities, while balancing liquidity requirements.

This chapter reviews the core tools used for financial planning and decision making. These topics include:

- The time value of money concept
- Capital budgeting metrics (e.g., net present value, profitability index, internal rate of return, and payback period)
- Cost behavior, including a discussion of classifications of costs, break-even analysis, the degree of operating leverage, and the degree of financial leverage
- The budgeting and forecasting process
- Financial statement and ratio analysis
- Performance measurement

II. TIME VALUE OF MONEY

The time value of money concept is a core principle of finance that recognizes that a certain amount of money received today is more valuable than if received at some other point in the future. This relationship holds because funds held today can be invested at a given interest rate, which gives rise to a larger deposit balance in the future. The time value of money concept is important in financial decision making as managers are frequently faced with trade-offs between present and future cash flows. For example, treasury professionals often have to decide whether to invest funds now to produce larger future cash flows. The time value of money establishes the relationship between cash flows received at different points in time and allows for a valid comparison between the two. Further, the time value of money concept is used to value bonds, stocks, and other assets.

The value of a cash flow at any point in time depends upon the expected timing of the cash flow and the rate at which the funds can be invested. The latter is commonly referred to as the *opportunity cost* of funds. In general, an opportunity cost is the value of the best alternative not taken when two or more mutually exclusive alternatives are available. In the context of the time value of money concept, suppose an investor with $100 in available funds can invest in a stock with an expected annual return of 10% or a CD with an interest rate of 3%. The investor's opportunity cost of investing in the stock is the forgone return on the CD (i.e., $3).

The opportunity cost concept is an important aspect of time value of money because investors look to alternative investments in a particular risk class to determine the best rate of return available for a given level of risk. Investors in a firm's securities have this rate available to them in the marketplace, so they lose the opportunity to invest in the available alternative when they invest in the given firm's securities.

An important item to note is the various terminology used to describe the opportunity cost of funds. This rate may be referred to as an *interest rate, investment rate,* or *discount rate,* among others.

The sections below describe two specific applications of time value of money: future values and present values.

A. Future Value

The future value of an investment represents the expected value of that investment at a specified future date. Calculating the future value requires compounding the interest earned on the investment during the holding period. That is, the income earned on the investment will be reinvested and grow at the assumed investment rate.

For example, investing $100 for two years at 10% per year yields a $10 return at the end of the first year. At the end of the first year, this $10 is added to the original $100. For the second year, $110 is invested at 10% and the investment earns $11 in interest. The $11 is added to the $110, which equates to an investment value of $121 at the end of year two. Future value computations are based on compounding the growth of an amount invested now in order to see what its value will be in the future.

A generalized formula for calculating future value (FV) follows:

$$FV = PV(1+i)^n$$

Where:

FV = Future value

PV = Present value (i.e., value today)

i = Annual investment rate

n = Number of periods

From the example above, the future value of $100 after two years invested at a 10% annual investment rate is:

$$FV = \$100(1+0.10)^2 = \$100 \times 1.21 = \$121$$

The term $(1 + i)^n$ is the future value interest factor. The future value interest factor provides an efficient method for calculating the compound interest earned on an investment. Here, the future value interest factor is 1.21. Without the benefit of compounded interest, the future value of the investment would be $120 (i.e., $100 + $10 + $10). However, with the benefit of compounded interest, the $10 received at the end of the first year is invested for the next year at a 10% investment rate.

As another example, assume $2,000 is invested for three years at 6% per year. In this case, the FV factor is $(1 + 0.06)^3$ and the calculation is as follows:

$$FV = \$2,000(1+0.06)^3 = \$2,000 \times 1.191 = \$2,382$$

The future value concept works for multiple cash flows as well as for lump sums. For example, assume that a business expects to receive a $4,000 payment today, $5,000 at the end of one year, and $6,000 at the end of two years. The goal is to determine how much the entire stream of payments will be worth at the end of the two years if the cash flows are invested and earn 8% per year. The future value at the end of two years can be calculated by recognizing that the payment received today will earn 8% interest for two years, the payment received in one year will earn 8% interest for one year, and the payment received at the end of year two will not have any time to earn interest. The following calculation illustrates this process:

$$FV = \$4,000(1 + 0.08)^2 + \$5,000(1 + 0.08)^1 + \$6,000$$
$$= \$4,000(1.1664) + \$5,000(1.08) + \$6,000$$
$$= \$4,665.60 + \$5,400.00 + \$6,000.00 = \$16,065.60$$

B. Present Value

The present value of a cash flow is the discounted value of a future expected cash flow. This concept is commonly used when an investor is asked to make an investment at the present time that will pay out future cash flows. For example, if an individual is offered the opportunity to buy a business, the buyer would estimate the net cash flows that the business is expected to generate in the future. Since $1 received tomorrow is less valuable than $1 received today, it is inadequate to compare the upfront cost of the business to the sum of the future cash flows that are expected to be produced by the business. Instead, the present value of the expected future cash flows must be calculated before they can be compared to the cost of the investment. Present value is the basis for several capital budgeting metrics, including net present value, internal rate of return, and profitability index. The values of long-term debt and equity securities are also dependent on present value. Specifically, the value of a long-term security will be equal to the present value of the expected future cash flows produced by the security.

Future values and present values have an inverse relationship. Future value starts in the present and moves forward in time, whereas present value starts in the future and moves back in time. To calculate the present value (PV) of a cash flow, the future value equation provided earlier can be rearranged to solve for the present value term. This results in the equation shown below:

$$PV = \frac{FV}{(1+i)^n} \text{ or } PV = FV \times \left[\frac{1}{(1+i)^n} \right]$$

Where:

$$\frac{1}{(1+i)^n} = \text{The present value interest factor}$$

Note that when performing present value calculations, the process of calculating the present value of a future amount in the present is called *discounting*. For this reason, the investment rate used for present value calculations is commonly referred to as the *discount rate*. As the equation shows, the present value is inversely related to the discount rate. That is, assuming all else constant, a higher discount rate leads to a lower present value.

Consider the cash flows used in the earlier example. The present value of $2,382 to be received three years from today, assuming a discount rate of 6%, is calculated as:

$$PV = \frac{\$2,382}{(1+0.06)^3} = \frac{\$2,382}{1.191} = \$2,000$$

This calculation indicates that an investor would be indifferent between receiving $2,000 today or $2,382 in three years, assuming a discount or investment rate of 6%.

The present value of a stream of payments is calculated by summing the individual present values of each payment. The present value of a series of future payments may be generalized for any number of periods as follows:

$$PV = \frac{C_1}{(1+i)^1} + \frac{C_2}{(1+i)^2} + \ldots + \frac{C_n}{(1+i)^n}$$

Where:

PV = Present value or value today

C_n = Cash flow C in time period n (i.e., C^3 represents the cash flow in period three)

n = Number of periods

i = Periodic investment rate or discount rate

As an example, assume the following annual cash flows: $200 in year one, $400 in year two, and $600 in year three. If the appropriate discount rate is 12%, the present value of the cash flow stream is:

$$PV = \frac{\$200}{(1+0.12)^1} + \frac{\$400}{(1+0.12)^2} + \frac{\$600}{(1+0.12)^3}$$

$$= \$178.57 + \$318.88 + \$427.08 = \$924.53$$

While the sum of the received cash flows is $1,200 (i.e., $200 + $400 + $600), the sum of the discounted cash flows is $924.53. This means that if a firm paid $924.53 now and received the future payments specified in the example, the firm will earn a 12% rate of return on the investment. As long as the firm can acquire this investment at a cost less than $924.53, it will earn a rate of return higher than 12%.

In cases where the investment period is less than one year, simple interest is frequently used instead of compound interest. Future value and present value equations that use simple interest follow:

$$FV = PV\left(1+(Days)\left(\frac{i}{Days\ in\ a\ Year}\right)\right)$$

$$PV = \frac{FV}{\left(1+(Days)\left(\frac{i}{Days\ in\ a\ Year}\right)\right)}$$

Where:

Days = Number of days in the period

i = Discount rate

And:
$$\left(\frac{i}{\text{Days in a Year}}\right) = \text{Daily Investment Rate}$$

As an example, suppose that a payment of $50,000 is scheduled to be received in 15 days and the annual discount rate is 6%. Assuming 365 days in a year, the present value is calculated as:

$$PV = \frac{50{,}000}{\left(1 + (15)\left(\frac{0.06}{365}\right)\right)} = \$49{,}877.02$$

Overall, the time value of money concept is an essential tool for managers who must compare the economic value of cash flows from different investment alternatives occurring at various times in the future. A consistent way to accomplish this is to compare their present values. Additional factors that should be considered include the current purchasing power of a dollar, the costs of current investment alternatives, and the amount of capital that can be currently raised for investment.

III. CAPITAL BUDGETING

Capital budgeting is the process of allocating funds for investments in long-term assets. Such capital investments are often strategic and commit the firm to a course of business that may not be easily changed. Examples include the purchase of new equipment, replacement of existing equipment, introduction of a new product line, or acquisition of another firm.

This section describes the essential aspects of capital budgeting, including:

· Identifying relevant cash flows

· Determining the cost of capital

· Using capital budgeting metrics

A. Identifying Relevant Cash Flows

The market value of an asset is determined by calculating the present value of the asset's future cash flows. For this reason, it is critical to identify the relevant cash flows that are associated with a proposed capital investment. Relevant cash flows are those that occur due to the acquisition of an investment; they can consist of cash inflows or cash outflows. Relevant cash flows are commonly referred to as *incremental* or *marginal cash flows*.

Common relevant cash flows include:

· **Initial Cash Outflow:** This is also known as the *upfront cost* of the investment, and therefore the initial investment is typically a cash outflow.

- **Operating Cash Flows:** These represent the periodic cash flows earned from the capital investment's operations. Operating cash flow can be calculated as revenues minus all deductible expenses minus taxes plus depreciation. The number of operating cash flows depends on the length of the holding period.

- **Terminal Cash Flow:** This cash flow is earned when the capital investment is sold at the end of the holding period.

When estimating the cash flows attributable to an investment, a common error is to include the effects of sunk costs (i.e., a cash outflow that was incurred in the past). However, once a cash outflow has occurred, it is no longer relevant to the analysis. For example, suppose management is considering a new project that will use a previously purchased piece of equipment that has no alternative use and no resale value. Suppose that the previously purchased equipment originally cost $200,000. It would be incorrect to account for this $200,000 when assessing the viability of the new project.

B. Determining the Cost of Capital

The cost of capital is closely related to the opportunity cost concept described in the section on time value of money. The cost of capital is the discount rate that is frequently used to discount the future cash flows generated by potential projects. The cost of capital is commonly referred to as the *weighted average cost of capital (WACC)*. A WACC of 10% implies that the firm must earn a return of at least 10% on its assets to satisfy investors' expectations. If the firm earns less than 10%, then investors will be disappointed and bid down the company's stock price, even if the firm reports accounting profits and has a positive cash flow. On the other hand, investors will be satisfied if the firm earns more than 10% on assets and may bid up the stock price. Because the ultimate goal of for-profit organizations is to create shareholder value, management should not invest in assets that earn less than the WACC. Conversely, projects that yield returns in excess of the WACC will increase shareholder value.

The WACC concept is related to opportunity cost because shareholders weigh the return earned on a given firm's shares against the return that could be earned on another firm with comparable risk. Consequently, shareholders will require that the firm provide a return that is commensurate with the firm's overall risk level. That is, the firm must provide a return equivalent to its WACC.

The WACC depends on several factors:

- **The mix of long-term debt and equity used to finance the firm's assets:** This mix refers to the firm's capital structure, where *capital* is defined as the sum of the long-term debt and equity. In practice, the term *capital* refers to permanent sources of funds, such as long-term debt, preferred stock, and common equity. Common equity includes money contributed by stockholders and earnings retained in the business.

- **The individual cost of each capital component:** The costs of debt and equity are determined by the market's collective perception of the firm's risk level. Each cost component represents the rate of return that could be earned by investing in the debt and equity instruments of other firms with similar risk. The primary cost associated with debt is the yield to maturity on the firm's most recent bond issuance. The cost of equity is the return stockholders expect to earn on stock issued by the firm. This rate is estimated using a number of techniques (e.g., capital asset pricing model).

C. Using Capital Budgeting Metrics

This section describes and illustrates several key capital budgeting metrics. In unique ways, each metric weighs the costs and benefits of a proposed capital investment. The metrics described include:

· Net present value

· Profitability index

· Internal rate of return

· Payback period

Each capital budgeting metric is illustrated using the information in Exhibit 9.1.

EXHIBIT 9.1 PROJECTED CASH FLOWS OF CAPITAL INVESTMENT PROJECTS

PROJECTED CASH FLOWS

	PROJECT A	PROJECT B
Year 0	$(1,000)	$(1,000)
Year 1	$300	$300
Year 2	$300	$300
Year 3	$400	$400
Year 4	$100	$1,000
Year 5	$100	$1,000

---

1. NET PRESENT VALUE (NPV)

For a proposed capital investment, the NPV is calculated by netting the present value of the expected cash outflows from the present value of the expected cash inflows. For many capital investments, the only cash outflow is the initial cost that occurs at the time the investment is made. In this case, the upfront cost is already in present value terms; that is, a time value of money adjustment is not required. Expected future cash inflows, however, are discounted at the WACC. The general formula for the NPV method is:

$$NPV = PV \text{ of Cash Inflows} - Cost$$

If the only cash outflow takes place in the present (as in the investments shown in Exhibit 9.1), then the equation is:

$$NPV = \frac{C_1}{(1+i)^1} + \frac{C_2}{(1+i)^2} + \frac{C_3}{(1+i)^3} + \dots + \frac{C_n}{(1+i)^n} - Cost$$

Where:

C = Net cash flow occurring in a given year n

i = WACC

Cost = Cash outflow

The value given by the NPV provides an estimate of the increase in firm value that is created if the investment is purchased. That is, the NPV indicates how much better off the firm would be if a capital investment is undertaken. A project's NPV is the present value of all future excess cash flows, with excess cash flow being the cash flow in excess of the initial project cost and financing costs. If the NPV for a project is positive, the cash inflows from the project more than cover the initial investment and all financing costs. If the NPV is negative, the future cash inflows fail to cover the initial investment and financing costs, and the NPV is the present value of the shortfall. Subsequently, capital investments with a positive NPV should be accepted, while those with a negative NPV should be rejected.

To illustrate the NPV concept, consider the capital investments presented in Exhibit 9.1. Assuming a WACC of 10%, the NPVs for Projects A and B, respectively, are:

$$NPV_A = \frac{\$300}{(1+0.10)^1} + \frac{\$300}{(1+0.10)^2} + \frac{\$400}{(1+0.10)^3} + \frac{\$100}{(1+0.10)^4} + \frac{\$100}{(1+0.10)^5} - \$1,000$$

$$NPV_A = \$272.73 + \$247.93 + \$300.53 + \$68.31 + \$62.07 - \$1,000 = -\$48.43$$

$$NPV_B = \frac{\$300}{(1+0.10)^1} + \frac{\$300}{(1+0.10)^2} + \frac{\$400}{(1+0.10)^3} + \frac{\$1,000}{(1+0.10)^4} + \frac{\$1,000}{(1+0.10)^5} - \$1,000$$

$$NPV_B = \$272.73 + \$247.93 + \$300.53 + \$683.06 + \$620.73 - \$1,000 = \$1,124.98$$

The NPV for Project A is −$48.43. Note that the NPV is negative even though the total nominal value of Project A's cash inflows is $1,200, and its upfront cost is only $1,000. This is due to the effect of time value of money. The negative NPV indicates that Project A should be rejected, as the firm would be better off keeping the $1,000 investment cost on hand.

Project B, however, should be accepted. This project will increase firm value by $1,124.98. That is, the firm would be better off by investing in the capital investment as opposed to investing the $1,000 at 10%.

2. PROFITABILITY INDEX (PI)

The PI represents the ratio of the present value of cash inflows to the present value of cash outflows. Subsequently, the PI quantifies the present value gained per invested dollar. The decision criterion for using PI is to accept a proposed project only if it contributes more value than it costs. That is, projects with a PI of 1.00 or greater should be accepted. Otherwise, the project should be rejected. The PI is calculated as:

$$PI = \frac{\text{Present Value of Cash Inflows}}{\text{Present Value of Cash Outflows}}$$

In many cases, the only cash outflow is the upfront cost (i.e., the denominator is simply the upfront cost).

The PIs for the projects appearing in Exhibit 9.1 follow:

$$PI_A = \frac{\$951.57}{\$1,000.00} = 0.952$$

$$PI_B = \frac{\$2,124.98}{\$1,000.00} = 2.125$$

Project A has a PI that is less than 1.00, so it should be rejected. This PI indicates that Project A contributes $0.952 of value for every $1.00 invested. Clearly, this would not be a good use of the firm's capital. Project B, on the other hand, contributes $2.125 of value for every $1.00 invested and should be considered for funding.

A couple of points on the PI metric should be noted. First, PI is not a rate of return measure; it is simply a multiple. Second, the PI leads to the same decision as the NPV. If the PI exceeds 1.00, then the NPV exceeds $0. Alternatively, if the PI is less than 1.00, then the NPV will be less than $0. Even though the PI and NPV result in the same decision, both metrics provide unique information. The NPV shows the overall change in firm value attributable to a project. Meanwhile, the PI quantifies how many times the upfront investment earns back its upfront investment value.

3. INTERNAL RATE OF RETURN (IRR)

The IRR earned on an investment is the discount rate or cost of capital that forces the present value of the cash inflows to equal the upfront cost of the investment. That is, the IRR is the discount rate at which the NPV equals $0. The decision rule associated with the IRR involves comparing the IRR to the WACC. If the IRR exceeds the WACC, then the investment should be accepted. Otherwise, the investment should be rejected.

Calculation of the IRR is illustrated with the following basic example. Suppose that a proposed investment will cost $100,000 and will produce a $120,000 cash inflow in one year. The following steps show the solution for the IRR:

$$\$0 = -\$100,000 + \frac{\$120,000}{(1+IRR)^1}$$

$$\$100,000 = \frac{\$120,000}{(1+IRR)^1}$$

$$\$100,000 \times (1+IRR)^1 = \$120,000$$

$$(1+IRR)^1 = \frac{\$120,000}{\$100,000}$$

$$1+IRR = 1.20$$

$$IRR = 20\%$$

This calculation indicates that the proposed investment has an IRR of 20%. That is, at a discount rate of 20%, the investment has an NPV of $0. This can be verified by recalculating the NPV with $i = 20\%$. The implication of this IRR is that the investment would be acceptable as long as the WACC is less than 20%.

Most capital investments have multiple cash flows, which makes solving for the IRR by hand impractical. Spreadsheet software determines the IRR using a trial-and-error approach by recalculating the NPV at various discount rates until the NPV equals $0.

Consider the investment projects shown in Exhibit 9.1. A financial calculator or a spreadsheet can be used to calculate the IRRs for each project, which are listed below:

$$IRR_A = 7.7\%$$

$$IRR_B = 38.1\%$$

When using IRR to evaluate investments, the accept/reject decision criterion involves comparing the IRR to the WACC. Since the firm's WACC is 10%, Project A is not an acceptable investment, but Project B is acceptable.

Note that the IRR does not provide information on the expected change in firm value associated with a project. Instead, it is a comparison of the project's investment yield (i.e., IRR) to the WACC. Firm value will increase if the IRR exceeds the WACC.

4. PAYBACK PERIOD

The payback period is the number of years required to recover the project's initial cost. There is no specific criterion for an acceptable payback period; it may be arbitrarily set by management. A shorter payback period is preferred as (1) funds recovered from the upfront cost can be more quickly reinvested in another project and (2) the riskiness of the project is lower.

Project A in Exhibit 9.1 has a payback period of three years because the cash flows earned in years one through three sum to $1,000 (i.e., the upfront cost of the project). Project B also has a payback period of three years. Despite the identical payback period, Project B is preferred, given the larger projected cash flows in years four and five (after payback).

For illustration purposes, suppose the total cost of each project increased to $1,500. In this case, Project A's payback period is unknown, since the projected cash flows never exceed the upfront cost. In the case of Project B, $1,000 of the $1,500 is still recovered in the first three years, and the remaining $500 is recovered in the first half of year four, meaning the payback period is 3.5 years.[1] Under this scenario, Project B has a shorter payback period than Project A.

The payback period method suffers from two shortcomings: (1) it does not consider the time value of money, and (2) it fails to consider cash flows beyond the payback period.

While the decision to accept or reject a proposed investment should not be made on the basis of payback alone, the method's shortcomings do not void its ability to assess the overall risk of the investment.

5. THE NEED FOR MULTIFACTOR COMPARISON

Since each of the aforementioned capital budgeting metrics examines capital investment from a unique perspective, it is usually helpful to consider a multifactor comparison. Note that consideration of the NPV, IRR, and PI metrics

---

1. This assumes that the cash flows occur equally throughout the year.

results in the same accept/reject decision regarding an individual capital investment. This holds because of the close relationships between the metrics. For example, if an investment's NPV is greater than zero, the investment's IRR must exceed the WACC.[2] This is due to the fact that the IRR is the discount rate that forces the NPV to equal zero. In addition, an investment with a positive NPV will also have a PI greater than 1.0.

Exhibit 9.2 summarizes results from the capital budgeting analysis. From Exhibit 9.2, it is clear that Project A should be rejected because it would reduce the value of the firm, while Project B is an acceptable capital investment. In summary, Project B has a(n):

- Positive NPV
- IRR in excess of the WACC of 10%
- PI greater than 1.0
- Reasonable payback period

Overall, analysts should place the greatest emphasis on the NPV metric as it accounts for all relevant cash flows as well as for the time value of money through the WACC. In addition, the NPV shows the change in overall firm value attributable to an investment.

EXHIBIT 9.2 **SUMMARY OF CAPITAL EXPENDITURE ANALYSIS**

METHOD	PROJECT ACCEPTANCE CRITERION	PROJECT A	PROJECT B
NET PRESENT VALUE (NPV)	NPV > 0	$(48.43)	$1,124.98
PROFITABILITY INDEX (PI)	PI > 1	0.952	2.125
INTERNAL RATE OF RETURN (IRR)	IRR > WACC*	7.7%	38.1%

*Weighted Average Cost of Capital (WACC) = 10% in the example

Typically, there will be more than two projects competing for capital resources (i.e., mutually exclusive projects).[3] Capital constraints may preclude managers from accepting multiple investments that have desirable capital budgeting metrics. As a result, projects that meet or exceed the basic decision criteria may not be funded in any given year. One way to evaluate competing or mutually exclusive projects is by using a capital budget constraints analysis, as shown in Exhibit 9.3. In this example, the firm had eight potential projects to evaluate (each represented by a diamond in the chart). The projects were first sorted by expected rate of return and then graphed based on cumulative budget requirements to fund the projects, starting with the highest IRR. Assuming a hurdle rate (i.e., required rate of return) of 5% (indicated by the horizontal dashed line in the chart), the firm would fund the top five projects, as they all have an IRR over 5%. In the example shown, the firm has a budget limit of $10 million (indicated by the vertical dotted line in the chart), and so will only fund the first two projects, as they both exceed the hurdle rate and fall within the budget constraints. Other projects may be funded in the future when more funds are available.

2. This holds for investments with *normal cash flows*, defined as a cash outflow followed by cash inflows.
3. In addition to capital constraints, investments may be mutually exclusive if the projects represent alternative ways of accomplishing the same objective.

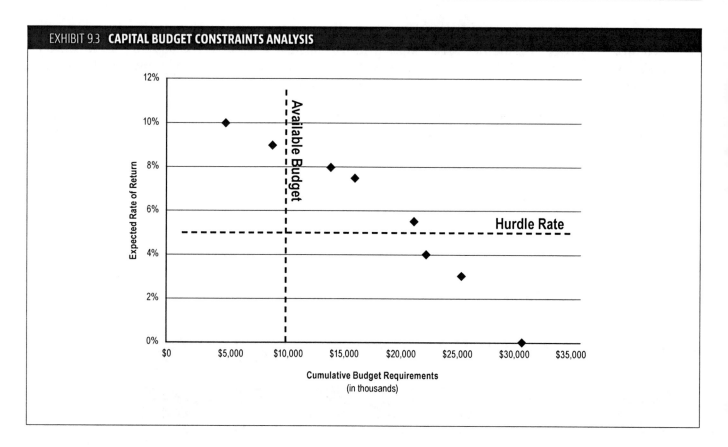

6. INVESTMENT RISK ANALYSIS

Capital investments are risky because their future cash flows are uncertain. This section describes the following methods for assessing investment risk:

· Sensitivity analysis

· Scenario analysis

· Simulation

· Risk-adjusted discount rate

· Risk-adjusted return on capital

a. Sensitivity Analysis

Sensitivity analysis determines the change in a financial value after varying the value of a particular input variable (e.g., recalculating a project's NPV after changing the value of the upfront cost). Sensitivity analysis can help the user to identify a project's areas of greatest vulnerability.

To illustrate the use of sensitivity analysis, consider the financial information provided in Exhibit 9.1. Suppose that the decision maker is uncertain about the firm's future WACC, possibly because long-term interest rates may increase. Sensitivity analysis can reveal the impact of varying the WACC while holding all other values constant. The baseline estimate for the WACC is 10%, but assume that it might increase to 15% in the future. The NPV is then recalculated as:

$$NPV_{B,15\%} = -\$1,000 + \frac{\$300}{1.15^1} + \frac{\$300}{1.15^2} + \frac{\$400}{1.15^3} + \frac{\$1,000}{1.15^4} + \frac{\$1,000}{1.15^5} = \$819.65$$

Moving from a WACC of 10% to 15% shows that the NPV drops from $1,124.98 to $819.65. The sensitivity analysis shows that the NPV is quite sensitive to the potential increase in the opportunity cost of capital.

The decision maker may also be interested in determining the NPV at a lower WACC, such as 5%:

$$NPV_{B,5\%} = -\$1,000 + \frac{\$300}{1.05^1} + \frac{\$300}{1.05^2} + \frac{\$400}{1.05^3} + \frac{\$1,000}{1.05^4} + \frac{\$1,000}{1.05^5} = \$1,509.59$$

Not surprisingly, the NPV increases as the WACC decreases.

There are numerous applications of sensitivity analysis. Essentially, any variable in the NPV model can be varied. The key point is that with sensitivity analysis only one variable at a time is changed, as opposed to multiple variables at a time. This allows the decision maker to identify the factor that drives the change in the NPV.

b. Scenario Analysis

Scenario analysis involves changing multiple variables at a time. This allows the decision maker to perform a what-if analysis that assesses possible outcomes under a range of circumstances. Scenario analysis is frequently used to establish the lower bound (or worst-case scenario) and the upper bound (or best-case scenario).

To illustrate, consider Project B. Assume the decision maker determines that the WACC may vary over the life of the project by as much as ±5% and that the future cash inflows may vary by ±25% from the baseline estimates, depending on market conditions. The best- and worst-case NPVs are calculated as follows:

$$NPV_{Best} = -\$1,000 + \frac{\$375}{1.05^1} + \frac{\$375}{1.05^2} + \frac{\$500}{1.05^3} + \frac{\$1,250}{1.05^4} + \frac{\$1,250}{1.05^5} = \$2,136.98$$

$$NPV_{Worst} = -\$1,000 + \frac{\$225}{1.15^1} + \frac{\$225}{1.15^2} + \frac{\$300}{1.15^3} + \frac{\$750}{1.15^4} + \frac{\$750}{1.15^5} = \$364.74$$

The scenario analysis indicates that the best-case scenario NPV is $2,136.98, while the worst-case scenario NPV is $364.74. The latter would provide the decision maker additional assurance of the safety and viability of an investment in Project B.

c. Simulation

Simulation techniques combine aspects of scenario and sensitivity analyses. Specifically, simulations allow the decision maker to specify certain assumptions regarding the uncertain variables used in the analysis. Further, multiple variables are allowed to change at a time. Simulation models are complex and are usually calculated using software programs.

The most commonly used simulation model is Monte Carlo analysis. It is an analytical technique in which a large number of simulations are run using random quantities selected from a probability distribution of values for specified variables. The simulated values can then be analyzed to determine potential financial outcomes.

d. Risk-Adjusted Discount Rate (RADR)

The RADR approach essentially requires high-risk endeavors to earn a higher rate of return in order to justify the investment. When properly applied, RADR allows managers to more closely match the firm's capital needs to available sources and to better manage the overall levels of risk and return.

For example, the discussion on specific capital budgeting measures used the firm's overall WACC for the associated calculations and decision analysis. While the firm's WACC is appropriate for large projects that are in line with the firm's overall risk level, it may not be the best to use for projects with significantly more or less risk. RADR is especially valuable for large, multidivisional firms, where each division has a distinctly different risk profile. In such cases, the analyst may want to adjust the WACC to match the risk of the investment. For example, assume a large corporation has determined that each of its divisions will be categorized as low, average, or high risk for capital budgeting purposes. Further, management has decided to use a risk adjustment factor of ±2% to the firm's overall WACC to determine the RADR for each division. If the firm's overall WACC is 10%, the divisional RADRs will be as follows:

- Low-Risk Divisions: RADR = 8%

- Average-Risk Divisions: RADR = 10%

- High-Risk Divisions: RADR = 12%

A similar adjustment could also be done at a project level within each division, with high-risk projects being allocated a higher required return level and low-risk projects being allocated a lower required return.

e. Risk-Adjusted Return on Capital (RAROC)

RAROC is a metric that measures the expected profitability of a project from a risk-adjusted standpoint. RAROC is primarily used by financial institutions to evaluate the profitability of investment opportunities and relationships. RAROC is a method of measuring the return on a project based upon the overall risk of the project.

As noted in the discussion of RADR, riskier projects should have higher returns than less risky projects. RADR accounts for this by setting a higher hurdle rate for riskier projects, but does nothing to adjust projected returns to account for the expected risk. RAROC estimates the risk of the project and uses that to adjust the return on capital calculations. In other words, RADR sets the evaluation bar, in terms of hurdle rate, higher for riskier projects, while RAROC actually adjusts the expected return from each project based on its project risk to permit projects to be compared to each other.

Although the actual calculation is beyond the scope of this book, RAROC adjusts the projected revenues of a project based upon some measure of how likely the project is to succeed and calculates a return on investment based on those adjusted revenues. The adjusted revenue used to calculate RAROC is revenue less interest on debt allocated to the project, operating costs, and the expected loss on the project. Adjusted revenue is then divided by allocated regulatory (or economic) capital to calculate RAROC. RAROC is then compared to a hurdle rate to determine the acceptability of the investment.

IV. BUDGETING

Strategic planning establishes the firm's overall goals and objectives and charts a course of action for achieving those objectives. To implement the desired strategies, appropriate budgeting is required. Treasury professionals typically have some degree of responsibility for the budgeting process, due to the budget's impact on the firm's cash flow streams and overall liquidity. In addition, treasury professionals may be required to assess the impact of budgets on debt covenants and credit ratings. This section describes the budgeting process.

A. Budgets and Financial Plans

A budget details how economic resources will be procured and deployed over a specific time period. Most budgets cover periods ranging from one month to a year. However, long-range financial plans can extend throughout many years. Most firms use a detailed annual budget for planning and control purposes. The annual budget provides specific details underlying the first year of the long-range plan and is comprised of shorter time divisions, such as quarters or months. An annual budget for the entire firm is called the *master budget*.

Long-range financial plans quantify the elements of the strategic plan in the form of forecasted financial statements over a five- to ten-year period. Longer-term budgets are usually less detailed and focus more on the big picture. These projected financial statements incorporate major debt and equity financing actions, as well as high-level business activities, such as acquisitions and/or divestitures of assets, products, services, divisions, or business lines. Since long-range financial plans quantify the business or strategic plan, projected balance sheets reflect the target capital structure, and projected income statements reflect the expected revenues and expenses. These pro forma financial statements serve as the basis for operating and financial budgets.

Most budgets are static plans that are frozen or fixed to serve as a specific frame of reference. To be truly effective, however, forecasts should be updated continually to reflect changes in the underlying economy, market conditions, and firm-specific characteristics, especially during times of financial uncertainty. Under these circumstances, static budgets can become meaningless and a more relevant forecast needs to be used as the new benchmark to measure progress, as well as to direct any necessary course correction.

B. The Budgeting Process

The master budget has two primary components: (1) the operating budget or profit plan and (2) the financial budget. The operating budget focuses on day-to-day operations, while the financial budget addresses financing and investing activities. The planning process begins by constructing the elements of the operating budget, including budgets for sales, production/purchases, and operating expenses.

Since the budgeted costs depend upon the expected sales level, the first step in developing an operating budget is to generate a sales budget. If a business sells goods or services on credit, this will have a critical impact on the cash collections schedule. This schedule details cash sales, accounts receivable balances, and cash collections of accounts receivable. The expenses necessary to support expected operations can be forecasted after the sales budget is established.

The financial budget can be constructed after the operating budget is complete.[4] The first step in constructing the financial budget is to develop the capital budget, which details the forecasted costs of expected capital investments (e.g., acquisition of new facilities, or replacement of aging or obsolete equipment) required under the long-range plan. The second step in constructing a financial budget is to develop the cash budget, which translates information from the operating and capital budgets into sources and uses of cash. The final step is to identify financing sources for any forecasted cash needs. If the cash budget projects a surplus, management must decide whether to use the cash for future investments, pay down debt, distribute cash to shareholders through dividends, or increase the share price through stock repurchases. If the cash budget projects a deficit, management must decide how to finance the deficit and/or reduce costs.

When combined, the operating and financial budgets form the master budget, which constitutes a set of pro forma financial statements for the budget period. Exhibit 9.4 illustrates how the information from the operating and financial budgets is used to construct financial statements.

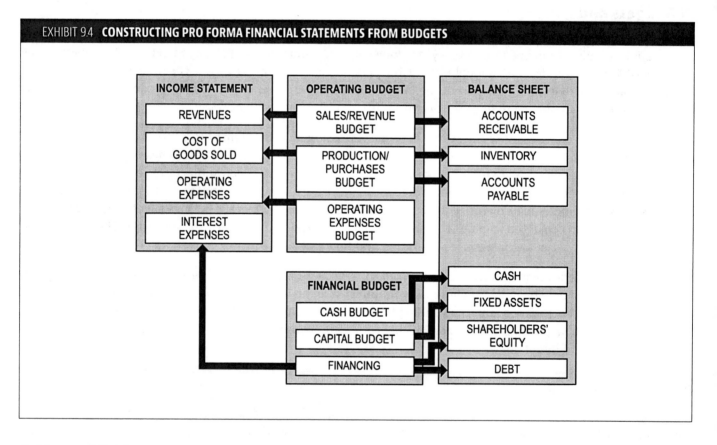

EXHIBIT 9.4 CONSTRUCTING PRO FORMA FINANCIAL STATEMENTS FROM BUDGETS

C. Uses of Budgets

Most budgets are used for planning and control purposes. Budgets discipline managers to plan for the resources required and to assess funding needs. Since managers are often evaluated based on their ability to stay within budget, the budgeting process also requires managers to anticipate changing conditions and contingencies.

---

4. The steps outlined here are primarily oriented toward large organizations. Smaller organizations may follow a more streamlined or informal process.

Another use of budgets is for resource allocation. All firms have resource constraints, so budgets are enlisted to assist in allocation decisions. For example, local, state, and federal government agencies use budgets to allocate funds raised from taxes and other sources, as well as to provide the requisite authority for the use of funds. Finally, a budget serves as a communication and coordination tool, informing all areas of an organization of each department's plans during a given budget period.

While the planning aspects of budgets are forward looking, the control aspects of the budget are retrospective in nature. A budget serves as the primary benchmark against which actual results are compared. The difference between the actual result and the budgeted figure is called a *variance*. The process of identifying and analyzing budget variances is referred to as *variance analysis*.

Small variances are inevitable in the course of business. Large variances, however, may be an early indicator of more serious problems, such as changes in economic conditions, the competitive environment, or customer buying patterns. Variances also may indicate a flaw in the forecasting method used. If the causes of the variances are identified and addressed quickly and effectively, it is more likely that the firm will achieve optimal performance.

Budgets are a type of forecast and should be updated and refreshed periodically as more current information becomes available. It is a common practice to update budgets on a quarterly basis as part of the variance analysis. Some firms update their budgets only if a major factor or assumption changes, such as the purchase or acquisition of a major subsidiary. While it is a best practice to update budgets periodically, some firms never update their budget outside of the annual budget cycle, and instead count on explanations of variances to cover major changes.

Modern enterprise resource planning (ERP) systems can simplify budget analysis by allowing for easy manipulation of budget numbers and assumptions. Managers can change assumptions and look at budget numbers in a variety of formats that can be useful for analysis purposes. For example, once a base budget is developed, pro forma budgets can easily be produced by product, department, or geographic unit to identify issues and trends and to isolate potential problems.

V. COST BEHAVIOR

This section describes types of costs, break-even analysis, and leverage (i.e., operating, financial, and total). These topics aid managers in determining the risks and returns associated with existing operations and future investment opportunities.

A. Types of Costs

Financial planning and analysis (FP&A) requires an understanding of cost behavior. Cost behavior describes the relationship between costs and *cost drivers*, defined as business activities that influence costs. Costs are classified as either *fixed*, *variable*, or *step-up*. Each type is described below:

- **Fixed costs** are expenses that do not vary over a certain range of activity. Examples of fixed costs include purchases of fixed assets, lease payments, interest expense, and property insurance. An example of a fixed cost that is specific to treasury management is a monthly account maintenance fee for deposit accounts charged by banks. The fee remains the same regardless of the number of transactions.

- **Variable costs** change in direct proportion to the level of production and/or sales. Examples of variable costs include direct materials, direct labor, and cost of goods sold (COGS).

- A **step-up cost** is fixed over a wide range of activity and is not immediately impacted by changes in business conditions. However, once output reaches a certain level, additional fixed costs will be required to facilitate an increased level of output. As an example, suppose that a $150,000 piece of equipment (i.e., a fixed cost) can produce 10,000 widgets. If management wants to produce more than 10,000 widgets, then additional equipment will be required. Subsequently, a step-up in fixed costs will be required.

Exhibit 9.5 displays the behavior of these types of costs in relation to production output. Note that the level of fixed costs does not vary with production volume (e.g., the fixed cost curve has no slope). Meanwhile, the positive slope of the variable cost curve indicates that variable costs increase with production output. The step-up cost curve increases in a stair-step fashion. Lastly, the total cost curve is the sum of each cost component for a given level of production.

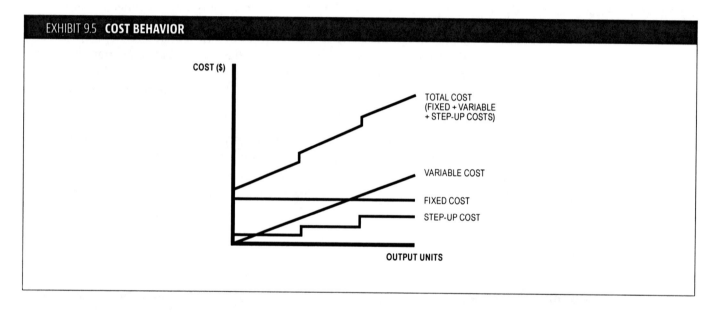

EXHIBIT 9.5 **COST BEHAVIOR**

B. Break-Even Analysis

Break-even analysis involves calculating the level of sales required to earn an operating profit of $0. This quantity is referred to as the *break-even quantity*.

Exhibit 9.6 provides a graphical illustration of the break-even concept. To simplify the graph, the step-up cost curve is omitted (both on its own and as part of the total cost curve). The graph also includes a revenue curve. The slope of the revenue curve is steeper than the total cost curve, which results from the markup earned on each unit sold. The point of intersection between the total revenue and total cost curves represents the break-even quantity of sales. At a sales level above the break-even quantity, an operating profit is earned, as shown by the vertical distance between the revenue and total cost line.

The break-even quantity can be calculated using estimates of the fixed costs, the per-unit sales price, and the variable cost per unit. A general formula appears below:

$$\text{Break-Even Quantity} = \frac{\text{Fixed Costs}}{\text{Selling Price per Unit} - \text{Variable Cost per Unit}}$$

The denominator of the formula is commonly referred to as the *contribution margin*, which represents the component of the sales price that offsets fixed costs.

An example will help illustrate the concept. Suppose that management is considering entering into a new product line that will require $10,000 in fixed costs. Each unit sold will also result in $6 in variable costs. Further, each unit will sell for $10. The break-even quantity is calculated as:

$$\text{Break-Even Quantity} = \frac{\$10,000}{\$10 - \$6} = 2,500 \text{ units}$$

The calculation indicates that the product line will earn an operating profit of $0 at a sales volume of 2,500 units. Note that this calculation can be verified by checking that the operating profit equals $0 at a sales level of 2,500 units.[5] If the firm sells more than 2,500 units, operating profit will expand by the contribution margin of $4 per unit.

Break-even analysis is quite helpful in financial planning and analysis. If management believes that future sales from the product line will fall below the break-even volume, then it would be advisable to avoid entering the product line. There are also numerous applications for break-even analysis in treasury management. One example is the calculation of the break-even amount of funds transferred that would justify a wire transfer versus an automated clearinghouse (ACH) network transfer. This could be accomplished via break-even analysis.

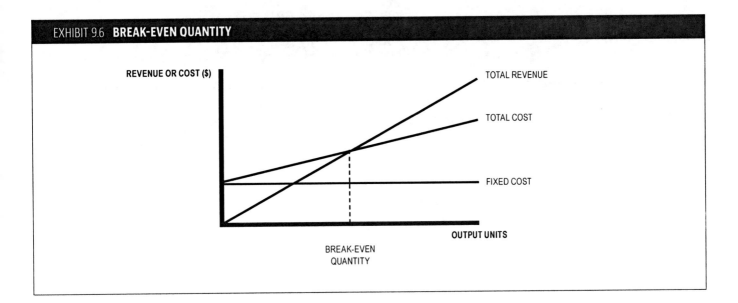

EXHIBIT 9.6 **BREAK-EVEN QUANTITY**

5. Operating profit equals quantity sold times the contribution margin minus fixed costs. This results in 2,500 × ($10 − $6) − $10,000, which equals $0.

C. Leverage

This section describes the three aspects of leverage, including:

- · Operating leverage
- · Financial leverage
- · Total leverage

1. OPERATING LEVERAGE

The relative levels of fixed and variable costs define the firm's operating cost structure and its degree of operating risk. The concept of *operating leverage* refers to the degree to which fixed costs comprise the cost structure. Both the high and low operating leverage strategies are described below:

- · **High operating leverage** refers to a cost structure with a higher proportion of fixed costs and a lower proportion of variable costs. The high operating leverage strategy is profitable when sales exceed the break-even quantity, due to the higher contribution margin earned per unit sold. However, high operating leverage will result in operating losses if sales are low since fixed costs are invariant to the sales level. For this reason higher operating leverage implies increased operating risk. Industries with high operating leverage generally have capital-intensive operations (e.g., auto manufacturing).

- · **Low operating leverage** refers to a cost structure with a lower proportion of fixed costs and a higher proportion of variable costs. With a high level of sales, lower operating leverage will result in lower profitability than would a higher level of operating leverage. Still, lower operating leverage implies less operating risk as this cost structure provides a lower break-even quantity of sales. Industries with low operating leverage usually have labor-intensive operations (e.g., restaurants or brokerage firms).

A measure used to quantify operating leverage is referred to as the *degree of operating leverage (DOL)*. DOL shows the responsiveness of operating profit, or EBIT (earnings before interest and taxes), to changes in sales and is computed as:

$$\text{Degree of Operating Leverage} = \frac{\%\ \text{Change in EBIT}}{\%\ \text{Change in Sales}}$$

The calculation and interpretation of the DOL is illustrated with the financial statement shown in Exhibit 9.7. Over the course of the fiscal year, sales increased from $10,000 to $12,000, implying sales growth of 20%. Due to the higher sales level, variable costs increased from $5,000 to $6,000. Fixed costs, however, remained at $2,000. EBIT increased from $3,000 to $4,000, which represents a 33% increase. For this particular level of sales and costs, the DOL is:

$$\text{Degree of Operating Leverage} = \frac{33\%}{20\%} = 1.650$$

This calculation indicates that the percentage change in EBIT is 1.65 times greater than the percentage change in sales. If next year's sales forecast calls for a 10% increase in sales, then EBIT should increase by 16.5%. However, if the sales forecast calls for a 10% decrease in sales, then EBIT should decrease by 16.5%. Overall, a higher DOL indicates higher operating risk, as EBIT is more volatile for a given change in sales.

EXHIBIT 9.7 OPERATING AND FINANCIAL LEVERAGE

OPERATING LEVERAGE (OL) IS THE RESULT OF FIXED COSTS IN OPERATIONS.
FINANCIAL LEVERAGE (FL) RESULTS FROM FIXED FINANCING COSTS (INTEREST).

ASSUMPTIONS:
VARIABLE OPERATING COSTS ARE 50% OF SALES.
FIXED OPERATING COSTS ARE $2,000.
INTEREST EXPENSE IS $1,000.
THE TAX RATE IS 40%.

ACCOUNT	YEAR 2015 $ AMOUNT		YEAR 2016 $ AMOUNT		CHANGE
SALES		10,000		12,000	+20%
LESS: VARIABLE COSTS (50%)	(5,000)		(6,000)	OL	
FIXED COSTS	(2,000)	(7,000)	(2,000)	(8,000)	
OPERATING PROFIT (EBIT)		3,000		4,000	+33%
LESS: INTEREST		(1,000)		(1,000)	
TAXABLE INCOME		2,000		3,000	FL
LESS: TAXES (40%)		(800)		(1,200)	
NET INCOME		1,200		1,800	+50%

---

2. FINANCIAL LEVERAGE

The concept of *financial leverage* refers to the impact of interest expense on overall profitability. Similar to fixed operating costs, interest expense represents a fixed cost that must be covered regardless of the sales level. Consequently, a higher level of interest expense implies more financial risk.

The degree of financial leverage (DFL) is used to quantify financial leverage. The DFL shows the responsiveness of net income to a change in EBIT. An increased level of debt implies more interest expense, which creates a larger wedge between EBIT and net income. DFL is computed as:

$$\text{Degree of Financial Leverage} = \frac{\% \text{ Change in Net Income}}{\% \text{ Change in EBIT}}$$

The financial statement provided in Exhibit 9.7 shows interest expense of $1,000 for both fiscal years. Net income increases from $1,200 to $1,800. The 50% increase in net income coupled with a 33% increase in EBIT results in the following calculation:

$$\text{Degree of Financial Leverage} = \frac{50\%}{33\%} = 1.515$$

This calculation indicates that net income will change 1.515 times the percentage change in EBIT. A higher DFL implies a higher level of financial risk.

3. TOTAL LEVERAGE

This section closes by showing that operating and financial leverage work together. Both operating and financing risk can be accounted for via the degree of total leverage (DTL), computed as:

$$\text{Degree of Total Leverage} = \frac{\% \text{ Change in Net Income}}{\% \text{ Change in Sales}}$$

This measure examines the sensitivity between overall earnings and sales. For this example, the DTL equals:

$$\text{Degree of Total Leverage} = \frac{50\%}{20\%} = 2.50$$

This calculation indicates that the change in net income will be 2.50 times that of the change in sales. Note that the DTL can also be expressed as the DOL multiplied by the DFL (1.650 × 1.515). Since the two types of leverage work together, managers must carefully choose the appropriate degrees for both operating and financial leverage.

VI. FINANCIAL STATEMENT ANALYSIS

This section reviews important aspects of financial statement analysis. Topics covered include ratio analysis and common-size financial statements.

Financial statement analysis provides critical information on firms' financial performance and use of economic resources. This information is of interest to a number of stakeholders, including suppliers, lenders, rating agencies, and investors.

The ratios described in this section consist of four types:

- **Liquidity or working capital ratios** measure the ability to meet financial obligations and whether cash is used effectively.

- **Efficiency or asset management ratios** measure how effectively assets are utilized.

- **Debt management ratios** measure the degree of indebtedness and the ability to service debt.

- **Profitability/performance ratios** measure profitability in relation to revenue and investment.

The sample calculations that follow use data (dollars expressed in thousands) from the financial statements provided in Exhibits 8.1, 8.2, and 8.3A from Chapter 8, Financial Accounting and Reporting. The calculations use period-end figures for all balance sheet items. An alternative approach is to use the average of the beginning balance and ending balance for balance sheet items. Using the average will help smooth fluctuations, but the averages may not be relevant if the firm's financial position has changed dramatically.

In addition to ratio analysis, common-size financial statements are also helpful when assessing performance. With common-size financial statements, balance sheet items are scaled by assets and income statement items are scaled by revenues. Common-sizing allows for comparability across firms of different sizes.

A. Liquidity or Working Capital Ratios

A firm's ability to meet current financial obligations when due is measured using liquidity or working capital ratios. These ratios are standardized and widely used formulas that allow management to:

- Determine adequate liquidity levels

- Establish liquidity policies and guidelines

- Continually monitor liquidity

Liquidity/working capital ratios are discussed in Chapter 11, Working Capital Metrics.

B. Efficiency or Asset Management Ratios

The ratios described in this section measure the efficiency with which assets are utilized. The principle underlying these ratios is that assets in place should be managed to maximize the revenues generated. Every dollar invested in assets must be supported by one dollar of financing, which comes with a cost. Investors that supply debt and equity capital expect to earn a rate of return on their investment. The more the firm invests in assets, the greater the cost.

Asset efficiency is measured with turnover ratios. The most common measures of asset utilization involve dividing revenues by assets.

1. TOTAL ASSET TURNOVER

Total asset turnover measures how many times the firm's asset base was used or turned over while generating the period's revenue. This is a measure of how effectively assets are used to generate revenue. Total asset turnover is calculated as follows:

$$\text{Total Asset Turnover} = \frac{\text{Revenues}}{\text{Total Assets}} = \frac{\$15,000}{\$16,000} = 0.938 \text{ times}$$

The higher the ratio, the more intensively assets were used. An alternative way to view the ratio is to observe that the firm generated $0.938 of revenue for every dollar of investment in assets.

2. FIXED ASSET TURNOVER

Fixed asset turnover focuses on how efficiently fixed assets or property, plant, and equipment are used. Sufficient productive assets are required to meet customer demand for products or services. Idle capacity does not generate revenue; rather, it generates operating and financing expenses. This ratio is calculated as follows:

$$\text{Fixed Asset Turnover} = \frac{\text{Revenues}}{\text{Net Property, Plant, and Equipment}} = \frac{\$15,000}{\$7,500} = 2.0 \text{ times}$$

This firm turned over net property, plant, and equipment two times during the year in question. Put another way, the firm generated $2.00 of revenue for each dollar invested in net fixed assets.

3. CURRENT ASSET TURNOVER

Current asset turnover measures how many times the firm turned over its stock of current assets to produce revenues. The equation and calculation for the current asset turnover ratio appear below:

$$\text{Current Asset Turnover} = \frac{\text{Revenues}}{\text{Current Assets}} = \frac{\$15,000}{\$8,000} = 1.88 \text{ times}$$

The firm turned over current assets 1.88 times over the course of the year. Alternatively, this ratio can be interpreted as the firm generated $1.88 of revenue per dollar invested in current assets.

4. CASH CONVERSION EFFICIENCY

Cash conversion efficiency measures the degree to which revenues are converted into cash flow. The cash flow generated by operations (i.e., operating cash flow from the statement of cash flows) is calculated as a percentage of revenue. The higher the cash conversion efficiency ratio, the greater the net cash generated per dollar of revenue. This ratio, also called the *cash profit margin*, can be calculated as follows:

$$\text{Cash Conversion Efficiency} = \frac{\text{Cash Flow from Operations}}{\text{Revenues}} = \frac{\$550}{\$15,000} = 0.037 \text{ or } 3.7\%$$

The calculation indicates that the firm retained $0.037 of cash from each dollar of revenue earned.

C. Debt Management Ratios

When used prudently, debt financing offers several advantages: (1) the cost of debt is generally less than the cost of equity, (2) the interest paid on debt is usually tax deductible, and (3) financing with debt does not dilute earnings.

Two types of ratios can help assess the appropriate level of debt. The first type examines the degree of indebtedness. The second type measures the firm's ability to service its debt.

1. DEBT RATIOS MEASURING INDEBTEDNESS

There are several ratios that can be used to measure a firm's level of indebtedness or use of leverage.

a. Total Liabilities to Total Assets

The total liabilities to total assets ratio measures the percentage of assets that are financed with debt. The higher the ratio, the more the firm relies on debt to finance its assets. The following example shows how to calculate the ratio:

$$\text{Total Liabilities to Total Assets} = \frac{\text{Total Liabilities}}{\text{Total Assets}} = \frac{\$7,300}{\$16,000} = 0.456 \text{ or } 45.6\%$$

This firm uses debt to finance 45.6% of its assets. In other words, for each $1 of assets acquired, the firm takes on $0.456 of debt financing.

b. Long-Term Debt to Capital

The long-term debt to capital ratio measures the percentage of long-term financing provided by long-term debt. *Capital* is defined as the sum of long-term debt and equity. Long-term debt includes such liabilities as long-term notes and bonds, term loans, capitalized lease obligations, and pension and retirement obligations. Equity capital consists of all preferred and common equity accounts. The higher the long-term debt to capital ratio, the greater the percentage of debt that is used in the firm's capital structure. This ratio is calculated as:

$$\text{Long-Term Debt to Capital} = \frac{\text{Long-Term Debt}}{\text{Long-Term Debt} + \text{Equity}} = \frac{\$3,900}{\$12,600} = 0.310 \text{ or } 31.0\%$$

The calculation reveals that long-term debt supplied 31.0% of the firm's total capital base.

c. Debt to Equity

The debt to equity ratio measures the degree of debt financing used per dollar of equity capital. The ratio uses total debt in the numerator, where total debt is the sum of short-term and long-term interest-bearing debt. A higher debt to equity ratio suggests more indebtedness and increased default risk. The calculation appears below:

$$\text{Debt to Equity} = \frac{\text{Total Debt}}{\text{Total Equity}} = \frac{\$1,800 + \$3,900}{\$8,700} = 0.655 \text{ or } 65.5\%$$

This calculation indicates that interest-bearing debt is 65.5% of equity. Another interpretation is that the firm uses $0.655 in debt financing per dollar of equity financing.

d. Debt to Tangible Net Worth

The debt to tangible net worth ratio is closely related to the debt to equity ratio. The sole difference in the ratios is the adjustment to the equity account for intangible assets. Some assets are difficult to value or are not easily converted into cash. Examples include goodwill, patents, trademarks, and copyrights. These items represent intangible assets because they are neither physical nor financial in form. Since their value is difficult to determine or is not realizable, it is reasonable to deduct their value from the equity value on the balance sheet.

When making this deduction, the remaining equity balance is called *tangible net worth*. For firms with significant levels of intangible assets, debt to tangible net worth typically shows debt to be a higher percentage of capital because of the adjustment to equity. Another noteworthy point about this ratio is that total debt consists of only interest-bearing debt (both short-term and long-term). For this reason, total debt is different from total liabilities. The calculation for this ratio appears as:

$$\text{Debt to Tangible Net Worth} = \frac{\text{Total Debt}}{\text{Total Equity} - \text{Intangible Assets}}$$

$$= \frac{\$1,800 + \$3,900}{\$8,700 - \$500} = \frac{\$5,700}{\$8,200}$$

$$= 0.695 \text{ or } 69.5\%$$

2. COVERAGE RATIOS: DEBT RATIOS MEASURING THE ABILITY TO SERVICE DEBT

While the measures above examine the level of debt relative to assets or capital, coverage ratios are primarily concerned with measuring the firm's ability to service its debt payments.

a. Times Interest Earned (TIE) Ratio

The TIE ratio measures the firm's ability to meet its interest payments. The numerator in the equation is EBIT. EBIT is used to isolate the amount available to pay interest expense. Moving down the income statement, revenues earned are used to cover cost of goods sold, operating expenses, and depreciation expense. The remaining funds equal EBIT, which can be used to pay interest expense. The following demonstrates the calculation:

$$\text{Times Interest Earned} = \frac{\text{EBIT}}{\text{Interest Expense}} = \frac{\$1,600}{\$300} = 5.33 \text{ times}$$

The TIE ratio indicates that the firm has 5.33 times the funds available to pay interest expense. The larger the TIE ratio, the greater the capacity for paying interest in the event EBIT were to decline due to a business downturn or competitive shock. For example, a TIE of 5.00 implies that EBIT could decline to one-fifth of its current amount and the firm could still pay the interest on its debt.

The TIE can also be calculated using earnings before interest, taxes, depreciation, and amortization (EBITDA) rather than EBIT. This configuration is often used by bondholders in bond covenant agreements, with one of the typical measures being the EBITDA to interest coverage ratio. Its application is similar to that of the TIE ratio, but it may be more appropriate for firms with high levels of depreciation and amortization. It was initially used by investment bankers financing leveraged buyouts to determine the ability of a new firm to service its debt in the short term.

b. Fixed-Charge Coverage Ratio

The fixed-charge coverage ratio is similar to the TIE, except that it also takes into account non-interest expense fixed charges, such as capitalized lease payments. The rationale is that lease payments represent a fixed obligation similar to debt service, so they should be included in examining a firm's indebtedness. The following calculation would result, assuming that the firm has annual lease payments of $500,000:

$$\text{Fixed-Charge Coverage} = \frac{\text{EBIT} + \text{Fixed Charges}}{\text{Interest Expense} + \text{Fixed Charges}}$$

$$= \frac{\$1,600 + \$500}{\$300 + \$500} = \frac{\$2,100}{\$800} = 2.625 \text{ times}$$

The interpretation of the fixed-charge coverage ratio is similar to that of the TIE. A larger ratio implies an improved capacity to meet its fixed-charge obligations. Note that the amount of the lease payments is added back to EBIT because these payments were deducted in the determination of EBIT.

D. Profitability Ratios

Profit is crucial to a firm's viability, but it is just an amount rather than a comment on financial performance. Performance is relative. In many cases, the relative basis for performance is revenues. For this reason many performance measures show some measure of profit expressed as a percentage of revenues. Several common performance ratios are described below.

1. GROSS PROFIT MARGIN

The gross profit margin shows the percentage of revenues remaining after the cost of goods sold is deducted from revenue. It is computed as:

$$\text{Gross Profit Margin} = \frac{\text{Gross Profit}}{\text{Revenues}} = \frac{\$5,800}{\$15,000} = 0.387 \text{ or } 38.7\%$$

This value indicates that COGS consumes 61.3% (1 − 0.387) of each $1 of revenue earned.

2. EBITDA MARGIN

The EBITDA margin is calculated as follows:

$$\text{EBITDA Margin} = \frac{\text{EBITDA}}{\text{Revenues}} = \frac{\$1,800}{\$15,000} = 0.120 \text{ or } 12.0\%$$

3. OPERATING PROFIT MARGIN

The operating profit margin shows the percentage of revenues remaining after COGS, operating expenses, and depreciation and amortization are deducted. The calculation for operating profit margin is:

$$\text{Operating Profit Margin} = \frac{\text{EBIT}}{\text{Revenues}} = \frac{\$1,600}{\$15,000} = 0.107 \text{ or } 10.7\%$$

4. NET PROFIT MARGIN

The net profit margin, also known as *return on sales*, shows the percentage of profits earned after all expenses and taxes are deducted from revenues. It is computed as:

$$\text{Net Profit Margin} = \frac{\text{Net Income}}{\text{Revenues}} = \frac{\$850}{\$15,000} = 0.057 \text{ or } 5.7\%$$

This value indicates that for each $1 of revenue earned, $0.057 is earned in net income.

To summarize, gross profit is $0.387 per dollar of revenue, EBITDA is $0.120 per dollar of revenue, operating profit is $0.107 per dollar of revenue, and net profit is $0.057 per dollar of revenue. Whether these results are satisfactory depends upon how they compare to the firm's profit plan at the beginning of the accounting year and how its competitors are faring, as determined by direct comparison with them or by comparing the firm to industry averages.

5. RETURN ON ASSETS (ROA)

ROA measures net income in relation to the investment in assets. A greater value for this ratio implies a larger net income generated per dollar invested in assets. For the sample firm, every dollar in total assets generates $0.053 in net income:

$$\text{ROA} = \frac{\text{Net Income}}{\text{Total Assets}} = \frac{\$850}{\$16,000} = 0.053 \text{ or } 5.3\%$$

6. RETURN ON COMMON EQUITY (ROE)

The return on common equity ratio measures the amount of earnings available to common shareholders relative to the level of their investment. If a firm issues preferred stock, the dividends due to its preferred shareholders must be paid before dividends are paid to common shareholders. Accordingly, the preferred share dividends must be deducted from net income to arrive at the value for the earnings available to common shareholders that is used in the numerator of the following calculation. The common equity measure in the denominator represents total equity less the book value of preferred equity. For the sample calculation, note that the sample balance sheet does not include preferred stock. Therefore, the earnings available to common shareholders equals net income, and common equity equals total equity. The equation and example calculation for ROE follow:

$$\text{ROE} = \frac{\text{Net Income} - \text{Preferred Dividends}}{\text{Total Equity} - \text{Preferred Equity}} = \frac{\$850 - \$0}{\$8,700 - \$0} = 0.098 \text{ or } 9.8\%$$

The calculation indicates that the firm earned $0.098 of net profit available to common shareholders per dollar of common equity.

E. Integrated Ratio Analysis

Important insights can be gained by examining the interaction effects among ratios. A common example of this is the DuPont approach, in which ROA is decomposed into a product of the net profit margin and total asset turnover. This relationship is expressed as:

$$\text{ROA} = \text{Net Profit Margin} \times \text{Total Asset Turnover} = \frac{\text{Net Income}}{\text{Revenues}} \times \frac{\text{Revenues}}{\text{Total Assets}}$$

$$= 0.057 \times 0.938 = 0.053 \text{ or } 5.3\%$$

This approach shows that ROA is influenced by earnings and the efficient use of assets.

The decomposition of ROA can help the user identify the cause for a change in ROA. For example, suppose that ROA was lower than normal because of a drop in the net profit margin. Analysts would then know to look deeper into the income statement. This process would identify expense categories that the company failed to control. If total asset turnover was too low, the firm produced a lower level of revenues given the asset base.

F. Service Industry Ratios

Ratio analysis is often taught using manufacturing firms as examples, but the service sector is now quite large. As a result, some contrasts in ratios merit mention. Pure service firms, such as executive search firms, software firms, or education and training companies, rely on human talent much more than physical assets. The following unique characteristics describe service firms:

· Small investments in buildings and land and an increased reliance on leasing

· Lower debt levels

· Balance sheets with proportionately higher levels of current assets, particularly accounts receivable, and lower levels of fixed assets

· Larger amounts for salaries and wages because employees are their biggest cost

These unique characteristics should be considered when examining the ratios of service firms.

G. Strengths and Limitations of Ratio Analysis

Financial ratio calculations provide information about a company's financial and operating condition. Their primary advantages include the following:

- They are easily computed and widely used.

- The required information is easily obtained.

- They facilitate trend or historical analysis, which allows the user to track the firm's performance over time.

- They facilitate comparisons between companies. This process is generally referred to as *comparative analysis* or *benchmarking*. Industry averages are widely available (e.g., Dun & Bradstreet, Moody's Investors Service, and Standard & Poor's) and are commonly used as benchmarks.

On the other hand, ratio analysis has limitations. The significant disadvantages include the following:

- Ratios assess historical performance at fixed points in time. Therefore, they do not capture intra-period variations, nor are they necessarily indicative of future performance.

- Ratios should not be used in isolation; instead, they must be analyzed on either a comparative basis or on a historical basis.

- Ratios summarize accounting information, but may not reflect economic value.

- Ratios do not reflect qualitative values, such as business strategies or managerial talent.

- The use of different accounting methods may reduce the validity of comparisons between firms.

H. Common-Size Financial Statements

Common-size financial statements result from scaling the financial statements to account for the scale or size of the firm. A common-size income statement expresses every line item as a percentage of revenue. Meanwhile, a common-size balance sheet expresses each account as a percentage of total assets. Exhibit 9.8 shows an example of a common-size balance sheet based on the sample balance sheet used throughout this chapter.

EXHIBIT 9.8 SAMPLE COMMON-SIZE BALANCE SHEET

AS OF DECEMBER 31

ASSETS	2016	2015
CASH	9.38%	7.09%
SHORT-TERM INVESTMENTS	8.13%	10.64%
ACCOUNTS RECEIVABLE	10.63%	9.22%
INVENTORY	16.25%	14.89%
PREPAID EXPENSES	5.63%	6.38%
TOTAL CURRENT ASSETS	**50.00%**	**48.23%**
GROSS PROPERTY, PLANT & EQUIPMENT	56.25%	57.45%
LESS: ACCUMULATED DEPRECIATION	9.38%	9.22%
NET PROPERTY, PLANT & EQUIPMENT	46.88%	48.23%
INTANGIBLE ASSETS	3.13%	3.55%
TOTAL ASSETS	**100.00%**	**100.00%**

LIABILITIES AND SHAREHOLDERS' EQUITY	2016	2015
ACCOUNTS PAYABLE	10.00%	8.51%
SHORT-TERM NOTES PAYABLE	11.25%	9.22%
TOTAL CURRENT LIABILITIES	**21.25%**	**17.73%**
LONG-TERM DEBT	24.38%	24.82%
TOTAL LIABILITIES	**45.63%**	**42.55%**
COMMON STOCK AT PAR VALUE	1.25%	1.42%
PAID-IN CAPITAL	22.50%	25.53%
RETAINED EARNINGS	30.63%	30.50%
TOTAL EQUITY	**54.38%**	**57.45%**
TOTAL LIABILITIES AND EQUITY	**100.00%**	**100.00%**

Common-size statements enable direct comparisons of financial data for firms of different sizes. Expenses as a percentage of revenues reveal which firm is the most efficient at controlling expenses. Asset categories expressed as a percentage of total assets can similarly be compared across companies, as can liability categories expressed as a percentage of total assets.

Some of the percentages in common-size income statements constitute profit margins, which are measures of profitability or performance. These include the gross profit, operating profit, net profit, and earnings before interest, taxes, depreciation, and amortization (EBITDA) margins.

VII. PERFORMANCE MEASUREMENT

This section describes common measures of performance. These include return on investment, economic value added, and free cash flow. The performance measures are calculated with the sample financial statements used throughout this chapter.

A. Return on Investment (ROI)

ROI is calculated as the profit per dollar of invested capital, as shown below:

$$ROI = \frac{Net\ Income}{Long\text{-}Term\ Debt + Equity} = \frac{\$850}{\$3,900 + \$8,700} = 0.0675\ or\ 6.75\%$$

The sample firm provided a 6.75% return on capital for the firm's shareholders and creditors.

ROI has a few key limitations:

- ROI does not include a charge for the cost of equity capital acquired from shareholders. This implies that the assets financed with equity are acquired at no capital cost.

- To maintain the firm's targeted ROI, managers may be tempted to reject a positive NPV project if the project leads to a decline in the business unit's ROI. Suppose a business unit experiences a 20% ROI, but a proposed addition to this unit promises a 16% ROI. If the investment is funded, it will increase the business unit's assets and reduce its ROI. If the WACC is 9%, the asset investment will increase firm value because it has a positive NPV.

- ROI may provide a misleading indication of performance in cases where earnings are not distributed evenly over time. For example, if the ROI in the example was calculated over a six-month period, and $520 of the $850 expected over the year occurred during that period, then the computed six-month ROI would be $520 ÷ $12,600 (or 4.1%), which would represent an 8.2% annual rate. An estimated ROI of 8.2% annually exaggerates the actual annual ROI.

B. Economic Value Added (EVA)

EVA is an important firm performance measure as it explicitly accounts for the cost of capital raised from creditors and shareholders. This metric involves subtracting an implied capital charge from the after-tax EBIT.[6] EVA will be positive only if the after-tax EBIT exceeds the capital charge. The formula for calculating EVA is:

$$EVA = EBIT \times (1 - Tax\ Rate) - WACC \times (Long\text{-}Term\ Debt + Equity)$$

Assuming a WACC of 9% and an implied tax rate of 34.615% (calculated as taxes divided by net profit before taxes, or $450 ÷ $1,300), the sample firm's EVA is:

$$EVA = \$1,600 \times (1 - 0.34615) - 0.09 \times (\$3,900 + \$8,700)$$

$$= \$1,600 \times 0.65385 - 0.09 \times \$12,600$$

$$= \$1,046 - \$1,134 = -\$88$$

---

6. This version of EVA uses EBIT as the measure of profit to reflect that required reinvestment in assets must occur via depreciation and amortization if the business is to continue in its present form and size. Other variations of the EVA use EBITDA in lieu of EBIT.

In this example, the company has a negative EVA. The negative EVA could be due to increases in the capital base that have not yet generated earnings. While growth can cause a negative EVA, a negative EVA is usually due to the expansion in capital base required to fund the growth. If revenue is growing, but the capital base is not expanding significantly and the company still has a negative EVA, it could indicate that the additional sales are not generating sufficient profit to add value.

In the absence of this growth, however, a different interpretation could be made. Based on the WACC and the level of capital, investors and creditors expect the firm to generate $1,134 as a return on their investment. When this capital charge is levied against the after-tax EBIT, EVA then equals –$88. While this may not be a problem in the short run, a trend of annual negative EVA might cause investors to bid down the firm's stock price. This would be the case even if the firm had positive returns on sales and assets. Overall, the EVA can be increased via improvements in operating efficiency and by investing in productive assets that earn returns exceeding the WACC.

EVA is a true measure of economic profit or loss, and is accepted in the professional financial community. EVA is commonly used to assess the performance of:

- The overall company
- Individual divisions and/or operating units
- Management

C. Free Cash Flow (FCF)

FCF indicates how much cash generated during the period is available to shareholders and creditors. FCF adjusts net income for noncash charges (i.e., depreciation and amortization), working capital, and capital expenditures. FCF is considered a fundamental component of assessing firm value.

A commonly used version of the FCF calculation follows:

$$FCF = Net\ Income + (Depreciation\ and\ Amortization) - Change\ in$$
$$Noncash\ Working\ Capital - Capital\ Expenditures$$

The FCF for the sample company is calculated as follows:[7]

$$FCF = \$850 + \$200 - \$500 - \$900 = -\$350$$

FCF can also be calculated using the operating cash flow figure from the statement of cash flows and then subtracting capital expenditures, yielding the same result:

$$FCF = \$550 - \$900 = -\$350$$

The FCF calculated above is negative, but it is important to note that negative FCF is not bad in and of itself. If FCF is negative, it could be a sign that a company is growing quickly and/or making large investments. If this growth can be supported and the investments earn a high return, then the strategy has the potential to pay off in the long run. In this example, the firm's revenues have grown by 20% from the prior to the current year, and the firm has made large investments in both working capital and fixed assets. Such investments may yield increased future revenues and cash flows.

---

7. The change in noncash working capital is the net of the changes in the working capital accounts (A/R, inventory, and A/P), as shown on the statement of cash flows.

VIII. SUMMARY

This chapter described tools that are commonly used by treasury personnel for financial planning and analysis tasks. These tasks often have a direct effect on shareholder value. The central tools described in this chapter include capital budgeting and ratio analysis.

Capital budgeting serves an important purpose by providing a framework for the allocation of capital that is available for investment. The primary capital budgeting technique is the NPV approach. In addition to the NPV approach, this chapter described other capital budgeting metrics that can be used to evaluate investments from multiple dimensions. These metrics can be applied to investments in long-term assets as well as to decisions that are specific to treasury management. Examples include switching from check to ACH disbursements and evaluating changes in trade credit policies, among others.

Ratio analysis is another key topic addressed in this chapter. Ratio analysis helps in assessing the firm's financial health. The financial health of a firm might encompass operating performance, efficiency metrics, and debt levels. In addition, treasury personnel can use ratio analysis to assess the firm's overall liquidity position.

Key Equations

$$\text{Future Value} = PV\left(1+i\right)^n$$

$$\text{Present Value} = \frac{FV}{\left(1+i\right)^n} \text{ or } PV = FV \times \left[\frac{1}{\left(1+i\right)^n}\right]$$

$$\text{Present Value} = \frac{C_1}{\left(1+i\right)^1} + \frac{C_2}{\left(1+i\right)^2} + \ldots + \frac{C_n}{\left(1+i\right)^n}$$

$$\text{Future Value} = PV\left(1+\left(\text{Days}\right)\left(\frac{i}{\text{Days in a Year}}\right)\right)$$

$$\text{Present Value} = \frac{FV}{\left(1+\left(\text{Days}\right)\left(\frac{i}{\text{Days in a Year}}\right)\right)}$$

$$\text{Net Present Value} = \text{PV of Cash Inflows} - \text{Cost}$$

$$\text{Net Present Value} = \frac{C_1}{\left(1+i\right)^1} + \frac{C_2}{\left(1+i\right)^2} + \frac{C_3}{\left(1+i\right)^3} + \ldots + \frac{C_n}{\left(1+i\right)^n} - \text{Cost}$$

$$\text{Profitability Index} = \frac{\text{Present Value of Cash Inflows}}{\text{Present Value of Cash Outflows}}$$

$$\text{Break-Even Quantity} = \frac{\text{Fixed Costs}}{\text{Selling Price per Unit} - \text{Variable Cost per Unit}}$$

$$\text{Degree of Operating Leverage} = \frac{\% \text{ Change in EBIT}}{\% \text{ Change in Sales}}$$

$$\text{Degree of Financial Leverage} = \frac{\% \text{ Change in Net Income}}{\% \text{ Change in EBIT}}$$

$$\text{Degree of Total Leverage} = \frac{\% \text{ Change in Net Income}}{\% \text{ Change in Sales}}$$

$$\text{Total Asset Turnover} = \frac{\text{Revenues}}{\text{Total Assets}}$$

$$\text{Fixed Asset Turnover} = \frac{\text{Revenues}}{\text{Net Property, Plant, and Equipment}}$$

$$\text{Current Asset Turnover} = \frac{\text{Revenues}}{\text{Current Assets}}$$

$$\text{Cash Conversion Efficiency} = \frac{\text{Cash Flow from Operations}}{\text{Revenues}}$$

$$\text{Total Liabilities to Total Assets} = \frac{\text{Total Liabilities}}{\text{Total Assets}}$$

$$\text{Long-Term Debt to Capital} = \frac{\text{Long-Term Debt}}{\text{Long-Term Debt} + \text{Equity}}$$

$$\text{Debt to Equity} = \frac{\text{Total Debt}}{\text{Total Equity}}$$

$$\text{Debt to Tangible Net Worth} = \frac{\text{Total Debt}}{\text{Total Equity} - \text{Intangible Assets}}$$

$$\text{Times Interest Earned} = \frac{\text{EBIT}}{\text{Interest Expense}}$$

$$\text{Fixed-Charge Coverage} = \frac{\text{EBIT} + \text{Fixed Charges}}{\text{Interest Expense} + \text{Fixed Charges}}$$

$$\text{Gross Profit Margin} = \frac{\text{Gross Profit}}{\text{Revenues}}$$

$$\text{EBITDA Margin} = \frac{\text{EBITDA}}{\text{Revenues}}$$

$$\text{Operating Profit Margin} = \frac{\text{EBIT}}{\text{Revenues}}$$

$$\text{Net Profit Margin} = \frac{\text{Net Income}}{\text{Revenues}}$$

$$\text{Return on Assets} = \frac{\text{Net Income}}{\text{Total Assets}}$$

$$\text{Return on Common Equity} = \frac{\text{Net Income} - \text{Preferred Dividends}}{\text{Total Equity} - \text{Preferred Equity}}$$

$$\text{Return on Assets} = \text{Net Profit Margin} \times \text{Total Asset Turnover}$$

$$= \frac{\text{Net Income}}{\text{Revenues}} \times \frac{\text{Revenues}}{\text{Total Assets}}$$

$$\text{Return on Investment} = \frac{\text{Net Income}}{\text{Long-Term Debt} + \text{Equity}}$$

$$\text{Economic Value Added} = \text{EBIT} \times (1 - \text{Tax Rate}) - (\text{WACC}) \times (\text{Long-Term Debt} + \text{Equity})$$

$$\text{Free Cash Flow} = \text{Net Income} + (\text{Depreciation and Amortization}) - \text{Change in Noncash Working Capital} - \text{Capital Expenditures}$$

PART IV
Working Capital Management

CHAPTER 10
Introduction to Working Capital

I. INTRODUCTION

II. OPERATING CASH FLOWS, CASH FLOW TIMELINE, AND FLOAT
A. Operating Cash Flows
B. Cash Flow Timeline
C. Float

III. THE CASH CONVERSION CYCLE (CCC)
A. Days' Inventory (DI)
B. Days' Receivables (DR)
C. Days' Payables (DP)
D. Calculating the CCC
E. Evaluating the Impact of Changes to the Cash Flow Timeline

IV. HOW CHANGES IN CURRENT BALANCE SHEET ACCOUNTS IMPACT EXTERNAL FINANCING
A. Changes in Current Assets
B. Changes in Current Liabilities
C. External Financing Requirements

V. WORKING CAPITAL INVESTMENT AND FINANCING STRATEGIES
A. Current Asset Investment Strategies
B. Current Asset Financing Strategies

VI. MANAGEMENT OF TRADE CREDIT AND ACCOUNTS RECEIVABLE (A/R)
A. Relationship between Treasury and Credit Management
B. Trade Credit Policies
C. Forms of Credit Extension
D. A/R Management

E. Cash Application

F. Considerations Pertaining to Terms of Sale

G. Financing A/R

VII. MANAGEMENT OF INVENTORY

A. Benefits and Costs of Inventory

B. Types of Inventory

C. Inventory Management Techniques

D. Inventory Financing Alternatives

VIII. MANAGEMENT OF ACCOUNTS PAYABLE (A/P)

A. Disbursement System Considerations

B. Types of A/P and Disbursement Systems

IX. MULTINATIONAL WORKING CAPITAL MANAGEMENT TOOLS

A. Multicurrency Accounts

B. Netting

C. Leading and Lagging

D. Re-invoicing

E. Internal Factoring

F. In-House Banking

G. Export Financing

X. SUMMARY

I. INTRODUCTION

Working capital management involves optimizing current assets and liabilities to ensure that the firm has sufficient liquidity. Optimization also includes releasing trapped cash from the working capital components, which will be discussed later in this chapter. Subsequently, working capital management is one of the primary responsibilities of treasury professionals.

Working capital management is influenced by the firm's daily operating activities, which consist of ordering and paying for goods and services, as well as making and collecting on sales. These operating activities result in the creation of various working capital accounts (e.g., inventory, accounts payable, and accounts receivable), which impact cash flows and liquidity. The ebb and flow of this operating cycle results in the cash conversion cycle, as illustrated in Exhibit 10.1.

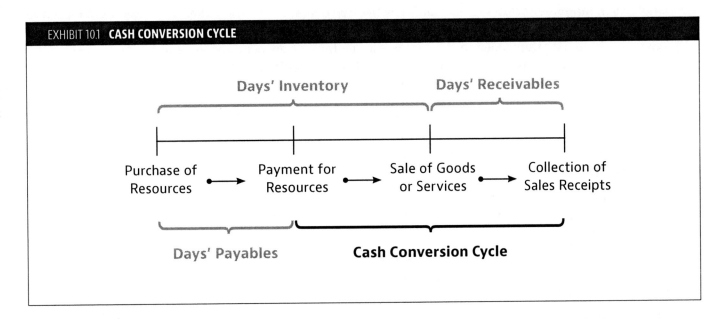

EXHIBIT 10.1 **CASH CONVERSION CYCLE**

The aspects of working capital management examined in this chapter include:

· Operating cash flows

· The concept of float

· The cash conversion cycle

· Working capital investment and financing strategies

· Management of accounts receivable (A/R), inventory, and accounts payable (A/P)

II. OPERATING CASH FLOWS, CASH FLOW TIMELINE, AND FLOAT

This section describes key operating aspects of working capital management. Specific topics include types of operating cash flows, the cash flow timeline, and float concepts that are pertinent to working capital.

A. Operating Cash Flows

Four types of cash flows that treasury professionals must consider include the following:

- **Cash outflows** include funds disbursed to employees, vendors/suppliers, lenders, tax agencies, bondholders, and shareholders. Cash outflows are typically described by the procure-to-pay timeline, as shown in the next section.

- **Cash inflows** include funds collected from customers, obtained from financial sources (e.g., loans or investment income), and/or received from other sources. Cash inflows are typically described by the order-to-cash timeline.

- **Concentration flows** (e.g., funding flows) involve internal transfers among operating units of a firm and the associated bank accounts. The primary objectives of concentration flows include the pooling of funds or the funding of disbursement accounts.

- **Liquidity management flows** refer to the effective deployment of the firm's liquidity reserves to maximize firm value. If there is a surplus of funds, treasury may either (1) invest in suitable investments, (2) pay down existing debt, or (3) return value to shareholders in the form of dividends or share repurchases. If there is a shortage of funds, treasury may either (1) sell off investments, or (2) draw on available debt sources (e.g., credit lines or commercial paper issuance).

This chapter focuses primarily on cash outflows and inflows. Concentration and liquidity management flows are described in later chapters.

B. Cash Flow Timeline

The cash flow timeline describes the conversion of noncash current assets and liabilities into cash. The cash flow timeline consists of the procure-to-pay period, the inventory period, and the order-to-cash period. Each aspect is shown in Exhibit 10.2.

- For most firms, the procure-to-pay timeline represents the time between the purchase of raw materials, retail goods, or services, and the point at which payment is received by the supplier. The procure-to-pay period represents an outflow of cash.

- Once the raw materials or retail goods have been received during the procure-to-pay period, the inventory timeline period begins. The inventory period includes the time needed to turn raw materials into finished goods and, subsequently, to sell the finished goods. For certain firms with efficient supply chains, the inventory timeline will be relatively short.

- The order-to-cash period is the final piece of the operating cycle and represents a cash inflow. This component includes all of the tasks involved in soliciting customers and converting inventory into sales and ultimately into cash.

The depiction of the timelines visually illustrates the creation of different working capital accounts, which ultimately impact firm liquidity. In terms of liquidity strategies, treasury professionals commonly seek to optimize liquidity by lengthening the procure-to-pay timeline and shortening the order-to-cash timeline. Note that the procure-to-pay and order-to-cash are opposite sides of the same coin; that is, one firm's procure-to-pay period is another firm's order-to-cash period. Actions that extend the first firm's procure-to-pay period will extend the second firm's order-to-cash timeline, and vice versa.

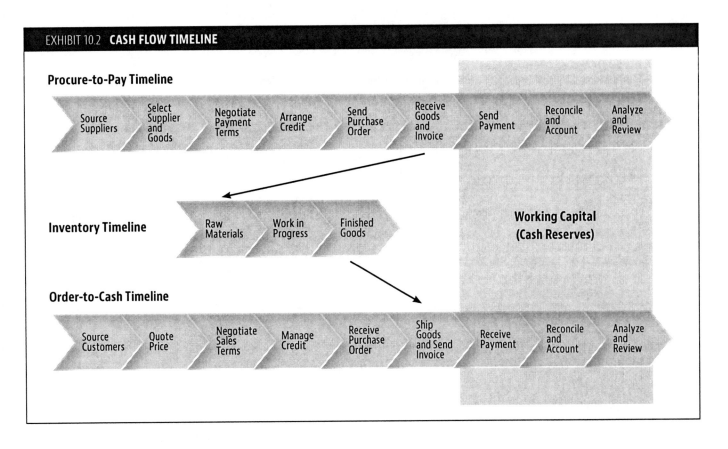

EXHIBIT 10.2 CASH FLOW TIMELINE

C. Float

The cash flow timeline spans the interval that begins with the purchase of raw materials or parts from vendors and suppliers at the start of the operating cycle and ends when payment is received from customers at the completion of the operating cycle.

Float refers to the time interval, or delay, between the start and the completion of a specific phase or process occurring along the cash flow timeline. Float is often the result of wait time (e.g., the time lost while waiting for someone else to take action or the time needed to transmit information between two parties) and inefficiencies within a specific process, but is also often increased by the use of paper processes and delivery systems, such as the mailing of invoices to a business's customers. As the use of e-commerce and related technology has expanded, the overall level of float created by paper processes has been declining for most companies. However, float may still be created if there are delays in a certain process. For example, invoices may be sent via e-mail or another electronic format, but if the seller is slow to create those invoices and send them out, then float will occur as part of that process. Exhibit 10.3 illustrates some of the typical types of float that treasury professionals have to manage, and shows their relative length in days.

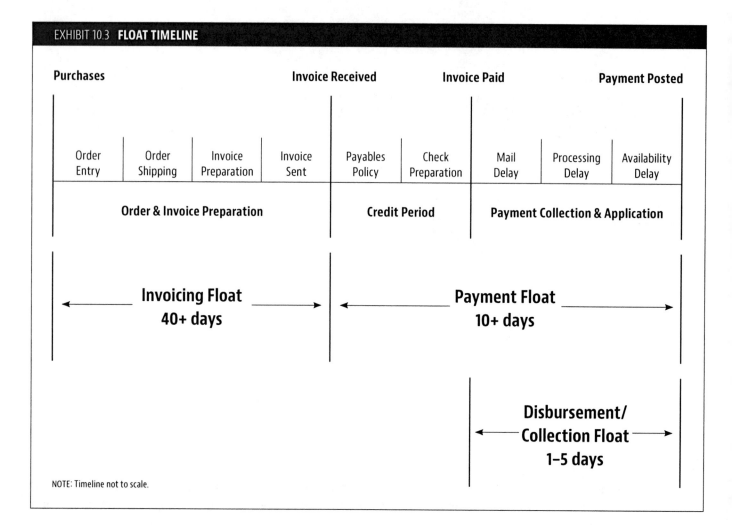

EXHIBIT 10.3 **FLOAT TIMELINE**

NOTE: Timeline not to scale.

The term *float* often is used just to refer to disbursement/collection float, the period of time that occurs between the payment generation and the actual time when the payee's account is credited with available funds. As can be seen in Exhibit 10.3, this type of float is typically the smallest piece of float with which a treasury professional needs to be concerned.

While e-commerce has moved quickly in many countries and in many industries, some countries still rely heavily on the use of paper processes for many of their business-to-business (B2B) transactions. While it may be typical for a global organization to use electronic billing and electronic payment of invoices, the common practice is still a mailed invoice to the buyer, with the remittance advice being mailed back to the seller. The delays inherent in this type of paper-based system result in numerous types of float that companies must manage.

1. DIFFERENT TYPES OF FLOAT

Different float terms may refer to the same or similar time intervals, but specific usage varies, depending upon whether the time period is viewed from the perspective of the seller/payee or the buyer/payor, as illustrated in Exhibit 10.4. For example, consider the term *payment float* when a check[1] is sent to pay an invoice:

1. Checks are used in this example because check payments illustrate types of float—for example, mail and clearing (check) float—not typically seen in electronic payments.

- From the seller/payee's perspective (order-to-cash), **payment float** (including mail, processing, and availability float, as well as any credit terms) represents the delay between the time an invoice is sent to the buyer and the time the seller/payee's account is credited with available funds.

- From the buyer/payor's perspective (procure-to-pay), **payment float** (including mail, processing, and clearing float, as well as any invoice processing time and credit terms) represents the delay between the time an invoice is received and the time the buyer/payor's account is debited.

- **Invoicing float** represents the delay between the ordering of goods or services and the receipt of an invoice by the buyer/payor.

- **Information float** refers to the inability to use or generate cash due to a delay in receiving related information, such as remittance information. (Since information float may occur in multiple processes, it does not appear at a specific point on the timeline in Exhibit 10.4.)

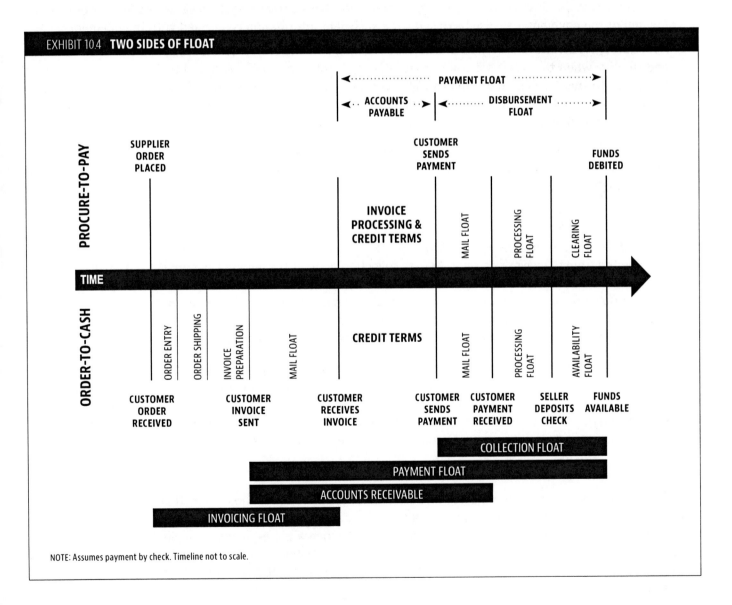

EXHIBIT 10.4 **TWO SIDES OF FLOAT**

NOTE: Assumes payment by check. Timeline not to scale.

a. Collection Float

Collection float is the time interval or delay between the time the buyer/payor initiates payment and the time the seller/payee receives good funds. Collection float applies principally to paper-based payment instruments that are subject to three types of float or delays:

- **Mail Float:** The time interval or delay between the day a payment (and any related remittance information) is mailed and the day it is received by a payee or at a payee's processing site. Mail float usually ranges between as little as a day or two to many days or even weeks in the case of international payments.

- **Processing Float:** The time interval or delay between the time the payee or the payee's processing site receives the payment and the time the payment (typically a check) is deposited into the payee's account. Processing time is required to capture remittance and payor information, and to prepare the deposit. Processing float is typically one day or less, but may extend for more days if the processing system is inefficient or has any built-in processing delays, such as receiving payments at branch locations but sending them elsewhere for final processing. Posting of the payment may also be delayed if insufficient information is received with the payment.

- **Availability Float:** The time interval or delay between the day when a payment is deposited into a bank account and the day when the payee's account is credited with collected funds. Availability float varies but ranges from zero to two business days domestically, and even longer for international payments. As discussed in Chapter 4, Payment Systems, availability is often negotiable and is determined by the depository institution's availability schedule or the availability schedule negotiated with the institution by its customer.

The primary cost associated with collection float is opportunity cost because uncollected funds cannot be invested or used to pay down debt. However, the cost of methods used to reduce or eliminate collection float, such as remote deposit capture (RDC) or lockbox services, should be weighed against the benefit of achieving those improvements.

b. Disbursement Float

Disbursement float is the time interval or delay between the day when a payment is initiated and the day when funds are debited from the payor's account. As with collection float, disbursement float applies principally to paper-based payment instruments, which are subject to three types of delays or float: mail, processing, and clearing. Disbursement float is analogous to collection float, except that it is viewed from the payor's perspective. As illustrated in Exhibit 10.4, the mail and processing float components of disbursement float are the same as in collection float. The primary difference between collection and disbursement float is availability versus clearing float.

Clearing float is the time interval or delay between the day when a check is deposited by the payee and the day when the payor's account is debited. In most cases, the payee's account is credited with collected funds at the same time the payor's account is debited. In some cases, however, there also may be clearing float considerations related to the use of disbursements with automated clearinghouse (ACH) network credits. Some banks require that certain customers fund ACH disbursements upon initiation rather than when the actual value transfer takes place.

c. Invoicing Float

Invoicing float is the delay between the day that a customer places an order and the day that the customer actually receives an invoice for that order that can be processed for payment. The major components of invoicing float are order entry and billing system delays, as well as mail float when a paper invoice is mailed to the customer. As shown in Exhibit 10.3, invoicing float is typically much larger than collection or disbursement float. The implementation of e-commerce and other technology tools, discussed in Chapter 15, Technology in Treasury, can significantly reduce invoicing float.

d. Payment Float

As discussed above, payment float is the period of time between the day that a bill or invoice is sent/received (depending on the perspective of the seller or buyer) and the day that payment is actually credited to the biller's bank account. By definition, payment float includes disbursement/collection float, but this is usually just a small part of the total payment float. The largest portion of payment float is typically related to the customer's payables policy and the trade (credit) terms that have been negotiated between the biller and the customer. While this delay can be the result of process inefficiencies related to receiving, verifying, and paying a specific invoice, it is more commonly caused by customers' deferring payment until a specific due date, as discussed below in the section on disbursement system considerations. Depending upon trade terms and the willingness of specific customers to delay payments, payment float can often be the largest float component in any commercial payment process. As a result, it can also provide the greatest opportunity for improvement and effective management. As with invoicing float, payment float can be significantly reduced by e-commerce, but effective management of trade terms can typically provide even greater benefit.

e. Information Float

Information float is different from other types of float in that instead of referring to delays in the actual collection of funds, it refers to lack of knowledge about the funds themselves. Information float is the time between receiving good funds and the time the organization knows that it has the funds available and can actually make use of those funds. This is especially critical for global organizations due to the significant time differences they must deal with. Even when daily balance information is available from a company's global banks, it is often prior-day balances, and value may be lost by not being able to move those balances until the next business day.

For a company receiving payments on A/R, there may also be delays between the receipt of the payment and the posting of that payment to a customer's account. This may trigger unnecessary collection activity. If the customer is close to its credit limit, this could, in turn, delay the ability of the company to sell more goods or services to that customer.

2. BENEFITS OF FLOAT REDUCTION

A company typically benefits from shortening all types of float associated with collections and lengthening all types of float associated with disbursements. However, it is important to note that suppliers have an incentive to engage in actions that minimize the company's payment float, while customers try to maximize the company's collection float. Traditionally, the rule in cash management is to collect quickly and disburse slowly, within the constraints of prudent business practices and the maintenance of good relations with trading partners and other stakeholders. Accordingly, partners along the supplier-producer-customer chain have opposing incentives. The introduction of electronic payment systems, including commercial cards, has changed this to an extent because the efficiency and benefits of the new payment methods outweigh the benefits of slowing paper-based payments, resulting in quicker disbursements.

In many industries, companies are taking a win-win approach by establishing strategic partner relationships with both suppliers and customers. In these industries, the focus has shifted away from the end of the operating cycle shown in Exhibit 10.1 (sale of goods or services through collection of sales receipts) and toward the beginning of the operating cycle (purchase of resources through sale of goods or services). In other words, the focus has shifted to the areas that represent the greatest possible gains in reducing cycle time, such as just-in-time (JIT) inventory and supply chain management.[2] For those industries and companies that have realigned trading partner relationships

2. Supply chain management is the integration of business processes with the entire chain of trading partners, which can include suppliers, intermediaries, third-party service providers, and customers.

and reengineered supply chain management, the trend is to replace checks with electronic payment methods and to replace paper invoices with electronic invoice presentment, thereby eliminating all paper-based float delays.

III. THE CASH CONVERSION CYCLE (CCC)

The continuous flow of cash through working capital accounts results in the CCC, which provides the amount of time that elapses between when funds are disbursed in direct support of a revenue-generating activity until the time when revenues are collected. The CCC shows how inventory, A/R, and A/P interact to affect cash flow.

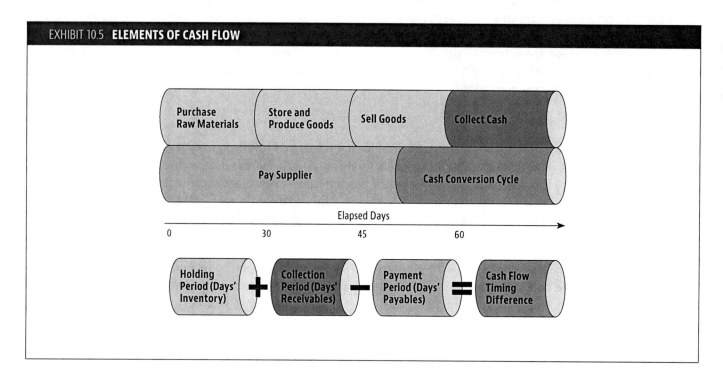

EXHIBIT 10.5 ELEMENTS OF CASH FLOW

Exhibit 10.5 lays out the various elements of the CCC in a linear fashion and shows that the cycle begins when inventory is purchased and ends when available funds are collected from A/R. The exhibit shows that the CCC is a function of days' inventory, days' receivables, and days' payables.

If all payments were settled in cash at the time of purchase or sale, the CCC would start with the purchase of raw materials and end with the sale of finished goods. However, inventory is typically purchased on credit, which creates an A/P entry. As a result, the CCC metric is the timing difference between the payment of A/P and the collection of cash from the sale of finished goods. In other words, the CCC is the period of time between disbursement for the A/P and collection of the A/R. Since the CCC represents the amount of time that it takes a firm to turn a cash outflow into a cash inflow, treasury professionals should strive to shorten the CCC.

The remainder of this section describes the individual components of the CCC and strategies that can be implemented to shorten the CCC.

A. Days' Inventory (DI)

For a manufacturing firm, days' inventory (i.e., inventory conversion period or days' sales in inventory) is the average number of days that elapse from the purchase of raw materials until the sale of finished goods. This period of time is the sum of the average number of days that:

- Raw materials remain in inventory
- Raw materials are converted into finished goods (work-in-progress inventory)
- Finished goods remain in inventory

Decisions that affect the raw materials, work in progress, or finished goods held in inventory impact days' inventory.

For a retailer, days' inventory is the average length of time that finished goods inventory is held before sale. For a service company, days' inventory is determined by the average length of time that materials are held in inventory until they are used to provide services.

B. Days' Receivables (DR)

For manufacturing, retail, and service firms, days' receivables (i.e., receivables conversion period) is the average number of days required to collect on credit. Changes in A/R policies (e.g., credit standards, credit terms, or collection efforts) impact days' receivables. Any changes in the competitive marketplace or general business conditions also may impact days' receivables.

C. Days' Payables (DP)

Irrespective of industry affiliation, days' payables (i.e., payables conversion period) is the average number of days between the purchase/receipt of materials, supplies, or services, and the accompanying payment.[3] Days' payables represents the actual trade credit period, which is often different from the stated trade terms. A firm with trade terms of net 30 will typically have days' payables that is higher than 30 days. The ability to purchase materials on deferred payment terms lets the buyer conserve cash by delaying payment. Any strategy that delays payment lengthens the buyer's days' payables, which shortens the CCC. Delaying payment until the end of the credit term or the credit discount period enables the firm to:

- Reduce debt
- Invest cash on a short-term basis
- Make other purchases

The proper management of payables is important and provides an effective source of liquidity for many firms. Deferring payments until the end of the established trade terms and negotiating improved trade terms are both good practices. Unilaterally paying suppliers late, while a practice of some firms, should be avoided. Stretching payables beyond agreed-upon credit terms can negatively affect relationships with suppliers.

D. Calculating the CCC

The formula for CCC is:

$$CCC = Days' \ Inventory + Days' \ Receivables - Days' \ Payables$$

---

3. For the purposes of the CCC discussion, this text is simply looking at when payment is issued, rather than getting involved in the details of disbursement or collection float, which are discussed in more detail earlier in this chapter.

CCC is the average number of days between the cash outflow for the acquisition of materials and supplies, and the cash inflow from the sale of products or services. Therefore, the CCC is a method for calculating the average length of time a firm must finance a cash outflow before receiving a cash inflow. Use the following information to calculate the CCC:

· Days' inventory = 45 days

· Days' receivables = 35 days

· Days' payables = 30 days

Therefore:

$$CCC = 45+35-30=50 \text{ days}$$

These assumptions result in a CCC of 50 days.[4]

Suppose that management reduces the days' inventory to 40 days by more carefully planning purchases, scheduling production runs, and managing finished goods inventories. Next, by encouraging slow-paying customers to pay within terms, the days' receivables is reduced to 32 days. Finally, the payables department discovers that payments were being made before the end of the credit period. By paying these obligations at the end of the trade credit term, the days' payables increases to 33 days. Through these improvements, the CCC is reduced to 39 days, as shown:

$$CCC = 40+32-33=39 \text{ days}$$

Decreased investment in inventory and A/R, and the increased process efficiency in A/P, are all sources of funds. Note that the firm's underlying business processes have not changed. Revenues, unit sales of the product or service, total purchases, and total billings remained constant. What has changed is that the firm now recovers a dollar invested in working capital in 39 days rather than 50 days, which significantly improves the firm's liquidity.

Another measure that is closely related to the CCC is the cash turnover measure. The formula for cash turnover is:

$$\text{Cash Turnover} = \frac{365}{\text{Cash Conversion Cycle}}$$

In the earlier example, when the CCC was 50 days, cash turnover was 7.3 (365÷50) times per year. Reducing the CCC to 39 days increases cash turnover to 9.4 (365÷39) times per year. The latter indicates that the firm goes through 9.4 CCCs per year. Subsequently, a higher cash turnover implies increased working capital efficiency.

Note that this example includes reducing the investment in inventory and increasing the funding provided by A/P. The net result is a reduction in current assets and in the amount of current liabilities needed to finance current assets. Increasing A/P may also help to reduce interest-bearing, short-term debt. All else held constant, shortening the CCC reduced the firm's investment in total assets and increased net income by lowering interest expense and inventory carrying costs.

Note also that the CCC calculation is based upon averages over a given period of time. To the extent that actual payment and receipt patterns are uneven (e.g., a firm may only make disbursements once a week or at the end of a month), the CCC calculation may not match actual values at a given point in time within the year.

---

4. The example provided is typical for most retail or manufacturing firms that have inventory. The calculation for service firms is identical, except that days' inventory may equal 0 days. For a service firm, the calculation becomes: CCC = 0 + 35 − 30 = 5 days.

The CCC can be shortened by reducing the receivables and inventory periods, and by extending the payables period. Taking these actions may improve profitability and the value of the firm. However, caution is warranted when pursuing operating policies that produce these results. The improvement in financial performance will be short-lived if the following occur:

- Lost sales due to overly strict credit and collection standards
- Production stoppages attributable to inadequate raw materials or parts inventories
- Payables stretched beyond the due date
- Forgone cost-saving trade discounts
- Higher prices assessed by suppliers because individual orders are smaller or payment is slower
- Refusal to sell to customers that are good credit risks, but occasionally slow in paying
- Excessive reliance on A/P in lieu of a stable base of short-term bank credit

The decision to implement policies that enhance short-term (and possibly long-term) profitability must be weighed against the considerations listed previously. If these lead to the loss of goodwill with a customer, supplier, or bank, then these strategies are likely to be counterproductive in the long run.

E. Evaluating the Impact of Changes to the Cash Flow Timeline

In several of the sections below, the impact of a change to the cash flow timeline is discussed. In evaluating different cash flow alternatives, the general approach is to determine the present value of each alternative at some interest rate and choose the best alternative for the organization (i.e., the lowest present value cost or highest present value benefit). The relevant interest rate is usually referred to as the *opportunity cost* for the decision in question.

In a general financial sense, the most common opportunity cost used is the weighted average cost of capital (WACC), which is discussed in Chapter 20, The Capital Structure Decision and Management. However, WACC may not be the proper cost to use for working capital decisions. WACC is primarily a cost of long-term capital, and for many organizations, it may be more appropriate to use some short-term measure for opportunity cost. The idea behind opportunity cost is to determine what the most attractive unused alternative is for any funds or balances that are generated as a result of the decision. Opportunity cost is discussed in more detail in Chapter 9, Financial Planning and Analysis.

For example, if an organization is offered different terms for paper versus electronic payments, the primary consideration on the proper opportunity cost is where will the organization get the funds for paying earlier via electronic means (assuming loss of clearing float as a result of electronic payment). If the organization is generally a net borrower (on a short-term basis), then the appropriate opportunity cost would be its short-term borrowing rate (assuming it would have to borrow in order to make an earlier payment). If, on the other hand, the organization is a net investor (in the short term), then the appropriate opportunity cost would be its short-term investment rate (assuming it would have to sell off some short-term investments to make an earlier payment).

Alternatively, some organizations may decide that using WACC for working capital decision evaluations is the best course for them. The rationale is that short-term rates may fluctuate rapidly in some economic situations, and an organization may prefer to have a rate that is more stable over time.

For the remainder of this chapter, the general term *opportunity cost* will be used to represent the cost of funds for any of the alternatives discussed. The actual opportunity cost used by an organization will vary depending on its circumstances.

IV. HOW CHANGES IN CURRENT BALANCE SHEET ACCOUNTS IMPACT EXTERNAL FINANCING

Many current asset and current liability accounts vary whenever sales activity occurs. These accounts are called *spontaneous* because no specific working capital management decisions are involved in increasing these accounts. Changes in account levels occur as account activity fluctuates with a change in the level of sales activity. The magnitude of spontaneous changes significantly impacts the amount of external financing necessary for working capital.

A. Changes in Current Assets

Generally, as the volume of sales activity increases, credit sales also increase, resulting in larger dollar amounts invested in A/R. Additional sales may require increases in raw materials and parts inventories to support the production of finished goods, thereby increasing both types of inventory. An increase in A/R and inventory may decrease the cash account or increase short-term borrowing to support the working capital requirement. If the increased level of sales activity is permanent, then it should result in a larger investment in cash and short-term securities to provide adequate liquidity in the business to match the new sales levels. Increases in noncash current assets must be supported by reducing cash and by increasing debt and other liabilities. Conversely, a sales decrease should cause a corresponding decrease in current asset accounts, although inventory may increase in the short term while production schedules are adjusted to reflect the lower sales level.

B. Changes in Current Liabilities

A decrease in A/P results in a decrease in cash or an increase in debt to pay off the accounts, because decreases in current liabilities must be offset by decreases in an asset account or increases in other liability accounts. For example, a larger volume of sales activity typically requires a higher volume of materials purchased. If these materials are purchased on vendor credit, then the A/P account increases. Likewise, the additional labor expenses associated with increased production would increase the accrued wages account. A tax increase due to a higher level of taxable income also would increase the accrued taxes account. On the other hand, a decrease in sales activity should cause corresponding decreases in these accounts.

C. External Financing Requirements

As current asset accounts increase, the need for working capital normally increases. Further, as the company generates additional profits, the retained earnings account increases. If the need for working capital exceeds the increase in funds generated by additional profits, the difference must be financed. Therefore, the total of net increases in current asset accounts represents the total amount of financing necessary to fund working capital, assuming cash flows do not change due to fluctuations in long-term assets or liabilities.

Suppose that a firm has annual sales of $20 million, A/R of $2 million, inventory of $3 million, and A/P of $1 million. The firm has $5 million of current assets (A/R and inventory) that must be financed. A/P provides $1 million of the required financing, but the remaining $4 million must be financed through debt and/or equity. Now suppose that annual sales increase to $30 million, and A/R, inventory, and A/P remain a constant percentage of sales. A/R will increase to $3 million and inventory will increase to $4.5 million, for a total of $7.5 million. This represents an increase of $2.5 million in required financing. A/P will increase to $1.5 million, providing increased financing of $0.5 million. The increase in sales therefore requires an additional $2.5 million in current assets, and $0.5 million of additional financing is provided by an increase in A/P. The firm will need to raise an additional $2 million in external financing (debt and/or equity) to support the increase in sales.

If current asset accounts decrease, funds have been released from investments in A/R and/or inventory, so the overall need for short-term liabilities to support current assets declines. If, however, there is a more-than-corresponding decline in non-interest-bearing current liabilities (e.g., A/P, and wages and taxes payable), then additional short- and/or long-term debt must support the current assets.

V. WORKING CAPITAL INVESTMENT AND FINANCING STRATEGIES

A treasury professional must establish a framework that addresses (1) the appropriate level of working capital and (2) the methods required to finance that level of working capital. Both decisions are related and should be made concurrently. The following sections address considerations surrounding how much to invest in working capital and how much working capital to finance.

A. Current Asset Investment Strategies

The appropriate investment in current assets should reflect the firm's operating needs and management's risk tolerance, with consideration given to industry practices. Two prominent current asset investment strategies include the restrictive and relaxed strategies.

1. RESTRICTIVE CURRENT ASSET INVESTMENT STRATEGY

Under a restrictive current asset investment strategy, management maintains low levels of current assets relative to sales. Inventory is managed as tightly as possible, and a restrictive credit policy enables reduced A/R. Likewise, cash holdings are reduced.

In general, a restrictive current asset investment strategy entails higher potential profitability, due to lower borrowing costs and lost interest on cash holdings. However, this strategy also implies more risk, as the firm will be more prone to:

- Face inventory stock-outs
- Turn down acceptable credit risks
- Run out of cash

Accordingly, a restrictive strategy is a more volatile strategy.

2. RELAXED CURRENT ASSET INVESTMENT STRATEGY

A relaxed current asset investment strategy is the inverse of the restrictive strategy. With a relaxed strategy, management maintains high levels of current assets relative to sales. Typically, this higher level of current assets occurs due to higher cash holdings and more liberal inventory and credit policies. While this larger investment in current assets is likely to lower investment returns, the firm operates with less risk.

3. SELECTING A CURRENT ASSET INVESTMENT STRATEGY

The appropriate current asset investment strategy depends upon management's risk tolerance. Likewise, the demands of the firm's creditors are also important. Creditors will likely account for the firm's current asset investment strategy when extending credit and when pricing the cost of credit (i.e., setting the interest rate).

A company's current asset strategy may also be influenced by industry practices. In industries with high gross profit margins on sales, a liberal credit policy may offer substantial benefits, especially if the potential for additional profit greatly outweighs potential costs. This observation assumes that profits gained from additional sales exceed the costs of carrying the additional receivables and any additional bad debt costs.

B. Current Asset Financing Strategies

Decisions on how to finance permanent and fluctuating current assets define the working capital financing strategy. While it may seem strange to talk about permanent current assets, the concept is important when considering financing. For a given firm, there will be a certain minimum amount of current assets that it must have to do business. This number will vary by company and industry, but one way of identifying it is to examine the balance sheet and determine the lowest amount of current assets that a given company has had in the past several years. This base is considered *permanent current assets* and anything over that amount is considered *fluctuating current assets*. It is then reasonable to use long-term debt to finance the permanent current assets.

Next, management must decide on how to finance the fluctuating current assets. Short-term debt, with an original maturity of less than one year (e.g., a line of credit), enables a firm to adjust the amount of financing to the fluctuation in current assets so it never has excess financing and never pays interest unnecessarily. On the other hand, if a multiyear revolving credit agreement (i.e., a revolver) cannot be obtained, then the line of credit must be renewed annually. Longer-term debt guarantees financing during those years. Under these conditions, however, excess financing and unnecessary interest expense may arise.

The choice of financing depends on management's risk orientation, but it also is influenced by interest rate differentials among short-, intermediate-, or long-term debt. A treasury professional must know whether it is less expensive to borrow from the money markets or banks, or to lock in an intermediate- or long-term rate by obtaining a term loan or accessing funds via capital markets.

Approaches to the financing decision may be classified as *maturity matching, conservative,* and *aggressive*. These policy approaches are shown in Exhibit 10.6. The top bar in the exhibit partitions current assets into permanent and fluctuating categories. The remaining bars depict the mix of short- and long-term financing associated with the three strategies. Depending on current interest rates, the forecast of future rates, and especially management's risk tolerance, any of these approaches may be appropriate at a particular time.

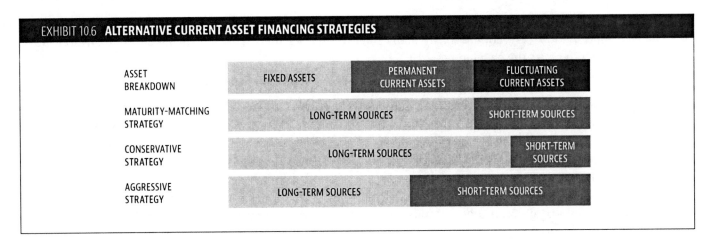

EXHIBIT 10.6 **ALTERNATIVE CURRENT ASSET FINANCING STRATEGIES**

1. MATURITY-MATCHING FINANCING STRATEGY

Under a maturity-matching financing strategy, the total of permanent current assets and fixed assets are financed with long-term financing (e.g., debt and equity). Short-term financing is used to finance fluctuating current assets. This means that the amount of short-term financing mirrors the level of fluctuating current assets at that time. This is the intention when financing with a line of credit. As fluctuating assets expand, drawing on the line increases to support that expansion. When the assets decline, funds are released and are used to pay down the line of credit.

2. CONSERVATIVE FINANCING STRATEGY

Under a conservative financing strategy, long-term financing supports fixed assets, permanent current assets, and some portion of fluctuating current assets. With this approach, it is common to finance the average level of fluctuating current assets with long-term sources. Short-term financing is used for the remainder of the fluctuating current assets. Since short-term financing is used for only a portion of the fluctuating current assets, this strategy generally involves the least use of short-term financing and, therefore, has higher financing costs than other approaches because long-term debt is carried when it is not needed.[5]

The relatively lower reliance on short-term financing results in a higher current ratio, but it also may result in lower profits because of increased interest expense. It is possible, however, that interest rate risk may be mitigated if long-term debt is borrowed on a fixed-rate basis and short-term financing is acquired on a floating- or variable-rate basis.

3. AGGRESSIVE FINANCING STRATEGY

Under an aggressive financing strategy, management finances all fixed assets with long-term debt and equity, but finances only a portion of permanent current assets with long-term financing. Short-term financing supports the remainder of permanent current assets and all of the fluctuating current assets. This strategy utilizes more ongoing short-term financing than other financing strategies.

Short-term financing typically costs less than long-term financing because the yield curve is generally upward sloping. Consequently, this strategy is often the most profitable because it is the least costly. However, the greater use of short-term financing results in greater liquidity risk, due to rollover or refinancing risk. The risk is associated

---

5. The higher financing costs result since there are times when the amount of funds borrowed on a long-term basis will exceed the required investment in fluctuating current assets. The excess amount will be invested in short-term investments and will most likely have a lower rate of return than the rate being paid on the long-term borrowing (assuming a normal yield curve).

with more volatile short-term interest rates and the need to renew credit frequently. In addition, if the lender has an annual "cleanup" period,[6] as is common with many short-term lines, management will need to find an alternative source of financing to cover the cleanup.

A poor business year could eventually occur due to a recession, a change in the firm's competitive environment, or other factors. When sales slump, inventory may not be converted into cash quickly enough to avert a cash shortage. Customers that normally pay on time may pay more slowly, causing a further drain on cash. The firm may find itself stretching its A/P beyond the credit term. Profit will decrease due to the sales slump and the profit-eroding influence of fixed operating expenses. Under this scenario, the firm needs to renew its short-term financing arrangement with its bank, but now the firm may appear to have more default risk. Thus, the bank may decide it must charge the firm a higher interest rate, but its analysis may reveal that the firm cannot support a higher interest payment. If the bank finds itself in a situation where it must ration credit among its customers, the firm may end up without financing at a critical moment.

4. SUMMARY OF INVESTING AND FINANCING STRATEGIES

Management that combines a restrictive current asset investment strategy with an aggressive financing policy may project increased profitability, but this is a risky strategy. Conversely, a relaxed current asset investment strategy combined with a conservative financing strategy may be excessively liquid, and thus be less profitable than it needs to be. Additionally, firms with large cash balances may be viewed as takeover targets by investors that are more interested in the value of the liquid assets than the operating value of the company itself. The overall decision involves trade-offs that need to be weighed in light of management's tolerance for risk, sales stability and predictability, lender concerns, the interest rate environment, the availability of funds, supplier reliability, and industry practices.

VI. MANAGEMENT OF TRADE CREDIT AND ACCOUNTS RECEIVABLE (A/R)

Trade credit is a contractual arrangement that allows a customer to immediately take possession of a good, product, or service and pay for it later. In turn, the seller receives a promise of future payment from the buyer. Payment is due per the agreed-upon trade credit terms extended to the customer by the seller. Sales made on trade credit terms create an A/R.

The primary reason for offering trade credit is to increase sales. Since most sales are made on an open account basis and many customers do not have access to other sources of financing, competition for customers usually requires that a selling firm grant trade credit. This is especially true in industries where credit extension is the norm. Credit terms are designed to lure customers away from competitors and to encourage existing customers to increase purchases. A liberal credit policy can increase sales, but it also increases account servicing costs, collection costs, and bad debt expense.

This section describes:

- The relationship between treasury and credit management
- Trade credit policies
- Forms of credit extension
- Accounts receivable management

---

6. Many lenders require their short-term borrowers to completely pay off or "clean up" the outstanding balance on an operating line of credit at least once a year to prove that the line is not really being used for long-term financing. Further details are discussed in Chapter 13, Short-Term Investing and Borrowing.

- Cash application
- Considerations pertaining to terms of sale
- Financing of A/R

A. Relationship between Treasury and Credit Management

In most firms, the treasury and credit management functions are separated. However, maintaining a good working relationship with departments and employees involved in credit management is important for treasury—especially because credit policies and A/R collection significantly impact the timing of cash inflows.

The credit manager administers policies that establish credit standards, defines the terms of trade credit extension, approves customers for credit sales, and sets individual and aggregate credit limits within policy guidelines. Since credit is used as a tool to increase sales, the credit manager usually works closely with the sales manager.

A/R is created once a sale is made and trade credit is extended. A/R management includes billing, posting remittance information, monitoring payment patterns, and collecting delinquent accounts. These duties typically fall under the responsibility of the credit manager. However, credit management and A/R management are sometimes outsourced to captive finance companies and/or factors. In either case, it is important that trade terms are negotiated and clearly established during the customer onboarding process. Failure to do so typically leads to collection problems and increased days' receivables.

B. Trade Credit Policies

To ensure consistent application and fairness, trade credit policies and procedures should clearly define the firm's:

- Credit standards
- Credit terms
- Customer discounts
- Methods of monitoring financial distress
- Collection policies

1. TRADE CREDIT STANDARDS

Establishing trade credit standards is a two-stage process. First, the credit acceptance criteria must be established to determine the maximum amount of acceptable payment risk. Second, the credit limit for each applicant must be determined.

There are two key considerations when determining credit extension policies:

- If credit standards are too strict, then potentially good customers may be lost.
- If credit standards are too lenient, then the firm may take on unacceptable credit risks.

Quantifying the costs of these risk considerations is difficult. However, credit is a sales tool and a zero default rate probably means that credit terms are too strict.

a. Information Sources

Management must consider the type, quantity, and cost of information when establishing a method for analyzing credit requests. Credit information is gathered in stages from internal and external sources. At each stage, costs are weighed against expected benefits. The most important sources of internally generated credit information include the credit application (agreement) completed by the applicant, and the firm's records regarding the applicant's payment history.

Various external sources can be used to help determine the applicant's creditworthiness. One primary source is an applicant's financial statements. Both audited and unaudited financial statements provide important information about corporate credit applicants as these statements can be compared to industry averages.

Trade references, or other suppliers from whom the applicant has purchased on credit, can provide a secondary source of information about the applicant's payment performance. Additionally, banks or other financial creditors (e.g., commercial finance or leasing companies) can provide standardized credit information about an applicant's payment history and available credit. Finally, there are various local and nationwide credit rating agencies that collect, evaluate, and report information about companies' credit histories. These credit reports include information such as payment history, financial information, maximum outstanding credit amounts, the length of time credit has been available, and any outstanding collection actions. Payment experience is provided to the rating agencies on a voluntary basis. That said, the sample used by the rating agency may be small and/or inaccurately represent the applicant's overall payment history.

b. The Five Cs of Credit

Credit analysis depends upon the type of information available and the trade-offs between the costs and benefits of the analysis. The traditional factors that lenders consider are known as the *five Cs of credit*, which include:

- **Character:** This is the perceived honesty or integrity of a borrower. Character indicates an intent or willingness to pay, as evidenced by personal or corporate payment history.
- **Capacity:** This represents the borrower's current and future financial resources that are available to repay obligations when due. This factor can be assessed using financial liquidity ratios and cash flow forecasts.
- **Capital:** This factor refers to the borrower's short- and long-term financial resources that could be accessed if the immediate cash flow is insufficient to meet payment obligations.
- **Collateral:** This identifies available assets or guarantees used to secure an obligation in the event that payment terms are not met.
- **Conditions:** This factor assesses the general, existing macroeconomic environment that impacts a borrower's ability to pay or the willingness of a lender to grant credit.

c. Quantitative Credit Analysis

The quantitative analysis of business credit information begins with an examination of a credit applicant's financial statements, usually using ratio analysis. The measures most often used include:

- Liquidity and working capital ratios (e.g., the current, quick, and cash flow to total debt ratios)
- Debt management and coverage ratios (e.g., times interest earned, long-term debt to capital, debt to total assets, and total liabilities to total assets ratios)
- Profitability measures (e.g., return on sales, return on assets, and return on equity)

Ratios provide valuable insight when evaluated in relation to industry and country standards published by credit rating agencies and other associations. Some commercial credit analysis involves credit scoring, which is evaluated by purchasing credit reports from third-party companies or by generating credit scores based on either internal or external databases.

In the consumer sector, quantitative credit scoring models are used extensively by major issuers of retail credit, such as department stores. Credit scoring involves a four-step process:

- Differentiating standard and high-risk accounts based on the applicant's monthly income, outstanding obligations, and employment history

- Weighting the characteristics of applicants that fit into each category to establish creditworthiness

- Setting cutoff scores for clear approval or denial of credit

- Applying further analysis to applicants whose scores fall between the cutoff points

These quantitative approaches are cost-effective and aid in complying with consumer credit legislation. A formal statistical method termed *discriminant analysis* can identify factors that effectively distinguish between paying and nonpaying customers, sometimes on a region-by-region basis. Consumer credit bureaus also assess creditworthiness based on proprietary models.

In business-to-business (B2B) transactions, quantitative credit scoring models[7] are becoming increasingly common, but are still not as widespread as in the consumer sector. There are several reasons for this, including the following:

- The available databases for building commercial credit scoring models are much smaller than those used for consumer models. This makes it more difficult to develop reliable models.

- The per-transaction exposure is usually much larger in the commercial sector than in the consumer sector. While a default by one large commercial customer could have a serious impact on a small seller, this is rarely the case in the consumer sector.

- It is sometimes difficult to obtain financial information for some customers, especially for smaller, private companies.

2. CREDIT TERMS

Establishing credit terms involves designing sales contracts or agreements that clearly specify under what conditions credit terms are granted. Creating collection policies involves determining the steps involved to collect delinquent accounts or bad debts.

A selling firm also must determine the aggregate amount of credit (i.e., the credit limit) to grant to each customer. New customers are usually granted credit at the lowest limit. After a period of satisfactory payment performance, credit limits increase. A customer's payment history is frequently reviewed in order to adjust these limits as necessary.

a. Credit Policy Constraints

A number of factors may constrain or influence a firm's credit policies. In many industries, credit terms and policies are based on industry standard practices. As a result, it is difficult for a company to vary its terms from those of its competitors. A company also must consider how offering trade credit may impact existing loan covenants. A change in A/R balances can affect working capital ratios, potentially resulting in failing to comply with covenants. There are also legal constraints that can vary significantly from country to country or even within a country.

---

7. An example of a B2B quantitative credit scoring model would be the Altman Z-Score (developed by Professor Edward Altman of New York University's Stern School of Business), which uses publicly available data to predict the probability that a publicly traded company will go bankrupt.

b. Financing Implications

A firm's credit terms, sales, and collection patterns determine its level of A/R. Since A/R must be financed, a firm's ability to extend credit relates directly to its ability to borrow. Mismanagement of receivables can cause liquidity problems due to delayed customer payments. However, A/R also may be a source of liquidity when used as collateral for asset-based loans, when used to securitize a debt instrument, or when sold for cash to factors. Factoring is discussed in more detail later in this chapter.

c. Income and Expenses Related to Granting Credit

Trade credit may increase a firm's income because the extension of credit increases sales. Another potential source of income arising from credit sales is interest earned from installment payment arrangements. This interest can be a significant source of profit, especially for retailers that provide direct financing to customers through their own private-label credit cards or installment contracts.

In addition to interest earned from credit sales, firms may assess a penalty fee for payments received after the due date. This fee is usually a percentage of the amount past due and must be stated clearly at the time of the sale and disclosed on the invoice.[8]

Further, there are costs associated with offering trade credit. On the expense side, the primary costs of A/R are carrying costs. This cost is typically the short-term borrowing cost or the weighted average cost of capital (WACC). Other costs refer to the expenses of operating and maintaining a credit department. Personnel costs, data and payment processing costs, and costs related to credit evaluation or obtaining credit information (if a third-party credit bureau is used) are all expenses associated with a credit department. These costs must be weighed against the cost of bad debt, which can be a significant element of A/R cost if not properly managed.

3. CUSTOMER DISCOUNTS

If a seller offers discount terms, then the "cost" of discounted payments affects income. If customers take advantage of the discount, but the discount offer does not produce a general increase in sales, then net revenue declines. The revenue loss may be fully or partially offset by a reduction in A/R carrying costs. Dynamic discounting takes traditional trade discounts a step further and includes the ability to vary the discount according to the date of early payment; the earlier the payment, the larger the discount. Finally, if discounts are offered, the company must determine a benchmark eligibility date. This can be the postmark date of the payment remittance or the date funds are received.

4. PAYMENT DISCREPANCIES

Payment discrepancies often arise from corporate customers paying multiple invoices—each with possible adjustments—with a single payment. The costs associated with monitoring, investigating, and resolving discrepancies between invoices and customer payments can be substantial. Discrepancies must be investigated, the legitimacy of shortfalls and deductions must be ascertained, and all related bookkeeping, invoicing, and payment adjustments must be recorded. Some customers may also use these discrepancies as a reason to delay payment, thus effectively increasing their credit period.

8. Interest and the interest calculation must be disclosed in the sales contract or on the invoice to allow the seller to collect interest in a court of law. Without disclosure, the seller's ability to collect is not enforceable.

5. MONITORING FINANCIAL DISTRESS

It is critical to monitor each credit account over time for potential financial distress. As financial distress for a particular customer increases, so does the probability of slower payments or default on the account. This monitoring should involve the tracking of payments and level of credit outstanding, as well as monitoring news and press releases issued by the customer. In many cases, the potential for financial distress may appear in the news before the customer is late on its payments.

6. COLLECTION POLICY

Costs related to delinquent account monitoring and bad debt collection impact income. Though accounting conventions may vary somewhat, it is generally the case that uncollectible A/R must be charged off as bad debt. Most firms use historical collection patterns to estimate the level of losses, and create a reserve account through periodic charges to bad debt expense. The timing and volume of bad debt expense and charge-offs are important aspects of a credit policy.

The cost of collecting delinquent accounts can be significant. Management can reduce the impact of bad debts by purchasing various types of insurance designed to cover receivables losses. Insurance premiums should be included in the cost/benefit analysis when assessing the potential profitability of credit sales.

C. Forms of Credit Extension

There are four basic forms of credit extension: open account or open book credit, installment credit, revolving credit, and letter of credit.

- **Open Account:** Open account, sometimes called *open book credit*, is the most common type of commercial trade credit. A seller issues an invoice as formal evidence of the obligation and records the sale as an A/R. The buyer is billed for each transaction by an invoice and/or monthly statement. Full payment of invoiced amounts is expected within the specified credit terms unless certain discounts or deductions are available to the buyer. A buyer's creditworthiness is reviewed periodically, but the buyer does not need to apply for credit each time it places an order.

- **Installment Credit:** Installment credit requires a customer to make equal periodic payments, each of which contains principal and interest components. Installment credit is used frequently for the purchase of high-value consumer durables, such as automobiles. Installment credit is liquidating, in that normal payments will eventually pay off the balance of the account over time. The seller requires the buyer to sign a contract, which specifies the credit terms of the obligation, discloses the interest rate, and lists all other costs.

- **Revolving Credit:** Under revolving credit terms, a seller grants credit without requiring specific transaction approval, as long as the account remains current. An account usually is considered current if the credit outstanding is below an established credit limit and minimum payments are made on time. If the account is not paid in full by the due date, an interest charge is calculated based on the average amount outstanding over the entire period. Unlike installment credit, revolving credit is not automatically liquidating, as new purchases are added to the balance even as payments for older purchases are received and processed.

- **Letter of Credit (L/C):** The most complex form of credit extension is a commercial L/C. With an L/C, a financial institution guarantees payment on behalf of the purchaser. L/Cs are most commonly used in import/export transactions.

D. A/R Management

The major objective of A/R management is to quickly convert A/R into cash, while minimizing collection expense and bad debt losses. The type of credit offered significantly impacts the collection method employed. Metrics for monitoring A/R balances and payment patterns are covered in the next chapter.

Effective A/R management includes reducing invoicing float, which is the interval between the time goods and services are sold to a customer and the time that a customer receives an invoice. The first step in collecting an account is sending accurate and timely invoices with clearly stated payment terms and remittance instructions. Delays in invoice preparation or errors on an invoice may extend the payment process. This is particularly an issue with customers that use "auto-match" processes that validate invoices against purchase orders and receiving statements (referred to as a *three-way match*) to authorize payment of invoices. Minor errors in an invoice can lead to lengthy delays in payment as a result. Sometimes, sellers send summary statements of outstanding invoices as a reminder that payment is due. Consumer billing typically involves sending statements listing goods or services purchased during the preceding month.

Electronic bill presentment and payment (EBPP) and electronic invoice presentment and payment (EIPP) are e-commerce tools that are increasingly being used to reduce invoice and payment float and improve overall collections.

When payment is not received by the due date, a seller can:

- Send a duplicate invoice, or mail a form letter or a series of form letters (i.e., dunning letters)
- Call the customer or pay a personal visit
- Suspend further shipment of goods or terminate services until past-due items are paid
- Negotiate with the customer for payment of overdue amounts

All of these measures are typically employed as collection efforts escalate. Once these methods are exhausted, the seller may pursue more serious actions, such as reporting the customer's delinquent status to credit bureaus, repossessing collateral, negotiating additional corporate or personal guarantees, obtaining a lien on specific assets, initiating direct legal action, or turning delinquent accounts over to a collection agency.

E. Cash Application

Cash application is the process of applying a customer's payment against outstanding invoices or receivables. This process occurs via an open item or a balance-forward system.

1. OPEN ITEM SYSTEM

An open item system is most commonly used in B2B sales. Each invoice sent is recorded in the A/R file. When a payment is received, it is matched with the specific invoices being paid. Any payment discrepancies are noted (e.g., discounts, allowances, adjustments, or returns). Remittance information, which typically accompanies payments, indicates the invoices that are being paid, as well as any adjustments to the payment. This application process may be manual, automated, or a combination of both. Most open accounts are cleared using the open item system.

Automated cash application programs take the payment and remittance information and, using a series of algorithms, apply the payments by matching them to specific invoices. These algorithms also determine the priority by which invoices are credited in the event of partial payments, which can have an impact on penalties and fees for overdue accounts. A high rate of successful, automated applications greatly reduces the manual effort required to complete the cash application process.

2. BALANCE-FORWARD SYSTEM

A balance-forward system is used most often by firms selling goods and services to individual consumers. A credit limit is established for each individual. A/R outstanding balances increase as purchases are made or services are provided. Similarly, A/R balances decrease as payments are received, but payments are not matched to specific purchases. The balance-forward system is most common in revolving credit situations, such as retail credit cards.

F. Considerations Pertaining to Terms of Sale

Buyers and sellers may choose from a variety of standard sales terms that are often specified in sales agreements, invoices, and other legal or commercial documents.

1. COMMON TERMS OF SALE

The most common sales terms are:

- **Cash before Delivery (CBD):** CBD terms, sometimes referred to as *prepayment terms*, require the buyer to make full and final payment before the shipment or receipt of goods. In business-to-consumer (B2C) sales, CBD is used frequently for catalog, telephone, or Internet transactions. In B2B sales, CBD is used when the seller does not know the buyer or when the seller considers the buyer a greater credit risk than the seller is willing to accept. A variation of this is to require a substantial prepayment of the sale prior to delivery, with the balance collected at some future date. While not as risk-free as CBD, it does reduce the potential for eventual bad debt.

- **Cash on Delivery (COD):** The seller ships the goods and the buyer pays upon receipt. If the buyer refuses to pay, the goods are returned and the seller must pay the shipping and handling costs.

- **Cash Terms:** The buyer generally has 7 to 10 days to make payment. Cash terms are used frequently in the sale of perishable items or in cases where the buyer has not established a credit history with the seller.

- **Net Terms:** The seller specifies a net due date by which the buyer must pay in full. For example, terms of net 30 require the buyer to pay within 30 days from the date of invoice, date of delivery, or some other specified date.

- **Discount Terms:** In addition to specifying a net due date, the seller may offer a discount on payments made prior to that date. Terms of 2/10 net 30 mean that the total amount is due within 30 days of the invoice date, but the buyer can take a 2% discount if it pays within 10 days.

- **Monthly Billing:** The seller issues a monthly statement covering all invoices prior to a cutoff date, typically toward the end of each month. If the seller extends proximo (or *prox*, meaning *in the following month*) payment terms, then the buyer must pay by a specified date during the following month. The seller may offer the buyer a discount for prompt payment. For example, if the terms are 1/10 prox 30, the buyer may take a discount of 1% if payment is made by the 10th day of the following month. However, the total due must be paid by the 30th day of the following month.

- **Draft/Bill of Lading:** Also known as a *documentary collection*, this credit term lets sellers collect payments through banking channels. Documentary collection is more common in international than domestic trade. The seller ships the goods to the buyer and sends the shipping and title documents to a bank, which transmits the documents to the buyer's bank. The buyer gains possession of the documents and thus ownership of the goods upon paying the bank or upon signing a draft agreeing to pay at a future date. Upon collection, the buyer's bank remits payment to the seller's bank. Note that a documentary collection is not guaranteed by the bank.

· **Seasonal Dating:** The seller agrees to accept payment at the end of the buyer's selling season. This lets a manufacturer provide short-term financing for a buyer's purchases and reduces the manufacturer's inventory costs. It is common in industries with distinct seasonality of sales, such as toys, greeting cards, garden supplies, sporting goods, or textbooks. Since the time between when goods are shipped to the buyer and when payment is received can be lengthy, the seller may offer a series of discounts to encourage the buyer to pay early.

· **Consignment:** Under a consignment agreement, the supplier (sometimes referred to as the *consignor*) ships goods to another party (sometimes referred to as the *consignee*) who has no obligation to pay until the goods have been sold. The supplier retains title to the goods until they are sold, at which time title is transferred to the ultimate buyer. The consignee will then deduct any commission or fees and forward the remainder to the supplier.

2. OFFERING DISCOUNTS

When offering cash discounts, the seller must evaluate the costs versus the benefits gained from receiving early payments. Standard practice involves using the gross or net method for discounted sales. Under the gross method, gross revenues are recorded on the income statement and in receivables, and discounts are recorded as an expense. In the net method, net revenues are recorded on the income statement and in receivables. Any discounts not taken are shown as income.

G. Financing A/R

Unsecured borrowing is a popular way to finance A/R. Alternatively, the supplier may pledge A/R as collateral and borrow on a secured basis. Commonly referred to as *asset-based lending*, this financing method is based on the quality of the receivables. A lender evaluates the A/R to determine those acceptable as collateral for a loan, which is repaid as the company collects the A/R. A related alternative is supply chain financing, which is discussed below in inventory financing, as it applies to both inventory and A/R for specific trading partners.

Large firms—particularly those with finance subsidiaries, such as mortgage, automobile, and credit card companies—bundle and issue securities backed by receivables in a process called *securitization*. Securitization is a financing method that frees up capital and enhances creditworthiness by using the buyer's installment payments to pay off the securitized instrument's principal and interest. A variation of this practice is the actual sale of the A/R to an intermediary financial institution who packages the accounts and securitizes them.

Some firms establish a wholly owned subsidiary known as a *captive finance company* to perform credit operations and obtain A/R financing for the sale of products. Since A/R represents a significant proportion of current assets, operating a captive finance company enhances the parent's liquidity and provides access to capital at a lower cost.

Third-party financing is another option, in which a selling firm collects the information necessary to complete a credit application from a customer and forwards it to a financial institution. The financial institution decides whether to grant credit. Due to the administrative costs involved, firms using third-party financing tend to manufacture and market big-ticket items, such as production machinery. Although third-party financing frees up capital, it does mean the seller relinquishes control over the credit-granting decision and forgoes direct marketing opportunities. It also means the seller may have to discount the price of goods sold to compensate the third party, thus forgoing potential income.

1. CARD PAYMENTS

Card payments are fairly common in consumer or retail transactions. Increasingly, suppliers are accepting cards as payment for goods and services from commercial customers. Typically, a supplier receives a payment, less fees, one to two business days following the transaction. The supplier may desire to be paid quickly in order to pay their own financial obligations (e.g., payroll). Fees charged by the acquiring banks, card network, and issuing bank will vary depending on the method of transmission (e.g., terminal, Internet, or paper), average size of the sale, total volume, type of card used (e.g., brand type, reward, corporate, foreign, or purchasing), and business or industry type.

The advantages of accepting credit cards rather than maintaining A/R in a B2B setting are as follows:

- The seller bears no direct costs of running a credit department.
- The seller does not have to finance A/R.
- Liability from customer bad debt shifts from the seller to the credit card issuer.
- Sales typically increase by making it easier for customers to charge purchases.
- The seller is paid more quickly—typically in one to two business days following the transaction.

The disadvantages of accepting credit cards include:

- The seller relinquishes control over the credit decision (e.g., the sale could be lost if the transaction is denied).
- The seller incurs discount costs and transaction fees.
- Charge-backs represent a business risk for the seller.
- There is an expense associated with maintaining compliance with credit card data security standards.

2. FACTORING

Factoring involves the outright sale of receivables to a factor, a firm that specializes in the financing and management of receivables. In most factoring arrangements, the buyer of the receivables has no recourse to the seller. *No recourse* or *without recourse* means that the factor must absorb the loss if a customer fails to pay. In some cases, however, the factoring arrangement stipulates that the factor has recourse, in which case the seller is liable for any bad debts the factor cannot collect. Most factoring is performed on a *notification* basis, meaning the seller must notify customers that the account has been sold because payment is remitted directly to the factor.

The primary benefit of factoring is that the seller can receive funds immediately upon completion of the factoring arrangement. The primary disadvantage is that the receivables will usually be sold at a significant discount. Where factoring is routinely used by a seller, the cost of this discount is usually incorporated into the sales price.

3. PRIVATE-LABEL FINANCING

In private-label financing, a third party operates the credit function in the seller's name rather than the seller administering a credit program in-house. From the customer's perspective, the credit appears to be arranged through the seller. Private-label financing lets sellers retain many of the promotional aspects of conducting credit functions while incurring none of the costs of maintaining a credit operation and/or financing A/R. However, the seller does not receive the full face value of the sale and may lose the authority to decide which customers receive credit.

VII. MANAGEMENT OF INVENTORY

The amount of inventory carried on the balance sheet impacts the firm's production and sales activities. The manner in which inventory is managed affects the length of the cash conversion cycle, the required liquidity level, and the cash flow forecast.

Although inventory management is generally the direct responsibility of marketing or manufacturing managers, treasury managers are responsible for obtaining inventory financing. The ability to use inventory as collateral for a loan is related directly to the type of inventory and how it is managed.

This section of the chapter describes the following:

- Benefits and costs of inventory
- Types of inventory
- Inventory management techniques
- Inventory financing alternatives

A. Benefits and Costs of Inventory

The primary benefit of inventory is to meet customer demand. Specifically, inventory helps shield suppliers from stock-out costs (e.g., lost sales due to a lack of sufficient inventory) that may arise from higher-than-expected customer demand or production problems throughout the supply chain. Consequently, inventory may provide a competitive advantage and increased customer goodwill. Further, inventory allows the holder to hedge potential price increases in required inputs.

Various costs also accompany inventory holdings. Specific costs include:

- **Holding Costs:** This component consists of physical storage and handling costs, insurance, taxes, and the opportunity cost of funds invested in inventory.

- **Obsolescence and Spoilage Costs:** *Obsolescence* refers to inventory that is no longer salable through normal channels because it is out of date or has been replaced with newer products. Obsolete inventory must either be written off or sold at a discount. *Spoilage* refers to inventory that is no longer salable due to damage or other defects that occur over time. Similar to obsolete inventory, spoiled inventory must eventually be disposed of through write-offs or through some form of discounted sale. Spoilage is distinct from scrap, which is a normal by-product of many manufacturing processes.

Generally, the objective of inventory management is to minimize the total costs associated with the inventory while meeting a desired level of production and/or customer service. Economic order quantity (EOQ) models are typically used to calculate the optimal level of inventory, given specified ordering and holding costs. However, EOQ models can be difficult to apply due to changing dynamics in the costs and benefits of inventory.

B. Types of Inventory

Most inventories are connected to the production process. Any item held in stock that links two or more production processes can also be thought of as inventory. Typical categories of inventory are described below:

- **Raw Materials:** Raw materials inventory represents the basic input to the manufacturing process and allows arrivals to be separated from production scheduling.

- **Work in Progress (WIP):** WIP inventory represents items or materials that are in the process of being manufactured. This type of inventory allows different phases of the production process to be separated. Further, WIP inventory also serves as a buffer between production stages with different processing speeds. The use and amount of WIP inventory is generally a function of the production process. A short, continuous process such as chemical production may have very little WIP, whereas a long batch-production process such as furniture manufacturing has a large level of WIP.

- **Finished Goods:** This type of inventory consists of completed items or materials available for sale. Finished goods allow a supplier to fill orders when received rather than depend upon product completion to satisfy customer demands. This allows firms to more easily manage highly variable or unpredictable demand levels, which is extremely valuable in a retail environment because it allows the retailer to maintain a wide variety of goods for customers. It is important to note a significant difference in the management of finished goods inventory for generic products versus customized products. Due to limited resale value, customized product inventories must be managed much more tightly than more generic, easily sold goods.

- **Scrap or Obsolete Items:** In industries such as steel and aluminum manufacturing, scrap from production can be reused in later batches or sold to recyclers. Also, a portion of inventory may become obsolete or damaged, especially in environments where there are rapid changes in existing products or introductions of new products. Obsolete or scrap inventories must be identified and dealt with independently. These inventories may be turned into cash through sales to scrap dealers or by taking tax deductions through write-offs.

- **Stores and Supplies:** Stores and supplies inventories are sometimes referred to as *indirect purchases*. These items are not used directly; rather, they support the production process. Examples include lubricating oils or maintenance materials for production machinery in a manufacturing business, or paper and other office supplies in a service business.

C. Inventory Management Techniques

Since excess inventory lowers profits, prudent inventory reduction is an ongoing management objective. Several techniques have been developed to reduce inventory, as described below.

One of the most popular inventory management approaches is the just-in-time (JIT) approach. This approach attempts to minimize inventory levels by reducing the costs or uncertainties that underlie the motives for holding inventory. The JIT methodology recognizes that excess inventory can be a liability rather than an asset. Therefore, JIT is not simply an inventory management system, but a production/business philosophy that treats inventory as being undesirable. Under this philosophy, excess inventory indicates poor inventory planning, poor inventory location and movement problems, inferior supplier quality, and/or unbalanced production processes. The unique demands of the JIT manufacturing environment have a major impact on a company's treasury and reporting functions, especially with respect to the information system for financial management.

Another technique is known as a *material planning system (MPS)*. With an MPS, a firm may negotiate arrangements with suppliers to provide a continuous level of production materials on short notice, resulting in reduced carrying costs for the raw materials used to create finished goods. JIT systems often are coupled with MPSs to bring together long-range production planning with the current flow of materials through the production process. Some retailers link point-of-sale (POS) equipment to suppliers so that specific merchandise sales can be tracked for automated reordering.

In supplier-managed replenishment programs, the supplier maintains and tracks the inventory of materials it provides to a customer. As the inventory is used, the supplier bills the customer for the items and replenishes the supply. Title to the product is transferred at the shipping dock. The rationale for this system is that the supplier can track trends in inventory usage and manage levels of inventory more efficiently, thus reducing costs for both the supplier and the customer.

The paid-on-production process is similar to supplier-managed replenishment programs, but has some specific implications for financial managers. Paid-on-production is the process by which a payment record is created for goods and/or services based on usage rather than shipment. It is similar to consignment sales in retail, but is employed in a manufacturing environment. Title to the product is transferred during the manufacturing process rather than at the shipping dock.

D. Inventory Financing Alternatives

Inventory financing alternatives include trade credit, supply chain financing, collateralized loans, asset-based loans, and floor planning.

Trade credit granted by suppliers is typically the least expensive financing alternative for inventory. This spontaneous source of financing varies with the level of inventory on hand. While some firms routinely delay payments to suppliers to extend the amount of financing provided, either because they cannot or chose not to pay on time, renegotiating appropriate trade credit terms is a better alternative. The opportunity cost of arbitrarily delaying trade payment is the cost of lost cash discounts, lost goodwill with suppliers, and lost sales due to delayed shipments. In many cases, suppliers refuse to ship additional products unless outstanding invoices are paid promptly. Such delays often cause production delays and sales problems, which can ultimately be more expensive than alternative methods of financing.

Supply chain financing is a related form of inventory lending where a seller receives financing based upon the existence of sales contracts and purchase orders with large, financially stable, trading partners. These types of programs are typically arranged for by the buyer rather than the seller and provide lower-cost loans based upon the buyer's credit rating and financial capabilities, rather than the seller's. The seller benefits by receiving a lower interest rate, and the buyer benefits by not having to directly finance the seller.

Collateralized loans are arranged using inventory as collateral for a loan, with the lender providing financing for some predetermined percentage of the inventory value. The buyer's cash flows are viewed as the primary repayment source, and inventory is viewed as a secondary repayment source. With this lending arrangement, a lien is placed on the inventory.

Another inventory financing alternative is an asset-based loan. Asset-based lending is based on the value of the inventory rather than the borrower's general financial strength. To enforce the claim on the inventory, the lender usually takes physical possession of it if defaults occurs. If this occurs, the lender may store the inventory at a public warehouse, which is a storage facility operated by an independent warehouse company on its own premises, or in a field warehouse rented by a company on another firm's premises. These warehouses are generally secure storage facilities where commodities, raw materials, or finished goods are held until a warehouse receipt is presented to claim them. In cases where the inventory directly supports a loan, a lender may release the materials only after the portion of the loan supported by inventory is paid.

Floor planning is a type of asset-based lending used for high-value durable goods, such as automobiles, trucks, or heavy equipment. Loans are made against each individual item, are recorded by serial number, and are not fully repaid until the item is sold. Floor plan lenders typically perform periodic inventory audits.[9]

VIII. MANAGEMENT OF ACCOUNTS PAYABLE (A/P)

A/P provides a major source of short-term financing for many firms. Both the treasury and A/P departments are involved with managing A/P. The treasury area generally oversees funding disbursement accounts and may manage the actual disbursement of payments. Meanwhile, an A/P manager's primary responsibility is to verify incoming invoices and authorize payments (i.e., vouchering). This process generally involves the traditional three-way match, in which an invoice is matched to both an approved purchase order, as well as to receiving and, in some cases, shipping information. This verification ensures that the items being billed are authorized purchases from an approved vendor and that all items are received in satisfactory condition. A three-way match will also reduce losses from invoice fraud, which occurs when false invoices are submitted or duplicate invoices are intentionally submitted for payment. The A/P function also monitors compliance with trade payment terms.

Once the approval process is complete, the invoice is vouchered for payment. In a typical B2B environment, multiple invoices are combined in a single payment. Once approved, the voucher is forwarded to the treasury manager or disbursements clerk who, in turn, generates payment.

There are two critical areas of coordination between treasury and A/P management. The first is the communication from A/P to treasury regarding the invoices vouchered for payment. The second is the communication from treasury back to A/P regarding the reconciliation of cleared items.

Firms with integrated enterprise resource planning (ERP) or accounting systems with treasury management modules often easily integrate these functions. However, many firms use either separate systems for disbursement management or treasury information software provided by banks. This software may not interface as easily with the A/P ledger. Customized interfaces or middleware (in a client-server environment) is required to facilitate the transfer of information between applications.

The net cost of making payments includes both opportunity costs and the administrative costs of managing A/P and disbursements processes.

This section describes:

· Disbursement system considerations
· Types of A/P and disbursement systems

A. Disbursement System Considerations

A disbursement system is a set of procedures that determines which parties may authorize payments, where and when the payments originate, how potential fraud is controlled, and how accounts are reconciled. In designing a disbursement system, an organization must keep several goals in mind:

· **Information Access:** Obtaining access to timely and accurate information regarding the status of disbursement accounts and disbursement clearings allows for more effective management of the cash position.

9. Depending on the lender, region, or industry, there may be requirements for interim payments on the loan if the item financed is not sold within some specified period of time.

- **Fraud Prevention:** Preventing fraud means protecting funds from unauthorized use, through written policies and internal controls, prompt bank reconciliation, and appropriate banking services (e.g., positive pay and debit blocks[10]).

- **Relationship Maintenance with Payees:** Maintaining good relationships with payees means ensuring timely payments to employees, vendors, suppliers, lenders, tax agencies, bondholders, and shareholders, as well as filing any necessary tax or other legal forms.

- **Timing of Payments:** While it is important to pay vendors in a timely fashion, it can be equally important that payments not be made before they are due. Scheduling of payments is an important function of any disbursement system. Making payments early reduces available working capital, while deferring payments increases working capital by maximizing trade credit.

B. Types of A/P and Disbursement Systems

A/P and disbursement systems may be centralized, decentralized, or a combination of both. Each system has distinct advantages and disadvantages in relation to the disbursement system goals just described.

1. CENTRALIZED A/P AND DISBURSEMENT SYSTEMS

- **Advantages:** In a centralized system, the A/P and disbursement functions are located in a single place—either at headquarters or at a centralized processing center. From this centralized location, a firm receives all inbound invoices, routes them to the appropriate area for approval, approves them for payment, issues payments, and funds and reconciles accounts. A centralized disbursement system makes it easier to maintain control, obtain information, concentrate excess cash, provide greater access to cash position information, and improve forecasting accuracy.

- **Disadvantages:** The principal disadvantage of a centralized A/P and disbursement system is its potentially negative impact on payee relationships. Centralized systems may result in delayed payments to vendors and suppliers and/or lost discount opportunities. Technology developments and improved access to information have reduced some of these problems. There is also a need for coordination between the central A/P department and the firm's field offices to resolve payment disputes.

2. DECENTRALIZED A/P AND DISBURSEMENT SYSTEMS

In a decentralized system, the A/P and disbursement functions are managed at the local or regional level. Field office managers approve invoices for payment, issue payments, and reconcile accounts. Additionally, payments are often made through a local or regional bank. Decentralized systems are often the result of mergers and acquisitions where the A/P and disbursement systems of the merging firms have not been combined.

- **Advantages:** This system gives greater autonomy to field office managers. As a result, the primary advantage is improved relationships with vendors and suppliers because items clear quickly and disputes can be resolved locally. In addition, it is easier to take advantage of discount terms that require payments to be made in a shorter time frame (typically 10 days).

- **Disadvantages:** The primary disadvantages of a decentralized system are the loss of control over information (possibly resulting in delayed payments); the lost opportunity to concentrate funds, reduce borrowing expenses, and increase investment returns; and the increased likelihood of unauthorized disbursements. Other disadvantages include the cost and complexity of redundant systems; loss of opportunities related to strategic sourcing and discounts; the increased possibility of excess or idle balances at the local bank level; increased

---

10. Positive pay and other fraud prevention tools are covered in more detail in Chapter 12, Disbursements, Collections, and Concentration.

difficulty in obtaining information about the daily cash position and cash outflows; difficulty in determining overall spend by vendor type; and increased transfer, reconciliation, and administrative costs.

3. DECENTRALIZED A/P AND DISBURSEMENT SYSTEMS WITH CENTRALIZED CLEARING

The advent of enterprise-wide software packages with distributed access and data entry has created the ability for some companies to use a hybrid system in which local or regional managers oversee the A/P process and authorize payments at a local level, but the actual disbursement of payments is managed centrally and drawn on a centralized disbursement bank.

In this type of system, invoices can be received and processed locally as well as at a common A/P processing location. This ability reduces the time lag required to send locally received invoices to a central A/P site for processing or to send centrally received invoices to local managers for approval. The distributed input capability, often coupled with workflow management software, allows managers to track and approve invoices as desired and ensures that all required approvals are received before an invoice is paid.

Disbursements are made by a central A/P system, which can generate payments from a central bank account or from subsidiary accounts as necessary. Payments can be made by any payment method desired, whether electronic or paper. The addition of remote printing capabilities makes it possible to actually print checks at local offices if needed or desired. Some companies take this process a step further and outsource the actual disbursement of payments using products such as integrated payables or shared services centers. This approach provides increased control along with reduced excess balances, improved cash position reporting and forecasting, and increased opportunities for volume discounts on bank disbursement services.

IX. MULTINATIONAL WORKING CAPITAL MANAGEMENT TOOLS

The previous sections have described general topics related to working capital management. Meanwhile, this section focuses on tools for multinational working capital management. Globalization motivates the coverage of these topics. Specific topics covered include:

- Multicurrency accounts
- Netting (bilateral and multilateral)
- Leading and lagging
- Re-invoicing
- Internal factoring
- In-house banking
- Export financing

A. Multicurrency Accounts

A multicurrency account is a special arrangement in which a bank allows a firm to receive or make payments in a range of currencies. A multicurrency agreement generally specifies four stipulations:

- The base currency in which the account is denominated
- The portfolio of currencies accepted
- The spread or margin over the spot rate to use in exchanging each currency back to the base currency
- The value date to apply to debits and credits for each transaction type and currency

Multicurrency accounts simplify multinational working capital management by allowing the firm to make and receive payments in a variety of currencies without having to worry about the associated foreign exchange (FX) implications.

B. Netting

Netting is a type of payables system that reduces the number of cross-border payments among the firm's units through the elimination or consolidation of funds denominated in different currencies.[11] This enhances "natural" hedging. Some countries impose restrictions on the use of netting systems due to their tax consequences; hence, central bank or government approval often is required.

Two distinct types of netting are bilateral netting and multilateral netting. Both are described below.

1. BILATERAL NETTING

In a bilateral netting system, purchases between two subsidiaries of the same firm are periodically netted against each other so that only the net difference is transferred. If the payments are in different currencies, then the total due to each subsidiary is converted to a common currency, usually that of the receiving country, to determine the net amount due.

As an example of bilateral netting, if one subsidiary of a multinational firm is located in France and another is located in the United Kingdom, then the payments are held until one or two regularly scheduled times during the month. Prior to a settlement date, payment flows in both directions are totaled and the net amount due to one of the subsidiaries is made available with a single transfer. The firm should hedge any material FX exposure that exists after netting.

2. MULTILATERAL NETTING

A multilateral netting system is similar to a bilateral system, but it involves more than two subsidiaries. Each subsidiary informs a central treasury management center of all planned cross-border payments through an electronic system. To determine netting transactions, payments between the subsidiaries are converted into a common currency and combined into a few larger transactions. Each unit is informed of the net amount owed or due in advance of the settlement date, and the central treasury management center makes the necessary FX conversions. Multilateral netting is used primarily for intercompany transactions between subsidiaries, but some firm's netting processes also include third-party payments and receipts. The mechanics of multilateral netting are illustrated in Exhibit 10.7.

11. Because the firm's units are usually separate legal entities, netting is considered an intercompany payables system.

EXHIBIT 10.7 MULTILATERAL NETTING

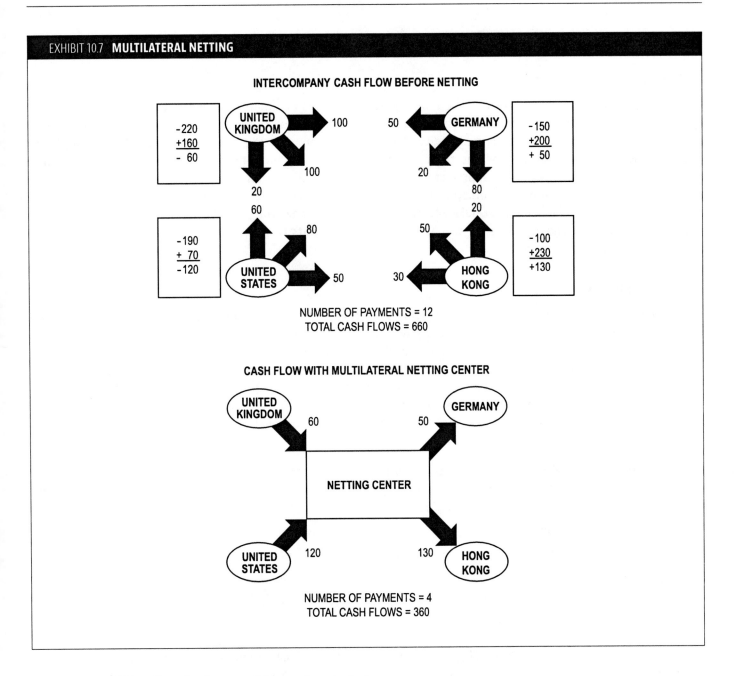

Three principal benefits of using a netting system include:

· A reduction in the number of FX transactions and cross-border wire transfers, and the resulting benefits from natural hedging

· More favorable FX rates due to the potential for larger FX trades resulting from consolidation

· Improved cash and currency exposure forecasting for both the subsidiary and the parent company as a result of the ability to preplan cross-border payments

The costs of netting, which include setup, administration, and maintenance expenses, must also be considered.

C. Leading and Lagging

Netting systems may be used to lead and lag payments. Leading and lagging involve executing cross-border payments between subsidiaries before the scheduled payment date (leading) or after the scheduled payment date (lagging). In both leading and lagging, liquidity is shifted from one subsidiary to another. Leading is employed when a subsidiary's currency is expected to depreciate relative to the parent's currency. Lagging is used when a subsidiary's currency is expected to appreciate relative to the parent's currency. For example, if a firm whose base currency is the euro has a subsidiary in Japan and expects the yen to depreciate in the near future, it will speed up (lead) payments from its Japanese subsidiary to avoid the depreciation in the yen. Likewise, if the same firm expects the yen to appreciate against the euro, it may delay (lag) payments from its Japanese subsidiary to collect the benefits of the gain in the yen.

D. Re-invoicing

Re-invoicing is a method of centralizing the responsibility for monitoring and collecting international A/R to more effectively manage related FX exposures. A re-invoicing center is a company-owned subsidiary that purchases goods from an exporting subsidiary and sells the goods to an importing subsidiary. The exporting unit invoices and receives funds from the re-invoicing subsidiary in its own currency, and the importing unit is invoiced and pays funds to the re-invoicing subsidiary in its own currency. Although the title to the goods passes through the re-invoicing center, the actual goods usually are shipped directly from the exporting subsidiary to the importing subsidiary. Establishing a re-invoicing center requires local government and tax approval, and negotiations with tax authorities in all involved countries to determine how the subsidiary is taxed.

One of the primary benefits of a re-invoicing center is the centralization of FX exposures, which allows for more effective financial risk management. The re-invoicing center also improves liquidity management by providing flexibility in inter-subsidiary payments. In addition, re-invoicing:

- Eases the implementation of leading and lagging arrangements
- Improves export trade financing and collections
- Reduces banking fees
- Minimizes FX risk and obtains advantaged FX rates by enabling larger trades
- Reduces payment costs

It is particularly beneficial to have the ability to set worldwide international pricing, but this practice may be regulated heavily by foreign taxation authorities. Major costs include the associated administrative costs as well as re-invoicing center expenses, which are incurred primarily when establishing a physical location. Re-invoicing is illustrated in Exhibit 10.8.

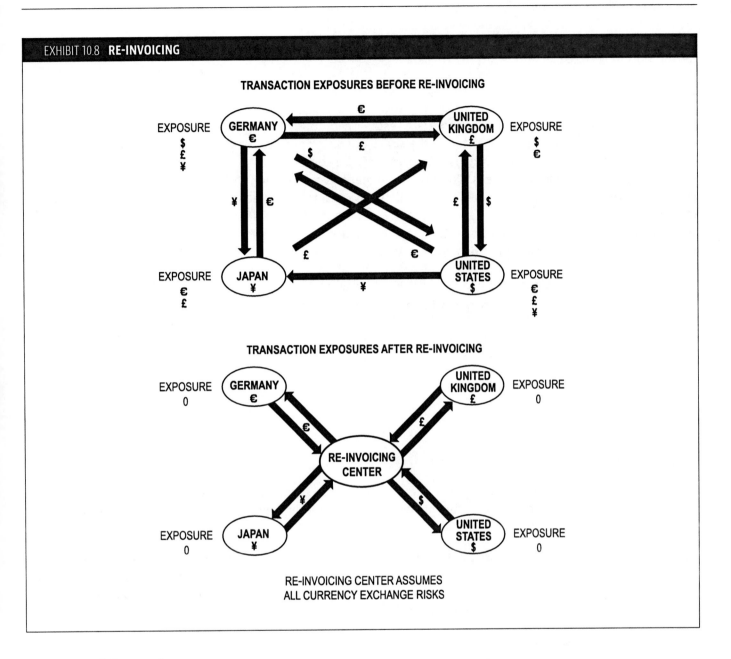

EXHIBIT 10.8 **RE-INVOICING**

E. Internal Factoring

Internal factoring is very similar to re-invoicing. However, rather than taking actual title to the goods, as is the case with re-invoicing, internal factoring involves buying A/R from the exporting unit and collecting funds from the importing unit. As with re-invoicing, internal factoring allows a firm to:

· Implement leading and lagging arrangements

· Centralize and improve export trade financing and collections

· Minimize FX risk

· Reduce banking costs

· Reduce payment costs

Most internal factoring is done on a *recourse* basis, meaning that the factor can return past-due A/R and bad debts to the subsidiary for collection.

F. In-House Banking

Many multinational firms have found it beneficial to establish in-house banks. In this arrangement, treasury becomes the main provider of banking services for all the firm's operating entities. Because treasury manages all banking services, individual transactions of various subsidiaries can be aggregated, netted, and processed in bulk, resulting in fewer transactions and lower fees. The primary benefit is a reduction in banking fees. Secondary benefits include improved visibility and control over subsidiary cash assets, minimized borrowing, and an improved ability to manage internal and external FX risk. There may also be potential tax benefits to using this type of structure, as it provides for better information and tax planning related to international transactions, and some countries provide tax advantages for in-house banking facilities.

The in-house bank normally is responsible for managing international treasury management solutions, including:

- Investments/debts, especially parent-to-subsidiary or subsidiary-to-subsidiary loans
- Netting
- Pooling
- Re-invoicing
- FX transactions and FX risk management
- Treasury management systems (TMSs)

G. Export Financing

In many countries, the government supports export activities through export loans, credit guarantees, or a combination of both.[12] The general term for entities that are established by governments to provide these services is *export credit agencies (ECAs)*.

ECAs are typically established to assist in the financing of goods and services from their country to international markets, often with a focus on smaller firms that are developing international capabilities. The basic services that the ECAs typically provide are working capital guarantees (i.e., pre-export financing), export credit insurance, and loan guarantees and direct loans (i.e., buyer financing).

The advantages of long-term export financing through an ECA include:

- The interest rate generally is fixed at a lower rate and for a longer term than would otherwise be available from commercial sources.
- Indirect government involvement can provide some protection against government appropriation or interference.

The disadvantages of long-term export financing through an ECA include:

- Additional time may be required to obtain the necessary approvals.
- The exporter may face currency exposure if the currency of the loan is different from that of the cash flow of the project being financed or the exporter's home currency.

12. Credit guarantees provided by export credit agencies will reimburse an exporter for sales to foreign buyers if those buyers default on payment to the exporter.

The Export-Import (EXIM) Bank of the United States is the official ECA of the United States. The EXIM Bank provides buyer financing, export credit insurance, and access to working capital for US exporters. In 2015, EXIM Bank financed approximately $17 billion in exports, and 25% of the authorizations (by dollar volume) provided direct insurance and financing support for small business exporters.[13]

While most ECAs are created to provide support for trade with their specific country, there are also a number of multilateral ECAs created to foster trade in multiple jurisdictions. The Multilateral Investment Guarantee Agency (MIGA), a subsidiary of the World Bank, was created to foster trade with developing countries and "South-South" trade (i.e., trade between developing countries).

X. SUMMARY

Working capital management refers to the processes and techniques needed to manage the firm's short-term assets and liabilities. Identifying and achieving an appropriate level of liquidity is a key goal of working capital management. This involves managing the impact of changes in a variety of working capital accounts and finding the appropriate balance between excess liquidity and investment needs.

This chapter introduced the concept of the cash conversion cycle and examined how that cycle affected the operating and financing activities. The concept of float was also introduced, and the various types of float were discussed. The chapter continued with a discussion of managing key working capital accounts: A/R, inventory, and A/P. The final section of the chapter discussed tools that are helpful in multinational working capital management.

Key Equations

$$\text{Cash Conversion Cycle} = \text{Days' Inventory} + \text{Days' Receivables} - \text{Days' Payables}$$

$$\text{Cash Turnover} = \frac{365}{\text{Cash Conversion Cycle}}$$

13. From "Export-Import Bank of the United States, Annual Report 2015" (http://www.exim.gov/sites/default/files/reports/annual/EXIM-2015-AR.pdf).

CHAPTER 11
Working Capital Metrics

I. INTRODUCTION

II. FUNDAMENTAL WORKING CAPITAL METRICS
    A. Current Ratio
    B. Quick Ratio
    C. Net Working Capital
    D. Summary of the Fundamental Working Capital Metrics

III. THE CASH CONVERSION CYCLE (CCC)
    A. Days' Inventory (DI)
    B. Days' Receivables (DR)
    C. Days' Payables (DP)
    D. Calculation of the CCC
    E. Cash Turnover

IV. CALCULATIONS FOR TRADE CREDIT DECISIONS
    A. Annualized Cost of Forgoing the Trade Credit Discount
    B. Financial Impact to a Seller of Offering a Cash Discount

V. ACCOUNTS RECEIVABLE (A/R) MONITORING
    A. Days' Sales Outstanding (DSO)
    B. A/R Aging Schedule
    C. A/R Balance Pattern

VI. SUMMARY

I. INTRODUCTION

Working capital management refers to the firm's use of current assets and current liabilities. Working capital management is important as it impacts a firm's liquidity, efficiency, and overall health. This chapter discusses several key metrics that provide treasury professionals with the tools needed to assess the effectiveness of working capital management practices.

The working capital metrics described in this chapter allow the user to determine the:

- Composition of current assets relative to current liabilities
- Dependence on short-term and long-term financing for funding current assets
- Length of time that funds are held in operating working capital
- Appropriate payment decisions when offered a trade credit discount
- Financial impact of extending a discount to customers
- Proportion of accounts receivable (A/R) that are past due

Specific metrics covered include the current ratio, quick ratio, cash conversion cycle, and cash turnover. Although a general discussion of the cash conversion cycle is presented in the previous chapter, the current chapter provides a more detailed discussion of the associated calculations. The chapter closes by examining specific calculations that are helpful when managing the use of trade credit financing.

II. FUNDAMENTAL WORKING CAPITAL METRICS

This section of the chapter presents fundamental metrics used to assess the efficiency of working capital management. These include the current ratio, quick ratio, and net working capital. These metrics collectively provide information regarding the firm's default risk (i.e., the risk of nonpayment by a borrower), which is why they are commonly referenced in debt covenants. Working capital metrics are also used internally to assess performance, adjust payment terms, forecast cash flows, and manage liquid resources. Understanding the firm's working capital position and related funding requirements provides the treasury professional with information necessary to make strategic decisions concerning short-term investments, borrowing, credit terms, and resource allocation. A number of working capital surveys are published annually. These survey results include metrics by industry and region, as well as trends in working capital.

When interpreting these metrics, it is important to realize that there is no right or wrong number for a particular metric. Instead, it is important to:

- Determine the metric's trend as well as to understand the factors underlying the trend.
- Realize that these metrics vary by industry and by country. Consequently, these metrics should be compared between firms operating in the same industry in similar countries.

A. Current Ratio

The *current ratio* is defined as total current assets divided by total current liabilities. This measure is intended to represent the ratio of liquid (or current) assets that are expected to become cash in one year or less to short-term (or current) liabilities that are due in one year or less. That is, the current ratio measures the degree to which a firm's current obligations are covered by current assets. Using the financial statements from Chapter 8, Financial Accounting and Reporting, the current ratio is calculated as:

$$\text{Current Ratio} = \frac{\text{Total Current Assets}}{\text{Total Current Liabilities}} = \frac{\$8,000}{\$3,400} = 2.35$$

This value for the current ratio implies that the firm's current assets are 2.35 times current liabilities. An alternative, yet consistent, interpretation is that the firm carries $2.35 of current assets for each $1 of current liabilities.

A higher current ratio generally indicates less default risk for creditors. For example, suppose that sales drop due to either increased competition or a decline in overall economic activity. Under these conditions a firm with a larger current asset base is better positioned to meet its current liabilities.

B. Quick Ratio

The *quick ratio* (i.e., the *acid test ratio*) is defined as the sum of cash, short-term investments, and accounts receivable, divided by total current liabilities. As with the current ratio, a higher value for the quick ratio implies less risk for creditors.

The quick ratio is a more stringent measure of liquidity than the current ratio, as it excludes inventory due to that current asset's lower liquidity. The quick ratio also excludes prepaid expenses, which have little to no likelihood of converting to cash. The quick ratio is calculated as follows:

$$\text{Quick Ratio} = \frac{\text{Cash + Short-Term Investments + Accounts Receivable}}{\text{Total Current Liabilities}}$$

$$= \frac{\$1,500 + \$1,300 + \$1,700}{\$3,400} = 1.32$$

The firm has $1.32 of liquid assets for each $1 of current liabilities. By definition, the quick ratio will not exceed the current ratio.

C. Net Working Capital

Net working capital (NWC) is defined as current assets less current liabilities. NWC is not a ratio: it is an absolute measure of the dollar amount by which current assets exceed current liabilities.

For the firm in question, NWC is calculated as:

$$\text{Net Working Capital} = \text{Current Assets} - \text{Current Liabilities}$$

$$= \$8,000 - \$3,400 = \$4,600$$

This value implies that if all current assets are converted to cash, then the firm would have $4,600 above what is needed to pay off current liabilities.

D. Summary of the Fundamental Working Capital Metrics

Overall, higher values for the current ratio, quick ratio, and NWC indicate that a firm has a stronger ability to cover its current obligations. However, it should be noted that it is not optimal for firms to have excessively high values for these metrics. This is because current assets earn a lower rate of return than fixed assets. Once the firm has an adequate base of current assets, additional investment in current assets lowers the overall return on assets, which translates into a lower profit per dollar of investment. Consequently, a key issue is to determine the appropriate balance of current assets and current liabilities based on the subject firm's unique characteristics. Industry averages for these metrics provide guidance, but senior management's risk tolerance should also be considered.

III. THE CASH CONVERSION CYCLE (CCC)

The CCC represents the time required to convert cash outflows associated with production into cash inflows through the collection of A/R. In short, the CCC is calculated as the average age of inventory (days' inventory) plus the average age of A/R (days' receivables) minus the average age of A/P (days' payables). The equation for the CCC follows:

$$\text{Cash Conversion Cycle} = \text{Days' Inventory} + \text{Days' Receivables} - \text{Days' Payables}$$

The CCC highlights the critical nature of monitoring the:

· Amount of time it takes to sell inventory

· Length of time between when a sale is made and when cash is collected

· Actual disbursement period

The following sections examine each component of the CCC. The calculations shown use the following financial data:

Annual Revenues	$15,000
Annual Cost of Goods Sold	$ 9,200
Cash Flow from Operations	$ 550
Ending Inventory	$ 2,600
Ending Accounts Receivable	$ 1,700
Ending Accounts Payable	$ 1,600

A. Days' Inventory (DI)

DI is calculated using inventory and cost of goods sold (COGS), which are taken from the balance sheet and income statement, respectively. Ending inventory is used here, although an average inventory figure is also commonly used. The COGS, rather than sales, is used in this formula because inventory is valued on the balance sheet at its purchase or manufacturing cost rather than at its selling price.

The equation and calculation for DI follow:

$$\text{Days' Inventory} = \frac{\text{Inventory}}{\text{Cost of Goods Sold}} \times 365 = \frac{\$2,600}{\$9,200} \times 365 = 103.15 \text{ Days}$$

This value indicates that it took the firm an average of 103.15 days to sell its inventory. All else constant, a shorter DI is preferred.

B. Days' Receivables (DR)

DR represents the number of days of sales held in the form of A/R. Accordingly, the period's ending value for A/R is divided by revenues, and the result is then multiplied by 365. Note that revenues are used rather than COGS because A/R is carried on the balance sheet based on the selling price. Year-end A/R is used here, but some users average the A/R balance from the two most recent fiscal periods.

DR is calculated as:

$$\text{Days' Receivables} = \frac{\text{Accounts Receivable}}{\text{Revenues}} \times 365 = \frac{\$1,700}{\$15,000} \times 365 = 41.37 \text{ Days}$$

This value indicates that the firm held 41.37 days of sales in A/R during the period in question. This value for DR can also be interpreted as the number of days required to convert a sale into a cash inflow.

C. Days' Payables (DP)

DP is calculated as accounts payable (A/P) divided by COGS, and the result is then multiplied by 365 days. COGS is used in the denominator as A/P reflects the cost paid for inventory. Year-end A/P is used here, but some users average the A/P balance from the two most recent fiscal periods.

DP is calculated as:

$$\text{Days' Payables} = \frac{\text{Accounts Payable}}{\text{Cost of Goods Sold}} \times 365 = \frac{\$1,600}{\$9,200} \times 365 = 63.48 \text{ Days}$$

This value indicates that the firm carried 63.48 days of COGS in A/P. That is, the firm took an average of 63.48 days to repay A/P. To ensure that prudent payment practices are being used, the DP value should be compared to the trade credit terms provided by suppliers.

D. Calculation of the CCC

Once the DI, DR, and DP are determined, the CCC can be calculated as:

$$\text{Cash Conversion Cycle} = \text{Days' Inventory} + \text{Days' Receivables} - \text{Days' Payables}$$

$$= 103.15 \text{ Days} + 41.37 \text{ Days} - 63.48 \text{ Days} = 81.04 \text{ Days}$$

This result indicates that, on average, 81.04 days elapsed from the time the firm disbursed cash until it recovered cash from a sale during the prior year.[1] The CCC can be improved by:

- Shortening DI through careful purchasing and production scheduling, and by removing excess finished goods inventory
- Shortening DR by monitoring customer payment habits and reducing delinquencies
- Increasing DP by managing A/P effectively through accepting supplier discounts only when it is economical (i.e., not paying earlier than is required)

E. Cash Turnover

The importance of the CCC becomes even more apparent when computing the *cash turnover ratio*, defined as the number of cash conversion cycles that a firm experiences per year. Cash turnover is calculated as:

$$\text{Cash Turnover} = \frac{365}{\text{Cash Conversion Cycle}} = \frac{365}{81.04} = 4.5 \text{ Times}$$

Based on the CCC calculation, it takes 81.04 days to recover each dollar invested in the production process. The recovered dollar can be spent again, which occurred 4.5 times during the last fiscal period.

If the cash turnover increased to 5.5 times, then the firm could spend, collect, and re-spend a dollar 5.5 times during an accounting cycle. This does not mean the volume of business has changed, but that the firm is more efficiently using working capital.

IV. CALCULATIONS FOR TRADE CREDIT DECISIONS

A. Annualized Cost of Forgoing the Trade Credit Discount

This section describes a methodology for treasury professionals to use when attempting to determine when to utilize a trade credit discount (also known as a *cash discount*). This methodology is important because of the trade-offs associated with the timing of vendor payments. On one hand, treasury professionals may opt to delay the payment of A/P until the day the invoice is due. However, suppliers sometimes offer two-part trade credit terms that provide the buyer a discount if payment occurs on or before a certain date. Trade credit discounts are offered to encourage earlier payment.

As an example, suppose that a supplier has offered trade credit terms of 2/10 net 30 to a buying firm for a $1,000 invoice. With these terms, the $1,000 invoice is due within the 30-day credit period, but the buyer may take a 2% discount if the invoice is paid within 10 days. That is, if the payment is made any time from day 11 through day 30, then the full invoice amount is due. Suppose that the buyer would need to borrow funds from its credit line to meet the early payment discount because the firm has very little operating cash. The annual borrowing cost on the credit line is 5%. To determine whether the discount should be taken, the buyer should compare the annualized cost of the cash discount to the interest rate on the credit line. The buyer should use the cheaper financing option.

---

1. Days' working capital (DWC) is similar to the CCC. The primary difference is that revenue is typically used as the denominator for all three DWC components (i.e., inventory, A/R, and A/P). As a result, DWC is interpreted as the number of days of sales invested in working capital.

Calculation Example: Annualized Cost of Forgoing the Trade Credit Discount

Before moving to the calculation, note that only two dates are material to the buyer: day 10 and day 30. That is, the buyer has no incentive to pay before day 10 or before day 30 (assuming that the buyer did not pay on day 10). These terms imply that the buyer can pay within 10 days and take a $20 discount ($1,000 × 2%). This means that the trade credit terms have provided the buyer with an option of paying $980 on day 10 or $1,000 on day 30. The implication is that the supplier charges $20 in implicit interest for the additional 20 days of financing. The annualized cost of forgoing the cash discount and paying at the end of the trade credit period is calculated using the following equation:[2]

$$\text{Annualized Cost of the Trade Credit Discount} = \frac{D}{100-D} \times \frac{365}{N-T}$$

Where:

D = Discount percentage

N = Net period

T = Discount period

The first term in the calculation, $D \div (100 - D)$, represents the interest rate applicable to the 10-day discount period. The second term, $365 \div (N - T)$, annualizes the interest rate.

Using the data in the above example, where the discount percentage is 2%, the net period is 30 days, and the discount period is 10 days, the annualized cost of the cash discount is calculated as follows:

$$\text{Annualized Cost of the Trade Credit Discount} = \frac{2}{100-2} \times \frac{365}{30-10} = \frac{2}{98} \times \frac{365}{20}$$

$$= 0.0204 \times 18.25 = 0.3723 \text{ or } 37.23\%$$

Payment can be "postponed" by 20 days by not taking the discount, and there are 18.25 20-day periods in a year. Therefore, the interest rate applicable to the discount period is annualized by multiplying it by 18.25.

The cost of not taking the discount can be compared with the buyer's 5% borrowing rate on the line of credit. Since the cost to borrow is less than the cost of bypassing the discount (i.e., 5% is less than 37.23%), the buyer should borrow funds from the credit line and take the discount.

To generalize, there are only two situations where it is economical to forgo the offered trade credit discount:

· If the buyer does not have cash available to take the discount, but has to borrow funds at an interest rate that exceeds the effective cost of the discount

· If the buyer has enough operating cash to pay the A/P by the discount date, but the buyer can earn a rate of return on its cash that exceeds the effective cost of the discount

---

2. This approach ignores the effect of compounding. A compounded interest approach will result in a higher rate, but the overall decision analysis will remain the same in most cases.

B. Financial Impact to a Seller of Offering a Trade Credit Discount

Sellers offer trade credit (cash) discounts to encourage their customers to speed up payments or to remain competitive with competitors. Before offering a cash discount, the seller must determine the net benefit of this strategy. The cost of offering a cash discount is the lower revenue per dollar of sales. This cost may be acceptable if the discount prompts increased sales. Regardless of sales growth, faster payments from customers allow the seller to more quickly reinvest the cash receipts. The following calculations show a net benefit analysis from the seller's perspective.

Calculation Example: Net Benefit of Offering a Trade Credit Discount

Assume that a seller has an opportunity cost of funds of 5%, and that the average credit sale is $1,000 on credit terms of 2/10 net 30. To determine the present value of receiving the discounted payment on day 10, begin by calculating the discounted payment amount, as follows:

$$\text{Discounted Amount} = \text{Credit Sale} \times (1 - \text{Discount Amount}) = \$1{,}000 \times (1 - 0.02) = \$980$$

As indicated in Chapter 9, Financial Planning and Analysis, the present value (PV) of a future cash flow is calculated by discounting the future cash flow using the daily opportunity cost of funds over the period in question, as follows:

$$PV = \frac{FV}{(1+i)^n}$$

And the interest rate (i) for the discount period can be calculated as:

$$i = \text{Days in Discount Period} \times \frac{\text{Annual Interest}}{365}$$

The present value of an invoice paid on day 10 (PV_{Day10}) is therefore calculated as follows:

$$PV_{Day10} = \frac{\$980}{1 + \left[10 \times \left(\dfrac{0.05}{365}\right)\right]}$$

$$= \frac{\$980}{1.00137}$$

$$= \$978.66$$

Alternatively, the PV of receiving the full payment after 30 days (PV_{Day30}) is calculated as follows:

$$PV_{Day30} = \frac{\$1{,}000}{1 + \left[30 \times \left(\dfrac{0.05}{365}\right)\right]}$$

$$= \frac{\$1{,}000}{1.00411}$$

$$= \$995.91$$

The seller can now calculate the net present value (NPV) of offering the discount as follows:

$$NPV = PV_{Day10} - PV_{Day30} = \$978.66 - \$995.91 = -\$17.25$$

This calculation indicates that the seller is better off if the buyer takes the full 30 days to repay the A/P. That is, for each $1,000 in credit sales, the seller loses $17.25 in present value cash flows when the buyer takes the discount by paying on the 10th day. In this case, the seller might reconsider its discount terms.

The seller can determine the discount that would leave the seller indifferent between the buyer's choice of payment timing. If the opportunity cost of funds and the credit terms remain the same as before, with the exception of the cash discount percentage, then the seller would solve for the cash discount percentage that causes PV_{Day10} to equal PV_{Day30} (i.e., $995.91). The solution is shown below:

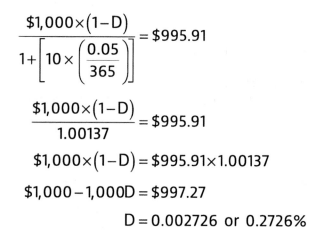

$$\frac{\$1,000 \times (1-D)}{1 + \left[10 \times \left(\frac{0.05}{365}\right)\right]} = \$995.91$$

$$\frac{\$1,000 \times (1-D)}{1.00137} = \$995.91$$

$$\$1,000 \times (1-D) = \$995.91 \times 1.00137$$

$$\$1,000 - 1,000D = \$997.27$$

$$D = 0.002726 \text{ or } 0.2726\%$$

Note that this is a substantially lower discount percentage than that provided on the original terms.

V. ACCOUNTS RECEIVABLE (A/R) MONITORING

To improve working capital efficiency, many firms actively monitor A/R at both an individual account and aggregate level.[3] It is important to monitor individual accounts in order to identify:

- Errors or delays in the invoicing or payment process that are slowing collections
- Customers that are intentionally delaying payment until follow-up is initiated
- A change in financial condition that may alter a customer's ability to make timely payments, which might require the curtailment of future credit sales

A/R should also be monitored on an aggregate level to identify the impact on overall firm liquidity and to determine the required level of external financing. Further, the analysis of aggregate receivables serves as the basis for forecasting future cash receipts.

Developments that may prompt significant changes in credit policies include variation in sales volumes, seasonality, modifications of trade credit standards, fluctuations in economic conditions, changes in foreign exchange rates, and promotions or other sales initiatives offered by competitors. Management should analyze these developments to determine the underlying causes and take corrective actions.

---

3. Notable exceptions include firms that receive payments via cash or credit cards.

Another consideration for management is to monitor the effectiveness of the application of payment and the overall level of write-offs or bad debt loss. The effectiveness of application of payments can be monitored by examining the discrepancies between amounts invoiced and the payments actually applied to those invoices. While some discrepancies may be related to invoicing errors or damaged goods, accounts may be adjusted in some cases due to customers paying less than what was owed. These adjustments should be accounted for as write-offs or bad debt losses in order to properly track the overall quality of A/R. A rise in write-offs could indicate the deterioration of A/R quality.

Three tools that are helpful in monitoring A/R include reports on days' sales outstanding, aging schedules, and A/R balance patterns.

A. Days' Sales Outstanding (DSO)

DSO (i.e., the average collection period) is one metric for measuring the quality of A/R. DSO is calculated by dividing A/R outstanding at the end of a fiscal period by the average daily credit sales for that period. This differs from DR, which is calculated using total sales rather than credit sales. Note that if there are no cash sales, then the two numbers are identical. DSO can be compared to stated credit terms, historic trends, or industry norms to indicate a company's overall collection efficiency. It may, however, be distorted by changing trends in sales volume or by strong sales seasonality.

DSO is calculated as:

$$DSO = \frac{Accounts\ Receivable}{Average\ Daily\ Credit\ Sales\ for\ Period}$$

Accounts receivable is the balance at the end of the specific accounting period (e.g., 30 days, 90 days, 365 days). Daily credit sales is calculated by dividing total credit sales during the accounting period by the number of days in the accounting period. For example, assume that a firm has recorded credit sales of $310,000 over the past 90 days and the current A/R balance is $285,000. Daily credit sales equal $3,444.44 ($310,000÷90). The DSO would be calculated as:

$$DSO = \frac{\$285,000}{\$3,444.44} = 82.74\ Days$$

In other words, the firm takes an average of just under 83 days to convert a credit sale into cash. This DSO value would be acceptable if the stated credit terms were net 90. However, if the credit terms were net 30, this DSO would be unacceptable as it would indicate that most of the credit sales were paid late. The average past due can be calculated as follows:

$$Average\ Past\ Due = DSO - Average\ Days\ of\ Credit\ Terms$$

$$= 82.74 - 30.00 = 52.74\ Days$$

B. A/R Aging Schedule

An aging schedule separates A/R into current and past-due receivables using set periods (typically, 30-day increments). An aging schedule provides helpful information on working capital efficiency as the likelihood of the account being uncollected increases with the age of the account. Managers can apply an aging schedule to aggregate receivables or on a customer-by-customer basis. Assuming credit terms of net 30, the aging schedule in Exhibit 11.1 reveals that 30% of the A/R is past due.

EXHIBIT 11.1 A/R AGING SCHEDULE		
AGE OF A/R	**AMOUNT OF A/R**	**% OF TOTAL A/R**
CURRENT	$1,750,000	70%
1–30 DAYS PAST DUE	375,000	15%
31–60 DAYS PAST DUE	250,000	10%
OVER 60 DAYS PAST DUE	125,000	5%
TOTAL	$2,500,000	100%

As compared to the DSO approach, an aging schedule is more indicative of trends as it illustrates a pattern of distribution, rather than just providing a single number representing an average. For example, the DSO value may be consistent with the stated trade credit terms, but certain individual accounts may be delinquent. The DSO will obscure the delinquencies, whereas the aging schedule immediately reveals them. However, an aging schedule can send the same misleading signals as DSO when sales vary significantly from month to month.

For both DSO and aging schedules, it is important to bear in mind how and when the time periods are calculated. Most firms start counting payment days once an invoice has been sent for a particular sale. Customers, on the other hand, may start counting payment days on the date they receive the invoice or the actual shipment, whichever is later. Practices vary by country and industry, and it is important to understand what the common practice is before assuming that payments are late. Whatever practice is used, the aging schedule should be calculated based on the "past-due date" (i.e., the date on which the payment actually becomes past due), not the invoice or mail date. For example, if terms are net 30 and the firm is tracking from the date of the invoice, then the payment is not past due until 30 days after the invoice date. On the 31st day after the invoice date, the payment is only 1 day past due, not 31 days past due.

C. A/R Balance Pattern

An A/R balance pattern is used to monitor customer payment timing. An A/R balance pattern specifies the percentage of credit sales during a time period (e.g., one month) that remain outstanding at the end of the current and each subsequent time period. A firm's collection history determines the normal balance pattern. Management evaluates any changes by comparing current patterns with historical norms. Balance patterns can also be used to project A/R at the end of a period, measure collection efficiency, and forecast future cash collections. Exhibit 11.2 provides an example of an A/R balance pattern report.

EXHIBIT 11.2 A/R BALANCE PATTERN REPORT		
SALES FOR MONTH	$200,000	
INTERVAL SINCE SALE	**AMOUNT OUTSTANDING AT END OF MONTH**	**PERCENTAGE OUTSTANDING AT END OF MONTH**
MONTH 0 (CURRENT MONTH)	$190,000	95%
MONTH 1	$110,000	55%
MONTH 2	$40,000	20%
MONTH 3	$10,000	5%
MONTH 4	0	0%

Looking at the pattern in Exhibit 11.2, it appears that 20% of sales remain in outstanding A/R two months after the sale. If payments from credit sales slow, the sales remaining in A/R for a given month will increase. Suppose that in subsequent months, the percentage of sales remaining in A/R after two months increases to 30%. This indicates that customers are taking longer to pay and as a result, A/R balances will increase. An increase in the company's aggregate A/R balance will require additional financing.

VI. SUMMARY

This chapter presented metrics that are frequently used by treasury professionals to assess working capital efficiency. The chapter opened with a review of the current ratio, quick ratio, and net working capital. Each measure provides unique information regarding the amount of coverage that current assets provide creditors. Next, the chapter described the cash conversion cycle, its components, and the cash turnover ratio. The final sections of the chapter examined decision analysis related to the receipt and extension of trade credit.

Key Equations

$$\text{Current Ratio} = \frac{\text{Total Current Assets}}{\text{Total Current Liabilities}}$$

$$\text{Quick Ratio} = \frac{\text{Cash} + \text{Short-Term Investments} + \text{Accounts Receivable}}{\text{Total Current Liabilities}}$$

$$\text{Net Working Capital} = \text{Current Assets} - \text{Current Liabilities}$$

$$\text{Cash Conversion Cycle} = \text{Days' Inventory} + \text{Days' Receivables} - \text{Days' Payables}$$

$$\text{Days' Inventory} = \frac{\text{Inventory}}{\text{Cost of Goods Sold}} \times 365$$

$$\text{Days' Receivables} = \frac{\text{Accounts Receivable}}{\text{Revenues}} \times 365$$

$$\text{Days' Payables} = \frac{\text{Accounts Payable}}{\text{Cost of Goods Sold}} \times 365$$

$$\text{Cash Turnover} = \frac{365}{\text{Cash Conversion Cycle}}$$

Annualized Cost of the Trade Credit Discount

$$= \frac{\text{Discount Percentage}}{(100 - \text{Discount Percentage})} \times \frac{365}{(\text{Net Period} - \text{Discount Period})}$$

$$PV = \frac{FV}{(1+i)^n}$$

$$i = \text{Days in Discount Period} \times \frac{\text{Annual Interest}}{365}$$

$$\text{Days' Sales Outstanding} = \frac{\text{Accounts Receivable}}{\text{Average Daily Credit Sales for Period}}$$

$$\text{Average Past Due} = \text{Days' Sales Outstanding} - \text{Average Days of Credit Terms}$$

CHAPTER 12
Disbursements, Collections, and Concentration

I. INTRODUCTION

II. DISBURSEMENTS

    A. Disbursement Management Products

    B. Electronic Disbursement Products

    C. Card Payments

    D. Outsourced Disbursement Services

    E. Managing Disbursement Information

    F. Payments Fraud

III. COLLECTIONS

    A. Collecting Payments

    B. Domestic Collection Products

    C. Cross-Border Collections and Trade Management Products

IV. CONCENTRATION OF FUNDS

    A. Domestic Concentration of Funds

    B. Global Concentration of Funds

V. SUMMARY

APPENDIX 12.1: US ACH STANDARD ENTRY CLASS (SEC) CODES AND PAYMENT TYPES

I. INTRODUCTION

Disbursements, collections, and *concentration* refer to the movement of funds throughout the various working capital accounts. Subsequently, these aspects represent the primary types of cash management services offered by banks to their customers. It is important to note that a given firm's disbursement of cash represents another firm's collection of cash. As a result, many of the same banking services and products are relevant to both disbursements and collections. *Concentration* refers to the movement of funds throughout the firm's various accounts following the collection of cash into one centralized account.

This chapter opens with a discussion of products and services commonly used by treasury professionals for the disbursement of funds. The disbursements section also describes tools used to deter payments fraud. Next, the chapter describes key aspects related to collections, including lockboxes and international collection issues. The chapter closes with a discussion of cash concentration, including the concepts of notional and physical pooling.

II. DISBURSEMENTS

Disbursements refer to the payment of funds to employees, suppliers, tax authorities, capital markets, etc. A primary concern in the management of disbursements is control. For example, treasury personnel will seek to ensure that disbursements are made exactly as requested by the accounts payable (A/P) department, that the required funds are available, and that the timing and risk of payments fraud is controlled. Disbursement processes include both the payment initiation and the reconciliation of the payment. The latter refers to verifying that the payment was correctly processed and debited from the disbursement account. Managing the information related to the disbursements and to the actual clearing and settlement of the payments is also an important part of the process.

A. Disbursement Management Products

Disbursement systems may range from a single bank account for a small business to a very complex system with multiple banks, accounts, payment methods, and products for a large corporation. This section describes many of the most common disbursement products.

1. DEMAND DEPOSIT ACCOUNTS (DDAs)

A DDA is used to facilitate business activity including the transfer of funds or other payment-related activities. Sample methods of payment include cash, check, debit card, internal book transfer, or electronic transfer.

2. ZERO BALANCE ACCOUNTS (ZBAs)

ZBAs are bank accounts in which the end-of-day balance is maintained at zero. Credits and debits that post to the ZBA are netted at the close of each business day. From the account holder's perspective, if there is a credit balance in the ZBA, then the ZBA will be debited and the master account will be credited. This brings the balance in the ZBA back to zero. If there is a debit balance in the ZBA, then the ZBA will be credited and the master account will be debited. Again, this end-of-day transaction returns the balance in the ZBA to zero. Funding of the ZBA is generally done automatically by the bank and the appropriate accounting entry is made by the bank and the company to reflect the transfer of funds.

ZBAs are typically disbursement accounts on which a company issues checks, initiates ACH[1] debits, or initiates wire transfers. In some cases, however, ZBAs can be used for both collections and disbursements.

---

1. The term *ACH transaction* is used in this text generically to include all pre-authorized, low-value debit and credit EFT transactions, including but not limited to ACH, SEPA, Bacs, ECG, and other country-specific transfer systems.

Multi-tiered ZBAs may be used by firms with multiple divisions or subsidiaries to initiate payments from separate accounts or segregate different types of payments (e.g., A/P, payroll, dividends, and taxes). A treasury professional can control the balances and funding of a master account and that account's associated ZBAs as if they were all one account. This approach reduces excess balances and the need for multiple, manual transfers, while maintaining distinct information and audit trails.

3. CONTROLLED DISBURSEMENT

Controlled disbursement is a bank service that provides same-day notification to a company of the amount of checks that will clear against its disbursement account on a given day. This product is unique to the United States and was developed due to the long-standing regulatory ban on paying interest on positive account balances and limitations on overdrawing current accounts. The amount of time it will take a check to be presented at a payor's bank can vary significantly due to such issues as mail and processing float. The historic inability of US banks to pay interest on checking accounts meant that if the account was funded on the day the checks were issued, funds would lie dormant until the checks were actually presented. With controlled disbursement, the account is typically not funded each day until after the daily notification is received. The daily clearings are normally available by early or mid-morning, allowing the treasury professional to more accurately determine the cash position. The disbursement bank generally receives its final cash letter of the day from the local Federal Reserve Bank early in the morning. This approach allows enough time for the payment items to be sorted and the firm to be notified of its funding requirement for the account. The firm must then provide adequate funds to the account to cover the value of the checks and other debits presented that day.

A controlled disbursement account is typically funded from a concentration account, in which case an automatic, internal bank transfer is made. This is usually accomplished by setting up controlled disbursement accounts as ZBAs. However, a wire transfer may be used when a firm negotiates the funding of a controlled disbursement account from another bank. In some cases, funding by ACH is negotiated, but this is the exception rather than the norm. For risk control purposes, most banks require that controlled disbursement accounts be funded either from another account at the same bank or by wire transfer. When the funding account for the controlled disbursement is not at the controlled disbursement bank, a balance equivalent to an average day's clearing or a sufficient line of credit is often required to reduce the bank's risk of nonpayment.

One of the principal advantages of a controlled disbursement account is that it allows the treasury department to calculate the daily cash position early enough to take advantage of better market rates for investing or borrowing. However, there are instances where discrepancies arise between the reported disbursement clearings and the actual amount of checks presented for payment. These discrepancies typically arise from same-day presentment, over-the-counter presentment, and rejected items. Some banks carry over these adjustments until the following business day.

4. IMPREST ACCOUNTS

An imprest account, which is sometimes used as a petty cash account, is an account maintained at a fixed amount for a particular purpose or activity. For example, a field office may have an imprest account for local disbursements, with a balance sufficient for one or two months' expenses. Based on either an established time frame or a designated level of imprest account balances, the field office submits expenses to headquarters for approval, and headquarters replenishes the imprest account and brings it back to the fixed amount.

B. Electronic Disbursement Products

Electronic funds transfers (EFT) via wire transfer and ACH are used for business-to-consumer (B2C) and business-to-business (B2B) payments, as well as for payments from governments to consumers (G2C), businesses to governments (B2G), and consumer to consumer (C2C). Results of an AFP survey indicate that 79% of companies are transitioning their B2B payments from checks to electronic methods.[2] One of the significant advantages of electronic disbursements is the ability to include remittance information with B2B payments. Additional information on specific types of electronic disbursements is provided below.

1. DIRECT DEPOSIT VIA AUTOMATED CLEARINGHOUSE (ACH)

Direct deposit via ACH has been used widely in the United States since the early 1980s for both government and commercial payments, and is now routinely used throughout much of the world. The introduction of the SEPA credit transfer scheme in the Eurozone and cross-border ACH in other countries (including the United States) has made global use of direct deposit simpler and more acceptable for many firms. Direct deposits are transfers made from a firm's account to the accounts of employees, shareholders, vendors, and trading partners using ACH credit transactions. Direct deposit via ACH can be used for payroll, employee expense reimbursements, interest payments, tax payments, dividend distributions, and B2B transactions. Some state labor departments allow firms to mandate direct deposit of payroll. For employees without bank accounts, an alternative to direct deposit of payroll is the payroll card.

In addition to corporate use of direct deposit, government agencies use direct deposit for benefits distributions, social security payments, and tax refunds. Two advantages of direct deposit via ACH are the low cost of the transactions and the certainty of timing.

2. TAX PAYMENTS

Many taxing authorities throughout the world allow (and in some cases mandate) electronic payment of various types of taxes. In the United States, the Electronic Federal Tax Payment System (EFTPS) is the primary method for collecting and accounting for federal taxes withheld by employers from individuals' salaries and wages, as well as corporate business, sales, and excise taxes.

Sub-sovereign or local taxing authorities are also moving toward electronic payment of taxes. In the United States, most states require companies with tax payments above certain amounts to remit them electronically. This is accomplished either by initiating an ACH credit or authorizing an ACH debit. The standard NACHA payment format for state and federal tax payments via ACH is known as the *tax payment (TXP) banking convention*, yet usage and specific formats vary from state to state. Some states also accept tax payments by wire transfer.

Many banks provide specialized systems that can support and maintain multiple tax payment formats and are specifically designed to handle the timing and information requirements of tax payments.

3. WIRE TRANSFERS

Wire transfers such as Fedwire in the United States or TARGET2 in Europe are an important disbursement tool for firms that need to make large-value payments that are immediate and final at the time of settlement. Most banks provide a number of methods for originating wire transfers, ranging from telephone initiation to online systems. To meet the needs of corporate users, banks generally classify wire transfers by usage category. This classification is based on which elements of information change from wire to wire. A summary appears below. Understanding the differences in the types of wires is important as the level of risk varies by type of wire:

---

2. The *2015 AFP Payments Cost Benchmarking Survey Report* is available through AFP's website (http://www.afponline.org/publications-data-tools/reports/survey-research-economic-data).

- **Repetitive Wires:** Repetitive wire transfers are used when frequent transfers are made to the same credit parties. In a repetitive wire, only the date and dollar amount of the wire change—all other information remains constant. The bank or treasury management system used by the treasury professional to originate the wire maintains a record of the debit and credit bank accounts and accepts instructions either electronically (most banks offer a web-based wire transfer system) or via telephone to initiate the transfer. A unique identifier is assigned to each instruction template that contains all of the standing information. Since only the date and the dollar amount can be changed on a repetitive wire, this type of transfer provides significant assurance that funds will not be sent to an unknown or fraudulent party.

- **Semi-Repetitive Wires:**[3] The debit and credit parties remain the same in a semi-repetitive wire transfer, but the description (e.g., a customer or an invoice number) may be changed, along with the date and the dollar amount. Semi-repetitive transfers combine the controls of repetitive transfers with the flexibility of non-repetitive transfers.

- **Non-Repetitive Wires:** With non-repetitive wires (also referred to as *free-form wires*), the debit and credit parties are different each time. Because all of the information is variable, this type of transfer has the highest degree of payment risk due to fraud or simple data entry errors. As a result, additional security measures are typically required to guard against both fraud and input errors. Examples of such measures are callbacks, secondary levels of approval, and segregation of duties.

- **Drawdown Wires:** A drawdown, or reverse, wire transfer is a request sent by a firm's bank to a second bank requesting that the second bank initiate a wire transfer from either the firm's account or another party's account at the second bank, sending the funds back to the first bank. The party being debited must pre-authorize the transfer; therefore, drawdown wires are most frequently used as part of a firm's concentration system, since the firm can authorize both sides of the transaction.

- **Standing Wires:** With a standing wire, repetitive transfer instructions are established to move funds between two specified accounts automatically when previously determined criteria are met. Standing wires typically are used for concentrating funds, and the criteria could address either timing (e.g., all funds in the account at the end of the day) or a designated balance level (e.g., all funds in excess of $50,000).

- **Book Transfers:** Wires between accounts at the same bank are referred to as *book transfers*. Since book transfers do not go through a system such as Fedwire, they are much less expensive than other types of wire transfers.

C. Card Payments

Card payments have become an important disbursement method for consumers and for businesses. If payment cards are used by the firm's employees, it is important to establish and document policies and procedures to provide appropriate controls. Cards used for disbursement purposes include purchasing cards, travel and entertainment (T&E) cards, virtual cards, and single-use cards. Characteristics of these types of cards, as well as others, are covered in Chapter 4, Payment Systems.

D. Outsourced Disbursement Services

Because of the complexity of many payment types and the need for extensive controls over disbursement activities, outsourcing disbursements is quite common. Products used to outsource disbursements include freight payment services, payroll services, and integrated or comprehensive A/P.

---

3. Depending upon the bank, the term *template wire* may be used to refer to either repetitive or semi-repetitive wires. This is based on the fact that a template is used to hold the fixed data for either type of wire.

1. FREIGHT PAYMENTS

Some banks and third parties offer a payment service called *freight payment* in which specialists pay all of a shipper's freight bills, audit bills for possible overcharges and duplicate payments, and provide reports that help a company compare costs for different routes and carriers. Manufacturers and wholesale distributors typically use this service.

2. PAYROLL SERVICES

Numerous vendors offer payroll services that handle many payroll functions, including check and direct deposit file issuance, payroll tax filing and payment, expatriate (expat) payroll, and retirement/pension account administration. Payroll services also provide employees with the required withholding forms for tax purposes. Many small- to medium-sized businesses outsource payroll because it is often a cost-effective and convenient service.

3. INTEGRATED OR COMPREHENSIVE ACCOUNTS PAYABLE (A/P)

An integrated or comprehensive A/P service allows a firm to outsource all or part of its A/P and/or disbursement functions. There are two common approaches to managing an integrated or comprehensive A/P service:

- In the first approach, a firm may send a data file to a financial service provider periodically, containing a list of all payments to be made. The file contains information on when to issue a disbursement and to whom, as well as instructions on the payment method to be used (e.g., check, wire, ACH, foreign draft, or foreign currency).

- In the second approach, the financial service provider may maintain a database of a firm's payees that includes detailed information, such as preferred payment methods, specific remittance information, and the names of receiving financial institutions. The database is updated periodically as payees are added or deleted, or as an existing payee's remittance profile changes. Under this method, when a company needs a disbursement, it sends only limited payment information to the financial service provider.

With either approach, the financial service provider issues the payments immediately or warehouses the items (i.e., holds payments until some future transaction date), according to the instructions in the data file.

4. PAYMENT FACTORIES

A payment factory is essentially a centralized A/P processing center. It is often part of a centralized treasury operation known as an *in-house bank*, or it may be set up as part of an organization's enterprise resource planning (ERP) system. Payment factories are often used in multinational organizations with a large number of cross-border payments. They can also be linked to multilateral netting systems or re-invoicing programs in order to reduce the number of transactions between subsidiaries of a company, as well as better control overall exposures from foreign currencies. To send payments outside the organization, a single payment file from all the operating units can be sent to a global or regional bank, which can then arrange for payments to be made in local currencies to the vendors.

E. Managing Disbursement Information

Accurate and comprehensive information management is central to an effective disbursement system. Obtaining timely and accurate information about the status of disbursement accounts and disbursement clearings lets a firm manage its cash position more effectively. In addition, information must be provided to the A/P function regarding the status of outstanding items.

1. BALANCE REPORTING SERVICES

Online balance or transaction reporting services allow a bank to report transaction and balance information to corporate customers. Information is typically classified as either *same day* or *prior day*. By providing current information, these services not only help treasury personnel manage bank accounts but are an important part of fraud control as they allow treasury professionals to see transactions in real or near-real time and question suspicious or unexpected transactions.

2. ACCOUNT RECONCILIATION PROGRAM (ARP)

Banks provide account reconciliation services to meet firms' information and control requirements. In a partial reconciliation program, the bank lists all items paid in numerical order by check serial number or in chronological order by date paid. For each item, the paid report generally shows the serial number (if applicable), dollar amount, and date paid.

With a full reconciliation program, a firm supplies the bank with an electronic file of all payments issued, and the bank matches items paid against the file. For firms using a bank's positive pay service, this can be the same file used for that service. In addition, many banks bundle ARP services with their positive pay services since the reconciliation is effectively being done as the items are presented to the account.

Related bank services that may be used for disbursement activities include stop payments and high-order prefix sorting. A stop payment is an order given to the paying bank instructing it not to honor a specific payment that has already been issued but has not yet cleared. These orders generally are given because a check is lost or stolen, or the payor determines after the payment is issued that there is a mistake and the payment must be rescinded. Stop payments may be initiated by voice, electronically, or in writing. Written confirmation may be required by the bank for telephone instructions. Stop payments usually remain in place for only six months and must be renewed, if necessary.

A high-order prefix (divisional) sort is a service that allows a firm with multiple units to use a single bank account for all of its payments and still identify individual payments by unit. Codes identifying the various units are included in the check serial number field at the beginning of the check number. The paying bank then sorts the payments by the high-order code and reports them to the firm either through account reconciliation or some other reporting service. This method is used to facilitate the identification and sorting of payments by operating unit.

3. CHECK IMAGES

Banks provide images of checks that have been presented for payment to help firms in researching payments and reconciling accounts. Images of both the front and the back of a paid check are captured during the check-processing cycle. (The check images may also be stored in a bank database that a company can access online for viewing or retrieving images.) Imaging provides a company with faster access to disbursement check information and is particularly beneficial when used in conjunction with controlled disbursement, payable through drafts, and/or positive pay services. Its primary use is to exchange information between the bank and customer.

F. Payments Fraud

Payments fraud is a key issue related to disbursements. This section describes disbursement products used to reduce payments fraud, including positive pay and reverse positive pay.

Positive pay is a disbursement service used to combat payments fraud related to both checks and ACH. With this service, the company transmits a file of payment information to the disbursement bank either at or before the time of the physical distribution of checks or anticipated ACH debits. The bank matches check serial numbers and dollar amounts of checks presented for payment against the issue database and pays only those checks or ACH transactions that match all relevant criteria. Many positive pay services also offer the ability to match against the payee field (i.e., payee positive pay), as well as the serial number and the amount, in an effort to detect an altered payee. In the case of ACH positive pay, transactions are matched based on dollar amount and originator.

The standard positive pay service is typically done on a batch basis as the bank processes checks or ACH payments. A related service, known as *teller positive pay*, allows for real-time inquiry on checks by tellers at all the branches of the bank, enabling the teller to match the item to the check issue file on a real-time basis and helping to prevent the cashing of fraudulent items.

Any exceptions to the positive pay match process are conveyed to the company for its decision whether to pay or return the item. Given the limited amount of time available to return items, exceptions typically must be reviewed and "decisioned" (i.e., a determination made to pay or reject the transaction) by an established deadline that same day. Because the bank cannot process the exception items without company authorization, it is common to set up accounts with a default status of either *pay all* or *return all*. In other words, if the company fails to notify the bank of its decision on any exception items by the deadline, the bank will either pay all of the exception items and post them to the company's account, or pay none of the exception items and return them all to the depositor. Most banks offer online access to payment transaction data and check images, to assist in this process of researching and identifying potentially fraudulent payments.

Reverse positive pay is a process whereby the bank transmits a file of the checks presented for payment to the company on a daily or intraday basis. Within a specified time deadline, the company matches this file to a list of checks issued and notifies the bank of any items to be returned. This service, however, does not prevent fraudulent checks from being cashed at the paying bank teller line (i.e., teller positive pay) since the bank does not have access to the issue file. As with regular positive pay, when using a reverse positive pay service, the company and bank must agree on a default action if the company does not meet the required deadline—that is, should the bank pay all or pay none, bearing in mind that in the case of reverse positive pay, pay none means that all checks presented that day will be returned, not just the exception items. Reverse positive pay is not available for ACH payments.

It is important to note that positive pay services cannot protect against a type of fraud known as *fraudulent endorsement*. Fraudulent endorsement occurs when an authorized check is stolen or intercepted by a third party, and then that party endorses and cashes the check. So long as the check amount, the check number, and potentially the payee are not altered, this type of fraud is not usually detected by positive pay. While positive pay services do detect duplicate checks (i.e., a valid check and a forged copy), they typically cannot distinguish between the original and a copy and will pay the first check presented. Fortunately, checks returned for forged or fraudulent endorsement are not subject to the normal next-day return deadline and may be returned upon discovery of the forged endorsement, subject to any agreed-upon limits with the paying bank.

An AFP survey reported that the majority of all organizations in the United States (73%) were the subject of attempted or actual payments fraud.[4] The survey also revealed that payments fraud is not limited to large companies, but is a concern for organizations of all sizes. It is very likely that this holds true throughout the world.

---

4. The *2016 AFP Payments Fraud and Control Survey Report* is available through AFP's website (http://www.afponline.org/publications-data-tools/reports/survey-research-economic-data).

The good news in the AFP survey is that the large majority of fraud attempts fail and that 70% of organizations that were attacked did not lose any money. Even better news is that while some of the methods used to perpetuate payments fraud are highly sophisticated, most of them are fairly simple, and some of the best methods of detection and prevention are fairly simple and easy to use. Positive pay (preferably with payee verification), ACH filters and blocks, and daily reconciliations are among the methods most used to help detect and control payments fraud. Other best practices for fraud control include:

· Use of check stock with built-in security features, such as microprinting, holograms, and other non-photo-reproducible features

· Appropriate segregation of duties so that the person reconciling accounts is not the person who can initiate transactions from the account

· The use of dual authentication for all EFT transactions, where one person originates a transaction and a second person reviews and releases the transaction

· The reduction or elimination of non-repetitive wires

· The use of separate accounts for deposits and disbursements

· Specific-purpose deposit-only ZBA accounts with debit blocks or filters

· Check blocks for ACH-only ZBA accounts

· The use of a dedicated computer (i.e., not used for other purposes) for the initiation of online EFT transactions

A problem related to check fraud that is typically not prevented by positive pay or daily reconciliation is known as the *"holder in due course" issue*. This is a uniquely US problem that results from US law regarding negotiable instruments such as checks. The problem occurs when a third party, someone other than the payee or the depository bank, accepts or cashes a negotiable instrument (e.g., a check) that subsequently turns out to be fraudulent. As long as the third party can show that it was a "holder in due course"[5] at the time that it accepted the check, the third party may be able to collect from the maker of the check even though the actual check was fraudulent or altered. A common example of this situation is when a check-cashing store that regularly accepts and cashes payroll checks for employees of a local company accepts and cashes a forged or altered payroll check, or a check with a stop payment placed on it, without having been given any notice or warning of any problems with the check. Positive pay will normally detect the item and allow its return, but the check-cashing store may be able to hold the company liable for the amount of the fraudulent check, assuming it is not an obvious forgery and the check casher had no reason to suspect that there was a problem with the check. While there is no sure defense against this problem, tamper-resistant check stock using non-photo-reproducible features may help reduce the problem. Another, more certain, alternative is to replace check payments with EFT or card payments.

III. COLLECTIONS

The efficient collection of funds is a key aspect of liquidity management. The collection system employed will depend upon the nature of the collecting firm and nature of the payee. For example, B2B collection systems will be very different from collection systems that are used for consumer payments and/or retail businesses. Firms that collect large amounts of cash and/or cash at a local level (e.g., fast food or retail) will require different collection

---

5. The Uniform Commercial Code § 3-302 defines a *holder in due course as* "...the holder of an instrument if: (1) the instrument when issued or negotiated to the holder does not bear such apparent evidence of forgery or alteration or is not otherwise so irregular or incomplete as to call into question its authenticity; and (2) the holder took the instrument (i) for value, (ii) in good faith, (iii) without notice that the instrument is overdue or has been dishonored...and (iv) without notice that the instrument contains an unauthorized signature or has been altered...." (From "UCC § 3-302" on Cornell University Law School's website, http://www.law.cornell.edu/ucc/3/3-302, accessed April 28, 2016.)

processes than a large service-type business (e.g., an accounting or consulting firm). There are a number of major issues that must be addressed in any collection system, including:

- **Speed of Collection:** The collection system should minimize the time it takes to collect the actual payment and have the funds available for use.

- **Security of the Payment:** The collection system should ensure that the payment is not diverted or stolen during the collection process.

- **Availability of Remittance Information:** It is important to know who made the payment and why, especially if the payment is for less than anticipated.

- **Cost of Collection:** Minimizing the cost of any collection system is important, but the cost must be balanced against the prior items.

A. Collecting Payments

In an effort to encourage timely payments, many collection systems are designed to handle many types of payments. For example, retail organizations receive most of their payments in the form of cash and cards, although some may accept checks. When the retailer has more than one location, the picture is complicated even further by the need to consolidate retail payments from the various locations into a central concentration account, as discussed later in this chapter.

The situation becomes even more complex when the organization has customers and trading partners in other countries. The organization must deal with foreign exchange risk, but it must also deal with the credit risk of foreign trading partners and cross-border payments, which often results in the need to deal with trade payments and letters of credit.

B. Domestic Collection Products

Domestic collection refers to payments received from customers and trading partners that are located within the same country as the collecting company. Just as there are a wide variety of products that support disbursements, banks and other vendors provide a number of products to support domestic collections, as described below.

1. ARMORED CARRIERS AND SMART SAFES

Firms with multiple retail locations use armored cars to collect deposits from their retail outlets to ensure the safety of both the collections and their staff. Because of the high cost of armored carriers, firms typically use them only for outlets with large amounts of cash receipts or where there are specific security concerns regarding the safety of employees taking deposits to local depository banks. The desire to speed up the collection cycle by having daily armored carrier pickups must be balanced against the cost of each individual pickup.

One solution to this problem that is becoming increasingly common is a product referred to as a *smart safe* (also known as a *virtual vault*). The armored carrier, working in conjunction with the firm's depository bank, provides a special safe (i.e., smart safe) to the retail outlet that records deposits into the safe and reports them to the armored carrier and the bank. The bank provides provisional credit at the time of the deposit into the safe, and the armored carrier picks up the contents of the safe on a reduced schedule, perhaps weekly instead of daily.

Smart safes also provide the ability for a bank to service retail outlets that are not near any of its branches. Working through the armored carrier, the bank can effectively accept deposits in any location that the armored carrier can service and is not limited to the geography of the bank's branches. As a result, this can also help geographically dispersed retailers handle their cash consolidation needs.

2. MERCHANT SERVICES

Merchant services refers to the services offered to help in processing credit and debit card transactions. While *merchant services* principally refers to the acceptance and processing of card transactions, it also often includes ancillary services such as returns and adjustments, point-of-sale terminals, supplies, and customer support.

Merchants that accept mail, phone, or Internet orders made with card payments may mitigate their risk of fraud by using an address verification service (AVS) that matches the address provided by the cardholder with the account billing address on record with the issuer. AVS and confirmation of the card verification value or card verification code (CVV/CVC) number printed on the reverse side of a credit card are two of the most common practices in reducing risks due to fraudulent credit card transactions.

3. REMOTE DEPOSIT CAPTURE (RDC)

RDC involves using a check scanner to capture an image of a check payment, which is then used to facilitate deposit at the depository bank(s) by image deposit. This service—available in the United States—eliminates the need to gather the checks and take them to the bank or send them via mail or overnight courier. This speeds up collection time, reduces the risk that the checks will be lost or stolen in transit, and typically reduces the overall cost of check processing. As with a smart safe, RDC allows a depository bank to service locations that are physically distant from a bank facility, alleviating the need for subsequent cash consolidation from a local field bank. In some cases, RDC scanners are being incorporated into the electronic safes used for smart safe services, providing a consolidated service for retail organizations. The product is limited to checks denominated in US dollars.

4. CHECK CONVERSION

Check conversion involves scanning the payor's check and converting it to an ACH debit. The benefit of this is that ACH transactions are typically less expensive than check processing. Checks can be converted at the point of presentment (e.g., the retail sales counter), in the back office or deposit-processing operation, or in a lockbox operation (see the discussion of lockbox below). Each type of conversion has a different standard entry class code.[6] As with RDC, check conversion is available only at US banks and is limited to checks drawn on US-domiciled accounts. Unlike RDC, which is available for both consumer and commercial checks, check conversion is limited to consumer checks under $25,000.[7]

5. MAIL PAYMENTS

Mail payments can be processed internally or outsourced to a lockbox processor as discussed in the next section. In an internal company processing center, check and/or payment card processing, along with deposit preparation, are performed in-house. For checks, the processing generally involves the following steps:

- Receiving and opening the mail
- Separating the check from the remittance advice, which provides information on who is paying and what they are paying

---

6. *Standard entry class* refers to a code that is used to distinguish different types of ACH transactions. A list of common standard entry class codes is provided in Appendix 12.1.

7. The technical limitation is to checks that do not contain an auxiliary on-us field in the MICR line, which is basically equivalent to consumer checks, as most business checks have an auxiliary on-us field. For complete details, refer to the current NACHA operating rules and guidelines.

- Forwarding the remittance advice, amount, and date of payment to the accounts receivable (A/R) department

- Preparing the check for deposit (i.e., endorsement and deposit preparation), or in the case of consumer payments, preparing the check for possible conversion into an ACH debit

- Transporting the check to the organization's deposit bank, employing remote deposit capture, or converting an eligible check into an ACH debit

For payment card collections, the card information and amount must be captured and sent to the merchant processor to start the collection process. Companies that choose to capture card information in-house and submit the information for collection must maintain compliance with the Payment Card Industry Data Security Standard (PCI DSS). A firm may decide to outsource the processing of card payment information received through the mail due to compliance requirements. If a firm does use in-house processing for card payments, it must meet PCI DSS requirements including the following:

- Install and maintain a firewall configuration to protect cardholder data.

- Do not use vendor-supplied defaults for system passwords and other security parameters.

- Protect stored cardholder data.

- Encrypt transmission of cardholder data across open public networks.

- Use and regularly update antivirus software or programs.

- Develop and maintain secure systems and applications.

- Restrict access to cardholder data by business need to know.

- Assign a unique ID to each person with computer access.

- Restrict physical access to cardholder data.

- Track and monitor all access to network resources and cardholder data.

- Regularly test security systems and processes.

- Maintain a policy that addresses information security for all personnel.

The primary advantage of an in-house processing center is that the firm maintains control of the collections operation. Maintaining control may be especially important if capture of detailed remittance information is required in order to allow the A/R department to properly apply the payments. The primary disadvantages are the need to provide appropriate controls (e.g., segregation of duties and security over payments), potential processing delays of internal processing, and the need to add staff to handle peak volumes of transactions.

Traditionally, in-house processing was performed either by very small firms with low volumes of check and card payments or by fairly large firms that could justify the expense of the automated equipment required to manage high volumes. The introduction of RDC and improved scanning technology, along with increased use of electronic payment and remittance transmission methods, has changed these guidelines. In today's collections environment, the choice between using an in-house processing center and a lockbox must be evaluated carefully to ensure the most cost-effective solution for the company.

6. LOCKBOX

A lockbox system is a collection tool in which a financial institution or third-party vendor receives mailed payments at specified post office box addresses, processes the remittances, and credits the payments into a payee's bank account. While lockbox services are available in a number of countries, they are most widely used in the United States, due to the widespread use of paper checks.

The major advantages of a lockbox system over an internal company payment-processing center include:

- Reduced mail and processing float

- Improved access to remittance information

- Reduced information float

- Reduced risk and improved security since payments are no longer received internally

- Improved control and record-keeping capabilities

- Uninterrupted service

- Scalability

- Proper segregation of duties

Lockbox procedures also establish an external audit trail for payments received and segregate check processing from other A/R functions. Generally, lockbox operators can establish business continuity plans and disaster recovery sites more readily than individual firms, which can result in a higher level of reliability in payment processing. Finally, a lockbox is generally easier to scale up or down as business volumes change, relative to an in-house processing center. This is especially advantageous for firms with seasonal product lines.

There are three basic types of lockboxes:

- **Retail lockboxes** process payments that involve machine-readable remittance documents (i.e., "coupons"), such as utility and credit card payments. These are typically consumer-to-business (C2B) payments and tend to be high volume, which may justify the cost of the equipment used to process and read the remittance documents.

- **Wholesale lockboxes** typically process B2B payments. Although wholesale lockboxes do not handle the payment volume of retail lockboxes, the former must handle remittance information that is usually not machine-readable. Subsequently, treasury professionals tend to use wholesale lockboxes when the dollar value of their payments is high, payment volume is lower, and the remittance information does not include a standardized remittance coupon.

- **Hybrid (or "wholetail") lockboxes** combine features of both wholesale and retail lockboxes. Specifically, a hybrid lockbox would handle smaller volumes but machine-readable remittance documents.

The increased volume of electronic remittance payments has spurred the creation of an electronic lockbox. This service combines and presents remittance information from electronic payments. While this service is not literally a lockbox since there is no actual mail involved, it does have many of the reporting features traditionally associated with lockbox processing.

As mentioned in the previous section, the introduction of RDC and related scanning technology has led a number of firms to move away from external providers and perform their own processing in-house. While in-house processing can reduce processing and collection float, and may be less costly than a bank or third-party provider lockbox, it does not provide all of the benefits of a standard lockbox service.

Assessing the suitability of using a lockbox system or network requires a cost/benefit analysis to determine whether the net benefit of reduced collection float and/or elimination of in-house processing outweighs the incremental costs of lockbox processing. The net benefit from a lockbox is the reduction in the opportunity cost of float adjusted for the difference between lockbox charges and internal processing costs. Three factors determine the opportunity cost of float:

- The dollar amount of the collected items

- The total collection time for items

- The firm's opportunity cost of funds (e.g., the short-term investment or borrowing rate)

Therefore, the first step in a lockbox cost/benefit analysis is to compare the differences in collection float (i.e., mail, processing, and availability float) for a company processing center versus a lockbox provider. Note, however, that in the case of a retail lockbox, float savings may not be as important as improved efficiency and lower per-item costs.

Collection float is usually measured in dollar-days and is a function of a transaction's dollar amount and the number of days of float delay. The dollar-days of float on an individual check are calculated by multiplying the dollar amount of the check by the number of days from the time the payor mails the check to the time when the payee is granted credit, or availability, of collected funds. Average daily float is calculated by dividing the sum of the dollar-days of float for all items received in a certain period by the number of days in the period. The cost of float is a product of the opportunity cost of funds and the average daily float.

An example of a lockbox cost/benefit calculation is shown in Exhibit 12.1. In the exhibit, the lockbox processor charges are the sum of a fixed cost and a variable cost based on the volume of items processed. Lockbox providers have many different methods of charging for services, but the costs can be classified as *fixed* or *variable*. Fixed monthly costs may include fees for renting the post office box, sending remittance data to the company, and providing balance reporting and account maintenance. Often, several of these costs are combined into a monthly lockbox maintenance charge. There also may be a charge for transferring funds to a concentration bank.

EXHIBIT 12.1 LOCKBOX COST/BENEFIT ANALYSIS

This exhibit shows the lockbox savings and associated costs for a company with $108,000,000 annual sales ($9,000,000 per month). Each of the items is assumed to be a batch of checks with an average check size of $9,000; the annual volume of checks is 12,000. The company's annual opportunity cost is 9%. The company's internal check-processing cost (assuming no lockbox) is $0.25 per item. The lockbox processor charges $10,000 per year plus a processing cost of $0.50 per item.

		WITHOUT LOCKBOX	
BATCH	DOLLAR AMOUNT	CALENDAR DAYS OF COLLECTION FLOAT WITHOUT LOCKBOX	TOTAL DOLLAR-DAYS
1	$1,500,000	x 4 =	$ 6,000,000
2	4,500,000	x 2 =	9,000,000
3	3,000,000	x 6 =	18,000,000
TOTAL DEPOSITS	$9,000,000	TOTAL FLOAT WITHOUT LOCKBOX	$33,000,000

DIVIDED BY: 30 CALENDAR DAYS =	$ 1,100,000
TIMES: OPPORTUNITY COST/INVESTMENT RATE	x 9%
EQUALS: ANNUAL COST OF FLOAT	$ 99,000

		WITH LOCKBOX	
BATCH	DOLLAR AMOUNT	CALENDAR DAYS OF COLLECTION FLOAT WITH LOCKBOX	TOTAL DOLLAR-DAYS
1	$1,500,000	x 3 =	$ 4,500,000
2	4,500,000	x 1 =	4,500,000
3	3,000,000	x 5 =	15,000,000
TOTAL DEPOSITS	$9,000,000	TOTAL FLOAT WITH LOCKBOX	$24,000,000

DIVIDED BY: 30 CALENDAR DAYS =	$ 800,000
TIMES: OPPORTUNITY COST/INVESTMENT RATE	x 9%
EQUALS: ANNUAL COST OF FLOAT	$ 72,000

ANNUAL COST OF FLOAT WITHOUT LOCKBOX	$ 99,000
ANNUAL COST OF FLOAT WITH LOCKBOX	(72,000)
LOCKBOX FLOAT SAVINGS	$ 27,000
FIXED LOCKBOX COST	$ (10,000)
VARIABLE LOCKBOX COST: 12,000 CHECKS x $0.50	(6,000)
ELIMINATION OF INTERNAL PROCESSING COST: 12,000 x $0.25	3,000
NET DOLLAR BENEFIT OF LOCKBOX	$ 14,000

Variable costs may include charges for deposits, per-item charges, and charges for transmission of remittance data, photocopying, and imaging. Usually, these and other customized processing charges are calculated on a per-item basis. Some costs may be either fixed or variable depending upon the lockbox processor. For example, some processors use a fixed monthly fee for deposit preparation while others charge by deposit. When preparing a cost/ benefit analysis, it is important to understand how the actual charges are being calculated.

Lockbox providers also differ in terms of service flexibility and quality. Only those providers meeting the firm's standard service criteria should be included in the final lockbox selection process.

A collection or lockbox study is conducted to estimate the float savings of implementing the lockbox. A collection study uses data from remittance envelopes and images of checks to obtain information, such as the location and geographic concentration of customers and the location of the customers making the largest check payments. Often, the company's existing depository institutions are asked to perform an endpoint analysis that provides information about availability on both an aggregate and item-by-item basis. Additional information necessary for the collection study includes intercity mail times and bank availability schedules.

Specialized treasury consulting companies and major cash management banks perform periodic studies to compare mail times for various combinations of cities.

Availability schedules, which can be negotiated, vary from bank to bank and must be obtained from all banks under consideration. The results of mail time studies are combined with information from availability schedules to compare providers. Banks or consulting firms use these data, in conjunction with an analysis of a company's actual remittances, to determine which cities or combinations of cities are the most effective collection sites. A computer analysis is performed to produce an optimal solution.

7. ELECTRONIC FUNDS TRANSFER (EFT) WITH REMITTANCE INFORMATION

As previously mentioned, the availability and reliability of remittance information is a key issue in processing collections. Historically, one of the problems with EFT transactions was the inability to transmit remittance information with the payment. As a result, firms received remittance information separately from the electronic payment and were forced to match the two. This is a particular problem when trading partners or customers are making partial payments or taking deductions from the face amount of an actual invoice. As a result, many of the EFT systems around the world have introduced extended remittance information capabilities largely modeled after the ISO 20022 payment standard supported by SWIFT.

For treasury areas, however, the focus often remains on the payment portion of the cycle. Efficiencies can usually be realized in the payment process by replacing paper document flows and payments with electronic methods. It may be difficult, however, for a selling firm to motivate its customers (i.e., buying firms) to switch from check-based payments to electronic payments, due to the loss of disbursement float for the buying firm. In these situations it is helpful to consider the payment terms that would make the buying firm indifferent between switching from check to electronic payments. Such payment terms (known as *float-neutral terms*) could involve adjusting the timing (i.e., value date) of the payment or negotiating a payment discount that would provide the same present value cost as the old terms. The payment discount would in essence maintain whatever float the buying firm was receiving with the paper payment, and can be calculated using the float-neutral calculation shown below.

To illustrate, consider a business transaction where the buyer can either pay by check or by electronic transfer. If the difference between the value date of the payment methods (from the buyer's perspective) is three days, then float-neutral terms would either allow the buyer to pay electronically three days later than by check or offer the buyer a discount that would make the electronic payment equivalent to the check payment. This example assumes no difference in the cost of the payment methods to the buyer.

If the discount approach is used, the amount of the discount will depend on the cost of funds (i.e., opportunity cost) for the buyer and the timing difference in days between check and electronic payments.

The general formula for determining the appropriate discount is as follows:

$$\text{Discount} = 1 - \frac{1}{\left[1 + TD\left(\dfrac{r}{365}\right)\right]}$$

Where:

TD = Total days' difference in timing between check and electronic payments

r = Annual opportunity cost rate

For this calculation, assume TD = 3 days, as suggested in the text above, and r = 5%. This results in the following discount for float-neutral terms:

$$\text{Discount} = 1 - \frac{1}{\left[1 + 3\left(\dfrac{0.05}{365}\right)\right]}$$

$$= 1 - \frac{1}{1.00041096} = 1 - 0.99958921$$

$$= 0.00041079 \text{ or } 0.041\%$$

This calculation indicates that a discount of 0.041% would result in the same present value cost for both payment types. Further, this implies that the buyer would be indifferent, at least with respect to present value costs, between paying via check or electronically. If the discount for paying electronically exceeds 0.041%, then the buying firm would prefer to pay electronically. However, if the discount is less than 0.041%, then the buying firm might prefer to maintain the extra three days of float and forgo the discount.

8. ELECTRONIC BILL PRESENTMENT AND PAYMENT (EBPP) AND ELECTRONIC INVOICE PRESENTMENT AND PAYMENT (EIPP)

Although often thought of as disbursement products since they allow consumers or firms to make payments electronically, EBPP and EIPP are actually a bridge between collections and disbursements that enable firms to send electronic statements and receive electronic remittances from their customers. With both products (EBPP for retail customers and EIPP for corporate customers), a firm sends billing data to its customer, typically through an e-mail with a link to the firm's billing portal or website. The customer can review the billing information, ask questions, and modify payment amounts as needed. Once satisfied, the customer authorizes payment electronically, typically triggering an EFT debit. Because the collecting company, or the third-party vendor, controls both the transmission of the billing data and the subsequent collection, the remittance information is already linked to the payment, simplifying subsequent posting to A/R and reducing any exception processing.

9. CONSOLIDATED REMITTANCE PROCESSING (CRP)

Because payments come in many forms and types, firms are often forced to deal with multiple sources of remittance information and payment data, often in widely different formats. This can result in processing delays and expensive exception item processing. One solution to this is CRP. The predecessor of CRP is a service often referred to as an *electronic lockbox*, which provides a single collection point for all ACH and wire payments; it can also process remittance advices from a variety of incoming formats into a single format for transmission to the firm's A/R department for posting and reconciliation. CRP takes this a step further by consolidating all remittance information into one stream of data in a common format. This can include payments made via EFT, check, and card. In some versions of CRP, the vendor (often a bank) also provides a service called *receivables matching*, in which the vendor matches a processed payment against the firm's open invoices, applies the payment, and updates the A/R record.

10. IMAGING TECHNOLOGY

In addition to being used for check processing (e.g., RDC), imaging technology can also facilitate the processing of both wholesale and retail remittance information. This technology allows paper documents, such as checks and remittance advices, to be scanned, converted to digital images, and stored for subsequent distribution, handling, and processing. Having this payment information readily available is especially beneficial for firms that must research a high volume of customer service inquiries (e.g., mortgage, insurance, and utility companies). Potential benefits of applying image technology to the remittance-processing function include:

- Reduced overall processing costs
- Reduced courier fees
- Increased productivity
- Improved accuracy
- Automated updating of A/R
- Improved response time to customer inquiries
- Faster resolution of lockbox discrepancies

C. Cross-Border Collections and Trade Management Products

International or cross-border payments add a significant degree of complexity to collections. In addition to all of the issues already discussed for domestic collections, cross-border collections add foreign exchange risk and heightened risk of credit management. As a result, a number of payment mechanisms have been developed to use in international business.

The most frequently used cross-border trade payment mechanisms (i.e., open account, documentary collection, and letters of credit) can be explained in terms of increasing levels of protection, complexity, and cost. Open account terms are the simplest and least costly, but offer the least protection for the seller. Documentary collections are more complex and costly, but offer some protection to both parties. Finally, letters of credit, which typically include documentary collection as part of the process, are the most complex and costly vehicles for international trade, but they provide the best combined security for both parties. Exhibit 12.2 shows the hierarchy of the primary international trade payment mechanisms in terms of protection for the buyer or seller.

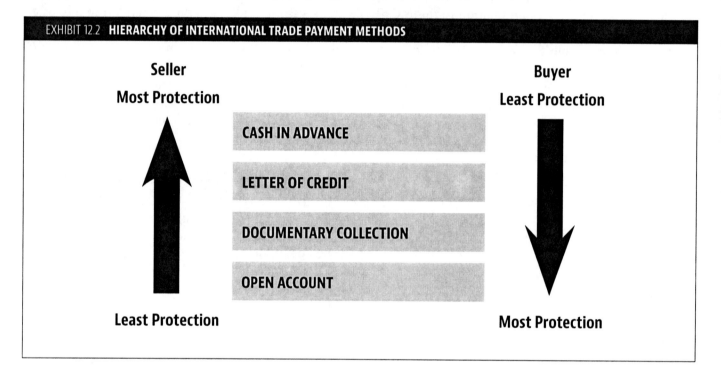

EXHIBIT 12.2 HIERARCHY OF INTERNATIONAL TRADE PAYMENT METHODS

Regardless of the method of trade payment, its use must be agreed upon by the buyer and the seller. The method of payment is usually specified in the buyer's or the seller's currency, but it may be in a third currency, if acceptable to both parties.

1. OPEN ACCOUNT

Open account is the most common form of credit extension and collection. It is widely used internationally when two trading partners have an existing relationship and essentially trust each other to complete their transaction obligations. When there is no such relationship, a seller will often require credit risk protection through either a letter of credit or documentary collection.

2. LETTER OF CREDIT (L/C)

An L/C is a document issued by a bank, guaranteeing the payment of a customer's draft up to a stated amount for a specified period, provided certain conditions are met. The L/C substitutes a bank's credit for that of the buyer, virtually eliminating the credit risk to the seller. L/Cs are a widely used method of payment for import and export shipments and are used frequently as a financing vehicle for cross-border trade transactions.

a. Commercial L/C

A commercial or documentary L/C is issued by a bank as the intended mechanism of payment in relation to a trade transaction involving the domestic or international shipment of merchandise. A commercial L/C typically requires presentment of a draft, commercial invoice, and related shipping documents; hence, it is documentary in nature. Because a bank's role in an L/C transaction is the examination of documents, not the underlying merchandise, it is the responsibility of the importer to specify the documentation required prior to payment, which reasonably ensures the receipt of the exact merchandise ordered. Additionally, since the bank's responsibility only extends to examining and approving documents, the buyer often pays for the goods prior to receiving them.

L/Cs may be revocable or irrevocable. A revocable L/C can be canceled by the bank or the buyer at any time. This limits the credit protection available to the beneficiary of the L/C (i.e., the exporter), who might ship goods only to find that the related L/C has been canceled. An irrevocable L/C can only be canceled if all parties to the transaction agree, thus providing maximum protection to the exporter. Most L/Cs are irrevocable.

Banks may serve a variety of roles in L/C transactions:

- The **issuing bank** is the importer's bank that issues the L/C in favor of the exporter.

- The **advising bank** advises the exporter of an L/C in its favor.

- Other banks that may be involved in the transaction are the **negotiating bank** and the **confirming bank**:

  o The advising and negotiating banks are frequently the same bank, performing dual roles. The advising/negotiating bank examines the documents presented by the beneficiary (i.e., the exporter), receives payment from the issuing bank, and pays the beneficiary.

  o If requested, the advising/negotiating bank may add confirmation, as the confirming bank, to an L/C. In doing so, the confirming bank commits to the exporter that payment will be made if documents meet the terms and conditions of the L/C, regardless of the issuing bank's ability to pay. If an L/C is confirmed, the confirming bank will be the negotiating bank, as well.

Once documentation has been presented, the L/C may provide either immediate payment (i.e., sight draft) or deferred payment (i.e., time draft) to the exporter. When the L/C requires the presentment of a sight draft, then the advising/negotiating bank pays the exporter immediately and is reimbursed by the issuing bank. When the L/C requires presentment of a time draft, the exporter provides credit terms to the buyer. The exporter may be able to receive payment prior to maturity by discounting (i.e., selling at a discounted value) the time draft to a local bank. At this point, the discounted L/C becomes a banker's acceptance, which is described in more detail later. A deferred payment L/C provides presentation of one or more sight drafts at specified dates in the future and sometimes extends over several years. When medium-term financing is provided for the export of capital goods, a deferred payment L/C may be used in conjunction with a term loan agreement. Exhibit 12.3 illustrates the participants in the issuance of a typical commercial L/C. The collection/payment process is identical to that discussed below and illustrated in Exhibit 12.4.

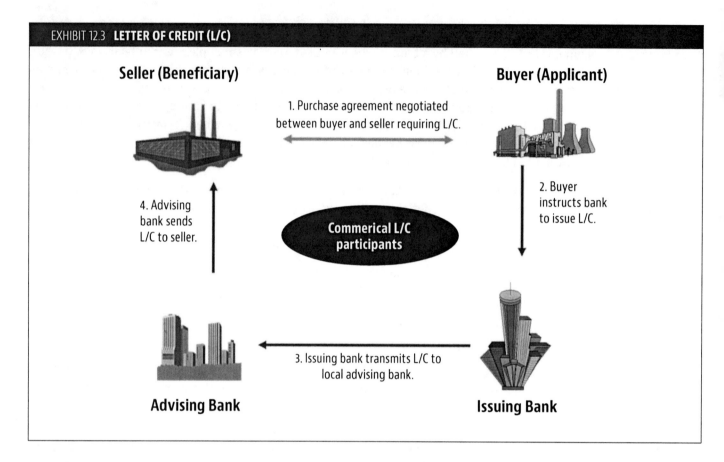

EXHIBIT 12.3 **LETTER OF CREDIT (L/C)**

The International Chamber of Commerce (ICC) has established rules governing commercial L/Cs, known as *Uniform Customs and Practice for Documentary Credits (UCP)*. The current rules are outlined under UCP 600, and these rules affect almost every credit issued under the ICC's UCP. Most notably, UCP 600 establishes an absolute deadline of five calendar days to review documents and pay or decline a draw.

In general, standard credit language in international trade agreements should be in compliance with and refer to UCP 600 to ensure proper administration and interpretation in the event of any legal disputes.

In conjunction with UCP 600, issuers should consider the administration of standby L/Cs and ensure that they are issued under the rules of ICC's publication *International Standby Practices: ISP98*. An increasing number of banks are issuing standby L/Cs under ISP98, because the guidelines offer a number of benefits to issuers. Most importantly, the ISP98 rules are often easier and clearer to apply than the UCP rules in the context of standby L/Cs.

b. Standby L/C or Guarantee

Standby L/Cs are variations of commercial L/Cs. While standby L/Cs can be issued by insurance companies in some countries, they are issued primarily by banks. In the United States they are referred to as *standby L/Cs* for regulatory reasons, while most of the rest of the world refers to them as *guarantees*. Once issued, a standby L/C serves as a vehicle to ensure the financial performance of a bank's customer to a third-party beneficiary. Unlike a standard L/C, which is paid upon presentment and validation of the required documents, a standby L/C or guarantee is only payable in the event that the primary entity fails to pay or perform some specified duty. A standby L/C typically requires the presentation of a sight draft and documentation that supports the beneficiary's claim of nonperformance on the part of the issuing bank's customer.

3. DOCUMENTARY COLLECTION

Documentary collection is a trade payment mechanism that processes the collection of a draft and accompanying shipping documents through international correspondent banks. Instructions regarding the transaction specifics are contained in a collection letter that accompanies the documentation. It is the responsibility of the exporter (i.e., the seller) to determine the instructions specified in the collection letter. As noted below, any discrepancies between the instructions and the actual documents presented for payment will delay and may bar any payment by the bank.

The typical information disclosed in a documentary collection letter includes:

- Name of the exporter

- Name and address of the importer

- Information regarding the collecting bank

- Details of the documentation accompanying the collection

- Date, tenor (i.e., length), and value of the collection

- Details of bank and other charges to be paid by the exporter, importer, or both

- Recourse procedures in the event of nonacceptance or nonpayment

- Any nonstandard terms or conditions

Absent a formal letter of credit, banks that are involved in a documentary collection normally act only as collecting and paying agents and assume no direct obligation for ensuring that payment is made. Banks involved in these transactions perform different roles:

- The **remitting bank**, which is the bank of the exporter, receives the collection documents from the exporter. These documents are then remitted (i.e., forwarded) to the importer's bank along with instructions for payment. The importer's bank is referred to as the *collecting* or *presenting bank* in this transaction.

- The **collecting or presenting bank** (the importer's bank, also referred to as the *issuing bank* when the transaction includes a letter of credit as discussed above) is the bank that presents the documents to the importer. In exchange for these documents, the bank collects either cash payment in the form of a bank draft or a promise of future payment in the form of a bill of exchange.

A collection letter specifies the exact procedures to be followed before shipping documents are released to the importer. The importer usually requires physical possession of the shipping documents in order to obtain the merchandise. Documents typically are released either against payment or acceptance:

- **Documents against payment (D/P)** use a sight draft, which is a draft payable on demand, that requires the collecting bank to receive full and final payment of the amount owed prior to releasing the documents.

- **Documents against acceptance (D/A)** use a time draft, which is a draft payable on a specified future date, that must be accepted by the importer before the collecting bank may release documents. Upon maturity of the time draft, it is presented to the importer for payment.

Once full and final payment is received from the importer, the collecting bank transfers funds to the remitting bank, as instructed, for payment to the exporter. Less commonly, the remitting bank advances payment to the exporter at a discount and then collects final payment on the due date. But this advance payment depends upon a preexisting credit relationship between the remitting bank and its exporter-customer.

In the event of nonpayment or nonacceptance, the exporter has the cost of remarketing the goods to another buyer or paying to have the merchandise returned. The exporter may request that the collecting bank initiate formal action against the importer for nonperformance. Exhibit 12.4 illustrates a documentary collection.

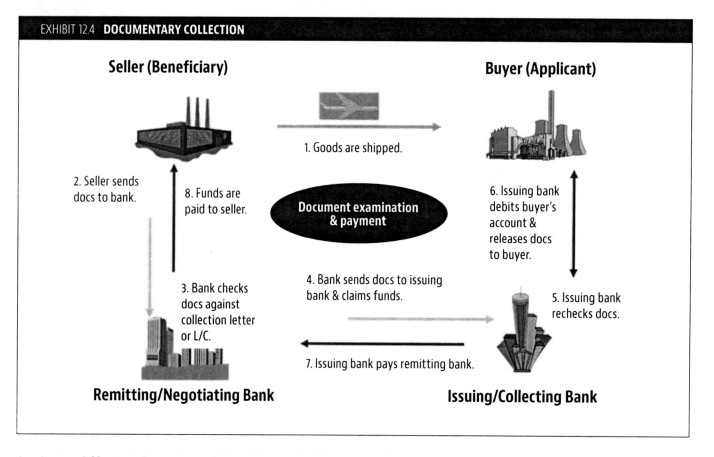

EXHIBIT 12.4 DOCUMENTARY COLLECTION

Seller (Beneficiary)

Buyer (Applicant)

1. Goods are shipped.

2. Seller sends docs to bank.

8. Funds are paid to seller.

Document examination & payment

6. Issuing bank debits buyer's account & releases docs to buyer.

3. Bank checks docs against collection letter or L/C.

4. Bank sends docs to issuing bank & claims funds.

5. Issuing bank rechecks docs.

7. Issuing bank pays remitting bank.

Remitting/Negotiating Bank

Issuing/Collecting Bank

A primary difference between a documentary collection and a letter of credit is that the collecting bank does not guarantee payment to the seller under a documentary collection. This is one reason why documentary collections are less expensive and less complicated than letters of credit.

An issue with both documentary collections and letters of credit is discrepant documents. Whenever the documentation does not match the terms and conditions of the documentary collection or letter of credit, either the documentation must be updated, the agreement must be amended, or the seller must waive the discrepancy. All of these actions take time and usually involve additional costs to both parties in the transaction.

It is important to realize that with both documentary collections and letters of credit, the banks are only reviewing documents for completeness and accuracy. There is no review of the physical merchandise and no guarantee that it is not defective. As a result, buyers often include an inspection requirement as part of the terms of the collection or letter of credit. The collecting bank will not process the transaction without presentation of an inspection document that indicates the goods have been inspected and meet the requirements of the collection. A current trend in the business is the ongoing consolidation and integration of logistics and trade solutions providers to allow for increased efficiency and risk reduction. These vendors provide a "one-stop shop" for customers by managing the physical movement of products as well as the information and documents needed for documentary collections and L/Cs.

4. BANKER'S ACCEPTANCE (BA)[8]

A BA can be used to finance the import, export, or domestic shipment of goods, as well as the storage of properly titled goods. BAs are used frequently in conjunction with L/Cs requiring a time draft drawn on a bank.

A BA is created when one person signs an unconditional written order directing a bank to pay a certain sum of money on demand or at a definite time to another person, usually to finance the shipment or temporary storage of goods. The unconditional written order, also known as a *time draft*, is stamped as *accepted* by the bank.

By accepting the draft, the bank agrees to pay the face value of the obligation if the buyer (i.e., the issuer that drew the draft) fails to make payment. Since the accepting bank assumes the risk of the buyer defaulting, it makes it easier for the buyer or seller to undertake international trade.

A BA is a less expensive form of short-term financing than a loan. BAs may be held by the bank until maturity or be sold at a discount in secondary markets as short-term negotiable instruments, where the bank's credit standing is substituted for the creditworthiness of the issuer.

The cost of BA financing has two components: the discount rate (i.e., the rate earned by the investor) and the commission. Most BA financing is accomplished with eligible BAs, which have a maturity not exceeding 180 days and are sold at a nominal spread over US Treasury bills. The rates at which they trade are known as *BA rates*. Eligible underlying transactions include the import or export of goods, domestic storage transactions with the documents conveying title attached, and storage of readily marketable staples secured by warehouse receipts.

5. TRADE ACCEPTANCE

A trade acceptance is similar to a BA except it is drawn on, and accepted by, an importer. It can be used to verify an importer's obligation to pay for purchased merchandise where the exporter is satisfied with the credit risk. Trade acceptances often are used by importers to secure financing from a bank or, similar to BAs, may even be sold to a bank or an investor at a discount prior to maturity.

6. OTHER TRADE PAYMENT METHODS

Other less frequently used cross-border trade payment mechanisms include cash in advance (i.e., cash before delivery) and consignment, as well as barter, countertrade, and trading companies:

- **Barter and Countertrade:** Barter involves the direct exchange of goods or services between two parties without the exchange of money. It is most frequently used when funds cannot be repatriated due to currency controls or other legal limitations. Countertrade is similar to barter but is used by firms that do not use currencies that are internationally traded to pay for imports from other countries. For example, an exporter ships merchandise to the countertrading country. In exchange, it takes merchandise that may be sold elsewhere in the world. Pricing and foreign exchange rates are established between the trading parties. This differs from barter in

---

8. This discussion refers to standard BAs created as an acceptance of a draft and related to a trade transaction. In Canada, the term *banker's acceptance* usually refers to a short-term investment instrument issued by banks, essentially similar to a negotiable certificate of deposit in the United States.

that the exporter is receiving valuable goods for resale locally to recoup its costs rather than a product that it intends to keep and use for its own purposes.

- **Trading Companies:** Trading companies are used when an exporter sells products at a discount to an export trading company, which then resells the products internationally. In some cases, a global parent company will create a trading company entity that purchases products and then resells to subsidiaries of the company.

IV. CONCENTRATION OF FUNDS

To the extent that a firm does all of its business with one bank in one country, collected cash receipts can be easily combined into a pool of usable funds via ZBA or internal book transfers. However, most firms deal with more than one bank and increasingly in more than one country. This results in pockets of money in different accounts in different banks and sometimes in different currencies. This creates a number of complexities for treasury professionals who are responsible for managing those funds. As a result, once cash is collected, the next step is to concentrate those funds into one or more concentration accounts at the firm's lead bank in preparation for future use, either for investment or disbursement. Exhibit 12.5 illustrates some of the potential transfers and accounts involved in a cash concentration system. This is a particularly complex example and includes multiple types of concentration. Most corporate systems are often much simpler.

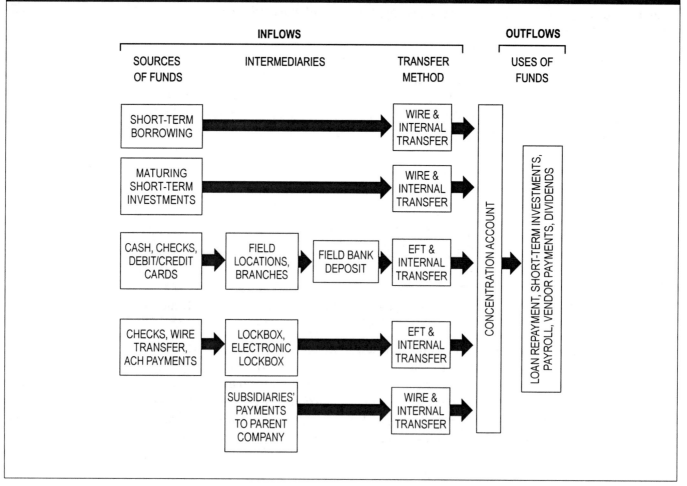

EXHIBIT 12.5 **CASH CONCENTRATION SYSTEM**

The two major objectives of a cash concentration system are to efficiently move the funds from deposit banks to the concentration bank and to minimize excess bank balances. Moving all the funds into a single concentration account enables those funds to be managed more efficiently and effectively, and facilitates daily liquidity management. Concentration of funds enables a firm to:

- Balance excess and deficit cash positions across multiple locations, entities, and currencies
- Optimize idle balances for offsetting fees or optimizing earnings credits
- Invest a larger amount of funds, potentially increasing interest income
- Pay down debt faster and minimize borrowings, potentially reducing interest expense
- Take advantage of supplier and/or vendor discount terms, potentially reducing the cost of goods sold or operating expenses

A. Domestic Concentration of Funds

Domestic cash concentration systems typically transfer funds from outlying depository locations, often at different banks, to a central bank account at a firm's primary bank, commonly referred to as a *concentration account*. This process is often referred to as *sweeping*.[9] While sweeping is particularly important in the United States due to the historically fragmented nature of the US banking environment, sweeping can occur in any country where an organization deals with more than one bank.

Many firms collect receipts at field locations (i.e., over-the-counter collections), which include local offices/branches and retail stores. Retailers accept cash, checks, and payment cards at the point of sale (POS). A wholesale customer or its agent may also deliver checks or cash to a vendor's office. Alternatively, a payee or a payee's agent may pick up cash or checks directly from a customer when making a delivery. Historically, these payments were all deposited into a bank located near each field location in the interest of security and convenience. These deposits were then swept into the firm's main concentration account, typically through the use of wire transfers or ACH debits. The introduction of banking services such as RDC and smart safes has simplified the process by allowing many firms to eliminate most field bank accounts and deposit funds directly into their concentration account. As a side note, it is worth mentioning that card transactions are automatically concentrated since the merchant services provider typically deposits the proceeds into a single account.

Most large retailers transmit information on local receipts from POS terminals to headquarters. Headquarters then transmits the ACH debit instructions to a concentration bank. In addition, some third-party providers specialize in gathering deposit information from field units by phone, POS terminal, or computer. After gathering the deposit data, the third party can create an ACH file that is sent directly to the concentration bank, which then processes the file through the ACH payments system. Alternatively, the deposit data can be sent to headquarters, allowing headquarters personnel to determine the transfer amounts and to prepare and transmit the ACH debit file. Some concentration banks also can receive deposit data reported by phone, e-mail, or other electronic communication directly from the field offices, and offer online access for headquarters to review deposit-reporting activity and identify non-reporting units.

One alternative to an ACH payment is a wire transfer. However, because wire transfers are an expensive funds transfer mechanism, they are used primarily to concentrate large dollar amounts when same-day value and finality are critical. Consequently, a break-even analysis is required to determine the appropriate funds transfer mechanism.

---

9. This should not be confused with sweep accounts used in the United States for the overnight investment of surplus funds.

When determining whether to use an ACH debit or a wire transfer to concentrate funds, the first step is to establish the value of funds acceleration. In this calculation, the relevant opportunity cost of funds is typically either a short-term investment rate (e.g., the US Treasury bill rate) or a short-term borrowing rate, depending upon whether the firm is a net investor or net borrower. By comparing the value of accelerated funds to the incremental cost of the wire, the appropriate transfer method can be identified.

Assume the following:

- The incremental cost of an ACH debit is $1.00.

- The incremental cost of a wire transfer is $10.00.

- The annual opportunity cost of funds is 3.5%.

- Funds are available one business day sooner with a wire transfer than with an ACH transfer.

The formula for computing the break-even wire transfer amount is as follows:

$$\text{Minimum Transfer} = \frac{\text{Wire Cost} - \text{ACH Cost}}{\text{Days Accelerated} \times \left(\dfrac{\text{Opportunity Cost}}{\text{365 Days}} \right)}$$

$$= \frac{\$10.00 - \$1.00}{1 \text{ Day} \times \left(\dfrac{0.035}{\text{365 Days}} \right)} = \frac{\$9.00}{1 \times 0.00009589} = \$93,858$$

Using the values provided above, the calculation indicates that the minimum funds transfer amount is $93,858. That is, as long as the wire transfer amount is larger than $93,858, the additional cost of the wire transfer is justified. If the transfer amount is less than $93,858, it is more cost effective to transfer funds via ACH.

B. Global Concentration of Funds

Multinational firms face a much more complex situation when concentrating funds. The additional complexities arise because of the need to juggle excess and deficit cash positions across multiple entities, regulatory environments, and currencies. As a result, multinational companies generally have to use a mix of different concentration techniques depending on the banking structures and regulations in the countries in which they operate. This section describes three pooling arrangements that are commonly used by multinational firms to concentrate cash.

1. PHYSICAL POOLING

In physical pooling, funds in separate subaccounts are automatically transferred to/from a concentration account in order to eliminate idle cash and fund cash outflows. The participating entities are either in surplus or deficit from a transactional perspective, but the bank accounts themselves have a balance of zero. Physical pooling can be used across multiple legal entities located in the same or different countries, but the funds must be in the same currency and all accounts must be with the same bank. The funds movement between the participating entities is accounted for via intercompany loans, which must be at an "arm's length" or market rate. This is somewhat analogous to a ZBA account structure, but differs in that there is no requirement that all the accounts belong to one entity, hence the need for intercompany loans.

2. NOTIONAL POOLING

Notional pooling is accomplished by making balancing entries on a set of virtual accounts with no changes to the bank accounts held by company entities. As with physical pooling, all of the accounts must be held at the same bank. The bank managing the notional pool provides an interest statement that reflects the net offset, which is similar to what would have been achieved with physical pooling. As there is no physical movement of money, intercompany loans are not required to account for the notional transactions. Banks usually require credit facilities to support any deficit balances in the pool, and notional pooling often requires extensive cross-guarantees among subsidiaries, which many firms find very difficult to implement.

Some countries, including the United States, Germany, Mexico, Japan, and Brazil, disallow notional pooling. In these cases, the physical pooling method must be used.

Recent tax, accounting, and regulatory changes may have negative implications for the future of notional pooling. For example, banks may not be able to net loans against deposition positions under Basel III.

The chart in Exhibit 12.6 summarizes the differences between physical and notional pooling.

EXHIBIT 12.6 **POOLING COMPARISON**		
NOTIONAL POOLING		**PHYSICAL POOLING**
Interest is earned/paid as bank interest.	COMPENSATION	Must use "arm's length" (or market) rate, track loans, and allocate interest.
Can provide tax efficiency.	TAX	Withholding taxes can apply to intercompany loans.
Is highly complex due to involvement of banks and multiple jurisdictions.	COMPLEXITY	Greater transparency generates less regulatory concern.
Can be implemented across multiple currencies.	APPLICABILITY	Must be done on a currency-by-currency basis.
Is restricted in many countries.	AVAILABILITY	Is widely available and most common form of pooling.

3. BANK OVERLAY STRUCTURE

A bank overlay structure is an approach that combines both sweeping and pooling. It is typically used when a firm's primary bank has branches in several countries, but the branches do not provide a full range of domestic banking services. A local bank is used to provide collection and disbursement transactions and accounts, and to sweep surplus funds to the primary bank. The primary bank (i.e., overlay bank) then notionally pools or physically transfers cash balances in overlay accounts, providing a multi-country solution. The exact structure of this arrangement will depend on the bank agreement and possible tax considerations. The concept is shown in Exhibit 12.7.

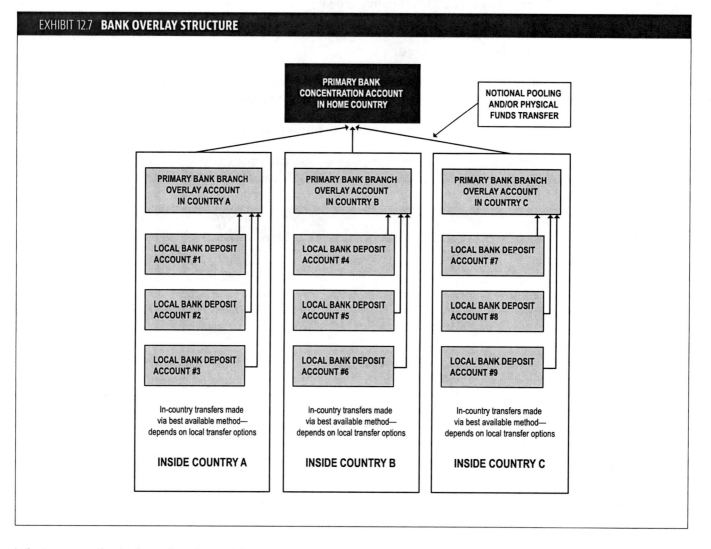

EXHIBIT 12.7 **BANK OVERLAY STRUCTURE**

Whatever method of pooling is used in managing multinational balances, it is essential to involve tax and legal counsel in any decision making. Although the basic concepts are fairly simple, the actual execution and the related legal documentation needed can be quite complex. Even small mistakes can result in large costs in the form of unexpected fees and taxes.

V. SUMMARY

Disbursements, collections, and concentration of funds represent key aspects of liquidity management and treasury operations. This chapter discussed specific products that are available to assist in efficient and cost-effective disbursement and collection management. It also covered some of the payments products utilized in international trade, including L/Cs and documentary collections. Domestic sweeps and multinational pooling were introduced as methods of concentrating funds and managing cash balances across international borders. Utilizing best practices in these areas will help improve firm liquidity and reduce the potential for losses stemming from fraud.

Key Equations

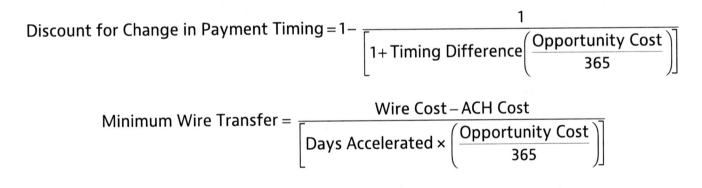

$$\text{Dollar-Days of Float} = \text{Dollar Amount} \times \text{Total Days of Float}$$

$$\text{Average Daily Float} = \frac{\text{Total Dollar-Days of Float}}{\text{Number of Days in Period}}$$

$$\text{Annual Cost of Float} = \text{Average Daily Float} \times \text{Opportunity Cost}$$

$$\text{Net Benefit of Lockbox} = \text{Lockbox Float Savings} - \text{Annual Cost of Lockbox}$$

$$\text{Discount for Change in Payment Timing} = 1 - \frac{1}{\left[1 + \text{Timing Difference}\left(\dfrac{\text{Opportunity Cost}}{365}\right)\right]}$$

$$\text{Minimum Wire Transfer} = \frac{\text{Wire Cost} - \text{ACH Cost}}{\left[\text{Days Accelerated} \times \left(\dfrac{\text{Opportunity Cost}}{365}\right)\right]}$$

APPENDIX 12.1: US ACH STANDARD ENTRY CLASS (SEC) CODES AND PAYMENT TYPES

The US ACH system uses standard entry class (SEC) codes to distinguish between various types of transactions. Transaction formats vary by SEC code. There are standard ACH formats for C2B, B2C, and B2B payments. All ACH payment formats move funds in essentially the same manner. The most appropriate format for a particular payment is determined by the relationship between the parties, the information exchanged, and the types of ACH payment services offered by the participating banks. The major ACH formats and their related SEC codes are as follows:

- **Accounts Receivable Conversion (ARC):** To increase funds availability and reduce check handling, eligible checks received at a lockbox can be converted into electronic debits and processed as ACH debits. The company receiving the checks must notify the check writer that checks will be converted. This typically is done by including a statement to this effect on bills or invoices.

- **Back Office Conversion (BOC):** Retailers and other entities that accept checks at the point of purchase (POP) or other manned bill payment locations can convert eligible checks to ACH debits in the back office. Explanatory signage must be present at the point of presentment, and the merchant/originator must put specific verbiage on the customer receipt indicating that the check may be converted and may clear as soon as the same day.

- **Corporate Credit or Debit (CCD) or CCD Plus Addendum (CCD+):** CCD is the basic electronic payment format used for the concentration and disbursement of funds within or between companies (i.e., B2B). Only a limited amount of remittance information can be sent with the CCD format. The CCD+ is essentially a CCD with an addendum record that can hold up to 80 characters of remittance data. CCD+ is one of the formats used for the US Treasury's Vendor Express program in paying commercial suppliers to federal agencies, and for B2B payments. It is useful when only a limited amount of information must be transmitted. The CCD+ addendum record also is used to report federal and state tax payment information, in which case the addenda data conform to the tax payment (TXP) banking conventions.

- **Customer-Initiated Entry (CIE):** The CIE format is used for pre-authorized payments that are initiated by consumers using telephone bill-paying services.

- **Corporate Trade Exchange (CTX):** The CTX format is designed for B2B trade payments. It consists of a standard ACH payment transaction and a variable-length message addendum designed to convey remittance information in the Accredited Standards Committee (ASC) X12 data standard. The addendum can accommodate 9,999 records of 80 characters each. CTX is useful for payments related to multiple invoices and those with substantial invoice detail.

- **International ACH Transaction (IAT):** An IAT is an ACH debit or credit entry that is part of a payment transaction originating from, or transmitted to, an office of a financial agency located outside the territorial jurisdiction of the United States. Corporate and consumer accounts may receive IAT entries.

- **Point-of-Purchase (POP) Check Conversion:** Many retail outlets have systems that allow customers to have checks scanned, capturing the account information from the MICR line at the POP. The MICR line data are converted into an ACH debit, and the check is voided and returned to the customer, who then signs a debit authorization in the form of a register receipt.

- **Prearranged Payment and Deposit (PPD):** The PPD format is the payment application by which consumers authorize a company or a financial institution to credit or debit an account for normally recurring payments in fixed amounts. Examples of consumer PPD credits (i.e., B2C and G2C) are payroll, expense reimbursements, dividends, social security benefits, and tax refunds. Examples of consumer PPD debits (i.e., C2B) are rent and mortgage payments, subscriptions, dues and memberships, insurance premiums, installment debt payments, and utility payments.

- **Re-Presented Check Entry (RCK):** The RCK format is used to transmit ACH debit entries in place of a paper check that has been returned for insufficient or uncollected funds. The general requirements are that the item be less than $2,500 and be drawn on a consumer account. RCK originators must provide advance notice to the check writer (e.g., in a customer statement or at the point of sale) that any check returned for insufficient or uncollected funds may be collected electronically. Originators may transmit a re-presented check entry no more than twice after the first return of a paper item and no more than once after the second return of a paper item.

- **Telephone-Initiated Entry (TEL):** The TEL format is used for payments that are not pre-authorized, but are approved by consumers over the phone. TEL entries are single payments used for telephone catalog sales, ticket sales, and other one-time purchases.

- **Internet-Initiated Entry (WEB):** The WEB format is used for payments that are not pre-authorized, but are initiated by consumers using the Internet. WEB entries can be either single payments for one-time purchases or recurring payments.

- **Destroyed Check Entry (XCK):** The XCK format is used to clear and settle items that originated as checks, but the original paper item was lost or destroyed due to a catastrophic event (e.g., fire, flood, or hurricane).

CHAPTER 13
Short-Term Investing and Borrowing

I. INTRODUCTION

II. MANAGING SHORT-TERM INVESTMENTS

A. In-House versus Outsourced Management of the Short-Term Investment Portfolio

B. Short-Term Investment Policies

C. Investment Strategies

D. Reporting

E. Securities Safekeeping and Custody Services

F. Investment Risk Considerations

III. PRICING AND YIELDS ON SHORT-TERM INVESTMENTS

A. Factors Influencing Investment Pricing

B. Yield Calculations for Short-Term Investments

C. Treasury Bill (T-Bill) Quotes and Yield Calculations

IV. MANAGING SHORT-TERM BORROWING

A. Short-Term Funding Alternatives

B. Pricing and Costs of Commercial Paper (CP) and Credit Lines

V. DEBT FINANCING

A. Basic Components of Interest Rates

B. Base Rates

C. Short-Term Interest Rates versus Long-Term Interest Rates

D. Loan Agreements and Covenants

E. Credit Rating Agencies

VI. SUMMARY

APPENDIX 13.1: LISTING OF SOME MAJOR CREDIT RATING AGENCIES

I. INTRODUCTION

The previous chapter described the importance of the collections, concentration, and disbursement policies in allowing the treasury department to determine the firm's current liquidity position. Once the liquidity position is known, treasury personnel can determine whether the firm has either excess cash available or a cash deficit.

This chapter begins with key issues related to short-term investing. Since the short-term investment portfolio consists of excess cash that the firm may require for future liquidity management purposes, most treasury professionals focus on the preservation of principal, as opposed to seeking higher yields by taking on more risk. For this reason, the vast majority of the short-term investment portfolio will consist of money market securities with a maturity of one year or less.

Next, the chapter describes topics that are pertinent to short-term borrowing, which may be required when the firm has a cash deficit. Specifically, the characteristics of several short-term borrowing instruments are covered, as well as the calculations involved in determining the effective borrowing cost for lines of credit and commercial paper. The chapter closes with a discussion of credit ratings and the agencies that provide them.

II. MANAGING SHORT-TERM INVESTMENTS

The first step in managing the short-term investment portfolio is the development of an investment policy.[1] Once the policy is developed, treasury personnel may choose to construct and manage the short-term investment portfolio in-house, externally via outsourced management, or using a combination of the two approaches. Each approach offers advantages and disadvantages. The sections below describe the different methods and discuss additional steps, such as investment policies, investment reporting, and securities safekeeping.

A. In-House versus Outsourced Management of the Short-Term Investment Portfolio

When using in-house management of short-term investments, an organization assumes responsibility for directly managing its own portfolio. Although investment decisions are guided by the organization's investment policy, management must be prepared to make specific decisions at all times based on current market conditions. Common investment objectives that should be considered include an investment's safety of principal, its liquidity, and the desired risk/return trade-off.

1. IN-HOUSE MANAGEMENT

In-house (or internal) management is generally appropriate only to the extent that the individuals charged with this responsibility have the training and experience required to effectively manage the portfolio. A further requirement is that appropriate controls are in place to approve and monitor investment activity.

The primary advantage of in-house management is that the firm maintains control over the investment process. However, a key disadvantage of in-house management is that it is costly to hire, train, and retain employees with the skills needed to execute the short-term investment strategy. Some firms deal with this issue by investing only in money market funds (MMFs). This practice may help alleviate some of the need for market knowledge and research, but does not relieve the firm of its overall responsibility to effectively manage its portfolio.

---

1. Chapter 18, Treasury Policies and Procedures, provides additional information on investment policies, as well as an example of a short-term investment policy.

2. OUTSOURCED MANAGEMENT

With outsourced management (or external management), the short-term investment portfolio duties are assigned to a third-party provider, such as an MMF manager or an outside money manager (e.g., an investment bank or registered investment advisor). While management costs or fees will be incurred (e.g., 10 to 100 basis points), these fees should be balanced against the cost needed to hire and maintain appropriate internal expertise. The use of external managers may also be dictated by the size and complexity of the organization's portfolio. External fund and money managers will typically have greater resources and experience than those usually found within an organization's treasury department. One of the most important of these resources is ready access to securities research. While in-house treasury managers can usually get access to research information from their broker-dealers, they must ask for it and in some cases may be required to pay for it.

A potential disadvantage of outsourcing is that investment policies and guidelines must be communicated clearly to the outside manager, who must be able to make individual, tactical investment decisions within a portfolio independent of the investor client and within the policy guidelines (or its exception provisions). This may become an issue when using MMFs, as the manager's investment choices may not be completely aligned with the client's preferences. Other issues can include compliance monitoring and general due diligence with regard to the safety and soundness of the outside management firm.

Another potential disadvantage of outsourcing is that the incentive structure faced by the outside investment manager may not align with the client firm's goals. For example, if a broker-dealer is hired to manage a firm's short-term investment portfolio, then the firm's management must recognize that the broker-dealer does not have a fiduciary duty to always act in its client's financial interest. Since a broker-dealer trades securities for its own account and on behalf of its customers, its investment recommendations may arise from securities that the broker-dealer has available for sale, which may not address the client's needs.[2] Alternatively, a firm's management may use a registered investment advisor to manage the short-term investment policy. An investment advisor has a fiduciary duty to its clients that a broker-dealer does not. Still, it is best practice for management to periodically review the portfolio with the outside manager to verify compliance with the short-term investment policy.

3. COMBINATION OF IN-HOUSE AND OUTSOURCED MANAGEMENT

Depending on the size of the investment portfolio, management of the portfolio may be split among more than one managing party, with the allocation of funds among the external managers being determined in-house. This strategy allows the firm's management to compare the cost and performance of the portfolio managers over time.[3] If one portfolio manager is significantly better or worse than the other, then the firm's management has an effective benchmark to use in renegotiating fees or reallocating the portfolio between portfolio managers. The downside of this approach is that the added cost of multiple managers may exceed the expected value of comparing the various managers. One alternative is to benchmark fund managers against industry indices, such as the Bank of America Merrill Lynch 3-Month T-Bill Index or the Barclays Capital 1–3 Year Global Treasury ex-US Capped Index. This approach is also helpful if the funds are allocated to various managers based on investment type or duration, making it difficult to directly compare the managers.

B. Short-Term Investment Policies

Short-term investment policies lay out the guidelines that must be followed when building and managing a short-term investment portfolio. Specifically, the short-term investment policy should regulate risk taking to ensure that

---

2. FINRA Rule 2111 holds US broker-dealers responsible for assessing the suitability of a given investment before recommending it to a customer, but this regulation says nothing about complying with a customer's investment policy.
3. When the short-term investment portfolio has multiple managers, separate service level agreements (SLAs) may be required for each manager.

the investment portfolio is aligned with firm's desired risk tolerance. Further, the investment portfolio should be constructed and regulated in a manner that is faithful to the goals of principal preservation and liquidity optimization.

Formulating a short-term investment policy requires (1) recognition of the primary short-term investment objective of preservation of principal and (2) determination of the firm's overall risk tolerance by the firm's board and management. Additionally, a board-approved investment policy should include the following:

- Investment objectives with respect to risk and return
- Permissible and prohibited investment vehicles or classes of investments
- Minimum acceptable security ratings
- Maximum maturity for individual securities
- Maximum weighted average maturity or duration for the portfolio
- Maximum amounts or concentration limits (either by percentage, total dollar amount, or both) of the portfolio that may be invested in individual securities, companies, instrument classes, geographic areas, or industries
- Policies/guidelines for investing in foreign securities
- Specific responsibilities for implementing the policy, by organizational title
- Methods of monitoring compliance with policies, procedures, and internal controls
- Provisions for performance measurement, evaluation, and reporting
- Responsibilities and reporting requirements for custodians, external investment managers, broker-dealers, and other investment counterparties
- Exception management and related approval processes

As previously noted, when using an MMF instrument, it will not always be possible to completely align the investment policy with the fund. Given the wide variety of MMFs, the investment manager should be able to find one that is fairly close in terms of investment objectives and policies. If MMFs are permitted investments, the policy should state this and clearly state the rules governing MMFs, including how the funds are to be selected, if they must be rated by one or more rating agencies, and whether their composition must adhere to the overall guidelines established in the investment policy.

In addition to the basic short-term investment policy, firms should have two other policies to round out the guidelines for the management of the short-term portfolio: a short-term investment valuation policy and a short-term investment impairment policy. While it is possible to combine these into one master policy, it often makes sense to leave them as separate policies due to their different purposes and potentially different owners (i.e., the latter two may be accounting policies rather than treasury policies).

The short-term investment valuation policy lays out the methodology that will be used to establish the fair market value of the various securities in the portfolio. While this is a rather routine process for the actively traded securities in the portfolio that have publicly quoted prices, the methodology used may not be as clear for securities that are not actively traded (i.e., those that do not have a publicly quoted market price). Although these other securities may represent only a small fraction of a given portfolio, the methodology that will be used to establish their fair value should be documented before questions are raised by auditors or other outsiders.

The impairment policy documents the actions that will be taken when a particular investment may be impaired, as discussed below in the section on reporting. The policy should clearly define the severity and duration of an unrealized loss that will cause an impairment review and identify the specific securities that need to be reviewed. An impairment review does not necessarily require a write-down, but leads to a quantitative analysis of the securities involved. There are always alternatives to be evaluated, and having a well-written and documented impairment policy can help avoid the unnecessary write-downs of securities that might otherwise be classified by the auditors as impaired.

C. Investment Strategies

A variety of short-term investment strategies are available to an organization, including a(n):

- Buy-and-hold-to-maturity strategy
- Actively managed portfolio strategy
- Tax-based strategy

These strategies may be used individually or in combination, depending on the organization's investment needs and strategic objectives. Each strategy is described below.

1. BUY-AND-HOLD-TO-MATURITY STRATEGY

A traditional strategy for investing excess cash and preserving capital is to (1) invest only in securities whose maturities can be expected to sufficiently fund any potential cash needs, (2) hold those securities to maturity, and (3) reinvest only if maturity proceeds are not needed for expenditures. This approach is referred to as a *buy-and-hold-to-maturity strategy*, which is a passive investment approach that might be favorable to conservative investors.[4]

The main advantages of the buy-and-hold strategy are that funding needs are always met, as long as securities are structured or laddered properly to meet cash needs, and interim price fluctuations can largely be ignored since the maturity will always fulfill the investment's initial return expectation. The disadvantage of this investment strategy is that the firm may forgo potentially lucrative alternative investments.

The buy-and-hold strategy is also referred to as a *matching strategy*. This stems from the fact that cash flows from maturing investments can be matched to future expenditures. This matching of cash flows generally allows for investing over extended periods (i.e., longer maturities), which may lead to increased yields. For this strategy to be effective, however, it requires careful forecasting of future cash flows and capital requirements. If cash is needed sooner than expected, the securities purchased to correspond with a specific cash outflow may have to be sold prematurely, perhaps at a loss. Firms that apply a matching strategy often will do so in a conservative manner, covering only a portion of the expected capital need.

2. ACTIVELY MANAGED PORTFOLIO STRATEGY

An active investment strategy (or a *total-return strategy*) is contrasted with the buy-and-hold strategy in that an active approach pursues enhanced returns by capturing capital gains that may arise on relatively longer-dated instruments. This strategy requires that an investor be prepared to sell holdings when their prices rise and is dependent on interest rates falling or on the relative creditworthiness of an issue improving. An actively managed investment strategy is typically used by investors to meet specific needs or to earn higher returns.

---

4. Investing in MMFs represents another type of passive investment strategy.

One advantage of an active investment approach is that for as long as the yield curve is positively sloped (i.e., short-term interest rates are lower than long-term interest rates), capital gains are possible. The yield curve, discussed in more detail later in this chapter, is the interest rate trend line that spans the full spectrum of maturities for a certain instrument. As time passes and longer-dated purchases approach maturity, their value in the secondary market increases because while their maturities are shortening, their stated interest rates remain at levels associated with longer-dated instruments. When this increase in value occurs, such securities can be sold for a premium because they now pay above the market rates for short-term investment instruments of identical maturity.[5]

The threats to cash assets from this strategy arise when time passes but prices do not rise—capital gains therefore do not materialize, and the investor's portfolio has a longer duration than intended due to the lack of capital gains. Investing in an actively managed portfolio, or using a total-return approach, is only appropriate for amounts of cash that are likely to be required no earlier than the longest-maturity security that might be purchased with such a strategy. An active short-term investment strategy requires that the in-house or outside investment manager forecast the course of interest rates over the very short term.

3. TAX-BASED STRATEGY

Corporate investors in high tax brackets may favor tax-based strategies that are designed to minimize income taxes on investment return. The success of tax-based strategies depends on the investor's location and applicable tax regulations. Where tax-advantaged investments exist, potentially higher returns may be available to certain investors. In most cases, the yield benefit of a tax-advantaged investment is related directly to an investor's marginal tax rate (see details in the yield calculation discussion in Section III.A.2 of this chapter). The use of such tax-advantaged investments can be employed in both passive and active strategies.

For global organizations, there may be advantages related to developing a globally based investment strategy. There are often tax advantages related to investing in one location or currency versus another, and an organization operating in many different currencies and countries must often maintain liquidity in many currencies and locations.

In India, for example, companies can earn higher yields by investing in tax-free infrastructure bonds. In the United States, there are several tax-advantaged investment strategies. Besides investing in specific and federally tax-exempt municipal securities, investors may buy shares in tax-advantaged mutual funds tailored to their state of domicile. Further, for firms with a mix of income from multiple US states, portfolios of municipal securities and/or bond funds can be used to match this income mix closely, thereby minimizing overall state taxation.

Dividend capture is another tax-motivated, short-term investment strategy also available to corporations that pay taxes in the United States. A firm may exclude from its taxable income 70–80% of the dividends received from stock owned in another corporation, as long as it owns the stock for at least 46 days of the 91-day period starting 45 days prior to the ex-dividend date.[6] Even though dividend capture requires an equity investment, the strategy is considered a short-term investment because the stock is held only long enough to capture the dividend and qualify for the dividend exclusion.

Assume, for example, that a firm purchases common stock in another firm after the dividend announcement, then sells it after the ex-dividend date, ensuring that at least 46 days of ownership elapse.[7] The investing firm has then captured the dividend and will receive it on the payment date. There is little risk that the dividend will not be paid because only stock in large, reputable firms is purchased for this purpose. However, there is a risk that the stock may have to be sold at a loss, but firms using this strategy employ it frequently so that gains and losses offset one

---

5. This would not be the case if the yield curve were inverted (i.e., short-term interest rates are higher than long-term interest rates), which has happened in the past.
6. For a 70% exclusion, the stock must be less than 20% owned by the corporation receiving the dividend. If a corporation owns more than 20% but less than 80%, then the exclusion is 80% of the dividend.
7. The ex-dividend date is the first date on which the stock is sold without entitlement to an upcoming dividend.

another over many transactions. The strategy should be avoided when the market is in a secular downtrend or if there is a sense that the market may be impacted adversely in the near future by a macroeconomic shock or political event.

D. Reporting

Reliable investment reporting is important in order to ensure that performance and risk management goals are met, as well as to satisfy any external reporting requirements. The investment report should clearly illustrate the composition of a portfolio according to maturity distribution, quality ratings, and security classes. This presentation furnishes a simplified means for assessing investment policy compliance and affords the reader a concise overview of the investment pool and its risk exposure.[8] If multiple fund managers are used, then each manager should provide a separate report for its portion of the overall portfolio.

Reporting is especially critical for publicly traded firms, due to regulatory and exchange requirements. In periodic filings, a firm must account for investment returns as allocated to a specific reporting period.[9] For money market and other fixed-income investment portfolios, this means reporting interest income on an accrual basis rather than a cash basis. For investment vehicles that pay interest on dates that do not coincide with a reporting period's beginning or ending dates, interest accrual reports must be prepared by the firm, and by its investment managers or brokers, that accurately show interest earned (even if unpaid) for any relevant reporting period.

An added component of investment reporting requires that unrealized gains or losses be shown. Because market values for money market and other fixed-income instruments may fluctuate during their lives until maturity, any difference between the current market value of a holding and its adjusted cost basis must be reported. This is referred to as *mark-to-market accounting*.

Under rules created by the Financial Accounting Standards Board (FASB) and the International Accounting Standards Board (IASB), a security is deemed to be impaired when its fair market value is less than its adjusted cost basis.[10] This difference is an unrealized loss unless the security is liquidated at that current price, whereupon it becomes a realized loss. However, under certain circumstances and according to IASB and FASB requirements, unrealized losses must be reported in the same manner as realized losses.

If a security is deemed to be impaired and this impairment is not or cannot be expected to be cured in the foreseeable future, then it must be further classified as *other-than-temporary impairment (OTTI)*. As such, the investment's carrying value must be reduced by the amount of the unrealized loss, and this loss amount must be subtracted from net earnings.[11] As discussed above, firms should have both valuation and impairment policies in place that spell out the actions that need to be taken to determine if specific securities are impaired and when or if a write-down is appropriate.

E. Securities Safekeeping and Custody Services

Once a security is purchased, it must be warehoused and tracked to ensure that any interest income, dividends, or other proceeds are credited properly to its owner. The common method for this is for securities to be registered in the name of an institution that holds securities on behalf of investors (sometimes referred to as the *nominee* or *street name*). In turn, these institutions are required to maintain separate books and records that evidence the specific, underlying ownership of the securities. The essential purpose of these processes is to facilitate fast and efficient transfers of securities from one broker to another.

8. In the United States, this reporting is covered under Accounting Standards Codification (ASC) Topic 820: Fair Value Measurement.
9. The relevant US guidelines in this area are ASC Topics 320, 820, and 825.
10. The FASB rules are covered in ASC Topic 320: *Investments–Debt and Equity Securities*, and the IASB rules are covered in International Accounting Standard (IAS) 39: *Financial Instruments: Recognition and Measurement*.
11. For securities deemed to be temporarily impaired, this unrealized loss amount must be accounted for on the firm's balance sheet rather than on its income statement.

Effective custody of securities can be accomplished by one of two basic means. The first choice is to engage a third party to provide custodial services for an investor. In this situation, the corporate trust department of a commercial bank serves as custodian of the securities, and collects income from the securities, redemption monies, and other cash flows associated with a particular investment on behalf of individual investor clients (including corporations). A custodian bank also serves as a conduit to the underlying investor for any notices, official information, or other actions regarding the securities it holds.

An alternative to fee-based, third-party custodians is to keep securities at the institution (usually a brokerage firm) from which they were purchased. This method affords all the same support as with a custodian bank, but such custody services are normally offered at no charge, which may be attractive to smaller organizations. This second approach is considered somewhat more risky than the first because there may be a potential for fraud, as the custodian is supposed to be the third-party control in the process.

The primary advantage of using a fee-based third party for securities custody is that reporting is consolidated and control over the investor's entire group of holdings is established. This is especially important when an organization uses multiple investment managers (as discussed earlier in this chapter), who otherwise might execute trades through their own brokerage. Since all of the portfolio's trades are handled by a single custodian, it is much easier to monitor compliance with policy and operating guidelines, and identify any irregularities in trading or undue concentration. Further, since this process requires managers (internal or external) to trade through a particular custodian rather than using their own facilities, it can be an important separation-of-duties control feature. While some firms may be able to take advantage of complimentary custody services extended by brokerage firms to reduce expenses, third-party custodians are often required for investors using outsourced investment management.

F. Investment Risk Considerations

A short-term investment portfolio will consist primarily of money market instruments, which are typically low-risk investments. Such low risk levels are accompanied by lower returns, but this is consistent with the primary short-term investment objective of preservation of principal. The major risk factors associated with short-term investments include:

- **Credit or Default Risk:** The risk that payments to investors of a security will not be made under the original terms of the security
- **Asset Liquidity Risk:** The risk that a security cannot be sold quickly without experiencing an unacceptable loss
- **Price/Interest Rate Risk:** The risk that arises when there are changes in interest rates for securities that are identical or nearly identical to portfolio securities
- **Foreign Exchange (FX) Risk:** The risk of a change in the exchange rate between the currency in which a security is denominated and the investor's local currency (applies to foreign currency investments only)

III. PRICING AND YIELDS ON SHORT-TERM INVESTMENTS

A. Factors Influencing Investment Pricing

Yield is a measure of the return an investor derives from a financial instrument. Typically, an investment yield is stated as an annual percentage rate of return. Many factors can influence the pricing and, ultimately, the yield of an investment. These factors include default, liquidity, and price risk; the general shape of the yield curve; and the tax status of the investment. The concept of yield curves and the impact of an investment's tax status are described below.

1. YIELD CURVES

A yield curve is a plot of the yields to maturity on the same investment instrument or class of instruments, but with varying maturities, as of a specific date. For example, a yield curve for US Treasury instruments is a plot of yields to maturity for US Treasury bond issues with varying maturities as of the close of business on a particular date. Similarly, a plot of yields to maturity for AA-rated industrial bonds with various maturities is a yield curve for that class of instruments.

Refer to Exhibit 13.1. The curve in the graphs of the various yields to maturity illustrates what is called the *term structure* of interest rates. In the left panel of Exhibit 13.1, the yield to maturity on the instrument or class of instruments increases with maturity, whereas it declines with maturity in the right panel.

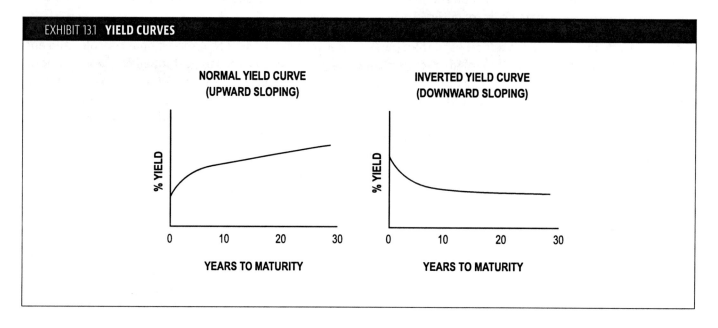

EXHIBIT 13.1 **YIELD CURVES**

The slope, or shape, of the yield curve at a point in time has decision implications for those managing the short-term investment portfolio. Since short-term interest rates are typically lower than long-term rates, an upward-sloping yield curve is referred to as a *normal yield curve*. The liquidity preference theory of the term structure of interest rates holds that investors demand a yield premium in compensation for the lower liquidity that is associated with a longer maturity. Thus, long-term rates are normally higher than short-term rates.

A downward-sloping yield curve is referred to as an *inverted yield curve*. In this case, investors are shifting their preferences to long-term securities (or conversely, issuers are shifting their preferences to short-term borrowing). This increased demand for long-term securities causes their prices to increase and long-term yields to decline, thus pushing down the long-term end of the curve and causing an inversion. An inverted yield curve is typically a sign that the market is expecting a recession in the near future and is investing in longer-term securities to attempt to lock in interest rates or avoid any reduced interest rate that may occur in the short run. It is also a sign of low expectations with regards to future inflation, as expectations of high inflation would automatically increase the yields required on long-term securities (to offset the expected inflation) and create a normal, upward-sloping yield curve. An inverted yield curve may occur as the result of Federal Open Market Committee (FOMC) open market operations in the United States. If the US Federal Reserve (Fed) is attempting to raise interest rates, and the target rate is a short-term interest rate, short-term rates will tend to increase before the actions affect longer-term interest rates. This may result in a downward-sloping yield curve until long-term rates increase.

2. TAX STATUS[12]

The tax status of an investment has a direct effect on the investment yield. Tax-exempt securities, such as US T-bills or Indian infrastructure bonds, provide a lower pretax yield than taxable securities of similar maturity and default risk because of their tax advantage. When comparing taxable and tax-exempt instruments, the tax-exempt yield should be converted to a taxable equivalent to allow proper comparison. The tax-exempt yield can be converted to a taxable equivalent yield as follows:

$$\text{Taxable Equivalent Yield} = \frac{\text{Tax-Exempt Yield}}{1 - \text{Marginal Tax Rate}}$$

For example, assume a treasury professional is choosing between a taxable security with a 4.60% yield and a tax-exempt security with a 3.20% yield. Both securities have similar risk and maturity. The firm's marginal income tax rate is 35%. In this case, the tax-exempt security has a taxable equivalent yield of 4.92%, calculated as follows:

$$\text{Taxable Equivalent Yield} = \frac{0.032}{1 - 0.35} = 0.0492 \text{ or } 4.92\%$$

Another approach for comparing these securities is to compute the after-tax yield on the taxable security, which can then be compared directly to the tax-exempt instrument. The calculation is as follows:

$$\text{After-Tax Yield} = \text{Taxable Yield} \times (1 - \text{Marginal Tax Rate})$$

$$= 0.0460 \times (1 - 0.35) = 0.0299 \text{ or } 2.99\%$$

Both approaches indicate that the tax-exempt security should be chosen because it has a higher taxable equivalent yield (4.92% versus 4.60%) and a higher effective after-tax yield (3.20% versus 2.99%) than the taxable security.

B. Yield Calculations for Short-Term Investments

This section provides examples that illustrate the calculations used to determine the yield on short-term investments. In general, a short-term investment yield is a function of the:

- Cash flows received from the investment
- Amount paid for that investment
- Maturity or holding period

---

12. This discussion is primarily from the perspective of a US investor, to illustrate the effects of tax status, but investors outside of the United States may also have access to tax-advantaged investments, depending on local tax codes.

One of the most basic types of yield is the holding period yield. The holding period yield is the return earned by an investor during the period in which the investment is held. Thus, a holding period yield can be calculated over investment periods (e.g., daily, weekly, monthly). A general formula for the holding period yield is:

$$\text{Holding Period Yield} = \frac{\text{Cash Received at Maturity} - \text{Amount Invested}}{\text{Amount Invested}}$$

As an example, assume that a $100,000 T-bill currently sells for $98,800 and matures in 90 days. The holding period yield is calculated as:

$$\text{Holding Period Yield} = \frac{\$100,000 - \$98,800}{\$98,800} = 0.01215 \text{ or } 1.215\%$$

Two yields that are commonly quoted for short-term investments include the money market yield (MMY) and the bond equivalent yield (BEY). In essence, both yields annualize the holding period yield. The key difference in the determination of these yields is the number of days used in the calculations. The MMY is based on a 360-day year, while the BEY is based on a 365-day year. The use of a 360-day year has its roots in historical convention. The year was treated as consisting of 12 months, each with 30 days. Rate quotes and interest payments on money market instruments are still computed using a 360-day year. An investor's effective annual yield is computed using a 365-day year.[13] The equations for the MMY and the BEY appear below:

$$\text{MMY} = \left(\frac{\text{Cash Received at Maturity} - \text{Amount Invested}}{\text{Amount Invested}} \right) \times \left(\frac{360}{\text{Days to Maturity}} \right)$$

$$\text{BEY} = \left(\frac{\text{Cash Received at Maturity} - \text{Amount Invested}}{\text{Amount Invested}} \right) \times \left(\frac{365}{\text{Days to Maturity}} \right)$$

The MMY and BEY for the T-bill from the previous example are calculated as shown below:

$$\text{MMY} = \left(\frac{\$100,000 - \$98,800}{\$98,800} \right) \times \left(\frac{360}{90} \right) = 0.04858 \text{ or } 4.858\%$$

$$\text{BEY} = \left(\frac{\$100,000 - \$98,800}{\$98,800} \right) \times \left(\frac{365}{90} \right) = 0.04926 \text{ or } 4.926\%$$

The higher yield on the BEY is logical because there are more 90-day periods in a 365-day year than there are in a 360-day year. That is, it takes the investor a smaller proportion of the year to earn $1,200 in a 365-day year than it does in a 360-day year, so the annualized yield over a 365-day year will be higher.

---

13. The decision to use 360 versus 365 (or in some cases 366) days in a year in various investment calculations is a standard convention based upon historical practice and is usually not left to the user's discretion. For consistency and comparability purposes, treasury professionals should comply with the appropriate convention. Further, the appropriate convention may vary by country.

Note that an investor can quickly convert from an MMY to a BEY by multiplying the MMY by the term *(365÷360)*. Further, the BEY can be converted to an MMY by multiplying the BEY by the term *(360÷365)*. This conversion works because the only difference in the MMY and BEY equations is the assumed days in a year (i.e., 360 versus 365). This short-cut approach is illustrated below using the previous example:

$$BEY = MMY \times \left(\frac{365}{360}\right) = 0.04858 \times \left(\frac{365}{360}\right) = 0.04925 \text{ or } 4.925\%$$

$$MMY = BEY \times \left(\frac{360}{365}\right) = 0.04925 \times \left(\frac{360}{365}\right) = 0.04858 \text{ or } 4.858\%$$

Another important concept related to short-term investment yields is the dollar discount. A security's *dollar discount* refers to the difference between its par value (i.e., the amount received by the investor at maturity) and the purchase price. The dollar discount is important in this context because many money market securities do not pay interest and instead sell at a discount from par value (e.g., T-bills, commercial paper, and banker's acceptances). These are referred to *discounted instruments*. In the preceding example, the dollar discount is calculated as:

$$\text{Dollar Discount} = \text{Par Value} - \text{Purchase Price} = \$100,000 - \$98,800 = \$1,200$$

A concept related to the dollar discount is the *discount rate*, which is defined as the dollar discount divided by the par value and then annualized using a 360-day year. The following example illustrates the calculation of the discount rate:

$$\text{Discount Rate} = \left(\frac{\text{Dollar Discount}}{\text{Par Value}}\right) \times \left(\frac{360}{\text{Days to Maturity}}\right)$$

$$= \left(\frac{\$1,200}{\$100,000}\right) \times \left(\frac{360}{90}\right) = 0.04800 \text{ or } 4.80\%$$

Note that the MMY and BEY will always exceed the discount rate because the holding period yield is calculated using the purchase price, which is less than par value, whereas the discount rate calculation uses par value.

C. Treasury Bill (T-Bill) Quotes and Yield Calculations

Dealers buy and sell T-bills in a secondary market and typically utilize a bid-ask quote framework. The ask quote is the discount at which the dealer will sell the T-bill, while the bid quote is the discount at which the dealer will purchase the T-bill. Both the bid and the ask quotes are based on a 360-day year basis because they are given in terms of a discount.

In addition to the bid and ask discounts, the ask yield is provided. The ask yield is the yield to an investor purchasing a T-bill at the ask discount. This yield is calculated on a 365-day year basis (i.e., it is quoted as a BEY). Sample quotes and calculations based on a March 13 purchase date are as follows:[14]

Maturity Date	Days to Maturity (Percent)	Bid Discount (Percent)	Ask Discount (Percent)	Ask Yield (Percent)
April 18	36	0.075	0.065	0.066
April 25	43	0.075	0.035	0.035
May 2	50	0.070	0.035	0.066
May 9	57	0.055	0.050	0.051

As an example, the purchase price an investor would pay for a $1,000,000 T-bill maturing on April 18 is based on the April 18 ask discount:

$$\text{Dollar Discount} = \text{Discount Rate} \times \text{Par Value} \times \left(\frac{\text{Days to Maturity}}{360}\right)$$

$$= 0.00065 \times \$1,000,000 \times \left(\frac{36}{360}\right) = \$65.00$$

$$\text{Purchase Price} = \text{Par Value} - \text{Dollar Discount}$$

$$= \$1,000,000 - \$65.00 = \$999,935.00$$

If the investor sold the T-bill, then the sale price paid to the investor by the dealer would be based on the April 18 bid discount of 0.075%:

$$\text{Dollar Discount} = 0.00075 \times \$1,000,000 \times \left(\frac{36}{360}\right) = \$75.00$$

$$\text{Sale Price} = \$1,000,000 - \$75.00 = \$999,925.00$$

The ask yield or BEY to the investor is determined as follows:

$$\text{Ask Yield} = \left(\frac{\$1,000,000 - \$999,935}{\$999,935}\right) \times \left(\frac{365}{36}\right) = 0.000659 \text{ or } 0.066\%$$

IV. MANAGING SHORT-TERM BORROWING

In this section the focus of the chapter turns from short-term investing to short-term borrowing. Topics covered include short-term borrowing alternatives, as well as methods for calculating the effective costs of lines of credit and commercial paper.

14. This is the format typically used for T-bill quotations in the financial press.

A. Short-Term Funding Alternatives

Short-term debt instruments mature within one year and are generally used by firms to finance current assets such as accounts receivable and inventory. There are a number of alternatives to short-term debt issuance, including trade financing, intercompany loans, and the sale of receivables. These are all potential sources of liquidity funding that should be considered as part of a company's short-term funding strategy, and are summarized below.

1. TRADE CREDIT

Trade credit arises when a customer receives goods or services but payment is not made to the supplier until a later date. Trade credit is the primary source of short-term financing used by many firms, since trade credit lets a buyer use the supplier's goods or services while simultaneously using the cash it otherwise would have had to pay in advance or upon delivery. Trade credit provides a tangible economic benefit as a source of financing because the buyer may avoid liquidating investments or incurring debt over the credit period. A firm that pays its suppliers before the invoice's due date (assuming no discount for early payment) may be forgoing an inexpensive source of short-term financing.

2. INTERCOMPANY LOANS

Intercompany lending may provide a low-cost source of funds. Multiple units of a firm—typically, separate subsidiaries of a multinational firm that are often in different countries—may borrow and lend among themselves through an in-house bank or other internal borrowing mechanism. Termed *intercompany lending*, these arrangements are formal and usually involve promissory notes or a memorandum of understanding. They are normally priced at market rates, or "arm's length" rates, to comply with tax and regulatory requirements; however, the entity as a whole retains the money.

Many laws and regulations affect domestic and cross-border intercompany lending.[15] For example, the length of time that intercompany loans are outstanding can affect whether the repayment of principal is treated as a return of capital or a dividend, for tax purposes. There are also significant issues pertaining to transfer pricing (which necessitates the use of market rates) and capitalization requirements. Many jurisdictions examine these loan programs very closely, and even minor compliance problems can result in large fines. As a result, policies and documentation related to intercompany lending transactions should be comprehensive and designed based on advice from legal, audit, and tax professionals to avoid possible problems.

3. SELLING OF RECEIVABLES

Receivables may be sold or discounted to raise cash in two ways. First, receivables may be sold at a discount from face value to a third party called a *factor*. The factor then collects on the receivable. This process is referred to as *factoring*. Second, receivables can be securitized. Through securitization, a firm issues debt securities backed by a pool of receivables. Receivables that are suitable for debt securitization have a predictable cash flow stream adequate to retire the issue and a historical record of low losses.

4. SUPPLY CHAIN FINANCE

In supply chain finance, a supplier receives loans based upon the credit rating and financial capabilities of its customer (i.e., the buying firm). Supply chain finance is typically arranged for by the buying firm rather than the supplier and allows the buying firm to extend its payables while providing lower-cost financing for its supplier. For example, suppose that a customer has historically paid suppliers 30 days after the receipt of invoices. Using supply chain

---

15. Such laws and regulations may vary by country.

finance, the firm may negotiate longer payment terms of 90 days. The new payment terms will increase the buyer's accounts payable, but it will also increase the suppliers' accounts receivable. Using supply chain finance, invoices are approved by the buyer when received. Suppliers may wait the full 90 days and receive the full amount of the invoice. Suppliers also have the option to receive a discounted amount prior to maturity. The primary advantage for the suppliers is that the invoices are discounted at a rate tied to the buyer's cost of capital. This rate may be much lower than the supplier's cost of capital, providing relatively low-cost financing for the supplier's accounts receivable.

5. COMMERCIAL BANK CREDIT

Bank borrowings represent an important source of working capital for most firms, especially middle-market and smaller firms. Larger, publicly traded firms often find bank credit attractive because banks can customize debt structures and use information not disclosed to the public to justify underwriting the debt.

Bank loans are offered on a secured or unsecured basis. Security, provided in the form of collateral or guarantees, may be used to obtain more favorable rates by some borrowers or to make credit available to businesses that cannot access unsecured credit facilities. In addition, a lender's use of private information may reduce borrowing costs.

The sections below describe the most common forms of bank credit. These include loan syndications and participations, as well as lines of credit. Note that loans and credit arrangements are often referred to as *credit facilities*.

a. Loan Syndications and Participations

For organizations requiring large credit facilities, banks may extend those facilities through loan syndications and participations.

In a loan syndication, multiple financial institutions share the funding of a single credit facility. The syndicate, or group of lenders, is led by an agent who acts as the intermediary between the firm and the syndicate to negotiate credit terms and documentation, make advances and collect payments on the loan, and disseminate information. The agent usually receives an annual fee for handling these tasks. All syndicate members share common documentation, but each lender has a promissory note, making it a direct lending relationship. The individual lenders in the syndicate are usually able to sell their shares with or without consent from the borrower.

In a loan participation, a financial institution purchases an interest in another lender's credit facility. The purchaser is called a *participant*, and the seller is the *lead institution*. The participant does not have a separate note and has only an indirect relationship with the borrower. A participation agreement specifies the participant's and lead institution's rights and obligations. In the case of a blind participation, the participation is not disclosed to the borrower, and the participant may not contact the borrower directly or disclose the participant's role in the credit facility.

The rationale for these arrangements is that they allow banks to offer larger loans than they could on their own, due to capital requirements, and to expand their loan portfolio beyond their usual market, creating a more diversified mix of loans. It is important for treasury professionals whose organizations have loans under syndication or participation arrangements to understand the structure of the arrangements since it will affect how they interact with the lenders.

b. Lines of Credit

i. Overview

A line of credit is an agreement in which the lender gives the borrower access to funds up to a maximum amount over a specific period of time. Lines of credit are usually *revolving* (see discussion below), meaning the borrower may borrow, repay, and borrow funds again up to the established limit during the commitment period. A line of credit can provide short-term financing, back up a commercial paper program, or provide temporary liquidity.

ii. Conditions and Covenants

Requirements and conditions frequently associated with lines of credit include cleanup periods, credit sub-limits, covenants, and material adverse change (MAC) clauses. To ensure that a line is used for temporary financing, a lender may require a period of 30 to 60 consecutive days with no outstanding borrowing on the line (i.e., a cleanup period). This requirement is used mostly for middle-market and small firms to ensure that they do not use short-term financing for needs more appropriately met by long-term sources. A lender also may establish sub-limits under the line for specific uses such as letter of credit issuance or drafts under banker's acceptances. Covenants used in short-term lending typically focus on maintaining certain minimum liquidity or coverage ratios, or maximum debt ratios. Finally, a MAC clause allows the lender to prohibit further funding or even declare the loan in default if there has been an adverse change in the borrower's credit profile.

Ensuring sound internal reporting protocols and implementing improvements in cash forecasting help to ensure that the firm remains compliant with the loan covenants. While reporting is normally a requirement of any covenant, it is also an important management tool. It is much easier to negotiate problems with covenant violations before they actually occur rather than after the fact. Since covenants typically apply to an entire organization, timely and accurate reporting from any subsidiaries is an essential part of this issue.

iii. Types of Lines

Lines of credit are secured or unsecured, and uncommitted or committed. Secured lines require the borrower to pledge some form of collateral, most often current assets such as receivables or inventory. Unsecured lines do not require any collateral as part of the borrowing arrangement. The availability under some secured lines is limited by a borrowing base (sometimes referred to as the *loan value*) that is negotiated as a percentage of the value of the collateral securing the line.

An uncommitted line is an agreement with a lender in which the lender offers to make funds available in the future but is not obligated to provide a specific amount. Usually, an uncommitted line is made available for a one-year period. However, funding may be refused at the lender's discretion or canceled outright, usually due to changes in the financial condition of the borrower. Hence, an uncommitted line is often called a *discretionary line of credit*. There is typically no fee for an uncommitted line unless funds are actually borrowed.

By contrast, a committed line usually involves a formal loan agreement that specifies the terms and conditions of the credit facility. It also typically requires compensation in the form of balances or fees because the lender is obligated to provide funding up to the credit limit stipulated in the agreement so long as the borrower is not in default. A commitment fee may be assessed based on the total amount or unused portion of the commitment. Typically, payment is made quarterly with varying fees, depending upon the company's creditworthiness, the stated purpose of the line, and the commitment term.

One of the most common types of credit lines is a revolving credit agreement, also known as a *revolver*. This is a committed line of credit, as opposed to an uncommitted line of credit, that is established for a specified period of time, often on a multiyear basis. Revolving credit lines are formal, contractual commitments with loan agreements, including covenants. Usually, there is a commitment fee on the unused portion, as well as a fee for use of the borrowing facility. Though often used for short-term borrowing, the commitment term typically ranges from two to five years and may be followed by a period in which the principal is repaid systematically. If more than one year remains on a multiyear revolver, accounting guidelines typically allow balances on this agreement to be carried as a long-term liability on the borrower's balance sheet.

Revolvers contain all the characteristics of committed lines. In addition, revolvers often feature short-term, fixed-rate funding options that offer fixed-rate loans for specified periods with penalties imposed for prepayment. An example is a funding option for 90-day advances fixed at a rate equal to some preestablished spread over the London Interbank Offered Rate (LIBOR). The amount of the spread varies depending on the credit risk.

Another type of credit line is referred to as a *guidance line* or *operating risk exposure limit*. Guidance lines are used by banks to accommodate the credit exposure created from operating activities, such as automated clearinghouse (ACH) operations, daylight overdrafts,[16] returned deposits, and foreign exchange exposure. Banks initiate this type of line, rather than the customer, in order to determine the overall level of exposure the bank has relative to all of the activities (borrowing and non-borrowing) that the customer has with the bank. Often, the bank will not disclose this type of line or credit limit. It is important, however, that treasury professionals ask about and actively manage any exposure limits to avoid potential problems with their firm's ability to send wires or ACH credits from its accounts or to obtain additional borrowing. This is especially true during periods of high growth or acquisitions, which may stretch or break limits that are not being managed. It is also important to note that while the guidance line is typically treated by the bank as a credit exposure that impacts overall lending to a specific customer, it does not represent any commitment on the part of the bank to lend funds to the organization in question.

iv. Compensating Balances

Compensating balances are balances maintained in the company's deposit accounts at the bank for the purpose of increasing the bank's overall revenue on the account. They generally do not earn interest or offset depository service charges. Under a compensating balance arrangement, the balance requirement can be specified as a percentage of one of the following:

- Total line commitment
- Unused amount of the commitment
- Outstanding borrowings

If compensating balances are required by the bank, their effect is to reduce the amount of borrowed funds that are available to be used by the borrower, thereby increasing the loan's effective annual interest rate. The practice of requiring compensating balances is becoming less common over time.

---

16. A daylight overdraft occurs when a customer's available account balance becomes negative during the day, but the needed funds are deposited or become available before the end of the business day. This may happen when a bank allows a customer to initiate wires or submit ACH payment files against funds that will be deposited or become available later in the day.

v. Pricing

Pricing for a line of credit is usually negotiable. The lender may take into account various aspects of the overall lender/borrower relationship in pricing the facility. There are three basic cost components for lines of credit:

- The all-in rate of interest
- Commitment fees, which can be on both used and unused balances
- Compensating balances

The all-in rate consists of a base rate, such as LIBOR, the US prime rate, or the Fed funds rate (all discussed later in this chapter), plus a spread that is added to, or occasionally subtracted from, the base rate. Rates on lines are normally variable and adjust immediately to changes in the base rate. While the actual rate on the loan will vary with the market, it is not unusual for a credit agreement to have a floor rate, which provides a bottom limit on how low the total interest rate can go.

The total interest paid is calculated as the all-in rate times the loan balance outstanding at any given time. Since both the rates and the loan balance can vary daily, the daily interest expense will also change. Annual (or period) interest is the total of the daily interest charges during the year (or period). Total fees paid include all commitment fees, placement fees, and any issuance costs. The average usable funds of the borrowed amount equal the average outstanding loan for the year less the required compensating balances. The impact of these rates and fees on loan pricing is covered later in this chapter.

6. SINGLE PAYMENT NOTES

Single payment notes are usually granted for a short period of time and specific purpose, with both the principal and interest amounts paid at maturity. Because of the limited duration and precise maturity of a single payment note, a specific cash flow event is frequently identified as the repayment source at the time the funds are advanced.

7. REPURCHASE AGREEMENTS

A repurchase agreement, or repo, is another source of short-term funds. With a repo, securities are sold, providing the seller with cash until the securities are repurchased. Repos let firms tap into the liquidity of their investment portfolio without having to permanently dispose of their short-term investments. An equivalent transaction may be structured by using a single payment note secured by marketable securities.

8. COMMERCIAL PAPER ISSUANCE

This section focuses on the use of commercial paper (CP) as a source of short-term financing. CP is unsecured promissory notes of highly rated corporations, financial institutions, or sovereigns. While the specific characteristics of CP programs vary by country, most CP markets are modeled after the US market, which is the oldest and still the largest CP market in the world.

In the United States, there are two types of CP programs, named after the sections in the Securities Act of 1933 that provide exemptions from registration of CP with the SEC. An issuer under a 3(a)(3) program can issue CP up to 270 days in minimum amounts of $100,000. The proceeds of 3(a)(3) CP may only be used for working capital purposes. An issuer under a 4(2) program can issue CP up to 397 days in minimum amounts of $250,000. There is no restriction on how the proceeds of 4(2) CP may be used, including for construction expenditures or acquisitions. In practice, most outstanding CP has a maturity less than 30 days, but issuers continually roll over the CP into a new issue at maturity.

Characteristics of 3(a)(3) and 4(2) CP programs are outlined in Exhibit 13.2.

EXHIBIT 13.2 CHARACTERISTICS OF 3(A)(3) AND 4(2) CP PROGRAMS

	3(a)(3)	4(2)
Type	Public	Private Placement
Proceeds	Working Capital	No Restrictions
Maximum Maturity	270 Days	397 Days
Minimum Issuance	$100,000	$250,000
Pricing	Spread to LIBOR	Spread to LIBOR (no premium)
Investors	Accredited Investors	Institutional Investors & Qualified Institutional Buyers (QIBs)

CP programs are rated by the major credit rating agencies, which normally require each program to have a liquidity backup in the event the market would not be available to issue or reissue CP for any reason. Typical backup facilities include a revolving credit facility or a letter of credit issued by a highly rated bank. Although common, not every CP issuer has to have a backup. Some firms with high liquidity and a strong credit rating are able to issue CP based solely on their own resources. CP can be issued directly by firms (i.e., sold directly to investors), but most CP is placed through dealers (selected by the issuer) who market the CP to investors for a nominal fee.

CP is sold at a discount, meaning the interest paid by the issuer on the CP is deducted from the CP's face value when determining the proceeds that are available for use by the issuing firm. The discount rate on CP is always calculated on a 360-day basis. Other costs associated with a CP program include the dealer fees, backup credit facility fees, rating agency charges, and any credit enhancement costs.

Because of the effort and high fixed costs involved in establishing a CP program, CP financing is desirable only when ongoing funding needs are large. Firms with the highest credit rating rarely issue CP for amounts below $50 million, although individual issues under an overall program may be for smaller amounts. In addition, firms without excellent credit ratings often find commercial bank credit more attractive than CP because banks have more flexibility in structuring credit (e.g., covenants, rate adjustments, and collateral) to mitigate risk and therefore lower costs to the borrower.

9. ASSET-BASED BORROWING

Commercial finance companies and some commercial banks specialize in asset-based lending. Asset-based lines of credit in the working capital area are typically secured by accounts receivable or inventory, and can support temporary financing needs.

B. Pricing and Costs of Commercial Paper (CP) and Credit Lines

A loan or other borrowing arrangement represents an investment by the counterparty (i.e., the lender or investor). Consequently, the factors that influence investment yield are the determinants of credit pricing. Pricing and fees on loans increase with default risk, price risk, liquidity, and length of maturity. A discussion of how these factors impact loan pricing via interest rates is provided in the following section of this chapter. Factors that enter into borrowing costs yet do not impact an investor's yields include dealer and placement fees, credit enhancement, and backup credit costs.

It should be noted that borrowing costs are commonly discussed in terms of basis points (typically abbrevieated as *bps*). One basis point is equal to a one-hundredth of 1%, which is 0.0001 or 0.01%. Thus, 50 bps is equivalent to 0.0050 or 0.50%.

In this section, the costs associated with CP and credit lines are covered, along with formulas and calculations for these sources.

1. ANNUAL COST FOR CP ISSUANCE

The all-in or total costs to issue CP include the interest rate implied in the discount, a dealer fee, and a fee for credit enhancement in the form of a backup or standby line of credit.

Assume that a firm issues $50,000,000 of CP with a 20-day maturity at a discount of 0.396%. To calculate the annualized cost of the paper, begin by finding the amount of usable funds, which is the face amount of the CP less the discount:

$$\text{Dollar Discount} = \text{Discount Rate} \times \text{Par Value} \times \left(\frac{\text{Days to Maturity}}{360} \right)$$

$$= 0.00396 \times \$50,000,000 \times \left(\frac{20}{360} \right) = \$11,000.00$$

$$\text{Usable Funds} = \text{Par Value} - \text{Dollar Discount}$$

$$= \$50,000,000 - \$11,000 = \$49,989,000$$

Assume that the annualized dealer fee is 0.12% (12 basis points) and the cost of a backup line of credit is 0.25% (25 basis points). The amount of the dealer fee and the amount of the backup line of credit fee are calculated as follows:

$$\text{Prorated Dealer Fee} = \text{Annual Fee Rate} \times \text{CP Issue Size} \times \left(\frac{\text{Days to Maturity}}{360} \right)$$

$$= 0.0012 \times \$50,000,000 \times \left(\frac{20}{360} \right) = \$3,333.33$$

$$\text{Prorated Backup} \frac{L}{C} \text{Fee} = \text{Annual Fee Rate} \times \text{CP Issue Size} \times \left(\frac{\text{Days to Maturity}}{360} \right)$$

$$= 0.0025 \times \$50,000,000 \times \left(\frac{20}{360} \right) = \$6,944.44$$

As a final step in determining the annual cost of the CP issuance, the periodic interest rate must be annualized based on the number of times in a year that CP could be issued assuming similar terms. When annualizing the cost of CP, note that a 365-day year is assumed. A general equation for this calculation appears below:

$$\text{Annualized Cost of CP} = \left(\frac{\text{Dollar Discount} + \text{Dealer Fee} + \text{Backup} \frac{L}{C} \text{ Fee}}{\text{Usable Funds}} \right) \times \left(\frac{365}{\text{Days to Maturity}} \right)$$

$$= \left(\frac{\$11,000.00 + \$3,333.33 + \$6,944.44}{\$49,989,000} \right) \times \left(\frac{365}{20} \right) = 0.0078 \text{ or } 0.78\%$$

The annualized cost of 0.78% applies to the issuer of the CP. However, the buyer's or investor's yield is based on how much is gained in relation to the amount of funds that are not usable because they are tied up in the investment. In this example, the nominal, or annual, yield to the investor (calculated on a 365-day basis) is:

$$\text{CP Nominal Yield} = \left(\frac{\text{Dollar Discount}}{\text{Purchase Price}} \right) \times \left(\frac{365}{\text{Days to Maturity}} \right)$$

$$= \left(\frac{\$11,000}{\$49,989,000} \right) \times \left(\frac{365}{20} \right) = 0.0040 \text{ or } 0.40\%$$

The investor's yield is lower than the borrower's cost because the investor does not receive the dealer fee or the backup line of credit fee paid by the borrower.

2. ANNUAL COST FOR A LINE OF CREDIT

A line of credit lender will typically charge interest on funds borrowed and charge a commitment fee on the line on an annual basis. While there may be other fees, they tend to be one-time charges rather than recurrent annual fees. Interest is charged on the used portion of the line. The commitment fee may be charged on the entire line or just its unused portion. The overall interest rate on the credit line is determined by the total interest paid on the line's used portion and the amount paid for the commitment fee relative to the average used portion of the credit line over the borrowing period. In the example that follows, the commitment fee applies to the unused portion of the credit line.

Assume that a firm expects to use $1,600,000 of short-term borrowings, but it wants to establish a $3,000,000 credit line to ensure adequate reserve borrowing capacity. A lender offers the firm LIBOR plus a risk premium of 2.50%. The lender requires a commitment fee of 0.30% (30 basis points) on the unused portion of the line. LIBOR at the time of the loan is 0.70%. The rate on the used portion of the line is LIBOR plus 2.50%, or 3.20% (the all-in rate). Begin by calculating all interest and fees paid:

$$\text{Interest Paid} = \text{Average Borrowings} \times \text{All-In Rate}$$

$$= \$1,600,000 \times 0.032 = \$51,200$$

$$\text{Fee on Unused Portion} = \text{Unused Portion} \times \text{Commitment Fee}$$

$$= (\$3,000,000 - \$1,600,000) \times 0.0030 = \$4,200$$

Next, the annual interest rate on the credit line is calculated as total costs relative to the amount used on the line:

$$\text{Annualized Cost of the Line} = \frac{\text{Interest} + \text{Fee on the Unused Portion of the Line}}{\text{Used Portion of the Line}}$$

$$= \frac{\$51,200 + \$4,200}{\$1,600,000} = 0.0346 \text{ or } 3.46\%$$

Now, suppose that the lender requires a 10% compensating balance. That is, the borrower must maintain a balance in its demand deposit account (DDA) that is not less than 10% of the amount borrowed on the credit line. Since the firm would have to hold 10% of $1,600,000, or $160,000, in its DDA, its usable funds would only be $1,440,000. The 10% compensating balance requirement means that the firm will have to borrow more than $1,600,000 on the line in order to have $1,600,000 available. The compensating balance has the following effect on the calculation of the annual interest rate:

$$\text{Annualized Cost of the Line} = \frac{\text{Interest} + \text{Fee on the Unused Portion of the Line}}{\text{Used Portion of the Line} - \text{Compensating Balance}}$$

$$= \frac{\$51,200 + \$4,200}{\$1,600,000 - \$160,000} = 0.0385 \text{ or } 3.85\%$$

The amount that must be borrowed on the line in order to have $1,600,000 available is calculated as:[17]

$$\text{Required Borrowings} = \frac{\$1,600,000}{1 - 0.10} = \$1,777,777.78$$

This larger amount borrowed increases the total interest and fees paid, as shown below:

$$\text{Interest Paid} = \text{Average Borrowings} \times \text{All-In Rate}$$

$$= \$1,777,777.78 \times 0.032 = \$56,888.89$$

$$\text{Fee on Unused Portion} = \text{Unused Portion} \times \text{Commitment Fee}$$

$$= (\$3,000,000.00 - \$1,777,777.78) \times 0.0030 = \$3,666.67$$

Then, the annual interest rate on the credit line can be recalculated as:

$$\text{Annualized Cost of the Line} = \frac{\text{Interest} + \text{Fee on the Unused Portion of the Line}}{\text{Used Portion of the Line} - \text{Compensating Balance}}$$

$$= \frac{\$56,888.89 + \$3,666.67}{\$1,777,777.78 - (0.10 \times \$1,777,777.78)}$$

$$= \frac{\$60,555.56}{\$1,600,000} = 0.0378 \text{ or } 3.78\%$$

The compensating balance requirement means that the firm will borrow more than it needs in usable funds. As a result, the firm will pay more in interest and fees ($60,555.56 versus $55,400.00) as well as a higher interest rate on the credit line (3.78% versus 3.46%).

---

17. This formula results from the algebraic approach of solving for the following: 90 percent of what level of required borrowings is equal to $1,600,000?

V. DEBT FINANCING

Debt financing is an important topic for treasury professionals to understand due to the impact of debt usage on profitability and firm value. Most of this section will cover this topic in a general framework, with some specific information provided on issues for US-based organizations. The major differences between countries are in the interest rate measures used and some specific regulations related to the credit and debt instruments.

A. Basic Components of Interest Rates

Interest rates depend on many factors. Some of these factors arise from general economic conditions, while others are dependent upon firm-specific variables (e.g., financial position, industry, overall debt use). To help form a basic understanding of these factors, the model below incorporates some of the most common factors into a calculation of an underlying interest rate on a specific debt issue.

For most borrowers, the underlying cost of debt (expressed as the variable r in the calculation below) is a function of the following factors:

$$r = r^*_{RF} + IP + DP + LP + MP$$

Where:

r^*_{RF} = Real risk-free rate of interest

IP = Inflation premium

DP = Default premium

LP = Liquidity premium

MP = Maturity premium

The *real risk-free rate of interest* is generally defined as the rate demanded by lenders (i.e., investors or savers) to compensate for delaying purchases made today, in the absence of any risk or inflation, for a one-year maturity. The real risk-free rate demanded by savers becomes the basis for the overall borrowing rate. Historically, the average real risk-free rate was approximately 1.2% between 1980 and 2016.[18] At the time of this writing, the real risk-free rate is at or close to zero in most major markets, due to long-term government intervention to lower rates.

The first adjustment to the real rate is for inflation, as lenders want to maintain the purchasing power of the money they lend to borrowers. The combination of the real risk-free rate and a short-term rate of inflation usually matches the rate on short-term government investments (e.g., a US T-bill) for the period in question. The sum of the real risk-free rate and the inflation premium (IP) is commonly referred to as the *nominal rate*.

The next adjustment is for default risk. For investments other than government securities, there is a risk of default on the part of the borrower that must be factored into the rate of interest. This is known as the *default risk premium (DP)*. As the level of default risk rises, so does the required interest rate.

While the markets for most securities issued by large governments[19] are very efficient and highly liquid, other securities are not as easily traded, resulting in higher transaction costs and, ultimately, lower liquidity. This results in a liquidity premium (LP).

---

18. This information is derived from the FRED® Economic Data resource provided by the Federal Reserve Bank of St. Louis (https://fred.stlouisfed.org, accessed August 8, 2016).

19. Examples include the governments of the G8 (or Group of Eight) countries, which consist of Canada, France, Germany, Italy, Japan, Russia, the United Kingdom, and the United States.

Finally, longer-term fixed instrument investments generally have more price risk (i.e., they fluctuate more in price for a given change in interest rates). As a result of this price risk, longer-term securities usually have a maturity premium (MP) in addition to the other interest rate adjustments.

To illustrate these concepts, Exhibit 13.3 shows the interest rate components for three basic types of notes or bonds: US Treasury issues, corporate issues, and municipal issues. Each type is shown with varying maturities. The rates displayed here are for illustration purposes only and are not necessarily representative of actual rates or spreads between different types of investments. In calculating the rates for each type of investment, the following assumptions are made:

· US Treasuries are perceived to be risk-free, with no default risk.

· US Treasuries are highly liquid and thus have no liquidity risk.

· Both corporate and municipal bonds have default and liquidity risk.

· Maturity risk increases with the issue's time to maturity.

This information is combined to calculate the total cost of borrowing for each investment type, which is shown in the final column of Exhibit 13.3.

EXHIBIT 13.3 COMPARISON OF INTEREST RATES OR YIELDS ON DIFFERENT TYPES OF INVESTMENTS

INVESTMENT	REAL RISK-FREE RATE	INFLATION PREMIUM	DEFAULT PREMIUM	LIQUIDITY PREMIUM	MATURITY PREMIUM	COST OF BORROWING
1-YEAR TREASURY	0.0%	0.5%	0.0%	0.0%	0.0%	0.5%
5-YEAR TREASURY	0.0%	2.5%	0.0%	0.0%	0.4%	2.9%
10-YEAR TREASURY	0.0%	4.0%	0.0%	0.0%	0.9%	4.9%
1-YEAR CORPORATE	0.0%	0.5%	2.5%	0.5%	0.0%	3.5%
5-YEAR CORPORATE	0.0%	2.5%	2.5%	0.5%	0.4%	5.9%
10-YEAR CORPORATE	0.0%	4.0%	2.5%	0.5%	0.9%	7.9%
1-YEAR MUNICIPAL	0.0%	0.5%	1.5%	1.0%	0.0%	3.0%
5-YEAR MUNICIPAL	0.0%	2.5%	1.5%	1.0%	0.4%	5.4%
10-YEAR MUNICIPAL	0.0%	4.0%	1.5%	1.0%	0.9%	7.4%

The impact of the various factors on the required rates for different types of bonds is shown in the exhibit. For example, for bonds with a one-year maturity, the T-bill rate is 0.5%, the corporate issue has a rate of 3.5%, and the municipal rate is 3.0%. The T-bill incorporates only the inflation premium as an adjustment to the real risk-free rate, while both the corporate and municipal issues reflect some amount of default risk and liquidity risk. Comparisons of the rates across the five- and ten-year maturities also show T-bills with the lowest rate, followed by municipal bonds and corporate bonds.

B. Base Rates

For most borrowers, the cost of funds is expressed as the sum of a base rate plus an appropriate adjustment or spread to account for other risks involved in the arrangement. The base rate will generally include the adjustments for inflation and maturity premiums, while the spread will factor in adjustments for the default and liquidity premiums. The difference between the common base rates discussed below and the T-bill rate is that the rates below are essentially interbank rates (i.e., the rate at which one bank will lend to another bank). The interbank rates will be slightly higher than the T-bill rate at any given time due to a small amount of default risk inherent in bank-to-bank borrowing arrangements.

Economic conditions and yield curves influence the general level of interest rates and base interest rates for borrowing, such as LIBOR and, to a lesser extent, the Fed funds rate and the US prime rate. The ICE Benchmark Administration (IBA) compiles LIBOR daily by averaging the interest rate quotes of at least eight banks chosen to reflect a balance by country, type of institution, reputation, and scale of marketing activity. LIBOR is quoted in numerous currencies and is released to the market in London each day.

The Fed funds rate is the interest rate US banks charge to borrow reserve balances from one another. The target rate for Fed funds is set by the Federal Open Market Committee (FOMC) on a periodic basis (about eight times per year), but the actual rate charged between banks is negotiated by those banks. This is known as the *Fed funds effective rate*. The prime rate is the interest rate commercial banks charge their best corporate customers, although strong, creditworthy borrowers usually can obtain rates below prime from their financial partners. Unlike LIBOR, which fluctuates on a daily basis, the US prime rate is typically set about three percentage points above the Fed funds rate and can remain fixed for extended periods of time.

C. Short-Term Interest Rates versus Long-Term Interest Rates

Historically, short-term interest rates are lower than long-term rates, so yield curves are usually normal, meaning they slope upward with maturity. This implies that there is a cost advantage to using short-term credit. When short-term rates are higher than long-term rates, the yield curve is inverted and slopes downward with maturity.

A significant responsibility for treasury professionals is to monitor interest rate cycles and the yield curve, in order to make effective decisions about short- versus long-term financing. Depending on interest rate cycles and the prevailing yield curve for interest rates, a company may secure long-term, low-rate bank or institutional financing and/or obtain fixed- versus floating-rate financing. There are also several short-term financing sources (e.g., accounts payable and accruals) that have little or no interest costs.

Borrowing on a short-term basis carries two types of risks to the borrower that are avoided in longer-term borrowing:

- The first risk relates to fluctuations in market interest rates. If the company borrows on a short-term, floating-rate basis, then it will borrow at the prevailing interest rate and risk dramatic rate swings in either direction. Such short-term borrowing risks can be reduced via interest rate caps, collars, swaps, and floors.

· The second risk of short-term financing concerns the availability of funds. If a company relies heavily on short-term borrowing, then the short-term funds may not be available at some future point due to tightening credit standards on the part of lenders. Also, a firm's credit quality may decline, thus endangering the future rollover or renewal of the credit arrangement. Some companies counter this risk by negotiating multiyear credit line commitments (e.g., revolving credit agreements), which guarantee the availability of funds over a longer term.[20]

In contrast to short-term borrowing, long-term borrowing on a fixed-rate basis stabilizes interest costs and provides funds for a longer term.

1. OPERATIONAL ADVANTAGES OF SHORT-TERM FINANCING

It is important to understand the advantages and disadvantages of short-term financing (i.e., credit facilities of less than one year) relative to long-term financing (i.e., credit facilities of at least one year). Aside from differences in cost and risk, there are operational differences in using short- versus long-term debt to finance current assets.

The primary operational advantages of short-term financing include ease of access, flexibility, and the ability to efficiently finance seasonal credit needs. In addition, short-term loans generally have less restrictive covenants than long-term loans because a lender's money is at risk for a shorter period of time. A short-term borrowing arrangement allows the borrower to maintain flexibility for future borrowing decisions. For example, to meet increased seasonal needs, a firm may need financing to increase inventory and/or accounts receivable. Short-term loans are a primary tool for financing seasonal (i.e., temporary) increases in current assets.

In addition to bank credit, short-term financing can also be obtained from spontaneous sources such as accounts payable and accruals, which are referred to as *spontaneously generated financing*. As sales grow, these sources spontaneously generate funds that can offset required investments in current assets.

2. OPERATIONAL DISADVANTAGES OF SHORT-TERM FINANCING

An operational disadvantage of short-term financing, especially sources such as lines of credit or commercial paper, is the continuing need to renegotiate or roll over the financing. This rollover risk is a disadvantage as a lender may decide not to roll over the loan or renew the credit line at maturity due to changes in the borrower's financial conditions or changes in general economic conditions. In addition, lenders that provide lines of credit typically require that loans used to finance short-term working capital deficits be paid in full for a minimum period of one to three months each year.

Many firms find that using short-term loans to finance permanent current asset requirements is risky. However, one approach to continued use of short-term debt that carries lower risk involves revolving loans secured by accounts receivable or inventory, referred to as *asset-based lending*. The downsides to this form of secured borrowing include:

· The assets used as security must be monitored.

· Key ratios related to the assets must often be maintained.

· Lending is generally limited to some percentage of the asset values.

---

20. During the global financial crisis of 2007–2009, many banks rescinded these guarantees using material adverse change (MAC) clauses. As the crisis continued, banks primarily offered credit agreements of less than one year in length, as the capital requirements on these agreements were lower than those for multiyear credit agreements.

D. Loan Agreements and Covenants

Loan covenants, discussed earlier in this chapter, impose either restrictions, known as *restrictive* or *negative covenants*, and/or obligations, known as *affirmative* or *positive covenants*, on the borrower. Loan covenants generally protect the lenders by preventing management from increasing the borrowing entity's credit risk, thereby reducing the value of existing debt securities. Because the lenders do not typically have a voice in the entity's management, they must protect themselves through covenants at the time the loan is made. For bonds, the covenants are typically determined from negotiations with the rating agency as part of the ratings process. The covenants may impose significant restrictions on the entity's financial decision making. These restrictions could include limits or restrictions on the:

· Ability to sell certain assets

· Right to issue additional bonds

· Use of second or junior mortgages

· Key ratios for the firm

· Payments made by the firm (e.g., dividends)

It is also important to understand that the terms of the loan agreements and covenants are generally negotiable between the borrower and the lender. The advantage that the borrower has is that it usually has a better idea about the amount of the line that will be used, as well as how often it will be used. In general, if only a small portion of the credit line will be used, then it would be advantageous to agree to a higher interest rate in return for a smaller commitment fee. If, on the other hand, the borrower thinks it will be using the bulk of the line, then a lower interest rate may be negotiated in return for a higher commitment fee, assuming the commitment fee is on the unused portion of the line.

In many cases, a multiyear revolving credit agreement may be counted as long-term debt on the firm's balance sheet, which can reduce the level of current liabilities, thereby improving key ratios (e.g., the current and quick ratios).

E. Credit Rating Agencies

Most publicly issued debt by firms and municipalities is rated by one or more of the credit rating agencies (CRAs).[21] CRAs assign credit ratings for issuers of short- and long-term debt obligations, as well as for the debt instruments themselves. Ratings can be on either a solicited or unsolicited basis. With a solicited rating, a borrower would ask one or more agencies to rate the borrower and may work with the agency to ensure an appropriate rating in anticipation of the future debt offering. With an unsolicited rating, a CRA would rate an entity based on publicly available information even when the entity has not requested a rating. This may result in a poor rating based on incomplete information. It is important to remember that a credit rating is not an investment recommendation; rather, it is an assessment of the potential for downside loss on the investment. A listing of some of the major credit rating agencies appears in Appendix 13.1.

CRAs generally have access to a borrower's internal information, and the CRA's analyses and subsequent rating are widely accepted by market participants and regulators. In most cases, the rating agencies have access to confidential, nonpublic information that the securities issuers provide to the agencies only for the determination of ratings. This information is not released to the general public without the issuer's permission. Financial institutions use these credit ratings when required by regulators to hold investment-grade bonds.

---

21. In the United States, CRAs are also known as *nationally recognized statistical rating organizations*.

Part of the US Dodd-Frank Wall Street Reform and Consumer Protection Act addresses CRAs and the potential for conflicts of interest arising because the CRAs receive their primary revenues from the entities they rate and not from the investors who use the information. Dodd-Frank requires the CRAs to provide greater disclosure of their rating models and methodologies, and subjects them to greater liability.

1. RATING CLASSES

There are two primary classes of ratings:

- **Issuer Credit Ratings:** This type of credit rating represents the CRA's opinion on the issuer's overall capacity to meet its financial obligations. These include counterparty, corporate, and sovereign credit ratings. Counterparty ratings are made for key counterparties in financial transactions (e.g., financial institutions and insurance companies). Corporate credit ratings are on corporate debt issuers, and sovereign ratings are on government debt issuers.

- **Issue-Specific Credit Ratings:** These ratings of specific long- and short-term securities consider the attributes of the issuer, as well as the specific terms of the issue, the quality of the collateral, and the creditworthiness of the guarantors.

2. THE RATINGS PROCESS

For issuers, the ratings process includes the quantitative and qualitative analyses of the issuer being assessed. The quantitative aspects focus mainly on financial analyses derived from the issuer's financial reports. In most cases, credit rating analysts examine the issuer's financials using proprietary models and may perform additional quantitative reviews if necessary. The qualitative side is concerned with aspects that are distinct from the financials. For a corporate issuer, this may include analyzing the quality of the management and the firm's competitiveness within its industry, as well as the expected growth of the industry and its vulnerability to business cycles, technology changes, regulatory changes, and labor relations.

For government issues, both sovereign and sub-sovereign, the typical analysis is based on the primary factors relating to government finance. These usually include the economy, overall debt levels, tax revenues, expenses, financial statements, and administration/management strategies for the government entity. Other factors would include the collateral for the debt and the primary source for repayment (e.g., general taxes or specific revenues, such as tolls for a bridge). Each factor is evaluated individually and in aggregate with respect to the total effect on the government entity's ability to repay its debt.

3. REVIEWS OF RATINGS

Ratings usually are reviewed by the CRAs once a year based on new financial reports, new business information, or review meetings with management. These review meetings are an important part of the ongoing relationship between the organization and the CRA. A credit watch or rating review is issued if there is a reason to believe that the review may lead to an unfavorable credit rating change.

4. CREDIT RATING SCALES

The scales used for bond credit ratings by the primary agencies recognized by the US SEC are shown in Exhibits 13.4 (long-term bonds) and 13.5 (short-term issues). Note that a different rating system is used to evaluate long-term and short-term credit ratings. The main reason for the difference in rating systems is that long-term debt has more possible options and variations that affect the ratings, and the maturity and seniority of the issue often play a major role in the ultimate ratings. Short-term issues, on the other hand, tend to be more standardized in their structure and options, so a narrow range of ratings is appropriate.

EXHIBIT 13.4 **LONG-TERM BOND CREDIT RATINGS**

Definitions	Moody's	S&P	Fitch	DBRS	JCR
Investment Grade					
Prime (Maximum Safety)	Aaa	AAA	AAA	AAA	AAA
High Grade (High Quality)	Aa1 to Aa3	AA+ to AA-	AA+ to AA-	AA	AA
Upper Medium Grade	A1 to A3	A+ to A-	A+ to A-	A	A
Lower Medium Grade	Baa1 to Baa3	BBB+ to BBB-	BBB+ to BBB-	BBB	BBB
Below or Non-Investment Grade					
Below Investment Grade	Ba1	BB+	BB+	–	–
Speculative	Ba2 to Ba3	BB to BB-	BB to BB-	BB	BB
Highly Speculative	B1 to B3	B+ to B-	B+ to B-	B	B
Substantial Risk	Caa	CCC+	CCC	CCC to C	CCC
In Poor Standing	–	CCC to CCC-	–	–	CC
Extremely Speculative	Ca	CC	CC	–	C
May Be in Default	C	C	C	–	LD
Default	–	D	DDD to D	D	D

EXHIBIT 13.5 **SHORT-TERM ISSUE CREDIT RATINGS**

Definitions	S&P	Moody's	Fitch	JCR
Investment Grade				
Highest Quality	A-1	Prime-1	F1	J-1
Good Quality	A-2	Prime-2	F2	J-2
Adequate Credit	A-3	Prime-3	F3	J-3
Speculative Grade				
Vulnerable to Changes	B-1 to B-3	NP	B	NJ
High Default Risk	C	NP	C	NJ
Under Regulatory Supervision	R	NP	RD	NJ
Default	SD or D	NP	D	NJ

VI. SUMMARY

Short-term borrowing and investing represent critical parts of the treasury function related to daily liquidity management. The first sections of this chapter discussed the various issues related to management of the short-term investment portfolio, including internal versus external management, investment strategies, reporting, and securities safekeeping. These sections also introduced key risks associated with short-term investments and presented pricing and yield calculations.

In the last half of the chapter, various forms of short-term borrowing were discussed, including effective borrowing cost calculations for lines of credit and commercial paper. The chapter concluded by describing the operational trade-offs of using short-term debt relative to long-term debt, as well as the role and importance of credit ratings.

Key Equations

Short-Term Investments:

$$\text{Taxable Equivalent Yield} = \frac{\text{Tax-Exempt Yield}}{1 - \text{Marginal Tax Rate}}$$

$$\text{After-Tax Yield} = \text{Taxable Yield} \times (1 - \text{Marginal Tax Rate})$$

$$\text{Holding Period Yield} = \frac{\text{Cash Received at Maturity} - \text{Amount Invested}}{\text{Amount Invested}}$$

$$\text{MMY} = \left(\frac{\text{Cash Received at Maturity} - \text{Amount Invested}}{\text{Amount Invested}} \right) \times \left(\frac{360}{\text{Days to Maturity}} \right)$$

$$\text{BEY} = \left(\frac{\text{Cash Received at Maturity} - \text{Amount Invested}}{\text{Amount Invested}} \right) \times \left(\frac{365}{\text{Days to Maturity}} \right)$$

$$\text{BEY} = \text{MMY} \times \left(\frac{365}{360} \right)$$

$$\text{MMY} = \text{BEY} \times \left(\frac{360}{365} \right)$$

$$\text{Dollar Discount} = \text{Par Value} - \text{Purchase Price}$$

$$\text{Discount Rate} = \left(\frac{\text{Dollar Discount}}{\text{Par Value}} \right) \times \left(\frac{360}{\text{Days to Maturity}} \right)$$

Short-Term Borrowing:

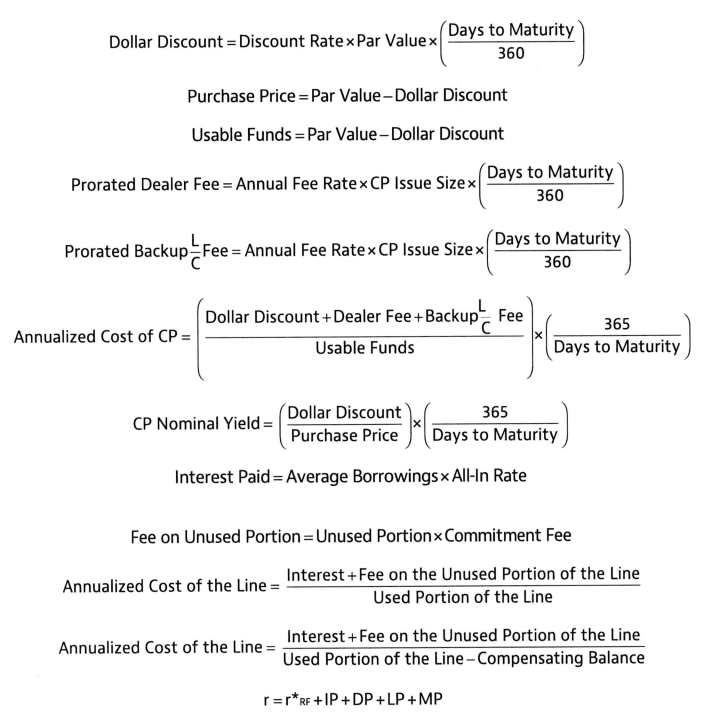

$$\text{Dollar Discount} = \text{Discount Rate} \times \text{Par Value} \times \left(\frac{\text{Days to Maturity}}{360}\right)$$

$$\text{Purchase Price} = \text{Par Value} - \text{Dollar Discount}$$

$$\text{Usable Funds} = \text{Par Value} - \text{Dollar Discount}$$

$$\text{Prorated Dealer Fee} = \text{Annual Fee Rate} \times \text{CP Issue Size} \times \left(\frac{\text{Days to Maturity}}{360}\right)$$

$$\text{Prorated Backup}\frac{L}{C}\text{Fee} = \text{Annual Fee Rate} \times \text{CP Issue Size} \times \left(\frac{\text{Days to Maturity}}{360}\right)$$

$$\text{Annualized Cost of CP} = \left(\frac{\text{Dollar Discount} + \text{Dealer Fee} + \text{Backup}\frac{L}{C}\text{ Fee}}{\text{Usable Funds}}\right) \times \left(\frac{365}{\text{Days to Maturity}}\right)$$

$$\text{CP Nominal Yield} = \left(\frac{\text{Dollar Discount}}{\text{Purchase Price}}\right) \times \left(\frac{365}{\text{Days to Maturity}}\right)$$

$$\text{Interest Paid} = \text{Average Borrowings} \times \text{All-In Rate}$$

$$\text{Fee on Unused Portion} = \text{Unused Portion} \times \text{Commitment Fee}$$

$$\text{Annualized Cost of the Line} = \frac{\text{Interest} + \text{Fee on the Unused Portion of the Line}}{\text{Used Portion of the Line}}$$

$$\text{Annualized Cost of the Line} = \frac{\text{Interest} + \text{Fee on the Unused Portion of the Line}}{\text{Used Portion of the Line} - \text{Compensating Balance}}$$

$$r = r^{*}{}_{RF} + IP + DP + LP + MP$$

APPENDIX 13.1: LISTING OF SOME MAJOR CREDIT RATING AGENCIES

- Moody's Investors Service [US]
- Standard & Poor's (S&P) [US]
- Fitch Ratings [US and UK]
- CRISIL Ratings [India]
- Japan Credit Rating Agency (JCR)
- Credit Analysis & Research (CARE) [India]
- DBRS (formerly Dominion Bond Rating Service) [Canada]
- Brickwork Ratings [India]
- A.M. Best [US-based insurance companies]
- ICRA (formerly Investment Information and Credit Rating Agency of India)
- Kroll Bond Rating Agency (KBRA) [US]
- Veda (formerly Baycorp Advantage) [Australia]
- China Credit Information Service (CCIS)
- RAM Holdings (formerly Rating Agency Malaysia Berhad)
- Egan-Jones Ratings Company [US]
- The Pakistan Credit Rating Agency Limited (PACRA)

CHAPTER 14
Cash Flow Forecasting

I. INTRODUCTION

II. PURPOSE OF CASH FLOW FORECASTING

III. ISSUES AND OPPORTUNITIES IN FORECASTING
  A. Simplicity
  B. Collaboration and Communication
  C. Consistency

IV. TYPES OF FORECASTS
  A. Purpose
  B. Forecasting Horizon
  C. Update Frequency
  D. Projected Closing Cash Position

V. THE FORECASTING PROCESS
  A. Cash Flow Components
  B. Degree of Certainty
  C. Data Identification and Organization
  D. Selection and Validation of the Forecasting Method

VI. FORECASTING METHODS
  A. Short-Term Cash Flow Forecasting Methods
  B. Medium- and Long-Term Forecasting Methods
  C. Statistical Methods in Forecasting

VII. BEST PRACTICES FOR CASH FLOW FORECASTING

VIII. SUMMARY

I. INTRODUCTION

The goal of cash flow forecasting is to optimize future cash resources. Cash flow forecasting assists a treasury professional in planning cash management activities. These activities include scheduling cash concentration transfers, funding disbursement accounts, making short-term investing and borrowing decisions, managing target balances for purposes of bank compensation, managing covenant restrictions, and abiding by regulatory requirements. Despite its importance, cash flow forecasting remains an inexact science, primarily because of the number of assumptions that must be made to forecast cash. For this reason, the assumptions underlying the cash forecast should be reviewed and updated frequently with the most current and complete information available.

Cash forecasts are different from the broader financial models that are often used for financial planning and analysis, because cash forecasts are more concerned with cash flow projections as opposed to accounting statements that must comply with US GAAP (US Generally Accepted Accounting Principles) or IFRS (International Financial Reporting Standards) requirements.

Cash flow forecasting requires a treasury professional to take four essential steps:

- Establish assumptions.
- Estimate future cash inflows and outflows.
- Generate a pro forma cash position.
- Identify how to finance cash deficits or invest cash surpluses. The shortfall or surplus is measured relative to the predetermined, minimum desired target cash balance.

This chapter describes the benefits of cash flow forecasting and the types of forecasts that are commonly performed by the treasury function. Next, the chapter provides an overview of the forecasting process and introduces some of the principal cash flow forecasting methods. The chapter concludes with a discussion of best practices in treasury forecasting.

II. PURPOSE OF CASH FLOW FORECASTING

The accurate prediction of cash inflows and outflows over time is an important part of a treasury professional's job and is essential to a variety of tasks:

- **Managing Liquidity:** Forecasting the net cash position at different intervals[1] to identify potential cash excesses or shortages is critical for scheduling investment decisions and anticipating borrowing requirements to meet daily obligations. Liquidity management is the most important motive for cash flow forecasting.

- **Maximizing Returns:** A cash forecast provides the timing and amounts of anticipated cash surpluses and cash deficits. Short-term investment returns are maximized when treasury professionals have time to select optimal investment instruments and maturities. If the firm follows a matching strategy for short-term investments, the maturity of an investment will be matched with the timing of future cash deficits. Knowing that the firm does not expect a cash deficit for a certain period of time allows the treasury professional to extend investment maturities and earn higher yields.

- **Controlling Financial Activities:** Variance analysis that compares actual cash flows with projected cash flows can help identify problems such as unanticipated inventory changes, delays in A/R collection, the mistiming of payments, and fraud or embezzlement. Early identification signals management to initiate corrective measures.

---

1. It is important to distinguish between the interval of a forecast, which is the period covered (e.g., daily, weekly, monthly), and the frequency with which the forecast is reviewed and updated. For example, a monthly forecast may be updated weekly as new information on actual cash flows becomes available.

- **Meeting Strategic Objectives:** Cash forecasts are used to project future funding requirements and make operating decisions to support the strategic plan.

- **Budgeting Capital:** Forecasts of revenue, expenditures, and funding are not only helpful for developing cash forecasts, but are also needed for the evaluation of capital investment alternatives (i.e., capital budgeting).

- **Managing Costs:** Cash forecasts can help minimize excess bank balances, reduce short-term borrowing costs, and increase short-term investment income.

- **Managing Currency Exposure:** Cash forecasts attributable to foreign operations are used to assess the degree of foreign currency exposure and provide information for policies designed to control currency risk.

- **Meeting Compliance Requirements:** Cash forecasts are frequently part of internal control procedures needed to comply with loan covenants, meet minimum capital requirements, or meet requirements for imprest tax accounts. Compliance is especially important for publicly traded companies.

III. ISSUES AND OPPORTUNITIES IN FORECASTING

A. Simplicity

The goal of a cash forecast is to create a reasonable snapshot of the projected cash position at a point in time. The key word here is *reasonable*. The necessary degree of accuracy is a function of the purpose of the forecast. A short-term forecast used to manage daily cash position should be more precise than a long-term forecast used to determine the availability of capital for future expansion of a production plant. But neither forecast needs to be accurate to the $0.01. The ultimate goal is to develop a cash forecast with a degree of detail that is commensurate with its ultimate purpose. That is, treasury personnel should weigh the benefits of a more accurate cash forecast versus the cost of improving accuracy.

It is important to note that for firms that conduct business in more than one currency or country, forecasts need to be made by currency. Shortfalls in one currency are not automatically offset by excesses in another currency unless specific plans to do so have already been made and put into place. One of the reasons for forecasting is to manage currency exposure, and this cannot be done if the forecasting model ignores the effects of other relevant currencies.

B. Collaboration and Communication

Treasury is dependent upon other business units to provide the information and assumptions needed to create an accurate forecast. Failure to know about impending payments or delays in collections can negatively affect a forecast from the outset. The need for collaboration with other units in the company, such as accounts payable, accounts receivable, tax, and financial planning and analysis (FP&A), creates a need for effective communication, clear expectations, and common terminology.

C. Consistency

Due to the many uses of a cash forecast and the similarity to financial statements, non-treasury departments often develop forecasts of their own. It is important to realize that while the end purposes of the forecasts are different, the information and assumptions used are usually similar and should be consistent. Unless the various departments that use forecasts cooperate, there is typically a duplication of time and effort. A less obvious issue is that the forecasts are developed by different people, using different inputs and assumptions. If the assumptions used are not consistent, the forecasts could be significantly different, resulting in large variances between the forecast and actual cash activity.

The important issue is the overall coordination of various areas in an organization that develop financial forecasts and models. It is a best practice to collaborate with other functional areas that develop forecasts to ensure access to the best available information and to help foster consistency in assumptions.

IV. TYPES OF FORECASTS

The choice of cash flow forecast method to be used depends on its purpose, the forecasting horizon or timeframe, and the frequency with which the forecast is updated. The type of forecast chosen may also be affected by the company's size and industry, as well as the available forecasting tools and sources of information.

A. Purpose

Forecasts serve a variety of purposes, from making short-term investing and borrowing decisions to making strategic decisions about long-term investments and funding. Whatever the actual purpose, forecasts can be broken down into two major categories:

- **Predictive forecasts** attempt to predict or project what will happen in the future. They can be used to answer questions such as "How much cash will I have available to invest over the next week?" or "Will I need to borrow money against my line of credit in the next week?"

- **Analytical forecasts**, also referred to as *simulations*, are used to answer what-if questions or to predict the financial impact of a given action. They are particularly useful in strategic planning around things like capital investments or tax planning.

B. Forecasting Horizon

The time interval over which information is to be forecasted is an important consideration because a method appropriate for a short-term forecast will not be appropriate for longer-term forecasts, and vice versa. In most companies, short-term forecasting is the responsibility of treasury while longer-term forecasts are often done by FP&A or the capital budgeting unit.

- **Short-Term Forecasting:** Short-term forecasts typically range from one to ninety days in length and predict cash receipts and disbursements, as well as the resulting balances, on a daily, weekly, monthly, or quarterly basis. They aid in scheduling cash transfers, funding disbursement accounts, and making short-term investing and borrowing decisions. Short-term forecasting is also important for establishing and managing target balances for purposes of bank compensation. To reduce potential overdrafts and other related bank fees, some firms create intraday cash forecasts. This practice is supported by the availability of intraday balance reporting data provided by many banks.

- **Medium-Term Forecasting:** Cash forecasts from three to twelve months in length are an integral part of cash budgeting and are considered *medium-term forecasts*. These forecasts project the inflows (i.e., collections from sales and other sources of funds) and outflows (i.e., expenses and other uses of funds) on a monthly or quarterly basis. Medium-term forecasts are used to determine the firm's need for short-term credit or the availability of excess cash for short-term investing. They also serve as a benchmark for performance by comparing actual cash flows to projected cash flows based on the cash budget.

· **Long-Term Forecasting:** Long-term forecasts cover any period beyond one year. These forecasts take into consideration projections of long-term sales and expenditures, as well as market factors. Long-term forecasts are of strategic importance because they help inform decisions about which type and amount of long-term financing to obtain, and the timing of obtaining funds. Financial institutions and rating agencies also use long-term forecasts for credit analysis and evaluation purposes.

C. Update Frequency

The frequency and type of update are also important factors to consider when working with cash forecasts:

· **Static Forecasts:** As the name implies, a static forecast is one in which the time period of the forecast does not change but remains static even though the actual numbers or data in the forecast change over time. The period of time used in the forecast remains constant, and the forecast is updated at the end of the forecast period to show the next period. A monthly (or quarterly) cash forecast that is done each month (or quarter) is an example of a static forecast. An annual budget is another common example of a static forecast in that the budget, which is a type of forecast, is normally always for the same 12-month period (e.g., January through December), even if the numbers are updated during the year.

· **Rolling Forecasts:** In contrast to a static forecast, a rolling forecast has a constant number of periods (weeks, months, etc.) and is updated on a regular basis. That is, this type of forecast "rolls" forward. An example of a rolling forecast would be a 13-month cash forecast that is updated monthly. Assume that the initial forecast covers the 13 months from January 2015 through January 2016. Sometime during January 2015, the forecast will be updated and will now cover the 13 months from February 2015 through February 2016. If nothing has changed, then January 2015 is dropped from the forecast and the projection for February 2016 is added. In reality, the forecast data for the other months in the report are typically also updated because newer information is now available.

D. Projected Closing Cash Position

A projected closing cash position statement, also known as the *daily cash forecast* or the *cash report*, is one particular type of cash forecast that is used by many treasury professionals. The projected closing position is used to determine whether there will be a cash surplus or a cash deficit in a particular bank account. A projected closing cash position is calculated by taking the day's opening available bank balance(s), plus expected settlements in the collection and concentration accounts (in depository banks), and minus projected disbursement totals. Information about receipts in the process of collection—whether checks, card payments, ACH, or wires—is typically available from the prior day's balance reports. Same-day receipts, such as wire transfers and controlled disbursement totals, are typically reported on a same-day basis.

Clearings of disbursements made from accounts other than controlled disbursement accounts must be estimated. Since wire transfers are real-time transactions, notice of incoming and outgoing wires is often available through a bank reporting system or treasury management system (TMS). Exhibit 14.1 is an example of a worksheet used to project the closing (or net) cash position.

EXHIBIT 14.1 DAILY CASH FORECAST

ACCOUNT NAME	Concentration Bank Acct	Regional Accounts				Total
		FL-1	FL-2	GA-1	LA-1	
OPENING AVAILABLE BALANCE (REPORTED BY BANK)	550,000.00	296,000.00	50,000.00	106,000.00	546,000.00	1,548,000.00
PLUS: CASH INFLOWS						
STORE RECEIPTS						
CREDIT CARD RECEIPTS	194,000.00	—	—	—	—	194,000.00
LOCKBOX RECEIPTS	1,375,000.00	—	—	—	—	1,375,000.00
CORPORATE RECEIPTS						
INCOMING CONCENTRATION WIRE TRANSFERS	930,000.00	(290,000.00)	—	(100,000.00)	(540,000.00)	—
MISC. INCOMING WIRE TRANSFERS	2,500,000.00	—	—	—	—	2,500,000.00
INVESTMENT MATURITIES	1,000,027.40	—	—	—	—	1,000,027.40
OTHER CASH INFLOWS	507,500.00	—	—	—	—	507,500.00
PROJECTED AVAILABLE BALANCE	7,056,527.40	6,000.00	50,000.00	6,000.00	6,000.00	7,124,527.40
LESS: CASH OUTFLOWS						
ACCOUNTS PAYABLE (CONTROLLED DISBURSEMENT)	—	2,003,000.00	1,742,000.00	—	—	3,745,000.00
PAYROLL	—	—	—	699,000.00	—	699,000.00
OUTGOING CONCENTRATION WIRES	4,444,000.00	(2,003,000.00)	(1,742,000.00)	(699,000.00)	—	—
MISC. WIRE/ACH PAYMENTS	—	—	—	—	—	—
SHORT- OR LONG-TERM INVESTMENT PURCHASES	—	—	—	—	—	—
DEBT AND INTEREST PAYMENTS	500,000.00	—	—	—	—	500,000.00
OTHER	800,000.00	—	—	—	—	800,000.00
TOTAL PROJECTED CASH OUTFLOWS	5,744,000.00	—	—	—	—	5,744,000.00
NET DAILY CASH POSITION	1,312,527.40	6,000.00	50,000.00	6,000.00	6,000.00	1,380,527.40

CREATED BY: _____

REVIEWED BY: _____

V. THE FORECASTING PROCESS

The forecasting process involves a number of steps, beginning with the identification of the cash flow components.

A. Cash Flow Components

To produce an accurate cash forecast, it is helpful to separate cash flow into its key components. One approach is to aggregate cash flows by type of activity: operating, investing, or financing. These categories can be segregated further into inflows and outflows. For example, operating cash inflows might be segregated by product line, type of customer, and sales region. Operating cash outflows can be segregated into large-dollar vendor payments, small-dollar vendor payments, payroll, taxes, and other expense categories. As a general rule, it is better to begin with broad categories then refine the categories as more information about the inflows and outflows becomes available.

B. Degree of Certainty

Another way to aggregate cash flows is based on a given cash flow's degree of certainty, as described below:

- **Known Cash Flows:** The timing and amounts of certain cash flows are fixed and known in advance. Common examples include interest expense, principal repayments, dividends, royalties, rent, and tax payments.

- **Predictable Cash Flows:** Cash collections from credit sales are an example of a cash flow component that can be predicted with reasonable accuracy. The cash flow on a given day depends on factors such as the level and pattern of past sales, age of accounts, number of customers, and payment histories. For certain firms, these factors enable reasonably accurate cash flow prediction. Disbursement for payroll and benefits tends to be very predictable because it is based on the number of employees, compensation method, and historical experience. Similarly, vendor check-clearing patterns can be predicted based on experience with clearing times.

- **Less Predictable Cash Flows:** Some cash flows are difficult to forecast. Examples include cash flows related to sales of a new product, unexpected repairs, or pending settlement of insurance claims. Less predictable cash flows also include the timing of marketing costs, travel, and bonuses. Collaboration with other functional areas of the organization may reduce the uncertainty associated with these cash flows. The experience and judgment of the forecaster are important in such situations.

C. Data Identification and Organization

Identifying suitable data is an important part of the cash flow forecasting process. Omitting relevant data may lead to unexpected cash shortages or surpluses. The following factors should be considered when identifying and organizing data:

- **Available Information:** Information may be gathered externally or internally. Sources include the firm's banks, field managers, sales managers, and the A/P, A/R, payroll, FP&A, and tax departments. In many cases much of this data is available from internal systems, such as general ledger (G/L) systems, enterprise resource planning (ERP) systems, or treasury management systems (TMSs).

- **Assumptions:** It is important to understand the assumptions underlying the various projected input data to determine how accurate and useful it may be. If sales managers are assuming that all accounts will be paid on time while the overall economy is slowing down, the treasury professional may need to adjust the underlying assumption to get an accurate cash forecast. Cash flows should be discussed with key participants to gain insight into any issues that need to be included in the forecast. For example, it may be important to know whether specific payments are made monthly, quarterly, or annually. As another example, retailers might expect that 80% of their projected annual sales occur in the last two months of the year.

- **Desired Type of Forecast:** The data collected should be dictated by the desired cash forecast, not simply by the data that are available. For example, in preparing a short-term cash needs forecast, immediate A/P data may be important, but long-term capital acquisitions and planned securities offerings are probably not needed.

- **Source of Information:** Source identification is affected by the degree of centralization in the firm's cash management structure. In a decentralized firm, field managers usually have the most current financial data related to their operations. However, a centralized firm is often less dependent on numerous field sources.

- **Bank Account Structure:** Bank account structure is also important in that it may help group cash flows in a meaningful fashion and help identify potential changes. For example, using a concentration account to collect cash inflows and disburse cash outflows via ZBAs helps to facilitate cash flow forecasting compared to a system of multiple, stand-alone accounts.

- **Reporting Requirements:** To ensure the usefulness of the data selected, it is essential that the data are defined precisely and reported accurately and in a timely manner. Reporting should include an analysis of variances between the forecast and actual results to help track accuracy and improve future forecasts. A growing number of firms use company intranets, treasury dashboards, and treasury websites to distribute management reports and cash forecasts.

- **Historical Data:** A variety of data from prior periods are useful in predicting the amount and timing of cash inflows and outflows. Credit sales, payment histories, purchases, and scheduled payments are examples. Historical data are used to analyze trends and seasonality in the firm's cash flows.

D. Selection and Validation of the Forecasting Method

Within the types of forecasts discussed above, there are more specific methods of forecasting. While those will be covered in a later section, this section focuses on selecting the forecasting method. The process of determining the most appropriate forecasting method involves several key steps. These include establishing data relationships, selecting the method, testing and validating relationships, documenting the process, and using technology.

1. ESTABLISHING DATA RELATIONSHIPS

Before selecting the appropriate forecasting method, treasury professionals should ascertain the statistical relationship between the available data and the cash flow components to be forecasted. For example, cash disbursements can be related quantitatively to invoices received for payment, and cash collections can be related to prior-period credit sales. Data relationships can be identified and evaluated using statistical procedures, or they can be estimated by graphing data or by employing the judgment of a treasury professional who has extensive experience with historical relationships.

2. SELECTING A METHOD

A forecasting method is selected after the data relationships are specified. For example, the treasury department may select a receipts and disbursements method for projecting the daily cash position, or an exponential smoothing method to forecast cash inflows from sales. (Both methods are discussed later in this chapter.) Forecasting methods should be cost effective. A forecasting system must be maintained along with the data required to produce the forecast. Forecasting software requires systems support. Time is required to collect and reconcile data, to interpret the data, and to input data to produce the periodic forecasts. The cost of increased sophistication of a forecasting system must be assessed in relation to the expected improvement in forecast accuracy.

3. TESTING AND VALIDATING RELATIONSHIPS

Ongoing testing and validation of the forecast are critical steps in the cash forecasting process. Initial validation of a cash forecast and its internal assumptions is needed to ensure that the forecast provides reasonable predicted values. Ongoing feedback and testing are also important to ensure that the forecast continues to produce reasonably accurate forecasts.

The following methods are often used for testing, validation, and refinement of the cash forecast:

- **In-Sample Validation:** The cash forecast is tested for accuracy using the historical data used to develop it. For example, if three years of monthly data are available, the first thirty months of data could be used to develop the forecast. The forecast could then be used to "predict" the cash flows for those same thirty months, and those predictions can then be compared to actual values for those months. If the forecast accurately predicts one data series from one or more other series, the relationships among the data series are deemed to be validated. When a forecast is initially developed, however, there typically are no other data available to test it.

· **Out-of-Sample Validation:** The cash forecast is tested using data that were not used to develop it. For example, if three years of monthly data are available, the first thirty months of data could be used to develop the forecast. The forecast could then be used to "predict" the cash flows for the subsequent six months, and those cash flows can then be compared to actual values for those months.

· **Ongoing Validation:** Continuing feedback from comparisons of projected versus actual values allows continuous evaluation and improvement of the cash forecast. This ongoing validation may be performed on a daily basis for critical forecasts. Any reporting should include an analysis of forecast errors to help foster this process.

4. DOCUMENTING THE PROCESS

It is important to document how the cash forecast process works, as well as documenting the sources of data, contact information for key personnel involved in the forecast, etc. This enables others to understand and work with the forecast, and allows future changes when needed.

5. USING TECHNOLOGY

Ranging from spreadsheets to sophisticated forecasting programs, technology provides tools to make forecasting faster and more accurate. Spreadsheets provide the ability to build simple to intermediate cash flow forecasting models. The advantages of spreadsheets include availability, ease of use, graphic capabilities, and relatively low cost. Spreadsheets can also accommodate various scenarios for the cash flow forecast. There is risk associated with the use of spreadsheets. Formula and logic errors, as well as broken links, may create undetected errors in the forecast. As the data and models grow more complex, treasury professionals turn to stand-alone forecasting applications, or forecasting tools in ERP systems and treasury workstations.

VI. FORECASTING METHODS

The cash flow forecasting method used often depends on the forecasting horizon. For example, the method most appropriate for making a daily cash forecast is probably not the best method for making a monthly forecast. Similarly, the best method for monthly forecasting will not be the best method for annual forecasting. It is also important to understand that while these forecasts provide a baseline for operational cash flow forecasting, any capital purchases, dividend payouts, debt repayment or collection, etc., must be layered onto these forecasts to obtain a more accurate projection of cash. For the purposes of discussion, this section will look at three basic categories of forecasting methods: (1) short-term methods, (2) medium- to long-term methods, and (3) statistical approaches.

A. Short-Term Cash Flow Forecasting Methods

For short-term cash forecasts, many firms use information that is related to expected receipts and disbursements in the near future. There are several methods to develop short-term cash projections that incorporate factors affecting cash flow. Three of the more important methods include an A/R balance pattern forecast, a receipts and disbursements forecast, and a distribution forecast.

1. ACCOUNTS RECEIVABLE (A/R) BALANCE PATTERN FORECAST

An A/R balance pattern may be used to forecast collections from credit sales. The A/R balance pattern specifies the percentage of credit sales during a time period (e.g., one month) that remain outstanding at the end of the current and subsequent time periods. The A/R balance pattern is used to determine a collection pattern that is used to forecast cash inflows. An average percentage collected during a given month is calculated by subtracting the percentage outstanding at the end of the month from the percentage outstanding at the beginning of the month. Exhibit 14.2 provides an example of an A/R balance pattern forecast.

EXHIBIT 14.2 A/R BALANCE PATTERN FORECAST

INTERVAL SINCE SALE	PERCENTAGE OUTSTANDING AT END OF MONTH	PERCENTAGE COLLECTED IN MONTH
Month 0 (current month)	95%	5%
Month 1	55%	40%
Month 2	20%	35%
Month 3	5%	15%
Month 4	0%	5%

FORECASTING CASH INFLOWS FROM CREDIT SALES

MONTH	SALES	MAY COLLECTIONS FORECAST	
January	$350,000	350,000 × 0.05 =	$17,500
February	$400,000	400,000 × 0.15 =	$60,000
March	$500,000	500,000 × 0.35 =	$175,000
April	$300,000	300,000 × 0.40 =	$120,000
May	$425,000	425,000 × 0.05 =	$21,250
Collections Forecast for May			$393,750

2. DISTRIBUTION FORECAST

A distribution forecast uses historical patterns to allocate proportions of total cash flow over a time period. For example, a retail store may have projected sales of $1,000,000 for a one-month period. Historical patterns indicate that in an average month, 20% of sales occur in week one, 40% of sales occur in week two, 30% of sales occur in week three, and the remaining 10% of sales occur in week four. This pattern may be used to forecast weekly sales of $200,000 in week one, $400,000 in week two, $300,000 in week three, and $100,000 in week four. The method is used widely for short-term forecasts. Distribution percentages are commonly calculated with simple averages and regression analysis.

With a simple average, the distribution percentages can be estimated by averaging past cash flows related to a particular category of disbursements. For example, a treasury professional may sample past clearings of A/P disbursements and discover that, on average, 40% of a certain category of disbursements cleared the day the payment was issued, 50% cleared the day after that, and 10% cleared after two or more days. The problem with taking a simple average is that actual payment posting dates may be influenced by more factors than the number of days after issuance.

While most distribution forecasts can be performed using a simple average approach, when there are multiple factors involved (e.g., day-of-the-week or -month effects, or holidays), a more sophisticated approach, such as regression analysis, may be needed. An overview of regression analysis is provided in the statistical methods section that follows.

Exhibit 14.3 provides an example of forecasting using the distribution method.

EXHIBIT 14.3 FORECASTING USING THE DISTRIBUTION METHOD

A company has used regression analysis based on historical data to estimate the proportion of dollars that will clear on a given business day. It has determined that this proportion depends on the number of business days since the checks were distributed. The estimated proportions are given below.

BUSINESS DAYS SINCE DISTRIBUTION	% OF DOLLARS EXPECTED TO CLEAR
1	13%
2	38%
3	28%
4	13%
5	8%
TOTAL	100%

Therefore, if $100,000 in checks is distributed on Wednesday, May 1, the checks are estimated to clear according to the schedule below.

DATE	BUSINESS DAYS AFTER DISTRIBUTION	DAY OF THE WEEK	PERCENTAGE OF DOLLARS CLEARING	FORECAST OF DOLLARS CLEARING
MAY 2	1	THURSDAY	13%	$ 13,000
MAY 3	2	FRIDAY	38%	$ 38,000
MAY 6	3	MONDAY	28%	$ 28,000
MAY 7	4	TUESDAY	13%	$ 13,000
MAY 8	5	WEDNESDAY	8%	$ 8,000
		TOTAL	100%	$100,000

---

3. RECEIPTS AND DISBURSEMENTS FORECAST

Projecting receipts and disbursements is the core of short-term cash flow forecasting. This forecast begins with separate schedules for cash receipts and disbursements. The schedules are prepared on a cash basis, rather than on an accrual basis, due to the need to forecast cash rather than earnings; this is especially important for firms with high levels of A/R and A/P. A good place to start is with the historic information provided in bank account statements, which by their nature are cash statements.

- **Receipts Schedule:** This schedule consists of a projection of collections from customers (e.g., cash sales or payments on A/R) and other cash inflows (e.g., interest or dividends received from investments). It should also include expected, nonrecurring cash inflows, such as the proceeds from asset sales and external financing activities.

- **Disbursements Schedule:** This schedule involves forecasting the cash disbursements for purchases and other cash outflows, such as payroll, taxes, interest, dividends, rent, and debt repayments. A/P systems are typically a good source for this information, but A/P data must be adjusted to recognize that payments typically do not clear immediately after the actual disbursement.

- **Completed Forecast:** A completed forecast combines the receipts and disbursements schedules, and compares the result to a desired minimum cash balance.

Exhibit 14.4 shows a receipts and disbursements forecast for a firm that has decided to maintain a $50,000 minimum cash balance to provide a cushion against unexpected expenses or enable the firm to take advantage of unanticipated opportunities. The beginning cash balance is the ending cash balance from the prior week. The final two lines of the forecast represent the forecasted deficit or surplus cash position in each week. With this information, treasury personnel can more accurately manage the firm's borrowing and investing activities. In the example, the forecast shows a surplus of funds in Week 1 that could be invested to earn interest. In Weeks 2 and 3, the forecast projects a cash shortage that would require short-term borrowings or liquidating a portion of the short-term investment portfolio.

EXHIBIT 14.4 RECEIPTS AND DISBURSEMENTS FORECAST

$ AMOUNTS IN THOUSANDS	WEEK 1	WEEK 2	WEEK 3
CASH RECEIPTS	$1,000	$ 1,000	$ 950
CASH DISBURSEMENTS	(870)	(1,350)	(1,000)
NET CASH FLOW	$ 130	$ (350)	$ (50)
BEGINNING CASH BALANCE	100	230	(120)
ENDING CASH BALANCE	$ 230	$ (120)	$ (170)
MINIMUM CASH REQUIRED (TARGET BALANCE)	50	50	50
FINANCING NEEDED (DEFICIT)		$ 170	$ 220
INVESTABLE FUNDS (SURPLUS)	$ 180		

B. Medium- and Long-Term Forecasting Methods

Medium- and long-term forecasting involves the development of pro forma financial statements. Such forecasts are typically used in strategic planning or FP&A functions. Coordinating collection of the required data and verifying the variable assumptions is important. The availability of internal accounting data provided by ERP or integrated accounting and reporting systems makes this task significantly easier. Many of the advanced reporting systems have sophisticated forecasting models as one of their options.

Projected income statements and balance sheets can be used to forecast cash flows over a longer time horizon. A common approach used to construct pro forma financial statements is based on the percentage-of-sales method, as illustrated in Exhibits 14.5A, 14.5B, and 14.5C.

The percentage-of-sales method involves projecting the income statement items as a percentage of sales. Likewise, certain items on the balance sheet, such as inventory, A/R, and A/P, are also projected as a percentage of sales.[2] These percentages are then used in conjunction with the forecasted sales level to produce a forecasted income statement, balance sheet, and statement of cash flows. This process is demonstrated in Exhibits 14.5A and 14.5B.

---

2. Other balance sheet and income statement accounts are forecasted based on miscellaneous factors (e.g., a known debt repayment schedule).

The percentage-of-sales method requires three steps:

- Forecast the income statement and balance sheet based on the relationships mentioned previously. (See Exhibits 14.5A and 14.5B.)

- Calculate the projected ending cash balance by determining how the forecasted income statement and balance sheet values impact cash (i.e., utilize a cash flow statement given the impact of changes to investments, changes to capital/depreciation, and potential slowing of cash collections or payments). (See Exhibit 14.5C.)

- Compare the projected ending cash balance with the firm's target cash balance, and adjust the pro forma statement to show the source of funding for a cash shortfall or the investment of a cash surplus. (See the note at the bottom of Exhibit 14.5C.)

EXHIBIT 14.5A FORECASTING WITH PRO FORMA FINANCIAL STATEMENTS (percentage- of-sales method)

Assume the following income statement and balance sheet (in thousands) represent a company's actual position as of December 31, 2016.

ACTUAL INCOME STATEMENT (IN THOUSANDS)—YEAR ENDING DECEMBER 31, 2016		
SALES	$ 2,000	
COST OF GOODS SOLD	(1,500)	[75% of sales]
SELLING & ADMIN. EXPENSE	(200)	[10% of sales]
DEPRECIATION	(100)	
INTEREST EXPENSE	(38)	[(0.12 × $150) + (0.10 × $200)]
INCOME BEFORE TAXES	$ 162	
TAXES	(55)	[34% tax rate]
NET INCOME	$ 107	

ACTUAL BALANCE SHEET (IN THOUSANDS)—YEAR ENDING DECEMBER 31, 2016			
CASH	$ 100	PAYABLES	$ 50
RECEIVABLES	300	NOTES (AT 12%)	150
INVENTORY	200	BONDS (AT 10%)	200
FIXED ASSETS	400	EQUITY	600
TOTAL ASSETS	$1,000	TOTAL LIABILITIES & EQUITY	$1,000

To generate the percentage-of-sales forecast, the following assumptions are made (all dollar amounts are in thousands) for the year 2017:

- Sales will increase by 10% to $2,200.
- Cost of goods sold, selling and administrative expenses, and current assets and liabilities (i.e., receivables, inventory, and payables) are a constant percentage of sales.
- Cash balance is derived from the cash flow statement.
- Additional fixed assets in the amount of $100 will be purchased.
- Depreciation will be $50.
- Notes will be reduced to $100 at the beginning of the year.
- Dividends will be $24.

EXHIBIT 14.5B FORECASTING WITH PRO FORMA FINANCIAL STATEMENTS (continued)

PROJECTED INCOME STATEMENT (IN THOUSANDS)—YEAR ENDING DECEMBER 31, 2016

SALES	$2,200	
COST OF GOODS SOLD	(1,650)	[75% of sales]
SELLING & ADMIN. EXPENSE	(220)	[10% of sales]
DEPRECIATION	(50)	
INTEREST EXPENSE	(32)	[(0.12 × $100) + (0.10 × $200)]
INCOME BEFORE TAXES	$ 248	
TAXES	(84)	[34% tax rate]
NET INCOME	$ 164	
DIVIDENDS	(24)	
RETAINED EARNINGS	$ 140	

PROJECTED BALANCE SHEET (IN THOUSANDS)—YEAR ENDING DECEMBER 31, 2016

CASH (FROM CASH FLOW STATEMENT)	$ 95	PAYABLES (2.5% OF SALES)	$ 55
RECEIVABLES (15% OF SALES)	330	NOTES (AT 12%)	100
INVENTORY (10% OF SALES)	220	BONDS (AT 10%)	200
NET FIXED ASSETS (NFA)		EQUITY	
(PRIOR NFA + NEW FIXED		(PRIOR EQUITY +	
ASSETS – DEPRECIATION)		RETAINED EARNINGS)	
($400 + $100 – $50)	450	($600 + $140)	740
TOTAL ASSETS	$1,095	TOTAL LIABILITIES & EQUITY	$1,095

All of the projected account balances except cash are calculated based upon the given assumptions. The ending cash balance is determined by evaluating the impact on cash of the income statement activity and balance sheet changes, and adjusting the beginning cash balance accordingly.

EXHIBIT 14.5C **FORECASTING WITH PRO FORMA FINANCIAL STATEMENTS** (continued)

PROJECTED STATEMENT OF CASH FLOWS (IN THOUSANDS)—YEAR ENDING DECEMBER 31, 2016		
BEGINNING CASH BALANCE		$ 100
CASH FLOWS FROM OPERATING ACTIVITIES		
NET INCOME	$164	
ADJUSTMENTS TO RECONCILE NET INCOME TO CASH		
DEPRECIATION	50	
INCREASE IN ACCOUNTS RECEIVABLE	(30)	
INCREASE IN INVENTORY	(20)	
INCREASE IN ACCOUNTS PAYABLE	5	
NET CASH PROVIDED (USED) IN OPERATING ACTIVITIES		$ 169
CASH FLOWS FROM INVESTING ACTIVITIES		
PURCHASE OF FIXED ASSETS	(100)	
NET CASH PROVIDED (USED) IN INVESTING ACTIVITIES		$(100)
CASH FLOWS FROM FINANCING ACTIVITIES		
NET REPAYMENT OF DEBT	(50)	
DIVIDENDS PAID	(24)	
NET CASH PROVIDED (USED) BY FINANCING ACTIVITIES		$ (74)
ENDING CASH BALANCE		$ 95

If the projected ending cash balance is less than the company's established target balance, the shortfall must be funded through taking on additional debt, issuing equity, or selling assets. Conversely, if the projected cash balance exceeds the target, the surplus may be invested in additional assets, used to reduce debt, and/or distributed to shareholders. In the above example, if the target cash balance were $110, then $15 in additional cash would need to be raised. If this were accomplished through an increase in notes payable, then the December 31, 2016, balance sheet would appear as before, except that cash would be $110 and notes payable would be $115.

C. Statistical Methods in Forecasting

Statistical methods are used for both short-term and long-term forecasting. There are many statistical approaches that are available for cash flow forecasting purposes. One of the most general statistical methods is that of time series, or extrapolation, where past trends are identified and used to predict the pattern of future cash flows. Simple moving averages and exponential smoothing are two of the most common applications of time series forecasting techniques. Other popular statistical techniques include correlation and regression analysis.

1. TIME SERIES FORECASTING

A time series is a serial chain of values for some variable, such as sales or cash flows. A time series contains a trend, seasonal pattern, cyclical pattern, and random movement. A trend is the general direction that the values are moving (e.g., sales are increasing 5% year over year). A seasonal pattern repeats with regard to time of year. A cyclical pattern repeats without regard to time of year. It is possible that the series is stationary (i.e., the trend value is zero). The seasonal and cyclical patterns may be strong, moderate, or weak. Random movement is a change in the series not identifiable as a trend, or a seasonal or cyclical influence. The source of random movement is usually unknown, but may be triggered by impactful random events (e.g., a terrorist attack).

The purpose of a time series model is to identify repetitive patterns in a historical series, so that this pattern can be used to predict future values of the series. There are many kinds of time series models, and two of the primary models are described below.

a. Simple Moving Average

A simple moving average bases a forecast on a rolling average of past values for a series. The method has the advantage of being easy to use, but since a forecast is developed using an average of past values, it will lag a trend if one exists and will tend to dampen or smooth turning points where seasonality or another irregular event is present. The larger the number of data points used to form the average, the greater the chance that random movement will be eliminated through averaging. However, the margin by which the trend will be missed will be greater, and the dampening of seasonal turning points will be stronger. An example of a five-day, moving average forecast is shown in Exhibit 14.6.

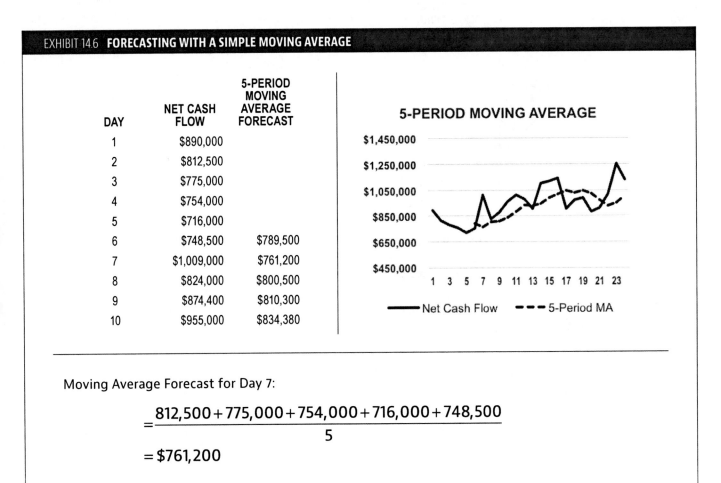

EXHIBIT 14.6 FORECASTING WITH A SIMPLE MOVING AVERAGE

DAY	NET CASH FLOW	5-PERIOD MOVING AVERAGE FORECAST
1	$890,000	
2	$812,500	
3	$775,000	
4	$754,000	
5	$716,000	
6	$748,500	$789,500
7	$1,009,000	$761,200
8	$824,000	$800,500
9	$874,400	$810,300
10	$955,000	$834,380

Moving Average Forecast for Day 7:

$$= \frac{812,500 + 775,000 + 754,000 + 716,000 + 748,500}{5}$$

$$= \$761,200$$

b. Exponential Smoothing

The exponential smoothing technique produces a forecasted cash value based on the most recent actual value, the most recent forecasted value, and a number between zero and one that is used to weight these two values. The weight, designated by the Greek letter *alpha* (α), is referred to as the *smoothing constant* and is calculated using a computer program such as a statistics package. This type of function is often built into many cash flow forecasting systems and TMSs. The program selects the alpha value that weights past actual values and past forecasted values to produce the most accurate forecast of the cash flow for the next period. The model is developed using in-sample validation, discussed earlier. An example of exponential smoothing is shown in Exhibit 14.7.

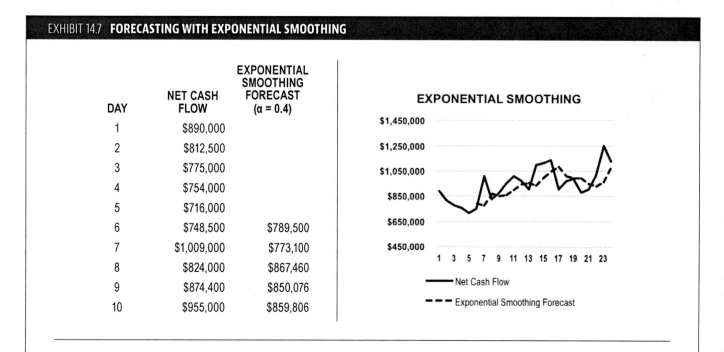

EXHIBIT 14.7 **FORECASTING WITH EXPONENTIAL SMOOTHING**

DAY	NET CASH FLOW	EXPONENTIAL SMOOTHING FORECAST (α = 0.4)
1	$890,000	
2	$812,500	
3	$775,000	
4	$754,000	
5	$716,000	
6	$748,500	$789,500
7	$1,009,000	$773,100
8	$824,000	$867,460
9	$874,400	$850,076
10	$955,000	$859,806

The exponential smoothing forecast begins with the moving average forecast of $789,500 for Day 6. Exponential Smoothing Forecast for Day 7 (α =0.4):

$$= (0.4)(748,500) + (1-0.4)(789,500)$$
$$= \$773,100$$

Exponential smoothing forecasted values are calculated using the following equation:

$$\text{Next-Period Forecast} = (\text{Alpha} \times \text{Current-Period Actual})$$
$$+ [(1 - \text{Alpha}) \times (\text{Current-Period Forecast})]$$

This formula can be expressed more formally as:

$$F_{t+1} = \alpha X_t + (1 - \alpha)(F_t)$$

Where:

t (subscript) = Time period (*t* = current period, *t + 1* = next period, etc.)

F_{t+1} = Cash flow forecast for the next period (*t + 1*)

F_t = Cash flow forecast for the current period (*t*)

α = Smoothing constant (0 < α < 1)

X_t = Actual cash flow for the current period (*t*)

As with a simple moving average forecast, exponential smoothing will yield a forecast that lags a trend in the series. If a trend in the series is mild, the lag effect will be minimal because, unlike a moving average, the forecast is made using values from the most recent period.

2. CORRELATION AND REGRESSION ANALYSIS

Correlation analysis involves identifying the degree of association between two variables. Understanding the variables that are strongly correlated with cash flow is important as these variables can be used to produce future cash forecasts. For example, there is usually a strong positive correlation between a firm's sales and its cash flows.

Once a correlation or relationship between cash flow and another variable is established, then cash flow can be forecasted using the other variable. This would typically be accomplished with regression analysis. Regression analysis is a statistical method that can be used to assess the impact that a given independent variable or driver variable has on a dependent variable.[3] To estimate the relationship using regression analysis, the user would need historical data values for the dependent and independent variable. Once the regression model is estimated using spreadsheet software or a statistical software package, the statistical output provides the values needed to forecast the dependent variable with an algebraic equation.

Exhibit 14.8 shows a scatter plot for a firm's net cash flow and sales, and a line that has been fitted to the data using regression analysis. Linear regression produces an intercept (-86,057) and slope (0.1698) for the line that best fit the data. The intercept is the net cash flow when sales equal zero, and the slope indicates the change in net cash flow when sales increase (or decrease) by one unit. Net cash flow is expected to increase (decrease) by 0.1698 for every one unit increase (decrease) in sales. The subsequent regression model used to forecast net cash flow is as follows:

$$\text{Net Cash Flow} = -86,057 + (0.1698 \times \text{Sales})$$

---

3. To be more precise, regression models can be estimated with multiple independent variables. Such regression models are referred to as *multivariate models*. Simple regression models include only one independent variable.

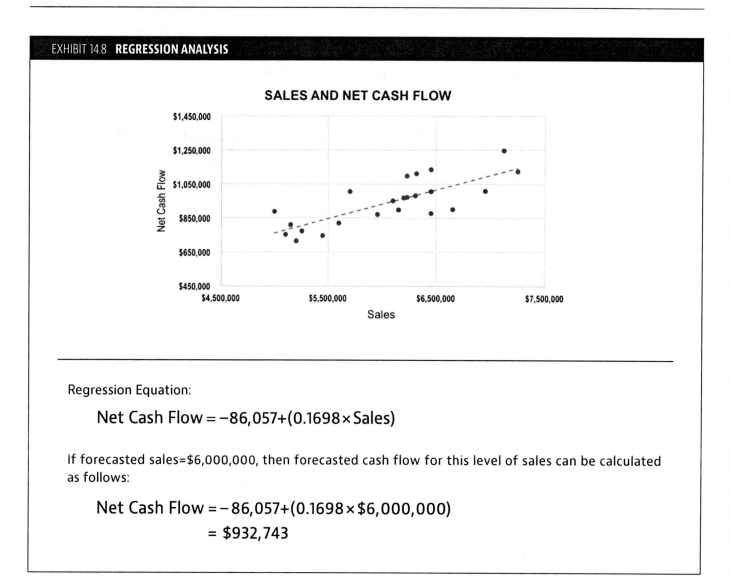

EXHIBIT 14.8 **REGRESSION ANALYSIS**

Regression Equation:

$$\text{Net Cash Flow} = -86{,}057 + (0.1698 \times \text{Sales})$$

If forecasted sales=$6,000,000, then forecasted cash flow for this level of sales can be calculated as follows:

$$\text{Net Cash Flow} = -86{,}057 + (0.1698 \times \$6{,}000{,}000)$$
$$= \$932{,}743$$

VII. BEST PRACTICES FOR CASH FLOW FORECASTING

There is a wide variation in cash flow forecasting methods used by treasury professionals. Despite this variation, there are a number of best practices that high-performing treasury operations tend to follow. Some of these include:

- **Use appropriate detail.** Perhaps the most important requirement is to make sure positions are forecasted in sufficient detail to meet the firm's requirements. If the forecast is to be used to determine whether there is sufficient cash to meet obligations in different currencies, positions need to be forecasted in each of those currencies. On the other hand, if the forecast is used to manage the firm's surplus balances, aggregated forecasts may be sufficient, even if this means that some funds sit idle in bank accounts overnight.

- **Disclose assumptions.** Significant assumptions (e.g., sales will increase by 5% per year) need to be disclosed, and the source of any information should also be documented. This is particularly useful in reviewing forecasts with someone who has not been involved in developing them.

- **Use the appropriate platform.** The most appropriate platform should be used to develop the forecast. When the cash flows are relatively stable and known in advance, there is very little need for sophisticated specialty tools to analyze the input data. On the other hand, where there are major fluctuations in data and significant variables involved, it may be necessary to use a system or software with greater processing power to generate the forecasted positions. Treasury personnel should always review the systems and solutions available to ensure they are being used to the maximum efficiency for the department as a whole. It might be appropriate when developing a global cash position forecast to use solutions that are already global in scope, such as an intranet, internal databases, or other proprietary tools. Alternatively, the organization could have access to additional functionality in its TMS or ERP system. Even if a treasury department has a sophisticated forecasting system, it will not necessarily be worth deploying in all situations.

- **Invest the appropriate amount of resources.** A forecast that takes a few minutes first thing every day and provides a result that is 90% accurate most of the time may be sufficient for many organizations. Only when there is more pressure for accuracy—to comply with covenants or manage limited liquidity, for example—will it be worthwhile to invest additional resources for a more accurate forecast. The costs of breaching a covenant or routinely overdrawing disbursement accounts may warrant the investment necessary to develop a forecasting system.

- **Validate the forecast.** Once the forecast period is over, treasury professionals should compare the forecast to actual results and determine the reason for any significant differences. Where possible, those reasons should be incorporated into future forecasts to improve long-term accuracy.

- **Cooperate and communicate.** Treasury depends on other business units for accurate and timely information, and in turn the business units are often dependent on the reliability of cash forecasts provided by treasury. Clear expectations and common terminology should be established from the start of any forecasting effort.

- **Ensure the forecast is usable.** The investment in developing the cash forecast has to be justified by the outcome. It is no use investing lots of time and effort producing a forecast that is unusable because it is too late to act upon it. In addition, the forecast must be sufficiently robust to provide meaningful data.

VIII. SUMMARY

Cash flow forecasting is an important part of treasury management. Everybody does it, but it is difficult to do well. This is primarily due to the large number of assumptions and estimates that are required in producing any forecast. Although technology has simplified the cash flow forecasting process, the forecasts are still only as accurate as the historical data and assumptions used in developing the forecast.

This chapter discussed the various types of forecasts used by treasury professionals and presented the typical forecasting processes and available methodologies. The chapter closed with a discussion of best practices in treasury forecasting. In general, cash forecasts should be as simple as possible, given the intended purpose of the forecast, and must be timely enough and accurate enough to be usable.

Key Equations

$$\text{Next-Period Forecast Using Exponential Smoothing} = $$
$$(\text{Alpha} \times \text{Current-Period Actual}) + [(1 - \text{Alpha}) \times (\text{Current-Period Forecast})]$$

CHAPTER 15
Technology in Treasury

I. INTRODUCTION

II. INFORMATION TECHNOLOGY FOR TREASURY
A. The Role of Information Management in Treasury
B. Information Security
C. Types of Information Management Technology Solutions
D. Information Management Technology Platforms
E. Workflow Management System Functionality
F. Technology Policies and Guidelines

III. TREASURY MANAGEMENT SYSTEMS (TMSs)
A. TMS Background
B. TMS Functionality
C. TMS Costs

IV. E-COMMERCE
A. Basics of E-Commerce
B. Electronic Data Interchange (EDI)
C. E-Commerce Communication Standards
D. Electronic Bank Account Management (eBAM)
E. Mobile Banking and Mobile Payments
F. Recent Developments

V. SUMMARY

I. INTRODUCTION

The treasury function manages its diverse responsibilities using various forms of technology. While many treasury professionals still rely primarily on spreadsheets and personal computers, the available technology has grown to include treasury management systems (TMSs), bank-specific workstations, cloud-based systems, company-wide enterprise resource planning (ERP) systems, and e-commerce.

The use of technology allows treasury professionals to retrieve, review, analyze, and transmit large amounts of financial data in a timely manner while minimizing the potential for operational and financial errors. Further, technology provides a standardized way to interact with various internal and external entities, including the accounting, payables, receivables, and corporate finance units, as well as financial institutions. Technology also helps facilitate visibility in treasury operations and allows organizations to leverage external capabilities, such as SWIFT, market rate providers, and online portals. Reliance on technology does, however, require an increased level of attention to controls and security to safeguard against intrusion and fraud.

This chapter introduces some of the basics of information management and technology as they apply to treasury, including a discussion of security, treasury applications, technology platforms, and information technology policies. Next, the chapter provides a detailed look at TMS functionality and cost. The chapter concludes with an overview of some of the issues associated with e-commerce and mobile or electronic banking, including a discussion of common information standards that are important to treasury.

II. INFORMATION TECHNOLOGY FOR TREASURY

Information technology and information management have become an integral part of treasury management and the driving force in the development of TMSs. Since the finance area is typically viewed as the clearinghouse for a wide variety of intracompany information flows, one of treasury's major responsibilities is to integrate treasury operations with other operational areas, including accounting, payables, receivables, and finance.

A. The Role of Information Management in Treasury

To add value to a company, treasury professionals continue to expand information management beyond the narrow focus of the daily cash position. The added value comes from using modern technology for tasks such as financial transaction initiation, as well as for effecting foreign exchange transactions, managing investment and debt, and implementing financial risk management programs. The benefits of an information technology-enhanced treasury department are magnified through collaboration with other departments and with various stakeholders and business partners. Acting as an information technology steward builds relationships between treasury and other areas, and enhances treasury's advisory role in strategic decision making.

With regards to information management, the treasury professional is commonly responsible for:

· Protecting financial assets

· Compiling data from a wide range of internal and external sources

· Sorting, analyzing, and storing information

· Initiating and validating transactions

- Obtaining account balances and transaction details from external sources
- Obtaining internal information that affects the cash flow timeline (e.g., receipts and disbursements)
- Consolidating information into the cash position worksheet
- Creating forecasts
- Generating journal entries for accounting
- Reporting information to management
- Assisting other areas with any treasury-related research

B. Information Security

1. BASICS OF INFORMATION SECURITY

Information security is the assurance that all information and messages are safe from intrusion, detection, and modification. Security is often required for regulatory and compliance purposes, and must provide a number of basic elements:

- **Privacy:** The assurance that information is only accessible by authorized individuals and will not be used for unintended purposes
- **Authentication:** The ability to know, with a reasonable amount of certainty, who is accessing information or initiating a transaction
- **Authorization:** The ability to know and control what functions and data an authenticated individual can access and use
- **Integrity:** The ability to ensure that a message was not modified in transit and that stored information has not been improperly modified or deleted (data integrity is especially important for financial transactions)
- **Non-repudiation:** The inability of the sender or receiver of a message to deny having sent or received the message

2. MULTIFACTOR AUTHENTICATION

Authentication methods for information technology and network purposes are based on four basic factors:

- Something the individual **knows**, such as a password or personal fact
- Something the individual **has**, such as a token or a cell phone
- Something the individual **is**, such as a fingerprint, voiceprint, retinal scan, or other biometrics
- Something the individual **does**, such as a the times of day that a person logs in or the IP (Internet protocol) address a person uses

Single-factor authentication uses only one of these factors, typically a password, to validate an individual attempting to access a system or network. Single-factor authentication is often acceptable for activities such as inquiries, which have no financial impact. Dual-factor authentication requires two of the four factors, such as a token and a password. A token is an electronic security device, and is discussed in more detail below. Since users demonstrate both possession of the token and knowledge of the password, they are meeting the first two factors. Dual-factor authentication is currently the accepted standard for most financial systems, especially when actual transactions are being processed. Four-factor authentication requires the use of all four factors and is the strongest authentication available. It is typically reserved for access to high-security systems and locations.

A multifactor authentication methodology may also include "out-of-band" controls. *Out-of-band* refers to the use of additional steps or actions taken beyond the technology boundaries of a specific transaction and includes such things as callback verification using a previously registered phone number or a cell-phone-based challenge, in which a one-time access code is transmitted to a previously registered cell phone and must be entered to authenticate the user.

The success of any given authentication method depends on more than just technology. An effective authentication method should have customer acceptance, reliable performance, scalability to accommodate growth, and compatibility with existing systems and future plans. Otherwise, users will look for ways to defeat the system. For example, requiring a long, complex, and random password as one factor is certainly more secure than short, simple passwords. However, this added security must be balanced against the tendency of many users to write long, random passwords down somewhere as they are difficult to remember, thereby defeating the purpose of the password length.

3. ENCRYPTION

Encryption refers to the process of transforming information using a computer-based model to make it unreadable to anyone except those possessing the key. Encryption addresses several of the security needs discussed above. First, encryption helps protect privacy. Second, properly designed encryption programs can also help with non-repudiation because the fact that a message has been encrypted and subsequently decrypted indicates that the originator possessed the specific key needed to originally encrypt the message. This also implies at least single-factor authentication. Both privacy and non-repudiation are important to treasury professionals when transmitting files related to investments, payments, and other financial transactions. The interception of an unencrypted ACH payroll file compromises the company's account information as well as the employee banking information.

Many popular encryption programs are designed using what is called *public-key infrastructure (PKI)*. PKI involves the use of dual keys. One of the keys is private and is kept by an individual user or organization. The other key is public and is distributed to trading partners. Information encrypted with one key can only be decrypted and read using the other key. As a result, individuals encrypting data with the public key know that no one but the holder of the private key can access the data. Conversely, individuals who are able to decrypt messages using the public key have some assurance that the information came from the holder of the private key. These keys are typically computer files or certificates that are protected by a local password. PKI is designed to provide security over traditionally unsecured networks, such as the Internet.

4. DIGITAL SIGNATURES

A digital signature is a message encoded with the sender's secret, private key that the receiver can use to identify the source. As long as the private key is never shared with anyone, forgery of a digital signature is extremely difficult. A digital signature is tied to a document and to the signer, meaning the signer's digital signature will be different for each document signed.

Note that a digital signature is different from a digitized signature such as that used as a facsimile signature on laser-printed checks. In the United States, the Electronic Signatures in Global and National Commerce Act (E-Sign Act) gave digital signatures the same legal status as paper/ink signatures, sometimes referred to as *wet signatures*.

5. DIGITAL CERTIFICATES

Digital certificates tie the identity of the user (private key) to the user's public key and may also authenticate the devices used to create documents or transactions. The identification information is secured by a trusted third party's digital signature on the certificate. The trusted third party is known as the *certificate authority*.

Banks and other third parties are partnering with security companies, certificate authorities, software providers, and other technology firms to administer their public-key infrastructure and issue digital certificates. These initiatives serve as virtual passports to subscribers.

The main objective of this type of partnership is for corporations to trust the identity of digital partners through real-time authentication and validation of the transmission under legally binding contracts. These associations also let users verify unknown buyers through a trusted financial institution and establish multilateral trust through one bilateral customer agreement. Oftentimes, certificates are stored in a smart card with dual authentication. A combination of the smart card and an assigned PIN (personal identification number) unlocks the card. The next section on tokens describes authentication devices in more detail.

6. TOKEN DEVICES

Token devices (or *tokens*) are electronic devices that contain circuitry that encodes assigned user-specific information or personal information to help ensure password protection. For example, one type of token contains a clock in a smart card that is synchronized to a clock on the host system where the data or application resides. When the user wants to log on to the system, whether locally or from a remote point, the token provides a unique dynamic code that, when entered with the user's PIN or password, ensures that the user is authorized to access the system. The unique dynamic code expires every few seconds and is replaced with a new code. Alternatively, the token may be a device that is plugged into a port on the user's computer and responds directly to the host system without the need for the user to enter, or even know, the challenge information. Devices specifically designed for this purpose are referred to as *hard tokens*. Soft tokens may also be used for authentication. Soft tokens rely on software installed on a computer, tablet, or mobile device. For example, the use of a soft token allows a treasury professional to access the unique dynamic code through a phone instead of requiring a separate hard token. The use of a token meets the "something they have" criteria of multifactor authentication.

7. SINGLE SIGN-ON (SSO)

An SSO permits an individual to enter one user name and password in order to access multiple applications on the same network or at the same host. SSO has broad applicability to all technology and can simplify access for treasury professionals that access multiple systems. For example, SSO is helpful when accessing a bank website or a hosted TMS provider with multiple applications, such as report generation and transaction initiation, because it allows an individual to sign on and authenticate one time and not have to be authenticated with each individual application.

C. Types of Information Management Technology Solutions

Treasury professionals use a wide variety of technology solutions, ranging from simple spreadsheets to complex TMS packages. Each provides a range of functionality and capabilities at varying cost levels.

1. SPREADSHEETS

Spreadsheets created with Microsoft Excel and other software programs remain an essential tool for consolidating and analyzing the data that are essential to treasury. The major advantages of spreadsheets are their low initial cost, ubiquity, and ease of access and use. The major drawbacks of spreadsheets include:

- Security limitations
- Potential for logic and formula errors
- Lack of auditability
- Poor version control
- Minimal integration with other applications
- Lack of organized information technology support and software maintenance
- Potential for corruption of data and internal formulas
- Lack of a common database, leading to duplication of data
- Lack of transaction initiation capabilities

While the spreadsheet software itself can be very inexpensive when compared to treasury-specific software, the total cost of ownership can be quite high based on the various drawbacks and the potential for problems or mistakes.

2. BANK PORTALS AND ONLINE BANKING SOLUTIONS

Historically, many banks supplied their commercial customers with online treasury applications that offered access to bank information and allowed for the initiation of various transactions. Most of these solutions started out as information reporting services. Over time, their capabilities were expanded in response to customer requests to provide broader access to information with inquiry capabilities, self-service capabilities for stop payments and other customer needs, and finally transaction initiation. In many cases, these bank-provided technology solutions offer functionality that can rival dedicated TMSs. Today, most of the bank-specific solutions have become online banking solutions typically offered over the Internet.

While bank-provided solutions overcome many of the drawbacks of spreadsheets, they are typically more expensive than spreadsheets over time due to ongoing fees for the use of the system. These fees are often based upon trans-action volumes and usage, and can become significant if multiple users are frequently accessing bank information. The major drawback to bank-provided solutions is that they are typically limited to dealing with only one bank. Although some of the bank products can consolidate and report data from multiple banks, transaction initiation and inquiry capabilities are normally limited to the bank that provides the application. As a result, treasury operations that have multiple bank relationships may need to use multiple bank solutions, all with different security requirements and different user interfaces.

3. TREASURY MANAGEMENT SYSTEMS (TMSs)

TMSs were initially developed in response to the need to use one system to access multiple banks. Today, most TMSs not only provide access to multiple banks, but they also typically provide expanded functionality in terms of managing debt, investments, foreign exchange, letters of credit, bank communications, and risk. TMSs often include the capability to directly connect with internal accounting and other financial systems. The expanded functionality comes at a higher cost, and often requires some form of internal information technology support to operate or configure the solution.

4. SPECIALTY SOFTWARE

In addition to full-featured TMSs, there are also a wide variety of specialty applications related to treasury. Although these tools may be less powerful or robust than TMSs, they are leveraged by many treasury professionals. These include packages such as investment management software; escheatment tracking and reporting software; front-/middle-/back-office trading systems; bank fee analysis tools; budgeting, forecasting, and foreign exchange exposure tools; and market rate data, risk management, and analytics/decision making packages.

5. ENTERPRISE RESOURCE PLANNING (ERP) SYSTEMS

ERP systems are sophisticated information management, production, and accounting software packages that link different functional areas or operational divisions of a company on an enterprise-wide basis. They integrate large amounts of data into a common database, which helps eliminate multiple, duplicate copies of information. The greatest advantage of ERP systems is that they can provide a single processing platform for all of an organization's accounting and finance software, reducing the number of integration points required with stand-alone packages. Many ERP systems include a TMS application, which may include the ability to directly connect to an organization's banks to initiate payments and other transactions from A/P and A/R, and to download and reconcile bank account information. One of the advantages of ERP-based TMS solutions is the built-in integration with a company's accounting and financial applications. The disadvantages can include a higher cost and a need for significant information technology support.

6. DASHBOARDS

A dashboard is a user interface or display that summarizes and presents information in a way that is easy to read and understand. Like a car's dashboard, it is often color coded to indicate the importance of specific information (e.g., green is normal and red requires immediate attention). Dashboards are intended to provide summary data that can be used to manage a function or process and often include the ability to drill down on specific pieces of information to get more detailed information about the specific item. For example, if one item on a dashboard is the number of payments over a specific dollar amount, clicking on the number would provide a detailed list of the individual payments.

A treasury management dashboard is intended to provide management immediate feedback on the overall status of treasury operations, while also publishing key financial information useful in running the business. The dashboard should be short and easy to read, and while the actual metrics and information published will vary across firms, general categories of information may include:

- Interest, investment, and foreign exchange rates
- Cash flow and/or borrowing statistics (including days' sales outstanding, days' payables outstanding, and cash conversion cycle)
- Accounts receivable amounts by currency and/or customer
- Projected and/or large-dollar disbursements

· Key performance indicators (KPIs) or metrics, such as reconcilements completed, cash forecasting accuracy, wire transfer timing and accuracy, or transaction volumes

· Key deadlines and operational alerts (e.g., bank holidays, disbursement calendars, employee stock option exercise dates, dividend payout dates, investment blackout periods, scheduled earnings announcements, and investor releases)

The principal challenges in implementing a treasury management dashboard include:

· Selecting the information and KPIs that are important to the specific organization

· Identifying the source(s) of information for each metric

· Automating the creation of the report so that it is produced and available in a timely manner

A sample treasury management dashboard is shown in Exhibit 15.1.

EXHIBIT 15.1 SAMPLE TREASURY MANAGEMENT DASHBOARD

XYZ Company Treasury Operations Dashboard

August 15, 2016

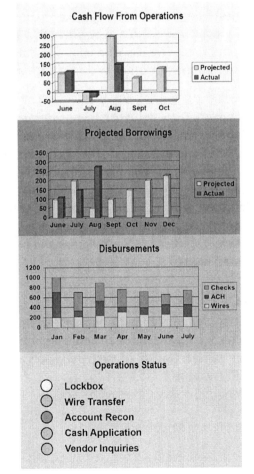

XYZ Co. (NYSE:XYZ)

29.18 -0.19 / -0.38%

Open:	29.31	Volume:	7,300
High:	29.49	Volume Avg:	411,700
Low:	29.12	P/E Ratio:	12.00
Prev. Close:	29.37	Div. Yield	3.99%

52-Week Range (Low - High): 23.83 - 30.72

Key Metrics

	June	July	Aug.
DSO	38	40	41
DI	20	15	14
DPO	45	40	41

Key Rates

	Tues.	Wed.
Treasury Bills (90-day)	4.97	4.97
Commercial Paper (Finl. 90-day)	5.27	5.27
Commercial Paper (Non-Finl. 90-day)	5.22	5.23
Federal Funds (Overnight)	5.24	5.23
Eurodollars (90-day)	5.40	5.40
One-Month LIBOR	3.17	3.18

Pending Disbursements (over $100K)

Payee	Amount	Date
James Doe	$155,000.00	Aug. 16, 2016
Huntington Reserve	$215,986.55	Aug. 16, 2016
IBM	$200,000.00	Aug. 18, 2016
IRS	$750,000.00	Aug. 20, 2016
Monroe Printers	$125,000.00	Aug. 31, 2016
PPG	$425,000.00	Sep. 15, 2016

D. Information Management Technology Platforms

Most of the technology solutions available to treasury professionals can be provided on a variety of technology platforms or architectures. The options range from stand-alone personal computers to enterprise technology platforms and the Internet. Each platform has different pros and cons ranging from ease of access to cost.

1. STAND-ALONE TECHNOLOGY

Stand-alone technology refers to software or applications that are installed on an individual computer or workstation. This is typically the type of platform used for word processing and spreadsheet software. Some of the special application packages available for treasury professionals are also often available as stand-alone applications. The drawbacks to this type of application include the fact that the application can only be used by one person at a time and, unless special provisions are made, the information and data are stored locally in the computer itself. Storing data on the computer creates a potential risk of loss if something happens to the computer and complicates any potential integration with other applications. If multiple copies of the software are installed on multiple computers to allow for use by more than one person at a time, there can be significant cost and effort involved in making sure that all copies of the application, as well as all versions of the data being used, are kept in sync and are identical.

2. INSTALLED CLIENT/SERVER SOLUTION

In a client/server solution, individual workstations or computers are connected to a common server (i.e., a computer designed to handle the computing requirements of multiple users) over a local or wide area network with a shared database. This allows multiple users to access the application at the same time. The use of a common database ensures that everyone is using the same information and simplifies integration with other systems, such as G/L, A/R, and A/P systems.

This type of environment is normally referred to as an *installed system*, because the software being used is actually installed and resides on the company's server. One of the advantages of this is that the software may be customized or configured to meet the specific needs of the company that has purchased and installed it. The disadvantage is that as newer versions of the software with expanded capabilities are developed, they must be installed on the server and any modifications made to the older software must be made to the newer version as well. The cost is typically higher than for a stand-alone solution, due to the need for database services and networks, but security and backup can be handled at the server and are typically easier to control. A client/server solution can be installed on a departmental basis and provide service to just one area, such as treasury, or it can be much larger and provide computing capabilities to an entire organization or enterprise, as discussed next.

3. ENTERPRISE TECHNOLOGY

Enterprise technology is functionally the same as a departmental client/server environment but is expanded and typically has more computing capability to handle the overall information technology needs of an entire organization. The result may look the same to an end user, but normally involves centralized control of systems, applications, and security. This is the type of technology platform usually used for ERP systems.

Organizations with enterprise technology solutions often have a dedicated information technology function that handles overall security, backup, and information control. Company policies typically include rules and requirements about the types of computers and software that can be installed on the enterprise network, as well as the types of data and information that can be stored on the network. In some cases, this information technology function is outsourced to an external vendor. Even if outsourced, enterprise technology is still considered installed software because the software is owned or licensed by a specific company and run on the company's equipment. The advantage to enterprise technology is that everything is centrally controlled and uniform across an organization. The disadvantages can be increased cost and the inability to get specific information technology resources when needed due to competing demands from other areas of the organization.

4. HOSTED SOLUTIONS

Many software vendors, including most TMS vendors, also provide their solutions in a hosted environment.[1] In fact, many vendors are now providing their solutions only in this fashion. In a hosted environment, the vendor runs the application on its own technology platform, and firms access the software over the Internet using personal computers. The vendor is responsible for updating and maintaining the software, as well as for providing appropriate backup and disaster recovery. Hosted solutions are also often referred to as *cloud computing*, since the applications are in the cloud[2] and accessed through the Internet.

Hosted software is typically charged for using a per-use fee, a per-user fee, or some combination of both. Some vendors also charge based on volume statistics, such as number of accounts or transactions, or services/modules actually used. This can result in higher ongoing processing fees but typically reduces or eliminates any up-front costs for software and hardware (since those belong to the vendor), as well as the cost and effort involved in installing new versions of the software as they become available. In most cases, the software is highly configurable so that individual users can customize their own input screens and reports. In addition, unlike an installed solution where a company may pay for capabilities that are provided in the purchased software but not actually used, with hosted software, companies typically only pay for what is actually used.

E. Workflow Management System Functionality

Workflow management is a function incorporated into many software packages that allows multistep processes to be automated, tracked, and actively managed. Although workflow software is available as independent software, it is more commonly seen as an integrated function of most TMS or ERP solutions.

Workflow management allows a company to use software to implement, monitor, and enforce the specific processes and procedures (i.e., the workflow) that it wants used throughout the company. For example, a company following best practices will normally require that all wire transfers be inputted by one individual and then approved and released by a second individual. Workflow management software will accept the initial transaction and then notify the appropriate approver(s) that a transaction is awaiting approval. Once the transaction is approved, the software will automatically release the transaction and may be set up to notify the original initiator that the transaction has been released. Management can view reports at any time to see how many transactions have been entered into the system and the current status of each transaction (e.g., entered, approved, or released). Workflow management systems are typically capable of managing processes with many steps and multiple decision points throughout the process. They not only help enforce proper procedures, but they also provide ongoing status reports that can be used to manage the overall process.

---

1. A hosted environment is also referred to as an *application service provider (ASP) model.*
2. The *cloud* is a term often used to describe distributed computing provided over the Internet that allows multiple users to access and use the same software from a variety of locations. The software is actually running on a number of servers or computers that can be scaled up or down depending upon the number of users and their usage at any particular time.

F. Technology Policies and Guidelines

Treasury policies and procedures are discussed in a separate chapter. There are, however, several policies that apply specifically to treasury technology. These aspects are described below.

1. END-USER COMPUTING

An organization's end-user computing policy is usually "owned" by the information technology department and not by treasury, and covers policies needed to control risk related to personal computers, laptops, tablets, mobile phones, and other portable devices. That being said, it is important for treasury to work with information technology as a partner in dealing with the various issues covered in the policy and not blindly assume that information technology is handling all of the details. An informed and cooperative treasury operation can help ensure that any problems related to technology are dealt with before becoming major issues. These policies typically cover:

- Password protection and update requirements
- Permitted use of company computer assets
- Permitted use of personal equipment, including "bring your own device" policies related to business continuity plans
- Software version control and documentation requirements, including updates and patches
- Backup and recovery procedures
- Data integrity
- Fraud and cybercrime security
- Use of antivirus software and update requirements
- Use of off-premise data controls for mobile devices and storage such as flash drives
- Permitted use of e-mail and Internet resources
- Documentation of end-user-developed software and spreadsheets

2. TREASURY SYSTEMS

In addition to end-user computing requirements, specific policies are needed regarding any TMS or other treasury-specific software an organization may have installed. While many of the issues involved are similar to those covered by a firm's information technology policies, these policies typically are owned and managed by treasury due to the ability to access the firm's financial assets and bank accounts. Concerns typically include:

- Access to treasury systems
- Password requirements
- Segregation of duties
- Reconcilement with accounting and other books of record
- Backup and recovery procedures
- Business continuity procedures
- Off-premise access and use
- Reporting requirements

III. TREASURY MANAGEMENT SYSTEMS (TMSs)

A. TMS Background

The simple treasury workstation of the 1980s that handled bank balance collection, daily cash positioning, and in some cases transaction initiation has expanded to an enterprise-wide TMS that now manages global liquidity, foreign exchange transactions, financial risk management, derivatives, and bank account access. Significant advances in technology have led to closer integration with other corporate applications, such as G/L and payroll, as well as single-function systems used for such things as escheatment and hedge accounting. While TMSs are available as independent solutions, many ERP systems now include TMSs as a part of their service offering.

Bank information is the core of a TMS regardless of how the data are received, and the real power of a TMS is the ability to collect, compile, synthesize, and relate the data to financial transactions and other treasury elements relevant to a particular organization. This section of the chapter describes the functionality that can be expected from a TMS and discusses some of the issues involved in selecting and implementing a TMS.

B. TMS Functionality

TMSs can provide a wide variety of capabilities and functionality that are of value to the treasury professional. This functionality can be broken down into the following major categories:

- Cash management
- Bank communications
- Payments
- Debt and investment transactions
- Accounting and G/L interfaces
- Bank account management
- Reporting
- Risk management (e.g., foreign exchange, interest rates, commodity prices)
- Cash flow forecasting and liquidity planning
- Invoice management
- Dashboards
- In-house banking

1. CASH MANAGEMENT

Daily cash management includes cash positioning, funding, and investment. It starts with bank reporting, using SWIFT, BAI2, BTRS, or other standards/formats (discussed below in more detail) to gather previous-day and current data from an organization's various banks. The TMS collects this information through direct bank connections (typically over the Internet), SWIFT, or some other secured third-party network. The value added by the TMS is that it eliminates the need for multiple bank communication tools to manage the connectivity process. TMSs typically manage the process so that users know if banks have failed to report, if files are incomplete, or if there are other problems collecting information (e.g., log-on or network issues).

Once data have been collected, TMSs typically prepare and reconcile an organization's daily cash position based on bank and cash flow forecasting information. Most TMSs have the ability to provide a real-time or near real-time view of positions across banks, accounts, entities, and geographies.

Cash flow forecasting is an area of critical importance for liquidity management and is a good example of how technology can provide significant benefits for treasury. A TMS should be able to accept direct input of forecast data (i.e., inputs) by teams in a variety of locations, import data from the ERP or a data warehouse, and build a forecast based on past results. Validating and consolidating the various inputs improves both the quality and ease of forecast assembly.

In-house banking is another part of the suite of cash management capabilities provided by many TMSs. *In-house banking* refers to the company, or more typically the treasury department, acting as a bank for a group of the company's operating businesses. Functions performed by an in-house banking function (IHB) can include cash pooling, inter/intracompany activity (including loans and license agreements), and foreign exchange. Having a technology-enabled IHB enables companies to benefit from functionality possible with an IHB without developing a large and expensive infrastructure to administer the operation. The IHB is the treasury structure that enables more strategic and flexible cash management for global-oriented businesses. Information technology is the mechanism that provides the ability to centralize cash management and function as an IHB without the use of an external service provider.

2. PAYMENTS

Meeting operational, compliance, and documentation demands for making basic payments can be time consuming, especially when multiple banks are involved, with a variety of access devices and user credentials. TMSs can help by providing the basic payment origination functionality and by connecting to a company's various banks. While many companies use their ERP systems for A/P, A/R, and payroll, and use the TMS for only treasury-related transactions, some organizations take this functionality a step further and use their TMS as a payment factory to collect payment transactions from across the organization and then sort/transmit them to the appropriate banks and payment channels. This requires special workflows that are included in the functionality of some TMSs.

Multilateral netting is a tool some companies use for managing inter/intracompany payment activity on a cost-effective basis. Most TMSs offer some form of netting system capable of working with payables, receivables, or a combination of the two (i.e., a hybrid system). In the event that the netting function is handled by an external provider such as a bank, the TMS can provide access to the transactions and information for posting and reporting purposes.

3. DEBT AND INVESTMENT TRANSACTIONS

Many TMSs provide the ability to manage debt and related derivative transactions. This includes portfolios of short- and long-term borrowings at fixed and floating rates, letters of credit, and lease contracts, as well as specialized functions such as calls, puts, and custom amortization schedules. Most TMS providers include a limited range of debt transactions within their base module. Additional capabilities not included in the base package are often available at an additional cost.

A TMS investment module supports the tracking and management of investment activity. Users can manage portfolios of short- and long-term investments, including money market funds and municipal bonds, as well as interest-bearing, fixed-rate, floating-rate, and amortizing contracts. As with debt, a limited amount of investment functionality is incorporated in the base TMS package, with additional functionality available as needed.

For those companies dealing in more than one currency, TMSs normally provide basic spot and forward foreign exchange transactions, and generally support the tracking and management of non-deliverable forwards, "plain vanilla" options, and other related products. Transactions can be imported from single-bank or multibank portals to help in reconciliation and to eliminate rekeying. Depending on the TMS, hedging and hedge effectiveness testing can be performed and mark-to-market valuations calculated.

4. ACCOUNTING AND G/L INTERFACES

Transactions created by or imported to the TMS can normally be automatically posted to the G/L through the generation of dual and multisided entries from the combination of bank and internal transactions within the TMS, increasing the potential for straight-through processing. Some systems support the independent reconcilement of bank transactions to accounting entries. Bank transactions imported each day are matched against accounting entries imported from the G/L based on user-defined rules, for a true bank-to-book reconciliation.

5. BANK ACCOUNT MANAGEMENT

Good treasury practices require a secure handle on details of bank accounts, including signatories. Many TMSs offer a complete review and approval workflow to manage signature authorities for all accounts and produce the appropriate management, bank, and compliance reporting. The addition of electronic bank account management (eBAM) capabilities provides an automated interface between the TMS and an organization's bank(s).

Additionally, some TMS vendors offer analysis and monitoring of bank fees. This capability is also available from certain specialized vendors but primarily for US banks, which typically use relatively standardized fee categories. The functionality allows users to analyze, reconcile, and manage bank fees to compare monthly fees against internal benchmarks.

6. REPORTING

Treasury management requires visibility of cash positions, bank account activity, risk exposure, payments, the cash forecast, investments, and debt. TMSs provide treasury professionals with automated customized reports for individual areas, such as bank account balances, payments, and audit reports. Dashboards are also available to consolidate multiple reports for an overview of treasury operations on a single screen.

7. FOREIGN EXCHANGE

TMSs offer foreign exchange modules to track and manage foreign exchange transactions, including spots, forwards, options, and swaps. The foreign exchange module may also include information on foreign exchange exposures, mark-to-market valuations for derivative contracts, and derivatives accounting and reporting.

C. TMS Costs

The initial costs of implementing a TMS are directly influenced by the type of TMS and the specific platform used, and can include one-time costs such as system selection, software, hardware, installation, start-up, implementation, and personnel training expenses. Implementation costs for a TMS may be significant, and care should be taken to ensure these costs are not underestimated.

Ongoing TMS costs can include licensing, maintenance, and software usage. Fixed costs typically include administration, overhead, software maintenance, licensing, and upgrades. Variable costs include transaction service charges, bank fees, and system security expenses.

When considering a TMS, it is important to consider the total cost of ownership for a particular solution. Installed systems often have higher up-front costs, but the ongoing costs can be significantly less since there are usually no usage fees. Hosted solutions, whether bank applications or TMSs, may have low initial costs, but ongoing costs can become significant for heavy users. Spreadsheets may appear to be a low-cost alternative until the lack of maintenance, security requirements, and auditability, and other risk factors are considered. ERP solutions can work well if the company already has an ERP system, but ERP solutions may not have all of the required functionality, leading to the need to purchase specialty software to fill any gaps.

The selection of a TMS should not be made using a strictly quantitative cost/benefit analysis, as many of the important benefits of a TMS are qualitative, including automation of processes, ease of use, the availability of ongoing support, stricter controls, and security.

Exhibit 15.2 provides a high-level comparison of the various TMS alternatives.

EXHIBIT 15.2 COMPARISON OF TMS ALTERNATIVES

Alternative	Features/Functions	Complexity	Ongoing Support	Security/Controls	Cost Visibility	Initial Cost	Ongoing Cost
Spreadsheets	Low	Low	None	Low/None	Low	Low	Potentially High
Bank Website	Medium	High	Medium	High	Low	Low	Medium to High
Installed TMS	High	High	Medium to High	High	High	Medium to High	Medium
Hosted TMS	High	High	High	High	Medium	Low	Medium to High
ERP	Medium to High	High	High	High	High	High	Medium

SOURCE: Treasury Alliance Group LLC, "Trends in Technology," published in 2013 (http://www.treasuryalliance.com/publications).

IV. E-COMMERCE

A. Basics of E-Commerce

E-commerce is defined as the application of information and secure network technology for the purpose of facilitating business relationships, including buying and selling, among trading partners. E-commerce encompasses many types of channels and communications protocols, including traditional electronic data interchange (EDI) and web-based commerce. In addition to treasury, other functional areas impacted by e-commerce include supply chain management, online marketing, online transaction processing, automated inventory management, and automated data collection, mining, and warehousing systems.

1. BENEFITS OF E-COMMERCE

E-commerce can offer several benefits, including:

- Improved productivity, thereby enhancing working capital management
- Reduced data reentry, thereby reducing error rates and enabling faster data processing
- The elimination of mail time, thereby enhancing cash flow processes
- Improved communication capabilities
- The ability to perform straight-through processing (STP)

Once data are entered at the beginning steps of any transaction, the same data can move from one business application system to another without manual intervention, so that information provided in a purchase order, for example, is automatically replicated in subsequent invoices, A/R systems, and A/P systems. E-commerce eliminates manual processes such as filing, matching, sorting, and retrieving material, as well as envelope stuffing, stamping, and mailing. It also significantly reduces cycle times because e-commerce transactions have no mail time delays, involve minimal processing time, and facilitate just-in-time (JIT) inventory management in many companies, all of which serve to meet key objectives of working capital management.

Since e-commerce makes data reentry unnecessary, it allows for straight-through processing, which reduces error rates and enables more efficient processing. For example, using e-commerce for the receipt of remittance information allows for greater accuracy in the posting of payments to the A/R ledger. E-commerce eliminates mail time in both receipts and disbursements, thereby reducing any uncertainty in cash flow timing, enabling more accurate cash flow forecasting, and improving working capital management.

It also offers improved communication capabilities. For example, acknowledgment that a customer has received an invoice helps to resolve issues of payment collection between buyers and sellers.[3]

2. USING THE INTERNET FOR E-COMMERCE

Increasingly, companies use the Internet as a payment and financial information channel. Because the Internet is accessible by virtually anyone in the world who possesses the necessary hardware, software, and communications systems, it is attractive to many businesses as a means to reach more customers and to facilitate sales and service. However, the openness and accessibility of the Internet makes security a major concern. In addition, some countries may have restrictions on data shared via the Internet or across international boundaries. Many proprietary, Internet-based systems have sophisticated security schemes to ensure the confidentiality of information, protect company networks and databases from unauthorized access, and prevent fraud. Properly secured systems can handle business-to-business (B2B) or business-to-consumer (B2C) transmissions, or a combination of both. Whenever new communications services are established, the file transmission formats and languages must be agreed upon by all parties prior to implementation. In addition, rigorous testing routines should be in place in order to verify that all transmissions are secure.

---

3. Delivery acknowledgment is typically standard in e-commerce communications; however, in mail-based systems, such acknowledgment is only available as a special, extra-cost option (e.g., certified mail).

A company must have a deep level of trust in its e-commerce partners. Reasons for this include the following:

- Business dealings with an e-commerce trading partner often involve access to the company's internal systems and information.
- Errors may be propagated quickly through the electronic trading channel.
- There are many financial, reputational, and operational consequences of security breaches to a company's system.

B. Electronic Data Interchange (EDI)

EDI is a traditional building block of e-commerce that is based on an infrastructure using standardized communication formats to exchange business data between two trading partners. The section below on e-commerce communication standards includes some of the common standards used in EDI and banking.

To send information electronically, companies must agree on a specific format and structure for electronic messages and data. In the early years of EDI, companies designed proprietary formats and communication interfaces, and either encouraged or mandated trading partners to participate. Proprietary data formats and technical requirements can be used when a company has a small number of partners. However, a common standard becomes necessary when a company has many EDI partners. EDI standards have evolved from proprietary standards to the current cross-industry and international standards.

An important part of EDI transactions is the concept of acknowledgment. The most basic form of acknowledgment simply indicates that a message was received and complied with the basic EDI format being used. This is generally referred to as a *functional acknowledgment*. A second level of acknowledgment relates to the contents of the message. For example, a buyer may send an electronic payment and remittance advice to a supplier. The supplier would send back a functional acknowledgment that simply says it received the remittance information and was able to read it. A second-level acknowledgment would provide details including whether payment was properly applied and would identify any open discrepancies in applying the remittance information. All EDI communication standards generally provide functional acknowledgments for all messages and then offer specific second-level or application acknowledgments for selected transactions or messages.

C. E-Commerce Communication Standards

Communication protocols, or standard languages, must be used in order for the many different types of systems to communicate with one another. Since treasury must often communicate with many internal and external entities in the conduct of its daily activities, it is important that treasury professionals have a basic understanding of the different communication standards they may encounter. Some examples of these languages are described below.

1. UNITED NATIONS/ELECTRONIC DATA INTERCHANGE FOR ADMINISTRATION, COMMERCE AND TRANSPORT (UN/EDIFACT) STANDARDS

UN/EDIFACT is a set of internationally agreed-upon standards, directories, and guidelines for e-commerce. UN/EDIFACT has been adopted by the International Organization for Standardization (ISO) as ISO Standard 9735. UN/EDIFACT standards are used widely in Europe and in some Asian countries. UN/EDIFACT standards are not compatible with ASC X12 EDI standards (discussed below), but there is translation software available that allows for integration of EDI data with either standard.

2. INTERNATIONAL ORGANIZATION FOR STANDARDIZATION (ISO) 20022

ISO 20022 is an XML-based messaging standard for the financial services industry, whose intended use is transmitting information related to securities, payments, financial reporting, account management, international trade, and foreign exchange transactions. It is part of the ongoing development of Single Euro Payments Area (SEPA) payments standards and the next generation of the SWIFT messaging format. ISO 20022 is used for communications between organizations and their banks, as well as between the banks themselves.

The ISO BSB (Bank Services Billing) electronic billing statement is an international standard electronic format used to transmit bank balance, service charge, and other information from a bank to commercial customers or other banks. The BSB standard was originally developed by the Transaction Workflow Innovations Standards Team (TWIST) but has been moved to ISO 20022. BSB allows the comparison of bank charges by category through the use of AFP Global Service Codes™.

3. SOCIETY FOR WORLDWIDE INTERBANK FINANCIAL TELECOMMUNICATION (SWIFT)

While SWIFT is primarily a messaging system, it is also responsible for helping to develop standards regarding the types of messages that are carried across various telecommunications networks. In addition to being heavily involved in the development and management of the ISO 20022 standard discussed above, SWIFT is also responsible for the SWIFT message type (MT) messaging standard that is still widely used around the world.

The SWIFT network supports two broad types of transactions. The first—file-level transfers, or FileAct—can be used to send and receive any type of bulk file that companies wish to transmit. The files transmitted using FileAct include both transaction data using the ISO 20022 standard, as well as bulk payment files and proprietary messages using nonstandard formats and data specifications agreed to by the various parties to the transmission. The second type of transaction is a traditional SWIFT MT message between two parties. Rather than bulk data, MT messages are predefined messages that provide specific information regarding individual transactions or specific information reporting. MTs are identified by number and cover such things as funds transfers, foreign exchange, securities, and bank balance and transaction reporting. Three of the most important messages from a treasury point of view are the MT 940, *Customer Statement Message*; the MT 941, *Balance Report*; and the MT 942, *Interim Transaction Report*. Traditionally, the MT 940 and MT 941 are used to provide previous-day and historical account information while the MT 942 is used to provide specific information regarding current-day transactions.

4. ASC X12 STANDARDS

The Accredited Standards Committee (ASC) X12 of the American National Standards Institute (ANSI) is the coordinating body that develops cross-industry EDI message standards in the United States. Development of the current US EDI standards began in 1968, with an initiative by the transportation industry to establish communication standards between and among railroads, ocean carriers, air carriers, and motor carriers. Following this lead, the grocery and retail industries also developed EDI standards. In 1979, ASC X12 was formed to develop general EDI standards that could be used cross-industry. Recently, the X12 groups have included XML standard usage in the financial services industry as part of their implementation and support efforts.

ASC X12's finance committee, ASC X12F, manages the following tasks:

- Develops and maintains X12 EDI and XML standards, including technical guidelines, focusing on financial e-commerce models

- Develops and maintains financial business models related to areas such as credit card processes, financial remittance delivery, and invoice and payment transactions (e.g., real estate and mortgage lending messages are developed and maintained using EDI and XML standards)

- Develops the payment systems architecture, which includes data security and data content management for financial standards

- Promotes the use of X12 EDI and XML standards across the financial services industry

5. ASC X12 FINANCIAL TRANSACTION SETS

By convention, numbers and letters are used to identify ASC X12 transaction sets. *Transaction sets* generally are defined as the electronic equivalent of a paper business document or form, with specific rules governing their formats. For example, the ACH CTX format is designed for B2B payments. The CTX format consists of a standard ACH payment transaction and an addendum designed to convey remittance information in the ASC X12 data format.[4]

6. BALANCE AND TRANSACTION REPORTING STANDARD (BTRS)[5]

BTRS is a communication protocol that has been developed by the ANSI ASC X9 committee to facilitate the transmission of balance and reporting information from banks and other financial institutions to their account holders. The predecessor to BTRS is the Bank Administration Institute (BAI) reporting format (often referred to as *BAI2* because it was the second such standard). BAI2 is not currently a standard; it is a commonly used format. BAI2 is widely used for information reporting of account balances, transactions, lockbox detail, and controlled disbursement detail. It has many optional fields and variations from bank to bank. Often banks require their clients to implement variations of the format, causing a large investment in scripting and resources to integrate these versions of the format into their back-office applications.

BTRS, the equivalent of BAI3, is a formal standard that is administered by the ASC X9 committee. BTRS is intended to increase standardization of and improve upon BAI2. Major changes include:

- Modernization of text to include developments in banking and technology over the past 25 years
- Additional structure to support extended wire remittance (in corporate trade payments)
- Rationalization and reduction of the number of supported transaction codes
- Additional SEPA transaction codes to support new European payment types
- Additional balance codes to facilitate SWIFT and ISO 20022 XML interoperability
- Modified currency rules to make them mandatory and allow for multicurrency applications
- New 900 series code categories to define debits and credits

The standard builds upon the older BAI2 information-reporting format while retaining forward compatibility. Although a BTRS file with the above changes could not be interpreted with a BAI2 reader, a BAI2 file could be interpreted with a BTRS reader.

---

4. More information regarding the implementation and usage of X12 transaction sets is available on ASC X12's website (http://www.x12.org/).
5. Much of the information on BTRS is taken from the ASC X9 website (https://x9.org/standards/btrs/, accessed May 13, 2016).

While the BAI2 code list is a domestic US format, many corporations have implemented the codes for their global reporting requirements. It is not uncommon to see information from other countries in a BAI format. The need for standardization of the BAI formats used for cross-border information is an industry objective and was one of the driving forces behind the transfer of the BAI format to the X9 committee and the globalization of BTRS. ASC X9 has international access and can promote national standards internationally to become ISO standards.

D. Electronic Bank Account Management (eBAM)

Bank account management refers to the management of the various facets of an organization's relationship with its bank(s), including opening and closing accounts, managing authorized signatories, and maintaining proper copies of documentation. Even though TMSs provide functionality to facilitate bank account management, this task can be a challenge for treasury operations due to the large amount of documents and paper that are typically part of the process. eBAM is an effort to replace the large amount of paper in the bank account management process with electronic messages and files exchanged between banks and their customers.

Conceptually, eBAM provides significant benefits to treasury operations, including:

- Eliminating the cost of creating, moving, reviewing, and storing paper
- Streamlining the process of managing complex, dispersed, bank account and signatory information
- Improving the ability to quickly change bank accounts and their signatories across banks and geographies
- Strengthening internal control and improving related auditing and management reporting

A key roadblock to eBAM is that it does not eliminate the work required to establish an initial relationship between an organization and a specific bank. Due to the various regulatory and documentation requirements of different countries, treasury personnel must first establish a relationship with a given bank before eBAM can be used to manage accounts and related information. SWIFT currently has a working group for eBAM that will be developing a standardized set of eBAM messages to facilitate the adoption of eBAM.

Exhibit 15.3 illustrates the key elements of a conceptual eBAM workflow.

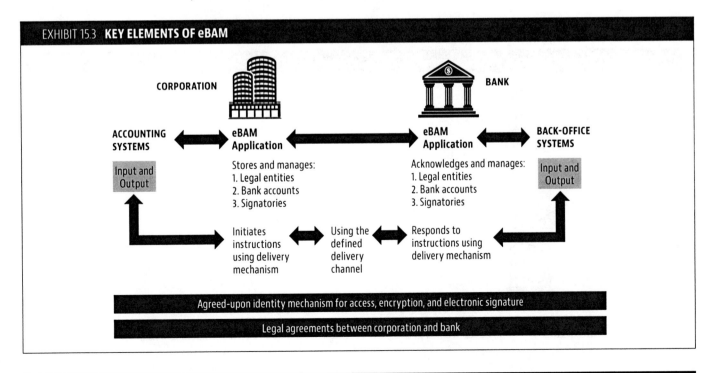

EXHIBIT 15.3 **KEY ELEMENTS OF eBAM**

There are currently three major models of eBAM:

- **Corporate-Centric:** The corporation controls the technology and communicates with multiple banks electronically.

- **Bank-Centric:** A specific bank controls the process and communicates with multiple corporate account holders electronically.

- **Utility:** A third party such as SWIFT manages the process and communicates between multiple banks and multiple account holders electronically. In this model, some third parties also provide the ability to create and mail hard-copy documents to banks that are not able or not willing to accept electronic transmissions.

These three models are illustrated in Exhibits 15.4, 15.5, and 15.6, respectively. The entities on the left of each exhibit are corporations, and the entities on the right are banks.

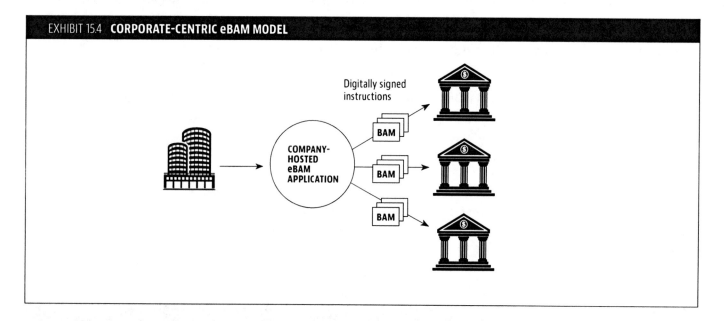

EXHIBIT 15.4 CORPORATE-CENTRIC eBAM MODEL

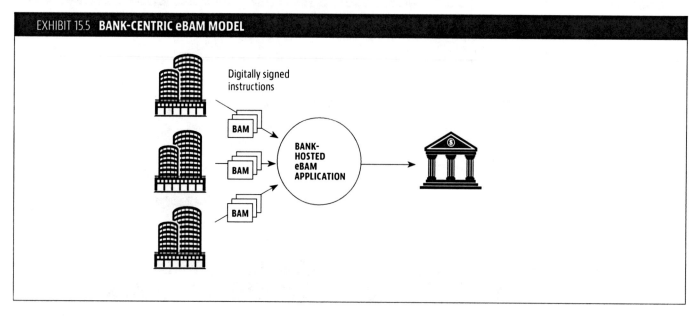

EXHIBIT 15.5 BANK-CENTRIC eBAM MODEL

EXHIBIT 15.6 **UTILITY eBAM MODEL**

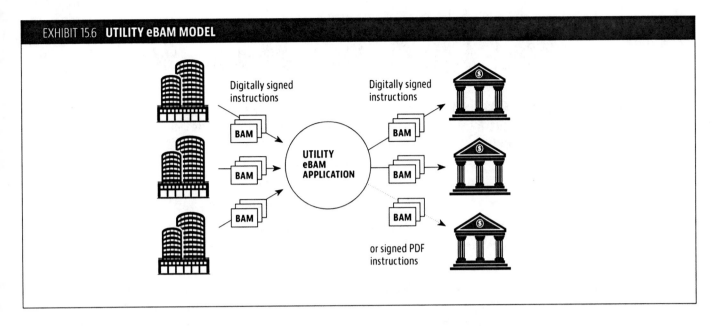

eBAM efforts are being led by SWIFT and a number of major multinational banks, providing a strong standards platform and a core base of bank users. A number of eBAM transaction sets have been added to the ISO 20022 format previously discussed. Although it holds significant promise, eBAM adoption rates have been much lower than anticipated. Several pilots have been in operation to test the concept, but more work is needed before eBAM becomes a broad reality.

E. Mobile Banking and Mobile Payments

Mobile banking refers to the provision of banking and financial services through mobile telecommunication devices (e.g., mobile smartphones and tablets). This service has become a reality for consumer banking, and as a result many corporate bank customers require mobile banking to address their needs. Mobile banking functions that relate specifically to treasury include transaction initiation and verification, remote deposit capture, and card acceptance. In addition to mobile banking, mobile payments (i.e., the use of mobile devices for payments or other transactions) are increasingly relevant for businesses as a growing number of consumers opt for mobile payments.

Currently, the primary mobile banking applications in the treasury area relate to information transmittal and transaction authorization. Treasury professionals are often on the go or are simply away from their desks at critical moments in the day when they need to control the disbursement of funds. Being able to do so from a mobile device is a significant benefit in terms of convenience. The informational feature of mobile computing provides instantaneous access to balance information, alerts on significant fund or market movements, and confirmation of important transaction events or credit line availability.

The major barriers to widespread acceptance of corporate mobile banking include (1) security requirements for both the networks and the mobile devices (especially for the initiation of large-dollar transactions), (2) technology issues related to the increased data and complexity associated with corporate transactions, and (3) the need to accommodate multiple users for a given bank account or relationship.

A number of technological advancements in communication standards are used in the mobile banking and payments space. These include:

- **Interactive Voice Response (IVR):** IVR allows the user to interact with computers via voice recognition and touch-tone signals from a telephone.

- **Short Message Service (SMS):** SMS is the text messaging service provided by most mobile telephones. It allows the exchange of short messages between mobile phones and other devices. While there are other messaging services available (e.g., multimedia messaging service or enhanced messaging service), SMS is more widely used as it is typically available on all modern mobile phones.

- **Wireless Application Protocol (WAP):** WAP is a technical standard for the use and exchange of information over a mobile wireless network. Most mobile devices access the Internet using a WAP-based browser.

- **Near Field Communication (NFC):** NFC is a short-range wireless proximity technology that uses radio frequency signals to communicate between two devices, such as a mobile phone and a payment terminal, or two mobile phones.

- **Radio Frequency Identification (RFID):** RFID uses noncontact wireless technology to transfer information, usually for the purposes of identifying and tracking ID tags attached to merchandise or other objects. RFID tags can be used to identify a specific mobile device for purposes of making and/or authenticating payments.

- **Quick Response (QR) Codes:** A QR code is a two-dimensional bar code that can be attached to an item or displayed on a mobile phone screen, and contains information that can be read by a QR reader or other optical scanner. When placed on an object, it can be scanned by a mobile phone and used to create an automated Internet link, which allows the user to obtain more information about the object or to purchase or pay for the object in a commercial transaction. When displayed on a mobile phone screen, it can be scanned at a point-of-sale terminal and used in place of a traditional payment card.

F. Recent Developments

A number of recent developments will likely reshape the future of the financial services industry. Application program interfaces (APIs) serve as software gateways between programs, allowing the data from one application to be used in another platform or service. Although APIs have been used for years, the impact on financial services is just beginning to unfold. Banks are beginning to share their APIs with outside partners for application development. These partnerships result in new applications related to services including payments, borrowing, investments, and insurance. Although an API may allow access to bank data, the bank may limit that access to a very narrow set of data points.

Banks opening up APIs to outside firms has helped fuel the rapid growth in the financial technology (i.e., FinTech) field. FinTech firms apply technology to provide services that are traditionally provided by banks, insurers, and investment companies. According to a recent survey by EY, 17.6% of respondents used FinTech services to make payments or transfer money overseas, and 16.7% of respondents used services for investments and budgeting.[6] Other commonly used services were insurance and borrowing. The same survey also indicated that only 15.5% of digitally active consumers had used at least two FinTech products in the six months prior to the survey, indicating significant potential for future growth.

6. From "EY FinTech Adoption Index," published by EY (http://www.ey.com/GL/en/Industries/Financial-Services/ey-fintech-adoption-index, accessed July 26, 2016). The survey was conducted in September–October 2015.

The past few years have also see the introduction of cryptocurrencies and related technological innovations. One of these innovations is distributed ledger technology, also known as *blockchain*. Distributed ledger technology creates transaction records that are linked and distributed across all participating network computers. Distributed ledger technology has the potential to increase transaction efficiency and lower costs. Blockchain is currently being used for some cross-border payments.

V. SUMMARY

The use of technology has become an essential part of treasury management, due to the large amount of information that must be managed, compiled, and synthesized as part of routine treasury operations. This chapter provided an overview of some of the key technology issues that treasury professionals face, including security and information management. It then discussed TMSs and provided an overview of the functionality and capabilities that modern TMSs provide. The chapter closed with a discussion of a number of issues related to e-commerce and mobile banking, including an overview of a variety of communication standards that are commonly used in treasury operations.

PART V
Risk Management

CHAPTER 16
Enterprise Risk Management

I. INTRODUCTION

II. GENERAL RISK MANAGEMENT
A. The Risk Management Process
B. Techniques Used to Measure Risk
C. Risk Management Policy and Governance

III. ENTERPRISE RISK MANAGEMENT (ERM)
A. Market Risk
B. Credit Risk
C. Operational Risk
D. Liquidity Risk
E. Legal and Regulatory Compliance Risk
F. Event Risk
G. Business Risk
H. Strategic Risk
I. Reputation Risk

IV. OPERATIONAL RISK MANAGEMENT
A. Internal Operational Risks
B. External Operational Risks
C. Cyberrisk
D. Fundamental Factors for an Operational Risk Management Strategy

V. DISASTER RECOVERY AND BUSINESS CONTINUITY
A. Developing Effective Disaster Recovery (DR) and Business Continuity (BC) Plans
B. Implementing the Plan
C. Performing Periodic Testing

VI. MANAGING INSURABLE RISKS
    A. Using Insurance Contracts to Manage Risk
    B. Dealing with Insurance Providers and Brokers
    C. Insurance Risk Management Services
    D. Risk-Financing Techniques

VII. SUMMARY

APPENDIX 16.1: DISASTER RECOVERY (DR) CHECKLIST

APPENDIX 16.2: TYPES OF INSURANCE COVERAGE

I. INTRODUCTION

Organizations are faced with a wide variety of potential negative or adverse outcomes. Such outcomes are referred to collectively as *risks* in this chapter. The purpose of this chapter is to provide an examination of the essential elements of risk management as well as the concept of enterprise risk management (ERM). *Enterprise risk management* refers to a comprehensive, organization-wide approach to identifying, measuring, and managing the various risks that threaten the achievement of the organization's objectives.

The topic of ERM is pertinent to treasury professionals since the treasury function is typically responsible for some of ERM's subcategories, such as financial risk management. In many organizations the board of directors has a risk management committee that provides oversight to management regarding the identification and evaluation of ERM-related issues. Some organizations have also added the position of chief risk officer (or chief risk management officer), whose primary responsibility is ERM. The chief risk officer is typically accountable to the board of directors for the measurement, management, and reporting of risks faced by the firm.

The chapter begins with a review of general risk management principles, including techniques used to measure and monitor risk. This section is followed by a discussion of the various types of enterprise and operational risks. The chapter closes with a brief discussion of disaster recovery and business continuity plans, and a discussion of insurance as part of the risk management process.

II. GENERAL RISK MANAGEMENT

In general, effective risk management helps minimize the adverse effects of actual and potential losses by either preventing such losses from occurring (i.e., risk control) or financing the recovery from any losses that do occur (i.e., risk financing). The purpose of an organization's risk management process is to:

- Help managers identify future events that create uncertainty
- Respond to negative possibilities by balancing the negative economic and/or regulatory effects of these possibilities with the costs that will be incurred to mitigate or eliminate them
- Guide recovery actions when serious negative events occur

A. The Risk Management Process

The risk management process involves six steps:

- Determine the organization's risk tolerance.
- Identify potential exposures.
- Quantify the impact and level of exposures.
- Develop and implement an appropriate risk management strategy to manage those exposures.
- Monitor the exposures and evaluate the effectiveness of the strategy.
- Review and modify the strategy as needed.

These steps are described below.

1. DETERMINE RISK TOLERANCE

The first step in developing a risk management strategy is to determine the organization's risk tolerance. The degree of risk tolerance will vary across organizations. Several examples are provided below:

- To gain a competitive advantage, a new company in a rapidly evolving industry may be more aggressive in taking significant risks.
- To protect an existing competitive advantage, an established company in a mature industry may be more cautious about taking risks.
- Government entities and not-for-profit organizations may be averse to assuming even small risks.
- A company's ability to accept risk may be limited by covenants or indentures in agreements or charters.

2. IDENTIFY POTENTIAL EXPOSURES

Risk exposures in all areas of the organization need to be identified clearly both in terms of their likelihood (i.e., probability of occurrence) and their potential impact on the organization. For example, financial risks such as interest rate variations, foreign exchange (FX) rate changes, or fluctuations in commodity prices will vary depending on the industry and form of the business organization or government agency. Operational risk is also an important consideration, especially for organizations with significant treasury operations. Timely and accurate exposure information is critical for effective risk management.

A company's *risk profile* refers to how the company's overall value changes as the price of financial variables changes. The basic risk profile for a public company shows how the firm's earnings per share, common stock price, or overall value responds to changes in interest rates, FX rates, or commodity prices.

The risk profile is an important tool used to identify key areas of exposure. Specifically, a risk profile analysis identifies the risks, classifies each risk into clearly defined categories, and quantifies the risks with respect to the probability of occurrence as well as the financial impact. The analysis can be used to evaluate the effectiveness of the risk reduction measures that are employed. In some organizations, this process is known as a *risk self-assessment*. To demonstrate compliance with the US Sarbanes-Oxley Act (SOX) and similar requirements in various countries, many companies perform risk self-assessments and test against them regularly. These assessments are sometimes referred to as *risk and control self-assessments (RCSAs)*. For organizations that are not publicly traded (i.e., privately held, not-for-profit, or governmental), a risk profile is used to assess the impact of a given risk on cash flow.

3. QUANTIFY THE EXPOSURE

Once an exposure is identified, it must be measured and assessed both quantitatively and qualitatively. The chief risk officer and/or other senior management must evaluate whether the organization can tolerate the risk, and whether the risk should be reduced, transferred, or eliminated.

Quantitative assessment is important in order to:

- Assess the materiality, or level, of the exposure (e.g., high/medium/low)
- Assess the estimated timing of the risk
- Identify the risk drivers or factors that cause the risk to materialize

· Determine the probability or likelihood for losses due to the exposure

· Provide a benchmark for assessing risk mitigation strategies, generally in a cost-versus-benefit framework

When quantifying materiality, a typical approach is to measure the cost or financial impact of a given risk. Material risks are those that exceed a predetermined level of financial impact or a predetermined level of risk to the organization. Materiality of risk exposure may vary significantly across firm characteristics (e.g., industry or product type), and should be assessed and reevaluated on a regular basis. The materiality of exposure will normally drive the frequency and amount of monitoring and testing needed.

Qualitative assessment is important to the overall design of appropriate risk mitigation strategies from both an economic and an accounting perspective. A qualitative assessment should:

· Examine basic operating procedures to determine where mitigation strategies, such as hedges, may be useful (e.g., a balance sheet hedge matches exposed liabilities against exposed assets and is referred to as *asset/liability management*)

· Determine how fundamental business processes contribute to risks and permit the identification of possible solutions

· Ensure that derivatives are structured and sized appropriately and proper accounting procedures are followed when derivatives are used as part of financial risk mitigation strategies

4. DEVELOP AND IMPLEMENT AN APPROPRIATE RISK MANAGEMENT STRATEGY

After identifying and measuring the risk exposures, the appropriate risk management strategy must be developed. There are four essential risk management approaches:

· **Avoid the Risk:** This approach may involve a company deciding not to enter into a certain line of business or utilize a particular business or manufacturing process due to the risks involved.

· **Mitigate the Risk:** Mitigating risk generally involves putting appropriate controls in place to limit the potential risk exposure. In financial risk management, approaches such as using derivatives or balance sheet hedges create a financial position that offsets the risk from an ongoing business process. For example, if a company expects to receive some amount of foreign currency as an accounts receivable, it could enter into a forward or futures contract that allows the company to convert the foreign currency into the home currency at a fixed rate, which is known today. Other risk mitigation approaches include process and facility design, project management, education, and compliance management.

· **Transfer the Risk:** With this approach, the organization moves a given risk to another party. The primary means of transferring risk is through insurance. A company may also contractually transfer risk by requiring that the risk be borne by another party in the supply chain.

· **Retain the Risk:** By their very nature, some lines of business carry inherent risks, and it may not be possible to completely avoid, transfer, or mitigate all the risks in certain types of operations. In these cases, it may be optimal to selectively bear some risks. For example, a utility firm operating in an area prone to hurricanes has to deal with the fact that its operations will likely be impacted by severe weather at some point. In this case, disaster recovery and contingency planning become a key part of the utility provider's risk management strategy. Since the risk of loss is retained and not transferred to another party, the firm must have the financial resources available to cover these losses.

A firm's risk management strategy may use a mixture of these approaches. Some risks may be retained while others are transferred. A combination of strategies may also be used when managing a single type of risk. For example, a firm may choose to mitigate some FX risk through the use of futures contracts, and avoid the risk where possible by invoicing in the home currency.

5. MONITOR THE EXPOSURES AND EVALUATE THE STRATEGY

An organization should monitor each material risk exposure. The monitoring frequency depends on the likelihood of the risk, the materiality of the risk, and the organization's appetite for risk. For example, the frequency may be shortened or lengthened if the underlying asset's volatility decreases or increases, or if management's risk tolerance changes. The effectiveness of each strategy must be periodically reevaluated as well. Such evaluations should be performed with the overall risk tolerance level in mind.

6. REVIEW AND MODIFY THE STRATEGY AS NEEDED

The risks that an organization faces change over time and its risk tolerance may also change. An effective risk management strategy must adapt to deal with these changes. Any risk strategy should be reviewed periodically in light of the quantitative results of the risk management program to determine what, if any, changes are needed. For example, if a company has decided to transfer risk through the use of insurance, it needs to review its insurance coverage to make sure that the coverage matches the current level of risk.

B. Techniques Used to Measure Risk

This section describes techniques used to evaluate the potential financial impact of certain firm-level risks. Specific techniques covered include:

- Sensitivity analysis
- Scenario analysis
- Value at risk (VaR)
- Cash flow at risk (CaR)
- Monte Carlo simulation

1. SENSITIVITY ANALYSIS

Sensitivity analysis examines the impact of a change in the value of a variable on a selected outcome measure, assuming all other variables are held constant. With sensitivity analysis, the value of a single input is varied and the change in the financial model is observed. For example, suppose that an analyst has estimated the cash flows associated with a potential investment. With an assumed value for the cost of capital, the analyst can calculate the net present value of the investment. Suppose that the analyst is interested in the sensitivity of the net present value to the cost of capital. To determine the degree of sensitivity, the analyst would simply recalculate the net present value assuming various values for the cost of capital. Since the cost of capital is the only variable in the financial model that changes, this example is an applied case of sensitivity analysis.

Sensitivity analysis helps to identify the variables that have the greatest influence on a financial model (e.g., net present value). Once identified, these variables can be categorized as *uncontrollable* or *somewhat controllable*. A monitoring protocol should be established to alert the user to unfavorable movements in the uncontrollable variables so that operations can be adjusted as needed.

2. SCENARIO ANALYSIS

Scenario analysis is similar to sensitivity analysis, but more than one variable is altered at a time. Scenario analysis usually starts with a base case (i.e., an expected value for each input variable affecting the final value). Employees who are most familiar with each variable should be asked to provide estimates of the best- and worst-case values for those variables. Overall best- and worst-case scenarios can then be constructed to assess the range of possible outcomes for a given financial model. Sometimes, scenario analysis is formalized by asking those who supply best- and worst-case values for the variables to provide a subjective probability distribution to accompany their estimates. This may improve the usefulness of the scenario analysis.

3. VALUE AT RISK (VaR)

VaR is a statistical technique that was developed in the trading rooms of financial institutions to estimate the trading losses for a given period of time. The VaR approach uses the probability and monetary impacts of specified events over a period of time to assess risk. Depending upon the circumstances, calculation of VaR can quickly become quite complex. A number of treasury and risk management systems offer VaR modules, and basic market risk management packages will sometimes provide VaR analysis for each hedge decision.

VaR was designed to incorporate a wide range of risk factors and summarize their impact in a single measure that answers the question, what is the maximum loss that can be expected over a given period of time with a reasonable amount of certainty? That amount is known as the *VaR*. A VaR is always stated in terms of a probability, an amount, and a time period.

For example, if a portfolio of securities has a one-day 5% VaR of $10 million, this means that there is a 5% probability that the portfolio value will drop in value by $10 million or more in a given trading day, absent any action by the owner of the securities (e.g., hedging or trading).

The most common approach to using VaR assumes that the future outcomes of some event are distributed normally. This approach only requires the estimation of two factors: an expected (i.e., average) value and a standard deviation for the distribution of these future outcomes.

For example, a treasury professional for a company whose functional currency is US dollars may want to determine the VaR of its FX exposure in its euro position, valued at $50 million, in order to determine whether the company needs to hedge the exposure. Assume that the treasury professional has determined, based on historical data, that the mean, or average, loss on any given day is zero. This is actually a reasonable result since the average change in currency value over a very short period of time is typically close to zero. Assume that it has also been determined that the standard deviation for the euro/dollar exchange rate is 0.60%. For this example, assume that the treasury professional wants to determine the VaR at the 5% level. In other words, the treasury professional is estimating the minimum dollar loss on 5% of the firm's trading days.[1] At the 5% level, the VaR is equal to 1.65 times the standard deviation of change in the currency. Using this information, the calculation becomes:

$$\text{VaR}(5\%) = \text{Portfolio Value} \times 1.65 \times \text{Standard Deviation}$$

$$= \$50,000,000 \times 1.65 \times 0.006$$

$$= \$495,000$$

---

1. VaR is typically calculated at the 1%, 2.5%, or 5% level.

Based on the information provided, the VaR at a 5% level for one day is $495,000. Another way to phrase this is to say that management should reasonably expect a foreign exchange loss of $495,000 or worse during 5% of the firm's trading days. Exhibit 16.1 provides an illustration of this VaR example.

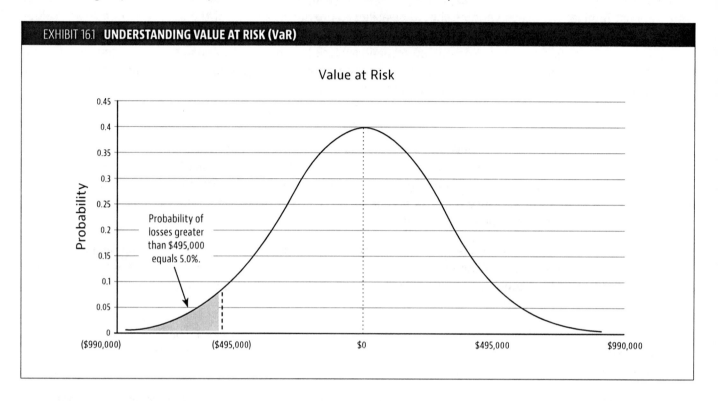

EXHIBIT 16.1 **UNDERSTANDING VALUE AT RISK (VaR)**

Another application of VaR is cash flow at risk (CaR). CaR is used to assess the risk of a cash shortfall over a longer period of time. If a firm's expected cash flow for the next year is $60 million, and the historical standard deviation of annual cash flow is $25 million, the firm's CaR would be calculated as:

$$CaR(5\%) = 1.65 \times Standard\ Deviation$$

$$= 1.65 \times \$25\ million$$

$$= \$41.25\ million$$

A CaR of $41.25 million indicates that there is a 5% probability that the firm's cash flow will fall short of the expected cash flow by $41.25 million or more next year. In other words, there is a 5% probability that cash flow for the next year will be $18.75 million or below.[2]

2. Expected Cash Flow − CaR(5%) = $60 million − $41.25 million = $18.75 million

4. MONTE CARLO SIMULATION

Monte Carlo simulation is a complex method that uses probability distributions and random numbers to simulate values for various models. This approach uses specialized software to quickly simulate thousands of iterated values. For example, consider the calculation of net present value from the sensitivity analysis discussion above. Monte Carlo simulation could be used to simulate the potential investment's net present value assuming various values for the cash flows as well as the opportunity cost of capital. The computer software chooses values for the random variables (e.g., cash flow or WACC) based on the probability distribution characteristics supplied by the user. Once the desired number of simulations is completed, the user can calculate the summary statistics. Key values of interest would include the minimum, maximum, mean, and median values. From these summary statistics, the user can make a more informed investment decision.

C. Risk Management Policy and Governance

Regardless of an organization's approach to risk, it is important for the firm's risk management committee and chief risk officer to have a clearly defined risk management policy endorsed and approved by the highest management level possible, preferably the board of directors. The policy should:

- Contain a concise statement of the risk management goals and the overall scope of the risk management policy (e.g., avoid, mitigate, transfer, or eliminate risk)
- Define authorities and responsibilities as well as the role of the chief risk officer
- Identify the types of exposures to be managed
- Delineate the mitigation techniques and products that may be used
- Outline the process for determining specific strategies to be employed and exposures to be mitigated
- Summarize the process for monitoring performance of the strategies
- Outline contingency plans
- Require periodic review of the policy and testing of plans

In many companies, the chief risk officer reports directly to the CEO, the board of directors, or both. This is important for two reasons. First, the high level within the company adds authority to requests and recommendations related to risk management. Second, reporting to the CEO as opposed to someone directly responsible for risk management activities (such as the CFO or treasurer) helps creates an appropriate segregation of duties and responsibilities.

III. ENTERPRISE RISK MANAGEMENT (ERM)

As previously mentioned, *ERM* refers to a comprehensive, organization-wide approach to identifying, measuring, and managing the various risks that threaten the achievement of the organization's strategic objectives. One purpose of ERM is to ascertain if and how each department contributes to, or is impacted by, a particular risk category. Traditionally, risks have been addressed at the business department or other organizational subdivision level. ERM's comprehensive approach allows the full scope of risk to be assessed across division lines. Methods and models of ERM have become important tools, and since they encompass the entire business, many aspects extend beyond the boundaries of treasury activities.[3]

---

3. An important standards organization in the area of ERM and related internal controls is the Committee of Sponsoring Organizations of the Treadway Commission (COSO). This group operates under the auspices of the American Institute of Certified Public Accountants (AICPA) and is responsible for establishing COSO's standards for ERM.

When examining an organization's overall enterprise risk, there are many types of risk that must be considered. Examples include:

Direct Responsibility of Treasury	Other Types of Risk
Market risk Credit risk Liquidity risk	Operational risk Legal and regulatory compliance risk Event risk Business risk Strategic risk Reputation risk

An ERM heat map may be used to assess the probability and impact of the various risks faced by a firm. Exhibit 16.2 provides a sample ERM heat map for illustrative purposes. The specified risks, probabilities, and impact levels will vary by organization.

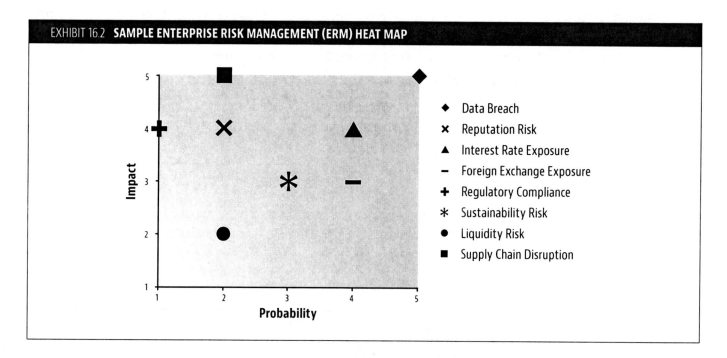

EXHIBIT 16.2 SAMPLE ENTERPRISE RISK MANAGEMENT (ERM) HEAT MAP

◆ Data Breach
✕ Reputation Risk
▲ Interest Rate Exposure
— Foreign Exchange Exposure
✚ Regulatory Compliance
✳ Sustainability Risk
● Liquidity Risk
■ Supply Chain Disruption

A. Market Risk

Market risk is the possibility that fluctuations in rates and prices in the financial markets will reduce the value of a security or portfolio. Market risk is usually divided into general risk (i.e., risk related to overall market rates and conditions) and firm-specific risk (i.e., risk related to individual firms). The four types of market risk are:

· Equity price risk

· Interest rate risk

· Foreign exchange (FX) risk

· Commodity price risk

The last three are referred to collectively as *financial risk*. From the perspective of a treasury professional, *financial risk* is the general term for the impact on an organization from unexpected changes in interest rates, FX rates, or commodity prices. In most cases, treasury looks at financial risk as the probability that the value of a given asset/ liability or some future transaction will be different from expectations. In many cases, these risks can be managed by some type of hedging, usually involving the use of a derivative contract or a natural hedge. *Natural hedging* refers to risk mitigation through the organization's activities. For example, a UK-based firm with FX risk due to cash inflows denominated in Japanese yen may borrow in yen or incur operating expenses in yen as a method of hedging.

Another view of financial risk is from the perspective of its impact on the overall market value of the firm or on a portfolio of investment assets. This view is somewhat broader in its approach and extends beyond just the transaction level. Here, the important issue pertains to the specific price impacts from changes in interest rates, FX rates, or commodity prices. For a portfolio manager of primarily domestic equities, equity price risk is of primary concern. On the other hand, for a manager of a portfolio that contains international equities/bonds and commodities (e.g., gold and silver), all four of the components of market risk are important.

1. EQUITY PRICE RISK

Equity price risk is usually associated with volatility in stock prices. The general form of this risk refers to the sensitivity of an instrument or portfolio value to a change in broad stock market indices, while the firm-specific portion of this risk relates just to the company in question. Firm-specific risk can be mitigated by holding a portfolio of stocks, while general risk cannot be eliminated.

2. INTEREST RATE RISK

Interest rate risk relates to changes in investment values and borrowing costs, and potentially in overall firm value, as interest rates change.

3. FOREIGN EXCHANGE (FX) RISK

FX risk arises from the exposure an organization has as a result of transactions, assets, and liabilities that are denominated in a foreign currency. As FX rates fluctuate, so too can the value of these items, ultimately impacting overall firm value.

4. COMMODITY PRICE RISK

Commodity price risk differs considerably from interest rate and FX risk since most commodities are traded in markets where supply is concentrated in the hands of a few suppliers, which can magnify price volatility.

Exhibit 16.3 provides examples of general and firm-specific market risk for each of the four risks described above.

EXHIBIT 16.3 **EXAMPLES OF MARKET RISK BY CATEGORY**

	GENERAL RISK	**FIRM-SPECIFIC RISK**
EQUITY PRICE RISK	The market as a whole declines due to general economic conditions.	The value of a company's stock declines due to a major product recall.
INTEREST RATE RISK	Interest rates increase broadly, impacting borrowing rates for all companies or, conversely, increasing yields on investments.	Interest rates for airplane leases rise, affecting the operating cost and related value of an airline whose entire fleet of planes is leased.
FX RISK	The value of the US dollar falls in relation to other major currencies, affecting the market value of US companies.	The value of the South African rand falls in relation to the US dollar, affecting the value of a US-based company with major South African operations.
COMMODITY PRICE RISK	Petroleum prices are rising significantly, impacting the value of any company that uses large amounts of petroleum, such as airlines and petrochemical companies.	Orange crops are wiped out by frost damage, impacting a company whose sole product is orange juice.

B. Credit Risk

Credit risk is a type of counterparty risk. Credit risk is related to how a change in the credit quality of a company would affect the value of a security or portfolio of investments. Default on an investment or security is the extreme case of credit risk, but downgrading of a security can also be an issue. In some cases, the creditor may recover some value after default, and the amount recovered is called the *recovery value* or *rate*. When given as a percentage, it is called the *loss given default*.

Credit risk arises both from transactions and from any risk in the portfolio due to concentration of similar assets. When the assets in a portfolio are all concentrated in a single area, industry, or type of security, the overall riskiness of the portfolio may increase significantly due to correlations between the investments (i.e., they all move together, thus increasing the overall volatility of the portfolio). For example, if a portfolio is comprised of bonds issued by firms in a single industry, declining demand in that industry would affect all of the debt issues in the portfolio. This risk may be reduced through diversification across industries and geographic regions. Other risks in the credit area include risks related to specific security issues, the risks from specific issuers, and the probability of large or multiple failures on the part of counterparties to the transactions.

C. Operational Risk

Operational risk refers to potential losses resulting from inadequate systems, management failure, faulty controls, fraud and human error, and other related issues. Management of operational risk exposure is covered in detail later in the section on operational risk management.

D. Liquidity Risk

Liquidity risk is typically divided into two areas: funding liquidity risk and asset liquidity risk. Funding liquidity risk relates to an organization's ability to raise necessary cash to meet its obligations as they come due. It is often linked to the ability to raise short-term and long-term capital in a timely manner, and it typically is managed by holding marketable securities or through available lines of credit. An example of funding liquidity risk would be a corporation with an active commercial paper program. Continually rolling over commercial paper exposes the company to considerable funding liquidity risk. This is because many factors can affect the ability to refinance commercial paper, such as a reduction in the credit rating of the company, narrowing spreads in short-term credit markets, or a deterioration in the credit markets themselves.

Asset liquidity risk relates to the ability to sell an asset quickly and at close to its true value. Asset liquidity risk is especially a problem for organizations holding portfolios of investment assets, particularly if those assets are not fully liquid due to the type of asset (e.g., mortgage-backed securities during the global financial crisis of 2007–2009) or general market conditions (e.g., having to sell securities in a downward-trending market).

E. Legal and Regulatory Compliance Risk

Legal and regulatory compliance risk is a type of operational risk and is typically managed by the compliance area of an organization. This topic is discussed later in this chapter's operational risk management section.

F. Event Risk

Event risk is the risk associated with unexpected events related to a given organization. Event risk includes an unplanned corporate reorganization or a large natural disaster.

G. Business Risk

Business risk refers to basic operating risks, such as uncertainty about the demand for products or services, the price that can be charged for those products or services, and the costs of producing and delivering the products or services. Business risk is primarily associated with the general day-to-day management of a company. Sometimes, strategic and reputation risks are viewed as components of business risk.

H. Strategic Risk

Strategic risk refers to the risk associated with major investments for which there is a significant uncertainty about success or profitability. Examples in this area would include entering into new markets, trying to spot and take advantage of trends, and investing in new technology. Strategic risks related to sustainability should also be considered. Among other factors, corporate leaders must assess and manage sustainability risks associated with the supply chain, the production methods, and the social impact of products. Investors and consumers have expectations concerning the environmental impact of a product and human rights issues related to the supply chain. Relationships with suppliers that have unacceptable environmental records can lead to a decline in demand for the firm's products and a decrease in the value of the firm.

I. Reputation Risk

Reputation risk is the risk that customers, suppliers, investors, and/or regulators may decide that a company has a bad reputation and decide not to do business with that company. For financial institutions, this type of risk is especially important. In some countries, companies are also under increasing pressure to demonstrate their ethical, social, and environmental responsibilities. Reputation risk also relates to how companies react to unexpected events that can impact their reputations and ultimately their futures.

Social media use by employees exposes the firm to reputation risk, and firms should develop a social media policy to protect against this risk. A social media policy should govern posts on the firm's social media accounts and employees' private accounts. Areas covered in the policy may include the disclosure of confidential information related to the firm or the firm's trading partners, disclosure of the employee's affiliation with the firm, and the requirement that employees clearly state when they are not speaking for the firm.

IV. OPERATIONAL RISK MANAGEMENT

Operational risk is defined as the risk of direct and indirect losses resulting either from external events that impact an organization's operations or from inadequate and failed internal processes, people, and systems. Operational risks do not ordinarily include market or credit risks. Usually, the internal sources of operational risk are related to the lack or failure of controls surrounding people, processes, or technology. External events can range from localized events (e.g., momentary communications failures) to negative global economic or political events.

Operational risk can be a significant cause of financial loss. Most financial disasters are attributed to a combination of exposure to market or credit risk, along with some failure of controls or the internal audit function. However, in many operational risk disasters, a single employee has been responsible for staggering losses that could have been prevented by appropriate oversight and controls. The problem is often the lack of management involvement in establishing financial controls and overseeing people who use financial tools such as derivatives or who have responsibilities relating to the trading of financial instruments and securities. The problem could also be related to spreadsheet risk. A broken link or formula error in a spreadsheet may lead to incorrect decisions regarding payments, investments, borrowing, or other mission-critical areas.

A. Internal Operational Risks

Internal risks involve an organization's employees, processes, or technology. Examples of each follow.

1. EMPLOYEE RISK

Employees can be a significant source of internal operational risk. The general risk of intentional employee fraud is known as *defalcation risk*, while the specific case of theft of money, securities, or property by an employee is known as *fidelity risk*. Employee fraud risk is not limited to the theft of company assets, but can also include the purposeful violation of company policies or procedures to improve performance ratings or compensation or to cover up errors and mistakes. An example of this type of fraud would be a rogue trader who violates company policy to indulge in risky and/or high-volume trades in an attempt to garner a larger year-end performance bonus. A more significant source of internal risk stems from unintentional actions by employees. Examples include employee errors in data entry or reentry, as well as transposition or deletion of numbers. Other potential sources of internal risk are the lack of knowledge or skills, and the loss of key personnel. Internal operational risk may arise from the employer's liability relative to employment law, as well as health and safety regulations. Once identified and assessed for materiality, most internal operational risks can be addressed by developing and implementing strong internal controls such as the segregation of duties, maker-checker controls,[4] periodic self-audits, and management oversight. In addition, insurance can help mitigate some of the impact from employee risk.

2. PROCESS RISK

Many organizations experience substantial exposure to losses related to the processes employed in day-to-day business operations. Process risk can arise from any functional area of a business, including procurement, manufacturing, sales, or fulfillment. The risk usually comes from a lack of proper controls or the failure of employees to follow procedures.

One source of process risk for the treasury area can result from accounting or financial reporting errors. Another source of process risk is a lack of timely reconciliation of bank accounts. These risks can be a potentially serious problem given the penalties introduced under SOX in the United States and similar regulations put forth by other national stock exchanges. Organizations with high levels of manual processes have a significant risk of potential errors in data entry.

Process risk is not limited to manual processes. It can also occur when processes are so technical and complex that the people using them do not understand the processes, how to use them, or more importantly, what their limitations are and when they should not be used. An example of this latter type of risk would be complex computer models used to make investment decisions. In many cases the models are very helpful, but when the decisions being made go beyond the capabilities of the various models, the resulting risk can be significant. This type of process risk was demonstrated through the various credit risk models that were used by many companies to manage the risk of auction rate securities in the early part of the century. The models, which indicated little or no risk of default for most of the securities, turned out to be based on incorrect assumptions that most investors did not understand, resulting in large losses for many companies.

Another type of process risk is incurred when an organization may not be able to meet the terms of contracts with customers and suppliers. This is often a problem in industries that deal in sparse commodities, where a supplier might not be able to meet demand. Also related to the production and delivery process is the risk of capacity error. Excess capacity increases overhead and fixed costs, which increases an organization's general business and operational risks. Conversely, insufficient capacity can lead to large backlogs, lost orders, increased errors, or unintended interruptions in the manufacturing and delivery process due to overtime or extra shifts.

---

4. The practice of maker-checker controls involves one person performing a task while another person checks for accuracy. For example, in most companies one person is responsible for creating or entering wire transfer information into a treasury workstation or bank terminal, and a second person is responsible for verifying and "releasing" the wire transfer.

Aside from the normal risk of nonpayment for goods or services, there can be errors in the actual clearing and settlement processes for financial transactions. On an internal basis, inbound payments may be posted to the wrong account or recorded improperly, which is sometimes a problem as organizations move from paper payment processes and implement new electronic processes. Outbound payments also may be misdirected, either unintentionally or as a result of employee fraud.

3. TECHNOLOGY RISK

As the treasury area of an organization increasingly relies on technology, the operational risk associated with the use of technology increases. Security breaches related to technology can be either internal or external types of risks. From an internal perspective, breaches are generally referred to as *security violations* and result when an employee bypasses or disobeys internal policies or guidelines related to technology use.

Another type of technology risk is the risk associated with the choice of a particular technology platform or vendor, including issues such as the need for after-sale installation and support or even the risk that a vendor may go out of business. A related issue is the risk associated with the potential failure or obsolescence of vendor-acquired hardware, software, and/or communications devices. This risk may also arise when a treasury system is selected without the support of, and consultation with, the organization's technology and legal staff.

For example, a treasury management system vendor may offer a product that is suitable for the organization, but the vendor's stability and long-term viability may be questionable. It is sometimes preferable to purchase a good, but perhaps second-choice, software product from a known and stable provider rather than a superior product from a new and untested provider. There could also be risks related to capabilities, capacity, and compatibility of treasury technology with other systems in the organization.

Technology risk may also involve extensive use of computer-based spreadsheets in many parts of an organization's day-to-day operations. Spreadsheets can be extremely useful for many business functions and for data management, but there are some issues when they are used for mission-critical applications that require transactional and information processing. Complex spreadsheet models mixed with formula protection are often difficult to monitor and audit with respect to reliability and may provide an avenue for potential mistakes, file corruption, or employee fraud.

While spreadsheets may be appropriate for some treasury functions if proper controls are in place, critical treasury functions, especially those related to the payment/settlement process, should be performed on treasury systems or bank-provided payment systems rather than on spreadsheets.[5]

B. External Operational Risks

There are numerous external sources of operational risk, resulting primarily from an organization's need to interact with many types of external parties. Generally, these sources are categorized as financial institution, counterparty, legal and regulatory/compliance, sovereign, supplier, external theft/fraud, physical and electronic security, natural disaster, and terrorism.

---

5. The ISO 27001 standard provides an excellent framework for evaluating and managing information technology security and risk.

1. FINANCIAL INSTITUTION RISK

Several key risks are associated with the use of financial institutions. The first is the potential failure of the financial institution and the resulting impact on the company (e.g., a loss of balances, diminished borrowing capabilities, or disrupted services). Other risks include potential operational failure on the part of the financial institution that performs daily transactions processing, communication failures between the company and the financial institution, risks related to the use of online banking portals, and the risk of loss or tampering with payment files.

2. COUNTERPARTY RISK

One of the key issues for treasury professionals in companies of all sizes is counterparty risk. Counterparty risk is the risk that the other party in a contract or financial transaction will not perform as promised. One component of counterparty risk is related to credit and default risk. In a generic context, however, the concept of counterparty risk extends to the risk related to any type of performance failure on the part of any of the counterparties with which an organization must interact. The failure of a supplier to deliver goods or the failure of a customer to pay for items purchased on credit would be examples of counterparty risk. Other examples include failure to deliver a currency on the maturity date of a forward contract or failure to make interest and principal payments on debt.

3. LEGAL AND REGULATORY/COMPLIANCE RISK

A significant source of external operational risk is potential lawsuits or other legal actions instigated by customers, trade partners, or governmental agencies and regulators. This is exacerbated by the continuing growth in governmental regulation in many countries around the world. Multinational companies need to understand and comply with regulatory authorities in every jurisdiction in which they operate. The growth of laws dealing with terrorism and anti-money laundering has added significant regulatory and compliance overhead for organizations with large numbers of financial transactions, especially those transactions that cross international borders.

4. SOVEREIGN RISK

Sovereign risk is the risk of interference by a foreign government in the settlement or payment of a foreign transaction, and *political risk* refers to the economic impact that businesses may face due to political changes or decisions within a country. This includes the risk of expropriation or other loss of foreign asset value. Also, tax risk (i.e., uncertainty about future tax liabilities) must be assessed, especially for multinational organizations that deal with a wide variety of sometimes conflicting tax codes and regulations. This risk can be substantial, given the penalties often assessed with missed filings or the underpayment of taxes.

5. SUPPLIER RISK

Risk related to an organization's suppliers and outsourcing arrangements is a specific type of counterparty risk that also entails significant operational risks. The more critical the supplier or commodity is in the production process, the more risk an organization faces if the supplier either fails to deliver according to plan or provides substandard products and services that result in customer dissatisfaction. These risks are even more important in an environment of shortened supply chains and just-in-time inventory management. Supplier failures or shortages quickly impact a company's customers, especially if the process being outsourced is critical to an organization's day-to-day operations. Also, the risk of a merger, acquisition, or divestiture of a particular supplier may result in disruptions in critical supplies or services. The trend toward outsourcing treasury functions has increased this aspect of operational risk significantly, as critical tasks are performed by outside parties rather than by company personnel.

6. EXTERNAL THEFT/FRAUD RISK

Traditionally, the primary source of risk in the area of external theft or fraud has been related to the payment process, often involving false invoices or check fraud. An organization should maintain an accounts payable environment with appropriate controls, such as proper authorization processes, segregation of duties, positive pay (preferably with payee verification), debit blocks, and daily reconciliation, to minimize losses due to invoice and check fraud.

Additionally, replacing paper-based payments with electronic payments can help to reduce potential check fraud. There are, however, potential fraud issues related to using electronic payments. To prevent potential automated clearinghouse (ACH) network fraud, organizations should use ACH debit blocks or filters, daily ACH reconciliation, and timely ACH returns. There are also fraud issues that can occur with business-to-business (B2B) card payments and for organizations that accept electronic payments from consumers.

Organizations also run the risk of a breach or compromise of electronic databases due to computer hackers or other sources. A data breach or compromise occurs when there is a loss of data or other digital media from an organization's computer systems. The data breach could involve either sensitive internal information from the organization, or information about the organization's suppliers or customers (e.g., a hacker steals customer credit card information). A related risk is that of corporate identity theft or account takeover, in which hackers use stolen information to access corporate bank accounts and financial assets.

There also may be the potential risk of loss from malfeasance, the collusion between external criminals and internal employees. Some of the typical crimes related to financial malfeasance include embezzlement, falsifying accounting data, corruption, money laundering, and counterfeiting. Among the preventative measures recommended by auditors are reinforcement of the corporate culture, ethical directives, and a strict code of conduct.

Retail environments routinely process large amounts of cash, and organizations dealing with large amounts of cash collections or disbursements run the risk of robbery or theft of those cash balances. The use of armored car services and automated store safes helps to reduce the risk of theft to the organization, and robbery of its employees, by controlling both the amount of available cash and the access to it.

7. PHYSICAL AND ELECTRONIC SECURITY RISK

Many organizations require physical security for their premises and employees to help prevent physical or electronic access to critical information (e.g., identity theft), as well as to ensure employees' safety. Security measures also may include biometric systems, using such technologies as fingerprint, face, or iris (eye) recognition to control physical access to facilities or key equipment. Physical security is especially important for financial institutions, utilities, and defense contractors.

In addition, many organizations have data-handling policies and procedures to address how staff should manage, store, and/or destroy restricted and sensitive information. Some organizations have records management officers and programs that address the review and classification of records and the controlled scheduled destruction of noncore records.

8. NATURAL DISASTER RISK

Natural disaster events leave organizations open to possible operational risk. These events could range from a temporary power outage to a major earthquake or hurricane. Every organization should have a contingency business resumption plan in place to manage and recover from impacts of such events. This plan should also be tested on a regular basis.

9. TERRORISM RISK

Terrorism has become a significant threat to the operations of many organizations. Many disaster recovery plans specifically include recovery from terrorist events, in addition to natural disasters. Most organizations try to manage exposure to terrorist activities by increasing the level of security for both their premises and employees.

C. Cyberrisk[6]

Security breaches involving employee, customer, and corporate data represent cyberthreats. These security breaches may come from both internal and external sources. Data may be corrupted, or stolen and sold to third parties. Security breaches also include denial-of-service attacks where data communication is blocked. Cybercrime costs the global economy $445 billion per year, according to estimates from the Center for Strategic and International Studies, and a recent AFP survey revealed that 34% of companies had been subjected to a cyberattack in the 18 months prior to the survey.

Current and former employees represent the primary source of cyberrisk for an organization, given the access that they have to information. Internal cyberattacks may be deliberate or the result of an employee error. Deliberate attacks may be initiated by disgruntled employees or former employees who still have access to the system. Other attacks may result from an employee opening phishing e-mails. Most business e-mail compromise (BEC) scams begin with a phishing e-mail that is used to gain access to an employee e-mail account. After monitoring that employee's e-mail account to determine who requests wire transfers and who initiates them, the fraudster will generate a fake e-mail from the CEO requesting the initiation of a wire transfer. The FBI reported that criminals stole nearly $750 million from US businesses through BEC scams between October 2013 and August 2015. When international businesses are included, the estimated total lost due to BEC scams during the period climbs to $1.2 billion. BEC scams have been reported in all 50 US states and in 79 countries.

Cyberthreats from external sources include hackers, activists, financial criminals, and intellectual property thieves. Firms will have various levels of risks associated with these threats. For example, a utility company may be the target of environmental activists who wish to disrupt operations through website takeovers or denial-of-service attacks. Financial criminals may be more likely to focus on retail firms to gain access to customer credit card information. Cyberrisk insurance may be purchased to cover third-party liability (e.g., liability for customer and employee losses due to an information breach) and losses incurred by the firm from theft, business interruption, and data loss.

D. Fundamental Factors for an Operational Risk Management Strategy

Four critical factors determine an operational risk management strategy for an organization: culture, internal controls, technology, and guidelines for the board of directors. The importance of each of these factors depends on the characteristics of the organization's business model.

---

6. The information on cyberrisk is taken from *CTC Guide—Cybersecurity: Setting a Cyberrisk Management Strategy* and *Treasury in Practice Guide—BEC Scams: Treasury's Number One Fraud Threat*, both published in 2015 by the Association for Financial Professionals.

1. ORGANIZATIONAL CULTURE

Organizational culture plays an important role in managing overall operational risk. Employees observing improper management behavior or board members who believe that senior management is not acting in shareholders' best interests must be free to report these activities without incurring significant personal or career risk. Both federal and state whistle-blower laws exist to protect employees who report unethical and illegal activities. A knowledgeable and independent board of directors is one of the best protections against managerial malfeasance.

Most risk management experts agree that the best approach is to develop a culture that promotes individual responsibility and is supportive of educated risk taking. One of the key characteristics of such a culture is a questioning approach to decision making that encourages anyone to ask legitimate questions or express genuine concerns related to the management of the organization. Another important characteristic is the willingness on the part of senior management to admit to a lack of sufficient information where applicable. Often, key decisions need to be made without complete information, but the decision maker must be aware of the information gaps and take some steps to mitigate this risk. Finally, the culture must provide all employees with written policies that set forth ethical behavior standards for every level of the organization.

2. INTERNAL CONTROLS

COSO[7] defines *internal control* as a process designed to provide reasonable assurance regarding achievement of objectives in the following categories: effectiveness or efficiency of operations; reliability of financial reporting; and compliance with applicable laws and regulations. In the United States, Sarbanes-Oxley (SOX) Section 404 requires that a firm establish internal controls over financial reporting to prevent material errors or misrepresentations in a firm's financial statements. Management is responsible for performing a formal assessment of the internal controls and including an assessment of internal controls in the annual report.

The firm's external auditors are required to provide an opinion on the effectiveness of the company's internal controls over financial reporting. For this reason, it is imperative that internal controls are well documented. In recent years, the failure rate for audits related to internal controls has averaged 39 percent.[8] Many of the issues centered on a failure to provide sufficient evidence that internal controls were operating effectively.

3. TECHNOLOGY

Technology is a critical factor in the formation of strategies related to operational risk management. Technology is necessary to help gather and analyze the information needed and then to monitor operational controls and procedures. Also, technology can help to reduce manual errors and, if properly implemented, can serve to limit access by non-authorized personnel.

4. GUIDELINES FOR THE BOARD OF DIRECTORS

Guidelines for the actions of the board of directors are especially important in reducing overall operating risk. For example, firms often place restrictions on how many board members and key executives may travel together in order to limit damage to corporate governance and control in the event of an accident. It is also important to address conflicts of interest, limit the number of internal board members, clarify personal responsibility, and facilitate the discussion and resolution of difficult or contentious issues. Many stock exchanges have explicit requirements regarding independence that must be adhered to if the company expects to continue to be listed on a given exchange. Lines of reporting should be clear, explicit, and known to all levels of the organization.

---

7. *COSO* is the acronym for the Committee of Sponsoring Organizations of the Treadway Commission.
8. From "FP&A—The Brave New World of Internal Control" (White Paper), published by Workiva (https://www.workiva.com/sites/workiva/files/FP&A–The Brave New World of Internal Control.pdf, accessed July 29, 2016).

The importance of procedures is especially critical to any organization involved in trading activities because of the essential need to monitor and control these activities in relation to limits placed on authority and risk taking. Procedures for board behavior must be outlined clearly in trading policies and guidelines, as well as remaining subject to regular review and monitoring by auditors.

Separate audit and risk committees may be formed by the board of directors. The risk committee will have oversight of the firm's risk management framework, including the establishment of a risk management policy, review of the firm's enterprise risk assessments, and oversight of the management of complex risks. Audit committees typically focus on risks related to financial reporting and other risks that may have financial reporting implications. For firms listed on the New York Stock Exchange (NYSE), the audit committee must meet with management to discuss risk assessment and management, even if the company has a separate risk committee.

V. DISASTER RECOVERY AND BUSINESS CONTINUITY

Disaster recovery refers to the restoration of systems and communications after an event causes an outage. *Business continuity* refers to the actions taken with regard to crisis management, alternative operating procedures, and communications to staff and customers. The intent of disaster avoidance, recovery, and remediation measures is to preserve the firm's revenue stream. It is important that these plans be tested and reevaluated on a regular basis to ensure that they are effective and current.

When organizations implement disaster recovery and business continuity plans, the focus is often on the business supply chain, ensuring that supplier linkages and production resources are restored and that customer service is maintained. While these are important factors, the business supply chain functions only as long as the related cash and information flows of the organization also continue.

The financial supply chain or procure-to-pay cycle is crucial to financial viability following a disaster. The treasury area plays a pivotal role in managing the organization's financial supply chain, through working capital management practices and by ensuring adequate liquidity sources. The key parties or resources involved in the financial chain generally are classified as either *internal resources* or *external counterparties*:

- **Internal resources** include treasury staff, computer systems, policies, procedures, processes (both automated and nonautomated), and office facilities.
- **External financial counterparties** include financial institutions, market information providers, vendors, and financial markets.

The infrastructure linking the two must be well designed and should include both internal and external networks, such as computers, servers, telecommunications, utilities, and vendor support services. An effective disaster recovery program encompasses each of these areas. Specific programs depend upon an organization's business, its treasury structure, and the specific risks the organization faces.

A. Developing Effective Disaster Recovery (DR) and Business Continuity (BC) Plans

1. IDENTIFY MISSION-CRITICAL FUNCTIONS

The first step in developing DR or BC plans is to identify mission-critical functions. An activity or function is mission critical when an interruption will create significant disruptions in an organization's business. Such disruptions have serious repercussions on an organization's ability to continue normal operations and ultimately to survive. Examples of mission-critical functions in treasury include the ability to initiate wire transfers for interest or bond payments, disbursement funding, and potentially payroll.

2. ASSESS RISKS

Once the critical functions have been identified, the potential risks that could disrupt these functions (e.g., inability to access a treasury workstation due to fire or flood) should be identified. The next step is to determine what would happen if the risk actually occurred. For example, what would be the impact if a denial-of-service attack by a hacker made it impossible to use the bank portal normally used to initiate wires?

In gauging risk levels, it is important to assess both the likelihood that something could go wrong and the consequences that would then occur.

3. EVALUATE CONTINGENCY MEASURES

After the risks have been assessed, the organization can then evaluate alternative measures to deal with the problem. For example, if a treasury professional is unable to access the organization's lead bank via the bank's portal, alternatives could include initiating transactions by telephone or originating transactions through a backup bank that has not been affected. The goal is to understand and catalog the measures currently in place and evaluate their effectiveness, considering mission-critical functions and current risk levels. Bear in mind that during a disaster, cash is truly king since banks, ATMs, and credit card systems may not be available. As a result, treasury has an important role in any DR or BC plan in making sure that sufficient funds are available to meet the needs of any specific contingency measures.

4. PRIORITIZE CORRECTIVE ACTION

Once the potential contingency measures have been identified, assessed, and cataloged, the organization can determine the appropriate actions to take in the case of specific problems. These actions need to be prioritized in light of the impact on the organization and the previously determined risk level. For example, implementing corrective action for wires for interest and bond payments may have higher priority than implementing corrective action for trade payments, which may be delayed for some period of time before becoming a critical problem. Implementing high-cost alternatives for low-impact problems is probably not a good idea.

5. CREATE A COMMUNICATION PLAN

A key element in developing and implementing any DR or BC plan is to develop a parallel communication plan. In many disasters, normal phone systems and e-mail are not immediately available, and alternatives need to be planned for. The communication plan should include critical telephone numbers and contingency instructions for all staff. The organization should consider providing local service partners, regulatory agencies, and local law enforcement agencies copies of the communication plan. Contingency websites and/or call-in lines for staff, customers, and other key stakeholders can be extremely valuable in providing updates, calming tempers, and avoiding constant requests for situation updates.

B. Implementing the Plan

Once the DR plan and the related communication plan are developed, they need to be documented, distributed, and implemented. Implementation should include notifying all staff, not just key players, and providing appropriate training. No one knows who will be available at the time of a disaster, so it is important that all staff understand the contingency plans, how the plans are implemented, and who they should contact for instructions and guidance. There are many excellent online systems for documenting plans, but there should also be hard copies of the DR plan and communication numbers available in the event that the electronic systems have been compromised in the disaster. Implementation of the DR plan should also consider employee welfare and provide appropriate support for both emergency staff and their families. Key staff are much more likely to follow company policy in an emergency if they know that their families are also being taken care.

C. Performing Periodic Testing

A plan without testing is no plan, as there is no proof that the plan will actually work. DR plans need to be tested on a periodic basis, at least annually and preferably semiannually. These tests fulfill two functions: first, they identify problems with the plan that need to be corrected, and second, they help train staff and ingrain appropriate emergency responses. Appendix 16.1 includes a DR checklist that may be helpful in developing and testing DR plans.

VI. MANAGING INSURABLE RISKS

Use of insurance is a specific form of risk management in which financial protection or reimbursement for possible losses is purchased from another party. It is essentially a method of transferring risk from one party to another, though the term *risk transfer* has a specific meaning in the insurance area and is discussed later.

Insurance management is a decision-making process that identifies the possible losses and determines if insurance should be purchased against the risk of that loss and how much insurance is needed. Every organization needs some insurance risk management due to the possibility of accidental loss (i.e., loss exposures) that can disrupt operations and lower overall efficiency and profitability. As their level of involvement in overall risk management increases, treasury managers are being asked to become managers of comprehensive risk. The issue no longer is about what the year-over-year increase is in premium cost; rather, as with overall risk management, it is about the company's risk tolerance threshold and involves looking at concepts like total cost of risk (TCOR)[9] rather than just purchasing insurance coverage. It is therefore becoming increasingly common for the risk manager to be part of the treasury staff at companies with a significant exposure to risk.

The four objectives of insurance management (as it applies to risk mitigation) are to:

- Insure against catastrophic loss
- Decide when and what to insure
- Manage the purchase and use of insurance
- Obtain efficient pricing for insurance needs

A. Using Insurance Contracts to Manage Risk

Insurance contracts offer a traditional approach to managing and controlling operational risk. Although risk management typically seeks to reduce the possibility of losses, insurance usually is designed to compensate for losses, especially accidental losses, after they occur. Accidental losses, even if all are covered by insurance, have broad implications for the treasury area. Management often finds that accidents tend to reduce the firm's profitability, increase liquidity requirements, and impair financial security.

---

9. TCOR is a metric that captures all the elements of risk management, including insurance premiums, self-retained losses, and any risk management administration expense.

1. WHY ORGANIZATIONS USE INSURANCE

Even if insurance eventually pays to repair or replace property, damage lowers the projected rate of return on the impaired assets. Any substantial business interruption is likely to lower profits because although an organization has business interruption insurance, cash inflows are slowed, putting pressure on the company's ability to meet its debt service obligations.

Liability losses can drain an organization's cash through the payment of uninsured claims, legal defense costs, or expenditures in negotiating with the involved insurers. Similarly, contractors' failure to complete projects deprives organizations of anticipated revenues and may impede growth, as can the death, disability, or resignation of a valuable, difficult-to-replace employee.

In addition to loss prevention and risk financing costs, the possibility of accidental losses imposes administrative costs on an organization. Management must decide where and how to apply loss prevention, select the proper types and amounts of insurance, and collect the insurance reimbursement when a covered loss occurs.

The total of all costs from both actual and potential losses constitutes an organization's cost of risk from losses. The total cost is often difficult to estimate. However, experts can assist organizations with this process by helping to identify the break-even point between the costs of insurance and the costs of uninsured losses for an organization.

2. TYPES OF LOSSES AND POLICIES

Effective risk management helps to control or prevent losses, and adequate insurance helps to finance an organization's recovery when a loss occurs. Events resulting in a major loss generally disrupt an organization's operating and financial plans. Losses occur for a variety of reasons, and as a result there are different types of policies designed to cover specific losses. Appendix 16.2 provides a partial list of the various types of insurance. Examples of potential insured losses include:

- Property loss (e.g., from internal or external theft)
- Business interruption or net income loss
- Surety or breach-of-contract loss (e.g., from a contractor's failure to perform)
- Liability loss (e.g., from lawsuits by injured customers)
- Personnel loss (e.g., loss of the president or other key employees)
- Workers' compensation claims
- Cyberrisk loss (e.g., loss caused by data or network security breach)

B. Dealing with Insurance Providers and Brokers

Most organizations purchase insurance through agents or brokers rather than directly from an insurance company. Although agents and brokers both receive commissions rather than salaries from insurers, an independent agent is legally an agent of the insurer while a broker is the legal agent of the applicant.

1. SELECTING INSURANCE—THE FINANCIAL PERSPECTIVE

When selecting among competing insurers, important factors to consider include:

- Long-term solvency of the insurer
- Rating for the insurer
- Service provided
- Cost versus exposure
- Industry knowledge and experience

a. Long-Term Solvency of the Insurer

Treasury professionals should investigate the financial solvency of the firm's insurers. Generally, state-guaranteed funds provide only limited protection when an insurer fails, and the delays involved in settling claims may be significant. Insurance coverage is only as good as the ability of the insurance company to pay claims, especially claims for large losses. Therefore, a firm's lenders may require credit agreements or loan covenants that stipulate minimum ratings for insurance carriers.

b. Rating for the Insurer

A.M. Best Company is the leading provider of ratings and financial information for the global insurance industry. It assigns two types of ratings: one for financial strength and one for indebtedness. Both are independent opinions based on the comprehensive quantitative and qualitative evaluation of an insurance company's balance sheet strength, operating performance, and business profile. Best's Financial Strength Ratings provide an opinion of an insurer's financial strength and ability to meet ongoing obligations to policyholders. Best's Issuer Credit Ratings provide the credit market with an opinion about the insurer's ability to meet its financial obligations to security holders when due. However, these are only opinions and do not guarantee a company's financial strength or its ability to meet obligations to policyholders and other financial claimants.

c. Service Provided

The ability of an insurer to provide loss control and/or claims service may help to reduce the overall cost of an insurance program. Service levels and specialization or expertise in a particular area of insurance should always be taken into consideration when selecting insurers, and many insurers will actually review operations and provide specific recommendations on risk mitigation. In some cases, failure to follow such recommendations can result in higher premiums and even termination of coverage.

d. Cost versus Exposure

The cost of an insurance policy or program should always be measured in relation to the financial stability, overall coverage, and quality of services offered by the prospective insurer.

e. Industry Knowledge and Experience

Insurance companies often specialize in specific industries and as a result have specific experience with the risks and issues faced by companies in that market segment. A prime example is Lloyd's of London, which got its start insuring against the loss of sailing ships and is historically known as an expert in the risks of the shipping industry.

2. SELECTING COVERAGE

Treasury professionals must select what to insure. The first step in this process is measuring risk exposures. A firm may decide to retain risks that are very improbable or that have a small cash flow impact if the event occurs. In other cases, firms may decide to retain a risk if the cost of insurance is equal to or greater than the expected loss.

When selecting insurance coverages, treasury professionals must consider the total cost of risk (TCOR). This measure includes the cost of insurance, the cost of losses that are retained, and the administrative costs associated with the firm's risk management program.

3. SELECTING A DEDUCTIBLE

By selecting insurance coverage that has a deductible (also referred to as a *retention*, depending upon the type of insurance), an insured party can obtain a significantly lower premium when compared to the cost of first-dollar coverage,[10] especially in the case of property insurance. In essence, the deductible forces the insured to share some of the front-end risk from potential losses. The higher the deductible is, the lower the cost of the premium for insurance. It is important to weigh the frequency and types of losses that could fall within the deductible, as well as the uncertainty that accepting a policy with a deductible introduces relative to the premium savings obtained. Deductibles may also be set on a combination of:

- **Per-Occurrence Basis:** The deductible applies for each occurrence during the policy period.
- **Aggregate Basis:** The deductible is set on a per-period basis, regardless of the number of occurrences.

4. SELECTING A LIABILITY LIMIT

Liability limits determine the maximum amount that an insurance policy will pay for a specific loss. Selecting an appropriate limit is important because higher limits increase cost while lower limits can reduce potential recovery if the loss is greater than the policy limit. The challenge of selecting a liability limit may be made more complex if the amount of liability insurance the organization wishes to purchase is not available to it. In selecting a policy limit, management should consider the total potential risk, cost versus limits, and cost versus exposure. It should be noted that in some cases the insured company may not have a lot of choice in either limits or deductibles; rather, certain limits or deductibles may be forced on them by the insurer.

5. CLAIMS PAYMENT

Most policies provide coverage on a basic occurrence basis, where the eligibility of a claim is primarily based on the date of occurrence of the insured event. This type of policy has a term period, with a specified start and end date for the coverage, to cover losses that occur during the designated policy period. A policy that provides coverage on a claims-made basis, on the other hand, is driven by when the claims are made, regardless of when the actual loss event occurs. Thus, a valid claims-made policy can process a claim made today for an incident from five years ago, as long as there is not a retroactive date[11] that precludes it.

C. Insurance Risk Management Services

Most organizations maintain an in-house risk management information system and a complete set of internal records on insurance and losses. In lieu of in-house risk management, or as a means to supplement in-house expertise, insurance risk management consultants offer additional services, on a fee basis and as needed, to make and carry out insurance risk financing, management, and control decisions.

10. A policy that offers first-dollar coverage provides reimbursement for losses without any deductible.
11. A retroactive date is a date in some claims-made insurance policies that limits coverage to events that occur after that date. Claims for issues that happened before the date will not be covered.

D. Risk-Financing Techniques

Risk-financing techniques involve resources that an organization may draw upon to finance recovery from losses and liabilities for which it is held responsible. Risk financing competes with other uses of corporate funds. Sound financial management requires integrating the organization's risk-financing needs with other more traditionally productive uses. This is necessary because without proper risk financing, profit-generating activities and assets are almost certain to be impaired, or even ruined, by accidents. As outlined below, the basic approaches to risk financing are risk retention and risk transfer.

1. RISK RETENTION

Risk retention involves the use of an organization's internal financial resources to provide funds to finance a recovery from losses. In other words, the organization retains some or all of the loss, rather than transferring it by paying someone else (e.g., an insurance organization) to take it.

a. Noninsurance

One approach to risk retention is known as *noninsurance*. This technique involves relying on normal revenues to pay for small, normal losses as current expenses. Noninsurance is appropriate for losses that an organization can absorb readily as costs of doing business, but not for highly disruptive, potentially ruinous accidents.

b. Self-Insurance

Self-insurance is not technically a form of insurance because it does not involve a transfer of risk to an insurer or another separate entity. Also, the term *self-insurance* can describe any risk retention program, even quite informal, unfunded arrangements. Self-insured retention (SIR) is the component of loss covered by the insured in a policy. SIR differs from a deductible in that the insured is responsible for all aspects of a claim up to the defined limit. Self-insurance requires careful forecasting to ensure that adequate funds are available to meet future losses and that these funds are systematically maintained by the organization. Self-insurance differs from noninsurance in that the organization had made a conscious decision to self-insure and typically allocates specific assets to fund or pay for the costs of self-insuring, as opposed to noninsurance where the risks are ignored or assumed to be negligible.

Many large organizations use self-insurance to manage their employee health care expenses. This usually works well for organizations with a sizeable pool of diverse employees. Typically, the organization will contract with a third party to manage the provider network and claims processing. In addition, the organization may purchase some type of excess coverage to protect against unexpectedly high claims in a given period.

c. Single-Parent Captive

Another approach to risk retention is the use of a captive insurance company. A single-parent captive is a subsidiary owned for the purpose of insuring the risk of a parent company or its affiliates. The captive provides guaranteed access to insurance, may be used to provide unique types of insurance coverage or favorable rates, and often generates tax advantages for the parent company. It should be noted that a major loss could result in insolvency for the captive, but the parent company would survive.

d. Group Captive

A group captive, also known as an *association captive*, resembles a single-parent captive except that it provides risk financing for multiple owners instead of just one. The captive may be owned jointly by each of the individual parents or by an association that the parent companies have formed. This shared ownership makes the group captive arrangement a form of insurance by virtue of the transfer of risk. In most cases, group captives are industry-based, which allows risk transfer across similar risks.

e. Risk Retention Group

A risk retention group is a special type of group captive formed under the terms of a federal law that is designed to enable business firms to work together to jointly finance product liability claims. To the extent that risks are shared, this is considered insurance. These plans often are used in industries with a high potential for catastrophic losses, such as the airline industry and certain professional occupations (e.g., physicians in high-risk practice areas, accountants, or lawyers).

f. Claims Management

Many companies that self-insure contract out the claims approval and payment process to an insurance company or another third party. The primary benefits of this relationship are cost reduction, availability of specialty skills and technology, and access to a system of providers.

2. RISK TRANSFER

The essence of any risk transfer is a contract between a transferring organization (i.e., the transferor) and another entity (i.e., the transferee), under which the transferee agrees to pay designated types of the transferor's losses within contractual limits. The transferor may have to pay the transferee a fee (e.g., an insurance premium) for this promise of indemnity, or the transferor may have the bargaining power to secure this promise as a condition for agreeing to do business with the transferee. Such risk transfer arrangements are made frequently for tax or regulatory reasons, and may be accomplished through the purchase of reinsurance, either from a broker or directly from the market. It is important to note that the transfer of risk is only as good as the transferee's, or the insurance company's, ability to pay claims. As part of the transfer, the insured gives up all of the rights it may have to recover the loss from other parties. This is typically referred to as *subrogation*.

a. Contractual Transfer

Under these contracts, typified by hold-harmless agreements, the transferee is not an insurer and the transfer contract may take any form permitted by applicable law. Such contractual transfers may not provide transferors the degree of financial security they could obtain from a true insurer because most hold-harmless transferees are not in business to bear others' risk of loss. Additionally, these contracts and business activities are not as strictly regulated as insurers. This is a form of risk transfer, where the burden of the risks in question is transferred to another party. The other party can choose to purchase insurance of some type to mitigate those risks if it wishes.

b. Guaranteed Cost Insurance Program

In this type of program, the insured pays a fixed premium at the beginning of the policy period, and the insurer assumes the risk for paying all losses occurring during the policy period that fall within the scope and amount of the policy. The premium paid by the insured cannot be changed until the next policy period, although either the insurer or the insured may cancel coverage in the middle of the policy period under certain conditions. An insured that cancels this type of policy mid-period may not be entitled to a refund of premiums paid.

c. Retrospectively (Retro) Rated Insurance Program

In this type of program, the insured's cost of coverage for a policy period varies with the insured's losses during that period. Such programs are used often for workers' compensation and product liability insurance plans. The insured pays a standard, or deposit, premium at the beginning of the coverage period. At the end of the period, the insurer computes a final premium based on an agreed-upon formula that varies with the insured's actual costs or losses (subject to limits) for the policy period.

VII. SUMMARY

Risk management is a complex topic that is becoming increasingly important to the treasury profession as a growing number of organizations are turning to treasury for risk management expertise. This chapter discussed the basic concepts behind risk management as well as the key components of enterprise risk management. The chapter also reviewed the major categories of operational risk management and considered how they might impact an organization. As part of this discussion, the chapter covered the need for a thorough disaster recovery plan and presented the steps involved in creating such a plan. An overview of some of the key concepts of insurance management were also provided.

Key Equations

$$\text{Value at Risk}\,(5\%) = \text{Portfolio Value} \times 1.65 \times \text{Standard Deviation}$$

$$\text{Cash Flow at Risk}\,(5\%) = 1.65 \times \text{Standard Deviation}$$

APPENDIX 16.1: DISASTER RECOVERY (DR) CHECKLIST[12]

The 2011 earthquake and subsequent tsunami in Japan have underscored once again the need for corporate treasurers no matter where they are located to always be ready to face unplanned service disruptions whether they be short-term outages or full-fledged disasters. Ensuring the business resiliency of your treasury operations is critical, and the processes for upgrading contingency plans should be ongoing, flexible, and dynamic. The questions below can help you assess your organization's readiness for business continuity in the event of a disaster—either man-made or natural.

Treasury Operations

· Have you reviewed your account information and your account structures—including authorized signers, security administrators, user IDs, and entitlements—with each of your banking partners to ensure that everything is accurate and up-to-date? Do you maintain this information off-site, as well as on-site?

· Are your locations geographically dispersed so you can rapidly shift treasury operations in the event of a crisis? Do your banking partners also have dispersed payments centers?

· If you lease your contingency site, how will space be allocated in the event of a major crisis (e.g., will it be on a first come, first served basis)?

· Will you have access to all necessary documentation and emergency procedures at off-site locations?

Contingency Plans

· Do you have contingency procedures in place so you can continue to process payments in the event of a crisis? Do you periodically test these procedures by logging on to your backup system and generating at least one real-time transaction? Are you reliant on a specific desktop PC, or do you maintain an alternate desktop PC as backup?

· Do you have an operational response plan? How often do you conduct a full end-to-end test to validate the recovery capabilities of staff and critical systems? Has the test been audited?

· In the event of a pandemic, which locations would be severely impacted if absentee rates were to reach between 30 to 50 percent of your organization? Having data on the number or percentage of your employees who rely on public transportation in high concentration areas will be helpful to you as you develop your contingency plans. In addition, as you review critical third-party organizations, be sure to check that they, too, have sufficient pandemic response plans.

· Have you tested your primary site against your contingency sites? Often, a single primary site requires recovery to multiple alternate sites. Recovery processes need to test coordination and communication procedures to ensure a full recovery of all components.

· In addition to contingency procedures for facilities, do you also have contingency procedures to ensure the security and protection of data?

· Do you have alternate power sources for your main server locations? Do you have a backup plan in the event your Internet provider goes down?

· Have you prepared other disaster contingencies, including a potable water supply, emergency food, flashlights, etc., on site?

---

12. Used with permission © 2013 JPMorgan Chase & Co. All rights reserved.

Crisis Communications

- Do you have an emergency management team in place? Do you have a clear, predetermined chain of command in the event of an emergency? Is this information documented and widely distributed within your organization? How often is it reviewed and updated?

- Does your crisis communication plan cover both internal and external procedures? Has it been documented and widely distributed throughout your organization?

- Have you provided your clients, colleagues, suppliers, financial and banking partners, and other key business contacts with emergency contact information?

- Have you established a dialogue with local fire, police, emergency medical services personnel, community leaders, government agencies, community organizations, and utilities regarding your disaster-preparedness procedures?

- Have you considered the emotional response your employees may have to a major crisis? A crisis could impact the ability of some of your employees to function. Consider cross-training personnel so that staff are ready to assume multiple roles if needed, and your organization is fully prepared to function in the event of an emergency.

- Have you reassessed all recovery plans to validate that assumptions and recovery solutions are still appropriate? An important step here is to include all constituents—both internal and external. In addition, business recovery time capabilities should be aligned with current recovery time objectives and should also ensure that the impact on clients is understood by all appropriate parties.

Other Factors for Consideration

- Have you considered how you would maintain liquidity if your primary provider were impacted by a disaster? How easily would you have access to cash in the event of a crisis?

- Have you conducted a comprehensive review of your insurance coverage? Does it include provisions for recovery and restoration?

- Do you use positive pay and stop payment capabilities to limit your exposure and help manage risk?

- Have you considered outsourcing your receivables collection to a provider with geographically dispersed network capabilities?

APPENDIX 16.2: TYPES OF INSURANCE COVERAGE

The list below describes some of the basic types of business insurance:

- **Business Interruption:** This coverage provides payments to an organization in the event it is unable to pursue a normal line of business for some period of time due to an unforeseen event. Business interruption insurance generally covers the loss of profits, as well as continuing fixed expenses (e.g., debt or lease arrangements), while the organization is temporarily out of business. For example, if an organization suffered a fire at a main production facility, property insurance would pay for rebuilding the facility, and business interruption insurance would make payments to compensate the organization for lost profits and increased costs during the rebuilding process.

- **Casualty:** Concerned primarily with the legal liability of losses caused by personal injury or property damage, casualty insurance provides specific coverage for a variety of losses. Examples of typical casualty insurance include plate glass, crime, robbery, boiler or machinery, and aviation insurance. Many casualty insurers also write surety bonds and other forms of insurance not classified as *property insurance*.

- **Commercial Crime:** A principal of common law is that there can be no coverage for intentional or criminal acts. As a result, someone who commits a criminal act, such as stealing inventory, assaulting a customer, or poisoning products, will not be covered by insurance. There can, however, be coverage for the organization that employs the person committing the act, as long as that action is taken without the knowledge or approval of the organization. A crime insurance policy can cover the organization for such acts (refer also to *fidelity* and *professional liability insurances*).

- **Difference in Conditions (DIC):** DIC insurance covers property for perils not covered by basic property insurance policies. It is often purchased to fill voids in policies purchased overseas and to insure property in transit. Typically used in conjunction with multiple basic policies to make them uniform, DIC insurance does not provide additional limits of coverage for basic property perils (as an umbrella policy does for liability insurance).

- **Directors and Officers (D&O):** D&O policies cover situations in which a director or officer of an organization commits a negligent act or omission, or makes a misstatement or misleading statement, and a legal action is brought against the organization as a result. The policy provides coverage (usually with a large deductible) for directors' and officers' liability exposure if these individuals are sued. Coverage also is provided for defense costs, such as legal fees and other court costs, and may include coverage for an organization's subsidiaries.

- **Excess or Umbrella:** This coverage supplements basic or primary liability coverage. Policies generally pay after the primary policy's limits have been exhausted. For example, if the primary insurance policy has a $250,000 limit and claims exceed this amount, then an umbrella or excess policy would pay the excess claims up to the limit of the policy. Excess or umbrella policies can also be used to fill gaps in coverage provided by basic liability policies (i.e., the difference in coverage between two policies).

- **Fidelity:** Fidelity bonds provide coverage that guarantees payment for money or other property lost through dishonest acts of bonded employees, either by name or position. Whether employees act alone or in concert, the bond generally covers all dishonest acts, such as larceny, theft, embezzlement, forgery, misappropriation, wrongful abstraction, or willful misapplication. Because a fidelity bond makes up only part of the protection against theft, other crime insurance is often mandatory. A blanket bond could be used to cover all employees of an organization, while crime insurance provides specific coverage for the perils of burglary, theft, and robbery by external parties.

- **Key Person:** This type of life insurance (also known as *key man insurance*) names the organization as the beneficiary to insure against the loss of key personnel, such as a CEO or owner. This type of policy can also be used by partnerships to cover potential estate tax issues for private companies, or by ownerships to avoid forced dissolution of the company upon the death of an owner or partner.

- **Liability:** This coverage insures against damage to other parties that can arise from product defects; business practices; accidents; actions of the organization's employees, officers, or board of directors; and general negligence in the operation of the organization. Liability insurance typically includes defense costs in the event of litigation.

- **Property:** This insurance provides for reimbursement in the event of a loss of or damage to some type of asset (e.g., buildings, equipment, or inventory). Policies often cover the replacement value of the items in question, paying the costs of completely replacing those assets at their current market prices rather than at their historical or book value.

- **Professional Liability:** Commonly referred to as *errors and omissions (E&O) policies*, these policies protect service- and advice-providing individuals and companies, such as consultants, accounting firms, and investment advisors, from the cost of defending against a negligence claim made by a client, as well as from the cost of any damages that may be awarded in a civil lawsuit. While E&O coverage typically includes defense costs, coverage normally excludes criminal prosecution.

- **Transit/Ocean Marine:** Property insurance typically restricts coverage to specified locations listed within the policy. Transit, or transportation, insurance covers products or property while in transit. Marine insurance specifically covers property while on a boat.

- **Workers' Compensation:** Required by most states, this type of insurance covers employees' job-related injuries or diseases as a matter of right (without regard to fault). It generally provides benefits in the areas of medical care, death, disability, and rehabilitation.

- **Other Types of Insurance:** There are a variety of additional specialized types of insurance policies designed to meet an organization's specific needs. These include such things as fiduciary insurance for pension plans, crop insurance, etc.

CHAPTER 17
Financial Risk Management

I. INTRODUCTION

II. OVERVIEW OF FINANCIAL RISK MANAGEMENT
    A. Interest Rate Risk
    B. Foreign Exchange (FX) Risk
    C. Commodity Price Risk

III. MANAGING FINANCIAL RISK
    A. Passive or Natural Hedging
    B. Active or Financial Hedging
    C. Speculation
    D. Arbitrage
    E. The Benefits of Financial Risk Management

IV. DERIVATIVE INSTRUMENTS USED AS FINANCIAL RISK MANAGEMENT TOOLS
    A. Forwards
    B. Futures
    C. Swaps
    D. Options
    E. Comparison of Forwards, Futures, and Options

V. FOREIGN EXCHANGE (FX) RISK MANAGEMENT
    A. Challenges in International/Global Treasury Management
    B. FX Rates
    C. Emerging Markets

VI. CURRENCY DERIVATIVES USED TO HEDGE FOREIGN EXCHANGE (FX) EXPOSURE

A. Currency Forwards

B. Currency Futures

C. Currency Swaps

D. Currency Options

VII. INTEREST RATE EXPOSURE AND RISK MANAGEMENT

A. Interest Rate Forwards

B. Interest Rate Futures

C. Interest Rate Swaps

D. Interest Rate Options

VIII. COMMODITY RISK EXPOSURE

IX. OTHER ISSUES RELATED TO FINANCIAL RISK MANAGEMENT

A. Accounting Issues

B. Tax Issues Related to Hedging

C. Hedging Policy Statement

X. SUMMARY

I. INTRODUCTION

The previous chapter introduced a standard process for enterprise risk management, which involved identifying, measuring, managing, and monitoring risks. This chapter builds on that framework by discussing the primary tools and techniques used to manage financial risks.

In most firms, the treasury department is responsible for financial risk management. Since the treasury department is a clearinghouse for daily financial information, treasury professionals are well positioned to understand and control a firm's exposure to financial risks. For domestic firms, financial risk has traditionally been driven by interest rate risk, but increased globalization and international trade has created a corresponding need for managing foreign exchange (FX) risk. Fortunately, the processes and tools available to manage FX risk are well developed.

This chapter begins with an overview of financial risk management, including a discussion of the three primary areas of financial risk. Next, the derivative products (e.g., forwards, futures, swaps, and options) used to hedge financial risks are described. Following this discussion, examples are provided that apply these derivatives to the management of FX risk and interest rate risk. The chapter closes with a discussion of the characteristics of commodity price risk and miscellaneous issues pertinent to financial risk management (e.g., accounting and tax issues, and hedging policy statements).

II. OVERVIEW OF FINANCIAL RISK MANAGEMENT

This section of the chapter describes three key categories of financial risk, including interest rate risk, FX risk, and commodity price risk.

A. Interest Rate Risk

Interest rate risk is the risk related to changes in investment values or borrowing costs due to changes in interest rates. For example, as interest rates change, a firm will find that the overall value of its short-term and/or long-term investment portfolio changes. A positive change is good, but without adequate planning or protection, a change may be negative and reduce the company's overall value. Alternatively, a company that finances operating expenses using bank credit will be exposed to changes in overall expense as interest rates charged by the bank change. An increase in rates will lead to an increase in expense, and consequently to decreased earnings.

B. Foreign Exchange (FX) Risk

FX risk arises from the exposure an organization has as a result of transactions, assets, and liabilities that are denominated in a foreign currency. As exchange rates fluctuate, so too can the value of these items, ultimately impacting the overall value of a firm. FX risk is further broken down into three types of risk: economic, transaction, and translation risk.

1. ECONOMIC RISK

Economic risk exposure is the long-term effect of changes in exchange rates on the present value of future cash flows. Multinational corporations that conduct business in several different currencies are, in the long run, always subject to fluctuations in cash flows because of exchange rate changes. Even companies that only operate domestically are exposed to economic risk whenever there is foreign competition within the local market.

A company that purchases supplies locally and sells products locally is not affected by transaction or translation exposure. However, if the local currency appreciates against a foreign competitor's currency, then the company's earnings in the long run may be impacted when domestic demand shifts toward the less costly product or service of the foreign competitor.

2. TRANSACTION RISK

Transaction risk exposure arises when a company creates receivables, payables, or other cash flows that are denominated in a currency other than its functional currency. Thus, the ultimate value of these receivables or payables when they are collected or paid may be different from when they were created, due to possible changes in the exchange rate between the currency of denomination and the company's functional currency.

FX transaction risk can also be divided into implicit and explicit risk:

- **Cash flow exposure (implicit risk)** is the risk that the value of future transactions will change due to changes in exchange rates. The firm has cash flow exposure from the time that a sale is expected until the sale occurs. For example, a company may publish price lists in a foreign currency or make a firm quote in a foreign currency. These result in a cash flow exposure until such time as a sale is actually made and the sale recorded. For this reason, companies with extensive foreign currency transactions often manage their FX risk based on projected sales to account for implicit risk.

- **Balance sheet exposure (explicit risk)** is the risk that occurs due to changes in FX rates between the time a transaction occurs and the time it is finally settled. For example, a Canadian-based company sells a product denominated in Japanese yen (JPY) for payment in 30 days. The company is subject to balance sheet exposure from the time of the sale until the receivable is actually collected.

Balance sheet exposure is the most common type of FX risk exposure to be hedged through the use of currency derivatives. Balance sheet exposure originates when a receivable or payable is entered on the balance sheet and remains until cash is received or paid. For example, when a Japanese exporter sells merchandise to a French buyer and agrees to accept payment in euros (EUR) in three months, the transaction is recorded in revenue and in accounts receivable using the JPY/EUR spot rate in effect at that time. However, the value of the receivable changes as the value of the euro changes against the yen over the following three months. These gains and losses are typically recorded on the income statement at the end of each accounting period, creating earnings volatility.

3. TRANSLATION RISK

Translation risk exposure is created when a foreign subsidiary's financial statements are converted (translated) into the parent company's reporting currency as part of the process of consolidating a company's financial statements into a common currency. Any company with an investment in operations in multiple countries and currencies must report its financial statements on a consolidated basis in its reporting currency. This exposure is sometimes referred to as *accounting exposure*. The exposure occurs because the value of the foreign assets and liabilities will change from one accounting period to the next as the underlying FX rates change. For example, if a German company has a subsidiary in the United Kingdom, then the value of that subsidiary's foreign currency financial statements will change as the exchange rate between the euro (EUR) and the British pound (GBP) changes over a given accounting period. If the GBP were to increase in value relative to the EUR over the course of a year, then there would be a translation gain as a result of that change.

In the United States, the prevailing guideline is Accounting Standards Codification (ASC) Topic 830: *Foreign Currency Matters*. For most global companies, International Accounting Standard (IAS) 21: *The Effects of Changes in Foreign Exchange Rates* provides guidance for determining the impact of changing FX rates on translating financial statements from one currency to another.

C. Commodity Price Risk

Commodity price risk is the risk that a change in the price of a raw material used by a company will impact the income (and hence value) of a company that uses that raw material. For example, a plastics manufacturer may find its expenses going up more than anticipated if the price of oil (a raw material for most plastic) goes up unexpectedly. Factors that can affect commodity prices include political and regulatory changes, weather, technology, and overall market conditions.

III. MANAGING FINANCIAL RISK

Managing the exposure to financial risk typically involves some form of hedging. This section discusses the general types of hedging. In addition, it covers the concept of arbitrage, which is used primarily to maintain efficiency in key financial markets.

A. Passive or Natural Hedging

The first step in managing financial risk in many companies is to use passive, or natural, hedging. A natural hedge (typically used to address FX risk) occurs when a company holds both assets and liabilities in the same currency, allowing them to offset each other in the event of market fluctuation. For example, a non-European company that expects to earn future revenue in euros might arrange to finance part of its facilities with a euro-based loan. To the extent that the future earnings in euros match the loan payments in euros, the company is economically unaffected by changes in the value of the euro. A company may also implement a natural hedging strategy by incurring revenue and expenses in the same currency. If a firms incurs manufacturing costs in Mexican pesos, it may intentionally price its products in pesos to avoid FX exposure. Passive hedging strategies include borrowing and investing using currencies other than the organization's reporting currency (i.e., creating natural hedges), and can also include decisions around fixed versus floating borrowing, balance sheet matching, and fixed-price supplier agreements.

B. Active or Financial Hedging

Active, or financial, hedging is the process of using various financial instruments (discussed in more detail in the section below on derivatives as financial risk management tools) to reduce or eliminate risks associated with future cash flows, or the values of assets or liabilities. This is a core principle of treasury financial risk management. Hedging is similar to the concept of buying insurance to protect an asset, and the purpose of the hedge is to insure the asset's value (or minimize the risk on a liability) when its market value fluctuates.

In hedging a transaction, an organization reduces the uncertainty associated with a future FX rate, interest rate, or commodity price to minimize the risk in a transaction. For example, if a Japanese company sold EUR 6 million of product to a foreign trading partner with payment due in six months, the Japanese company might purchase a forward contract to deliver EUR 6 million in six months. By buying a forward contract now (discussed in more detail later in this chapter), the company is locking in an FX rate so that if the value of the euro (EUR) declines in the next six months, the company will not lose any value on the deal.[1] On the other hand, the company is also giving up any potential gain it might have made if the euro had gained in value over those same six months.

---

1. Alternatively, this transaction can be hedged by buying a futures contract or option, both of which are also discussed later in this chapter.

C. Speculation

Speculation goes beyond hedging and involves taking a position on the direction of the market in the attempt to make a profit, which is not usually a treasury objective. Most companies use hedging to minimize risk, not to make a profit. But some companies go a step further and attempt to use the products to make a profit. This is referred to as *speculation*. In many companies, corporate hedging policies forbid this type of speculation. For some organizations, however, speculation in certain markets may be a treasury objective, as determined by the board of directors. For example, financial institutions often have a trading floor for stocks, FX contracts, or interest contracts where speculation is encouraged as a means of revenue generation. Another example might be an energy company that speculates in certain energy markets (e.g., oil and gas) as part of its corporate objectives.

D. Arbitrage

Arbitrage is the process by which an asset is purchased in one market and simultaneously sold in another market to produce a riskless profit. While making a profit is not usually a treasury objective, it is important for a treasury professional to understand the arbitrage process because arbitrage is the primary mechanism that ensures efficiency in financial markets.

An example of arbitrage is referred to as *covered interest arbitrage*. In this case an investor takes advantage of differences in the interest rates in two different currencies by using a forward contract (discussed later in this chapter) to eliminate any exposure to changes in the currencies (i.e., to "cover" the investor). In theory, the exchange rates (both long and short) in the two currencies should be such that an investor would earn exactly the same amount no matter which currency was used for the investment. This is referred to as *interest rate parity*. Although it is uncommon, there can be situations where interest rate parity does not exist and investors can improve their returns by selecting the right currency.

For example, suppose the current spot exchange rate[2] is 1.1265 US dollars (USD) per euro (EUR), the six-month forward exchange rate is 1.1221 USD per EUR, and an investor has EUR 1,000,000 to invest. Assume also that the current euro deposit rate is 1.2% and the dollar deposit rate is 1.3% for six-month deposits. An investor can deposit the euros and earn EUR 6,000 in interest. However, the investor could also convert the euros to US dollars at the current spot rate and invest the resulting $1,126,500 at 1.3% for six months, returning $1,133,822.25, or EUR 1,010,446.71, for a profit of EUR 10,446.71. By investing in a covered forward, the investor increases his/her revenue by EUR 4,446.71 (less any fees charged for the forward), or 74%. As market participants buy US dollars in the spot market and sell US dollars in the forward market, the FX rates will move toward interest rate parity.

E. The Benefits of Financial Risk Management

Managing a company's risk helps to reduce the variability of both a company's future cash flows and its profitability due to external changes in FX rates, interest rates, and commodity prices, which consequently increases the company's value. Hedging enables treasury to smooth uneven cash flows due to unexpected external changes and forecast financial results with greater confidence. Less variability in expected future cash flows increases a firm's value in three ways:

- Greater predictability in future cash flows makes the company more attractive to shareholders.

- The company gains an enhanced borrowing advantage in credit markets because lenders view the firm as being less risky.

---

2 A spot exchange rate, or just spot rate, is the rate quoted for an immediate exchange of currencies, or "on the spot" delivery. In reality, spot deals are normally consummated with a one- or two-day lag.

· The company's probability of financial distress decreases because the firm can assess costs and revenues more accurately.

IV. DERIVATIVE INSTRUMENTS USED AS FINANCIAL RISK MANAGEMENT TOOLS

A derivative instrument is a financial product that acquires its value by inference through a formulaic connection to another asset. The other asset is termed the *underlying asset*, and can be a financial instrument (e.g., a stock or bond), currency, or commodity. For treasury professionals, the primary uses of these instruments are for managing FX (i.e., foreign currency), interest rate, and commodity price risks.

The use of derivatives may have an immediate impact on cash flow that is either favorable or unfavorable. Derivatives are complex and not always easy to understand, analyze, apply, account for, and report on. In considering the use of derivatives, a treasury professional must also consider the added cost of tax, regulatory, and reporting requirements related to the use of these instruments, which may dilute their value. Accordingly, many treasury professionals seek the advice of outside experts.

It is highly recommended that an organization that enters into a derivative contract execute an agreement with the counterparty to that contract. The International Swaps and Derivatives Association (ISDA) is a trade organization made up of companies, dealers, and service providers that participate in the market for over-the-counter (OTC) derivative instruments. The organization created a standardized contract, the ISDA master agreement, and most derivatives in the global derivatives market are documented using ISDA agreements and related documentation. The master agreement consists of standardized items, which include general terms and conditions, and a schedule. The schedule is an integral part of the master agreement. It is used to customize the master agreement by amending the standard terms and specifying certain details for the standard terms. When the agreement is signed, it governs all past and future transactions entered into between the parties. Consequently, it must be negotiated with great prudence. It should be noted that the standard terms normally include an agreement to comply with Dodd-Frank requirements regarding derivatives (which are discussed in Chapter 2, Legal and Regulatory Environment), making them binding on both US and non-US organizations that sign an ISDA agreement. The master agreement has no fixed term—it is open ended. If the parties want to end their relationship, they may terminate the master agreement formally or simply not enter into further contracts with one another. In dealing with derivatives, any organization must also consider the potential for counterparty risk, which is discussed in Chapter 16, Enterprise Risk Management.

The four basic types of derivative instruments are forwards, futures, swaps, and options.

A. Forwards

A forward contract is an agreement between two parties to buy or sell a fixed amount of an asset to be delivered at a future date and at a price agreed upon today. The underlying asset can be a financial instrument (e.g., a stock index fund or debt instrument), a currency (e.g., the euro or pound), or a commodity (e.g., gold or coffee). This contrasts with a spot contract, which is an agreement between two parties to buy or sell a fixed amount of an asset immediately or in the very near future (settlement is typically two days for currencies). The major difference between a forward and an option (discussed below) is that a forward transaction *must* occur while an option transaction *may* occur. In other words, settlement of a forward is mandatory, while the settlement of an option is optional at the discretion of the option holder. The future date is referred to as the contract's *maturity date*, and the price is called the *delivery price*. A company that purchases or sells a forward contract is one party to the contract; the other party to the contract is referred to as the *counterparty*. In forward currency contracts, the counterparty is typically a bank or dealer in the FX markets. The party that intends to purchase the underlying asset is said to be in a *long forward* contract position; the counterparty is in a *short forward* contract position. The long position in a forward contract gains value when the price of the underlying asset rises and loses value when the price of the underlying asset falls. Conversely, the short position gains value when the underlying asset price falls and loses value when it rises. Exhibits 17.1A and 17.1B depict the payoff profiles in a forward contract from a long and a short position, respectively. Note how a gain in the value of one contract is offset by the loss of value in the other.

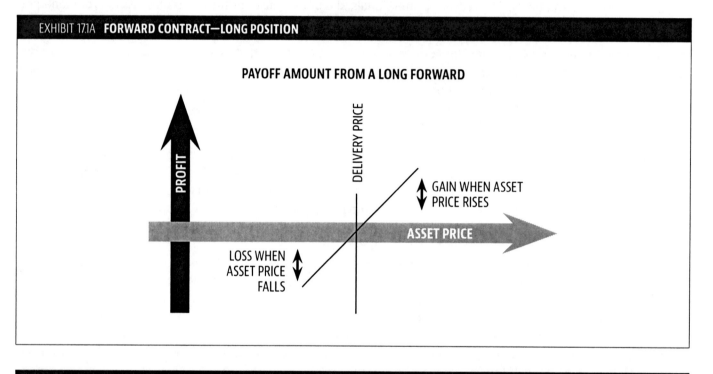

EXHIBIT 17.1A   FORWARD CONTRACT—LONG POSITION

PAYOFF AMOUNT FROM A LONG FORWARD

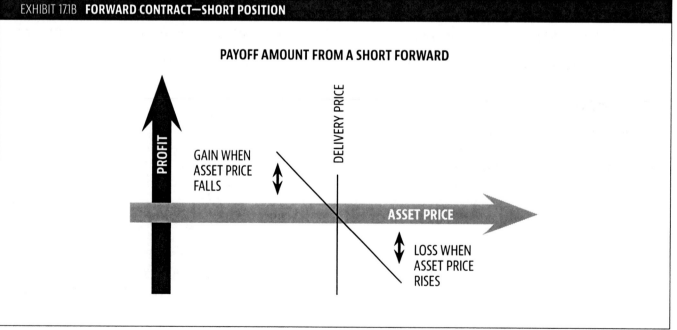

EXHIBIT 17.1B   FORWARD CONTRACT—SHORT POSITION

PAYOFF AMOUNT FROM A SHORT FORWARD

Forward markets are managed and supported by a group of banks, dealers, and traders that act as market makers (i.e., they quote both a bid and an ask price whenever requested to do so). Forward contracts are private contracts between two parties and are customized to each party's needs. The amount of the underlying asset and the maturity date of the contract are established when the contract is negotiated. In some cases, delivery of the underlying asset takes place at the maturity of the forward contract. There are many different types of forwards, with currency forwards and interest rate forwards being the most common.

B. Futures

Futures are similar to forwards in that the payoff profile from a long or short position in a futures contract looks exactly the same as the payoff in the respective forward contract (see Exhibits 17.1A and 17.1B). The main differences between futures and forwards are that (1) futures are standardized contracts traded on organized exchanges and (2) the counterparty to all futures contracts is the exchange itself. The fact that the exchange is the counterparty increases the liquidity of the contract and virtually eliminates counterparty risk.

Futures contracts are standardized by the exchanges with respect to contract size and delivery dates. As a result, a limited range of delivery dates is available, which may not always match the exact needs of an organization. Relative to forward contracts, futures contracts are easier and less expensive to acquire. On the other hand, since contract sizes and maturities are standardized, it is probably not possible to create a "perfect" hedge,[3] as may be accomplished with a forward contract. For example, the size of a typical British pound (GBP) futures contract on the Chicago Mercantile Exchange is GBP 62,500, and delivery dates are listed for March, June, September, and December. If an organization has an exposure that is not a multiple of this number and/or the delivery date on the contract is not the date when pounds are required, using a futures contract to hedge will not precisely mitigate the exposure.

Futures trading requires a margin account that is marked to market on a daily basis using the closing price of the previous business day. *Marked to market* means that the hedger's gains or losses on the position are reflected on a daily basis. If the margin account drops below a specified amount, termed the *maintenance margin*, then a margin call is issued. A margin call requires the account holder to deposit cash sufficient to replenish the account to the initial level, or to close out the position with the exchange. Rarely are futures contracts settled by delivery; instead, they typically are closed out (i.e., settled financially between the two parties) prior to maturity. Currency futures are discussed in detail later in this chapter.

C. Swaps

A swap is an agreement between two parties to exchange (or swap) a set of cash flows at a future point in time. The most common type of swap is an interest rate swap. In this type of swap, Party X agrees to pay Party Y a stream of cash flows equal to a floating rate of interest on some mutually agreed-upon amount. This amount is referred to as *notional principal* because the principal amount does not exchange hands; instead, only interest payments are exchanged. At the same time, Party Y agrees to pay Party X a stream of cash flows equal to a fixed rate of interest on the same notional principal at the same future dates. In other words, Party X is swapping a fixed-rate loan for a floating-rate loan while Party Y is doing exactly the opposite (and the swap is therefore commonly referred to as a *fixed-floating swap*).

Other types of swap arrangements include currency swaps, commodity swaps, and a type of interest rate swap called a *basis rate swap*. Currency swaps are agreements to convert an obligation in one currency to an obligation in another currency. Commodity swaps involve the exchange of a floating price on a commodity for a fixed price on the

---

3. A *perfect hedge* is defined as a hedge that eliminates all market risk from a given transaction. In other words, the hedge is exactly the inverse of the base transaction. Perfect hedges are hard to create since many derivatives are traded in standard amounts or have standard settlement dates.

same commodity over a specified period of time. The actual commodity is not exchanged—the swap is a purely financial transaction based on any change in the price of the commodity. Basis rate swaps are used to manage interest rate risk and typically involve swapping one rate base for another (e.g., swapping the US prime rate for the London Interbank Offered Rate [LIBOR]). Examples of currency and interest rate swaps are discussed later in this chapter.

One of the risks in using swaps, as with any derivative, is counterparty risk. The value of the swap depends upon the other party fulfilling its obligation to make the agreed-upon payment stream. If the other party (the counterparty) does not make the payments, then the first party may still be liable for the original payment stream or cash flow. Using a trusted third party, such as a bank or FX dealer, helps mitigate the counterparty risk as the third party is responsible for evaluating the credit quality of each party involved in the swap.

D. Options

An option is a contract giving the buyer of the contract the right, but not the obligation, to buy or sell a fixed amount of an underlying asset at a fixed price on or before a specified date (see the discussion in the next paragraph regarding European versus American styles of options). The counterparty is called the *writer* of the option and receives the premium (price) paid for the contract. Options may be exchange-traded contracts or contracts negotiated with a specific counterparty. Exchange-traded options share many of the characteristics of futures contracts. They are standardized with respect to the quantity and delivery dates covered by the contract. In financial risk management, options can be used to manage FX, interest rate, and commodity risk for an organization. This section covers the basics of options and their valuation. The specific types of options used for FX and interest rate management are covered later in this chapter.

Unlike an American option, which allows the contract to be exercised at any time on or before the delivery date, a European option may be exercised only on the delivery date. Under similar conditions, an American option will sell for a larger premium than a European option because the American option may be exercised at any time on or before its expiration date. Alternatively, a Bermuda option's exercise feature places it between American and European option contracts. It is exercisable only on specified dates that are spaced evenly over the option's life. Since its exercise feature is less liberal than an American option's but more liberal than a European option's, its premium is lower than the premium on an American option, but higher than the premium on a European option, for like circumstances.

1. CALL VERSUS PUT OPTIONS

A call option gives the contract owner the right, but not the obligation, to buy (call) the underlying asset from the contract writer at a fixed price through the delivery date. A put option gives the contract owner the right, but not the obligation, to sell (put) the underlying asset to the contract writer at a fixed price through the delivery date. This fixed price is called the *strike price* or *exercise price* of the contract. A call option is said to be "in the money" when the current market price is higher than the contract's strike price.

Assume for example that the current market price for oil is $55 per barrel. If an organization expects the price of oil to go up (or merely wants to protect against a rise in the price of oil since oil is used in production), it can purchase a call option to buy a specific quantity of oil, say 1,000 barrels, at $60 per barrel. The strike price of the contract is $60, and the company will pay a premium of approximately $5 per barrel, or $5,000, for the contract. If the price of oil does not go up or actually falls, the option is not exercised, and the company loses the $5,000 option premium.

Assume instead that oil goes up to $70 per barrel. The company will exercise its option to buy oil at $60 per barrel and then sell it at $70, for a gross profit of $10 per barrel, less the premium, for a net profit of $5 per barrel, or $5,000. (If this had been a commodity hedge for raw materials, the company would have saved $5,000 in expense rather than making a profit.)

The break-even price for the company in this case is $65 per barrel, since that is the point at which the profit on the contract will offset the premium paid for the contract.[4] It should be noted that this is a simple example to illustrate how an option might be used to hedge price risk. Options are much more complex in practice.

2. OPTION PREMIUMS

The option buyer pays a premium to the option writer in exchange for the ability to call or put the option (i.e., buy or sell the underlying asset). The premium for an American option contract will assume a larger time value[5] than will a European option contract because the American contract may be exercised any time through the delivery date. The owner of a European contract cannot gain from a rise in the price of the underlying asset until the delivery date because the contract may be exercised only on the delivery date. Thus, the time value of a European option will be smaller. As discussed above, a Bermuda option will fall somewhere between these two extremes.

The premium (or price) of an option contract represents a combination of the intrinsic value (i.e., the amount by which the option is in the money) and the time value. Suppose a call contract on a commodity has been written with a strike price of $50 per ton. If the commodity is now selling for $54 per ton, the intrinsic value of the option contract is $4. Suppose that the option expires tomorrow. If the owner sells the contract at this point, a buyer will pay at most $4 per ton for the contract because at that price the contract can be used to purchase the commodity at $50, resulting in a $54 per-ton cost to the buyer of the contract if it is exercised (the total of the $4 price for the option and the $50 cost to exercise the option)—the same as the price of the commodity in the open market. The seller of the contract will not accept less than $4 because the contract can be used to purchase the commodity for $50. If it is sold, the seller of the contract will have to pay $54 for the commodity in the open market. Therefore, if the option expires tomorrow, the option premium will be approximately $4. If the option has three months left until maturity, the price of the commodity may increase more during the remaining time and the premium will be above $4 due to the time value. As the option approaches maturity, the time value of the option will decrease and the option price will move toward the intrinsic value. Overall, the price of the option will depend on the price of the underlying asset, the strike price, the time to maturity, and the volatility of the asset price. Option pricing models, such as Black-Scholes, incorporate all of these variables to calculate the fair value of an option.

There are five possible relationships between an option's premium and its strike (exercise) price:

- A call or put option is "at the money" if the underlying asset price is equal to the strike price of the option.
- A call option is "out of the money" if the asset price is less than the strike price of the option.
- A put option is "out of the money" if the asset price is greater than the strike price of the option.
- A call option is "in the money" if the asset price is greater than the strike price of the option.
- A put option is "in the money" if the asset price is less than the strike price of the option.

Option pricing examples that illustrate the possible relationships between an option's premium and its strike price are shown in Exhibits 17.2A and 17.2B. The time value of the option is not included; only the relationship between the price of the underlying asset, the option premium, and the profit or loss position on the option is shown.

---

4. For purposes of illustration, this example ignores any broker's fees or other transaction costs that would typically increase the cost of the option to the buyer.
5. Time value is that part of the premium that is based on the probability that the value of the underlying asset will increase or decrease over the life of the contract. The amount of the premium is based on the amount the writer of the option expects the price of the commodity to change over the life of the option.

Exhibit 17.2A follows the call option example given earlier in the section on option premiums, and Exhibit 17.2B examines the corresponding put option.

EXHIBIT 17.2A CALL OPTION PRICING

A CALL OPTION WITH A $50 STRIKE PRICE IS PURCHASED WHEN THE UNDERLYING ASSET IS SELLING FOR $46 PER UNIT. THE PREMIUM PAID IS $1.

PRICE OF UNDERLYING ASSET ($)	PREMIUM PAID ($)	$50 CALL OPTION VALUE ($)	PROFIT (+) OR LOSS (-) ($)	CALL OPTION IS IN, AT, OR OUT OF THE MONEY
46	1	0	-1	OUT
47	1	0	-1	OUT
48	1	0	-1	OUT
49	1	0	-1	OUT
50	1	0	-1	AT
51	1	1	0	IN
52	1	2	+1	IN
53	1	3	+2	IN
54	1	4	+3	IN
55	1	5	+4	IN

EXHIBIT 17.2B PUT OPTION PRICING

A PUT OPTION WITH A $50 STRIKE PRICE IS PURCHASED WHEN THE UNDERLYING ASSET IS SELLING FOR $54 PER UNIT. THE PREMIUM PAID IS $1.

PRICE OF UNDERLYING ASSET ($)	PREMIUM PAID ($)	$50 PUT OPTION VALUE ($)	PROFIT (+) OR LOSS (-) ($)	PUT OPTION IS IN, AT, OR OUT OF THE MONEY
54	1	0	-1	OUT
53	1	0	-1	OUT
52	1	0	-1	OUT
51	1	0	-1	OUT
50	1	0	-1	AT
49	1	1	0	IN
48	1	2	+1	IN
47	1	3	+2	IN
46	1	4	+3	IN
45	1	5	+4	IN

A call option is purchased by a party that wishes to control its effective cost paid for a commodity (note that the actual cost will still vary but the company has limited its exposure to this change through buying an option). A put option is purchased by a party that wishes to control the effective price for which the commodity can be sold. This party may be in possession of the asset or may be speculating that the market price of the asset will decline.

In practice, the purchaser of a call contract normally does not exercise the option to buy, and the purchaser of a put contract normally does not exercise the option to sell. The actual commodity transaction occurs in the spot market. The option contract is sold and its value is used to offset losses if the asset price is higher (call option) or lower (put option) than the strike price. If a party writes (sells) a call option contract, it is setting a ceiling on the asset price it will receive in exchange for the premium obtained. The writer of a put contract is ensuring a floor on the price at which it is willing to sell the asset in exchange for the premium.

Options are also useful for a company that is bidding on a business contract that would result in exchange rate exposures if the bid is accepted. For example, a US company bids on providing products or services priced in euros (EUR) to a French company. The US company is uncertain whether it will win the bid, but if its bid is accepted, then the company will have an exposure that results from euro-denominated receivables.

A currency call option lets the company lock in a minimum value of euros for a known premium amount. If the company does not win the bid, then the option can be closed out or allowed to expire if it is out of the money. The company is not obligated to exchange the currencies as it would be had it entered into a forward contract, nor has it exposed itself to possible losses as would be true had it purchased a futures contract. The price of these advantages is the premium paid for the currency call option contract.

It is important to realize that the option premium is paid at the time the option contract is written, even if the underlying transaction is never completed because it is not in the money. This is in contrast with a forward contract, where the underlying transaction is always completed, either through delivery of the asset or through unwinding, or buying out, the transaction.

E. Comparison of Forwards, Futures, and Options

	FORWARD CONTRACT	FUTURES CONTRACT	OPTION CONTRACT
DEFINITION	An agreement between two parties to buy or sell an asset at a fixed point in time for a specified price	A standardized contract to buy or sell an asset at a certain point in the future for a specified price	A contract that gives the buyer the option to buy (call) or sell (put) an asset at some point in the future for a specified price
CONTRACT SIZE	Customized to the needs of the customer	Standardized size and time periods	Standardized if exchange-traded but customized if individually contracted
EXPIRATION DATE	Negotiable	Standardized	Standardized and negotiable are both available.
MARKET	Negotiated directly between the parties with no initial payment	Traded on an exchange with an initial margin deposit required	Exchange-traded or negotiated directly between two parties; if exchange-traded, typically requires a margin deposit
REGULATION	Not regulated	Government-regulated (CFTC in the United States)	Exchange-traded options are regulated by the exchange rules.
SETTLEMENT	Mandatory	Mandatory	Optional

V. FOREIGN EXCHANGE (FX) RISK MANAGEMENT

Managing the risks related to changing FX rates is a critical part of managing global treasury operations. This section discusses the risks and issues related to managing FX rate fluctuations.

A. Challenges in International/Global Treasury Management

The objectives of global treasury management are similar to those of domestic treasury management, with the main objective being the efficient use of an organization's global cash resources in a manner consistent with its strategic goals. A global treasury operation must also manage cross-border funds movement and use FX and liquidity management techniques that are different from those used within just one country. The selection of financial service providers that are capable of assisting a company with international operations is a critical aspect of the global treasury management process.

1. FX RISK

International companies with cash flows in various foreign currencies are exposed to FX risk. A company must assess the volatility of the different types and levels of FX rate fluctuations for each specific currency involved and how changes in FX rates can impact its balance sheet and income statement. Methods for managing FX risk are covered elsewhere in this chapter. Companies that conduct business globally but only in their base, or reporting, currency sometimes falsely assume that they have eliminated their FX risk. In reality, they have only transferred the risk to their global trading partners, who will typically include the cost of any FX risk in making their trading decisions. As a result, companies that demand payment in their reporting currency may limit their explicit (balance sheet) FX risk, but assume an implicit (cash flow) FX risk that can reduce the market competitiveness of their products.

2. CASH FLOW COMPLEXITY

A global company must manage the cash flows from subsidiaries, suppliers, and customers in each country in which it operates. Due to widely differing regulations, banking practices, payment systems, and levels of information availability, global companies must often manage treasury transactions in different currencies, as well as those transactions that cross national boundaries.

3. TAX ISSUES

Global companies face a myriad of tax laws and regulations. Global treasury operations often are required to seek expert tax and legal advice to interpret the rules and regulations of different, and sometimes conflicting, tax authorities. It is important to involve tax and legal experts in the development of any FX or global trading strategy.

B. FX Rates

1. FOREIGN CURRENCY QUOTATION FORMATS

FX rates, or spot rates, are quoted in several ways, depending on the currencies and the markets involved. An FX rate is typically expressed as the equivalent unit of one currency per unit of another currency at a given moment in time.

Foreign currency quotation formats tend to be structured as:

[Currency X] / [Currency Y] Rate

This can be read as "one unit of Currency X is equal to rate multiplied by one unit of Currency Y." To determine the cost in Currency Y of a given number of units of Currency X, just multiply that number by the rate. Conversely, to determine the amount of Currency X that could be purchased with a given amount of Currency Y, divide the amount of Currency Y by the rate.

From a US perspective, there are two ways to quote FX rates: the US dollar (USD) equivalent of one unit of foreign currency, or the foreign currency equivalent of one US dollar. If Currency Y is the US dollar, this is called a *USD equivalent quote*. If Currency X is the US dollar, this is called a *foreign currency equivalent quote*. To convert a foreign currency equivalent quote to a USD equivalent quote, use the following formula:

USD Equivalent = 1 ÷ Foreign Currency Equivalent

In the spot market, the standard market convention for quoting most currencies in comparison to the USD is the European quotation convention (i.e., the number of foreign currency units that one US dollar will purchase). The British pound (GBP), euro (EUR), Australian dollar (AUD), and New Zealand dollar (NZD) are exceptions to this rule and are quoted as USD equivalent rates (i.e., the number of USD that one GBP or EUR will purchase), which is known as the *American quotation convention*. The following table displays examples of both types of quotation formats for selected foreign currencies, with the most common format used for each currency indicated in italic/bold type.

Sample Foreign Currency Quotation Formats

CURRENCY	AMERICAN CONVENTION (USD EQUIVALENT)	EUROPEAN CONVENTION (NON-USD EQUIVALENT)
British pound (GBP)	*GBP/USD 1.3199*	USD/GBP 0.7576
Canadian dollar (CAD)	CAD/USD 0.7744	*USD/CAD 1.2914*
Euro (EUR)	*EUR/USD 1.1307*	USD/EUR 0.8844
Japanese yen (JPY)	JPY/USD 0.009976	*USD/JPY 100.24*

Calculation Example: FX Conversion

In the table above, the quote for British pounds is:

GBP/USD 1.3199

This expression means that every British pound costs $1.3199. Since the US dollar (USD) cost of a single British pound is known, the USD cost of 250,000 pounds can be calculated by multiplying 250,000 by the rate, as in the following calculation:

$$GBP\ 250,000 = 250,000 \times 1.3199 = USD\ 329,975$$

Similarly, to determine how many pounds can be purchased with $100,000, the following calculation would be used:

$$USD\ 100,000 = 100,000 \div 1.3199 = GBP\ 75,763.32$$

2. BID-OFFER QUOTES

Banks and other dealers quote both bid and offer rates for foreign currency. The bid rate is the rate at which a dealer is willing to buy currency. The offer rate is the rate at which a dealer is willing to sell currency. The difference between the bid rate and the offer rate is referred to as the *bid-offer spread* or *bid-ask spread*. The spread covers the dealer's exposures, expenses, and profits.

The bid-offer quote is usually structured in the following format:

[Currency X] / [Currency Y] Bid Rate–Offer Rate

The bid rate is the rate at which the dealer is willing to buy Currency X and sell Currency Y. Conversely, the offer rate is the rate at which the dealer is willing to sell Currency X and buy Currency Y.

Calculation Example: Bid-Offer Quote

For this example, assume a dealer provides a bid-offer quote of USD/JPY 100.22–100.26 (often just abbreviated as USD/JPY 100.22–26). This means the dealer is willing to buy (bid) one US dollar (USD) at JPY 100.22 and sell (offer) one USD at JPY 100.26.

If a US organization wants to sell $50,000 to the dealer in exchange for Japanese yen (JPY), then the dealer buys (bids) the $50,000 from the organization for JPY 5,011,000. This is calculated as:

$$\text{JPY Amount} = \text{USD}\,50,000 \times 100.22 = \text{JPY}\,5,011,000$$

However, if the same US organization sells the JPY 5,011,000 back to the dealer in exchange for dollars, the dealer sells (offers) the organization only $49,980.05, calculated as:

$$\text{USD Amount} = \frac{\text{JPY}\,5,011,000}{100.26} = \text{USD}\,49,980.05$$

The difference of $19.95 (i.e., $50,000 − $49,980.05) represents the dealer's spread, or earnings, on the round-trip transaction.

3. HOW RATES ARE OBTAINED

Most companies that are active in the FX markets subscribe to one of the real-time rate reporting and/or electronic trading services, such as Bloomberg, EBS BrokerTec, or Reuters. Companies trading in the FX market on a less frequent basis may access FX rates through a bank or FX dealer or through online trading platforms such as FXall and 360 Treasury Systems AG (360T). Rates also are available on the Internet from a variety of sources. However, free services generally have a slight time delay. If a treasury professional is using a website for free market rate information, it is essential to understand the timing lags between the rates quoted online and the current market rate. The timing difference may vary from a 15-minute delay to a one-day lag.

4. FX SPOT VERSUS FORWARD QUOTES

There are two basic FX markets: the spot market and the forward market. A rate quoted in the spot market is called the *spot FX rate* (also referred to as a *spot rate* or *spot contract*). Regular spot settlement is one or two days, depending on the currency pair selected. Faster settlement may be possible, but it is often at a less favorable rate than the spot rate.

A forward FX rate (*forward rate*) is a rate quoted for the delivery (or settlement) of currency beyond the terms of a spot contract. Most FX forward contracts mature within one year, but they can go beyond one year depending on a company's FX risk profile.

The forward rate is based on the spot rate, plus or minus forward points. Forward points reflect the difference between two countries' short-term money market interest rates (e.g., rates on short-term government borrowing or interbank rates) at the time the trade is executed. The interest rate differential between two countries determines if respective currencies will trade at par, at a discount, or at a premium in the forward market:

- **Par:** If the spot rate and forward rate are the same, then the forward rate is at par with the spot rate. In theory, this implies that the interest rate structure between the two countries is the same. Because this occurs only rarely, currencies generally trade at a discount or premium.

- **Discount:** A currency is at a discount when it is worth less in the forward market than in the spot market. The currency with the higher interest rate will trade at a discount in the forward market against a currency with a lower interest rate.

- **Premium:** A currency is at a premium when it is worth more in the forward market than in the spot market. The currency with the lower interest rate will trade at a premium in the forward market against a currency with a higher interest rate.

· **Points:** Premiums and discounts are commonly quoted in points (basis points, or 1/100th of a percent). In the jargon of the industry, forward points are added to the spot rate when there is a premium and are subtracted from the spot rate in the case of a discount.

The relationship among the spot, forward, and interest rates is known as *interest rate parity* (discussed earlier in this chapter). As long as FX and interest rate markets are efficient,[6] it should not be possible to take a loan in one country with lower interest rates, invest those funds in another country with higher interest rates, return the funds to the original country, and generate a higher rate of return than could have been earned in the original country's money market. If an advantage to investing in another country's money market exists, it will be eliminated quickly because spot rates and forward rates adjust to the cross-border money flows created by investors as they attempt to capture the advantage. Thus, the difference observed between spot and forward market rates is not a prediction of the future movement of the spot rate; rather, it represents an adjustment of the exchange rate that gives economic recognition to the difference between short-term interest rates in the two countries.

C. Emerging Markets

For global companies operating in emerging markets, there may be some special challenges to managing the risk related to dealing with local currencies and governments in these markets. Some emerging economies have very tightly managed currencies, in terms of both exchange rates and availability. Management of FX exposures and risk in these situations may be very different from the more traditional FX risk management in more commonly traded currencies. It is important to be aware that organizations actually introduce greater elements of financial uncertainty when they fail to take adequate measures to address FX-related risk. Considering that emerging market FX risk is becoming more common within international enterprises, this is now more relevant to more businesses than ever before.

1. EMERGING MARKET/EXOTIC CURRENCIES

On a broad level, emerging market currencies (often referred to as *exotic currencies* because they are not commonly traded) fall into one of several different categories contributing to the underlying risk profile:

· Free-floating currencies that are traded with some degree of transparency

· Currencies that trade subject to strict regulations imposed by monetary authorities in the country

· Currencies that are pegged to another currency in some form

· Currencies that trade within a band against other currencies

· Currencies that are not freely convertible

Examples of exotic currencies currently include the New Belarusian ruble (BYN), the Lebanese pound (LBP), the Samoan tala (WST), and the Iraqi dinar (IQD).

2. ISSUES WITH EXOTIC CURRENCIES

Emerging market FX risk may be a consideration for some multinationals, especially in view of the growth in business in emerging markets. Although FX exposures in major economies can be addressed using mainstream risk management instruments and techniques, the same is not necessarily the case with emerging markets. In particular, exotic currencies have unique characteristics that often impede more commonplace approaches to controlling FX risk.

---

6. In this context, efficient markets would mean zero (or at least very low) transaction costs, perfect and costless information, no barriers to entry, and the ability of market participants to borrow or invest at some risk-free rate. While these conditions are not likely for the average investor, they may be possible for large institutional players, such as global banks and central banks.

The characteristics of exotic currencies typically include the following:

- Illiquidity

- Volatility

- Reduced transparency

- Limited derivative availability

- Capital controls

- Government intervention in FX markets

- Heightened carrying risk

- Pricing distortions

- Limited risk-sharing options

- Minimal internal hedging alternatives

- Transfer risks

VI. CURRENCY DERIVATIVES USED TO HEDGE FOREIGN EXCHANGE (FX) EXPOSURE

Once a company has identified and quantified material exposures to exchange rate changes, it must decide whether to hedge each exposure. There are several instruments that a company can use to manage FX rate risk. While these tools were discussed briefly above, they are discussed in more detail in this section.

A. Currency Forwards

A currency or FX forward is a commitment to buy or sell a specified amount of foreign currency on a future date at an agreed-upon exchange rate today. FX forwards are available through banks and other FX traders in most major currencies and in commonly available maturities of one, two, three, six, nine, and twelve months. Since these contracts are sold in the OTC market, they may be negotiated for most currencies and maturities, given a willing counterparty. Because forwards are credit instruments that relate to a company's ability to deliver at the end of the contract, the dealers or counterparties in FX forwards are often banks. As a result, the legal documentation concerning FX forwards usually involves credit-related risk issues and, in many cases, the dealer or counterparty may require the company to execute an ISDA master agreement before FX forward contracts can be initiated. The forward rate, or the rate at which the two currencies will be exchanged, depends upon three factors:

- The current spot rate

- The term of the forward contract

- The current interest rates in the two countries during the term

Forward contracts are useful tools for managing currency exposure because uncertainty is exchanged for a certain outcome. The company is protected against losses if the currency moves against the underlying exposure, although it forgoes any benefit if the currency moves in favor of the underlying exposure. Forward contracts are best suited for known (or contracted) exposures and when there is a need to lock in the rate to eliminate uncertainty.

Calculation Example: Currency Forward

The following example assumes that a US importer has agreed to pay in British pounds (GBP). The US importer must pay an invoice for GBP 125,000 in 90 days.

- · The importer could purchase a forward contract today for GBP quoted at $1.3243 in US dollars (USD) per GBP (i.e., GBP/USD 1.3243), deliverable in 90 days.

- · At the end of 90 days, the importer would pay $165,537.50, calculated as follows:

$$\text{USD Amount} = 1.3243 \times \text{GBP } 125,000 = \text{USD } 165,537.50$$

- · Upon payment of this amount on the contract, the US importer would receive GBP 125,000 to pay the invoice.

- · Therefore, no matter what fluctuation occurred in the exchange rate during the next 90-day period, the purchase of the forward contract locks in the exchange rate for British pounds.

A window forward is a variation on the standard forward contract. In a window forward, rather than settling on a specific date, the forward allows settlement during a given period (or "window") of time. This type of forward allows some flexibility in dealing with potential production or legal delays but will typically cost more than a standard forward since the counterparty does not know exactly when the contract will settle and will typically price on the worst-case scenario.

An average-rate forward is a tool that is used when the hedger will be trading funds at some point in the future, but does not know the exact dates and volumes of the individual trades. An average-rate forward allows the buyer the ability to create a hedge rate for this unknown future exposure by locking in forward points and a spot rate today. At some specified point in the future, there is an averaging period of daily spot observations to determine an average rate that, when compared to the hedge rate, will set the payout.

The principal derivative of choice for exotic currencies is the non-deliverable forward (NDF). The NDF is considered a synthetic instrument in that it is cash-settled in a major base currency (i.e., USD, EUR, etc.).[7] It is used as a proxy hedge in a situation in which an exotic currency is not actively traded in the forward market. In this case, a *proxy hedge* is defined as a hedge in an alternate currency that is actively traded and that typically moves in the same direction as the desired currency. The challenge is finding an appropriate proxy currency.

As NDF contracts are cash-settled, there is no actual exchange of the underlying currencies on settlement. Settlement simply reflects the difference between the previously agreed-upon NDF rate and the existing spot rate at the time of fixing. This difference should approximately offset what occurred over the same time with respect to the underlying exotic currency relative to the base currency.

For example, a Canadian company is importing products from China. The Canadian company is billed in Chinese renminbi (CNY) but pays its invoices in US dollars (USD). The company can purchase a USD/CNY NDF based on the amount and terms of its current invoice from its Chinese supplier to hedge against possible changes in the USD/CNY FX rate. At settlement time, the company will pay its supplier in USD and settle with its counterparty on the NDF in USD for any change in the FX rate. No renminbi will ever change hands.

In addition to NDFs (and similar to basic, "plain vanilla" option contracts), non-deliverable option (NDO) contracts can be used to address exotic FX risk. The NDO extends to the buyer the right, but not the obligation, to buy (via a call option) or sell (via a put option) a set amount of foreign currency at a specified rate, or strike price, on a

---

7. A synthetic security is created by combining one set of securities (usually including some type of derivative) to mimic the properties of another security.

predetermined future date. Fundamentally, the NDO serves as an insurance policy against undesirable market trends. The significant difference between an NDF and an NDO is that the NDO gives the user the right, but not the obligation, to buy or sell a prearranged amount of foreign currency at a specified rate and on a predetermined future date, while the NDF requires that the contract be consummated.

B. Currency Futures

Currency futures contracts are similar to currency forwards except that futures are traded on organized exchanges and are standardized in terms of their amount and maturity date. Currency futures were initially offered at the Chicago Mercantile Exchange (CME), now known as CME Group, which is still the largest regulated currency futures marketplace in the world, but they are now offered by a number of exchanges around the world. Typically, the market price for a currency futures contract will be relatively the same no matter which broker is used.

Currency futures, like any other futures contracts, are marked to market and require the investor to maintain a margin account to protect against potential adverse changes in the value of the contract. With a margin account, currency traders are able to purchase contracts for some multiple of the amount in their margin account. Therefore, rather than paying the full purchase price at the time they purchase a contract, traders can purchase contracts for multiples of their margin account. In effect they "borrow" money from their broker to buy futures contracts and repay the loan on settlement. If the value of the contract ever falls below the amount in the margin account, the trader will be asked to deposit additional funds due to the margin call. If the trader is unable to do this, the broker or exchange will normally liquidate the trader's position immediately and charge any loss to the margin account. The size of the margin is dependent upon the rules of the specific exchange and broker, and in some cases the type of contract. For example, the Montreal Exchange requires a larger margin for speculative accounts than it does for hedging transactions.

An illustrative listing of some of the more common contracts available on the CME and their required margins is provided in Exhibit 17.3. Contracts are generally offered for six-month maturities on a quarterly cycle (i.e., March, June, September, and December).

EXHIBIT 17.3 SELECTED CURRENCY CONTRACTS ON CME

CURRENCY PAIR	CONTRACT SIZE	MARGIN REQUIRED
EUR/USD	EUR 125,000	$3,350
USD/JPY	JPY 12,500,000	$4,100
GBP/USD	GBP 62,500	$3,600
USD/CHF	CHF 125,000	$3,600
USD/CAD	CAD 100,000	$1,450

Note: CHF is the designation for the Swiss franc.

Calculation Example: Currency Futures

Consider the example of a US import company that must pay an invoice for GBP 125,000 in 90 days. The company is uncertain regarding the future exchange rate and wishes to prevent exposure due to fluctuations in the value of the British pound (GBP). The company decides to purchase a futures contract for pounds today and hold the contract until the currency must be purchased in the spot market.

- If the value of the pound rises, causing an increase in the company's cost to pay the invoice, then the company could sell the futures contract (the price of which would also rise) for a profit. The profit gained on the futures contract is then used to offset the higher purchase price of the pounds in the spot market.

- Assume that a futures contract allows the company to purchase pounds at a rate of GBP/USD 1.3251, and assume that the information in Exhibit 17.3 is currently valid. The company would need to purchase two GBP futures contracts (at GBP 62,500 each) to fully hedge its exposure of GBP 125,000. In this case, the margin requirement for the position would be $3,600 per contract, for a total margin requirement of $7,200.

- If the GBP futures contracts decrease in value on a given day, money will be taken from the margin account. If the contracts increase in value on a given day, money will be added to the margin account when the position is marked to market.

- For example, suppose that at the end of the first day, the contract price settles at GBP/USD 1.3403. The value of the two contracts has increased by a total of $1,900, and the new value on the margin account after marking to market is $9,100, calculated as follows:

$$\text{Change in Contract Value} = (1.3403 - 1.3251) \times \text{GBP}\,125,000 = \text{USD}\,1,900$$

$$\text{New Margin Account Value} = \$7,200 + \$1,900 = \$9,100$$

- If the futures contract price decreases to GBP/USD 1.3354 the next day, then the resulting change in fair (or mark-to-market) value will be a negative $612.50, which must be subtracted from the margin account when it is marked to market. The value of the margin account after the second day will be $8,487.50, which still exceeds the minimum margin requirement. These calculations are illustrated below. Note that the process of marking the position to market at the end of each day will continue as long as the position is open.

$$\text{Change in Contract Value} = (1.3354 - 1.3403) \times \text{GBP}\,125,000 = -\text{USD}\,612.50$$

$$\text{New Margin Account Value} = \$9,100 - \$612.50 = \$8,487.50$$

- Assume that when the company needs to buy pounds in 90 days, the exchange rate has risen to GBP/USD 1.3934. In this scenario, the company could buy the pounds in the spot market, paying GBP/USD 1.3934. The futures contract that the company holds to buy at GBP/USD 1.3251 has a profit of $0.0683 per pound, calculated as follows:

$$\text{Profit on Contract} = \$1.3934 - \$1.3251 = \$0.0683\,\text{per GBP}$$

The company sells the contract back to the exchange and uses the profit of $0.0683 per GBP to offset the purchase price on the spot market, effectively achieving a net price of $1.3251 per pound.

- If, instead, the exchange rate has dropped to GBP/USD 1.2951, then the company would still buy the needed GBP in the spot market and would close the futures contract (i.e., sell the contract back to the exchange) at a loss of $0.0300 per pound, calculated as follows:

$$\text{Loss on Contract} = \$1.2951 - \$1.3251 = -\$0.0300 \text{ per GBP}$$

- In either case, the net cost of GBP to the company would still be GBP/USD 1.3251, and the total cost to pay the invoice would be $165,637.50 (1.3251 × GBP 125,000).

C. Currency Swaps

A currency swap typically involves the exchange of a cash flow denominated in one currency with a cash flow denominated in another currency, as well as an exchange of principal. The two cash flows can be at either fixed or floating rates. In the example below, both are fixed. A swap can also be used to change the value date of a forward when a company cannot meet the original delivery date due to unexpected circumstances, such as a late payment from a foreign customer.

Calculation Example: Currency Swap

Consider the following example of a currency swap, as illustrated in Exhibit 17.4. A US-based firm (Company A) wishes to borrow JPY 100 million for 10 years to fund an investment in Japan, and the current exchange rate is USD/JPY 99.0099. Since Company A is based in the United States, it has better access to the US capital markets and can borrow at a relatively lower interest rate in the United States. In this case, Company A may be able to lock in a lower interest rate by borrowing in US dollars (USD) and converting to Japanese yen (JPY) at the spot rate.

However, the company will face exchange rate risk throughout the life of the loan if yen-denominated cash flows from the Japanese investment are the anticipated source for interest and principal payments. Company A may use a currency swap to manage the FX exposure.

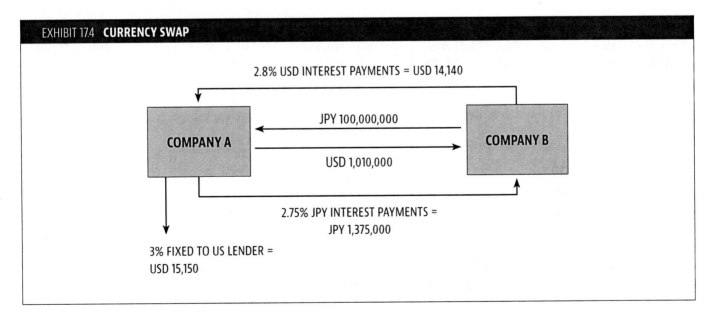

EXHIBIT 17.4 **CURRENCY SWAP**

2.8% USD INTEREST PAYMENTS = USD 14,140

COMPANY A

JPY 100,000,000

USD 1,010,000

COMPANY B

2.75% JPY INTEREST PAYMENTS = JPY 1,375,000

3% FIXED TO US LENDER = USD 15,150

Suppose that Company A borrows $1,010,000 (the USD equivalent of JPY 100 million) for 10 years at a fixed interest rate of 3%. The company can then enter into a currency swap with a counterparty (Company B, typically a bank) to obtain the yen-denominated funding while limiting the exchange rate risk. Under the terms of the swap, Company A will make semiannual payments in yen to Company B (the counterparty) at a fixed rate of 2.75%, and Company B will make semiannual payments in US dollars to Company A at a fixed rate of 2.8%. A currency swap will typically specify that the company and counterparty exchange the notional principal at the beginning and end of the swap.

Therefore, the currency swap will consist of the following transactions:

· Company A will pay $1,010,000 to Company B, and Company B will pay Company A JPY 100 million. Company A can then use the JPY 100 million to make its investment in Japan.

· Every six months for 10 years, Company A and Company B will make the following payments:

  ○ Company A will pay Company B JPY 1,375,000 from local yen currency that it has obtained from its Japanese investment, calculated as:

$$0.0275 \times \text{JPY } 100,000,000 \times (180 \div 360) = \text{JPY } 1,375,000$$

  ○ Company B will pay Company A $14,140, calculated as:

$$0.028 \times \$1,010,000 \times (180 \div 360) = \$14,140$$

At the end of 10 years, the Japanese investment will mature, returning to Company A the JPY 100 million principal, which Company A will then pay to Company B. Company B will pay Company A $1,010,000.

This structure will allow Company A to borrow in the market in which it has a competitive advantage (i.e., the United States), obtain the yen needed to finance operations in Japan, and minimize the risk associated with changes in the FX rate. Since Company A issued USD debt at 3%, the semiannual interest payment to the US creditors will be $15,150, calculated as:

$$0.03 \times \$1,010,000 \times (180 \div 360) = \$15,150$$

Assuming the exchange rate continues to be USD/JPY 99.0099, Company A will also make semiannual interest payments of $13,887.50 (JPY 1,375,000 ÷ 99.0099) to Company B, and will receive $14,140.00 every six months from Company B, under the terms of the swap. As a result, the net semiannual interest expense for Company A will be $14,897.50, calculated as:

$$\$15,150.00 + \$13,887.50 - \$14,140.00 = \$14,897.50$$

D. Currency Options

A currency option gives the buyer the right to buy (call) or sell (put) a fixed amount of a foreign currency at a fixed exchange rate (the strike price) on or before a specific future date. For example, a foreign currency call option sets a ceiling price to buy a foreign currency in terms of the domestic currency. The ceiling price is the strike price plus the premium paid for the call. Assume a call option on euros (EUR) has a strike price of $1.20 with a premium of $0.10. The maximum price, or ceiling, for this arrangement will be $1.30 (i.e., $1.20 + $0.10) per euro. Stated another way, the buyer will pay no more than $1.30 (net) to purchase EUR 1.00.

On the other hand, a foreign currency put option establishes a floor value to sell a foreign currency in terms of the domestic currency. The floor value is the exercise price less the premium paid for the put. Assume a put option on euros has a strike price of $1.05 with a premium of $0.05. The minimum value, or floor, for this arrangement will be $1.00 (i.e., $1.05 − $0.05) per euro. Stated another way, the seller will receive no less than $1.00 (net) for each euro sold.

As another example, assume a UK importer has an account payable due in three months in euros. The importer can ensure a maximum cost to obtain those euros by buying a call option on euros. If, at the time of payment, the spot market price of the euro is less than the strike price of the call option, the importer does not exercise the option and loses only the premium paid. The net cost of the euros to the importer is the spot price of the euro plus the option premium. The option acts as insurance against the spot price of the euro rising above a specific level. For this form of insurance, the importer pays the option premium (price). Note that as previously discussed, the buyer of the option will pay the option premium even if the contract is never exercised.

Calculation Example: Currency Option

Suppose a call option contract on British pounds (GBP) has been written with a strike price of $1.40 per pound (i.e., exchange rate is GBP/USD 1.40).

- Assuming this is an American option, if the spot exchange rate is GBP/USD 1.4372, then the option contract is said to be in the money by $0.0372 (i.e., spot rate minus the strike price, or $1.4372 − $1.40).

- A buyer of the contract will pay at least $0.0372 per GBP because at that price, the contract can be used to purchase GBP at $1.40, resulting in a GBP/USD 1.4372 cost to the buyer of the contract if it is exercised. This is the same price that would be paid for British pounds in the spot market. The seller of the contract will not accept less than $0.0372 per GBP because the contract can be used to purchase British pounds at GBP/USD 1.40. If the contract is exercised, the seller of the contract will have to pay GBP/USD 1.4372 in the spot market to purchase the British pounds for delivery.

- If there is some time until the contract expires, the premium for the contract will exceed $0.0372 per GBP[8] because the party buying the contract has locked in a maximum price of GBP/USD 1.40 through the delivery date. No matter how much the value of the pound rises prior to the delivery date, the option holder can exercise the contract at GBP/USD 1.40. Accordingly, a buyer of the contract will be willing to pay some amount more than $0.0372 per GBP (the time value) for the option. If the market value of the British pound rises above GBP/USD 1.4372, then the option holder may gain by buying the currency at GBP/USD 1.40 or by selling the contract for more than was paid for it.

- For example, if the exchange rate rose to GBP/USD 1.5245 prior to the delivery date, then the option contract would sell for at least $0.1245 (intrinsic value) plus a time value premium because the option is in the money by $0.1245 (i.e., $1.5245 − $1.40). The time value portion of the price is a function of the time to maturity and the volatility of the underlying asset price. The time value of an option will generally decline as the premium (option price) rises. As rising exchange rates cause the premium on the call option to increase, an option buyer who pays the higher price to acquire the contract has more money at risk should the value of the British pound subsequently decline. Accordingly, a call option buyer will be willing to pay a smaller time value premium as the price of the option increases.

- In the case of the call option in this example, the market value of the British pound may drop below GBP/USD 1.40, in which case the option is out of the money. If the price never recovers to rise above GBP/USD 1.40 by the delivery date, then the option will not be exercised because British pounds can be purchased in the spot market for less than $1.40 per pound. In this case, the party that purchased the option contract will experience

---

8. In extreme circumstances, negative interest rates may result in an option premium that is less than the intrinsic value.

a loss equal to the premium (price) paid for the contract. Again, as the price paid for the call contract increases as the exchange rate rises above GBP/USD 1.40, a buyer who pays the higher price to acquire the call contract has more money at risk should the exchange rate drop below GBP/USD 1.40 after the contract is purchased. Accordingly, a buyer will be willing to pay a smaller time value premium the higher the price of the option.

· The opposite is true of a put option. If a put option contract is purchased that permits the contract owner to sell GBP at $1.40 per pound, then the value of the contract will not increase as the exchange rate rises above GBP/USD 1.40. This is because an owner of the underlying asset (i.e., British pounds) will sell the pounds in the market for the higher price rather than exercise the right to sell (put) the pounds at GBP/USD 1.40. If the spot exchange rate falls below GBP/USD 1.40, then the put contract will gain value because it lets the option's owner sell the currency at $1.40 per pound. The more the exchange rate declines below GBP/USD 1.40, the more value the put option gains.

VII. INTEREST RATE EXPOSURE AND RISK MANAGEMENT

Many organizations face financial risks attributable to interest rate changes. The risk exposure arises from the nature of the firm's operating and/or financing activities. Organizations with variable interest rate investments face the possibility of lower earnings when interest rates fall, while organizations with debt tied to variable interest rates face higher borrowing costs when interest rates rise. Interest rate forwards (including forward rate agreements), futures, swaps, and options are typical instruments used to manage interest rate risk.

A. Interest Rate Forwards

1. BASICS OF INTEREST RATE FORWARDS

A forward contract allows its buyer to lock in today the future price of an asset, such as an interest-linked security. The buyer has to pay the agreed-upon price on the settlement date, whether or not the interest rate has moved in the buyer's favor. The seller is also required to deliver the asset on the settlement date, whatever that asset's price is in the spot market. There is generally no up-front fee or margin required on these types of contracts and no cash changes hands before the settlement date.

Interest rate forwards are typically cash-settled rather than settled through delivery. That is, one party is obligated to pay the other the difference between the contract value of the forward and its spot value at the maturity date. The most popular of these is the forward rate agreement (FRA) outlined below.

2. FORWARD RATE AGREEMENTS (FRAs)

An FRA is a forward contract on interest rates in which two parties agree that a certain interest rate will apply to a certain principal during a specified, future period of time. The notional principal amounts are agreed upon, but they are never exchanged. If the actual rate is different from the agreed-upon rate in the contract at settlement, then one party pays the other a cash amount equal to the difference. The majority of FRAs are based on Eurodollar rates (typically LIBOR), although other rates are available. FRAs that are based on US Treasury yields are referred to as *Treasury locks*, or *T-locks*. FRAs are very popular with short-term borrowers who are trying to fix today the effective interest rate they will have to pay at a future date. A corporation may use such an arrangement to lock in an interest rate today for future working capital financing scheduled in six months.

For example, a company may project that it will need to borrow $1,000,000 for six months starting three months from now. Because the company is concerned that current interest rates will rise over the next three months before it borrows the needed funds, it can purchase a 3x9 FRA to lock in current rates. In a 3x9 FRA, the 3 indicates that the effective or starting date of the FRA is three months from now, and the 9 indicates that the termination of the FRA will be nine months from now. The term of the FRA will be six (9 − 3) months.

B. Interest Rate Futures

Interest rate futures are contracts on an underlying asset whose price is dependent solely on the level of interest rates. The most popular short-term interest rate contracts are US Treasury bill (T-bill) contracts, and Eurodollar contracts traded on the Chicago Mercantile Exchange as bank certificates of deposit (CDs). The underlying asset in a T-bill futures contract is the 90-day T-bill rate. The underlying asset in a Eurodollar contract is the interest earned on a Eurodollar deposit (CD) at three-month LIBOR. The most actively traded long-term interest rate contracts are the 5- and 10-year US Treasury notes.[9]

Like other futures contracts, interest rate futures contracts are typically traded on an exchange and require a margin account. Each day, the gains or losses on the contract are posted to the account (marked to market), and if the losses are large enough, the holder of the contract may receive a margin call, requiring the holder to either post additional funds to the account or have the position liquidated.

Investors will use these types of contracts because they allow the investors to protect open positions from adverse price movements. Any gains or losses on the open positions held by the investors are offset by the payoffs from the derivative contracts. If the actual interest rate at maturity is different from the predetermined rate, then money is paid or received, depending on whether the difference is positive or negative.

This type of contract allows a company to hedge a one-period rate change and is similar to the FRA discussed above. While short-term contracts are cash-settled, some long-term futures contracts involve settlement by delivering specific long-term bonds. The market for all these contracts is typically very competitive, with fairly narrow spreads.

An example of a typical interest rate futures contract is provided below.

Calculation Example: Interest Rate Futures

Futures contract pricing on a three-month Eurodollar deposit is defined as 100 minus LIBOR.

- Assuming that three-month LIBOR is expected to be 0.92% when the contract matures, the futures contract price will be quoted at 99.08 (100 − 0.92).

- However, if the actual rate for a three-month Eurodollar deposit is 1.25% when the contract matures, then the realized value is only 98.75 (100 − 1.25). The holder of the long position (i.e., the one who bought the futures contract) pays the seller of the contract the difference between the contracted rate of 0.92% and the actual rate of 1.25%, or the difference of 99.08 − 98.75, which equals 0.33 per unit of the contract.

- If the rate had moved in the other direction, and instead of 0.92%, the interest rate on a three-month Eurodollar deposit was 0.50%, then the realized value would be 99.50 (100 − 0.50). In this case the holder of the long position (i.e., the purchaser of the contract) would be paid by the seller of the contract the difference between the contracted rate of 0.92% and the actual rate of 0.50%, which equals 0.42 per unit of the contract.

---

9. From "Leading Products Q2 2016," published by the CME Group, 2016 (http://www.cmegroup.com/education/files/cme-group-leading-products-2016-q2.pdf).

C. Interest Rate Swaps

An interest rate swap is an OTC agreement between two parties to exchange the cash flows of two different securities throughout the life of the contract. Interest rate swaps can be viewed as a series of forwards and, as with forwards, the contract is binding on both sides of the contract. Interest rate swaps are very flexible hedging instruments used by treasury professionals for asset/liability management, as well as by bond portfolio managers to reduce or extend the average maturity or exposure of an open position.

The most common type of interest rate swap is the fixed-floating swap, which is the exchange of a fixed interest rate cash flow for a floating interest rate cash flow (or vice versa), with both interest rates in the same currency. The fixed side pays a fixed interest rate on a notional amount, usually quarterly or semiannually, while the floating side pays a floating rate on the same notional amount. The reference rate is generally LIBOR, but could be any mutually agreed-upon rate. This is often referred to as a *vanilla swap*. If both interest rates are floating, then the exchange of cash flows is called a *basis rate swap*, which is less commonly used. An example of a basis rate swap is the exchange of interest payments based on LIBOR for interest payments based on the US prime rate. Note that there is no exchange of principal as it cancels out both at inception and at maturity.

Interest rate swaps are often used by treasury professionals to convert a fixed-rate investment or obligation into a floating-rate investment or obligation (or vice versa) in order to better match the particular needs of a company and the current offerings of the market.

Calculation Example: Interest Rate Swap

Assume two parties (A and B) enter into a five-year swap with a notional value of $100 million. Party A will take the fixed side of the transaction because it wants to have certainty about its future interest rate expense, and Party B will take the floating side of the transaction because it believes interest rates are likely to fall over the five-year period.

- In this example, Party A is exchanging its floating-rate exposure for a fixed rate, and Party B is exchanging its fixed-rate exposure for a floating rate. As a result, Party A will pay a fixed rate to Party B, and Party B will pay a floating rate to Party A. The reference rates are 3.75% on the fixed side and LIBOR + 3.50% on the floating side. This means that at the end of each year, Party A will owe Party B $100 million × 3.75%, while Party B will owe Party A $100 million × (LIBOR + 3.50%).

- In practice, there is a netting procedure and only the difference is settled. That is, if LIBOR is less than 0.25% (or 3.75% − 3.50%), then Party A pays Party B, and if LIBOR is greater than 0.25%, then Party B pays Party A. For example:

  ○ If LIBOR is 0.15%, then Party A pays Party B as follows:

$$[0.0375-(0.0015+0.0350)]\times \$100,000,000 = \$100,000$$

  ○ If LIBOR is 0.45%, then Party B pays Party A as follows:

$$[(0.0045+0.0350)-0.0375]\times \$100,000,000 = \$200,000$$

Alternatively, assume that the same two parties enter into an interest rate swap agreement because Party A has a comparative advantage in the fixed-rate market and Party B has a comparative advantage in the floating-rate market. The two parties agree to split the rate advantage 50/50. The following chart shows the fixed and floating rates available to each party:

	FIXED RATE	FLOATING RATE
Party A	2.25%	6-month LIBOR + 0.75%
Party B	3.25%	6-month LIBOR + 1.25%

Party A will enter into a fixed-rate loan for 2.25%, and Party B will enter into a floating-rate loan for LIBOR + 1.25%. Since the difference in their effective rates at the time of the swap is 0.50%,[10] they will split the advantage 50/50, or 0.25% each. Each party pays its lender directly. Party A will also pay Party B LIBOR + 0.25%, while Party B will pay Party A 2.00% fixed, based on their swap agreement.

Party A's net interest rate can be determined using the following calculation:

$$\text{Net Interest Rate} = \text{Rate Paid to Lender} + \text{Rate Paid for Swap} - \text{Rate Received from Swap}$$
$$= 2.25\% + (\text{LIBOR} + 0.25\%) - 2.00\%$$
$$= \text{LIBOR} + 0.50\% \, (\text{saving } 0.25\% \text{ over the offered floating rate of LIBOR} + 0.75\%)$$

Similarly, Party B's net interest rate can be calculated as:

$$\text{Net Interest Rate} = \text{Rate Paid to Lender} + \text{Rate Paid for Swap} - \text{Rate Received from Swap}$$
$$= (\text{LIBOR} + 1.25\%) + 2.00\% - (\text{LIBOR} + 0.25\%)$$
$$= 3.00\% \, (\text{saving } 0.25\% \text{ over the offered fixed rate of } 3.25\%)$$

D. Interest Rate Options

Interest rate options are option-type derivatives where the payoff depends on the level of interest rates. There are three basic types of interest rate options: caps, floors, and collars. They are similar to currency options (discussed earlier in this chapter), which can also be purchased as caps, floors, and collars, but their purpose is to help protect the user from unwanted interest rate fluctuations rather than currency fluctuations.

1. INTEREST RATE CAPS

Caps ensure that the borrower of a floating-rate loan pays no more than a predetermined maximum rate if interest rates rise above a ceiling level. This level is known as the *cap rate*. If rates fall, then the borrower is not obligated to exercise the option and can still enjoy the benefits of lower borrowing costs. The price of this insurance is the premium paid for the cap.

For example, assume a German firm is negotiating a borrowing agreement for a 10-year term loan that will have a floating rate set at the European Central Bank (ECB) benchmark lending rate plus 250 basis points. At the time the agreement is being signed, the ECB rate is only 0.25%, resulting in an all-in rate on the loan of 2.75%. The firm is worried that interest rates will rise in the future and asks for a cap of 6.00% on the all-in rate for the agreement. This cap will be in the form of an up-front premium based on the loan amount, typically for the period of the loan

---

10. The net advantage of the swap is calculated by taking the difference between the differences in the fixed and floating rates, as follows: (3.25% − 2.25%) − [(LIBOR + 1.25%) − (LIBOR + 0.75%)] = 0.50%.

agreement. Assume a loan amount of EUR 50 million and a premium for the cap of 50 basis points. In this case, the firm will pay EUR 50,000,000 × 0.0050 = EUR 250,000 to obtain the cap.

2. INTEREST RATE FLOORS

Floors ensure that the owner of a floating-rate asset receives a minimum rate if interest rates fall below a floor level. If rates fall below this level, then the floating-rate asset is protected by a put option on interest rates. If interest rates rise, then the company can still benefit because it is not obligated to exercise the put option. The cost of this insurance is the premium paid for the interest rate floor.

For example, a Japanese investor is looking to purchase a JPY 100 million, five-year investment with a variable rate that is based on the Bank of Japan prime lending rate plus 200 basis points. At the time of the purchase, the Bank of Japan rate is 1.00%, resulting in a return to the investor of 3.00%. If the investor is worried that rates will fall in the future, the investor may wish to purchase a floor on the rate paid. If a floor of 2.75% (return to the investor) is offered for a premium of 5 basis points, then the investor would pay JPY 100,000,000 × 0.0005 = JPY 50,000 to obtain the floor.

3. INTEREST RATE COLLARS

A combination of an interest rate cap and an interest rate floor is called an *interest rate collar*. A company that buys an interest rate cap and sells an interest rate floor is effectively locking in a range for borrowing costs. The cap establishes a maximum borrowing rate, thereby protecting the company against higher interest rates, while the floor sets a minimum borrowing rate. A collar has no costs when the income received from selling the floor matches the premium paid for the cap. Costless collars are popular hedging vehicles providing some interest rate protection at zero cost. Besides caps, floors, and collars, there are other complex derivatives constantly being developed and marketed that are beyond the scope of this book.

VIII. COMMODITY RISK EXPOSURE

Commodities used in production or operations processes are sold in commodities markets. The most common commodities markets are for agricultural and meat products, oil and gas, minerals, and metals. There are two major types of commodities risk: price exposure and delivery exposure.

The primary commodity exposure that organizations face is the potential for changes in the price of a commodity. If an organization uses commodities in the production process, then rising prices create an exposure for the organization. Conversely, if an organization sells the product, then falling prices create an exposure.

For certain organizations that are large users of energy products (e.g., oil, gas, and coal), a regular supply of the commodity is crucial. As examples, airlines depend upon the availability of jet fuel, and electricity-generating plants require natural gas or coal. In addition to price exposure, these organizations also may face delivery exposure, if the supplier is unable or unwilling to deliver when needed. Entering into a long-term agreement with a reliable and trusted energy producer can help to mitigate these exposures.

Like interest rate and FX risks, commodity price risk can be managed using forwards, futures, swaps, options, or combinations of these derivative instruments. Consider the following example. In an oil swap, two parties would agree on a notional principal expressed in barrels of oil (not dollars). Similar to currency or interest rate swaps, the parties make regular settlements on the basis of fixed and floating oil prices. The floating price used in an oil swap is usually the average price of oil over a specified period. To reduce the uncertainty associated with the change in the price of oil, a treasury professional may attempt to construct a costless collar (i.e., a combination of a cap and a floor).

IX. OTHER ISSUES RELATED TO FINANCIAL RISK MANAGEMENT

A. Accounting Issues

Due to the strict rules around many of the instruments used in FX and other types of financial risk management, there are exacting accounting issues to consider. These are addressed by the International Accounting Standards Board (IASB) globally and by the Financial Accounting Standards Board (FASB) in the United States. Global and US accounting standards that relate to derivative and hedge accounting are discussed in more detail in Chapter 8, Financial Accounting and Reporting.

One of the primary problems in the valuation of, and subsequent accounting for, derivatives is determining their accurate value. For many years, especially as both financial markets and asset prices rose rapidly, the valuation approach of mark-to-market was used. This approach allowed buyers of derivatives to report large profits related to their trading activities and subsequently increase their compensation significantly. The problems came as the markets fell and these same assets had to be written down, sometimes very quickly, resulting in large losses for these institutions. The question sometimes comes down to something as simple as, what is the real market price of an asset?

As a general guideline, ASC Topic 820-10: *Fair Value Measurement—Overall* offers some updated guidance on this issue, especially in volatile or illiquid markets. A rapid deterioration in an asset class (e.g., specific commodities) can make market participants risk averse and cause illiquidity in otherwise liquid markets. These conditions set the stage for a very challenging environment for establishing reliable assumptions and inputs. Additional detail on ASC Topic 820 is provided in Chapter 8, Financial Accounting and Reporting.

With respect to improving the transparency of information disclosure relating to the use of derivatives and hedging, ASC Topic 815: *Derivatives and Hedging* is the prevailing guideline for US companies (with updates to International Financial Reporting Standards [IFRS] essentially matching these guidelines). ASC Topic 815 is designed to give a more accurate picture of a company's financial position by requiring additional information about how and why any derivative contracts are being used.

B. Tax Issues Related to Hedging

Tax issues surrounding the use of hedges are complex, and errors in the accounting treatment of hedge transactions can be very costly. If an improper accounting treatment is used or documentation does not meet tax authority requirements, then the organization may not be able to treat the gains/losses from derivative holdings as an offset to operational gains/losses. This could result in a significantly higher tax liability from hedging activities. A treasury professional must be aware of these issues and should approach entering into hedge transactions with caution. In general, advice should be obtained from legal, tax, and accounting experts who specialize in this area.

Other tax-related problems are the tax liabilities that are incurred as a result of a restatement of financial information due to errors in applying very complex accounting guidelines for derivative instruments and hedging. This problem makes it even more imperative that global companies involved in active hedging strategies keep abreast of current developments in these areas and ensure that their external accountants and auditors are experts in tax issues related to their business.

C. Hedging Policy Statement

An effective hedging strategy requires both approval of the general hedging policy (typically at the board of directors' level) and implementation of that policy (usually in the treasury area of the organization). This policy should provide general directives, targets to be achieved, or a mixture of both, and is essential for management oversight as well as regulatory compliance. As previously noted, most hedging policy statements will bar the use of derivatives for speculative purposes. The hedging policy statement should address the following items in the three key financial risk management areas:

For foreign currency hedging:

- Known foreign currency exposures on the balance sheet (transaction-related)
- Balance sheet exposures
- Cash flow exposures (forecasted)
- Net equity investment exposures
- Translation exposures

For interest rate hedging:

- Known interest rate exposures on existing short-term investments and borrowing
- Known interest rate exposures on existing long-term investments and borrowing
- Interest rate exposures on forecasted investments and borrowing

For commodity hedging:

- Known and forecasted exposures related to commodity pricing
- Known and forecasted exposures related to commodity availability

Accounting issues related to hedging and the use of cash flow versus fair value approaches are covered in Chapter 8, Financial Accounting and Reporting.

X. SUMMARY

Financial risk management is a complex and important part of treasury management. In particular, the management of FX risk is growing increasingly important as business expands globally. Because treasury is often a central clearinghouse for financial information in many companies, it is well positioned to help manage financial risk.

Proper financial risk management reduces the uncertainty surrounding a firm's cash flows, asset values, and the value of liabilities. Reducing uncertainty will result in better access to capital and a lower cost of capital due to lower risk. Managing financial risks associated with foreign currencies, interest rates, and commodity prices allows treasury professionals to more accurately forecast future cash flows, and lowers the company's probability of financial distress.

This chapter discussed the basics of financial risk management, covered the three types of financial risk exposure, and presented some of the tools that are used to manage financial risk, including commonly available derivatives such as forwards, futures, swaps, and options. Lastly, some of the key issues associated with hedge accounting, tax issues, and hedging policy statements were reviewed. Treasury professionals will want to monitor developments in these areas to remain compliant with the appropriate regulations.

CHAPTER 18
Treasury Policies and Procedures

I. INTRODUCTION

II. OVERVIEW OF TREASURY POLICIES AND PROCEDURES

III. GUIDELINES FOR CREATING POLICIES AND PROCEDURES
    A. Key Control Considerations
    B. Writing the Policy
    C. Approval of the Policy
    D. Policy Reviews, Updates, and Revisions
    E. Procedure Development and Implementation

IV. POLICY DEVELOPMENT EXAMPLE: SHORT-TERM INVESTMENT POLICY
    A. The Importance of Having an Investment Policy
    B. Setting Investment Objectives
    C. Developing a List of Permitted Investments
    D. Investment Requirements
    E. Other Issues in Developing an Investment Policy

V. OVERVIEW OF KEY TREASURY POLICIES
    A. Liquidity Policy
    B. Bank Account and Financial Services Authority Policies
    C. Payments Policy
    D. Wire Transfer Policy
    E. Collection and Concentration Policy
    F. Cash Flow Forecasting Policy
    G. Investment Valuation and Impairment Policies
    H. Payment Card Policies

I. Merchant Card Policies

J. Outsourcing Policy

K. Financial Risk Management Policies

L. Regulatory Compliance Policies

M. Funding/Financing Policies

N. Treasury Systems Policy

VI. SUMMARY

APPENDIX 18.1: SAMPLE SHORT-TERM INVESTMENT POLICY

I. INTRODUCTION

Organizations use policies to identify and describe key risks and to establish essential limits, guidelines, account-abilities, and risk management practices. A policy guides activities in a particular area and establishes performance evaluation guidelines and process measurements. Meanwhile, a procedure is a specified series of actions or operations that should be executed in a consistent manner to achieve the desired results identified in the policy. In other words, procedures should follow the guidelines of the policy. Policies and procedures should be clearly stated and enforced, as they are the basic principles, often approved by the board of directors, by which an organization operates.

This chapter provides an overview of treasury policies and procedures and discusses the key elements needed in developing an effective policy statement. To provide an overall example of policy development, the chapter presents a detailed discussion of a specific policy statement. The chapter concludes by providing a list of key treasury policies and the elements that should be considered when developing them. Appendix 18.1 provides a sample short-term investment policy.

II. OVERVIEW OF TREASURY POLICIES AND PROCEDURES

Treasury policies and procedures provide a framework for the design of workflows and controls that support operational, financial, and treasury management objectives. The behavior of treasury staff cannot be regulated merely by declaration. However, assigning specific duties and documenting the assignment of those duties to designated parties provides a baseline for acceptable behavior. The addition of specific penalties in the event of violations of that behavior also helps set appropriate expectations.

The formalization of policies and procedures is one way for an organization to inform employees, agents, contractors, and vendors of the expected behavior related to certain specific treasury activities. The standards outlined in an organization's treasury policies and procedures should be reviewed regularly for continued appropriateness and to make sure they incorporate relevant legislative, regulatory, or process changes/revisions. In addition, policies and procedures are often used as training tools to help document best practices and expectations.

There are four primary reasons why treasury policies and procedures are necessary:

- **Organizational Needs:** To provide a documented guide to best practices to ensure fundamental operational processes are performed in a consistent manner that meets the organization's needs. Additionally, policy statements are needed to grant and delegate the authority required to conduct treasury procedures.

- **Risk Management:** To provide a control process to mitigate identified risks in the operation.

- **Roles and Responsibilities:** To provide a clear definition of the roles and responsibilities within the treasury function. When problems occur, documented policies and procedures can provide some degree of protection for staff that follow the approved procedures. Policies and procedures also provide clarity when dealing with accountability issues.

- **Compliance:** To provide an effective internal audit and control tool that helps ensure compliance with regulatory and legal requirements.

III. GUIDELINES FOR CREATING POLICIES AND PROCEDURES

This section discusses guidelines for the development of formal policies and procedures governing treasury operational activities. At the start of the development process, it is important to determine the primary objective relating to each treasury function (e.g., investment management or foreign exchange [FX] risk management). Determining the objectives for each treasury functional area helps focus the development of the related policies and procedures. In addition, by including the objectives in the formal policies and procedures, the objectives can be communicated throughout the organization, which helps ensure that the practices employed will support the desired objectives. It is also important to understand that the processes in each functional area are generally influenced by factors outside that area, and perhaps even outside the treasury function. For example, processes related to the use of lockbox services and the management of remittance information passing through the lockbox are often influenced by requirements of the accounts receivable and credit departments.

A. Key Control Considerations

Regardless of the firm's organization or the structure of its treasury operations, there is a need for some fundamental level of controls, which should be in place and operating at all times. Well-written policy statements help document that these controls have been given appropriate consideration. Ultimately, a board of directors (or the owner/ governing body of the organization) is responsible for ensuring that adequate internal controls are established and maintained to protect the company's assets. An example of a specific treasury department policy statement with supporting controls is provided in Appendix 18.1.

1. STRUCTURE OF CONTROLS

There is no standard structure for determining the optimal levels of control that should be in place, but there are certain best-practice standards that should be followed, especially from an audit perspective. The analysis and understanding of operations give rise to controls that can be implemented in a targeted and effective manner. Proper documentation of those controls in board-approved policy statements is a key step in that implementation. Correctly designed, operated, updated, and monitored controls can not only assist in preventing financial losses, but can also result in more effective management of the organization. In establishing and documenting controls, some of the items to consider are:

- Internal and external controls
- Reporting and audit trails
- Controls on third-party service providers
- Compliance with regulatory requirements of major stock exchanges (e.g., the Sarbanes-Oxley Act [SOX] Section 404[1] for organizations listed on a US exchange)

2. DELEGATION OF AUTHORITY

Policies and procedures should address the delegation of authority. Generally, this is accomplished by a board of directors' resolution outlining the responsibilities that are delegated to a particular management position within the treasury operations area and identifying any designated limits, such as signing limits, on that authority. As an example, all decisions regarding the selection of financial institutions and related services might be delegated to the CFO or treasurer. The CFO or treasurer (with board approval) might then further delegate the authority for managing the request for proposal (RFP) and vendor selection process. The assistant treasurer or treasury manager

---

1. SOX Section 404 requires managers to state their responsibility for establishing and maintaining adequate internal controls for financial reporting.

might have the authority to select or manage certain services (e.g., lockboxes or controlled disbursement accounts) with a requirement that the CFO or treasurer provide final approval in the selection process. Signature authority on bank accounts (i.e., check-signing authority) is a common example of delegation of authority.

3. SEGREGATION OF DUTIES

Segregation of duties is another key control that should be addressed in policies and procedures. Segregation of duties is the concept of having more than one individual involved in a process to complete a task, which significantly reduces the risks of fraud and human error. This is a key concept of internal control in any financial operation. A typical example of a process requiring the segregation of duties would be the execution of a wire transfer, where one individual initiates the wire while another individual reviews and approves the wire. At least two individuals should generally be involved in wire transactions. However, for large wire transfers, there are typically several levels of approval required to ensure the accuracy of the transaction. Another example is the approval of expense reports. An individual submitting an expense report should never be allowed to approve his/her own expense reimbursement request.

4. ROLES AND RESPONSIBILITIES

Another key control to be addressed by policies and procedures is the role of key personnel in the treasury organization, specifically identifying responsibilities and authority for each position and function. For example, the treasurer of an organization would be required to approve the hiring of an investment manager for the organization's short-term portfolio, but the assistant treasurer would be responsible for the day-to-day oversight of the investment manager.

5. RECORDS RETENTION

There are many regulations relating to the retention of records, especially for compliance with regulatory and tax authorities. There are also severe penalties for failure to maintain proper workpapers, especially those related to audit activity, bankruptcies, and many government investigations. Retention policies also frequently include when and how specific key records should be destroyed. For example, a firm may have a records retention policy that states, "Disbursement requests and supporting documentation will be destroyed five years after payment has been made." In addition to a general records retention policy, other treasury policies and procedures documents should contain requirements for the appropriate retention, safekeeping, and destruction of records, where appropriate.[2]

6. MOVING FROM CONTROLS TO POLICIES AND PROCEDURES

Given the importance of controls to the treasury area, the treasury policies development process should build in the desired controls for each function. As control requirements change over time in response to new developments and technology, so should the related policies and procedures.

B. Writing the Policy

1. PREDEVELOPMENT STAGE

It is essential to get authorization and support for the entire policy development process at the highest level possible in the organization before development begins. A vital step is to appoint an individual or group to take the lead and to whom primary responsibility for the development process can be assigned. Targeted individuals to fill this

---

2. Treasury professionals should consult with their organizations' attorneys and tax professionals regarding appropriate record retention requirements since these may vary by country.

role typically include the general managers of the functional areas directly impacted by the policy. In addition, the active involvement and support of senior management will contribute greatly to the success of the development process and to producing a policy that is acceptable to all of the areas involved. Staff from the various functional areas directly affected by the policy should also be included in the policy development process.

2. IDENTIFYING ISSUES AND CONDUCTING ANALYSES

Prior to drafting the policy, the issues relating to the proposed policy should be identified and analyzed. If membership on the development team includes all of the affected areas, then the chances of creating a policy that will be accepted by those affected are very good. The owners of all related processes should be included, and an agreed-upon flowchart, including workflows and organization charts, should be created for the proper execution of those processes.

3. DRAFTING THE POLICY

In the drafting stage, the development team creates the new basic policy or modifies an existing policy, using a common format and set of definitions. The policy should represent a consistent, logical framework for organizational action. Some general guidelines for the creation of the policy include:

- Use clear, concise, simple language.
- Address what the rule will be, rather than how to implement it.
- Make the policy readily available to the organizational area.
- Describe clear lines of authority.
- Designate expert resources to interpret the policy if questions arise.
- Identify the parties who will review and approve the policy, and define any ongoing review process (e.g., "this policy will be reviewed and updated annually by the treasurer").

4. BASIC ELEMENTS OF A POLICY

Each organizational or functional area will have different needs for its policies, and the format will most likely vary considerably. There are, however, some general guidelines that should be followed regarding basic policy elements:

- **Objectives:** The objectives for the policy should be clearly stated at the beginning of the policy document.
- **Scope:** The scope of the policy should define, as precisely as possible, the areas and processes the policy will cover.
- **Basic Guidelines:** This section should provide a listing of all the areas covered by the policy, along with procedures for how each of the related processes should be performed and managed. These guidelines should also include how to manage exceptions (i.e., what constitutes an exception and how to handle it).
- **Roles and Responsibilities:** This section should provide a clear listing of the roles and responsibilities of the key participants in each policy. Included in this section should be an outline of the lines of authority, delegation, and segregation of duties.
- **Performance Measurement and Reporting:** This is an important part of the policy, especially when investments, derivatives, or trading activities are involved. The metrics or benchmarks used for performance measurement should be defined clearly, as well as the expectations for meeting the performance objectives. Any required reports should be discussed, including formats, timeframes, and deadlines.

- **Required Controls and Compliance Considerations:** One of the key aspects of developing policies and procedures is to ensure proper controls for processes used in the area in question. Mandating a policy will not ensure compliance without appropriate oversight and controls. This section should also specify the external regulatory requirements that are addressed by the policy.

- **Exception Management:** Even with a comprehensive policy statement, the possibility for required exceptions will still exist. It is important that a policy statement identify who can approve exceptions and how they will be tracked and managed once they have been approved.

- **Review Cycle:** As discussed below in the section on policy review and updates, procedures change and evolve over time and the related policies must also change. An essential item in any policy is a statement of how frequently the policy will be reviewed and what approvals will be required (e.g., "this policy will be reviewed by the CFO annually and all changes approved by the board of directors"). The date of the last review should be included in the policy itself.

- **Definitions:** A policy should define all significant terms. Definitions are important to clarify the specific meaning of certain terms (e.g., whether the term *year* refers to a calendar year or fiscal year, or whether the term *employee* refers to all employees or full-time employees only).

- **Policy Attachments:** A policy is most effective when it provides comprehensive information in the form of exhibits and appendices. These normally consist of glossaries, distribution lists, procedures manuals, organization charts, standard reports, and any other information needed to support or clarify the information provided in the body of the policy. It is important to keep the attachments as current as the policies.

C. Approval of the Policy

Once a policy has been developed, it should be reviewed as part of a four-level formal approval process:

- **Treasury Department Review:** Senior treasury staff should review and approve the policy, ensuring that it meets the intended purpose and objective, and that its content includes the required controls and consequences associated with the policy and related procedures. This review should include an assessment of reasonableness and functionality, as unreasonable policies are typically ignored.

- **Review by Other Functional Area Managers:** The policy should be reviewed and approved by the accounting and legal areas, as well as by any areas other than treasury that are impacted by the policy. In addition, the policy should be reviewed by key financial managers in decentralized operating units. The focus of this review should be on the operational implications of the policy.

- **Review by Internal Audit and/or Compliance Group:** The internal audit group typically reviews policies for compliance with financial controls and regulatory requirements, including SOX in the United States. Many organizations have a compliance group that is separate from the internal audit function and is responsible for reviewing the firm's adherence with existing laws and regulations. In the investment area, the compliance (and/or audit) group is often a required level of control, monitoring trading restrictions and licensing.[3] General operational policies may not require this review, especially if they have no direct impact on the financial statements.

- **Final Approval:** Most treasury policies will need to be formally approved by the board of directors (or appropriate board committee) or equivalent, since they typically involve delegation of board authority and prerogatives (e.g., the authority to open or close a bank account). Policies with a lower impact may only require approval at a designated executive level. Final approval authority will vary depending upon existing delegations of board authority.

---

3. The compliance and/or audit group makes certain that items such as business licenses, securities licenses, and professional certifications are current and that any continuing education requirements are being met.

D. Policy Reviews, Updates, and Revisions

As organizations change and grow with the addition of staff and/or new products or services, the practices related to a given area may also undergo change. Policies should be reviewed, updated, and reapproved periodically, driven by the internal protocol, the regulatory environment, and the size and type of the organization. The structure of the review and the level(s) of review required should be outlined in the policy. A good practice, as illustrated in Appendix 18.1, is to include a revision-tracking section as part of the document. This should list all changes and updates in order to provide historical context and document any necessary regulatory compliance.

Policies should also be reevaluated and updated immediately following any major reorganization of the company's structure, material change in banking services, or relevant regulatory change. Implementation of the operational requirements dictated by a policy is most effectively accomplished through a detailed procedures manual, discussed in the next section, which can serve as a reference for daily activities and duties.

Policy compliance reviews are also important to the success of the policy. These reviews may be included within the scope of internal and/or external audits, but practice may vary by the type and size of the organization. The policy should clearly specify who is responsible for compliance testing, the scope of the testing, and to whom the results should be reported.

To ensure adequate compliance evaluation, many organizations assign compliance measurement to a specific person or unit outside the policy-related functional area. This is generally considered a best practice, as it ensures objectivity in the review process.

E. Procedure Development and Implementation

It is important to understand that policies drive the development of day-to-day procedures (often referred to as *standard operating procedures*, or *SOPs*). At the same time, procedures reinforce compliance with policy. An organization should make this relationship explicit by tying procedures to their underlying policies. Also, management should communicate how those procedures help the organization achieve its goals or strategic plan, and should ensure understanding and compliance on the part of managers and employees. The managers and employees affected should be involved in developing the procedures, as this will create a sense of ownership and, it is hoped, better compliance.

Some of the more specific considerations in the development of procedures include the following:

- Procedures should be written so that they are clear and understandable to both existing and new managers and employees. They should be written in a concise manner with a minimum of verbiage, and all acronyms and technical terms should be spelled out clearly.

- Procedures that are unnecessarily restrictive may limit their usefulness, so when feasible, they should offer alternatives. For example, a process that is highly automated should include alternative manual procedures in the event of a systems failure.

- Documentation should be factual and reviewed for accuracy. Where possible, information that may become quickly outdated should not be included in the procedures.

- Where applicable, the procedures manual should include step-by-step instructions for completing any required forms (both paper and electronic).

- The procedures document itself should be structured so that users can focus quickly on the aspect of the procedure relevant to their decision/task at hand. Many organizations use a flexible, modular outline to make the document easy to modify and keep up to date.

IV. POLICY DEVELOPMENT EXAMPLE: SHORT-TERM INVESTMENT POLICY

A discussion of the elements of a short-term investment policy is provided to illustrate the various issues involved in developing a policy. This section describes how the key short-term investment issues are converted into an actual policy statement. A sample short-term investment policy is provided in Appendix 18.1 to support this discussion.

In the treasury area, the investment policy guidelines generally address management policies for the different types of securities that can be held by a company. The guidelines discussed in this section relate to the creation of a general investment policy and are appropriate for most types of organization.

A. The Importance of Having an Investment Policy

A formal investment policy establishes a clear understanding of the firm's investment philosophy and objectives. This allows the treasury team to better manage liquidity, monitor compliance, and minimize risk, regardless of its structure (e.g., centralized or decentralized). The investment policy also serves to protect staff in case any discrepancy arises.

In general, the more decentralized and geographically widespread the investment decision making, the more crucial an investment policy becomes to ensure a consistent, enterprise-wide approach. Formal written policies also help to delineate the relationship between the parent/holding company/corporate office and the subsidiary in decentralized operations.

B. Setting Investment Objectives

A common objective of most investment policies is to minimize the exposure to financial loss while ensuring cash availability and maximizing returns. For this reason, the short-term investment policies for most firms will focus on the preservation of principal and the liquidity of potential investments. The objectives of an investment policy reflect the organization's philosophy about risk and return. Therefore, the objectives must be appropriately written to reflect the organization's structure, competitive environment, and overall goals and objectives. For example, the objectives should reflect the business and environmental factors affecting the organization, such as company size, capital structure, and industry competition and regulation.

1. SAFETY

Investment safety is usually viewed from the perspective of preservation of principal, but related factors such as credit quality and price volatility must also be considered. Credit quality can be measured in various ways and often indicates the probability of default, which means it can also be used to help measure the safety of the principal. Additionally, credit ratings are the primary mechanism used in measuring the quality of an investment portfolio. Oftentimes, minimum acceptable ratings levels for a portfolio or investment type are defined in the policy. Investment research is also used to evaluate credit risk. A wide variety of resources are available to help evaluate portfolio risk. Volatility, or the variability in the pricing of an investment, is also an important measure of both liquidity and safety. For fixed-income investments, volatility is usually related to maturity (i.e., longer maturity equates to higher price volatility). For equity investments, a commonly used measure of volatility is the beta (ß) for the stock.

2. LIQUIDITY

For a short-term investment portfolio, maintaining adequate liquidity is usually defined as the ability to quickly convert an asset into cash without a significant loss. For long-term portfolios, especially where the maturity of the investments can be matched closely to the need for funds, liquidity may not be a primary objective. Liquidity needs may vary significantly across companies. For example, some firms (e.g., broker-dealers) require daily liquidity, while others (e.g., pension funds or insurance companies) may have long-term liquidity requirements. Even firms within a specific industry may have differing liquidity requirements depending on their cash flow cycles, current profitability, and investment opportunities. Some firms may not have sufficient investment balances to consider alternatives such as external management or long-term investment horizons. Seasonality may also define the required liquidity needs (e.g., higher cash flows in the summer months). It is critical that both static and dynamic liquidity concerns be considered in the development of the investment policy.[4]

3. RISK/RETURN TRADE-OFF

An important objective of any investment policy is to achieve an acceptable return on invested capital. Careful consideration must be given when ranking investment return in relation to the other objectives of safety and liquidity. A key determinant in the return/safety/liquidity balance is the firm's risk tolerance. *Risk tolerance* refers to the willingness to take on additional risk in order to increase the expected rate of return on a portfolio. Risks that should be considered include credit, counterparty, interest rate, reinvestment, prepayment, FX, and sovereign risk. The investment policy should address specific procedures that must be followed to minimize the various types of investment risk. Like many elements of the investment policy, guidelines pertaining to risk tolerance must be tailored to each organization.

Some firms are more sensitive and susceptible to certain risks than others. Firms that engage in international commerce may face significant FX risks while other firms face none. Furthermore, every firm has its own perspective on and benchmarks for risk taking, principal preservation, and investment return, and ranks them in order of importance. Investment benchmarks are covered later in this chapter.

C. Developing a List of Permitted Investments

Once the investment objectives are established, the firm must decide which securities/instruments are suitable for investment and develop an approved list of permitted investments. Many firms include the approved list in their investment policies. The list may name specific securities approved for investment (e.g., ABC Company commercial paper) or it may simply specify categories of qualified investment instruments (e.g., commercial paper). Lists are sometimes based on minimum credit ratings (e.g., commercial paper with a minimum rating of A-1/P-1). For global companies, the approved list may further specify acceptable issuer countries and in some cases specific industries within countries. As an example, investment in African manufacturing companies may be approved, but not mining companies in Africa, due to concerns about conflict minerals. Regardless of the approach taken to establish the list, it is important to review each approved instrument periodically to ensure that it remains compatible with the stated investment objectives.

---

4. Static liquidity is measured at a particular point in time while dynamic liquidity is a measure of liquidity over a future period of time.

D. Investment Requirements

1. DIVERSIFICATION

Diversification is one of the most important tools an investment manager possesses to protect the organization from the risks to which it is exposed. Diversification approaches include:

- Allocating by asset class (e.g., fixed income, equity, and cash), or among a variety of investment management firms (e.g., 25% with Company A and 75% with Company B)

- Holding a certain percentage of foreign securities so the company can minimize the impact that movements in a specific currency may have on the portfolio (e.g., the US dollar weakens by 5% against the euro)

- Limiting investments in issues from the same organization to a certain percentage of the total portfolio (e.g., 10% of the portfolio)

- Limiting investments from specific issuers and/or instruments in order to limit concentration risk (e.g., can invest up to $10 million in ABC Company commercial paper, or can invest up to 10% of the portfolio in a single currency or country)

Whatever approach is used, the diversification strategy should be defined clearly in the investment policy.

Many instruments in an investment portfolio may make periodic coupon or dividend payments. The organization must decide how the payments should be reinvested in order to achieve optimal asset allocation. The investment policy should stipulate guidelines and procedures governing the receipt of payments and their use. These rules may have important tax implications and should therefore be drafted in consultation with a corporate tax advisor.

2. INVESTMENT OR EXPOSURE HORIZON

The investment horizon is the total length of time that an investment will be held before the investment matures or is sold. The longer the average time to maturity (i.e., duration) of investments in the portfolio, the greater the exposure to interest rate risk. An investment policy should specify any limitations that a firm may have regarding the maximum and average duration of the investments in its portfolio. This exposure horizon is a function of both the organization's risk philosophy and the total interest rate exposure already present in other areas of the organization. Short- and medium-term investment portfolios often consist of fixed-income securities and money market funds (MMFs). Since the price and/or return on those securities and MMFs are largely a function of the market interest rate, the portfolios are subject to significant interest rate exposure.

3. OTHER LIMITATIONS ON INVESTMENTS

In addition to decisions regarding diversification and investment/exposure horizons, organizations must consider several other investment-related issues and outline decisions regarding these issues in their investment policies. For example, an investment policy should:

- Clearly state the organization's attitude toward maintaining simultaneous outstanding debt and investment positions. Some companies prohibit any investment activity while the organization has outstanding debt that can be paid off.

- Clearly specify any limits on the holding of less-than-liquid assets. These are assets for which there is a limited secondary or resale market.

- List financial and/or credit rating requirements for financial institutions and other companies in which investments are made.

- Define any special credit requirements and guidelines if foreign investments are allowed in the policy (e.g., direct investment in foreign companies or indirect investment through brokers/funds).

- Ensure that collateralization and guarantee guidelines are specified clearly. Collateralization partially protects the purchaser of the securities from loss of invested principal. When accepting securities or other assets as collateral, the purchaser must consider not only the value of the collateral, but also its liquidity.

- Specify how mutual funds are to be selected and whether their composition must adhere to the guidelines established in the investment policy (e.g., approved investments, diversification, and exposure horizon) when mutual funds are utilized for an investment portfolio.

E. Other Issues in Developing an Investment Policy

1. VALUATION OF INVESTMENTS

The investment policy should state the process to be used for the valuation of investment portfolios and how to manage investments that may become impaired. This must comply with appropriate accounting guidelines, but it also helps document and support management choices where there are alternatives.

2. EXCEPTION MANAGEMENT

The investment policy must include provisions to accommodate exceptions. For example, when an investment opportunity arises that falls outside the approved list, the policy should dictate the appropriate procedure for obtaining exception approval. This can be as simple as obtaining a senior financial officer's written consent, or it may require a more formal approval. In addition, there should be guidelines on how to handle an investment that is downgraded, especially if the rating falls below investment policy guidelines.

There may be other cases where exceptions to the guidelines may be required. The investment policy should identify the individual or group whose approval is required for these exceptions. In addition, the policy should detail actions and procedures for dealing with exceptions found during compliance testing. For example, the policy might require that any exceptions found and determined to be high risk should be reported to the audit committee of the board of directors.

3. USE OF EXTERNAL MONEY MANAGERS

As an alternative to managing investments in-house, some firms may elect to use outside money managers. External money managers should be subject to the provisions of the corporate investment policy.

It is critical that the policy clearly describe the roles and responsibilities of those involved in the investment process.[5] These include the roles of the person(s) involved in:

- Investment selection (investment manager, treasurer)

- Investment execution and reporting (treasury staff)

---

5. A functional organizational chart or investment flowchart can also be very helpful in this process.

- Investment policy approvals or modifications, and exception management (CFO, board of directors)
- Accounting and reconciliation of investment activity (controller)
- Overall management of the investment process (senior management)

Furthermore, the roles and responsibilities of internal or external parties that have peripheral or infrequent involvement with the process should be identified. A description of their related duties and when they are performed should also be listed (e.g., annual external audit of the investment balances).

4. PERFORMANCE MEASUREMENT AND REPORTING

The policy should specify the appropriate benchmarks used for performance evaluation, as well as essential aspects of the required reports.

a. Performance Measurement

Portfolio performance should be evaluated against established benchmarks to measure and validate the success of the investment policy's objectives. The benchmarks selected should be consistent with the company's agreed-upon goals and should be based on investment vehicles permitted by the investment policy. Common benchmarks include yields on US Treasury securities and 30-day commercial paper. Indices of a particular segment of the market may also be used as benchmarks. Some common indices are the Lipper Money Market Funds Index, Barclays Capital 1–3 Year US Government/Credit Bond Index, and the Merrill Lynch 6-Month US Treasury Bill Index. Depending on the composition of the portfolio, a customized or blended benchmark, such as a weighted average of the 30-day T-bill yield and the 2-year Treasury note yield, may be best.

Firms that authorize the use of foreign investment instruments should also select benchmarks that reflect their global market exposure. These might include reference rates such as the London Interbank Offered Rate (LIBOR) and Sterling Overnight Index Average (SONIA), as well as specific international bond rates (e.g., Eurobonds). The impact of currency movements on the portfolio should also be reported.

b. Reporting

Reporting should be designed to accomplish specific goals. Accordingly, there should be different levels of reporting depending on the goals. For example, in a large organization with a significant investment portfolio, daily investment summaries may be prepared by the treasury or investment unit. Such reports are intended to provide financial managers with basic information about the daily portfolio composition, related interest rates, and maturities. Any breaches of investment limits and how those breaches were remedied should also be reported as quickly as possible. Weekly or monthly performance reports are another common form of investment reporting that provide a snapshot of portfolio holdings at a specific time. They also contain weekly or monthly average return information on the portfolio, comparisons to benchmarks, and narrative explanations of why the portfolio over- or underperformed relative to the benchmarks.

Furthermore, these reports often contain explanations of any fluctuation in average rates or invested balances, and may include projections for the next period. This type of report would be distributed to financial managers, but might also be directed to senior management. Other reports may be designed to address issues for discussion at quarterly or annual meetings of the board of directors, or to meet regulatory and rating agency financial statement reporting requirements (including narrative in the notes to consolidated financial statements, as well as in the management's discussion and analysis section required in reports such as US SEC Form 10-K reports).

c. Calculating Returns

As a concluding point in the discussion of performance measurement and reporting, it is important to note that a variety of methods exist for calculating the return associated with a security or portfolio. Total return, current yield, and yield to maturity are the most popular methods.

When comparing performance across time periods or across portfolios, it is essential that the portfolio returns are calculated in a consistent manner. Therefore, the investment policy should clearly state the method(s) that must be used to measure performance. Any differences related to taxable versus tax-exempt investments should also be considered, and any external investment managers should be required to report the same way.

5. POLICY COMPLIANCE

As with all policies, an investment policy should incorporate the need for regular policy compliance review and evaluation. Furthermore, it should identify the parties responsible for fulfilling this role. This may be a responsibility of internal or external auditors or a specific person or area outside the policy-related functional area, such as the compliance department. In certain firms, the internal or external auditors include investment policy compliance testing in their audits. When this is the case, the internal or external auditors should evaluate and review procedures, test individual transactions for compliance with the policy, confirm effectiveness and validity of selected investment reports, and make any appropriate recommendations to amend the policy or procedures. At the very least, auditors should test compliance and policy effectiveness annually, as well as immediately following periods of significant change in the company or following periods of major economic upheaval.

If internal or external auditors do not review investments for compliance with the policy, the responsibility for investment policy compliance measurement should be assigned to a specific person or unit outside the policy-related functional area. This approach clearly represents a best practice, as it ensures objectivity in the review process and does not rely on internal or external audit resources that may have other responsibilities that take precedence over compliance testing.

6. INTERNAL AND EXTERNAL CONTROLS

Controls should be established to ensure that assets and market-sensitive inside information are protected from loss, theft, or misuse. These controls should be described clearly in the investment policy. Segregation of duties is critical to ensuring sound internal controls. The separation of transaction authority from accounting and record keeping is essential to enforcing the checks and balances of the treasury department. Investment-related accounting activities should be segregated from the person and/or area responsible for managing investments. In addition, sound internal controls over the wire transfer process must be established and maintained. Again, these activities should be performed by someone outside the investment management process.

The monthly reconciliation of investment statements and records to an organization's internal general ledger accounts is considered a best practice and another significant safeguard in maintaining strong internal control. In addition to establishing internal safeguards against fraud and/or negligence, it is also important to understand the controls that third-party service providers have in place. Another recommended best practice is to conduct periodic audits of service providers to evaluate not only their service capabilities but also their internal controls. One approach for monitoring internal controls for providers is to require SSAE 16[6] audits of the providers' relevant operational controls.

---

6. Statement on Standards for Attestation Engagements (SSAE) No. 16 is formerly Statement on Auditing Standards No. 70, or SAS 70.

a. Custodial Service Providers

The investment policy should describe under what conditions a third-party custodian or safekeeping bank would be required to perform settlement of all investment transactions for external control purposes. A custodian will typically take possession of securities, receive delivery or book entry of principal and interest payments, perform record keeping, and provide maintenance services for the investment portfolio. These providers also play an important role in furnishing current electronic reporting on portfolio composition and performance. The custodian selection process usually includes reference checks and an analysis of financial stability, operating capabilities, quality of service, and services the custodian offers other than safekeeping (e.g., securities lending, reporting, FX, and short-term investment management services). Custodian performance is typically measured by the timeliness, completeness, and accuracy with which the custodian carries out its prescribed duties, and by compliance with established guidelines. As previously discussed, an organization may consider requesting an SSAE 16 report to help in the evaluation and review of any custodians.

b. Limitation of Liability

Limitation of liability is an area that should be addressed in the investment policy. For the purposes of an investment policy, limitation of liability relates to the measures designed to protect an organization involved in investment activity from financial loss due to negligence or crime. As such, it is important for organizations to specify in the investment policy what risk management steps should be taken (both internally and by outside parties) to limit exposure from negligence and crime (e.g., liability insurance).

7. EXTERNAL RESTRICTIONS

Regulatory or legal restrictions that may impact investment practices should be clearly described in the investment policy. Certain regulated entities (e.g., insurance companies, government agencies, and public utilities) may have specific investment constraints. For example, an insurance company may be required by NAIC (National Association of Insurance Commissioners) guidelines to limit investment activities to specific types of investments or impose concentration limits on permitted investments. Similarly, depending upon their legal structure and prevailing regulations, insurance companies, regulated entities, or state-sponsored institutions (e.g., universities and hospitals) may need to segregate their investments in separate accounts to comply with statutory commingling guidelines. The investment policy should clearly define all restrictions that affect the investment practices of the organization. Debt covenants may also place specific limitations on how a company manages investments. Restrictions may require the debt issuer to pay down the debt with any available cash, effectively prohibiting the company from making any short-term investments until the debt is retired.

V. OVERVIEW OF KEY TREASURY POLICIES

This section presents a list of key treasury policies that should be considered for all organizations. An overview of the major factors that should be addressed in drafting the specific policies is also provided.

A. Liquidity Policy

One of the primary objectives of treasury management is maintaining liquidity. A firm may limit the probability of a cash shortage by developing and implementing a liquidity policy. The liquidity policy should include the following components:

- Purpose of the policy
- Liquidity management objectives

- Reporting
- Sources of liquidity
- Liquidity measurement
- Methods to identify potential events that can create liquidity shortages
- Exception management
- Roles and responsibilities
- Definitions

B. Bank Account and Financial Services Authority Policies

Bank account and financial services authority policies are essential for providing the appropriate delegation of authority regarding opening, closing, and managing accounts. Key items to be addressed in these policies include:

- Delegation of authority allowing treasury to manage financial service provider relationships
- Delegation of authority to open and close bank accounts
- Oversight and governance of banking relationships
- Duties and tasks involved in managing relationships
- Qualifying types of financial institutions
- Signing authority and reporting requirements
- Financial institution evaluation and reporting requirements
- Documentation requirements
- Records retention requirements

C. Payments Policy

A payments policy is important in order to provide consistent management of payments and payments risk across all payment processes.[7] Key elements of a payments policy include:

- Delegation of authority
- Permitted payment methods
- Payment and approval limits
- Joint approval requirements
- Payment authorization requirements
- Payment risk management
- Required documentation

---

7. In addition to an overall payments policy, many companies provide a separate electronic funds transfer policy and/or an international payments policy, due to the increased potential risks associated with these areas.

D. Wire Transfer Policy

A wire transfer policy is important due to the risks associated with wire payments. A wire transfer policy should provide guidance to ensure that wire transfers are executed in a secure manner. Key elements of the policy may include:

- Objective of the policy
- Minimum wire transfer amount
- Required documentation
- Processing times
- Individual responsibilities for initiators and approvers
- Permitted wire systems (e.g., Fedwire, CHIPS)
- Segregation of duties

E. Collection and Concentration Policy

A collection and concentration policy covers the issues involved in collecting customer payments and converting the receipts into accessible, available funds. Concerns to be addressed in this policy include:

- Control objectives
- Segregation of duties
- Customer satisfaction
- Acceptable payment types (e.g., cash or credit cards)
- Performance measurement
- Reporting requirements
- Exception management
- Incident response

F. Cash Flow Forecasting Policy

Organizations should establish a cash flow forecasting policy to ensure that a current, consistent, and accurate cash flow forecast is available. The cash flow forecast is an essential tool for liquidity planning and risk management. A cash flow forecasting policy should include:

- Goals of the cash flow forecast
- Roles and responsibilities
- Forecast frequency (e.g., daily, weekly, monthly)
- Format
- Definitions
- Schedule for updating the forecast

· Acceptable forecasting methods

· Variance analysis

· Directions for forecasting cash flows in foreign currencies

G. Investment Valuation and Impairment Policies

In addition to a general short-term investment policy, it may also be beneficial to develop policies regarding investment valuation and impairment. These policies should address:

· Identification of impaired investments, including other-than-temporary impairment

· Mark-to-market requirements

· Valuation of impaired securities

· Reporting requirements

· Exception management

· Security breaches and incident response

H. Payment Card Policies

Policies for payment cards should include:

· Types of cards issued

· Eligibility and approved uses

· Definition of responsibilities

· Card and transaction limits

· Review and reconcilement requirements

· Purchase restrictions, if any

· Rules regarding cash advances

· Exception management

· PCI DSS compliance requirements[8]

· Payment and fraud risk management

I. Merchant Card Policies

Policies for receipt of card payments from customers should include:

· Types of cards accepted

· Approved card acceptance methods

· Definition of responsibilities

· Transaction limits, if any

· Review and reconcilement requirements

---

8. The Payment Card Industry Data Security Standard (PCI DSS) is discussed in Chapter 4, Payment Systems.

- PCI DSS compliance requirements

- Payment and fraud risk management

- Any requirements regarding merchant services providers

- Compliance with network rules

- Compliance with state and local laws

- Incident response

J. Outsourcing Policy

The growing trend of firms outsourcing various operating units underscores the need for outsourcing policies that help manage risk and maintain control. Key issues to be addressed in an outsourcing policy include:

- Delegation of authority

- Reporting requirements

- Vendor and operational risk management

- Information security and confidentiality requirements

- Performance measurement

K. Financial Risk Management Policies

Financial risk management falls under the umbrella of enterprise risk management, but warrants a separate policy due to its unique nature. Financial risk management policies apply to any financial instruments but are especially necessary if financial derivatives are used, as policies may be a requirement for proper accounting and tax purposes. Firms involved in hedging or otherwise using derivatives may want to consider specific policies covering just their use. Key items to be incorporated in financial risk management policies include:

- Scope of permitted hedging and derivative activities

- Delegation of authority

- Segregation of duties

- Authorized derivatives

- Performance measurement and evaluation

- Management reporting

- Accounting and disclosure

- Trade/deal limits and monitoring

- Exception management

- Approved counterparties and related limits

L. Regulatory Compliance Policies

Regulatory compliance policies cover activities needed to comply with regulatory requirements that exist in a growing number of countries, including regulations related to money laundering, trade, and corruption. Corporations should implement policies to ensure compliance with labor laws, environmental regulations, antitrust laws, securities laws, and many others. Key policy elements include:

- Statement of policy and required compliance
- Subcontractor and vendor compliance requirements
- Compliance monitoring activities
- Audit requirements
- Exception management
- Disciplinary processes

M. Funding/Financing Policies

Funding/financing policies pertain to the execution of strategies for long-term funding of the organization and should include:

- Funding objectives
- Limits and targets for committed funding
- Limits and targets for different sources of funding (e.g., banks and capital markets)
- Structural considerations of fixed- versus variable-rate debt
- Covenants
- Regulatory restrictions, if any
- Tax and other compliance mandates
- Authorization/approval processes and any related delegation of authority
- Refinancing or prepayment processes
- Arbitrage rules (which may precipitate spend-down requirements)
- Uses of derivatives
- References to standard documentation

N. Treasury Systems Policy

In addition to end-user computing requirements, firms may want a specific policy regarding any treasury management systems (TMSs) they have installed. Concerns to be addressed in this policy include:

- Access to treasury systems
- Granular security to limit access to specific areas (e.g., wire transfer modules and cash balance visibility)
- Password requirements
- Segregation of duties

· Reconcilement with accounting and other books of record

· Backup and recovery

· Off-premise access and use

· Reporting requirements

· Timeline for disabling access of employees leaving the firm

VI. SUMMARY

Written treasury policies and procedures are an important part of an organization's internal controls and risk management activities. This chapter covered the key elements of a well-written policy statement and how to develop and document treasury policies and procedures. A short-term investment policy was provided as a sample policy and used to illustrate the development of a policy statement. The chapter closed with a high-level description of essential treasury policies, including key items that should be addressed in those policy statements. A sample investment policy is provided in Appendix 18.1 for further illustration and reference.

APPENDIX 18.1: SAMPLE SHORT-TERM INVESTMENT POLICY

Policy Title: Short-Term Investment Policy for ABC Inc.
Created: January 3, 2013

Revision History		
Version	**Board Approval**	**Comments**
1.0	January 3, 2013	Initial policy
1.1	January 4, 2014	Revised list of approved investments
2.0	July 5, 2015	Compliance update
3.0	March 17, 2016	Revised roles and responsibilities

Table of Contents

1.0 PURPOSE

The purpose of this policy is to set guidelines for the parameters, responsibilities, and controls for the short-term (12 months or less) investment of corporate funds.

2.0 OBJECTIVES

A. To ensure the safety and preservation of principal

B. To maintain adequate liquidity to meet cash flow requirements

C. To obtain the best available return consistent with safety and liquidity

D. To maintain standardized guidelines throughout the company

3.0 SCOPE

This policy applies to ABC Inc. and all of its wholly owned subsidiaries, including foreign subsidiaries. Investments are restricted to short-term investments as defined in the policy and as governed by ABC Inc.'s treasury department for all of its subsidiaries. For the purposes of this policy, the chief financial officer (CFO), treasurer, assistant treasurer, manager of treasury operations, and any of their appointees have the roles and responsibilities as defined in the policy for the investment activities of the company as a whole. This policy does not cover 401(k), profit-sharing, deferred compensation, stock purchase, or deferred director fee plans of ABC Inc., which are covered by separate policies.

4.0 APPROVED LIST OF SHORT-TERM INVESTMENTS

The following instruments are approved for short-term investment:

- Bank deposits
- Domestic certificates of deposit
- Domestic commercial paper (rated A-1/P-1)
- Banker's acceptances
- US Treasury bills and notes
- Collateralized repurchase agreements
- Eurodollar time deposits
- Mutual funds that invest exclusively in securities approved under this policy

5.0 INVESTMENT REQUIREMENTS

- Active investments with outside money managers are prohibited, with the exception of mutual funds (as stated in Section 4.0).
- To minimize foreign exchange exposure, all investments must be denominated in the functional currency of the entity making the investment.
- All issuers of commercial paper must be US corporations.
- Repurchase agreements must be fully collateralized by any of the securities approved under this investment policy. The current market value of the collateral must cover the principal amount of the investment at all times during the term of the investment.
- The composition of any mutual fund must meet the criteria for approved securities.
- The average duration of any short-term investment portfolio must not exceed nine months.
- ABC Inc. may take simultaneous debt and investment positions. The CFO has full discretion in determining the size of those positions.
- No more than 25% of the portfolio may be invested in securities lacking an active secondary market. Securities that have no active secondary market must mature in periods during which the company has high working capital requirements. Selection of the appropriate maturity schedule is left to the discretion of the CFO.
- All new types of investments must pass a formal review process that evaluates all related risks.
- Cash receipts from coupon and interest payments shall be handled by the accounting department. An accrued tax liability shall be recorded and the proceeds returned to the portfolio for reinvestment.

Investments in banks and domestic corporations under this policy are subject to the following additional limitations:

- US banks must have total assets of at least $40 billion or have a credit relationship with the company.
- Foreign banks must have total assets of at least $50 billion or have a credit relationship with the company. Foreign banks must have an agency, branch, or representative office with a domestic US license.
- Issuing corporations must have a commercial paper rating of P-1 or better by Moody's Investors Service and A-1 or better by Standard & Poor's, or an equivalent rating by another nationally recognized rating agency. (At least two ratings are required.) If the rating is supported by a bank letter of credit (L/C), then the L/C must be issued by a bank having a minimum long-term debt rating of Aa by Moody's and AA by Standard & Poor's.

Any exceptions to the above must be approved by the CFO.

Diversification

The approved types of investment instruments must be allocated among the following three categories, but not exceed the percentages indicated:

Category	Not More Than % of Total	Portfolio Instrument Types
US Government	95%	Treasury bills, Treasury notes, collateralized repurchase agreements backed by Treasuries
Corporate	55%	Domestic commercial paper, collateralized repurchase agreements backed by commercial paper
Bank	95%	Bank accounts, Eurodollar time deposits, money market accounts, banker's acceptances, certificates of deposit, collateralized repurchase agreements backed by any of the above bank-related securities
Concentration per Organization: To provide for diversification, investments are limited to $5 million per issuing entity for corporate-related instruments.		
Concentration per Mutual Fund: Up to $60 million may be invested in any single well-diversified mutual fund that invests exclusively in securities authorized under this investment policy.		

6.0 CUSTODY OF SECURITIES

All of the financial institutions in which the company is eligible to invest, subject to the investment requirements listed in Section 5.0 of this document, are also authorized to hold investments in custody on behalf of the company. The company shall not take physical possession of investment securities.

7.0 EXCEPTION MANAGEMENT

Any exceptions to this policy must be approved in writing. For minor exceptions, such as exceeding investment limits on approved investments, the written approval of the CFO or treasurer is required. For major exceptions, such as purchasing a new investment instrument or exceeding portfolio diversification requirements, the written approval of the board of directors is required.

8.0 PERFORMANCE MEASUREMENT AND REPORTING

The performance of the short-term investment portfolio shall be benchmarked against the total return and yield to maturity of the Lipper Money Market Funds Index, the Merrill Lynch 1–3 Year US Corporate/Government Bond Index, and the Barclays Capital US Aggregate Bond Index. Money market mutual funds shall be benchmarked against the iMoneyNet Money Fund Report All-Taxable Average.

The treasury staff shall prepare weekly performance reports under the guidance of the assistant treasurer. The manager of treasury operations shall deliver a monthly report to the CFO and board of directors detailing the short-term investment portfolio's composition and performance. In addition, the manager of treasury operations is charged with disclosure of portfolio holdings in the 10-K and 10-Q reports that must be filed with the US Securities and Exchange Commission.

9.0 ROLES AND RESPONSIBILITIES

Roles and responsibilities of the parties involved are specified below:

ROLE: **Board of Directors**

- Approving the policy
- Approving major policy exceptions (e.g., new investment types)
- Approving policy revisions
- Setting performance metrics

ROLE: **Chief Financial Officer**

- Developing the investment strategy
- Approving minor policy exceptions (e.g., amounts and terms)

ROLE: **Treasurer**

- Serving as policy custodian
- Developing the investment strategy
- Distributing the policy and revisions

ROLE: **Assistant Treasurer**

- Overseeing investment activities
- Recommending variations in set amounts and/or terms
- Collecting performance information

ROLE: **Manager of Treasury Operations**

- Keeping abreast of developments in the money market
- Keeping the treasurer and assistant treasurer informed of developments in the money market
- Providing investment reports to management as requested
- Investing excess funds as provided herein
- Determining the amount and maturity of an investment
- Distributing performance information

10.0 INTERNAL CONTROLS

The following internal controls must be enforced:

- The separation of transaction authority from accounting and record keeping shall be enforced.
- The separation of wire transfer and investment transaction duties shall be maintained. Wire transfers must be performed by a party outside the investment management process.
- All physical deliveries or book entries of principal and/or interest shall be performed by a third-party custodian.
- A monthly reconciliation of investment statements to the general ledger accounts shall be performed, and the results shall be delivered to the CFO and the treasurer.
- All investment portfolios must be covered by the company's liability and crime coverage insurance policies.
- All banks, brokers, and custodians must carry adequate liability and crime coverage, and provide a detailed review and assessment of their internal controls.

The manager of treasury operations shall have responsibility and authority over internal controls; however, controls may be removed only with the written consent of the CFO.

11.0 COMPLIANCE

Internal auditors shall include policy compliance in their audits. Auditors shall review procedures and performance and make recommendations for changes, as appropriate. Compliance testing shall be performed annually.

A copy of the policy and related procedures manual shall be placed on file in the treasurer's office, and an electronic version shall be posted on the company's intranet.

PART VI
Financial Management

CHAPTER 19
Long-Term Investments

I. INTRODUCTION

II. VALUATION OF CAPITAL MARKET SECURITIES
    A. Bond Valuation
    B. Preferred Stock Valuation
    C. Common Stock Valuation

III. MANAGING CAPITAL MARKET INVESTMENTS
    A. Asset Allocation
    B. Managing the Bond Portfolio
    C. Managing the Equity Portfolio

IV. SUMMARY

I. INTRODUCTION

This chapter describes key elements associated with the valuation of bonds and equity securities (i.e., long-term or capital market investments). As compared to money market instruments, capital market investments are less liquid and have increased price volatility. Treasury professionals should therefore be familiar with the returns and risk characteristics associated with long-term investments.

The return objective for most capital market investment portfolios will be a mix between current income (e.g., coupon payments for bonds and dividends for stocks) and capital gains arising from an increase in the market price of the security. The investment return objective may also be impacted by the intended use for those returns. For example, if the portfolio is to be used for pension fund purposes, then the portfolio manager may use asset/liability management to structure the cash flows and maturities of the portfolio to match the projected needs for the pension payments. As another example, if the projected use for the investment returns is to provide a sinking fund for repayment of a debt issue's principal, then investments would be structured specifically to meet the large, future cash outflow.

Key issues that treasury professionals should consider when determining their capital market investment objectives include:

- Risk tolerance
- Return objectives
- Liquidity needs
- Time horizons or future needs for funds
- Tax issues
- Asset/liability matching
- Legal or regulatory factors (especially for pension fund investments)

Also, firms will find it helpful to have a capital market investment policy. The primary differences between the short-term and capital market investment policies will be the overall investment guidelines and the permitted investments. These differences result from capital preservation being the primary objective of the short-term investment portfolio. This objective, however, may not fit the guidelines for capital market investments, where it is usually assumed that the firm has the ability to weather short-term volatility in the prices of bond and equity securities.

This chapter opens with a discussion of the techniques used to value bonds, preferred equity, and common equity. Next, the asset allocation decision is discussed, followed by a description of key aspects of bond portfolio management. The chapter concludes with a discussion of the key areas of risk that are associated with each type of capital market investment.

II. VALUATION OF CAPITAL MARKET SECURITIES

Securities that are issued by publicly traded firms are valued by capital providers in financial markets. The market value of a financial security equals the present value of the expected cash flows derived from the security. To arrive at the present value, the expected stream of cash flows is discounted by the required rate of return that the market believes is commensurate with the security's level of risk. This valuation approach is written using the following formula:

$$PV_0 = \frac{CF_1}{(1+k)^1} + \frac{CF_2}{(1+k)^2} + ... + \frac{CF_n}{(1+k)^n}$$

Where:

PV_0 = Present value of the security's cash flow stream

CF_n = Annual cash flow produced by the security in year n

k = Required rate of return or opportunity cost for the security

If the present value exceeds the security's current price, then the investor would seek to purchase the security. Meanwhile, the investor would seek to sell the security if the present value is less than the security's current price. This generalized valuation approach is used to calculate the market price for bonds, preferred stock, and common stock.

A. Bond Valuation

The valuation of bonds is fairly straightforward because the amount and timing of future cash flows are specified. In fact, this is why bonds are commonly referred to as *fixed-income securities*. The cash flows derived from a bond include periodic coupon payments and the payment of par value at maturity. In effect, these cash flows are similar to those that are common with other types of loan agreements in that the payment of coupons is comparable to the payment of interest expense, and the payment of par value at maturity is comparable to the repayment of principal.

A bond's market price is the present value of the stream of coupon payments plus the present value of the par value. The cash flows are discounted at the market's required rate of return, which is the interest rate the market is demanding over the remaining life of the bond at a particular point in time. This rate is called the *yield to maturity (YTM)*.

For example, suppose that a three-year $1,000 bond with a 10% annual coupon rate has a YTM of 5%.[1] This bond will provide the investor with a current income stream of $100 (i.e.,$1,000 × 10%) at the end of each of the next three years. Further, the bond issuer will repay the bond's par value of $1,000 at maturity. The market price of the bond is therefore calculated as:

$$\text{Market Price of Bond} = \frac{\$100}{(1+0.05)^1} + \frac{\$100}{(1+0.05)^2} + \frac{\$1,100}{(1+0.05)^3} = \$1,136.16$$

In some cases, an investor would be interested in determining the YTM on a bond, given the bond's coupon payments and current market price. For coupon-paying bonds, there is no closed-form solution for the YTM; an investor would therefore need to use a financial calculator or spreadsheet software (e.g., Microsoft Excel) to solve for the YTM. Once the YTM is determined, the investor can compare it to the rate of return that the investor would require before buying the bond. If the YTM exceeds this required rate, then the investor would consider purchasing the bond. However, if the YTM is less than the required return, the investor would consider selling the bond.

---

1. Many bonds pay semiannual coupons. For valuation, the coupon payment and required rate of return are divided by two, while the number of coupons received is doubled. The investor receives the same aggregate level of coupons, but the timing of receipt changes. For ease of calculation, the quantitative example assumes annual coupon payments.

If a bond has a call provision, which allows the issuer to redeem the bond prior to maturity, then an investor will also be interested in the yield to call (YTC). This is the yield that the bond would provide if the issuer calls it prior to maturity. The YTC is determined much like the YTM but uses the call date instead of the maturity date. Since callable bonds usually are called only if interest rates have fallen, the YTC is typically lower than the YTM. One approach to analyzing callable bonds is known as *yield to worst (YTW)*, where all the possible YTC values are determined and the lowest of the potential values is the YTW. This process provides a range of possible outcomes that helps the investor better understand the risk parameters of the investment. Exhibit 19.1 illustrates the YTM, YTC, and YTW concepts.

EXHIBIT 19.1 YIELD TO MATURITY, YIELD TO CALL, AND YIELD TO WORST

The yield on a bond is the rate of return that is earned if the bond is purchased at a given price and held until maturity, or some other specific call date. Suppose that the market price of a $1,000 par value bond with a 6% annual coupon is $1,063, and the bond matures in five years. The yield to maturity (YTM) is the rate of return earned if the bond is purchased at $1,063 and held for five years. The yield to maturity for this bond is 4.56%.

Now assume that the bond is callable at the end of each year prior to maturity. The yield to call (YTC) is the rate of return earned if the bond is purchased at $1,063 and then called on a specific date. The call schedule, call prices, and corresponding yield to call for each call date are given below.

END OF YEAR	CALL PRICE	YIELD TO CALL (YTC)
1	$1,050	4.42%
2	$1,040	4.59%
3	$1,020	4.35%
4	$1,010	4.48%

Given the yield to maturity on the bond and the yields to call, the lowest yield is earned if the bond is called at the end of Year 3. Therefore, the yield to worst (YTW) is 4.35%.

The YTW concept can also be used with other types of bonds. In this context, YTW is the lowest possible yield that can be received on a bond without the issuer actually defaulting. This yield is calculated by making worst-case scenario assumptions on the issue by calculating the returns that would be received if all potentially negative provisions (e.g., prepayments, calls, or sinking funds) are used by the issuer.

B. Preferred Stock Valuation

Preferred stock is a hybrid security that has features of both debt and equity. Preferred stock offers investors a steady stream of income via preferred dividends, much like the coupon payments offered on bonds. The annual preferred dividend is stated as a percentage of the preferred stock's par value, but it is distributed in quarterly installments. Like debt, preferred stock has a claim above common stock in both going concern and liquidation situations.

Preferred stock is like common equity in that bankruptcy is not a possible consequence of missing a dividend payment. Further, preferred stock generally does not mature and its claim on earnings or asset liquidation values is subordinate to all debt claims. From a valuation standpoint, preferred stock is viewed as a perpetuity. To value a perpetuity, the perpetual cash flow is simply divided by the required rate of return on the security.

As an example, assume that a share of preferred stock has a $50 par value and pays a 6.6% annual dividend. Further, the market currently requires an 8.0% return on the firm's preferred stock. The preferred stock annual dividend is calculated as:

$$\text{Annual Preferred Stock Dividend} = \text{Preferred Stock Dividend Rate} \times \text{Par Value}$$

$$= 0.066 \times \$50 = \$3.30$$

The present value of the perpetual stream of preferred dividends is calculated as:

$$\text{Price of Preferred Stock} = \frac{\text{Annual Preferred Stock Dividend}}{\text{Required Rate of Return}}$$

$$= \frac{\$3.30}{0.08} = \$41.25$$

Note that the present value of preferred stock is inversely related to the market's required return. For example, an increase in the required rate of return from 8% to 10% results in the following price:

$$\text{Price of Preferred Stock} = \frac{\$3.30}{0.10} = \$33.00$$

As these calculations reveal, the market price of preferred stock falls when the required rate of return increases. The only way a higher return can be earned from a fixed dividend stream is to pay less for the right to receive that stream of dividends.

C. Common Stock Valuation

Common stock valuation differs from that of bonds and preferred stock because the timing and level of cash flows associated with common stock ownership are not fixed. A firm's dividend policy is set by its board of directors, and the actual dividend paid may change over time. In fact, one of the primary advantages of investing in common equity is the growth potential in earnings and dividends.

To value common stock, an investor must estimate the present value of the future dividend stream. This involves estimating the future dividends and determining the appropriate required rate of return on the issuer's equity. One of the most common approaches is to assume that the dividends will grow at some constant rate in the future.

If this is the case, then the future dividend in period *t+1* (D_{t+1}) is simply the current dividend (D_t) multiplied by one plus the estimated growth rate (*g*), as stated below:

$$D_{t+1} = D_t(1+g)$$

After using the above formula to calculate the next expected dividend (D_{t+1}), the following equation can be used to estimate the present value of a share of common stock:[2]

$$\text{Price of Common Stock in Period } t = \frac{D_{t+1}}{k-g}$$

In the equation, *k* represents the required rate of return, while *g* represents the growth rate in dividends. This valuation model is commonly referred to as the *Gordon growth model* or *dividend discount model*. This model works well for firms that pay a steadily growing dividend. In many cases, growth can be determined from either historical growth patterns or via estimates provided by analysts. The required rate of return on the stock can be determined using the capital asset pricing model (CAPM), which is discussed in further detail later in this chapter.

As an example, this approach can be applied using the following assumptions:

- Current dividend paid (D_t) = $2.00
- Expected dividend growth rate (*g*) = 6%
- Required return on common equity (*k*) = 13%

In this example, the price of a share of common stock is calculated as:

$$\text{Price of Common Stock in Period } t = \frac{\$2(1.06)}{0.13-0.06} = \$30.29$$

Note that an individual investor may calculate a different price than that for which the share currently trades. For example, suppose that an investor believes that future dividend growth will only be 3%, as opposed to the consensus of 6% in the capital market. The investor would then calculate the price as follows:

$$\text{Price of Common Stock in Period } t = \frac{\$2(1.03)}{0.13-0.03} = \$20.60$$

This estimate of value is lower than in the previous example due to the assumed lower growth rate in dividends.

In closing this section, it is important to note that the Gordon growth model should only be used to value common stock when the following assumptions are met:

1. The required return must exceed the dividend growth rate (i.e., k > g).
2. The dividend growth rate must be expected to be constant in perpetuity.

---

2. By dividing D_{t+1} by *k-g*, the equation calculates the present value of the perpetual stream of growing dividends.

III. MANAGING CAPITAL MARKET INVESTMENTS

A. Asset Allocation

One of the key decisions in managing a capital market investment portfolio is that of asset allocation, or the mix between bonds and equities.[3] A careful analysis of the investor's risk tolerance is a starting point for determining the optimal asset allocation. After determining the risk tolerance, the investor's return objective should be considered. The return objective may be stated in terms of:

- An absolute return, such as an annualized return of 2.5%

- A general goal (e.g., current income, capital appreciation, capital preservation, or total return)

- A relative benchmark return, such as exceeding the return on 10-year US Treasuries by 50 basis points

The firm's liquidity needs will also influence the asset allocation decision. A firm that will need cash from the portfolio in the near future will hold a higher percentage of short-term bonds, while a firm without near-term liquidity needs may allocate more capital to equities.

This section describes key issues associated with managing both bond and equity portfolios. An improved understanding of these issues will help guide the management of the overall capital market portfolio.

B. Managing the Bond Portfolio

Risk refers to the possibility that actual results may differ from expected results. Bonds are generally considered less risky than equity investments. This is because bonds provide a fixed income stream. Despite this, bonds are not risk-free investments. In fact, interest rate volatility is one of the key risks associated with investments in bonds.

This section describes several aspects that should be considered when managing the bond portion of a capital market portfolio. These risks are particularly relevant to investors that operate as insurance companies, financial intermediaries, or educational institutions.

Further, many of the policy and procedure issues related to the management of a bond portfolio are the same as those related to short-term investments. A key difference, however, is that the associated maturities of bonds represent a greater concern, relative to the shorter maturities of short-term investments.

1. INTEREST RATE RISK

The fixed-income nature of bonds implies that the price of these securities is highly sensitive to interest rates. To illustrate, examine the price action[4] for the bond from the earlier example that had a par value of $1,000, a 10% annual coupon rate, and a maturity of three years. At a market rate of interest, or YTM, of 5%, the bond would be priced at $1,136.16. Suppose that interest rates suddenly increased to 6%. The bond price would decrease to $1,106.92, as shown below:

$$\text{Price of Bond} = \frac{\$100}{(1+0.06)^1} + \frac{\$100}{(1+0.06)^2} + \frac{\$1,100}{(1+0.06)^3} = \$1,106.92$$

---

3. A long-term portfolio may generate some cash due to normal operations (also referred to as *residual cash*), but cash and cash equivalents are normally considered part of short-term investment management until invested in a capital asset.

4. *Price action* refers to the movement of a security's price in response to various market factors.

This example illustrates a fundamental aspect of bond pricing: bond prices are inversely related to interest rates. That is, as interest rates increase, bond prices drop. Likewise, as interest rates drop, bond prices increase (e.g., the bond price is $1,198.00 at a YTM of 3%).

An important measure that can be used to approximate a bond's price change is referred to as *duration*. Duration represents the bond's weighted average time to maturity. In short, bonds with longer durations are more sensitive to changes in interest rates. The following steps are used to calculate duration:

1. Calculate the present value of each annual cash flow generated by the bond.

2. Multiply the values from Step 1 by the year in which the cash flow occurs.

3. Divide each product from Step 2 by the bond price.

4. Sum the values from Step 3.

These steps are illustrated below:

$$\text{Step 1} = \frac{\$100}{(1+0.06)^1} + \frac{\$100}{(1+0.06)^2} + \frac{\$1,100}{(1+0.06)^3} = 94.34 + 89.00 + 923.58 = \$1,106.92$$

$$\text{Step 2} = (1)94.34 + (2)89.00 + (3)923.58 = 94.34 + 178.00 + 2,770.74$$

$$\text{Step 3} = \frac{94.34}{1,106.92} + \frac{178.00}{1,106.92} + \frac{2,770.74}{1,106.92} = 0.0852 + 0.1608 + 2.503$$

$$\text{Step 4} = 0.0852 + 0.1608 + 2.503 = 2.75$$

$$\text{Duration} = 2.75$$

These calculations indicate that this bond has a duration[5] of 2.75 years, which means that the bondholder recoups its invested capital in 2.75 years. Another implication of duration is that it allows the investor to approximate a bond's price sensitivity to interest rate movements. In general, the approximate percentage change in bond price can be calculated using the following equation:

$$\text{Approximate \% Change in Bond Price} = -\text{Duration} \times \text{Change in Interest Rate}$$

The equation shows that an increase in the interest rate (i.e., a positive change in interest rate) will lead to a lower bond price. Further, the equation shows that bonds with longer durations will have larger price drops, given an increase in interest rates.

---

5. This example provides the calculation for Macaulay duration. Modified duration is another frequently used measure that is calculated by dividing the Macaulay duration by *(1+YTM)*. In this example, modified duration would be calculated as: 2.75÷(1+0.06) = 2.59.

To illustrate, consider the earlier example in which the market interest rate increased from 5% to 6% and the bond price decreased from $1,136.16 to $1,106.92, which represents a percentage decrease of 2.57%.[6] If the approximation approach above is used to calculate the percentage change in the bond price, the result would be slightly different, as shown below:

$$\text{Approximate \% Change in Bond Price} = -2.75 \times 0.01 = -0.0275 \text{ or } -2.75\%$$

The approximation approach slightly overestimates the implied percentage decrease in the bond price.[7] Note that the equation can also be used to estimate the price change if interest rates are expected to decrease. For example, given an anticipated 2% decrease in interest rates, the approximate percentage change in this bond's price is 5.50%.

A helpful attribute of the approximation approach is that it provides the investor with a quick method for determining the price volatility of the bond. Duration helps treasury professionals understand the concept of interest rate risk, or the risk from changes in market value for fixed-income investments when the general level of market rates fluctuates. For risk management purposes, some investors may avoid bonds with longer durations. Meanwhile, other investors with a greater risk tolerance may seek out bonds with longer durations if they believe that future interest rates will drop.

Factors that affect bond duration include:

- **Time to Maturity:** Consider two bonds, each with a cost of $1,000 and a YTM of 5%. A bond that matures in one year would have a shorter duration than a bond that matures in 10 years. As a result, the shorter-maturity bond would have less price risk.

- **Coupon Rate:** The coupon payment (i.e., the coupon rate multiplied by the par value) is a key variable that influences duration. All else equal, bonds with larger coupon rates will have shorter durations and less price risk, relative to comparable bonds with smaller coupon rates. This relationship holds because the larger coupon speeds up the repayment of the investor's capital. In an extreme case, consider the duration of a zero-coupon bond (i.e., the coupon payment is $0). A zero-coupon bond has a duration equal to the maturity of the bond.

Exhibit 19.2 demonstrates the impact on the pricing of the one-year and ten-year bonds given a change in YTM. Due to its longer maturity, and therefore longer stream of coupon payments, the ten-year bond shows a much greater change in price than the one-year bond. As discussed above, the duration measure provides a rough estimate of the impact of changes in interest rates on the price of the bond. For the one-year bond, the duration of 0.978 would predict a drop in the bond price of about 0.978% for a 1% interest rate increase, which is close to the actual percentage change. For the ten-year bond, the duration of 8.295 indicates a much greater price drop (approximately 8.3%) for a 1% increase in interest rates—close to the 7.85% actual drop in price. Thus, higher duration equates to higher interest rate risk.

---

6. The percentage decrease is calculated as: ($1,106.92–$1,136.16)÷$1,136.16.
7. The duration approach does not provide the exact percentage change in bond price due to the convex relationship between bond prices and the YTM.

EXHIBIT 19.2 **DURATION'S IMPACT ON INTEREST RATE RISK**

PAR VALUE	COUPON RATE	MATURITY	DURATION	MARKET PRICE AT 3.5% YIELD	MARKET PRICE AT 4.5% YIELD	PERCENTAGE CHANGE
$1,000	3.00%	1 YEAR	0.978	$995.13	$985.49	−0.969%
$1,000	4.00%	10 YEARS	8.295	$1,041.88	$960.09	−7.850%

2. DIVERSIFICATION

Just as with stocks, diversification across issuers can help reduce the overall risk of a fixed-income portfolio. Credit risk diversification reduces the overall risk of the portfolio as long as credit rating changes and defaults are not highly correlated. However, diversification may not fully insulate investors from losses during periods of extreme market turmoil.

3. RATIO OF FIXED-RATE INVESTMENTS TO FLOATING-RATE INVESTMENTS

In addition to using interest rate risk, many fixed-income portfolio managers also use the ratio of fixed-rate obligations to floating-rate obligations to monitor their portfolios. This relation is usually expressed in terms of a target fixed/floating ratio. In general, the ratio of fixed-rate to floating-rate investments tends to correspond to management's views on long-term interest rates. If interest rates are expected to rise, then it would be optimal to hold more floating-rate than fixed-rate investments in the portfolio. There are two reasons that a firm will benefit from holding more floating-rate bonds in a rising interest rate environment. First, coupon payments received from the investment will increase as rates rise. Second, floating-rate bond prices are less sensitive to interest rate changes, as the durations for floating-rate bonds are shorter than for fixed-rate bonds with the same maturity. Therefore, if interest rates increase, the price of a floating-rate bond will have a smaller decrease than the price of a fixed-rate bond. Alternatively, if rates are expected to drop, then fixed-rate obligations should be locked in.

The drawback to managing a portfolio solely on the ratio of fixed-rate investments to floating-rate investments is that it only considers one operational target and fails to take into account the terms of the actual securities in the portfolio. Since bonds come in various maturities, the ratio of fixed-rate debt to total debt reveals very little about the debt's maturity profile and the associated risks. As a result, it is also important to take into account the average term to maturity of the portfolio, as well as the overall duration of the portfolio.

4. FOREIGN-CURRENCY-DENOMINATED BONDS

An additional complication associated with managing a bond portfolio arises when bonds are held that are denominated in a foreign currency. When investing in foreign-currency-denominated bonds, the investment manager must consider the impact of fluctuating exchange rates on the value of the bond portfolio. This means that in addition to default and interest rate risks, foreign exchange volatility must also be considered. This topic is discussed in detail in Chapter 17, Financial Risk Management.

5. USING DERIVATIVES TO HEDGE RISKS

Due to the risks associated with investing in bonds, a portfolio manager will typically utilize derivative instruments to mitigate these risks. For example, futures, forwards, options, and swaps can be used to manage interest rate and foreign exchange rate risks. Credit default swaps[8] can be used to manage credit risk. Nothing comes without a cost, however. While proper use of derivatives can reduce overall risk, the cost of using them will also reduce the potential profit. These instruments are discussed in more detail in Chapter 17, Financial Risk Management.

6. ASSET/LIABILITY MANAGEMENT

Whenever an investment portfolio utilizes borrowed funds as part of its overall strategy, the issue of asset/liability management arises. This is primarily an issue for banks and large financial institutions that fund their investments with either deposits or borrowed funds. In many cases, the issue is expressed in terms of a maturity mismatch; that is, the institution may be borrowing funds in the short-term markets (e.g., by using commercial paper) while using the proceeds from the financing to create or purchase long-term assets. This results in liabilities with shorter durations and investments with longer durations. Therefore, any changes in interest rates will have a larger impact on the value of the assets than on the value of the liabilities.

An asset/liability mismatch will also have an effect on profit margins. If liabilities have shorter maturities than investments, liabilities are repriced as the interest rates rise, increasing the cost of funds. The return on the longer-term investments will remain constant and the profit margin will decrease.

This strategy can be profitable as long as the yield curve is upward sloping (i.e., when short-term rates are lower than long-term rates), the value of the long-term assets remains stable, and short-term credit is readily available. In the global financial crisis of 2007–2009, however, all of these factors turned unfavorable at the same time, resulting in serious valuation and liquidity problems for many large financial institutions.

Asset/liability management is also important for treasury professionals who manage defined benefit pension plans. The projected benefit obligation associated with a defined benefit pension plan is equal to the present value of the expected future payments to retirees. Pension plan assets include cash and investments, and these assets are reported at market value. If the duration of the assets is longer than the duration of the projected benefit obligation and interest rates increase, the decrease in the market value of assets will exceed the decrease in the pension benefit obligation. This will result in the plan being underfunded and the corporation's balance sheet will report a pension liability equal to the amount of underfunding.

7. SECURITIES LENDING

One technique that is available to help manage investments in bonds (and other long-term assets) is securities lending. Securities lending is a practice where the owner of specific securities lends them to another party. The terms of the securities lending agreement normally require the borrower to provide the lender of the securities with collateral, in the form of other securities or a letter of credit, equal to or greater in value than the securities that are being lent. The primary purpose of the loan is to allow the borrower to hedge or short-sell securities that it does not own, in anticipation of the value of the security declining. In return, the borrower pays the lender a

---

8. A credit default swap, or CDS, is an arrangement whereby the seller of the CDS will pay the buyer in the event of a loan default or other credit event (e.g., bankruptcy) on the part of a particular issuer. It is, in effect, a form of insurance against loss due to credit issues. A "naked" CDS is a CDS where the buyer does not actually have any investment in or exposure to the firm covered by the CDS, and is an investment vehicle rather than an insurance or hedging tool.

negotiated fee. Loaned securities are also used to cover or eliminate "failed transactions."[9] The practice allows owners of long-term securities to earn additional income on holdings that they cannot or do not want to actually sell out of their portfolio.

C. Managing the Equity Portfolio

The passive and active approaches are two common strategies for managing the equity portfolio. The passive approach is basically a buy-and-hold strategy, while an active management approach attempts to outperform, on a risk-adjusted basis, a benchmark portfolio.

It is beyond the scope of treasury management to delve into the details of managing the equity portfolio. Rather, this section discusses the basic concepts of equity portfolio management, as well as methods for determining the relative risk and return of equity securities, all of which should be considered in developing an overall investment strategy.

1. DEFINING AND MEASURING INVESTMENT RISK

The risk associated with an investment in common stock is the possibility that the realized return on the stock may differ from the expected return. Stocks with higher return variability are riskier than stocks with lower return variability. The variability in returns is typically measured with the statistic known as the *standard deviation*.[10] A *standard deviation* refers to the average deviation from the expected value. For example, suppose that an analyst is considering adding to the investment portfolio a common stock with a historical mean or average annual return of 10% and a standard deviation of annual returns equal to 2%. These statistics may be used to infer that next year's expected return on the stock is 10%, but that it is also quite likely that the stock will earn a return between 8% (i.e., 10% − 2%) and 12% (i.e., 10% + 2%). One of the benefits of the standard deviation is that it allows the user to develop bands around an expected value. Overall, when a stock is held in isolation, the expected return and standard deviation are adequate for evaluating the merits of an investment in the common stock.

However, when a common stock is owned in combination with other common stocks in a portfolio, a different perspective on risk is needed. This is because the overall risk level of the portfolio depends on the covariance between the various stocks. In this context, *covariance* refers to the degree to which the returns on stocks move together. When two stocks have a negative covariance, their returns move in opposite directions. This is a desired property for stocks in a portfolio as this can significantly reduce the portfolio's risk. This occurs through the principle of diversification. As more stocks are added to a portfolio, the overall riskiness and variability of the portfolio is reduced. Studies show that company-specific return variation is almost completely eliminated when portfolios hold between 25 and 40 stocks across various industries.

2. CAPITAL ASSET PRICING MODEL (CAPM)

The CAPM is a widely accepted method for establishing a relationship between a common stock's required rate of return and its risk level. The total risk associated with an equity investment can be broken down into idiosyncratic risk and systematic risk. Idiosyncratic risk is the result of events that affect a specific firm. Examples include strikes, product recalls, and new product innovations. Idiosyncratic events are uncorrelated across firms. Since some events will increase stock prices and others will decrease stock prices, these effects may cancel each other

---

9. A failed transaction occurs when the seller of securities is unable to deliver them on the settlement date for some reason. The seller, or its broker, can borrow the proper security to avoid the failed transaction. The borrowed securities are typically returned when the seller is able to actually deliver the originally promised securities.
10. Technically, the standard deviation is the square root of the variance of the distribution of a particular variable. It usually is calculated from the historical or past values of that variable.

out when stocks are held in a diversified portfolio. Systematic risk is generated by macroeconomic events that affect all firms. Examples of systematic risk factors include recession, inflation, oil prices, and political instability. Since the CAPM assumes that investors hold a diversified portfolio of stocks, only systematic risk is relevant in stock pricing. An individual stock's degree of systematic risk is measured using beta (ß). Beta indicates the sensitivity of the individual stock's returns to the returns earned on the overall stock market and is calculated by estimating the historical relationship between the returns on the specific stock and the stock market (e.g., the S&P 500) using regression analysis. A firm's beta will change over time. Because of this, it is important to periodically reestimate beta.

Since beta measures a stock's volatility relative to the overall market, it is important to note key values for beta:

- **Beta equal to 1.00:** A stock with a beta of 1.00 has the same level of risk as the overall market. Thus, as the market increases (or decreases), the stock's return will likewise increase (or decrease) in the same proportion.

- **Beta greater than 1.00:** This implies that the firm has more risk than the overall market. Consequently, the expected return on the stock should exceed that of the market. For example, a beta of 1.20 implies that the stock's return tends to rise and fall 120% as fast as the market. Firms in high-growth industries with volatile earnings tend to have beta values greater than 1.00.

- **Beta less than 1.00:** Stocks with a beta less than 1.00 are considered less risky than the overall market. This leads to an expectation of a lower return, relative to that earned in the overall market. A beta of 0.60 implies that the return on the stock will rise or fall only 60% as fast as the overall market. Utility companies tend to have beta values less than 1.00.

Exhibit 19.3 provides average beta values for a number of industries.

EXHIBIT 19.3 AVERAGE BETAS FOR SELECTED INDUSTRIES	
APPAREL	1.06
BANKS	0.51
DRUGS (PHARMACEUTICAL)	1.02
FOOD WHOLESALERS	0.73
HOUSEHOLD PRODUCTS	1.05
OIL/GAS DISTRIBUTION	1.22
RETAIL (GENERAL)	1.16
SEMICONDUCTOR	1.39
UTILITY (WATER)	0.47

SOURCE: "Total Betas by Sector (for computing private company costs of equity) – US" as of January 2016, from NYU Stern School of Business's website (http://pages.stern.nyu.edu/~adamodar/New_Home_Page/datafile/totalbeta.html).
NOTE: Betas for firms are estimated by regressing weekly returns on the stock against a local index, using five years of data or the listed period. The betas provided in this exhibit are average levered betas.

Once an analyst has obtained a common stock's beta, the CAPM can be used to estimate the required rate of return for the stock in question. In addition to beta, the required rate of return is also a function of the risk-free rate of return and the expected return on the market. The CAPM is a linear relationship expressed algebraically as:

$$r_E = r_{RF} + (r_M - r_{RF})\beta$$

Where:

r$_E$ = Required rate of return on a common stock

r$_{RF}$ = Expected rate of return on the risk-free asset (e.g., US Treasury yield)

r$_M$ = Expected rate of return on the market portfolio (e.g., S&P 500 index)

ß = Beta value for firm

The return on the risk-free asset is sometimes measured by the return on short-term government securities, such as the US Treasury bill. Another approach is to use a risk-free rate with a maturity that matches the asset's maturity. In this case, a long-term government security rate could be used as a risk-free rate for long-term bonds or stocks. The choice depends upon the analyst's viewpoint.

To illustrate, suppose that the risk-free rate of return is 2.0%, and the expected rate of return on the overall stock market is 8.0%. Further, Company X has a beta of 1.50. Company X's required rate of return is estimated as:

$$r_E = 0.02 + (0.08 - 0.02)1.50$$
$$= 0.11 \text{ or } 11\%$$

Given these assumptions, the return on Company X's stock must equal 11% or higher to satisfy investors. The required return of 11% exceeds the expected return on the market of 8% because Company X's stock has a higher level of risk than the market, as evidenced by the beta of 1.50.

Consider another example in which Company Y has a beta of 0.60. Company Y's required return is estimated as:

$$r_E = 0.02 + (0.08 - 0.02)0.60$$
$$= 0.056 \text{ or } 5.60\%$$

The CAPM indicates that a 5.6% return on Company Y's common stock is commensurate with the firm's level of systematic risk (i.e., a beta of 0.60).

3. DETERMINING PORTFOLIO RISK AND RETURN

A benefit of using the CAPM for managing the equity portfolio is the ability to determine a portfolio's average return and risk by simply taking the weighted average of the returns and the betas of the individual stocks held in the portfolio. This is illustrated in the example below, using the values for Companies X and Y provided in the prior section.

Assume that an analyst has developed a two-stock portfolio with a 70% weighting on Company X's common stock and a 30% weighting on Company Y's common stock. The calculations for the portfolio beta and expected return are as follows:

$$\text{Portfolio Beta} = (\% \text{ of Co. X Stock} \times \text{Co. X Beta}) + (\% \text{ of Co. Y Stock} \times \text{Co. Y Beta})$$

$$= (0.70 \times 1.50) + (0.30 \times 0.60) = 1.23$$

As would be expected, the portfolio beta is above 0.60 but lower than 1.50. With a value of 1.23, the portfolio beta implies that the expected return on the portfolio should exceed that of the overall market, which is verified below:

$$\text{Portfolio Return} = (\% \text{ of Co. X Stock} \times \text{Co. X Return}) + (\% \text{ of Co. Y Stock} \times \text{Co. Y Return})$$

$$= (0.70 \times 0.11) + (0.30 \times 0.056) = 0.094 \text{ or } 9.40\%$$

It should also be noted that the same portfolio return is obtained if the portfolio beta is used to calculate the required rate of return with the CAPM equation:

$$\text{Portfolio Return} = 0.02 + (0.08 - 0.02)1.23$$

$$= 0.094 \text{ or } 9.40\%$$

IV. SUMMARY

Managing capital market investments is very different from managing a short-term investment portfolio. In managing a short-term portfolio, the primary objective is capital preservation, since the assets may need to be liquidated at any time. As a result, rate of return, while important, is a secondary concern. When managing the capital market investment portfolio, a greater degree of risk is acceptable in return for a higher long-term return on investment on the overall portfolio.

This chapter discussed the valuation of capital market investments as the present value of the expected cash flows received in return for the investment. Examples were provided with respect to bonds, preferred stock, and common stock.

The chapter also discussed the concept of balancing risk and return for capital market investments. It presented an overview of how that risk/return balance impacts capital market investment objectives and described a number of tools that are available to help manage the long-term investment portfolio, including duration, beta, and CAPM—all of which help predict how the value of a particular investment may change with changes in the overall market.

Key Equations

Value of a Long-Term Security $=$ Present Value of Expected Future Cash Flows $=$

$$PV_0 = \frac{CF_1}{(1+k)^1} + \frac{CF_2}{(1+k)^2} + \ldots + \frac{CF_n}{(1+k)^n}$$

Annual Preferred Stock Dividend $=$ Preferred Stock Dividend Rate $\times$ Par Value

$$\text{Price of Preferred Stock} = \frac{\text{Annual Preferred Stock Dividend}}{\text{Required Rate of Return}}$$

$$\text{Price of Common Stock in Period } t = \frac{D_{t+1}}{k-g}$$

Approximate % Change in Bond Price $= -$ Duration $\times$ Change in Interest Rate

$$r_E = r_{RF} + (r_M - r_{RF})\beta$$

Portfolio Beta $=$
$(\text{% Invested in Stock A} \times \text{Beta of Stock A}) + (\text{% Invested in Stock B} \times \text{Beta of Stock B})$

Portfolio Return $=$
$(\text{% Invested in Stock A} \times \text{Return on Stock A}) + (\text{% Invested in Stock B} \times \text{Return on Stock B})$

CHAPTER 20
The Capital Structure Decision and Management

I. INTRODUCTION

II. CAPITAL STRUCTURE

    A. Characteristics of Debt and Equity Capital

    B. Capital Structure Theory

    C. Factors Influencing the Target Capital Structure

    D. Capital Structure for Not-For-Profit Organizations

III. RAISING AND MANAGING LONG-TERM CAPITAL

    A. Raising Capital

    B. Managing Outstanding Capital

IV. THE WEIGHTED AVERAGE COST OF CAPITAL (WACC)

    A. The Cost of Debt

    B. The Cost of Common Equity

    C. Equation for Calculating the WACC

    D. The WACC and Economic Value Added (EVA)

V. LEASE FINANCING

    A. Motivations for Leasing Assets

    B. Types of Leases

    C. Estimated Residual Value

    D. Tax Considerations for Leases

    E. Lease versus Borrow-and-Buy Decision

VI. EQUITY FINANCING AND MANAGEMENT

    A. The Initial Public Offering (IPO)

    B. The Decision to List Stock

    C. Choice of Exchanges

    D. Types of Stock

    E. Shareholder Rights

    F. Mergers and Acquisitions

    G. At the Market (ATM) Programs

VII. MISCELLANEOUS CORPORATE FINANCE TOPICS

    A. Dividend Policy

    B. Tax Strategies

    C. Repatriation of Capital for Multinational Companies (MNCs)

    D. Market Analysis and Research Tools

VIII. SUMMARY

I. INTRODUCTION

Capital structure refers to the mix of debt and equity used to fund the assets held by a firm. When choosing a capital structure, the goal is to find the financing mix that minimizes the overall cost of capital, thus maximizing shareholder value. For this reason, it is important that treasury professionals have a grasp of the basic issues associated with capital structure.

This chapter opens with a review of capital structure. In addition, the chapter reviews other important areas of financial management, such as lease financing, equity management, an overview of tax strategy, shareholder rights, and dividend policy. Each topic can have a direct bearing on firm value.

II. CAPITAL STRUCTURE

New capital is required to finance a firm's growth strategies. Capital can be acquired externally through debt issuance (e.g., term loans and bonds) or stock sales (e.g., preferred and common stock), or internally through profit retention. The mix of long-term debt and equity used by a firm influences its overall cost of capital. The firm's *target capital structure* refers to the mix of long-term debt and equity that produces the minimum weighted average cost of capital (WACC).[1] A lower WACC allows the firm to be more competitive when pursuing investment opportunities. Although much research has been conducted on the theory of optimal capital structure, what has emerged is, at best, a general understanding of how debt and equity interplay to influence the WACC. It may be optimal for certain firms to be financed entirely with equity, while it may be optimal for other firms to be financed primarily with debt.

This section discusses:

- The characteristics of debt and equity capital
- Capital structure theory
- Factors influencing the target capital structure
- Capital structure for not-for-profit organizations

A. Characteristics of Debt and Equity Capital

The unique aspects of long-term debt and equity make it important for managers to consider the characteristics of both sources of financing when setting capital structure.

The characteristics of long-term debt financing include:

- **The Cost of Debt:** Debt financing is usually cheaper than the cost of equity. This characteristic arises from the fact that creditors are paid before equity holders, in the event of liquidation. For this reason, creditors require a lower yield than equity holders.

- **Tax Benefits of Debt:** Interest payments paid by corporations are generally tax deductible. Subsequently, a firm's after-tax cost of debt is considered to be more relevant than the firm's before-tax cost of debt. The tax deductibility of interest expense is often referred to as a *tax shield*.

- **Efficiency of Debt Markets:** The capital markets for long-term debt are generally efficient, especially for debt issues that are highly rated. In normal markets, there is typically an adequate supply of investor funds to purchase large debt issues across a broad range of risk and repayment characteristics.[2]

---

1. The target capital structure is also commonly referred to as the *optimal capital structure*.
2. The global financial crisis of 2007–2009 demonstrated that efficient operation of capital markets can be impacted severely by unusual economic conditions. Markets in developing countries may also be inefficient due to the local conditions and market participants. Over the long run, however, most capital markets (especially those in developed countries) have proven to be broad-based and efficient.

- **Restrictions on Managerial Flexibility:** The use of debt financing can reduce managerial flexibility. For example, required interest and principal payments on debt must be paid in full and in a timely fashion or creditors have cause for action against the firm. In the extreme, an inability to make required debt payments may lead to bankruptcy. Also, debt can be accompanied by liens on assets (e.g., mortgages), which limit management's flexibility.

- **Monitoring Requirements:** Creditors monitor borrowing firms to ensure that they adhere to the covenant and reporting requirements specified in the indenture or loan agreement. These monitoring requirements entail a cost borne by the firm.

The characteristics of equity financing via stock issuance or retained earnings include:

- **The Cost of Equity:** Equity is often one of the most expensive sources of capital. This is attributable to the greater level of risk for equity holders compared to debt holders (i.e., equity provides a cushion against creditor losses) and the fact that there is no tax benefit associated with equity issuance.

- **Managerial Flexibility:** Equity financing does not obligate the firm to make fixed payments to investors; dividend payments are optional. Furthermore, stock does not mature.

- **Voting Rights:** The sale of common stock may extend voting rights and control to a wider base of shareholders.

- **Costs of Issuance:** The cost of underwriting or issuing common equity is significant when compared with other sources of capital.

- **Earnings Dilution:** Increasing the outstanding number of common shares will automatically reduce earnings per share in the short run, assuming that earnings remain constant. This is referred to as *dilution*. Dilution can lead to a reduction in stock price if investors believe that management will not be able to use the new capital to increase earnings enough to maintain or increase the expected earnings per share.

- **Retained Earnings:** Reinvesting earnings is a lower-cost source of equity than the issuance of new common stock. By retaining earnings instead of paying dividends, the firm raises equity capital without the under-writing cost associated with issuing new stock.

B. Capital Structure Theory

There are several theories that attempt to explain how management determines a firm's capital structure. In terms of research and discussion in traditional financial management texts, the trade-off theory is the approach most often used to illustrate corporate capital structure.

The trade-off theory's essential idea is that management "trades off" the use of debt and equity in capital structures until the lowest WACC is obtained. The mix of debt and equity that provides the lowest WACC is considered the optimal capital structure. Suppose a firm was financed entirely by equity. The capital cost is simply the cost of equity. If a small amount of debt was then substituted for equity in the capital structure, the WACC would decrease because debt is cheaper than equity. The debt ratio would still be very low, while the coverage ratios (e.g., times interest earned) would be very high. However, at some degree of indebtedness, adding more debt will cause the WACC to increase. From the perspective of shareholders, an increase in debt may signal a reduction in the firm's ability to distribute earnings via dividends. To compensate for this, shareholders will require a higher return on their capital. Thus, the cost of equity increases. Furthermore, an increase in debt may cause creditors to increase the interest rate on future loans. Both effects result in an increased WACC. The dynamic nature of the WACC is illustrated in Exhibit 20.1.

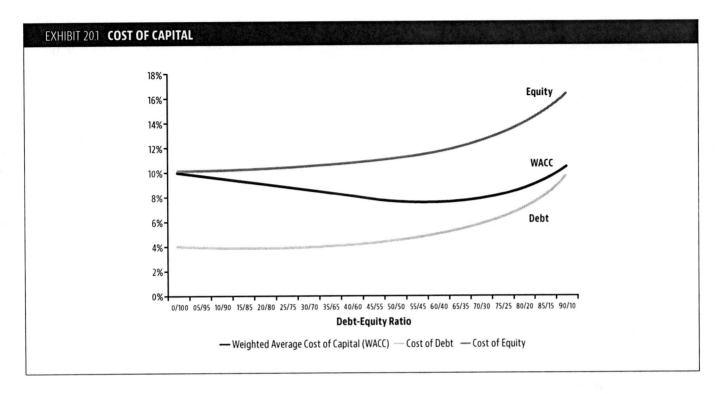

EXHIBIT 20.1 **COST OF CAPITAL**

While the idea of an optimal capital structure based on this trade-off between the benefits and costs of debt is appealing as a theory, there are other practical factors that must be considered. For most firms, the trade-off approach is used along with other factors relevant to both the firm and its industry, which are then used to arrive at a target capital structure. This target is used to raise new capital as required. For example, some industries (e.g., regulated power utilities) often have generally high debt ratios due to a large asset base that can be used as collateral and as a stable stream of cash flow.

Several general factors that CFOs and treasurers should consider when assessing capital structure include the following:

· The firm's operating risks and earnings volatility

· The immediate and expected long-term financing needs

· The relative costs of debt and equity at the time funds must be raised

· The risk tolerance of the board of directors and senior management

· The impact on the firm's credit rating

Based on an analysis of all of these factors, the board and management will determine a target capital structure that will be used for raising new capital as it is needed. The target capital structure will generally range between 40% and 60% debt, with remaining financing provided by equity. Though this range may vary considerably between industries and from firm to firm within an industry, the range is set so that the value of the firm and its WACC will not vary significantly within this range. When firms are toward the lower end of their debt range, they are usually said to have *significant debt capacity*. This means that they can add debt easily without negatively impacting the company's value. Firms that are toward the high end of this range are said to have *little debt capacity*, meaning that issuing more debt will likely cause a decrease in the firm's value.

Managers would generally choose to be at the lower end of the debt range, as this offers the most flexibility in terms of being able to raise capital in the future. The other consideration, however, is that there are many forces over which management may have little or no control that move it along this range. A period of high profitability might move the firm toward the lower end, as it has more retained earnings and thus higher levels of equity financing. The availability of long-term investments will also have an impact. A firm that is growing quickly, and is making large investments in fixed assets and working capital, may not be able to generate sufficient internal funding (i.e., retained earnings). It therefore may have to raise external debt and/or equity to maintain its growth. The general costs and market availability of debt and equity capital will also have an impact on how capital is raised. And while the obvious goal is to minimize the WACC, this must often be balanced against the need to preserve overall financial flexibility to meet future needs. In the end, the capital structure observed for a given firm at any point in time may be more a function of historical profits, investments, and markets than a conscious decision on management's part to maintain a specific mix of debt and equity.

C. Factors Influencing the Target Capital Structure

There are a number of factors that should be considered when determining the best mix of debt and equity for raising new capital. These include:

- **Business and Financial Risk:** Business risk is related to the stability and predictability of the overall revenue stream. The greater the revenue volatility, the greater the business risk. Financial risk is related to variability in net income. Firms with lower levels of business risk or financial risk are able to carry higher levels of debt. Business and financial risk can be measured with the degree of operating leverage and the degree of financial leverage, respectively.

- **Asset Structure:** The ability to use assets as collateral for loans can allow management to choose higher levels of indebtedness. Assets that provide favorable collateral include liquid assets with reasonably certain market values.

- **Shareholder Control and Dilution:** When capital is raised by issuing equity securities, the firm's earnings and the voting power of existing shareholders are diluted. For this reason, managers may prefer to raise capital via debt to maintain the current level of control and distribution of earnings.

- **Profitability:** If operations are profitable, then additional funds are available as an internally generated financing source. All else constant, profitable firms will have increased access to debt financing. Profitability helps ensure creditors that the firm has sufficient earnings capacity to service the debt.

- **Market Conditions:** Management should consider current and expected conditions in the macroeconomic environment (e.g., Brexit and other geopolitical events) when choosing the appropriate capital structure. The US equity market has been through numerous bubble periods in which stock prices were excessively high, making equity cheaper than normal (i.e., a lower number of shares can be issued when share prices are higher). Investment bankers can be a good source of expertise in assessing current and projected market conditions.

- **Lender and Rating Agency Considerations:** Regardless of what management or shareholders believe is the target capital structure, lenders may require a more conservative level of debt to protect their interests. For example, debt covenants may specify a required maximum debt ratio, minimum coverage ratios, conditions to be met before dividends can be paid or increased, and limitations on increased indebtedness or the types of debt that can be issued. Rating agencies will also provide guidelines on capital ratios needed to qualify for particular ratings. As a result, management has to bear in mind the impact on its credit rating when evaluating a change in the firm's capital structure.

· **Regulatory Restrictions and Minimum Capital Requirements:** Countries often have regulatory restrictions that must be met to do business within that country. A major concern in this area is so-called *thinly capitalized* (i.e., *thin cap*) subsidiaries of multinational companies. A thin cap company has more debt and therefore makes higher interest payments than would normally be possible if it were a stand-alone company. Thin capitalization is typically seen in multinational companies that have a choice of how much debt and how much equity to use in financing foreign subsidiaries since much of the debt and equity is coming from the parent company. The subsidiary is only able to carry the debt load because it is either borrowing from related parties or borrowing from third parties on the strength of group support in the form of guarantees from the parent company. The high level of debt leads to high interest expense paid to the parent, which in turn leads to excessive interest deductions when determining local taxes. Subsequently, many countries have restrictions on thin capitalization and either require higher rates of capital or limit the interest deductions that may be taken by the subsidiary. In some cases, the interest payments of thin cap subsidiaries are treated as a deemed dividend to the parent company. Deemed dividends are discussed in more detail later in the chapter.

In addition, various countries—or even regional governments such as states or provinces—may have specific capital requirements for certain industries. Many government entities also impose minimum capital requirements on various types of insurance companies operating within their boundaries. Such requirements ensure that insurance companies have adequate capital and reserves to meet any claims made against their policies. Other industries that typically have regulatory restrictions on capital include utilities, education, and transportation services.

D. Capital Structure for Not-For-Profit Organizations

In not-for-profit organizations (NFPs), capital structure is just as important an issue as it is in for-profit corporations. Though NFPs cannot issue common stock for equity financing, they often have equity via accumulated retained earnings. NFPs can also raise the equivalent of equity capital (i.e., net assets) through government grants and charitable contributions. For example, many governments are concerned about the provision of health care services to their general population. As a result, they often make grants to NFP providers to help offset the costs of services rendered to patients who cannot pay for those services.

In terms of debt financing, the availability of tax-exempt financing provides some NFPs with tax-based incentives to issue debt.[3] Depending on the projects the NFP is pursuing and its other sources of capital, the directors of the organization will most likely arrive at a target level of debt for the organization. There may also be targets for the levels of short-term versus long-term debt in the overall financing of the NFP.

III. RAISING AND MANAGING LONG-TERM CAPITAL

This section describes the key aspects of raising and managing long-term capital. The treasury department will often play a vital role in these areas.

A. Raising Capital

For any firm, the ability to raise capital at a reasonable price is one of the primary determinants of long-term success. While smaller firms primarily use personal capital and funds borrowed from banks, most midsize to large firms issue debt or equity securities. Further, some firms sell debt and equity instruments in the private market rather than to the general public (i.e., private placement). The purchaser in a private sale is usually an institutional investor (e.g., pension fund, insurance company, bank, or trust company).

---

3. While many NFPs are tax exempt (e.g., most charities), many are not. The latter includes unions or homeowners associations, among others.

Raising capital through the private placement of securities may be preferred over public issuance due to:

- Less restrictive covenants

- Relatively small issue size

- Reduced time to issuance

- Fewer reporting and disclosure requirements

- Lower costs

- Control over who holds the debt

- Greater flexibility of terms and maturities

There are also disadvantages associated with the private placement of securities:

- Cost to locate appropriate investors

- Limited information about the company

- Investors' desire for more equity in exchange for assuming greater risk and lower liquidity

There are advantages and disadvantages to raising capital through public offerings. One of the principal advantages is that access to capital markets offers the potential to raise large amounts of debt and equity at prevailing rates. One of the primary disadvantages is the significant cost involved in managing the reporting, disclosure, and rating agency requirements for public security issues.

Initial public offerings (IPOs) require significant disclosure of a firm's ownership, business activities, and financial statements. Publicly held firms are required by various regulators, such as the Securities and Exchange Commission (SEC) in the United States, to file a wide variety of forms and reports (e.g., SEC Forms 10-K, 8-K, and 10-Q) on a regular basis.

When raising and managing capital, management must deal with various external parties, including investment bankers, corporate bankers, regulatory agencies, market analysts, rating agencies, auditors, shareholders, and bondholders. Each of these parties requires different types and degrees of information, and each views the firm from a different perspective. In order to successfully raise the required capital, treasury professionals must be able to respond to the involved parties' needs and expectations.

B. Managing Outstanding Capital

Once the debt or equity securities have been issued, the payment requirements accompanying each security must be managed. To meet this need, treasury professionals must often manage trustee relationships and responsibilities relative to the securities, as well as act as a disbursing agent for shareholder or bondholder payments. Shareholders may receive dividends as declared for preferred and common stock. Meanwhile, bondholders may receive interest and principal payments. Also, any sinking fund obligations (i.e., funds accumulated in a custodial account to retire debt instruments according to a predetermined schedule) or covenants on bond issues must be met. Financial reports must be completed and sent to interested parties in a timely manner, and various reports must be prepared and sent to regulatory agencies. Management must also plan for the future retirement or refinancing of maturing issues and manage bank credit relationships.

In addition to its trustee and disbursing responsibilities, the treasury department may be involved with investor relations, including such responsibilities as:

- Participating in presentations to potential investors to raise capital (also known as *road shows*)

- Maintaining shareholder lists

- Sending out financial statements, annual reports, and other required filings

- Communicating with shareholders and bondholders

- Addressing investors' questions

IV. THE WEIGHTED AVERAGE COST OF CAPITAL (WACC)

The WACC has many applications in the evaluation of capital investment decisions and in assessing overall firm value. It is the basic target number that asset returns must exceed if the firm is to create value for shareholders. Otherwise, creditors and shareholders will reallocate their holdings to ensure that an appropriate return is earned for the given level of investment risk. Such expectations must be met or the market will reduce firm value by bidding down stock and bond prices.[4] The return expectation for a security becomes that source's cost of funds from the firm's perspective.

The WACC is calculated by weighting the costs of the primary funding sources of permanent capital by their proportionate dollar contribution to the firm's capital base.

The primary sources of permanent capital are long-term debt, primarily in the form of bonds, and equity capital in the form of common stock and retained earnings. The relevant cost of these sources is their marginal cost (i.e., the rate of return the market would demand if funds were raised today).

The following sections provide:

- A description of the individual costs of debt and equity

- An equation for calculating the WACC

- A discussion of the link between the WACC and firm value

A. The Cost of Debt

The appropriate proxy for a firm's before-tax cost of debt is the yield to maturity (YTM) on the firm's most recent bond issue. The YTM is the return that investors currently demand for a given bond investment. Since interest expense is tax deductible, the after-tax cost of debt is the relevant or marginal cost of issuing debt that should be accounted for in the WACC equation.

The YTM is converted to an after-tax rate using the firm's marginal tax rate, as follows:

$$\text{After-Tax } r_D = r_D(1-T)$$

---

4. It is important to note that firm value can be affected (often negatively) by industry perceptions or anticipated future trends, even though the company's own financials may be strong.

Where:

After-Tax r_D = After-tax cost of debt

r_D = Yield to maturity on newly issued debt on a before-tax basis

T = Firm's marginal income tax rate

Calculation Example: After-Tax Cost of Debt

Assume that a firm's bond is currently trading at a YTM of 5% and the firm's marginal tax rate is 30%. With these specifications, the calculation of the after-tax cost of debt is as follows:

$$\text{After-Tax } r_D = 0.05(1-0.30) = 0.035 \text{ or } 3.50\%$$

For this firm, the after-tax cost of debt is 3.5%, which means that the ability to treat interest as a tax-deductible expense has effectively lowered the cost of debt from 5% to 3.5%.

When calculating the after-tax cost of debt, a couple of additional points should be considered:

- For firms with complicated tax liabilities, the marginal tax rate may be difficult to estimate from standard financial statements. If the analysis is performed internally, then the tax department may be able to provide an appropriate figure.

- Issuance or flotation costs may be significant for certain bond issuers. When appropriate, these costs should be included in the determination of the cost of debt.

B. The Cost of Common Equity

Funds from common equity can be raised via retained earnings or by issuing new common stock. The market's required rate of return on equity applies to retained earnings and common stock. The board of directors has the option to distribute earnings to shareholders as dividends. If the board chooses to reinvest all or some of the earnings inside the firm (i.e., retained earnings), shareholders expect a rate of return on this investment just as they do when they purchase shares in the stock market.

The capital asset pricing model (CAPM) may be used to estimate the market's required rate of return on a firm's equity. This is the cost that applies to equity funds that are obtained through retained earnings. The cost of issuing new, additional common stock will be a bit higher because the company will receive less per share when shares are sold, due to issuance expenses.[5] The CAPM formula follows:

$$r_E = r_{RF} + (r_M - r_{RF})\text{ß}$$

Where:

r_E = Required rate of return on equity

r_{RF} = Expected rate of return on the risk-free asset (e.g., US Treasury yield)

r_M = Expected rate of return on the market portfolio (e.g., S&P 500 index)

ß = Beta value for the company's stock

---

5. Flotation costs are not considered in the CAPM formula.

Calculation Example: Equity Cost of Capital

Assume that the risk-free (e.g., Treasury yield rate) is 4%, the return on the overall stock market is 10%, and the beta for the firm is 1.20. In this case, the cost of equity capital would be calculated as follows:

$$r_E = 0.04 + (0.10 - 0.04)(1.20) = 0.112 \text{ or } 11.2\%$$

For this firm, the cost of equity capital is 11.2%. This means that funds raised via equity issuance or through retained earnings effectively cost the firm 11.2%.

C. Equation for Calculating the WACC

To calculate the WACC, the costs of long-term debt and equity should be weighted by each component's proportion of the capital structure. These weights can be quickly approximated using the book value method, in which the debt weighting equals total debt divided by total assets and the equity weighting equals equity divided by total assets. The equation used to calculate the WACC follows:

$$WACC = w_D r_D (1 - T) + w_E r_E$$

Where:

w_D = Weighting of debt financing

r_D = Yield to maturity on newly issued debt on a before-tax basis

T = Firm's marginal income tax rate

w_E = Weighting of equity financing

r_E = Required rate of return on equity

Calculation Example: WACC

The following example uses information for the cost of debt and equity as determined in the earlier examples. It also assumes that one-third (33.3%) of total long-term financing is provided by debt and two-thirds (66.7%) is provided by equity:

$$WACC = w_D r_D (1 - T) + w_E r_E$$

$$= [0.333 \times 0.05 \times (1 - 0.30)] + (0.667 \times 0.112) = 0.0864 \text{ or } 8.64\%$$

For this firm, the WACC is 8.64%. By construction, the weighting process results in the WACC falling between the after-tax cost of debt and the cost of equity. In general, the WACC represents the overall return that the market expects for the firm to provide.

D. The WACC and Economic Value Added (EVA)

The concept of EVA emphasizes that the firm must earn a rate of return on assets that exceeds the WACC in order to create value for shareholders. Therefore, the firm in the preceding example must earn a rate of return on assets equal to or above 8.64%. If it earns less, then firm value will fall because market return expectations were not met. This can be illustrated via the EVA metric.

Calculation Example: EVA

In addition to the previously calculated WACC and an assumed tax rate of 30%, assume that $50,000,000 of capital (i.e., long-term debt and equity) is employed and that the company generated an operating profit (i.e., earnings before interest and taxes, or EBIT) of $6,800,000. EVA in this case would be:

$$EVA = EBIT(1-T) - (WACC)(\text{Long-Term Debt} + \text{Equity})$$

$$= \$6,800,000 \times (1-0.30) - (0.0864 \times \$50,000,000)$$

$$= \$4,760,000 - \$4,320,000 = \$440,000$$

The positive EVA of $440,000 indicates that the firm over-performed in the previous year, which means that the firm's share price should increase. Another way to view this concept is that the firm earned a return of 9.52% on its assets for the year (i.e., $4,760,000 ÷ $50,000,000), while the WACC is 8.64%. Just like the EVA calculation, this comparison indicates value was created because the return on capital exceeded the WACC.

Note that the EVA is influenced by the WACC. At a higher WACC, the EVA drops, and vice versa. A key takeaway from this is that a higher WACC makes it more difficult for managers to create value for shareholders. This same takeaway is evident from the relationship between the NPV and the WACC. At a higher WACC, the NPV of a given investment will drop. Thus, firms with higher WACCs are less competitive than competitors with lower WACCs.

V. LEASE FINANCING

This section describes the important aspects of lease financing. Leasing allows managers to venture into new product markets without purchasing the required capital assets. If adequate revenues are not earned in the product market, then lease financing allows the firm to quickly exit the product line. For many types of equipment acquisitions, leasing may be considered a substitute for debt. Subsequently, the lease versus borrow-and-buy decision is one of the most important types of analysis for firms acquiring capital assets.

Before proceeding, the following leasing terminology is clarified:

- The **lessor** is the individual or entity that owns the assets being leased. The lessor provides the asset and receives lease payments during the lease.

- The **lessee** is the individual or entity that leases the asset. The lessee has access to the asset over the length of the lease and provides lease payments to the lessor.

A. Motivations for Leasing Assets

A key reason for leasing is the tax benefit for both the lessor and the lessee.[6] There also may be an advantage to using leasing as a source of off-balance-sheet financing. In most cases, long-term lease arrangements may be considered a direct substitute for debt. This is especially true for firms with poor credit, which might limit their access to traditional borrowing instruments. Also, loan and debt covenants may dictate the form and structure of leases for many firms, although in return, leases may offer fewer restrictions than direct lending covenants.

Leasing is generally an appealing choice for lessees that require assets with a high potential for technological obsolescence, such as computers, medical equipment, and communications equipment. Leasing also may be attractive to start-ups or firms beginning sales in a new area that have a high level of uncertainty about future demand and where the cancellation provisions of a lease may offer substantial protection.

Management may also choose to lease assets that are needed to conduct business but that fall outside the firm's area of expertise. For example, a food wholesaler may choose to lease a fleet of delivery trucks rather than purchase the assets. The lessor provides financing and maintains the fleet while the wholesaler focuses on operating its business. In many cases, lease financing may be offered simultaneously to the acquisition of the asset, making it an easy, one-stop shopping arrangement. While this type of arrangement may not be available for all types of leases, it can be a desirable option if available.

Finally, leasing may be considered purely from a desire for more flexible financing options. The actual terms available on a lease, combined with the ability to "walk away" from the asset at the end of the lease term, may be more valuable than the asset's residual value.

B. Types of Leases[7]

The primary differences among lease types include the:

- Length of lease period
- Party responsible for asset maintenance and upkeep
- Residual value of the asset (i.e., the estimated value of the asset at the end of the lease)
- Relevant tax treatment (though this may differ significantly for not-for-profits and municipalities)
- Party retaining the asset at the end of the lease and the lease terms

Specific types of leasing arrangements are described below.

1. SALE-AND-LEASEBACK ARRANGEMENTS

Under a sale-and-leaseback arrangement, equipment is sold to another party (lessor) and then immediately leased back by the original owner (lessee). A sale-and-leaseback aids firms that need cash or that cannot take full advantage of the tax benefits from depreciation due to excessive operating losses. The sale-and-leaseback arrangement can move the cash flow stream (income or costs) to different periods as well.

---

6. Tax advantages from leasing are dependent on the tax codes in effect for the organization. Lease financing and tax advantages under US Generally Accepted Accounting Principles (US GAAP) and International Financial Reporting Standards (IFRS) are explained later in this chapter.

7. For discussion purposes, this book will focus on ASC Topic 840-10-15, issued by the Financial Accounting Standards Board (FASB). The International Accounting Standards Board (IASB) has comparable requirements in International Accounting Standard (IAS) 17: *Leases*. On February 25, 2016, FASB issued an Accounting Standards Update (ASU) that will require both capital and operating leases to be presented on the balance sheet. The goal of this ASU is to improve the understanding for users of financial statements with respect to the amount, timing, and uncertainty of cash flows that arise from leases. For public companies in the United States, this ASU will be enforced beginning after December 15, 2018. For nonpublic entities, enforcement begins after December 15, 2019. The IASB issued a comparable standard (IFRS 16) on January 13, 2016. More information on this topic is available on FASB's website (www.fasb.org).

---

2. OPERATING LEASES

Operating leases are established so that the lessor retains ownership of the leased assets at the end of the lease period. Further, the lessor provides maintenance for the equipment. Operating leases are often done on an off-balance-sheet basis, meaning that the lease payment is only reflected on the lessee's income statement. That is, neither the assets nor the lease appears on the lessee's balance sheet, while the lease payments simply appear as an expense on the income statement.

Operating leases usually extend for periods shorter than the life of the asset (e.g., 3–5 years for equipment and up to 20 years for real estate). Consequently, lease payments usually are not sufficient to fully pay for the original cost of the asset, meaning there is some residual value of the asset at the end of the lease term. Significant operating lease arrangements and the financial value of future lease commitments must be reported in a footnote to the financial statements, further ensuring that no investor or lender is unaware of leasing arrangements. In analyzing operating leases, it is important to carefully consider the flexibility of cancellation policies.

3. CAPITAL LEASES

Capital leases, or financial leases, have different terms than those of operating leases. Capital leases are essentially an alternative to borrowing the funds and purchasing the asset.

For US firms, Accounting Standards Codification (ASC) Topic 840-10-15: *Leases: Scope and Scope Exceptions* specifies that a lease meeting any one of the following four conditions must be classified as a *capital lease*:

- The length of the lease is at least 75 percent of the estimated useful life of the asset.
- There is a transfer of ownership to the lessee at the end of the lease.
- The lease agreement contains a provision that allows the lessee to purchase the asset per a bargain purchase option during or at the end of the lease's life. A bargain price is one that is sufficiently less than fair market value, such that an expectation is created at the outset that the option will be exercised.
- The present value of the discounted lease payments at the beginning of the lease term exceeds 90 percent of the asset's fair market value.

A lease that does not meet any of these conditions may be classified as an *operating lease*.

The residual value is generally the estimated value of the asset at the end of a capital lease. The amortization of the asset's value considers the residual value in the computation of lease payments. The lessee generally is responsible for maintaining the asset and must pay any applicable taxes and insurance.

A capital lease is sometimes referred to as a *double-net lease* because the lessor receives payment after expenses are paid (e.g., maintenance, operating, and insurance expenses). When this type of lease is used in real estate, it may be referred to as a *triple-net lease* because the lessee agrees to make the payments for taxes, insurance premiums, and utilities. This type of lease is an alternative to borrowing funds to finance the acquisition of a capital asset.[8]

Under certain conditions, leases may be considered a source of off-balance-sheet financing, thus avoiding the appearance of additional debt on a company's balance sheet, as well as increasing its return on assets. To correct this problem, the FASB issued ASC Topic 840-10-15, which requires US firms entering into financial leases to capitalize the lease. This process restates the balance sheet to show the leased asset as a fixed asset and the present value of the lease payments as a liability.

The logic behind the FASB requirement is that the financial lease agreement makes the obligation to make lease payments just as binding as in a long-term loan agreement. Thus, for most purposes, capitalized leases are a direct substitute for long-term debt financing.

---

8. Double- and triple-net leases may also be operating leases if properly structured, but are more likely to be capital leases due to the lessee's acceptance of maintenance and risk.

Exhibit 20.2 summarizes lease characteristics by type of lease.

EXHIBIT 20.2 **CHARACTERISTICS OF LEASES BY TYPE**			
CHARACTERISTIC	**SALE AND LEASEBACK**	**CAPITAL LEASE**	**OPERATING LEASE**
LEASE CRITERIA:* OWNERSHIP	N/A. Can be either capital or operating lease based on lease agreement.	Ownership of the asset is transferred to the lessee at the end of the lease term.	Ownership is retained by the lessor during and after the lease term.
LEASE CRITERIA: BARGAIN PURCHASE OPTION	N/A. Can be either capital or operating lease based on lease agreement.	The lease contains a bargain purchase option to buy the asset at less than fair market value.	The lease cannot contain a bargain purchase option.
LEASE CRITERIA: LENGTH OF LEASE PERIOD	N/A. Can be either capital or operating lease based on lease agreement.	The lease term equals or exceeds 75% of the asset's estimated useful life.	The lease term is less than 75% of the estimated useful life of the asset.
LEASE CRITERIA: PRESENT VALUE	N/A. Can be either capital or operating lease based on lease agreement.	The present value of the lease payments exceeds 90% of the total original cost of the asset.	The present value of the lease payments is less than 90% of the asset's fair market value.
MAINTENANCE	Depends upon the lease agreement.	Transferred to lessee. Lessee pays maintenance, insurance, and taxes.	Right to use only. Lessor takes risks and benefits, and often pays maintenance costs.
ACCOUNTING	May be sale and financial leaseback, or sale and operating leaseback. If the lessee classifies the leaseback as an operating lease, any gain or loss on sale is recognized immediately. If the leaseback is classified as a *financial lease*, the lessee defers and amortizes any gain on sale over the lease term.	Lease is considered an asset (leased asset) and a liability (lease payments). Payments are shown in the balance sheet.	No risk of ownership. Payments are considered operating expenses and shown in the income statement.
TAX TREATMENT	Depends upon the type of lease.	Lessee is considered to be the owner of the equipment and therefore claims depreciation expense and interest expense.	Lessee is considered to be renting the equipment and therefore the lease payment is considered a rental expense.

* A lease that meets any one of the four lease criteria must be characterized as a *capital lease*.

C. Estimated Residual Value

A depreciable asset's residual value is the amount remaining after all allowable depreciation charges have been subtracted from the asset's book value. In most cases, the estimated residual value is built into the leasing arrangement. Assets with potentially high residual values generally have lower lease payments than assets with lower residual values.

Setting the residual value may impact the lease's tax status, as well as requirements for listing the lease as an on- or off-balance-sheet item. In lease analysis, it is critical to know the asset's assumed residual value at the end of the lease. There might be a requirement that the lessee reimburse the lessor for any difference between the estimated residual value and the actual residual value of the asset (e.g., if it is lower than the estimate). In vehicle leases, this requirement may be tied to the mileage (e.g., requiring the lessee to pay for any mileage above the agreed maximum) or to the general condition of the vehicle, especially if the lessee failed to properly maintain the vehicle according to the lease agreement.

D. Tax Considerations for Leases

Tax considerations for leases can vary by country. In the United States, the full amount of an annual operating lease payment is a tax-deductible expense for the lessee, provided the Internal Revenue Service (IRS) agrees that a particular contract is a genuine operating lease (based upon the US GAAP requirements) and not simply an installment loan in the guise of a lease. The primary reason for IRS restrictions on lease terms is to prevent a lessee from setting up a lease arrangement that allows for the more rapid write-off of an asset than that allowed by the IRS's depreciation rules.

Other countries have similar requirements that distinguish between capital or finance leases (also referred to as *funding leases* or *hire-purchase agreements*) and operating leases, typically now based upon IFRS guidelines. IFRS lease guidelines focus on the overall substance of a particular transaction. Lease classification as an operating lease or a finance lease (i.e., the equivalent of a capital lease under US GAAP) depends on whether the lease transfers substantially all of the risks and rewards of ownership to the lessee. Although lease classification criteria are similar to those identified in US GAAP, there are no quantitative breakpoints in IFRS (e.g., 90 percent of the total cost). A lease of special-purpose assets that only the lessee can use without major modification generally would be classified as a *finance lease*, as would any lease that does not subject the lessor to significant risk with respect to the residual value of the leased property.

In general, most tax legislation related to leases is intended to deny deductions for interest (i.e., require treatment as a capital lease) when the avoidance of tax is deemed one of the main purposes for the lease transaction. Local tax treatment should always be confirmed before making any lease versus borrow-and-buy decision.

E. Lease versus Borrow-and-Buy Decision

After deciding to acquire a capital asset, a critical decision then must be made in terms of purchasing or leasing the capital asset. The appropriate way to evaluate this decision is to compare the present value of the costs of leasing with the present value of the costs of owning the asset. The decision maker should then select the alternative that maximizes firm value. In terms of asset acquisition, this usually implies choosing the option that provides the lowest present value cost. An example illustrates the analysis.

Calculation Example: Lease versus Borrow-and-Buy

Assume that a firm needs to buy a new piece of machinery with a total cost of $50,000. The firm will only need the machine for three years and can then resell it for its residual value of $20,000. The firm can borrow the needed funds at 6%, with annual interest payments and a final principal repayment at the end of three years. For tax purposes, assume that the firm has a marginal tax rate of 30% and that depreciation for the machine will be $10,000 the first year, $16,000 the second year, and $6,000 the third year. Maintenance expenses on the machine will be $5,000 per year.

Alternatively, the firm can lease the machine for $16,000 per year for three years with the payment due at the beginning of each year. With this option, there will be no maintenance expense, and the firm will return the machine to the lessor at the end of the three years.

The decision maker should calculate the annual cash flow associated with each option and then calculate and compare the NPV of the two sets of cash flows, as illustrated below.

Cost to Own:

		YEAR 1	YEAR 2	YEAR 3
1	Interest Payments ($50,000 × 6%)	(3,000)	(3,000)	(3,000)
2	Less: Tax Savings @ 30%	900	900	900
3	Equals: After-Tax Interest Cost	(2,100)	(2,100)	(2,100)
4	Principal Repayment			(50,000)
5	Maintenance Expense	(5,000)	(5,000)	(5,000)
6	Less: Tax Savings @ 30%	1,500	1,500	1,500
7	Equals: After-Tax Maintenance Expense	(3,500)	(3,500)	(3,500)
8	Depreciation Expense	(10,000)	(16,000)	(6,000)
9	Tax Savings on Depreciation (30% × Depreciation)	3,000	4,800	1,800
10	Residual Value of Machine			20,000
11	Book Value of Machine (Purchase Price Less Depreciation)			18,000
12	Taxable Gain on Sale			2,000
13	Tax on Gain @ 30%			(600)
	Net Cash Flow (Line 3+4+7+9+10+13)	(2,600)	(800)	(34,400)

The net present value of owning can be calculated as:

$$\text{NPV of Owning @ 6\%} = \frac{-\$2,600}{(1 + 0.06)^1} + \frac{-\$800}{(1 + 0.06)^2} + \frac{-\$34,400}{(1 + 0.06)^3}$$

$$= -\$2,453 + -\$712 + -\$28,883 = -\$32,048$$

Cost to Lease:

Note that the lease payments are made at the beginning of each year instead of the end, so the first payment is made immediately, which is considered Year 0.

		YEAR 0	YEAR 1	YEAR 2
1	Lease Payments	(16,000)	(16,000)	(16,000)
2	Less: Tax Savings @ 30%	4,800	4,800	4,800
3	Equals: Net Cash Flow	(11,200)	(11,200)	(11,200)

The net present value of leasing can be calculated as:

$$\text{NPV of Leasing @ 6\%} = \frac{-\$11,200}{(1 + 0.06)^0} + \frac{-\$11,200}{(1 + 0.06)^1} + \frac{-\$11,200}{(1 + 0.06)^2}$$

$$= -\$11,200 + -\$10,566 + -\$9,968 = -\$31,734$$

Comparison of Cost to Own versus Lease:

$$\text{Difference} = \$32,048 - \$31,734 = \$314$$

Based on the information in this example, the firm will save $314 by leasing the machine instead of buying it. Although not quantified in this example, the firm will also save the time and effort involved in reselling the machine at the end of the period.

VI. EQUITY FINANCING AND MANAGEMENT

This section covers some of the key topics related to equity financing and management. Specific topics include issuing stock, choosing exchanges or over-the-counter (OTC) trading, and financing mergers and acquisitions.

A. The Initial Public Offering (IPO)

Although the common usage of the term tends to be limited to common stock, an *IPO* describes an issuer's first public offering of a security of any class. For firms with equity securities that are not currently available to the public or are not listed on one of the various exchanges, the decision to go public and/or to list the firm's securities can be critical to future growth.

1. ADVANTAGES OF GOING PUBLIC

The decision to go public offers several advantages. Examples include:

- **Diversification for Owners:** Owners of closely held firms may have a large proportion of their wealth invested in the firm. By selling a portion of stock to the general public, owners may invest the proceeds in other areas and increase their personal diversification, as well as raise capital.

- **Increased Liquidity:** The stock of closely held firms is very illiquid. It can be sold only to certain types of investors; hence, there is no intermediary to help in the sale. As a result, such firms have a weakened ability to raise capital when needed. Going public can help resolve this liquidity problem.

- **Increased Transparency:** A firm must meet certain disclosure thresholds (as determined by the SEC in the United States or by similar regulatory agencies in other countries) in order for its stock to become listed publicly. Transparency and outside regulation make investors more willing to purchase the stock of a publicly traded firm and enhance a firm's ability to raise equity capital.

- **Improved Ability to Spin Off Divisions:** IPOs can also be used to spin off a division or wholly owned subsidiary of a firm that is already public. This process is often used by large, diversified firms when it is determined that a particular part of the firm might be more valuable as a stand-alone entity. For example, the information technology section of a large manufacturing firm may have developed highly regarded software for computer-aided design. In order to realize the full value of this software, management may find it advantageous to spin off that part of the firm so that it can more easily sell the software.

2. DISADVANTAGES OF GOING PUBLIC

Going public does have some disadvantages, primarily related to the disclosure required for the public issue. Disadvantages of going public include:

- **Regulatory Disclosure:** The level of disclosure required for an IPO can be costly and can reveal information that managers might prefer to keep unobservable. For example, competitors may gain access to proprietary information, and outsiders may learn the compensation and net worth of the owners.

- **Managerial Flexibility:** When a firm's stock is held closely, the owners have greater flexibility. For example, large management salaries or generous perks do not produce the kinds of conflicts between management and shareholders that may occur in a publicly held company.

- **Control:** Owners of closely held firms surrender some control by going public, even if majority ownership is retained. In publicly held firms and/or firms in industries with strong labor union representation, minority shareholders may have significant rights with respect to the firm's operations and representation on the board of directors. Also, there are many examples of publicly held firms being taken private by management to increase control. This is especially true when a firm is incorporated in a state where cumulative voting is allowed. This type of voting provides minority interests with a better opportunity to gain board representation.

· **Exposure to Market Conditions:** When a firm is publicly traded, the value of its equity shares are sensitive to capital market conditions. Even though a particular firm may be exceeding expectations, a broad sell-off in an industry or geographical region can reduce the value of the firm's shares of equity. In turn, this can increase the likelihood of a takeover or merger.

B. The Decision to List Stock

For most firms, the decision to go public coincides with the decision to list the stock on one of the organized exchanges (e.g., the New York Stock Exchange [NYSE] or the London Stock Exchange Group). Although the various national and regional exchanges have much in common, rules and requirements can vary by exchange and by country. In addition, tax consequences can vary by country. Therefore, it is important to consider the cost of complying with the regulatory requirements and tax regimes when choosing an exchange. Increasingly, firms are forgoing organized exchanges and listing securities on automated quotation systems, such as NASDAQ or JASDAQ, which started out as computer-based OTC trading systems and are now officially recognized exchanges. Whichever market is chosen, it is important to work with sell-side analysts to help ensure that the stock is followed and rated in a manner consistent with the firm's objectives.

1. ADVANTAGES OF LISTING STOCK

The primary advantage of listing a stock on one of the organized exchanges is to increase marketability. In general, listing is advantageous to both the firm and the public because the stock can be traded more widely and more investors can access it. Listing can also result in higher sales for the firm in question because of increased public exposure. Additionally, the increased level of disclosure required for public listing has a tendency to reduce the firm's perceived market risk, which in turn may lower the WACC, thereby increasing overall firm value.

2. DISADVANTAGES OF LISTING STOCK

Most organized exchanges have their own rules and regulations, typically reporting and governance requirements, that can go well beyond any government regulation of public companies. Given these additional requirements and the higher costs charged by the exchanges, some firms remain in the OTC market rather than on an organized exchange.

3. DELISTING OF STOCK

Stocks can be delisted from an exchange. In some cases, a stock is forced to be delisted (i.e., involuntary delisting) because it has fallen out of compliance with the exchange's requirements. For example, an exchange may require that the share price be equal to or greater than $1. If the share price drops below $1, then the share may be delisted. Most exchanges have procedures for firms that want to maintain their listing to try to get back into compliance. However, if the requirements are not met within a set time period, then the firm will be dropped from the exchange. Delisted stock may still be traded on the OTC market.

Some firms choose to have their stock delisted (i.e., voluntary delisting). For example, the added disclosure requirements and expense of audit and reporting compliance on the NYSE have caused some smaller firms to go through the delisting process. Some foreign companies also have delisted their American depositary receipts (ADRs) to avoid exchange compliance requirements.

C. Choice of Exchanges

Once management has decided to list its stock rather than use the OTC market, it must decide on which exchanges the stock will be listed. There are requirements for joining the various exchanges, and firms must abide by the rules of each exchange on which they want their stocks traded.

For firms desiring to raise capital globally, there are stock exchanges in most of the world's money centers, including New York, Toronto, London, Tokyo, Frankfurt, Paris, Zurich, Singapore, and Hong Kong. Stocks of major US firms may be listed and traded on stock exchanges outside the United States. Similarly, stocks of large, foreign multinational companies may be listed and traded in the US markets (e.g., ADRs).

D. Types of Stock

In addition to deciding where and when to list, management must determine what types of stock to issue. Stock can be issued in various classes, referred to as a *dual-* or *multi-class stock*. These stock classes may provide different rights to different shareholders. This is typically done to try to retain voting control of the firm while raising capital in the market. In a dual-class system, two types of stock are issued: typically Class A and Class B stock. One class is sold to the general market and has limited voting rights, but may have preferential dividends in compensation. The second class is typically reserved for the original owners and executives, and has greater voting power to maintain majority control of the firm.

E. Shareholder Rights

Treasury professionals should be familiar with shareholder rights and privileges because (1) equity is a key funding source and (2) investor relations sometimes becomes part of treasury's responsibilities. Generally, common stockholders have all or some of the following legal rights and privileges:

- **Control:** As owners of the firm, shareholders have the right to elect directors, who in turn select the officers to manage the business. There are numerous regulations, which can vary by legal jurisdiction, concerning the election of directors and accompanying procedures.

- **Cumulative Voting:** Corporate bylaws typically permit one vote per share of stock and, sometimes, cumulative voting. Cumulative voting allows a shareholder as many votes per share owned as there are open positions on the board in the same election. It also allows shareholders to cast these votes in any way they see fit. For example, if six board seats are to be filled, then the holder of one share receives six votes. The shareholder could cast all six votes for one candidate or split them among candidates in any way desired. The purpose of cumulative voting is to increase the possibility that a minority of shareholders can elect a board member. Since they are concentrating their votes on one or two candidates, they virtually ensure that they will elect at least one board member and thereby have a minority position on the board of directors, allowing their viewpoints to be expressed during board deliberations.

- **Proxy:** The right to vote at the annual meeting can be assigned to another individual through a proxy. When shareholders are satisfied with the board's conduct and management's performance, they assign their proxies to the CEO or another designated company executive. If a shareholder group is dissatisfied, then it will retain its votes and solicit the proxy votes of other shareholders in an attempt to elect candidates it favors to the board. When shareholder groups aggressively solicit the proxies of other shareholders, it is referred to as a *proxy fight*.

- **Staggered Election of Directors:** A system of staggered elections is when board members hold office for multiple years, but a minority of board seats are open in a single election. For example, on a twelve-person board, members may be elected to serve for three years, with four members elected to three-year terms each year. Staggered elections are used either to make it difficult to take over the board or because it is felt that continuity on the board is conducive to its making well-considered decisions.

- **Preemptive Right:** A preemptive right provides that existing shareholders will have the first right to purchase shares of any new stock issue on a pro rata basis that is based on the current proportion of shares owned. Existing shareholders do not have to exercise the right, but they do possess a right of first refusal. The stock issue is usually conducted through a rights offering, in which existing shareholders declare their intention to subscribe to a certain number of shares when they are issued. The right conveys the opportunity to purchase shares at the subscription price. Rights are negotiable, so a shareholder who does not wish to purchase stock can sell the rights to third parties. A rights offering provides existing shareholders with the opportunity to maintain their proportionate share of ownership if they choose to do so. It is not a requirement in all jurisdictions, but it is incorporated into many corporate charters in places where it is not required.

F. Mergers and Acquisitions

Mergers and acquisitions (M&As) refer to corporate consolidations involving either two or more firms combining together (in a merger) or one firm being purchased or acquired by another (in an acquisition). Given the dollar amounts involved, M&As represent significant financial decisions that will have a major impact on the futures of the firms involved. Motives for M&As may include tapping into growth potential, reducing costs, and strengthening balance sheets (e.g., acquiring a firm with substantial cash holdings). This section describes several key aspects related to M&As.

1. TYPES OF TRANSACTIONS

Whether a purchase is considered a merger or an acquisition depends on whether the purchase is friendly or hostile, and how it is announced. In other words, the real difference lies in how the purchase is communicated to and received by the target firm's board of directors, employees, and shareholders.

a. Merging Two Firms

In the pure sense of the term, a *merger* happens when two firms, often of about the same size, agree to go forward as a single new company rather than remain separately owned and operated. This kind of action is more precisely referred to as a *merger of equals*. The stocks for both firms are surrendered, and new stock is issued in its place. In practice, however, actual mergers of equals do not happen very often. Usually, one firm, the acquirer, will buy another and, as part of the deal's terms, simply allow the acquired firm to proclaim that the action is a merger of equals, even if it is technically an acquisition. Being bought out often carries negative connotations; therefore, by describing the deal as a merger, deal makers and top managers try to make the takeover more appealing to the market.

b. Acquisition of a Firm

An acquisition results when one firm buys a majority of the voting shares of another firm. An acquisition may be friendly or hostile. Each type is described below:

- **Friendly Acquisition:** In this case, the bidder will typically inform the other firm's board of directors of its intention to acquire. In a friendly acquisition, with the board of the target firm cooperating, the acquiring firm may conduct extensive due diligence into the financial and other affairs of the targeted firm. The potential acquirer may negotiate directly with the target firm's management.

· **Hostile Takeover:** This usually occurs when the target is expected to fight the acquisition attempt. In this case, the acquirer will normally make a tender offer directly to the target firm's shareholders, bypassing management. A tender offer represents a cash offer for common shares. Generally, tender offers are more expensive than negotiated M&As, due to the resistance of target management and the fact that the target is now "in play" and may attract other bidders. A second approach is to engage in a proxy fight prior to the target's annual shareholders meeting. If the acquiring firm can obtain enough of the proxies, then it can elect a new board of directors that, presumably, will approve the acquisition. Another approach is known as a *creeping tender offer*, which involves quietly purchasing sufficient stock on the open market to enable a change in the management. Regardless of the approach, the key similarity is that the existing board and management are resistant to the acquisition.

c. Leveraged Buyout (LBO)

An LBO occurs when an acquisition is financed primarily by using the acquired firm's assets as collateral. The debt is normally carried on the balance sheet of the acquired firm, and the debt is serviced by the acquired firm's operating cash flows. In limited cases, an LBO may be made when the acquirer uses its own assets as security for the loan. An LBO can also be used if management wishes to take a firm private, in which case borrowed funds are used to buy back the acquired firm's outstanding stock. In most cases, the shareholders of the acquired firm will receive a premium for their shares. An LBO often involves more risk than an acquisition paid for through the issuance of equity securities, due to the high level of debt and the need to generate ongoing operating cash flows to make the debt payments.

LBOs differ from ordinary acquisitions in two major ways:

· First, a large fraction of the purchase price is debt-financed. Typically, a large portion of the debt is junk (i.e., below investment grade).

· Second, the LBO goes private, and its shares no longer trade on the open market. The LBO's stock is typically held by a partnership of investors. When this group is led by the company's management, the acquisition is called a *management buyout (MBO)*.

Many LBO investor groups hope to capture value by selling off the acquired firm's assets in pieces. Some groups try to raise cash by selling poorer performing assets, and building sales and profits of the remaining assets, hoping to sell them for a substantial profit at a later date. Though some LBOs may remain private for an extended period, most tend to be more of a short-term duration of less than five years.

2. FINANCING THE TRANSACTION

M&A transactions can be financed using existing cash, equity, debt, or a combination of all three. Common structures include:

· All-cash transactions

· Stock transactions, financed through the exchange of stock

· Mixed stock/cash transactions

· Leveraged cash transactions, financed through debt issue

· Leveraged buyouts, with the majority of equity replaced by debt

· Debt transactions, financed through debt offered to the acquired company's shareholders

· Mixed cash/debt transactions

· Preferred stock transactions

When cash is involved in paying for the acquired firm, it may come from a variety of sources:

- · Cash from the acquiring firm
- · Excess cash from the acquired firm
- · Cash from the sale of some of the acquired firm's assets
- · Issuance of investment-grade bonds
- · Issuance of below-investment-grade bonds (i.e., junk bonds) that have an amortization schedule supported by a forecast of operating cash flows[9]

G. At the Market (ATM) Programs

As an alternative to a traditional underwritten offering of a fixed number of shares at a fixed price all at once, some organizations have turned to ATM programs. An ATM program allows for the issuance of up to a specific amount of equity over time that is sold into the existing secondary market at the current market price on an as-needed basis.

In an ATM program, the issuer still needs to file appropriate disclosure documents, but in this case files a shelf registration to cover the potential issuance of stock. Once the registration and prospectus are approved, a specific broker-dealer is authorized to issue new stock for sale at current market prices as the firm needs additional capital. Since the stock is issued in small increments to avoid impacting the market price of the stock, these plans are also sometimes referred to as *dribble plans*.

VII. MISCELLANEOUS CORPORATE FINANCE TOPICS

A. Dividend Policy

Dividend policies are typically set by the CEO or board of directors, often with input from the treasurer. Dividend policies can have a significant impact on treasury operations due to the accompanying impact on cash flows and capital structure. In terms of the latter, steadily increasing dividends may make a firm's common stock more attractive to certain institutional investors and may increase the stock price.[10] However, increasing dividends reduces the amount of cash flow available for reinvestment. This may slow growth and, hence, capital appreciation. A firm may then become less attractive to investors that have a preference for capital gains relative to dividends. In effect, dividend policy determines the type of investor that is likely to be interested in being a shareholder. This is referred to as *dividend catering*.

The optimal dividend policy is one that:

- · Maximizes shareholder value
- · Allows for the sufficient retention of funds for future asset expansion
- · Provides information to investors about the future earnings of the firm, which is commonly referred to as *dividend signaling*[11]

---

9. The low rating usually results from higher debt ratios, a lower interest coverage ratio (e.g., times interest earned), and less than full confidence on the part of the rating agency that the forecasted operating cash flows will be sufficient to meet amortization requirements.
10. A popular way to value dividend-paying stocks is with the dividend discount model. With this model, an increase in dividends results in an increase in stock price, all else constant.
11. Signaling can be either positive or negative, and often depends upon the context of the dividend. For example, is the company returning capital that will not be needed in the future, or is the company expecting growth in overall earnings?

---

1. DIVIDEND PAYMENT PROCEDURES

When a dividend is planned, the board of directors declares a dividend amount, a payment date, and a shareholder-of-record date. This results in four dates:

- **Declaration Date:** This is the date when the board of directors announces or declares the dividend.

- **Record Date:** Also known as a *shareholder-of-record date* or a *holder-of-record date*, this is the date when the firm looks at its records to determine its shareholders of record that are entitled to receive the declared dividend.

- **Ex-Dividend Date:** This is the first date on which the stock is sold without entitlement to the upcoming dividend. The ex-dividend date is usually two business days prior to the shareholder-of-record date, thereby enabling brokerage firms to send an updated list of shareholders to a company on time. Theoretically, there should be a drop in the stock price equivalent to the dividend on the ex-dividend date. However, this is difficult to measure because other factors may influence the market price.

- **Payment Date:** This is the date when the dividend is paid, which is usually a week or more after the record date, to allow the firm time to process and disburse the dividend.

As an example of these dates, on June 3, 2017, a firm announces that it will pay a $0.25 quarterly cash dividend on July 1, 2017, to shareholders of record on June 14, 2017. In this example:

- The declaration date is June 3, 2017.

- The record date is June 14, 2017.

- The ex-dividend date is June 12, 2017.[12]

- The payment date is July 1, 2017.

2. DIVIDEND REINVESTMENT PLANS (DRIPs)

DRIPs may be used to allow investors to increase their ownership of the firm's shares. A DRIP enables existing shareholders to purchase additional shares directly from the firm on a when-desired basis, normally with no commission or with only a small processing charge. DRIPs also allow investors to reinvest dividends automatically in additional shares. Shares that the firm distributes under these plans may be held in the treasury (i.e., treasury stock), be repurchased by the company in the market and intended for this purpose, or be new, authorized shares of stock that have not been issued yet (i.e., shelf-registered stock).

DRIPs benefit smaller shareholders because transaction costs are low or nonexistent. Also, a few firms sell shares to DRIP investors at a discount to market price. From the firm's point of view, this method of raising capital is significantly less expensive than issuing new stock to the general public (due to no underwriting costs), thus saving cash for the issuer. One negative aspect of DRIPs, however, is that they may increase the number of small shareholders, resulting in more expensive investor relations through an increased cost of maintaining shareholder records.

3. TYPES OF DIVIDENDS

Many different methods can be employed to pay dividends to shareholders. Regular cash dividends are the most common, but there are other types, including stock, special, and liquidating dividends. Although not technically dividends, stock splits often are considered part of dividend policy.

---

12. June 12, 13, and 14 are assumed to be business days.

---

a. Cash Dividends

As mentioned previously, the most common form of dividend payment is a regular cash dividend. Cash dividends usually are paid on a quarterly basis. Historically, they were paid by check, but are increasingly paid electronically.

b. Stock Dividends

Stock dividends occur when shareholders are paid dividends with additional shares of stock, as opposed to cash. The stock's per-share price in the market is reduced because additional shares are in circulation, but there is no real impact on shareholder wealth since the added shares do not alter the firm's overall value. However, there may be additional costs for managing the record keeping for the new shares. The dilution in earnings caused by the stock dividend will cause a fall in share price that is proportionate to the increase in the number of shares outstanding. If a firm is in a period of rapid growth and needs to retain all earnings for reinvestment, stock dividends may be a means of compensating shareholders for their loyalty. For example, a firm that follows a stable dividend policy and that has many attractive but expensive investment alternatives will be faced with a dilemma: shareholders have been conditioned to expect a cash dividend. One solution to this dilemma is to pay the dividend in stock rather than cash. This does not impart added value for shareholders, but may make shareholders feel as though they have benefited. In addition, the shareholders will not owe taxes on the stock dividend until the shares are sold.

c. Special Dividends

Dividend policy provides information to shareholders, especially if dividends change unexpectedly. For this reason, most firms that pay regular dividends attempt to avoid sudden dividend changes. If a firm has a one-time earnings spike, paying a higher dividend for just one period will send mixed signals to shareholders. It may also cause a false expectation that dividends were increased permanently, which eventually will negatively impact the stock price. In such cases management may opt for a special dividend, in which the dividend is meant to be a one-time payment rather than an ongoing dividend increase.

d. Liquidating Dividends

A liquidating dividend[13] is paid out of capital rather than earnings. This sometimes occurs when a firm or one of its divisions is going out of business and management decides to pay off shareholders through a liquidating dividend. As the name implies, the remaining assets of the failed firm or division are liquidated to pay the dividend. This approach may also be used by the acquiring firm in an LBO to liquidate the acquired firm in order to meet debt service requirements.

e. Stock Splits

A stock split occurs when an existing share is split into more than one share at a reduced share price. The basic idea behind a stock split is that an optimal trading range exists for a stock's price. When management deems that the share price has become too high for smaller shareholders to purchase the stock in round lots (multiples of 100 shares), it will recommend to the board of directors that the stock be split to reduce the share price. By reducing the price, it is possible that latent demand may become active and trigger an increase in share price. A negative aspect of a stock split is the subsequent earnings dilution.

Firms with declining share prices occasionally initiate a reverse split to increase share price. A primary motivation for a reverse split is to avoid having the firm's shares be delisted by an exchange under the exchange's minimum price policy.

---

13. Securities laws in some jurisdictions have specific regulations about the term *liquidating dividend* versus *return of capital.*

4. STOCK REPURCHASES

As an alternative to paying cash dividends, the board of directors can authorize a stock repurchase, whereby internally generated funds are used to enter the market and buy back the firm's own shares. For non-dividend-paying firms this is an important means of returning value to shareholders. There are typically regulatory and potentially covenant restrictions with which firms must comply when repurchasing shares.

5. INTERCOMPANY DIVIDENDS

Intercompany dividends are a movement of funds between related firms that may be subject to taxes or regulatory restrictions. Large firms with wholly owned subsidiaries often use intercompany dividends to transfer profits from subsidiaries to the parent. Subsidiaries may be required to pay a stated percentage of earnings to the parent, although these may be subject to thin capitalization rules, which restrict payments to the parent if this would cause the subsidiary to become undercapitalized. Intercompany dividend payments may impact covenants with lenders. It should be noted that cross-border repatriation of dividends may not always be permitted by local regulators, and where permitted, may be heavily scrutinized. Tax consequences must be balanced with the profit potential, and firms should seek advice from qualified tax professionals. Global financial institutions often offer services in this area for their customers.

6. TAXES ON DIVIDENDS

There are numerous tax considerations for dividend payments, mainly impacting recipients. For the average investor, dividends are usually taxable income and may be taxed at a different rate than capital gains. In some countries, tax rates on dividends received by corporations may be adjusted to reduce the potential double-taxation effect on those dividends. Tax regulations on dividends change constantly, and tax experts should be consulted for the latest information.

7. RESTRICTIONS ON DIVIDENDS

There may be restrictions on the dividends that can be paid from different types of firms. Many borrowing arrangements include restrictive covenants on the payment of dividends unless certain financial ratios are maintained.

There may also be dividend restrictions oriented toward certain industries or classes of companies imposed by financial and regulatory authorities. Financial institutions and insurers often have restrictions on their dividends to protect their capital base in the event of loan or policy losses.

B. Tax Strategies

Tax and accounting issues have a major impact on financial decision making. This section focuses primarily on general tax strategies typically used by multinational firms.

Multinational firms need an effective global tax strategy or they risk incurring highly unfavorable tax consequences. Effective international tax planning can reduce taxes by minimizing the potential for double taxation (i.e., to a foreign jurisdiction and the firm's home country). An effective global tax strategy will balance home country and foreign tax considerations in the context of the firm's broader business and financial objectives.

Taxing jurisdictions carefully monitor firms' transfers of funds between subsidiaries across borders. An example of this is the development of international transfer pricing rules, which require firms to document their annual compliance with strict "arm's length" standards for the pricing of intercompany transfers of goods and services. Another problem area is that of deemed dividends, where payments on loans, sales of stock, or other transactions may be interpreted by tax authorities as a corporate attempt to avoid paying taxes on dividends. The payments may then be determined to be deemed dividends, and appropriate taxes charged. These and other international tax rules are constantly changing, which poses a challenge.

Proper international tax planning requires a global tax strategy that facilitates the firm's global business objectives. The starting point is to develop a solid understanding of the firm's business and financial position, its international operating strategy, and where and how it intends to operate outside its home country. With this knowledge, an overall global tax strategy can be developed. International tax planning for specific situations can then be approached in a coherent manner, taking into account the firm's broader global tax and operating strategies.

C. Repatriation of Capital for Multinational Companies (MNCs)

An important issue for the treasury departments of MNCs is whether or when to repatriate cash from foreign subsidiaries to the domestic parent's country. Repatriation involves the transfer of funds between countries. Most repatriation policies are related to the transfer of funds back to the parent from wholly or partially owned global subsidiaries. The objectives are to ensure that the MNC is compensated fairly for the foreign investment and that the host country benefits from the local reinvestment of funds.

The principal method of repatriation is the use of dividends. However, the relative differences in tax policies across the involved countries impact this approach. Therefore, other methods can be used for repatriation purposes. These include management fees, royalties, licensing, transfer pricing, and intercompany loans.

1. MNC DIVIDENDS

The use of dividends to transfer profits from global subsidiaries is often restricted by host governments. Usually, there are either significant taxes (e.g., a 35% tax in the United States) charged on cross-border dividend payments, or outright restrictions on the repatriation of funds via dividend payments. Dividend payments to the parent company take subsidiary profits out of a country, but host governments prefer to see earnings reinvested locally.

To counter this problem, MNCs unbundle the cash flows from subsidiaries into separate items that are justified more easily to foreign governments than outright dividends. The techniques for separating items are management fees, transfer pricing, and intercompany loans.

2. MANAGEMENT FEES

Many MNCs charge global subsidiaries licensing and/or management fees in order to justify to host governments the flow of funds from a subsidiary to the parent company. Oftentimes, these fees are negotiated with the host government prior to when the MNC invests in the country.

3. TRANSFER PRICING

Transfer pricing is the price that subsidiaries of a large corporation charge one another for components sold among them. The benefit for MNCs is that transfer pricing can be used as a mechanism to locate profits in subsidiaries in low-tax countries and to move them out of subsidiaries in high-tax countries. Host governments resent these actions;

hence, they frequently place restrictions on transfer pricing or changes in transfer prices made by MNCs within their jurisdictions. The implication for management is that most transfer pricing for global subsidiaries must be done at "arm's length." This means setting transfer prices at the same level at which a firm would buy or sell similar products from an unaffiliated entity. This assures host governments that the profits from the MNC will be distributed fairly among all global subsidiaries. The complexity of transfer pricing is such that MNCs often seek the advice of highly specialized tax consultants to establish policies and procedures.

4. INTERCOMPANY LOANS

Another way to transfer funds between foreign subsidiaries is to use intercompany loans.[14] When funds are required by a foreign subsidiary in a country whose government permits the transfer of funds for the servicing of a loan, the parent or subsidiary may loan funds rather than contribute equity. Subsequent loan and interest payments effectively replace the dividends that the subsidiary cannot pay the parent company. Should repayment of intercompany loans also be restricted, an MNC can sometimes bring a third-party intermediary into the process. Intercompany loans often produce tax advantages because foreign governments do not impose taxes on loan repayments, as would be the case with cross-border dividend payments. Management must be cautious that repeated intercompany loans are not viewed as deemed dividends by the relevant tax authorities and taxed as such. This is particularly likely to happen if the loans are not paid back in a timely or routine fashion. Intercompany loans may be supported by tax treaties between the countries involved.

5. DEEMED DIVIDENDS

Deemed dividends occur when payments on loans, sales of stock, or other transactions may be interpreted by tax authorities as an attempt by a company to avoid paying taxes on dividends. The payments may be deemed, or considered, dividends and appropriate taxes may then be charged.

For example, a US MNC with offshore-controlled foreign corporations (OFCs) may face some of the following issues with deemed dividends:

- Borrowings from OFCs by the parent may be considered dividends rather than borrowings, and thus taxable distributions as far as the tax authorities are concerned.

- Under Section 956 of the US tax code, a US shareholder of an OFC is currently required to include in income (as a deemed dividend) its pro rata share of any increase in the earnings of the OFC that are invested in US property.

D. Market Analysis and Research Tools

Financial professionals can use various market analysis and research tools to help them make financial decisions. These are typically resources that are available to help with (1) portfolio investment decisions (e.g., when purchasing/ selling investments or managing the portfolio), (2) acquisition and divestment decisions, (3) evaluation of trading partners for credit and counterparty risk, and (4) comparisons with other firms or industry averages.

Some of the analysis and research tools, such as Bloomberg, FactSet, Thomson Reuters, and Dow Jones Financial Information Services, provide a wide range of services, including real-time news and information on financial markets (e.g., interest rates, foreign exchange rates, and market indices), as well as historical data. Some of the services also include platforms that allow for the execution of trades for stocks, bonds, currencies, and derivatives.

---

14. At the time of this writing, the US Treasury Department has proposed revisions to Internal Revenue Code Section 385. These provisions may require that firms reclassify some inter-company loans as equity in the future.

Other analysis and research tools focus more on the provision of historical data for research purposes (e.g., Standard & Poor's and Mergent). Fee-based companies like Dun & Bradstreet (D&B) and CreditRiskMonitor provide information for those wanting to perform a credit analysis on potential customers or borrowers. Financial information on publicly traded companies is available from a wide range of sources as well. While many financial reporting services charge fees, there are also a large number of free sources, such as Google Finance, Yahoo! Finance, CNBC, and MSN Money. Financial statements of US publicly traded firms are also available at no charge through the SEC's Electronic Data Gathering, Analysis, and Retrieval (EDGAR) system. In addition, information on municipal bonds, including official disclosures, refunding documents, and market information, may be obtained from EMMA (Electronic Municipal Market Access), which is a service of the Municipal Securities Rulemaking Board (MSRB).

VIII. SUMMARY

This chapter covered various topics related to corporate financial management. Although treasury professionals may not have direct responsibility for some of these topics, it is important that they are aware of their potential impact on treasury, especially on cash flows and payments. The topics covered in this chapter include capital structure, raising and managing capital, leasing, and equity financing.

The chapter closed with a discussion of a number of related issues that impact MNCs, including international tax strategies, deemed dividends, and repatriation of international earnings. A common element in this discussion is that while there are similarities in the treatment of these issues in many countries, local treatment—especially of tax issues—can vary. It is important that treasury professionals be aware of how local authorities and regulators will react before making specific decisions.

Key Equations

$$\text{After-Tax } r_D = r_D(1-T)$$

$$r_E = r_{RF} + (r_M - r_{RF})\beta$$

$$\text{WACC} = w_D r_D(1-T) + w_E r_E$$

$$\text{EVA} = \text{EBIT}(1-T) - (\text{WACC})(\text{Long-Term Debt} + \text{Equity})$$

LIST OF ACRONYMS AND ABBREVIATIONS

A/P	Accounts Payable
A/R	Accounts Receivable
ABA	American Bankers Association
ABCP	Asset-Backed Commercial Paper
ABL	Asset-Based Lending
ABS	Asset-Backed Security
ACCA	Association of Chartered Certified Accountants
ACH	Automated Clearinghouse
ADR	American Depositary Receipt
AICPA	American Institute of Certified Public Accountants
Amex	American Express
ANSI	American National Standards Institute
API	Application Program Interface
APIC	Additional Paid-In Capital
ARP	Account Reconciliation Program
ASB	Auditing Standards Board
ASC	Accounting Standards Codification
ASC	Accredited Standards Committee
ASP	Application Service Provider
ASU	Accounting Standards Update
ATM	At the Market [Program]
ATM	Automated Teller Machine
AVS	Address Verification Service
B2B	Business to Business
B2C	Business to Consumer
B2G	Business to Government
BA	Banker's Acceptance
BAI	Bank Administration Institute
BAN	Bond Anticipation Note

BBAN	Basic Bank Account Number
BC	Business Continuity
BCBS	Basel Committee on Banking Supervision
BEC	Business E-mail Compromise
BEY	Bond Equivalent Yield
BIC	Bank Identification Code
BIS	Bank for International Settlements
BNF	Beneficiary Information
BSA	Bank Secrecy Act
BSB	Bank Services Billing
BTRS	Balance and Transaction Reporting Standard
C2B	Consumer to Business
C2C	Consumer to Consumer
C2G	Consumer to Government
CA	Chartered Accountant
CAPM	Capital Asset Pricing Model
CaR	Cash Flow at Risk
CBD	Cash before Delivery
CBES	Commercial Book-Entry System
CCC	Cash Conversion Cycle
CD	Certificate of Deposit
CDARS	Certificate of Deposit Account Registry Service
CDS	Credit Default Swap
CEO	Chief Executive Officer
CFO	Chief Financial Officer
CFPB	Consumer Financial Protection Bureau
CFTC	Commodity Futures Trading Commission

CGFS	Committee on the Global Financial System	**DIDMCA**	Depository Institutions Deregulation and Monetary Control Act
CHAPS	Clearing House Automated Payments System	**DIF**	Deposit Insurance Fund
Check 21	Check Clearing for the 21st Century Act	**DOJ**	Department of Justice
		DOL	Degree of Operating Leverage
CHIPS	Clearing House Interbank Payments System	**DP**	Days' Payables
CIP	Customer Identification Program	**DP**	Default Risk Premium
CLS	Continuous Linked Settlement	**DR**	Days' Receivables
CNAPS	China National Advanced Payment System	**DR**	Depositary Receipt
		DR	Disaster Recovery
COD	Cash on Delivery	**DRIP**	Dividend Reinvestment Plan
COGS	Cost of Goods Sold	**DSO**	Days' Sales Outstanding
COSO	Committee of Sponsoring Organizations of the Treadway Commission	**DTC**	Depository Trust Company
		DTCC	Depository Trust & Clearing Corporation
CP	Commercial Paper	**DTL**	Degree of Total Leverage
CPA	Certified Public Accountant	**DWC**	Days' Working Capital
CPA	Chartered Professional Accountant	**E&O**	Errors and Omissions
CPSS	Committee on Payment and Settlement Systems	**EBA**	European Banking Authority
		eBAM	Electronic Bank Account Management
CRA	Credit Rating Agency	**EBIT**	Earnings Before Interest and Taxes
Credit CARD Act	Credit Card Accountability Responsibility and Disclosure Act	**EBITDA**	Earnings Before Interest, Taxes, Depreciation, and Amortization
CRP	Consolidated Remittance Processing	**EBPP**	Electronic Bill Presentment and Payment
CSD	Central Securities Depository	**EC**	European Commission
CTP	Certified Treasury Professional	**ECA**	Earnings Credit Analysis
CTP	Customer Transfer Plus	**ECA**	Export Credit Agency
CVV/CVC	Card Verification Value/Code	**ECB**	European Central Bank
D&B	Dun & Bradstreet	**E-Commerce**	Electronic Commerce
D&O	Directors and Officers	**ECR**	Earnings Credit Rate
D/A	Documents against Acceptance	**EDGAR**	Electronic Data Gathering, Analysis, and Retrieval [Database]
D/P	Documents against Payment		
DDA	Demand Deposit Account	**EDI**	Electronic Data Interchange
DFL	Degree of Financial Leverage	**EFT**	Electronic Funds Transfer
DI	Days' Inventory	**EFTA**	Electronic Fund Transfer Act
DIC	Difference in Conditions		

EFTPOS	Electronic Funds Transfer at the Point of Sale	**FATCA**	Foreign Account Tax Compliance Act
EFTPS	Electronic Federal Tax Payment System	**FATF**	Financial Action Task Force
EIOPA	European Insurance and Occupational Pensions Authority	**FBAR**	Report of Foreign Bank and Financial Accounts
EIPP	Electronic Invoice Presentment and Payment	**FBI**	Federal Bureau of Investigation
		FCA	Financial Conduct Authority
EMIR	European Market Infrastructure Regulation	**FCF**	Free Cash Flow
		FCPA	Foreign Corrupt Practices Act
EMMA	Electronic Municipal Market Access	**FDIC**	Federal Deposit Insurance Corporation
EMS	European Monetary System	**Fed**	Federal Reserve Bank/System
EMU	Economic and Monetary Union	**FFIEC**	Federal Financial Institutions Examination Council
EMV	Europay, Mastercard, and Visa		
EOQ	Economic Order Quantity	**FHC**	Financial Holding Company
EPC	European Payments Council	**FHLMC (Freddie Mac)**	Federal Home Loan Mortgage Corporation
EPC	External Processing Code		
EPN	Electronic Payments Network	**FI**	Financial Institution
EPS	Earnings Per Share	**FinCEN**	Financial Crimes Enforcement Network
EPU	European Payments Union		
ERM	Enterprise Risk Management	**FINRA**	Financial Industry Regulatory Authority
ERP	Enterprise Resource Planning		
E-Sign Act	Electronic Signatures in Global and National Commerce Act	**FinTech**	Financial Technology
		FIU	Financial Intelligence Unit
ESMA	European Securities and Markets Authority	**FNMA (Fannie Mae)**	Federal National Mortgage Association
ESRB	European Systemic Risk Board	**FOMC**	Federal Open Market Committee
ETF	Exchange-Traded Fund	**FP&A**	Financial Planning and Analysis
EU	European Union	**FRA**	Forward Rate Agreement
Euribor	Euro Interbank Offered Rate	**FRN**	Floating-Rate Note
EVA	Economic Value Added	**FRR**	Financial Reporting Release
EXIM	Export-Import Bank of the United States	**FSB**	Financial Stability Board
		FSOC	Financial Stability Oversight Council
FACT	Fair and Accurate Credit Transactions Act		
		FSP	Financial Service Provider
		FTC	Federal Trade Commission
FAS	Financial Accounting Standard	**FV**	Future Value
FASB	Financial Accounting Standards Board	**FX**	Foreign Exchange
		G/L	General Ledger

G/NFP	Governmental and Not-For-Profit [Organizations]		**IP**	Inflation Premium
G2B	Government to Business		**IP**	Internet Protocol
G2C	Government to Consumer		**IPO**	Initial Public Offering
GAAP	Generally Accepted Accounting Principles		**IRD**	Image Replacement Document
GAAS	Generally Accepted Auditing Standards		**IRR**	Internal Rate of Return
			IRS	Internal Revenue Service
GASB	Governmental Accounting Standards Board		**ISAE**	International Standard on Assurance Engagements
GDR	Global Depositary Receipt		**ISDA**	International Swaps and Derivatives Association
GHOS	Group of Governors and Heads of Supervision		**ISO**	International Organization for Standardization
GLB	Graham-Leach-Bliley Act		**ISP**	International Standby Practice
GNMA (Ginnie Mae)	Government National Mortgage Association		**IT**	Information Technology
			IVR	Interactive Voice Response
GSE	Government-Sponsored Enterprise		**JGB**	Japanese Government Bond
HR	Human Resources		**JIT**	Just-in-Time [Inventory/Method]
IAASB	International Auditing and Assurance Standards Board		**KPI**	Key Performance Indicator
			KYC	Know Your Customer
IADI	International Association of Deposit Insurers		**L/C**	Letter of Credit
			LBO	Leveraged Buyout
IAIS	International Association of Insurance Supervisors		**LIBOR**	London Interbank Offered Rate
			LIFO	Last-In, First-Out
IAS	International Accounting Standard		**LP**	Liquidity Premium
IASB	International Accounting Standards Board		**LVTS**	Large Value Transfer System
			M&A	Merger and Acquisition
IBA	ICE Benchmark Administration		**MAC**	Material Adverse Change
IBAN	International Bank Account Number		**MBO**	Management Buyout
			MBS	Mortgage-Backed Security
IBRD	International Bank for Reconstruction and Development		**MCC**	Merchant Category Code
ICC	International Chamber of Commerce		**MD&A**	Management's Discussion & Analysis
IFAC	International Federation of Accountants		**MFN**	Most Favored Nation
			MICR	Magnetic Ink Character Recognition
IFRS	International Financial Reporting Standards		**MIGA**	Multilateral Investment Guarantee Agency
IHB	In-house Bank/Banking Function		**MLCA**	Money Laundering Control Act
IMF	International Monetary Fund		**MMDA**	Money Market Deposit Account
IOSCO	International Organization of Securities Commissions		**MMF**	Money Market Fund
			MMY	Money Market Yield

MNC	Multinational Company	**OECD**	Organisation for Economic Co-operation and Development
MNPI	Material Nonpublic Information	**OFAC**	Office of Foreign Assets Control
MOTO	Mail Order or Telephone Order	**OFC**	Offshore-Controlled Foreign Corporation
MP	Maturity Premium		
MPS	Material Planning System	**ORG**	Originator Information
MSRB	Municipal Securities Rulemaking Board	**OTC**	Over the Counter
		OTTI	Other-Than-Temporary Impairment
MT	Message Type		
Muni	Municipal Bond/Note	**P2P**	Person to Person
NAIC	National Association of Insurance Commissioners	**PCAOB**	Public Company Accounting Oversight Board
NASD	National Association of Securities Dealers	**P-Card**	Procurement Card
		PCI DSS	Payment Card Industry Data Security Standard
NAV	Net Asset Value		
NBES	National Book-Entry System	**PI**	Profitability Index
NCI	Noncash Item/Not Cash Item	**PIN**	Personal Identification Number
NCUA	National Credit Union Administration	**PKI**	Public-Key Infrastructure
		POD	Proof of Deposit
NCUSIF	National Credit Union Share Insurance Fund	**POP**	Point of Purchase
		POS	Point of Sale
NDF	Non-Deliverable Forward	**PSD**	European Payment Services Directive
NDO	Non-Deliverable Option		
NFC	Near Field Communication	**PTD**	Payable Through Draft
NFP	Not-for-Profit [Organization]	**PV**	Present Value
NPV	Net Present Value		
NRSRO	Nationally Recognized Statistical Rating Organization	**QIB**	Qualified Institutional Buyer
		QII	Qualified Institutional Investor
NSCC	National Securities Clearing Corporation	**QR**	Quick Response [Code]
		RADR	Risk-Adjusted Discount Rate
NSF	Non-sufficient Funds	**RAROC**	Risk-Adjusted Return on Capital
NWC	Net Working Capital	**RCC**	Remotely Created Check
NYSE	New York Stock Exchange	**RCSA**	Risk and Control Self-Assessment
OBI	Originator to Beneficiary Information	**RDC**	Remote Deposit Capture
		RDFI	Receiving Depository Financial Institution
OBSA	Off-Balance-Sheet Arrangement		
OCC	Office of the Comptroller of the Currency	**Repo**	Repurchase Agreement
		RFB	Reference to Beneficiary
OCR	Optical Character Recognition	**RFI**	Request for Information
ODFI	Originating Depository Financial Institution	**RFID**	Radio Frequency Identification
		RFP	Request for Proposal

RFQ	Request for Quotation/Quote	**TCOR**	Total Cost of Risk
ROA	Return on Assets	**TDA**	Time Deposit Account
ROE	Return on Common Equity	**TIE**	Times Interest Earned [Ratio]
ROI	Return on Investment	**TIF**	Tax Increment Financing [Bond]
RTGS	Real-Time Gross Settlement	**TILA**	Truth in Lending Act
RTM	Refer to Maker	**TMS**	Treasury Management System
RTN	Routing Transit Number	**TRADES**	Treasury/Reserve Automated Debt Entry System
S&P	Standard & Poor's		
SAS	Statement on Auditing Standards	**TWIST**	Transaction Workflow Innovation Standards Team
SDR	Special Drawing Right		
SEC	Securities and Exchange Commission	**TXP**	Tax Payment [Banking Convention/ACH Format]
SEC	Standard Entry Class	**UBPR**	Uniform Bank Performance Report
SEO	Seasoned Equity Offering	**UCC**	Uniform Commercial Code
SEPA	Single Euro Payments Area	**UCF/UF**	Uncollected Funds
SIR	Self-Insured Retention	**UCP**	Uniform Customs and Practice for Documentary Credits
SLA	Service Level Agreement		
SMS	Short Message Service	**UFH**	Uncollected Funds Hold
SOC	Service Organization Controls	**UN/EDIFACT**	United Nations/Electronic Data Interchange for Administration, Commerce and Transport
SOE	State-Owned Enterprise		
SONIA	Sterling Overnight Index Average		
SOP	Standard Operating Procedure	**USA PATRIOT Act**	Uniting and Strengthening America by Providing Appropriate Tools Required to Intercept and Obstruct Terrorism Act
SOX	Sarbanes-Oxley Act		
SPDR/Spider	Standard & Poor's Depositary Receipt		
SSAE	Statement on Standards for Attestation Engagements		
		UTL	Unable to Locate
SSC	Shared Services Center	**VA**	Department of Veterans Affairs
SSO	Single Sign-On	**VaR**	Value at Risk
STP	Straight-Through Processing	**VAT**	Value-Added Tax
SVC	Stored-Value Card	**VRDO**	Variable-Rate Demand Obligation
SWF	Sovereign Wealth Fund	**WACC**	Weighted Average Cost of Capital
SWIFT	Society for Worldwide Interbank Financial Telecommunication	**WAP**	Wireless Application Protocol
		WIP	Work in Progress [Inventory]
T&E Card	Travel and Entertainment Card	**XML**	eXtensible Markup Language
TAN	Tax Anticipation Note	**YTC**	Yield to Call
TARGET2	Trans-European Automated Real-time Gross settlement Express Transfer (2nd generation)	**YTM**	Yield to Maturity
		YTW	Yield to Worst
		ZBA	Zero Balance Account
T-Bill	Treasury Bill		

LIST OF GLOSSARY TERMS

acceptance: A drawee's signed agreement to pay a negotiable instrument (typically a letter of credit or related draft) as presented. Acceptance acknowledges that all of the terms of the instrument, other than time, have been met and the instrument will be paid at the proper time. – CH12

account analysis: Largely unique to the US banking system, this is a record of the services provided to the customers of a bank, along with detailed information on balances and credits earned for those balances. The terms *account analysis* and *account analysis statement* are often used synonymously. *Account analysis* can also refer to the process used by the bank to determine earnings credits and service charges in creating this statement. – CH7

account analysis statement: A periodic statement that lists the fees for banking services provided to the account holder and any offsetting credits for deposited funds. – CH7

account reconciliation program (ARP): A service offered by a financial institution that matches issue information to paid check information and reports outstanding/unpaid items. – CH12

account resolution: Usually made at the board of director's level, this is the basic account or service authorization empowering a representative of the business to enter into agreements for financial services. It usually specifies the functions that can be performed by specific individuals or job titles, the persons authorized to open and close accounts, and the entire scope and limitations of the relationship. An account resolution is a specific type of board resolution. – CH7

account takeover: A type of fraud in which a hacker gains access to a company's bank account information and uses that information to remove funds from the account. – CH16

Accounting Standards Codification (ASC): The detailed set of rules in the United States, referred to as *Generally Accepted Accounting Principles*, that are developed, agreed upon, and published in the form of ASC Topics by the Financial Accounting Standards Board, an independent, self-regulating organization formed in 1973. – CH8

accounts receivable (A/R) balance pattern: A forecasting tool that specifies the percentage of credit sales during a time period (e.g., one month) that remain outstanding at the end of the current time period and each subsequent time period. – CH11

Accounts Receivable Conversion (ARC): A US automated clearinghouse (ACH) format used to convert eligible checks received at a lockbox into electronic debits and process them as automated clearinghouse (ACH) transactions. The company receiving the checks must notify the check writer that checks will be converted. *ARC* is the standard entry class (SEC) code for this format. – CH12

account-to-account transfer: Under the FedGlobal ACH Payments system, this is the standard option for distributing payments between deposit accounts. – CH3

account-to-receiver transfer: Under the FedGlobal ACH Payments system, this type of transfer allows funds from accounts at a US depository financial institution to be retrieved by any receiver either at a participating bank location or at a trusted, third-party provider in certain receiving countries. – CH4

Accredited Standards Committee (ASC) X12: A not-for-profit organization chartered by the American National Standards Institute (ANSI), responsible for developing and maintaining cross-industry electronic data interchange (EDI) message standards in the United States. – CH15

Accredited Standards Committee (ASC) X12 822: A major standardized format currently in use for the transmission of commercial account analysis information and used primarily by US financial institutions. The ASC X12 title is *Account Analysis Transaction Set 822.* – CH7

Accredited Standards Committee (ASC) X9: A not-for-profit organization chartered by the American National Standards Institute (ANSI), responsible for developing and maintaining financial industry standards, such as the size of a paper check and protocols for messaging, electronic security systems, and paperless contracts. ASC X9 is responsible for the Balance and Transaction Reporting Standard (BTRS), which has replaced the prior Bank Administration Institute reporting standard (BAI2). – CH15

accrual accounting: The accounting approach under which expenses must be reported when the revenues with which they are associated are recognized. Long-lived or fixed assets are capitalized (i.e., recorded as assets on the balance sheet) and depreciated over time because they produce revenues over many accounting periods. This practice matches an asset's cost to the revenues it produces. Under the revenue recognition and matching principles, sales are reported even though cash has not been received. Similarly, expenses are reported even though cash has not been paid out. – CH8

accumulated depreciation: An asset account that records the amount of depreciation previously expensed on a company's assets. It appears on the asset side of the balance sheet, but it is a source of funds when it increases. While depreciation is technically a noncash expense (i.e., there is no actual payment for depreciation), it does have a cash flow impact because it reduces the company's income taxes by lowering pretax income. – CH8

active hedging: The process of using various financial instruments (in particular, derivatives) to reduce or eliminate risks associated with future cash flows, or the values of assets or liabilities. A core principle of treasury financial risk management, hedging is similar to the concept of buying insurance to protect an asset, and the purpose of the hedge is to insure the asset's value (or minimize the risk on a liability) when its market value fluctuates. Also known as *financial hedging.* – CH17

additional paid-in capital (APIC): An equity account that reflects the difference at the time of issue between the par value and the issuance price (less underwriting costs) of any new stock sold by a company. – CH6

address verification service (AVS): A system used to verify the identity of the person claiming to own the credit card being used in a transaction. The system will check the billing address of the credit card provided by the user with the address on file at the credit card company. – CH12

advising bank: In a letter of credit (L/C) transaction, this is the bank that advises the seller of an L/C in its favor. – CH12

aggregate basis: A method of establishing insurance policy deductibles in which the deductible is set on a per-period basis, regardless of the number of occurrences (claims). – CH16

aggressive financing strategy: A current asset financing strategy that involves a company financing all fixed assets with long-term debt and equity, but financing only a portion of permanent current assets with long-term financing. Short-term financing supports the remainder of the permanent current assets and all temporary current assets. – CH10

aging schedule: A schedule that separates accounts receivable (A/R) into current and past-due receivables using set periods (typically 30-day increments) and is used for measuring A/R. – CH11

all-in rate: An interest rate that consists of a base rate, such as the London Interbank Offered Rate (LIBOR), the US prime rate, or the Fed funds rate, plus a spread that is added to, or occasionally subtracted from, the base rate. Rates on lines of credit are normally variable and adjust immediately to changes in the base rate. – CH13

alpha (smoothing constant): In an exponential smoothing forecasting methodology, this is the weight assigned to the most recent actual value and the most recent forecasted value. It is calculated using a computer program. The program selects the alpha value that weights past actual values and past forecasted values so as to produce the most accurate forecast of the variable's value in the next period. – CH14

American Bankers Association (ABA) number: In the United States, the ABA number (also known as the *routing transit number*) is a nine-digit number that identifies the paying bank for a check and provides the depository bank with the information it requires to route the check back to the paying bank through the clearing system. – CH4

American option: A type of option contract that can be executed or settled on or any time prior to the stated expiration date of the contract. Contrast with *European option* and *Bermuda option*. – CH17

analytical forecast: A type of forecast that can be used to answer what-if questions or to predict the financial impact of a given action. Also referred to as a *simulation*. – CH14

application program interface (API): A set of routines, protocols, and tools for building software applications. An API acts as a software gateway between programs, allowing data from one application to be used in another platform or service. – CH15

application service provider (ASP): A business that provides computer-based services to customers over a network. – CH15

arbitrage: The process by which an asset is purchased in one financial market and sold in another market to produce a riskless profit. Arbitrage is the primary mechanism that ensures efficiency in financial markets. – CH17

ask price: The price or yield at which a dealer will sell a security. – CH5

as-of adjustment: The practice of a bank adding additional time as part of the collected-balance calculation when a check takes longer to clear than the initial availability that was granted. – CH4

asset allocation: The mix between bonds and equities in a capital market investment portfolio. A careful analysis of the investor's risk tolerance is a starting point for determining the optimal asset allocation. – CH19

asset-backed commercial paper (ABCP): An investment that has most of the features of standard commercial paper (CP), but is secured against specific assets—usually short-term trade receivables from a single company or a range of companies. ABCP may be classified as either *single seller* if it is backed by assets from a single institution or *multi-seller* if it is backed by assets purchased from a number of issuers. – CH5

asset/liability management: The process of managing and coordinating the assets and liabilities held in an investment portfolio to maximize earnings and minimize risk. Whenever an investment portfolio utilizes borrowed funds as part of its overall strategy, the issue of asset/liability management arises. This is primarily an issue for banks and large financial institutions that fund their investments with either deposits or borrowed funds. In many cases, the issue is expressed in terms of a maturity mismatch; that is, the institution may be borrowing funds in the short-term markets (e.g., by using commercial paper) while using the proceeds from the financing to purchase long-term assets. – CH19

asset liquidity risk: The risk that a security investment cannot be sold quickly without experiencing an unacceptable loss. This risk can also affect the yield and pricing on a security. By definition, a *liquid security* is one that can be converted quickly and easily into cash with very little exposure to market price risk and for a small transaction cost. Also referred to as *liquidity risk*. – CH5

asset tax: A tax owed on the value of accumulated real property or business equipment, or on the value of a financial portfolio. This tax may be charged in some countries in order to impose tax liabilities on a business even through that business may not show a profit or owe income tax on an international project. – CH2

asset-based lending: A type of lending that involves commercial loans or lines of credit that are backed by liens on specific assets of the borrowing company. Asset-based lines of credit in the working capital area are typically secured by accounts receivable or inventory, and can support temporary financing needs. – CH10

at the market (ATM) program: A type of stock sales program that allows listed companies to sell additional shares of company stock over time through a designated broker-dealer at the current or prevailing market price to raise additional capital. – CH20

auditor's opinion: An opinion on a company's financial statements that is provided by an independent auditor (or audit firm) based on a financial audit. The purpose of conducting an audit is to produce an audit report in which an independent audit firm indicates the scope of the audit and renders an opinion regarding the relevance, completeness, and accuracy of the income statement, statement of financial position, statement of cash flows, any other statements, and all supporting material. In addition, the auditor will examine the strengths of the organization's internal controls and processes. The auditor's opinion does not comment on the company's financial fitness, but rather on whether the financial statements fairly reflect the company's financial position and are comparable to prior periods. – CH8

authentication: In electronic payment security, this is the ability to know, with a reasonable amount of certainty, who is accessing information or initiating a transaction. – CH15

automated clearinghouse (ACH): An electronic network for financial transactions in the United States. ACH processes large volumes of low-value credit and debit transactions in batches. – CH4

automated clearinghouse (ACH) credit transaction: An electronic message that instructs the originating depository financial institution to move funds from the originator's account to the receiver's account at the receiving depository financial institution. – CH4

automated clearinghouse (ACH) debit transaction: An electronic message that instructs the originating depository financial institution to move funds from the receiver's account to the originator's account. – CH4

availability: In a payment system, this is the point in time when the payee can use the funds provided by the payment, even though the payment may not be final. – CH4

availability float: The time interval or delay between the day when a payment is deposited into a bank account and the day when the payee's account is credited with collected funds. – CH10

availability schedule: A schedule that specifies, for each drawee endpoint, when a bank grants available credit or collected balances for deposited items. – CH4

available balance: The available balance (sometimes referred to as the *investable balance*) represents the balances in the customer's account that the bank was able to invest in income-producing assets during the account analysis period. *Available balance* is also defined as the amount of funds available for withdrawal from an account, based on the bank's availability schedule and/or local regulations that require specific availability for certain funds (e.g., Federal Reserve Regulation CC in the United States; other countries typically have similar regulations). – CH4

average collected balance: The sum of the daily ending collected balances (both positive and negative) divided by the number of days in the analysis period. In many account analysis statements, this item is calculated as the average ledger balance minus the average deposit float. – CH7

average collection period: The average number of days required to convert a credit sale into a cash inflow. Also referred to as *days' sales outstanding*. – CH11

average daily float: The sum of the dollar-days of float for all items received in a certain period divided by the number of days in the period. – CH12

average deposit float: The sum of the daily dollar amount of items in the process of collection (primarily checks) divided by the number of calendar or business days in the account analysis period. – CH7

average ledger balance: The sum of the daily ending ledger balances (both positive and negative) divided by the number of days in the account analysis period. Balances used in the calculation are net of any current-period adjustments. – CH7

Back Office Conversion (BOC): A US automated clearinghouse (ACH) format used to convert eligible checks received by retailers at the point of sale or presentment into electronic debits and process them as ACH transactions when the conversion is not done at the point of sale. Retailers and other entities that accept checks at the point of purchase or other manned bill payment locations can convert eligible checks to ACH debits in the back office. Explanatory signage must be present at the point of presentment, and the merchant/originator must put specific verbiage on the customer receipt indicating that the check may be converted and may clear as soon as the same day. *BOC* is the standard entry class (SEC) code for this format. – CH12

Balance and Transaction Reporting Standard (BTRS): A standard communication protocol used by financial institutions for reporting bank balance and transaction information to corporate customers. BTRS is administered by the American National Standards Institute (ANSI) via its Accredited Standards Committee (ASC) X9, and replaces the previous Bank Administration Institute reporting standard (BAI2). – CH15

balance-forward system: A cash application process (most commonly used in consumer transactions) in which payments are applied to the total outstanding balance on an accounts receivable account rather than to specific items. The remaining balance, if any, is then carried forward to the next billing cycle. The balance-forward system is most common in revolving credit situations, such as retail credit cards. – CH10

balance sheet: A financial statement that reports a company's financial condition—including assets, liabilities and stockholders' equity—at a point in time. Also called a *statement of financial position*. – CH6

Bank Administration Institute (BAI) BAI2 format: An electronic reporting format used widely for reporting information about account balances, transactions, and lockbox and controlled disbursement details. BAI2 is superceded by the Balance and Transaction Reporting Standard (BTRS). – CH15

bank capital requirements: Rules or regulations that specify the amount of capital (usually defined as equity funds) the owners of a bank must contribute to the business. This is typically in the form of a ratio of capital to at-risk assets (loans and other investments). The higher the ratio of capital to assets, the lower the risk on the part of the bank. – CH2

Bank for International Settlements (BIS): An organization that fosters international monetary and financial cooperation and serves as a bank for central banks. The BIS is also the sponsoring organization for the Basel Committee on Banking Supervision. – CH2

Bank Identification Code (BIC): An international standard for uniquely identifying financial institutions included in a financial transaction. Identifiers for the bank, country, location, and sometimes branch are included in the code. – CH3

bank obligation: A debt instrument issued by a bank to raise funds. Banks raise funds in the money markets through time deposits, repurchase agreements (repos), and banker's acceptances, collectively referred to as *bank obligations* or *bank paper*. Examples of time deposits include savings accounts, certificates of deposit (CDs), and negotiable CDs. Negotiable CDs are large-value time deposits issued by banks and other financial institutions that are bought and sold on the open market. – CH5

bank of first deposit: In processing checks, this is the bank in which a check is initially deposited as part of the clearing process. Also known as the *depository bank* or *collecting bank*. – CH4

bank overlay structure: A type of pooling structure that combines both sweeping and pooling. It is typically used when a company's primary bank has branches in several countries, but the branches do not provide a full range of domestic banking services. A local bank is used to provide collection and disbursement transactions and accounts, and to sweep surplus funds to the primary bank. The primary bank (overlay bank) then notionally pools or physically transfers cash balances in overlay accounts, providing a multi-country solution. – CH12

Bank Secrecy Act of 1970 (BSA): A US legislative act under which US banks (and, in many cases, companies and individuals) are required to perform due diligence by determining a customer's identity and monitoring transactions for suspicious activity. The primary intent of the BSA is to deter money laundering and the use of secret foreign bank accounts. – CH2

banker's acceptance (BA): A cross-border financing instrument that can be used to finance the import, export, or domestic shipment of goods, as well as the storage of properly titled goods. BAs are used frequently in conjunction with letters of credit (L/Cs) requiring a time draft drawn on a bank. A BA is created when one person signs an unconditional written order directing a bank to pay a certain sum of money on demand or at a definite time to another person, usually to finance the shipment or temporary storage of goods. The unconditional written order, also known as a *time draft*, is stamped "accepted" by the bank. – CH12

banker's acceptance (BA) rate: The rate at which BAs trade in the secondary market. BAs are sold at a nominal spread over US Treasury bills. – CH12

bankruptcy: A condition of financial failure involving the inability to pay one's debts in a timely manner. This form of financial distress affects many organizations each year. In addition to the typical financial problems that may force a firm into bankruptcy, many management teams use the bankruptcy laws in innovative ways to protect either the firm's stakeholders or its management. In the United States, the bankruptcy process is under the control of federal bankruptcy laws and generally begins when the firm has not been able to meet scheduled payments on its debt. Bankruptcy may also occur when a firm's projections of cash flows indicate that it will not be able to meet debt payments at some time in the near future. – CH2

barter: A trade payment method that involves the direct exchange of goods or services between two parties without the exchange of money. It is most frequently used when funds cannot be repatriated due to currency controls or other legal limitations. – CH12

Basel Accords: A series of recommendations, issued by the Basel Committee on Banking Supervision, regarding the creation of international standards and regulations for how much capital financial institutions must put aside to reduce risks associated with investing and lending, as well as operational risk. There are currently three sets of Basel Accords, referred to as *Basel I*, *Basel II*, and *Basel III*. – CH2

Basel Committee on Banking Supervision (BCBS): A standards-setting body that operates under the Bank for International Settlements and provides a forum for regular cooperation on banking supervisory matters. – CH2

beneficial ownership (beneficial interest): Control over funds or accounts, which may be separate from signature authority or legal title. It recognizes that the entity in whose name an account is opened with a bank is not necessarily the person who ultimately controls the funds or who is ultimately entitled to the funds. – CH7

Bermuda option: A type of option contract that is exercisable only on specified dates that are spaced evenly over the option's life, in contrast with both American and European options. – CH17

beta: A measure of the volatility, or systematic risk, of a security or a portfolio in comparison to the market as a whole. – CH19

bid-offer quote: A price quote in which a dealer or other entity provides both the price at which it is willing to purchase (bid) and sell (offer) a specific commodity or security. The difference between the two is referred to as the *bid-offer spread* or *bid-ask spread*. – CH17

bid price: The price or yield at which a dealer will purchase a security. – CH5

bilateral netting system: A type of netting system in which purchases between two subsidiaries of the same company are netted against each other so that periodically only the net difference is transferred. – CH10

blockchain: A type of distributed ledger technology consisting of data structure blocks that may contain data or programs, with each block holding batches of individual transactions and the results of any executables. Each block contains a time stamp and a link to a previous block. – CH15

blocked currencies: A type of political risk, this is the practice of a government not allowing the conversion from the local currency into a major trading currency. – CH7

board/corporate resolution: A resolution usually approved by an enterprise's board of directors that gives a specific individual (or individuals) the authority to facilitate the business of the enterprise. See also *account resolution*. – CH7

board of directors: A group of individuals that are elected as, or elected to act as, representatives of the stockholders to establish corporate management-related policies and to make decisions on major company issues. Such issues include the hiring/firing of executives, dividend policies, options policies, and executive compensation. Every public company must have a board of directors. – CH1

Board of Governors: The controlling entity for the US Federal Reserve System; the Board of Governors is responsible for the discount rate and reserve requirements. – CH2

bond: A debt investment in which an investor loans money to an entity (corporate or governmental) that borrows the funds for a defined period of time at a fixed interest rate. – CH6

bond anticipation note (BAN): A short-term, interest-bearing security issued in the anticipation of future revenues (e.g., tax anticipation notes and revenue bonds). – CH5

bond equivalent yield (BEY): A calculation for restating semiannual, quarterly, or monthly discount bond or note yields into an annual yield. This type of yield is calculated on a 365-day year basis, while the money market yield is based on a 360-day year. – CH13

bond indenture: A legal document that outlines the rights and obligations of the borrower (bond issuer) and lender (bondholder). It is a contract between the company and the bondholders, which includes various restrictive covenants that impose constraints on the actions of a company's management. – CH6

bond rating: A quality rating that is assigned to a bond issue to reflect both the probability of default and the loss given default on the issue. – CH6

book value per share: Total common stockholders' equity divided by the number of shares outstanding. – CH6

break-even analysis: A type of cost/benefit analysis that establishes the level of activity at which benefits and costs are equal. – CH9

broker-dealer: A company or other organization that serves as an intermediary in the purchase and sale of capital market securities. – CH6

brokerage firms: Institutions/firms that specialize in the sale of securities to institutional and retail customers by executing the distribution, or selling, side of an investment bank's intermediation function. – CH3

budget: An in-depth plan that details how economic resources will be procured and deployed over a specific time period. Budgets typically cover periods ranging from one month to two years. – CH14

business continuity: Actions taken with regard to crisis management, alternative operating procedures, and communications to staff and customers. The intent of disaster avoidance, recovery, and remediation measures is to preserve the firm's revenue stream. – CH16

business interruption insurance: A type of insurance coverage that provides payments to an organization in the event it is unable to pursue a normal line of business for some period of time due to an unforeseen event. Business interruption insurance generally covers the loss of profits and continuing fixed expenses (e.g., debt or lease arrangements) while the organization is temporarily out of business. – CH16

business risk: A type of risk that represents the classic risks to success in operating a business venture, such as uncertainty about the demand for products or services, the price that can be charged for those products or services, and the costs of producing and delivering the products or services. Business risk is primarily associated with the general day-to-day management of a company. – CH16

call option: A type of option contract that gives the contract owner the right, but not the obligation, to buy (call) the underlying asset from the contract writer at a fixed price through the delivery date. – CH17

call premium: See *call provision.* – CH6

call provision: A bond provision that gives the issuing entity the right to call in a bond or other issue for redemption prior to the original maturity. As compensation to investors for early redemption, a call premium is generally paid when a bond is called. The call premium usually is set on a sliding scale, with larger premiums above par required the earlier an issue is called. – CH6

capacity: As part of the five Cs of credit, this represents the borrower's current and future financial resources that are available to repay obligations when due. – CH10

capital: The more permanent sources of funds used by a company, such as long-term debt, preferred stock, and common equity. – CH1

capital adequacy: A factor that measures whether the amount of capital maintained relative to the nature and extent of an institution's risks is sufficient given management's ability to identify, measure, monitor, and control these risks. – CH2

capital asset pricing model (CAPM): A model that describes one possible relationship between risk and the required rate of return on an asset. In the case of common stock, the CAPM is based on the concept that a sensible investor holds a diversified portfolio of stocks to mitigate risk. As more stocks are added to a portfolio, the overall riskiness and variability of the portfolio is reduced. – CH19

capital budgeting: The process by which proposed large-dollar investments in long-term assets are evaluated. – CH9

capital investment: Money used by a business to purchase long-term, typically fixed assets, such as land, machinery, or buildings. Capital investment may also refer to investments in long-term securities that are typically used to finance the purchase of such assets. Also known as *long-term investment.* – CH6

capital lease: A type of lease that has terms that are different from those of operating leases. Capital leases are essentially an alternative to borrowing the funds and purchasing the asset in question. Also known as a *financial lease* or *finance lease.* – CH20

capital market: A market in which individuals and institutions trade financial securities. Organizations/institutions in the public and private sectors also often sell long-term (debt and/or equity) securities on the capital markets in order to raise funds. Thus, this type of market is composed of both the primary and secondary markets. – CH6

capital preservation: An investment goal in which investors want to maintain the purchasing power of their investments while minimizing the risk of loss. While this is a suitable short-term investment management strategy, it may not always fit into the guidelines for capital investments. – CH19

capital structure: The mix of long-term debt (in the form of term loans and various types of bonds) and equity (in the form of preferred stock, common stock, and retained earnings). – CH20

capital structure theory: A systematic approach to financing business activities through a combination of equities and liabilities. – CH20

capital tax: In some foreign countries, particularly those experiencing an upsurge in economic growth, companies are assessed a capital tax on the initial capital used to establish a new venture, and on subsequent incoming capital or repatriated capital. – CH2

captive finance company: A type of industrial bank that is a subsidiary of a large industrial corporation and whose sole purpose is to finance purchases of the corporation's products. – CH3

"card not present"/MOTO transaction: A payment card transaction accepted over the phone or via the Internet. Originally called *MOTO* transactions from *mail order or telephone order*, these transactions may be assessed higher fees due to increased risk (e.g., fraud and data errors). – CH4

card verification value/code (CVV/CVC): A number usually printed on the reverse side of a payment card and used as an anti-fraud security feature to help verify possession of the actual payment card by the individual using the card. – CH12

cash application: The process of applying a customer's payment against outstanding invoices or receivables. – CH10

cash basis accounting: A major accounting method that recognizes revenues and expenses at the time physical cash is actually received or disbursed. – CH8

cash before delivery (CBD): A term of sale that requires the buyer to make full and final payment before the shipment or receipt of goods. Also known as *prepayment terms*. – CH10

cash concentration system: A system typically used to transfer funds from outlying depository locations (often at different banks) to a central bank account at a company's primary bank, commonly referred to as a *concentration account*. These systems are used in situations where companies may have to deal with a number of separate banks in disbursed geographic locations. – CH12

cash conversion cycle (CCC): In working capital management, this formula explains and calculates how much time elapses from when funds are disbursed in direct support of a revenue-generating activity until the time when funds are recovered from revenues. It is calculated as days' receivables plus days' inventory minus days' payables. The result is the average number of days between the cash outflow for the acquisition of materials and supplies, and the cash inflow from the sale of products or services. – CH10

cash conversion efficiency: An efficiency/asset management ratio that measures how effectively a company has converted sales (or revenues) into cash. It is computed as cash flow from operations divided by revenues. – CH9

cash dividend: The most common form of dividend payment, typically paid on a quarterly basis either by check or electronically. – CH20

cash flow at risk (CaR): A type of value at risk (VaR) calculation used to assess the risk of a cash shortfall over a longer period of time. – CH16

cash flow statement: See *statement of cash flows*. – CH8

cash flow timeline: The interval that begins with the purchase of raw materials or parts from vendors and suppliers at the start of the operating cycle and ends when payment is received from customers at the completion of the operating cycle. – CH10

cash flow to total debt ratio: A ratio that measures the liquidity of a company as a function of cash flow and the level of total debt. It is calculated as net income plus depreciation (and other noncash expenses, such as amortization and depletion), divided by total long- and short-term debt. – CH10

cash inflows: Funds collected from customers, obtained from financial sources (e.g., loans or investment income), and/or received from other sources. – CH10

cash letter: In a check-clearing process, a file of check images or a bundle of checks accompanied by a list of individual items and other control documents. – CH4

cash management: The subset of treasury management that specifically deals with managing the daily liquidity (available cash) of a company or organization to ensure the company or organization can meet its short-term obligations. – CH1

cash on delivery (COD): A term of sale whereby the seller ships the goods and the buyer pays upon receipt. If the buyer refuses to pay, the goods are returned and the seller must pay the shipping and handling costs. – CH10

cash outflows: Funds disbursed to employees, vendors, and suppliers; lenders; local, state, and federal tax agencies; bondholders; and shareholders. – CH10

cash position: The quantity of cash that a company is holding at a given point in time. – CH10

cash terms: A term of sale whereby the buyer generally has 7 to 10 days to make payment. – CH10

cash turnover ratio: A ratio that indicates the number of cash cycles a firm experiences in one year, generally defined as the days in the year (365) divided by the cash conversion cycle. – CH10

cashier's check: A payment instrument in the form of a check drawn on a bank's own funds. Also known as an *official bank check*. – CH4

casualty insurance: Concerned primarily with the legal liability of losses caused by personal injury or property damage, this type of insurance provides specific coverage for a variety of losses. Examples of typical casualty insurance include plate glass, crime, robbery, boiler or machinery, and aviation insurance. Many casualty insurers also write surety bonds and other forms of insurance not classified as *property insurance*. – CH16

central bank: An entity that is responsible for implementing and managing a country's monetary policy—in other words, the country's money supply and interest rates. – CH2

central securities depository (CSD): A financial services company that holds securities, in either certificated or noncertificated (dematerialized) form, on behalf of their actual owners in order to enable book-entry transfer of securities. – CH5

century bonds: Bonds with a term of 100 years or greater. – CH6

certificate authority: A trusted third party that secures the identification information used in a digital certificate. – CH15

certificate of deposit (CD): A type of time deposit account that pays the bearer some stated rate (either fixed or variable) of interest over its maturity. It may be issued in any denomination, with maturities generally ranging from one month to five years. CDs under $100,000 are usually not negotiable, but large-denomination CDs, also referred to as *jumbos*, issued to corporations, banks, and institutional investors may be negotiable. In the United States, CDs are covered by the Federal Deposit Insurance Corporation up to the current deposit limits. – CH3

Certificate of Deposit Account Registry Service (CDARS): A private service that makes it possible to receive full Federal Deposit Insurance Corporation insurance coverage on amounts up to $50 million by distributing the funds among certificates of deposit issued by a participating network of banks. – CH5

certificate of incumbency: A document (authorized by the board of directors) confirming the authority of a corporate officer to perform certain actions on behalf of the enterprise. – CH7

certified check: A payment instrument drawn on a depositor's checking account; funds are withdrawn from the depositor's account at the time of certification, to assure payment with a certification or guarantee by the bank. It carries the signature of a bank officer certifying the check to be genuine and guaranteeing payment. Due to the higher processing costs of certified checks, most banks have replaced them with cashier's checks. – CH4

Chapter 7 bankruptcy: A US bankruptcy petition for liquidation filed by a company, which protects the debtor from legal actions by creditors. In a Chapter 7 bankruptcy, all remaining assets are liquidated, and the company ceases to exist. – CH2

Chapter 11 bankruptcy: A US bankruptcy petition filed by a company that allows it to reorganize under court protection to restructure debts and emerge from bankruptcy after meeting certain conditions imposed by the court. – CH2

Chapter 13 bankruptcy: A US bankruptcy petition filed by a consumer that allows the consumer to file for bankruptcy and reorganization. – CH2

character: As part of the five Cs of credit, this is the perceived honesty or integrity of an individual applicant or a corporate applicant's officers. Character indicates an intent or willingness to pay, as evidenced by personal or corporate payment history. – CH10

charge-back: The reversal of a prior outbound transfer of funds from a consumer's bank account, line of credit, or credit card. – CH4

Check Clearing for the 21st Century Act of 2003 (Check 21): A US law that provided the basis for electronic clearing of checks by allowing the substitution of a copy or image of a check for the original document in the clearing process. It created a new negotiable instrument called an *image replacement document*. – CH2

check conversion: The process of converting a paper check to an electronic form, typically an ACH debit. It does not include an image used for check image processing. – CH12

chief executive officer (CEO): The highest ranking executive in a company whose main responsibilities include developing and implementing high-level strategies, making major corporate decisions, managing the overall operations and resources of a company, and acting as the main point of communication between the board of directors and the corporate operations. – CH1

chief financial officer (CFO): The senior manager who is responsible for overseeing the financial activities of an entire company. This includes signing checks, monitoring cash flow, and financial planning. – CH1

chief risk officer: The executive accountable to the board of directors for the efficient and effective governance of significant risks—and related opportunities—for an organization and its various segments. Sometimes known as the *chief risk management officer*. – CH16

cleanup period: In relation to a commercial line of credit, this is a period of time, usually annually, during which the borrower must pay down all outstanding borrowings and reduce the balance of the loan to zero. – CH13

clearing: The process in which FIs use the information contained in a payment instruction, such as a check or wire transfer, to transfer money between themselves on behalf of the payor and the beneficiary, either directly or through some external network. – CH4

clearing channel: In a payment system, this is the method used to move either the payment instrument or information related to the instrument between parties involved in the transaction, as well as their banks. – CH4

clearing float: The time interval or delay between the day when a check is deposited by the payee and the day when the payor's account is debited. – CH10

Clearing House Interbank Payments System (CHIPS): A bank-owned, large-dollar funds transfer network operated by The Clearing House Payments Company. – CH4

clearinghouse: In a payment clearing process, this is a group of banks or other financial institutions that agree to exchange payment instruments (paper or electronic) drawn on the member participants. – CH4

client/server solution: A type of information management technology setup where individual workstations or computers are connected to a common server (i.e., a computer designed to handle the computing requirements of multiple users) over a local or wide area network with a shared database. This allows multiple users to access the application at the same time. The use of a common database ensures that everyone is using the same information and simplifies integration with other systems, such as G/L, A/R, and A/P systems. – CH15

closed-loop card: A card issued by a gas company, department store, or other retailer that is accepted only by the issuing company. – CH4

cloud computing: The storing and accessing of computer software and data through an Internet browser rather than running installed software on a local computer. The software and data are typically housed on a distributed network managed by a third-party vendor. The vendor is responsible for updating and maintaining the software, as well as providing for appropriate backup and disaster recovery. – CH15

collateral: Assets used as security for a loan or bond issue. They may include physical assets (e.g., plant, equipment, and inventory) or financial assets (e.g., receivables and marketable securities). – CH6

collateral trust bond: A type of bond backed by securities of other companies that are owned by the firm issuing the bond. – CH6

collateralized loan: In inventory financing, this is a type of loan that is arranged using inventory as collateral for the loan, with the lender providing financing for some predetermined percentage of the inventory's value. – CH10

collected balance: An aggregate of bank account balances that is calculated as the average ledger balance minus the deposit float. – CH4

collecting bank (presenting bank): (1) In the check clearing process, this is the bank that accepts a check for deposit and collects the funds from the payee's bank. The collecting bank is also referred to as the *bank of first deposit* or *depository bank*. (2) In a documentary collection process, this is the bank (the buyer's bank) that presents the documents to the buyer. The collecting bank is also referred to as the *presenting bank*. – CH12

collection float: The time interval or delay between the time the buyer/payor initiates payment and the time the seller/payee receives good funds; it consists of mail float, processing float, and availability float. – CH10

collection letter: A document in a documentary collection process that specifies the exact procedures to be followed before shipping documents are released to the importer. – CH12

comfort letter: A letter from another party stating actions that it will or will not take on behalf of the borrower. This type of agreement is not legally enforceable. – CH6

commercial bank: A financial institution that accepts deposits from both businesses and consumers, and then lends some portion of those deposits to other businesses and consumers. – CH2

Commercial Book-Entry System (CBES): A multi-tiered, automated system for purchasing, holding, and transferring marketable securities. CBES exists as a delivery system that provides for the simultaneous transfer of securities against the settlement of funds. Securities owners (or their brokers on their behalf) receive interest and redemption payments wired directly to their linked accounts. CBES is operated by the US Treasury and is also known as the *Treasury/Reserve Automated Debt Entry System*, or *TRADES*. – CH5

commercial letter of credit (L/C): A commercial (or documentary) L/C is issued by a bank as the intended mechanism of payment in relation to a trade transaction involving the domestic or international shipment of merchandise. L/Cs are most commonly used in import/export transactions and are sometimes referred to as *trade L/Cs*. – CH12

commercial paper (CP): Tradable promissory notes issued by companies, as opposed to banks. Companies raise funds in the short-term money market through the issuance of CP. Maturity can range from overnight to 270 days for publicly traded CP and up to 397 days for private-placement CP, but most paper issued matures in less than 45 days. CP does not usually pay interest during its term. Instead, it is issued at a discounted price and the face value is paid at maturity. – CH5

commitment fee: A fee assessed based on the total amount or unused portion of a committed line of credit. A committed line usually involves a formal loan agreement that specifies the terms and conditions of the credit facility. – CH13

Committee on Payment and Settlement Systems (CPSS): A standards-setting body for payment and securities settlement systems. The CPSS is hosted by the Bank for International Settlements. – CH2

Committee on the Global Financial System (CGFS): A central bank forum for the monitoring and examination of broad issues relating to financial markets and systems. It helps to elaborate appropriate policy recommendations to support the central banks in the fulfillment of their responsibilities for monetary and financial stability. In carrying out this task, the committee places particular emphasis on assisting central bank governors in recognizing, analyzing, and responding to threats to the stability of financial markets and the global financial system. – CH2

Commodity Futures Trading Commission (CFTC): An independent US government agency with the mandate to regulate commodity futures and option markets in the United States. – CH2

commodity price risk: A type of risk related to the impact of changing commodity prices on the value of an organization. It differs considerably from interest rate and foreign exchange risk since most commodities are traded in markets where the concentration of supply in the hands of a few suppliers can magnify price volatility. – CH16

common equity: The capital contributed by stockholders and earnings retained in the business. Also refers to an account on corporate financial statements that reflects this amount. – CH2

common-size financial statement: A financial statement analysis technique that involves stating line items as percentages rather than amounts. A common-size income statement expresses every line item on the statement as a percentage of revenue, and a common-size balance sheet expresses each account as a percentage of total assets. Common-size statements enable direct comparisons of financial data for firms of different sizes. – CH9

common stock: A security that represents ownership in a company. The management of a company acts as an agent for shareholders to protect their interests. Equity in the form of common stock usually represents a significant portion of a publicly traded company's capital base. – CH6

company processing center: A business function where check and payment card processing, along with deposit preparation, are performed in-house. – CH12

compensating balance: A balance maintained in a company's deposit accounts at a bank for the purpose of increasing the bank's overall revenue on the account. Compensating balances generally do not earn interest or offset depository service charges. – CH13

comprehensive income: The sum of net income and other items that must bypass the income statement because they have not been realized, including items like an unrealized holding gain or loss from available-for-sale securities and foreign currency translation gains or losses. – CH8

concentration account: An account used by an organization to receive funds from collection accounts or to provide funding for disbursement accounts. These accounts are sometimes referred to as *master accounts*, especially when used in conjunction with a zero balance account. – CH12

concentration flows (funding flows): A practice involving internal transfers among operating units of a company and between a firm's various bank accounts, with the objectives of pooling funds for other purposes or to fund various disbursement accounts. – CH10

conditions: As part of the five Cs of credit, this factor assesses the general, existing macroeconomic environment that impacts a borrower's ability to pay or the willingness of a lender to grant credit. – CH10

confirming bank: In a letter of credit (L/C) transaction, this is the bank that commits to the seller that payment will be made if documents meet the terms and conditions of the L/C, regardless of the issuing bank's ability to pay. – CH12

conservative financing strategy: A current asset financing strategy that involves using long-term financing (e.g., debt and equity) to finance fixed assets, permanent current assets, and some portion of fluctuating current assets. Short-term financing is used for the remainder of the fluctuating current assets. – CH10

consignment: A term of sale whereby the supplier (sometimes referred to as the *consignor*) ships goods to another party (sometimes referred to as the *consignee*) who has no obligation to pay until the goods have been sold. – CH10

consolidated remittance processing (CRP): A service that provides a single collection point for all types of remittance payments (both electronic and paper) and consolidates all remittance information into one stream of data in a common format. – CH12

Consumer Financial Protection Bureau (CFPB): An independent consumer protection entity within the Federal Reserve that was created as part of the Dodd-Frank Act. The primary reason behind the CFPB's creation was to consolidate and strengthen consumer protection responsibilities and oversee the enforcement of federal laws intended to ensure the fair, equitable, and nondiscriminatory access to credit for individuals and communities. – CH2

continuous linked settlement (CLS): A process that allows a simultaneous exchange of the payments for both sides of underlying financial transactions (e.g., foreign exchange contracts, non-deliverable forward contracts, and over-the-counter derivative contracts), thereby eliminating settlement risk. – CH4

contractual transfer: A form of risk transfer in which the burden of the risks in question is contractually transferred to another party. – CH16

controlled disbursement: A bank service (unique to the United States) that provides same-day notification to a company of the amount of checks that will clear against its disbursement account on a given day. The disbursement account is typically not funded each day until after the daily notification is received. – CH12

convertible bond: A type of corporate debt security that can be converted by the holder, or sometimes the issuer, into shares of common or preferred stock at a fixed ratio of shares per bond. – CH6

Corporate Credit or Debit (CCD) or CCD Plus Addendum (CCD+): A US automated clearinghouse (ACH) format used for the concentration and disbursement of funds within or between companies (business-to-business). Only a limited amount of remittance information can be sent with the CCD format. The CCD+ is essentially a CCD with an addendum record that can hold up to 80 characters of remittance data. *CCD* and *CCD+* are the standard entry class (SEC) codes for these formats, respectively. – CH12

Corporate Trade Exchange (CTX): A US automated clearinghouse (ACH) format designed for business-to-business trade payments. It consists of a standard ACH payment transaction and a variable-length message addendum designed to convey remittance information in the Accredited Standards Committee (ASC) X12 data standard. The addendum can accommodate 9,999 records of 80 characters each. *CTX* is the standard entry class (SEC) code for this format. – CH12

correlation: As part of regression analysis (a statistical cash forecasting methodology), correlation calculations involve a statistical identification of the degree of association between a cash flow and another variable. Once this relationship is established, the cash flow can be forecasted based on the actual or expected behavior of the other variable. – CH14

correspondent bank: In a payment clearing process, this is one of two banks that have accounts with each other for the purpose of clearing and settlement of payment items between the banks. The collecting bank maintains a depository account with another bank, called a *correspondent bank*. The collecting bank sends cash letters to the correspondent bank, which presents the items to the paying bank through a local clearinghouse or the Fed. The collecting bank's depository account at the correspondent bank is then credited with the proceeds of the checks. – CH4

cost/benefit analysis: A business decision process that assesses whether the relevant economic benefits of a given course of action exceed the relevant economic costs. – CH12

cost of capital: A measure of the cost a company would incur to raise funds to make investments in assets. The overall cost of capital for a company is a function of the mix of capital components used and the individual costs of each component. – CH6

cost of goods sold (COGS): The expense associated with providing the goods or services whose sale is recognized as revenues. COGS includes labor and material directly used in manufacturing the product sold, as well as any indirect or allocated manufacturing expenses. – CH8

counterparty risk: The risk that the other party in a contract or financial transaction will not perform as promised. One component of counterparty risk is related to credit and default risk. In a generic context, however, the concept of counterparty risk extends to the risk related to any type of performance failure on the part of any of the counterparties with which an organization must interact. – CH7

countertrade: A trade payment method used by companies that do not have access to sufficient hard currencies (i.e., internationally traded currencies) to pay for imports from other countries. As an example, an exporter ships merchandise to the countertrading country. In exchange, it takes merchandise that may be sold elsewhere in the world. – CH12

covariance: A measure of the degree to which returns on two assets/stocks move in tandem. A *positive covariance* means that asset returns move together, while a *negative covariance* means that returns move inversely. Negative covariance is a desired property for stocks in a portfolio as this can significantly reduce the portfolio's risk. – CH19

covenant: An additional requirement that is placed on debt or bond issues and that imposes constraints on the actions of the company's management. Covenants may be negative (i.e., actions the company cannot take, such as the double pledging of collateral) or affirmative (i.e., actions the company must take, such as providing regular financial statements or maintaining certain financial ratios). – CH6

coverage ratios: Financial ratios concerned primarily with measuring a company's ability to make payments on (i.e., service) its debt. – CH9

cram-down procedure: A type of procedure for formulating a reorganization plan in a US Chapter 11 bankruptcy filing. This procedure is generally executed by secured creditors and comes into play when a reorganization plan fails to meet the standard for approval by all classes of creditors under the unanimous consent procedure, or when the firm is insolvent and the old equity must be eliminated. In a cram-down case, if at least one class of creditors has voted in favor of a plan, then the court may confirm the plan (or a modified version of it) as long as each dissenting class is treated fairly and equitably. – CH2

credit card: A payment card issued by a company that provides the holder of the card the ability to borrow funds, typically at the point of sale, to pay for a transaction. – CH4

Credit Card Accountability Responsibility and Disclosure Act of 2009 (Credit CARD Act): A US law designed to protect consumers from arbitrary pricing and notification practices by credit card companies. – CH2

credit enhancement: An addition to a borrowing arrangement or debt securities issue meant to improve the overall credit rating on the loan or issue. It generally provides either a guarantee of payment in the event of default or an agreement to provide financing to roll over the debt issue. – CH6

credit manager: A credit management function/position that administers policies that establish credit standards, defines the terms of trade credit extension, approves customers for credit sales, and sets individual and aggregate credit limits within policy guidelines. – CH10

credit scheme: The term used in the Single Euro Payments Area (SEPA) initiative to describe a pre-authorized credit program in which one person or company authorizes another to automatically credit its bank account for payments that are due. – CH4

credit transfer: In an electronic payment system, this is the process of a payor pushing funds from its account to the account of the payee. – CH2

credit unions: Member-owned not-for-profit financial corporations in the United States, chartered by either federal or state agencies that originally were intended to restrict membership to individuals with a common affiliation (e.g., an employer, association, community organization, or geographic location) but may now include businesses as members. – CH3

cumulative voting: A form of voting that allows a shareholder as many votes per share owned as there are open positions on the board in the same election. – CH20

cure period: A period of time, often specified in a loan agreement, in which an event of default may be corrected before the lender may pursue default remedies. – CH6

currency derivative: A derivative instrument that allows trading partners to establish predetermined exchange rates for set periods, which effectively hedges against foreign exchange risk. Currency derivatives include options, futures, swaps, and forwards contracts. – CH17

current account: A bank depository account that is both a store of value (deposits) and, perhaps more importantly for treasury management purposes, a vehicle through which an account holder uses a bank to transfer funds to, and receive deposits from, a third party. Referred to as a *checking* or *demand deposit account (DDA)* in the United States. – CH3

current asset turnover ratio: An efficiency/asset management ratio that measures how many times the firm has turned over the stock of its most liquid assets with the flow of revenue. It is computed as revenues divided by current assets. – CH9

current assets: A term that generally refers to assets that are expected to be converted into cash within one year. – CH10

current liabilities: A term that generally refers to liabilities that are required to be paid for within one year. – CH10

current ratio: A ratio defined as total current assets divided by total current liabilities. It is therefore the ratio of cash and assets expected to become cash in one year or less, to short-term liabilities that must be paid in one year or less. – CH10

custodian: A third party that typically takes possession of securities, receives delivery or book entry of principal and interest payments, performs record keeping, and provides maintenance services for an investment portfolio. – CH18

customer identification program (CIP): The processes used by a financial institution to verify and validate the stated identity of a customer. CIP is normally part of the anti-money laundering processes of a financial institution. – CH7

Customer-Initiated Entry (CIE): A US automated clearinghouse (ACH) format used for pre-authorized payments that are initiated by consumers using telephone bill-paying services. *CIE* is the standard entry class (SEC) code for this format. – CH12

Customer Transfer Plus (CTP): A Fedwire format implemented in late 2010 that provides the ability to send large amounts of remittance data in either a structured or unstructured format along with the payment. – CH4

cutoff time: A time by which a specific process, such as depositing payments, must be completed for processing in the current cycle. For example, checks deposited after the current day's cutoff time will typically be processed the next day. – CH4

cyberrisk: A type of risk associated with security breaches involving employee, customer, and corporate data. These security breaches may come from both internal and external sources. Data may be corrupted, or stolen and sold to third parties. Security breaches also include denial-of-service attacks where data communication is blocked. – CH16

dashboard: An easy-to-read, typically graphical, report or online display that shows the current status of key performance indicators. – CH15

daylight overdraft: A type of overdraft position that occurs when a financial institution permits a corporation to make payments that exceed the available balance on the corporation's account. These overdraft positions are usually eliminated by funds that arrive later in the day. – CH4

days' inventory (DI): In the cash conversion cycle, this is the average number of days that elapse from the purchase of raw materials until the sale of finished goods. Also referred to as *days' sales in inventory* or *inventory conversion period*. – CH10

days' payables (DP): In the cash conversion cycle, this is the average number of days between the purchase/receipt of materials or supplies and issuance of payment for them. Also referred to as *payables conversion period*. – CH10

days' receivables (DR): In the cash conversion cycle, this is the average number of days required to collect on credit. Also referred to as *receivables conversion period*. – CH10

days' sales outstanding (DSO): The average number of days required to convert a credit sale into a cash inflow. Also referred to as *average collection period*. – CH10

debentures: Unsecured bonds that represent general claims against the issuer organization's assets and/or cash flows and may carry a higher interest cost (to the issuer) than secured bonds. – CH6

debit card: A card that allows access to funds directly from a cardholder's checking or savings deposit account and can be either signature-based or personal identification number (PIN)-based. Often referred to as *EFTPOS* in many parts of the world. *EFTPOS* refers to electronic funds transfer (EFT) at the point of sale (POS). – CH4

debit scheme: The term used in the Single Euro Payments Area (SEPA) initiative to describe a pre-authorized debit program in which one person or company authorizes another to automatically debit its bank account for payments that are due. – CH4

debit transfer: In an electronic payments system, this is the process of a payor authorizing payees to initiate value transfers from the payor's account to the account of the payee. – CH2

debt indenture: The contract between the issuing entity of a bond and the bondholders. – CH6

debt management ratio: A type of ratio that measures the firm's degree of indebtedness and its ability to service its debt. – CH9

debt market: A financial market in which participants can issue new debt, or buy and sell debt securities. – CH6

debt to tangible net worth ratio: A type of debt management ratio that reflects the impact of intangible assets (e.g., goodwill, patents, trademarks, and copyrights) on the balance sheet. It is computed as total debt divided by total equity minus intangible assets. – CH9

deemed dividend: A situation that occurs when payments on loans, sales of stock, or other transactions are interpreted by tax authorities as an attempt by a company to avoid paying taxes on dividends. The payments may be considered (i.e., "deemed") dividends and appropriate taxes charged. Deemed dividends are a potential issue for any global company and can vary significantly from country to country. – CH20

default/credit risk: A form of risk that is related to how a change in the credit quality of a company, including its ability to make payments in a timely manner, would affect the value of a security or portfolio of investments. Default/credit risk arises both from transactions and from any risk in the portfolio due to concentration of similar assets. Higher yields are typically associated with higher risk, as investors will require a higher return to compensate for a higher chance of loss. – CH5

default premium: An adjustment to the base interest rate to account for possible default on an investment. – CH13

defeasance of debt: A financial management method that removes debt from an organization's balance sheet without actually retiring the debt issue. In this arrangement, the borrower places sufficient funds in escrow, usually in government securities, to pay for interest and principal on the debt issue. Because control of both the debt and escrow funds is relinquished, and payment and retirement of the debt issue is now guaranteed, this debt and the related securities can be removed from the balance sheet and do not need to be considered in relation to any restrictive covenants the organization may have regarding debt. – CH6

degree of certainty: In the cash flow forecasting process, this is the practice of designating cash flows as certain flows, predictable flows, or less predictable flows. – CH14

demand deposit account (DDA): An account through which an account holder uses a bank to transfer funds to, and receive deposits from, a third party. Also known as a *checking account* or a *current account*. – CH3

departmental (unnamed) card: A variation on the purchasing card in which each department is given its own purchasing card for general use by that department. – CH4

deposit deadline: The time within the banking day when an item must be ready for transit at the depository bank's processing center to qualify for the availability stated in the availability schedule. – CH4

deposit insurance (deposit guarantee): A regulatory safeguard that protects the assets of smaller deposit customers (typically consumers, although corporate accounts are also typically covered up to a certain amount) who would be most harmed by a bank failure. – CH2

depositary receipt (DR): A type of negotiable financial instrument (typically equity securities) that trades on a local exchange but actually represents stock ownership in a foreign, publicly listed company. There are American and global DRs (ADRs and GDRs, respectively). – CH6

depository bank: The bank or financial institution in which a check is deposited for processing and clearing. Also known as the *bank of first deposit, collecting bank,* or *payee's bank.* – CH4

Depository Institutions Deregulation and Monetary Control Act of 1980 (DIDMCA): A US legislative act that provided for a phase-out of interest rate ceilings for financial institutions, mandated that all depository institutions hold reserves at the Federal Reserve (Fed), and mandated that the Fed price or eliminate its float in the check-clearing system. The act is also referred to as the *Monetary Control Act.* – CH2

Depository Trust & Clearing Corporation (DTCC): An investment-industry-owned corporation that works through its subsidiaries to provide clearing, settlement, and information services for equities, corporate and municipal bonds, government and mortgage-backed securities, money market instruments, and over-the-counter derivatives. It was formed in 1999 by the combination of the Depository Trust Company (DTC) and the National Securities Clearing Corporation (NSCC). – CH5

derivative: A financial product that acquires its value by inference through a formulaic connection to another asset. The other asset is termed the *underlying asset*, and can be a financial instrument (e.g., a stock or bond), currency, or commodity. – CH8

Destroyed Check Entry Format (XCK): A US automated clearinghouse (ACH) format used to clear and settle items that originated as checks, but the original paper item was lost or destroyed due to a catastrophic event (e.g., fire, flood, or hurricane). *XCK* is the standard entry class (SEC) code for this format. – CH12

difference in conditions (DIC): A type of insurance that covers property for perils not covered by basic property insurance policies. It is often purchased to fill voids in policies purchased overseas and to insure property in transit. Typically used in conjunction with multiple basic policies to make them uniform, DIC insurance does not provide additional limits of coverage for basic property perils (as an umbrella policy does for liability insurance). – CH16

digital certificate: An electronic commerce security product that ties the identity of the user (private key) to the user's public key and may also authenticate the devices used to create documents or transactions. – CH15

digital signature: A message encoded with the sender's secret, private key that the receiver can use to identify the source. A digital signature is essentially an electronic signature used in place of a written signature and is tied to a document and to the signer, meaning the signer's digital signature will be different for each document signed. – CH15

digitized signature: A scanned version of a written signature. A digitized signature should not be confused with a digital signature, which is an electronic signature used in place of a written signature. – CH15

direct deposit: A transfer made from a company's account to the account of an employee, shareholder, vendor, or trading partner using an automated clearinghouse credit transaction. – CH12

direct exchange: A process in which collecting banks arrange to send cash letters directly to a paying bank or to a nonlocal Federal Reserve Bank (in the United States) rather than using typical clearing channels. This process enables banks to meet various deposit deadlines and achieve faster clearing times. Also referred to as *direct send* or *direct presentment*. – CH4

directors and officers (D&O) insurance: A type of insurance that covers situations in which a director or officer of an organization commits a negligent act or omission, or makes a misstatement or misleading statement, and a legal action is brought against the organization as a result. The policy provides coverage (usually with a large deductible) for directors' and officers' liability exposure if these individuals are sued. Coverage also is provided for defense costs, such as legal fees and other court costs, and may include coverage for an organization's subsidiaries. – CH16

disaster recovery: The restoration of systems and communications after an event causes an outage. – CH1

disbursement float: The time interval or delay between the day when a payment is initiated and the day when funds are debited from the payor's account. – CH10

disbursements schedule: A schedule that involves forecasting the cash disbursements for purchases and other cash outflows, such as payroll, taxes, interest, dividends, rent, and debt repayments. It is a component of the receipts and disbursements forecast process. – CH14

discount (discount rate): Used in the valuation of discount investments such as US Treasury bills, commercial paper, and banker's acceptances, this is the rate used to determine the present value or purchase price of the instrument. In calculations, the discount rate is defined as the dollar discount divided by par, or maturity, value and then annualized using a 360-day year. – CH11

discount brokerage: A brokerage firm that lets investors make trades at reduced prices, but provides little or no investment advice. – CH3

discount terms: A term of sale whereby the seller offers a discount on payments made prior to the net due date. Terms of 2/10 net 30 mean that the total amount is due within 30 days of the invoice date, but the buyer can take a 2% discount if it pays within 10 days. – CH10

distributed ledger technology: A distributed database that maintains a continuously growing list of records secured from tampering and revision. Data is geographically spread across multiple sites, countries, and/or institutions. – CH15

distribution: An investment bank function that involves a securities sale to investors by an investment bank or syndicate of investment banks. – CH3

distribution forecast: A short-term forecasting methodology that estimates the daily impact that a single event has on cash flows over a specified period, based on historical patterns. – CH14

diversification: A method of managing risk by including a wide variety of investments with differing characteristics in a portfolio so that the risk of loss due to the failure of any one individual security is minimized. – CH19

dividend capture: A tax-motivated, short-term investment strategy that is available to corporations that pay taxes in the United States. A corporation may exclude from its taxable income 70–80% of the dividends received from stock owned in another corporation, as long as it owns the stock for at least 46 days of the 91-day period starting 45 days prior to the ex-dividend date. Even though dividend capture requires an equity investment, the strategy is considered a short-term investment because the stock is held only long enough to capture the dividend and qualify for the dividend exclusion. – CH13

dividend declaration date: The date when the board of directors announces (declares) a dividend. – CH20

dividend payment date: The date when a dividend is paid. – CH20

dividend policy: A company's policy regarding whether to pay dividends and, if so, how much and when to pay. Dividend policies are typically set by the CEO or board of directors, often with input from the treasurer. – CH20

dividend record date: The date when shareholders of record are entitled to receive a declared dividend. Also known as a *shareholder-of-record date*, or just *holder-of-record date*. – CH20

dividend reinvestment plan (DRIP): A plan that enables existing shareholders to purchase additional shares directly from the company on a when-desired basis, normally with no commission or with only a small processing charge. These plans also allow investors to elect to reinvest dividends automatically in additional shares of company stock. – CH20

dividend signaling: A theory that dividends have information content or a signaling effect. Dividends are observed to contain information that signals management's intentions to investors and may provide information regarding expected future earnings. – CH20

documentary collection: A trade payment mechanism that processes the collection of a draft and accompanying shipping documents through international correspondent banks. Instructions regarding the transaction specifics are contained in a collection letter that accompanies the documentation. It is the responsibility of the exporter (i.e., the seller) to determine the instructions specified in the collection letter. – CH3

documents against acceptance: A type of collection letter (in a documentary collection process) that uses a time draft, which is a draft payable on a specified future date, that must be accepted by the importer before the collecting bank may release documents. Upon maturity of the time draft, it is presented to the importer for payment. – CH12

documents against payment: A type of collection letter (in a documentary collection process) that uses a sight draft, which is a draft payable on demand, that requires the collecting bank to receive full and final payment of the amount owed prior to releasing the documents. – CH12

Dodd-Frank Wall Street Reform and Consumer Protection Act of 2010: Legislation enacted in the United States in response to concerns related to the financial services industry in the wake of the global financial crisis of 2007–2009. The act had a major impact on the regulation of banks and other FIs, and brought financial consumer protection under a single authority. – CH2

dollar-days: A unit of measurement that reflects both a transaction's dollar amount and the number of days of float delay. The dollar-days of float on an individual check are calculated by multiplying the dollar amount of the check by the number of days from the time the payor mails the check to the time when the payee is granted credit, or availability, of collected funds. – CH12

dollar discount: The difference between the purchase price and the par, or maturity, value on discounted investment instruments, such as US Treasury bills, commercial paper, and banker's acceptances. This difference represents interest earned on the investment. – CH13

draft/bill of lading: A term of sale whereby sellers collect payments through banking channels in what is known as a *documentary collection*. – CH10

drawdown wire: A type of wire transfer that is a request sent by a company's bank to a second bank requesting that the second bank initiate a wire transfer from either the company's account or another party's account at the second bank, sending the funds back to the first bank. The party being debited must pre-authorize the transfer. – CH12

dual- or multi-class stock: Stock issued in more than one class (e.g., Class A and Class B). – CH20

DuPont equation: An integrated ratio analysis technique that looks at the return on assets (ROA) ratio as a product of the return on sales (i.e., net profit margin) and total asset turnover. – CH9

duration: A measure of the number of years required to recover the true cost of a bond, considering the present value of all coupon and principal payments received in the future. Duration, in its simplest form, is the weighted average time to receipt of all future cash flows associated with a bond investment, but it can also provide a measure of the sensitivity of the investment to changes in underlying interest rates. This is one of the primary measures of risk for a bond or fixed-income portfolio. – CH19

Durbin Amendment: An amendment to the Dodd-Frank Act in the United States that restricts interchange fees, or fees that financial institutions may charge for processing debit card payments. – CH2

earnings before interest and taxes (EBIT): A measure of operating income or profit that is calculated as gross profit less operating expenses, depreciation, and amortization. EBIT has traditionally been the measure used to evaluate a firm's ability to generate operating profits and to meet its financial and tax obligations. – CH8

earnings before interest, taxes, depreciation, and amortization (EBITDA): A measure of operating profitability that is calculated as gross profit less operating expenses (but not subtracting depreciation and amortization). EBITDA first came into common use with leveraged buyouts in the 1980s, when it was used to indicate the ability of a company to service debt. As time passed, it became popular in industries with expensive assets that had to be written down over long periods. Many companies, especially in the technology sector, now commonly quote EBITDA. – CH8

earnings credit allowance: The total dollar value of earnings credit (imputed interest) that can be used by a company to offset the bank service charges incurred during the account analysis period. – CH7

earnings credit rate: A short-term rate (most commonly the 90-day US Treasury bill rate) that is multiplied by the investable balance to determine the earnings credit allowance for the period, as part of the account analysis process. – CH7

EBIT: See *earnings before interest and taxes.* – CH8

EBITDA: See *earnings before interest, taxes, depreciation, and amortization.* – CH8

EBITDA margin: A measure of operating profitability calculated by dividing EBITDA (earnings before interest, taxes, depreciation, and amortization) by total revenues. – CH9

e-commerce (electronic commerce): The application of information and secure network technology for the purpose of facilitating business relationships, including buying and selling, among trading partners. E-commerce encompasses many types of channels and communications protocols, including traditional electronic data interchange (EDI) and Internet-based commerce. – CH15

economic development bond: A type of bond typically issued by a developing country or sponsoring organization, such as the World Bank or the International Monetary Fund, for the express purpose of fostering development of infrastructure and related projects. – CH6

economic order quantity (EOQ) model: A model used to calculate optimal inventory levels, given specified ordering and holding costs. – CH10

economic risk exposure (economic exposure): A form of risk that represents the long-term effect of changes in exchange rates on the present value of future cash flows. Multinational corporations that conduct business in several different currencies are, in the long run, always subject to fluctuations in cash flows because of exchange-rate changes. Even companies that only operate domestically are exposed to economic risk whenever there is foreign competition within the local market. – CH17

economic value added (EVA): A performance measurement ratio that isolates the funds available to all suppliers of capital and then relates that total to the amount of capital supplied. It can be computed as earnings before interest and taxes (EBIT), times one minus the company's tax rate, and then subtracting the product of the weighted average cost of capital and long-term debt and equity. – CH9

economies of scale: A relationship that occurs when an increase in sales lowers the average cost per unit sold. – CH1

efficiency/asset management ratios: A type of ratio that measures how effectively assets are utilized. – CH9

electronic bank account management (eBAM): A type of bank account management process that attempts to replace the large amount of paper in the process with electronic messages and files exchanged between banks and their customers. *Bank account management* refers to the management of all of the various facets of an organization's relationship with its bank(s), including opening and closing accounts, managing authorized signatories, and maintaining proper copies of documentation. – CH15

electronic bill presentment and payment (EBPP): A system for integrating the billing and payment processes, thereby enabling companies to send electronic statements and receive electronic remittances from customers. It is the retail consumer version of electronic invoice presentment and payment. – CH12

electronic commerce: See *e-commerce*. – CH15

Electronic Data Gathering, Analysis, and Retrieval (EDGAR) database: A database that contains a searchable listing of US Securities and Exchange Commission filings for public companies. – CH8

electronic data interchange (EDI): A traditional building block of e-commerce that is based on an infrastructure using standardized communication formats to exchange business data between two trading partners. – CH15

Electronic Federal Tax Payment System (EFTPS): A system that serves as the primary method for collecting and accounting for US federal taxes withheld by employers from individuals' salaries and wages, as well as corporate business, sales, and excise taxes. – CH12

electronic invoice presentment and payment (EIPP): A system for integrating the billing and payment processes, thereby enabling companies to send electronic statements and receive electronic remittances from customers. – CH12

electronic lockbox: A variation of the lockbox approach that provides a single collection point for all automated clearinghouse (ACH) and wire payments for organizations with a large number of electronic funds transfer (EFT) collections. It can also process remittance advices from a variety of incoming formats into a single format for transmission to the organization's accounts receivable department for posting and reconciliation. – CH12

Electronic Signatures in Global and National Commerce Act of 2000 (E-Sign Act): US legislation that was enacted to support electronic commerce (e-commerce) initiatives and grant digital signatures the same legal status as handwritten ink signatures. It establishes the legal certainty of e-commerce transactions and provides a measure of confidence around the enforceability of electronic transactions. – CH2

employee risk: A type of risk that is related to employees and represents a significant source of internal operational risk. The general risk of intentional employee fraud is typically referred to as *defalcation risk*, while the specific case of theft of money, securities, or property by an employee is known as *fidelity risk*. A more significant source of internal risk stems from unintentional actions by employees. Examples include employee errors in data entry or reentry, as well as transposition or deletion of numbers. – CH16

EMV: An acronym for *Europay, MasterCard, and Visa* that refers to a global standard for the use of smart cards (or chip cards) as either debit or credit cards. – CH4

encryption: The process of transforming information using some type of computer-based model to make it unreadable to anyone except those possessing special knowledge, similar to a password, usually referred to as a *key*. – CH15

enterprise resource planning (ERP) system: A sophisticated information management, production, and accounting software package that links different functional areas or operational divisions of a company on an enterprise-wide basis. – CH15

enterprise risk management (ERM): A comprehensive, organization-wide approach to identifying, measuring, and managing the various risks that threaten the achievement of an organization's strategic objectives and therefore its overall operations. It is characterized as having a viewpoint that encompasses all areas of the organization. – CH16

equipment trust certificate: A type of bond that is secured by movable equipment (e.g., a fleet of trucks or railroad equipment). Each certificate is backed by a specific asset or group of assets (i.e., there is no blanket lien securing the issue). – CH6

equity capital: The invested capital of an organization (as contrasted with borrowed or debt capital). From an accounting point of view, equity capital consists of all preferred and common equity accounts, including retained earnings, and is typically represented by securities such as shares of common and preferred stock. – CH9

equity market: A market where shares are issued and traded. Consisting of both primary and secondary markets, it is also known as the *stock market*. – CH6

equity price risk: A type of risk usually associated with volatility in stock prices. The general form of this risk refers to the sensitivity of an instrument or portfolio value to a change in broad stock market indices, while the firm-specific portion of this risk relates just to the company in question. – CH16

equity securities: Stock (shares) that represent the ownership of publicly owned corporations. – CH6

escheatment: The process of turning over unclaimed assets to the government, in specific instances. In the business world, escheat statutes primarily impact banks or companies that hold unclaimed assets of customers or employees. The most general occurrence of escheat is when an entity (e.g., a bank) holds money or property (e.g., an account in that bank) and the property goes unclaimed for some specified period of time (generally referred to as a *dormant account*). In many jurisdictions, if the owner cannot be located, such property must be escheated to the government. – CH2

Eurobond: A type of bond sold simultaneously in many countries outside the country of the borrower and denominated in a currency other than that of the country in which it is issued. Usually, a Eurobond is issued by an international syndicate and categorized according to the currency in which it is denominated. Sometimes called an *external bond*. – CH6

eurodeposit: Originally defined as the deposit of non-euro currency in a European bank, this term has come to mean the deposit of any type of currency in a financial institution outside of the currency's home market (e.g., the deposit of US dollars or Japanese yen in a London bank account). – CH17

Eurodollar: A deposit denominated in US dollars held in a financial institution outside of the United States, typically in Europe. It may be issued as a negotiable Eurodollar certificate of deposit or as a nonnegotiable Eurodollar time deposit, both of which are interest-bearing. – CH5

European Central Bank (ECB): The central bank for the Economic and Monetary Union (EMU). The ECB conducts a unified monetary policy for the euro zone, which includes all EMU members that have adopted the euro as their common currency. – CH2

European option: A type of option contract that may only be executed (settled) on the actual option date specified in the contract. European options can be contrasted with American options, which may be settled any time before or on the specified option date. Contrast also with *Bermuda option*. – CH17

European Payments Council (EPC): The coordination and decision-making body of the European banking industry in relation to payments. The purpose of the EPC is to support and promote the Single Euro Payments Area (SEPA). The EPC develops payment schemes and frameworks that help to realize the integrated euro payments market. In particular, the EPC defines common positions for the cooperative space of payment services. – CH2

European Union (EU): A union of more than two dozen member countries in Europe that have organized to work toward common political, social and economic interests. – CH2

event of default: An action or circumstance by which a borrower breaches or violates any term or condition under a debt agreement. – CH6

excess (umbrella) insurance: A type of insurance coverage that supplements basic or primary liability coverage. Policies generally pay after the primary policy's limits have been exhausted. For example, if the primary insurance policy has a $250,000 limit and claims exceed this amount, then an umbrella or excess policy would pay the excess claims up to the limit of the policy. Excess or umbrella policies can also be used to fill gaps in coverage provided by basic liability policies (i.e., the difference in coverage between two policies). – CH16

excess balance: A situation that occurs in an account when its average collected balance is greater than either the amount that the financial institution requires as a compensating balance or the target level that a company has chosen to maintain. – CH7

ex-dividend date: The first date on which a stock is sold without entitlement to the upcoming dividend. The ex-dividend date is usually two business days prior to the shareholder-of-record date, thereby enabling brokerage firms to send an updated list of shareholders to a company on time. – CH20

exotic currency: A foreign exchange term used for a currency that is not widely traded (sometimes referred to as a *thinly traded currency*). These currencies can be difficult and expensive to trade due to a lack of liquidity or available counterparties. – CH17

exponential smoothing: A statistical cash forecasting technique that produces a forecasted value based on the most recent actual value, the most recent forecasted value, and a number between zero and one that is used to weight these two values. The weight, designated by the Greek letter alpha (α), is referred to as the *smoothing constant* and is calculated using a computer program such as a statistics package. – CH14

export credit agencies (ECAs): The general term for entities that are established by governments to support export activities through export loans, credit guarantees, or a combination of both. – CH10

export financing: Government support of export activities through export loans, credit guarantees, or a combination of both. – CH10

Export-Import (EXIM) Bank of the United States: The official export credit agency of the United States. – CH10

expropriation: A government takeover of a single company, with or without compensation. – CH7

eXtensible markup language (XML): A computer-based language that is an extension of hypertext markup language (HTML) that allows the content and structure to be defined. – CH15

external controls: Measures that affect a company's operations, but which are enacted by the government or other organizations rather than by the company itself. These may include any rule or regulation that has an effect on the actions of the company, any tax law enacted by the government which affects the flow of money, a lease that restricts what a company can or can not do with its office space, or other such measures. – CH18

external theft/fraud risk: The risk of theft or fraud involving individuals external to the targeted company. Traditionally, the primary source of external theft or fraud has been related to the payment process, often involving falsified invoices or check fraud. – CH16

extrapolation: One of the most general statistical methods, this process identifies past trends and predicts the pattern of future cash flows using these trends. – CH14

factor: A type of nonbank financial intermediary that provides short-term financing to companies by purchasing accounts receivable at a discount. – CH3

factoring: An accounts receivable (A/R) financing process that involves the outright sale of receivables to a factor, a company that specializes in the financing and management of receivables. The factoring may be performed on a with or without recourse basis. In a with recourse arrangement, the factor may return any uncollectible A/R to the seller for full credit. In a without recourse factoring arrangement, the factor takes all the risk of default on the A/R. – CH10

fair value: Under Accounting Standards Codification (ASC) Topic 820, the fair value of an asset or liability is defined by determining the price that would be received in an asset sale or the price paid to transfer a liability. The valuation price must be market-based and take into consideration all observable valuation inputs, such as competition and risk. ASC Topic 825 expands this application by stating that fair value should be applied to all financial assets and liabilities except for certain specified types of assets. – CH8

fair value hedge: A type of hedge in which the risk being hedged is a change in the fair value of an asset or a liability. Changes in fair value may arise through changes in interest rates (for fixed-rate loans), foreign exchange rates, equity prices, or commodity prices. – CH8

Federal Deposit Insurance Corporation (FDIC): An independent agency of the US federal government whose primary role is to protect depositors from losses caused by bank insolvency. The FDIC preserves and promotes public confidence in the US financial system by insuring deposits in banks and thrift institutions up to a maximum of $250,000 per depositor; by identifying, monitoring and addressing risks to the Deposit Insurance Fund; and by limiting the effect on the economy and the financial system when a bank or thrift institution fails. – CH2

Federal Home Loan Mortgage Corporation (FHLMC, or Freddie Mac): A stockholder-owned, government-sponsored enterprise chartered by the US Congress in 1970 to keep money flowing to mortgage lenders in support of homeownership and rental housing for middle-income Americans. The FHLMC purchases, guarantees, and securitizes mortgages to form mortgage-backed securities (MBSs). – CH5

Federal National Mortgage Association (FNMA, or Fannie Mae): A US government-sponsored enterprise that was created in 1938 to expand the flow of mortgage money by creating a secondary mortgage market. Fannie Mae is a publicly traded company that operates under a congressional charter that directs Fannie Mae to channel its efforts into increasing the availability and affordability of homeownership for low-, moderate-, and middle-income Americans. – CH5

Federal Open Market Committee (FOMC): The committee of the US Federal Reserve that runs the open market operations which help to implement US monetary policy and control the money supply. – CH5

Federal Reserve (Fed): The central bank for the United States, from the perspective of monetary policy. – CH2

FedGlobal ACH Payments: A service offered by the US Federal Reserve Bank to provide a framework for sending cross-border automated clearinghouse (ACH) transactions to countries around the world (over 35 countries as of 2015). – CH4

Fedwire: A large-value, real-time gross settlement (RTGS) transfer system operated by the US Federal Reserve. – CH4

fidelity bond: A type of insurance coverage that guarantees payment for money or other property lost through dishonest acts of bonded employees, either by name or position. Whether employees act alone or in concert, the bond generally covers all dishonest acts, such as larceny, theft, embezzlement, forgery, misappropriation, wrongful abstraction, or willful misapplication. Because a fidelity bond makes up only part of the protection against theft, other crime insurance is often mandatory. A blanket bond could be used to cover all employees of an organization, while crime insurance provides specific coverage for the perils of burglary, theft, and robbery by external parties. – CH16

fiduciary: An individual or institution to which certain property is given to hold in trust according to a trust agreement. – CH3

finality: In a payment system, this is the point in time when a payment can no longer be taken back or retracted by a payor or payor's bank, and the payee has full use of the funds. – CH4

Financial Accounting Standards (FASs): The former name of Accounting Standards Codification (ASC) Topics. – CH8

Financial Accounting Standards Board (FASB): An independent, self-regulating US organization made up of accounting professionals that establishes financial accounting and reporting standards in the United States, collectively referred to as *Generally Accepted Accounting Principles (GAAP)*. – CH8

Financial Action Task Force (FATF): An international, intergovernmental organization composed of members from more than 30 countries, whose primary purpose is the development and promotion of policies, at both national and international levels, to combat money laundering and terrorist financing. – CH3

financial budget: A component of a master budget, this budget addresses an organization's financing and investing activities. – CH9

Financial Crimes Enforcement Network (FinCEN): The primary US government agency (operating as a bureau of the US Treasury) that oversees and implements policies to prevent and detect money laundering by criminal or terrorist organizations. FinCEN serves as the US financial intelligence unit (FIU). – CH2

Financial Industry Regulatory Authority (FINRA): The largest independent regulator for all securities firms and registered securities representatives doing business in the United States. FINRA's mission is to provide investor protection and market integrity through effective and efficient regulation, as well as through compliance and technology-based services. – CH2

financial institution (FI): An organization that provides some type of financial services to the public. A commercial bank is the most common type of FI. – CH3

financial institution risk: The risk of loss to an organization associated with the failure, either operational or financial, of a financial institution used by an organization. – CH7

financial intelligence unit (FIU): A specialized government agency established in many countries to monitor and deal with the problems of money laundering and similar financial crimes. FinCEN in the United States is an FIU. – CH2

financial lease: See *capital lease*. – CH20

financial leverage: A concept that examines the fixed costs of financing. Generally, the higher the level of debt capital used in a company, the higher the interest costs and the greater the amount of financial leverage. Financial leverage is also the measure of a company's use of debt in its capital structure. – CH9

financial planning: An organizational function that involves determining the need for present and future funding to support operations. An important part of this function is the forecasting of revenues, income, and external financing required to support the company's planned growth. – CH1

financial risk: The risk that the overall value of an organization may change in response to a change in interest or foreign exchange rates. – CH7

financial service provider (FSP): A vendor that provides treasury-related services. – CH7

Financial Stability Board (FSB): A board established to provide international coordination of national financial authorities and international standard-setting bodies. It is based in Basel, Switzerland, and works to develop and promote the implementation of effective regulatory, supervisory, and other financial sector policies. – CH2

Financial Stability Oversight Council (FSOC): A US agency created under the Dodd-Frank Act, whose primary responsibility is to prevent systemic risk from threatening the financial system by identifying threats to financial stability and gaps in regulations, and facilitating coordination across federal and state agencies. FSOC oversees the primary bank regulators. – CH2

financial statements: Accounting reports that summarize a company's operating results and financial position at a point in time. Analyzing these statements provides insights into (1) how well the company has managed its liquidity position, (2) how effectively it used and financed its assets, (3) whether it had a proper balance between debt and equity financing compared to peers, (4) how well it controlled operating and financing costs, and (5) whether the profit it earned was satisfactory in relation to the levels of revenue it experienced and the investment in assets that support its operations. – CH8

financial supply chain: The connection of trading partners from order placement to receipt of payment. It refers to the flow of financial information and money in counterpoint to the flow of goods and services. The financial supply chain is crucial to financial viability following a disaster. The treasury area plays a pivotal role in managing the organization's financial supply chain, through working capital management practices and by ensuring adequate liquidity sources. – CH7

finished goods: A type of inventory that consists of completed items or materials available for sale. It lets a company fill orders when received rather than depend upon product completion to satisfy customer demands. – CH10

firm value: An economic measure reflecting the market value of a business. It is a sum of claims by all claimants: creditors (secured and unsecured) and shareholders (preferred and common). – CH20

five Cs of credit: A credit analysis process that considers the character, capacity, capital, collateral, and conditions of the potential borrower. – CH10

fixed asset turnover ratio: An efficiency/asset management ratio that measures how efficiently fixed assets (or property, plant, and equipment) are used. It is computed as revenues divided by net property, plant, and equipment. – CH9

fixed-charge coverage ratio: A coverage ratio that is similar to the times interest earned ratio but also takes into account fixed charges other than interest, such as payments on leases. It is computed as earnings before interest and taxes (EBIT) plus fixed charges, divided by interest expense plus fixed charges. – CH9

fixed costs: Costs that do not vary in total over a wide range of activity and are not immediately impacted by changes in business activities. In cost accounting, fixed costs are contrasted with variable costs, which do change based on volume or activity levels. – CH9

fixed/floating ratio: A ratio that provides a measure of interest rate risk utilizing a debt portfolio's mix of fixed-rate obligations relative to floating-rate obligations. Though duration is a more common measure of interest rate risk, many debt portfolio managers also use this ratio. This relationship is usually expressed in terms of a target fixed/floating ratio. – CH19

fixed-income capital: A type of capital that has fixed payments and includes capital such as bond securities and term loans. – CH6

fixed-to-fixed—foreign currency to foreign currency: A transaction currency option available as part of the FedGlobal ACH Payments service, in which payments are both transferred and received in foreign currency. The foreign exchange rate and settlement are managed and processed by participating US financial institutions and the respective foreign gateway operators via their foreign correspondent banks. – CH4

fixed-to-fixed—US dollar to US dollar: A transaction currency option available as part of the FedGlobal ACH Payments service, in which payments are both transferred and received in US dollars. Settlement is between participating US financial institutions and the Federal Reserve Banks, in US dollars. – CH4

fixed-to-variable currency: A transaction currency option available as part of the FedGlobal ACH Payments service, in which US dollars are converted to a variable amount of a destination currency based on a competitive exchange rate. Settlement is between participating US financial institutions and the Federal Reserve Banks, in US dollars. – CH4

float: The time interval, or delay, between the start and the completion of a specific phase or process occurring along the cash flow timeline. – CH10

float-neutral terms: Sales terms offered for electronic payment in which either the timing (i.e., value date) of a payment is adjusted or a discount is offered so as to maintain whatever float the buyer was receiving with the paper payment. – CH12

floating-rate debt: A type of debt issue that carries interest payments that reset periodically based on movement in a representative interest rate index, such as the London Interbank Offered Rate (LIBOR) or the US Treasury bill. – CH6

floating-rate note (FRN): A note with a variable interest rate. The adjustments to the interest rate are made periodically (usually every six months) and are tied to a certain money market index. FRNs typically have a maturity of one year or longer. – CH5

floor planning: In inventory financing, this is a type of asset-based lending used for high-value durable goods, such as automobiles, trucks, or heavy equipment. Loans are made against each individual item, recorded by serial number, and are not fully repaid until the item is sold. – CH10

flotation costs: The costs of issuing a security (usually the underwriting costs), not related to direct interest or equity costs. – CH20

forced reinvestment: A type of political risk in which funds cannot be transferred out of a country in any form, or the amount that can be transferred is limited. – CH7

forecasting horizon: In the cash forecasting process, this is the time interval over which information is to be forecasted. – CH14

foreign bond: A type of bond sold in a particular country by a foreign borrower, but usually denominated in the domestic currency of the country where issued. These bonds are primarily regulated by the authorities in the country of issue. – CH6

foreign check: A check deposited at a bank in one country that is drawn on a bank in another country. – CH4

Foreign Corrupt Practices Act (FCPA): US legislation that specifically prohibits payments to foreign officials or their family members for the purpose of gaining any improper business advantage. – CH7

foreign currency account: A bank account where deposit balances may be held in a currency other than that of the country in which the bank is located. – CH3

foreign currency translation: A process used to convert the financial results of a parent company's foreign subsidiaries to its reporting currency. – CH8

foreign exchange (FX): The conversion of one country's currency into that of another. – CH3

foreign exchange (FX) risk: A type of risk that arises from the exposure an organization has as a result of transactions, assets, and liabilities that are denominated in a foreign currency. As exchange rates fluctuate, so too can the value of these items, ultimately impacting the overall value of a firm. – CH16

foreign tax credit: A type of tax credit available to a company with foreign income that has already been taxed by the foreign jurisdiction. For example, a US company's income derived from its non-US operations typically is included in its tax return to determine the amount of US income tax due. If income from foreign sources has already been subjected to foreign income taxes, the same income is taxed twice. To relieve the effect of double taxation, US tax law grants a US company a tax credit against its total US income tax liability for foreign income taxes paid by the parent and its subsidiaries. This credit is called the *foreign tax credit*. – CH2

forward: An agreement between two parties to buy or sell a fixed amount of an asset to be delivered at a future date and at a price agreed upon today. The underlying asset in a forward contract can be a financial instrument (e.g., a stock index fund or debt instrument), a currency (e.g., the euro or pound), or a commodity (e.g., gold or coffee). – CH17

Forward foreign exchange (FX) rate: A rate quoted for the delivery (or settlement) of currency beyond two business days following the date of the trade. – CH17

forward market: A financial market in which contracts for future delivery (futures) of currency or commodities are bought and sold. – CH3

forward rate agreement (FRA): A forward contract on interest rates in which two parties agree that a certain interest rate will apply to a certain principal during a specified, future period of time. The notional principal amounts are agreed upon, but they are never exchanged. If the actual rate is different from the agreed-upon rate in the contract at settlement, then one party pays the other a cash amount equal to the difference. – CH17

free cash flow (FCF): A performance measurement ratio that is similar to residual income analysis but which—in addition to accounting for capital costs—also includes adjustments for noncash items and for working capital investments. Its primary objective is to determine the amount of effective cash flow available to a company after all necessary investments have been accounted for. To this end, it is used extensively in the analysis of new or high-growth companies, especially by the providers of venture capital. It is most commonly computed by adding net income to depreciation and amortization, less the change in working capital and capital expenditures. – CH9

free-fall bankruptcy: A type of bankruptcy in which a firm goes (or is forced) into bankruptcy and has no structured plan for coming out of bankruptcy. – CH2

freight payment services: An outsourced form of accounts payable wherein specialists pay all of a shipper's freight bills, audit bills for possible overcharges and duplicate payments, and provide reports that help a company compare costs for different routes and carriers. – CH12

friendly acquisition: A situation in which a target company's management and board of directors agree to a merger or acquisition by another company. – CH20

full guarantee: A level of guarantee for a subsidiary in which the guarantee party (the parent organization or another party) fully guarantees any borrowing arrangement by the subsidiary and agrees to take over the loan if the subsidiary fails to make timely payments. – CH6

full-service brokerage: A brokerage that has research analysts who are industry specialists and provides investment advice to institutions and individual investors. – CH3

functional currency: For determining foreign exchange translation exposure, this is the currency of the primary economic environment in which the entity operates. Normally, the majority of the entity's business activities are transacted in that currency. – CH8

future value (FV): For an investment made today, this is the expected value of the investment at a specified, future date. – CH9

futures: Similar to forwards, futures are agreements between two parties to buy or sell a fixed amount of an asset to be delivered at a future date and at a price agreed upon today. Futures differ, however, in the following ways. First, they are standardized contracts (i.e., standard contract sizes and delivery dates). Second, they are typically traded on organized exchanges rather than over the counter. Third, they are generally not settled with delivery of the underlying asset; instead, they typically are closed out (i.e., settled financially between the two parties) prior to maturity. – CH17

Generally Accepted Accounting Principles (GAAP): A detailed set of rules that govern US accounting standards. These principles are developed, agreed upon, and published in the form of Accounting Standards Codification (ASC) Topics by the Financial Accounting Standards Board (FASB). – CH8

ghost card: A variation on the purchasing card that does not involve the use of an actual card. With a ghost card system, a card number is given to a specific vendor and is then used for electronic purchasing and billing purposes. Also known as a *virtual card.* – CH4

giro: A method of transferring money by instructing a bank to directly transfer funds from one bank account to another without the use of checks. Giro payments are initiated by the payor and can be one-time payments or can be recurring standing instructions for a series of payments. A giro payment is the functional equivalent of an ACH credit. Also known as *postal giro*, since many giro systems are run by the postal system within a country. – CH4

global financial institution (FI): A financial institution that operates in multiple countries in more than one part of the world, providing services to both domestic and multinational corporations. – CH3

good funds: Collected funds in an account that are immediately usable by the owner of the account. – CH10

goodwill: An account that can be found in the assets portion of a company's balance sheet. Goodwill can often arise when one company is purchased by another company. In an acquisition, the amount paid for the company over book value usually accounts for the target firm's intangible assets. – CH8

Gordon growth model: A common stock valuation model used to determine the intrinsic value of a stock based on a future series of dividends that grow at a constant rate. This model works well for firms that pay a steadily growing dividend. Also referred to as the *dividend discount model.* – CH19

Government National Mortgage Association (GNMA, or Ginnie Mae): A wholly owned agency of the United States that provides liquidity for government-sponsored mortgage programs through its mortgage-backed securities plan. – CH5

government paper: A range of short-term paper, generally referred to as *treasury bills* or *government-issued promissory notes*, issued by state and local government agencies and authorities, as well as other government entities, in order to raise funds in the short-term money market. – CH5

government-sponsored enterprise (GSE): A company that is created by a national government in order to participate in or help support various commercial activities on the government's behalf. These organizations are generally formed for a specific purpose and are designed to support a certain economic sector. In the United States, examples would include Freddie Mac and Fannie Mae. *GSE* is a US term; the more generic global term is *state-owned enterprise.* – CH6

government warrant: In government finance, this is an order to pay that instructs a treasurer to pay the warrant holder on demand or after a maturity date. Warrants deposited in a bank are routed (based on the magnetic ink character recognition line information) to a collecting bank that processes them as collection items. The collecting bank presents the warrants to the government entity's treasury department for payment each business day. – CH4

Governmental Accounting Standards Board (GASB): The authoritative standard-setting body for US state and local governments, as well as for public schools, state universities, and other government-affiliated agencies. – CH8

governmental and not-for-profit (G/NFP) organization: A type of organization that does not have shareholders or other owners, but is organized to serve a collective group. Governmental agencies provide goods, services, or information to benefit the public as a whole or its particular segments. They raise cash primarily through taxes and fees paid by members of the community, regardless of whether those paying such taxes and fees derive any benefit from the resulting goods or services. Nongovernmental, not-for-profit organizations serve specific constituencies who pay for some or all the benefits provided. – CH8

green bond: (1) A type of bond used by federally qualified organizations to raise funds to promote sustainability by developing underutilized or abandoned properties (e.g., brownfield sites). (2) A type of corporate bond that designates proceeds for environmental projects, renewable energy projects, or making buildings more energy efficient. – CH6

gross profit margin: A performance ratio that shows the percentage of revenues remaining after the cost of goods sold is deducted from revenue. It is computed as gross profit divided by revenues. – CH9

gross settlement: A type of settlement in a payment system in which each transaction results in a separate value transfer between the payor and payee. In most gross settlement systems, the settlement is on a real-time basis, resulting in a real-time gross settlement (RTGS) system. – CH4

group captive: An approach to risk retention in which a subsidiary is owned by multiple owners for the purpose of insuring the risk of the parent owners or their affiliates. Also known as an *association captive*, it provides risk financing for the owners of the subsidiary. This shared ownership makes the group captive arrangement a form of insurance by virtue of the transfer of risk. In most cases, group captives are industry-based, which allows risk transfer across similar risks. – CH16

Group of Governors and Heads of Supervision (GHOS): The governing body of the Basel Committee on Banking Supervision. The GHOS is comprised of central bank governors and (non-central-bank) heads of supervision from member countries. – CH2

guarantee of payment or collection: A guarantee by one party (usually a parent company) that another party (usually a subsidiary) will make payment on a loan or collection. The guarantor is only responsible in the event that the subsidiary formally defaults on the loan. – CH6

guaranteed cost insurance program: A type of insurance program in which a fixed premium is paid at the beginning of the policy period and the insurer assumes the risk for paying all losses occurring during the policy period that fall within the scope and amount of the policy. – CH16

hedging: A risk management strategy used to limit the probability of loss from changes in the prices of commodities, currencies, or securities. In active hedging, an organization uses various financial instruments to reduce or eliminate risks associated with uncertain future cash flows. In passive (or natural) hedging, an organization holds both assets and liabilities in the same currency so that fluctuations offset each other. – CH17

Herstatt risk: Foreign or cross-currency settlement risk, especially between bank counterparties; the risk that one party to a transaction defaults and is not able to fulfill its obligation to settle the transaction, potentially triggering a string of other defaults. Herstatt risk is named after a German bank that failed in 1974, causing a cascading string of payment defaults. – CH2

high-yield bond: A high-paying bond with a lower credit rating than investment-grade corporate bonds, Treasury bonds, and municipal bonds. Because of the higher risk of default, these bonds pay a higher yield than investment-grade bonds. Also referred to as *junk bonds* or *below-investment-grade bonds* (i.e., an investment quality rating of BB+ or less from S&P, or Ba1 or less from Moody's). – CH6

"holder in due course" issue: A situation that arises when a third party, someone other than the payee or the depository bank, accepts or cashes a negotiable instrument (i.e., a check) in good faith that subsequently turns out to be fraudulent. This is a uniquely US problem that results from US law regarding negotiable instruments such as checks. – CH12

holding period: The expected period of time that a particular investor will hold a given investment or asset, generally the time between when the asset is purchased and when it is sold. – CH13

holding period yield: The yield computed for the time a security is held. However, yields are quoted on an annualized basis, so the holding period yield is adjusted by determining how many holding periods occur in one year and using that number to annualize the yield. – CH13

home currency: The currency of the country in which an entity's headquarters are located. In foreign exchange translation, if the functional currency of the subsidiary is the home currency, then the current method is used to translate financial statement line items to the parent company's currency. The current method translates all assets and liabilities at the current spot rate at the date of translation. – CH8

hosted solution: A type of software solution in which the vendor runs the application on its own technology platform, and firms access the software over the Internet using personal computers. – CH15

hostile takeover: The acquisition of one company (called the *target company*) by another (called the *acquirer*) that is accomplished by going directly to the company's shareholders or fighting to replace management to get the acquisition approved. – CH20

hybrid lockbox: A lockbox system (sometimes referred to as *wholetail*) that combines features of wholesale and retail lockboxes, and is configured, usually on a customized basis, to process both business-to-business and consumer-to-business payments. – CH12

hybrid security: A type of security that is generally created by combining the elements of two or more different types of securities into one. Typically, a hybrid will behave like a fixed-income security (bond) under certain circumstances and an equity security (stock) under other circumstances. – CH6

image processing: Processing of a document, such as a check, using an electronic image of the document in place of the original physical instrument. – CH4

image replacement document (IRD): In the United States, this is a paper reproduction of the original check that contains an image of the front and back of the original check and is the legal equivalent of the original check. – CH4

imaging technology: A technology that allows paper documents, such as checks and remittance advices, to be scanned, converted to digital images, and stored for subsequent distribution, handling, and processing. Also known as *image technology*. – CH12

impairment of capital rule: A regulatory restriction on the amount that an FI can lend or invest in a particular company or industry, based on the quality of the FI's existing loan portfolio. – CH2

imprest account: An account maintained at a fixed amount for a particular purpose or activity. Sometimes used as a petty cash account. – CH12

in-house banking: The practice of having treasury become the main provider of banking services for all the company's operating entities. – CH10

in-sample validation: In the selection and validation of a forecasting model, this process tests a forecast for accuracy using the historical data used to develop it. If the forecast accurately predicts one data series from one or more other series, the relationships among the data series are deemed to be validated. When a forecast is initially developed, however, there typically is no other data available to test it. – CH14

income bond: A type of bond that pays interest only if a company has profits, thus reducing some of the risk of issuing debt from a company's viewpoint. – CH6

income statement: A financial statement that summarizes revenues earned, expenses incurred, and gains and losses arising from conversions of assets and liabilities over an accounting period. Also called a *statement of earnings*, a *statement of operations*, or a *profit and loss statement*. – CH8

incumbency certificate: See *certificate of incumbency*. – CH7

indebtedness/debt ratio: A ratio used to measure the level of indebtedness or use of leverage (i.e., debt usage) by a company. – CH9

independent auditor: An external auditor with a certified public accounting designation that qualifies him or her to provide an auditor's report. May also be used to refer to a public accounting firm that employs qualified external auditors. – CH8

independent director: Under New York Stock Exchange standards, this is a director who has no material relationship with the listed company, either directly or as a partner, shareholder, or officer of the organization. – CH1

index bond: A type of bond that has interest rates tied to an economic index. Index bonds are used most often when a high level of price inflation is present or possible. – CH6

indirect purchases: Purchases of stores and supplies inventories, which are not used directly in a manufacturing/production process. Rather, they support the production process. – CH10

industrial bank/industrial loan company: An FI with a limited scope of services. Industrial banks sell certificates that are labeled as *investment shares* and can also accept customer deposits. They then invest the proceeds in installment loans for consumers and small businesses. Industrial banks differ from commercial lenders because they accept deposits. They also differ from commercial banks because they do not offer checking accounts. Because of their limited scope of services, they do not fall under general banking regulatory authority, are locally chartered, and may be owned by nonbank holding companies. – CH3

inflation premium: An adjustment to the base interest rate to account for projected inflation over the investment period. – CH13

informal bankruptcy: A form of bankruptcy handled outside the bankruptcy courts. In bankruptcy proceedings, it is possible to perform a reorganization or a liquidation informally. An informal reorganization typically involves a firm that is fundamentally sound, but is undergoing temporary financial difficulties. This is often done outside of bankruptcy in an agreed-upon write-off of some portion of the firm's debts by its creditors. – CH2

information float: The time between receiving good funds and the time the organization knows that it has the funds available and can actually make use of those funds. For a company receiving payments on accounts receivable, there may also be delays between the receipt of the payment and the posting of that payment to a customer's account. If the customer is close to its credit limit, this could, in turn, delay the ability of the company to sell more goods or services to that customer. – CH10

initial public offering (IPO): The first sale of stock by a private company to the public. IPOs are often issued by smaller, younger companies seeking the capital to expand, but can also be done by large privately owned companies looking to become publicly traded. – CH6

insolvency: The inability to pay one's debts in a timely manner. The terms *bankruptcy* and *insolvency* are often used interchangeably, but in some jurisdictions, such as the United Kingdom, *bankruptcy* refers only to personal insolvency while the general term *insolvency* applies to both corporate and personal insolvency. – CH2

installment credit: A form of credit extension that requires a customer to make equal periodic payments, each of which contains principal and interest components. – CH10

insurance company: A type of nonbank financial institution that sells insurance products. From a corporate perspective, insurance companies are primarily long-term lenders to companies. They are significant investors in real estate, particularly commercial real estate (e.g., shopping centers), as well as long-term bonds. Insurance companies have started to compete with banks for short- and medium-term loans. They provide mortgage funding, leasing services, guaranteed investment contracts (similar to bank certificates of deposit, generally paying interest for one to five years), and universal life insurance policies with long-term savings features. – CH3

insurance management: A decision or problem-solving process that identifies possible risks and losses, and determines if insurance should be purchased against the risk of each loss and how much insurance is needed. – CH16

insurance risk management: A risk management technique in which financial protection (or reimbursement) for possible loss is purchased from another party in the form of insurance. It is essentially a method of transferring risk from one party to another. – CH16

intangible assets: Assets that lack physical substance and for which there is often a high degree of uncertainty concerning their future value. Examples are goodwill, trademarks, and patents. An intangible asset with a finite and useful life is amortized over its legal or useful life, but if the intangible asset has an indefinite useful life, it is not amortized. However, it must be evaluated annually for any decline in value, which must be charged against income when identified. – CH8

integrated/comprehensive accounts payable (A/P) service: A function in which a financial service provider (FSP) provides outsourced disbursement services to a company based on a transmission of payment information. The service allows a company to make multiple types of payments (e.g., check, electronic funds transfer, or card) through one channel. – CH12

integrated ratio analysis: The practice of looking at various financial ratios in pairs or groups to gain better insight into a company's financial performance. – CH9

integrity: In information security, this is the ability to ensure that a message was not modified in transit and that stored information has not been improperly modified or deleted. Data integrity is especially important for financial transactions. – CH15

interchange fees: Fees established by the payment card brands that go directly to the issuing bank to cover its costs in issuing cards and in processing card transactions. These fees typically account for the largest portion of overall card fees and represent a fee that is paid to the issuing bank for each transaction. – CH4

intercompany dividend: A type of dividend used in large companies with wholly owned subsidiaries to transfer profits from subsidiaries back to the parent company. – CH20

interest rate forward: A type of forward contract, similar to a forward rate agreement, that allows its buyer to lock in today the future price of an asset, such as an interest-linked security. The buyer has to pay the agreed-upon price on the settlement date, whether or not the interest rate has moved in the buyer's favor. The seller is also required to deliver the asset on the settlement date, whatever that asset's price is in the spot market. – CH17

interest rate option: An option-type derivative where the payoff depends on the level of interest rates. – CH17

interest rate risk: A type of risk that relates to changes in investment values and borrowing costs, and potentially to overall firm value, as interest rates change. – CH16

intermediate-term note: A note with a maturity of two to ten years. In most cases, interest is paid at periodic intervals, and the notes are similar to long-term bonds except for the shorter maturity. – CH6

internal controls: Measures taken by an organization to provide reasonable assurance regarding achievement of the organization's objectives related to operational effectiveness and efficiency, reliable financial reporting, and compliance with laws, regulations, and policies. – CH18

internal factoring: The practice of a company's internal factoring unit buying accounts receivable from the exporting unit and collecting funds from the importing unit. – CH10

internal rate of return (IRR): The discount rate that makes the net present value equal to zero or, equivalently, makes the present value (PV) of cash inflows equal to the PV of cash outflows. – CH9

International Accounting Standards Board (IASB): An international standards-setting body that determines general accounting standards and is made up of board members from nine countries. Based in London, England, the IASB's mission is to develop a single set of global accounting standards published as pronouncements called *International Financial Reporting Standards*. – CH8

International ACH Transaction (IAT): A US automated clearinghouse (ACH) format that is part of a payment transaction originating from, or transmitted to, an office of a financial agency located outside the territorial jurisdiction of the United States. *IAT* is the standard entry class (SEC) code for this format. – CH12

International Association of Deposit Insurers (IADI): An international not-for-profit organization formed to enhance the effectiveness of deposit insurance systems by promoting guidance and international cooperation. Members of IADI conduct research and produce guidance for the benefit of those jurisdictions seeking to establish or improve a deposit insurance system. Members also share their knowledge and expertise through participation in international conferences and other forums. – CH2

International Association of Insurance Supervisors (IAIS): The standards-setting group that represents insurance regulators and supervisory entities of some 190 jurisdictions in nearly 140 countries, constituting the great majority of the world's insurance premiums. – CH2

International Bank Account Number (IBAN): An international standard for identifying bank accounts across national borders. – CH3

International Chamber of Commerce (ICC) Publication UCP 600: An ICC publication that deals with international standby practices and governs the administration of standby letters of credit. The current version is International Standby Practices (1998), or ISP98, which is contained in ICC Publication UCP 600. *UCP* is an acronym for Uniform Customs and Practice for Documentary Credits. – CH12

International Financial Reporting Standards (IFRS): A set of international accounting standards stating how particular types of transactions and other events should be reported in financial statements. IFRS are issued by the International Accounting Standards Board. – CH8

International Organization for Standardization (ISO): The world's largest developer of voluntary international standards for a variety of products and services, including financial reporting and payments. – CH3

International Organization for Standardization (ISO) 20022: An XML-based global messaging standard for the financial services industry whose intended use is transmitting information related to securities, payments, financial reporting, account management, international trade, and foreign exchange. – CH15

International Organization of Securities Commissions (IOSCO): An organization that is recognized as the international standard setter for securities markets. Its membership regulates more than 95% of the world's securities markets, and it is the primary international cooperative forum for securities market regulatory agencies. – CH2

International Standard on Assurance Engagements (ISAE) 3402: A global assurance standard for reporting on controls at service organizations. – CH7

International Swaps and Derivatives Association (ISDA): A trade organization made up of companies, dealers, and service providers that participate in the market for over-the-counter derivative instruments. – CH17

Internet-Initiated Entry (WEB): A US automated clearinghouse (ACH) format used for payments that are not pre-authorized, but are initiated by consumers using the Internet. *WEB* is the standard entry class (SEC) code for this format. – CH12

inventory conversion period: See *days' inventory.* – CH10

investment bank: A financial intermediary that performs a variety of services, such as: (1) underwriting, by acting as an intermediary between an issuer of securities and the investing public; (2) facilitating mergers, acquisitions, divestitures, and other corporate reorganizations; and (3) acting as a broker/financial advisor for institutional clients. – CH3

investment banker: A professional who is responsible for assisting issuers in the design and placement of securities issuances. – CH6

invoicing float: The delay between the day that a customer places an order and the day that the customer actually receives an invoice for that order that can be processed for payment. – CH10

issuer credit rating: A credit rating that represents a rating agency's opinion on the obligor's (issuer's) overall capacity to meet its financial obligations. – CH13

issue-specific rating: A credit rating of a specific long- or short-term security that considers the attributes of the issuer, as well as the specific terms of the issue, the quality of the collateral, and the creditworthiness of the guarantors. – CH13

issuing bank: In a letter of credit (L/C) transaction, this is the buyer's (importer's) bank that issues the L/C in favor of the seller (exporter). – CH12

just-in-time (JIT) inventory: An inventory management approach that attempts to minimize inventory levels by reducing the costs or uncertainties that underlie the motives for holding inventory. – CH10

know your customer (KYC): The due diligence procedures that a financial institution must follow to determine or verify the identity of its customers. KYC is considered a key part of anti-money laundering compliance activities. – CH7

lagging: The executing of cross-border payments between subsidiaries after the scheduled payment date. Lagging is used when a subsidiary country's currency is expected to appreciate relative to the parent company's currency. – CH10

Large Value Transfer System (LVTS): A system in Canada for electronic wire transfers of large sums of money. It allows the participating institutions and their clients to send large sums of money securely in real time with complete certainty that the payment will settle. – CH4

layering: The attempt to conceal the source of ownership of money by creating a complex series of transactions (layers) in order to provide anonymity. Used in relation to money laundering. – CH2

lead bank/institution: The financial institution that is responsible for managing a syndicated loan or securities sale that is funded by multiple financial institutions. The lead bank/institution receives most of the fees from the sale. – CH3

leading: The executing of cross-border payments between subsidiaries before the scheduled payment date. Leading is employed when a subsidiary country's currency is expected to depreciate relative to the parent company's currency. – CH10

ledger balance: A bank balance that reflects all entries to a bank account, regardless of whether the deposited items have been collected and are available for withdrawal. – CH4

ledger cutoff: The time of day when a bank deposit must be received in order to be posted to the ledger balance of the depositor's account. – CH4

legal risk: A type of operational risk that relates to legal actions against a company. Given the increasingly litigious business environment, a significant source of external operational risk is potential lawsuits or other legal actions instigated by customers, trade partners, or governmental agencies and regulators. Insurance may be used to mitigate this risk in some cases. – CH16

less predictable cash flow: In the cash flow forecasting process, this is a cash flow component that is difficult to forecast. Examples of these types of cash flows would be those related to sales of a new product, unexpected repairs, pending settlement of insurance claims, or the cost of settling a strike. – CH14

letter of credit (L/C): A promise by the issuing bank to pay a certain amount under specific circumstances. A commercial L/C (see definition earlier in glossary) is related to a business transaction, while a standby letter of credit (see definition later in the glossary) is typically used as a guarantee. – CH12

leveraged buyout (LBO): A type of transaction in which an entity buys or acquires a firm using a significant amount of borrowed funds in the process. In many cases, the assets of the acquired company may be used as collateral for the borrowed funds. – CH20

liability insurance: Any type of insurance policy that protects against damage to other parties that can arise from product defects; business practices; accidents; actions of the organization's employees, officers, or board of directors; and general negligence in the operation of the organization. Liability insurance typically includes defense costs in the event of litigation. Intentional damage and contractual liabilities are typically not covered in these types of policies. – CH16

lien: A legal claim on an asset or assets. In most types of secured lending, the lender has a lien or legal claim on the assets used as collateral in the event it cannot take physical possession of the assets. – CH6

line of credit: An agreement in which the lender gives the borrower access to funds up to a maximum amount over a specific period of time. Lines of credit are usually revolving, meaning the borrower may borrow, repay, and borrow funds again up to the established limit during the commitment period. – CH13

liquidating dividend: A dividend that is paid out of capital rather than earnings. This sometimes occurs when a company or one of its divisions is going out of business and management decides to pay off shareholders through a liquidating dividend. As the name implies, the company liquidates the remaining assets (capital) of the failed company or division to pay the dividend. This approach may also be used by the acquiring company in a leveraged buyout to liquidate the acquired company in order to meet debt service requirements. – CH20

liquidity: The ability of an organization to convert assets into cash quickly and without a significant risk of loss. – CH1

liquidity management flows: Cash flows that are employed to use an organization's liquidity reserves in the most effective manner. If there is a surplus of funds, treasury may either (1) invest them in suitable investments, or (2) pay down existing debt. Alternatively, if there is a shortage of funds, then treasury may either (1) sell off investments, or (2) draw on available debt sources (e.g., credit lines or commercial paper issuance). – CH10

liquidity premium: An adjustment to the base interest rate to account for the lack of liquidity on an investment. – CH13

liquidity risk: A type of risk that is typically divided into two areas: *funding liquidity risk* and *asset liquidity risk*. *Funding liquidity risk* relates primarily to an organization's ability to raise necessary cash to meet its obligations as they come due. It is often linked to the ability to raise capital (both short- and long-term) in a timely manner, and it typically is managed by holding marketable securities or open (i.e., available) lines of credit. *Asset liquidity risk* is defined earlier in the glossary. – CH5

liquidity/working capital ratio: A type of ratio that measures the firm's ability to meet its payment obligations on short-term debt and helps ascertain whether cash is being used effectively. – CH9

loan covenant: A requirement included in a loan agreement that serves to protect the lender. Loan covenants impose either restrictions (known as *restrictive* or *negative covenants*) and/or obligations (known as *affirmative* or *positive covenants*) on the part of an organization's management. They typically have a significant impact on an organization's financial decision making. – CH13

loan participation: A type of lending arrangement in which a financial institution purchases an interest in another lender's credit facility. The purchaser is called a *participant*, and the seller is the *lead institution*. The participant does not have a separate note and has only an indirect relationship with the borrower. – CH13

loan sales: An offering of commercial banks that involves the structuring of lending facilities so that short-term loans can be sold to other banks and investors. – CH3

loan syndication: A type of lending arrangement in which multiple financial institutions share the funding of a single credit facility. The syndicate, or group of lenders, is led by an agent who acts as the intermediary between the company and the syndicate to negotiate credit terms and documentation, make advances and collect payments on the loan, and disseminate information. – CH13

lockbox system: A collection tool in which a financial institution or third-party vendor receives payments at specified post office box (lockbox) addresses, processes the remittances, and credits the payments into a payee's account. – CH12

London Interbank Offered Rate (LIBOR): An interest rate at which banks can borrow funds, in marketable size, from other banks in the London interbank market. LIBOR is fixed on a daily basis by the British Bankers' Association. LIBOR is derived from a filtered average of the world's most creditworthy banks' interbank deposit rates for larger loans with maturities between overnight and one full year. – CH13

long-term bond: A bond with a maturity of 10 to 30 years. – CH6

long-term debt to capital ratio: A type of debt management ratio that measures the percentage of a company's capital (where *capital* is defined as the sum of long-term debt and equity) that is provided by long-term debt. It is computed as long-term debt divided by long-term debt plus equity. – CH9

long-term forecasting: A type of cash forecasting in which the forecast covers any period beyond one year. It takes into consideration projections of long-term sales and expenditures, as well as market factors. – CH14

long-term investment: Any investment with a term greater than one year. See *capital investment*. – CH19

magnetic ink character recognition (MICR): A data capture process that translates the machine-readable information on a check into a digital data entry. See also *MICR line*. – CH4

mail float: The time interval or delay between the day a payment (and any related remittance information) is mailed and the day it is received by a payee or at a payee's processing site. – CH10

maker: The entity that creates a check or other negotiable instrument. Also referred to as a *payor*. – CH4

mark to market: The accounting act of recording the price or value of a security, portfolio, or account to reflect its current market value rather than its book value. – CH6

market risk: A type of risk that involves the possibility that fluctuations in financial market prices and rates will reduce the value of a security or a portfolio. It is usually divided into general risk (i.e., risk related to overall market rates and conditions) and firm-specific risk (i.e., risk related solely to an individual firm). – CH16

market value per share: The current price at which a share of stock is traded. Though this is not technically part of the accounting statements, it is often included in reports issued by a company and various financial reporting services. – CH6

marketability: A measure of the ability of a security to be bought and sold. Along with maturity, it is one of the primary determinants of liquidity. The existence of an active secondary market ensures that short-term securities suitable for liquidity management purposes are readily marketable. – CH5

master account: An account used by an organization to receive funds from collection accounts or to provide funding for disbursement accounts as part of a zero balance account (ZBA) arrangement. These accounts are sometimes referred to as *concentration accounts*. – CH12

master budget: An annual budget for an entire organization. The master budget has two chief components: (1) the operating budget or profit plan, and (2) the financial budget. – CH9

matching: An internal control method that involves the matching of an invoice to the original purchase order to help confirm the order was placed and that the invoice complies with the agreed terms. A further match against receiving records ensures the order was fulfilled. – CH10

material adverse change (MAC) clause: A clause in a loan agreement that allows a lender to refuse funding or declare a borrower to be in default, even if all agreements are in full compliance, if the lender believes a material adverse change has occurred in the borrower's condition. – CH6

materiality: An accounting concept that involves determining the significance of the impact of information on the financial position of the entity being reported. In most accounting applications, there is usually a significant degree of judgment involved in the preparation of the accounts. Where decisions are required about the appropriateness of a particular accounting judgment, the materiality convention suggests that this should only be an issue if the judgment is significant or material to the presentation of the accounts. The concept of materiality is therefore an important issue for auditors of financial accounts. – CH8

maturity-matching financing strategy: A current asset financing strategy that involves using long-term financing (e.g., debt and equity) to finance permanent current assets and fixed assets. Short-term financing is used to finance fluctuating current assets. – CH10

maturity-matching investment strategy: An investment strategy that involves matching the maturity of an investment to the future need for funds. – CH6

maturity premium: An adjustment to the base interest rate of a longer-term security to account for the increased price risk created by the longer maturity. – CH13

medium-term forecasting: A type of cash flow forecasting in which the forecasts are for periods of one to twelve months. These forecasts are an integral part of cash budgeting. They project the inflows (e.g., collections from sales and other sources of funds) and outflows (e.g., expenses and other uses of funds) on a monthly basis. They are used to determine the company's need for short-term credit or the availability of funds for short-term investing. They also serve as a benchmark for performance by comparing actual cash flows to projected cash flows based on the cash budget. – CH14

merchant acquirer: The financial institution that processes and settles payment card transactions on behalf of a merchant. – CH4

merchant discount: A type of bundled merchant card processing fee in which the merchant is charged one fee by its card processor that covers all of the cost components of the transaction. The term *discount* is used because this type of fee is typically subtracted directly from any card settlement. – CH4

merchant services: The term typically used to describe the products offered by a bank, Internet service provider, or other firm (referred to as a *merchant processor*) that processes credit and debit card transactions. While the term principally refers to the acceptance and processing of card transactions, it also often includes ancillary services such as returns and adjustments, point-of-sale (POS) terminals, supplies, and customer support. – CH12

message authentication: An electronic commerce security element that provides the ability to know, with a reasonable amount of certainty, who sent or received a message. – CH2

MICR line: The machine-readable information on the bottom of a check. A MICR line is printed using a special font and magnetic ink. *MICR* is an acronym for *magnetic ink character recognition*. While initially read using special magnetic scanning equipment, many MICR lines are now processed using optical character recognition. – CH4

middleware: Computer-based software that links two different applications. – CH10

mobile banking: The provision of banking and financial services with the help of mobile telecommunication devices, such as mobile phones and tablets. – CH15

mobile payments: Electronic payments made using mobile devices, such as mobile phones or tablets. – CH15

mobile wallet: An emerging payment type that uses smartphones and tablets equipped with near field communication (NFC) chips or a bar code. Examples include Alipay, Google Wallet, and Apple Pay. – CH4

Monetary Control Act: See *Depository Institutions Deregulation and Monetary Control Act of 1980 (DIDMCA)*. – CH2

monetary policy: Government policy related to monitoring and controlling a country's money supply and interest rates. – CH2

money laundering: Any financial transaction that generates an asset or a value as the result of an illegal act, which may involve actions such as tax evasion or false accounting. – CH2

money market: That part of the global financial market that deals with financial instruments that are easily converted to cash (highly liquid) and have very short maturities, typically one year or less. In addition, most money market instruments are debt-type securities, which are also known as *fixed-income securities*. – CH5

money market deposit account (MMDA): A type of demand deposit account that pays an unregulated rate of interest determined by individual institutions. Generally, there can be no more than six transfers or pre-authorized withdrawals per calendar month or statement cycle. Although transfers and pre-authorized debits are limited, in-person teller transactions are unlimited. – CH3

money market fund (MMF): A commingled pool of money market instruments, typically held by banks or investment firms, in which fund investors have an ownership interest. The funds may be offered in the local currency or, where allowed by local regulators, in a foreign currency. They generally have a net asset value set at one unit of the currency of the offering. Known as a *unit trust* in the United Kingdom and Europe. – CH5

money market yield (MMY): A calculation for restating semiannual, quarterly, or monthly discount bond or note yields into an annual yield. This type of yield is calculated on a 360-day year basis, while the bond equivalent yield is based on a 365-day year. – CH13

money order: A prepaid instrument issued by various third parties such as banks, postal services, or consumer outlets (e.g., convenience stores and check-cashing agencies), where the purchaser is the instrument's payor and the money order is the obligation of the issuer. – CH4

Monte Carlo simulation: A type of simulation/analytical technique in which a large number of simulations are run using random quantities selected from a probability distribution of values for specified variables. The resulting probability distribution is analyzed to infer which values are most likely to occur. – CH16

monthly billing: A term of sale whereby the seller issues a monthly statement covering all invoices prior to a cut-off date, typically toward the end of each month. – CH10

mortgage-backed security (MBS): A type of asset-backed security that uses pools of mortgages (mainly residential) as the source of cash flows to the investors. – CH5

mortgage bond: A type of bond used to finance specific assets pledged as security against the issue. Mortgage bonds usually include substantial financial covenants or indenture agreements. – CH6

multicurrency account: A special arrangement between a bank and a company, in which the bank lets the customer receive or make payments in a range of currencies from a single account or multiple subsidiary accounts. – CH10

multicurrency bond: A type of bond that is usually issued as (1) a currency option bond that allows investors to choose among several predetermined currencies, or (2) a currency cocktail bond that is denominated in a standard basket of several currencies (e.g., special drawing rights). – CH6

multifactor authentication: An authentication method for information technology and network purposes requiring the presence of different factors of authentication. – CH15

multilateral netting system: A type of netting system that is similar to a bilateral system but it involves more than two subsidiaries. Each subsidiary informs a central treasury management center of all planned cross-border payments through an electronic system. Multilateral netting is used primarily for intracompany transactions. – CH10

municipal bond (muni): A sub-sovereign bond issued by a municipality, typically in the United States and usually in the form of a general obligation or revenue bond. General obligation bonds are paid from the proceeds of general tax revenues. Alternatively, revenue bonds are linked directly to, and repaid from, the revenues generated from specific public projects or services (e.g., stadiums, toll roads and bridges, or public utilities). Most municipal bonds are exempt from federal and, in some cases, state and local income taxes. – CH6

municipal securities: Types of debt (bonds or notes) issued by city, county, or state government entities that generally have some type of income tax exemption for any interest paid on them. Commonly called *munis*. – CH3

mutual fund: A company that brings together money from many people and invests it in stocks, bonds, or other assets. The combined holdings of stocks, bonds, or other assets the fund owns are known as its *portfolio*. – CH5

mutual fund company: A company that brings together money from many people and invests it in stocks, bonds, or other assets. Each investor in the fund owns shares, which represent a part of these holdings. – CH6

NACHA, the Electronic Payments Association: A US membership organization of financial institutions and other stakeholders that establishes and administers the rules, standards, and procedures that enable members to exchange automated clearinghouse (ACH) payments on a national basis. The organization also levies fines for violations of the rules. NACHA membership includes a number of regional ACH associations that provide various educational, rules guidance, and other support services to their local members. Formerly known as the *National Automated Clearing House Association*. – CH4

National Book-Entry System (NBES): A real-time gross settlement system used for the transfer of US Treasury, government agency, and other securities. – CH5

National Credit Union Administration (NCUA): An independent, US federal agency that charters and supervises federal credit unions. The NCUA is backed by the full faith and credit of the US government. It also operates the National Credit Union Share Insurance Fund, insuring the savings of account holders in all federal credit unions and many state-chartered credit unions. – CH2

nationalization: A government takeover of all companies in a particular industry, often involving ore extraction, petroleum, transportation, or power generation and distribution businesses. – CH7

nationally recognized statistical rating organizations (NRSROs): Companies that assign credit ratings for issuers of certain types of short- and long-term debt obligations, as well as for the debt instruments themselves. Ratings can be on either a solicited or unsolicited basis. Also known as *credit rating agencies*. – CH13

natural disaster risk: A type of risk related to losses resulting from naturally occurring events, such as storms, floods, or earthquakes. Natural disaster events leave organizations open to possible operational risk. These events could range from a temporary power outage to a major earthquake or hurricane. Every organization should have a contingency business resumption plan in place to manage and recover from impacts of such events. This plan should also be tested on a regular basis. – CH16

natural hedge: The practice of offsetting foreign asset exposures effectively by borrowing funds to finance the assets in the same currency. This approach reduces the net exposure of the parent company. Also called a *balance sheet hedge*. – CH17

near field communication (NFC): A short-range wireless connectivity standard that uses magnetic field induction to enable communication between devices when they are touched together or brought within a few centimeters of each other. – CH4

negotiating bank: In a letter of credit transaction, this is the bank that examines the documents presented by the beneficiary, receives payment from the issuing bank, and pays the beneficiary. – CH12

net asset value (NAV): A value that represents the price per share of a mutual fund or an exchange-traded fund. It is generally calculated as the total value of all the securities or assets in the fund (less any liabilities) divided by the number of shares outstanding. For most funds, the NAV will fluctuate as the market values of the securities in the fund portfolio change. The primary exception is a money market fund, which generally has a fixed NAV equivalent to one unit of the currency of denomination. – CH5

net investment hedge: A type of hedge designed to hedge currency risk associated with the translation of subsidiary (or other foreign operations) financial statements into the parent firm's functional currency. – CH8

net present value (NPV): A type of financial analysis, this value is calculated by netting the present value (PV) of anticipated cash inflows with the PV of cash outflows. – CH9

net profit margin: A performance ratio that shows the percentage of profits earned after all expenses and taxes are deducted from revenues. It is defined as net income divided by revenues. Also known as *return on sales* or *return on revenues*. – CH9

net terms: A term of sale whereby the seller specifies a net due date by which the buyer must pay in full. – CH10

net working capital (NWC): A working capital metric that is defined as current assets less current liabilities. NWC is not a ratio: it is an absolute measure of the dollar amount by which current assets exceed current liabilities. – CH11

netting: An internal company (intercompany) payables system that is designed to reduce the number of cross-border payments among company units through the elimination or consolidation of funds denominated in different currencies. – CH10

nonbank intermediary: A financial services firm that does not accept deposits from the general public but may offer a variety of financial services including leasing, factoring, pension funds, mutual funds, and insurance plans. – CH4

noninsurance: An approach to risk retention, this technique involves relying on normal revenues to pay for small, normal losses as current expenses. Noninsurance is appropriate for losses that an organization can absorb readily as costs of doing business, but not for highly disruptive, potentially ruinous accidents. – CH16

non-repetitive (free-form) wire: A type of wire transfer where both the debit and credit parties can be changed for each transaction. As a result, additional security measures are typically required. Examples of such measures are callbacks, secondary levels of approval, and segregation of duties. – CH12

non-repudiation: The inability of the purported maker or originator of a statement, document, or payment to challenge the validity of the original item. The term may also be used to refer to the inability of a receiver to deny having received the item. – CH15

nonresident account: An account with a global financial institution that is owned by a nonresident of the country in which the global financial institution is chartered. – CH3

notional pooling: A type of pooling that requires a company's subsidiaries to use branches of the same bank. All excess and deficit balances in the company's subsidiary accounts are summed each day to calculate the net interest earned or due. Funds are not actually transferred; rather, they are simply totaled for the purpose of calculating interest. – CH12

notional principal: The base amount of a financial transaction, used to calculate interest payments. The notional principal is never actually exchanged, but is only used for calculation purposes, hence the term *notional*. In an interest rate swap, the notional principal is the dollar amount used to calculate the interest rate payments that are exchanged as part of the transaction. – CH17

off-balance-sheet arrangement (OBSA): A US Securities and Exchange Commission (SEC) term used to refer to any transaction, agreement, or other contractual arrangement that obligates the reporting company but does not appear on the balance sheet. It is intended to include off-balance-sheet arrangements for which a company may have contingent liabilities or obligations that are not readily apparent to an investor. These arrangements must be disclosed in the discussion portion of financial statements. – CH2

off-balance-sheet financing: A type of arrangement designed to provide financing that does not appear on the balance sheet. This is one type of off-balance-sheet arrangement. Examples of off-balance-sheet financing include joint ventures, research and development partnerships, and sales of receivables (factoring). Historically, operating leases have been included; however, in February 2016, the US-based Financial Accounting Standards Board (FASB) issued an Accounting Standards Update (ASU) that requires operating leases with terms of more than 12 months to be capitalized on the balance sheet. – CH2

Office of Foreign Assets and Control (OFAC): An office of the US Department of the Treasury that administers and enforces economic and trade sanctions based on US foreign policy and national security goals. Its objective is to identify and target threats to the national security, foreign policy, or economy of the United States. – CH2

Office of the Comptroller of the Currency (OCC): A bureau of the US Treasury Department that was established by Congress in 1863 to regulate the national banking system. It is the primary chartering authority and regulator for national banks. – CH2

official bank check: A type of check that is issued by the bank that draws on the bank's own funds. Also known as a *cashier's check*. – CH4

on-us check clearing: A type of check-clearing process that involves a single bank and occurs when a payee deposits a check in an account at the same bank on which it is drawn. – CH4

on-we check clearing: A type of check-clearing process that occurs when checks are deposited at a financial institution that are drawn on related financial institutions or on financial institutions that share a common check-processing system, thus eliminating the need to clear the checks through another bank. – CH4

ongoing validation: In the selection and validation of a forecasting model, this process involves using continuing feedback from projected versus actual comparisons and allows continuous evaluation and improvement of the forecast. – CH14

open account (open book credit): A form of credit extension that is the most common type of commercial trade credit. A seller issues an invoice as formal evidence of the obligation and records the sale as an account receivable. The buyer is billed for each transaction by an invoice and/or monthly statement. Full payment of invoiced amounts is expected within the specified credit terms unless certain discounts or deductions are available to the buyer. A buyer's creditworthiness is reviewed periodically, but the buyer does not need to apply for credit each time it places an order. – CH10

open item system: A cash application process most commonly used in business-to-business sales. Each invoice sent to a customer is recorded in the accounts receivable file. When a payment is received, it is matched with the specific invoices being paid. Any payment discrepancies are noted (e.g., discounts, allowances, adjustments, or returns). – CH10

open-loop card: A credit card—either bank-issued credit card, American Express, or Discover—that is accepted anywhere the card logo is displayed. – CH4

operating budget: A component of a master budget, this budget focuses on day-to-day operations. Also known as a *profit plan*. – CH9

operating cycle: A representation of the flow of funds through a company from the acquisition of raw materials, through the production cycle and the sale of products or services, and finally to the collection of payments from customers. – CH1

operating lease: A type of lease that is established in such a way that the lessor may maintain the equipment and retain ownership thereof at the end of the lease. These arrangements are often done on an off-balance-sheet basis, meaning that lease payments are reflected only on the income statement. – CH6

operating leverage: A concept that examines the responsiveness of operating profits to changes in sales. Operating leverage is determined by the extent to which fixed costs are used in a company's operating cost structure. The higher the proportion of fixed costs, the higher the company's operating leverage. – CH9

operating profit margin: A performance ratio that shows the percentage of revenue remaining after both the cost of goods sold and all operating expenses are deducted from revenue. It is computed as earnings before interest and taxes (EBIT) divided by revenues. – CH9

operational risk: The risk of direct and indirect losses resulting either from external events that impact an organization's operations or from inadequate and failed internal processes, people, and systems. Operational risk can be a significant cause of financial loss. – CH16

opportunity cost: The value of the best alternative not taken when two or more mutually exclusive alternatives are available. – CH9

optical character recognition (OCR): A processing method for data entry that reads preprinted information on remittance documents and creates a digital data file. – CH4

optimal capital structure: The mix of long-term debt and equity that produces the lowest overall weighted average cost of capital for a firm. Also known as a *target capital structure*. – CH20

option: A contract giving the buyer of the contract the right, but not the obligation, to buy or sell a fixed amount of an underlying asset at a fixed price on or before a specified date. – CH17

option premium: The price paid for the option contract. – CH17

order-to-cash timeline: The process or steps involved in converting orders or sales of goods into cash or good funds in the merchant's bank account. – CH10

originating depository financial institution (ODFI): In an automated clearinghouse transaction, this is the financial institution that initiates the transaction on the originator's behalf. – CH4

origination: An investment bank function that involves consultation with a company raising funds about the characteristics of a securities issue and any underlying documents. The investment bank also monitors market conditions and advises the company about the best time to bring the issue to market in order to maximize the price per issued share and the amount of funds the firm wishes to raise. – CH3

origination desk: A subset of trading professionals who are charged with evaluating, pricing, and managing the placement of new security issues. Also known as *originators*. – CH6

originator: (1) The party that creates an automated clearinghouse (ACH) transaction. (2) In investment banking, a subset of trading professionals who are charged with evaluating, pricing, and managing the placement of new security issues. Also known as an *origination desk*. – CH4

other-than-temporary impairment (OTTI): A classification for securities that are impaired (i.e., market value is less than adjusted cost) and whose impairment is not or cannot be expected to be cured in the foreseeable future. If a security is considered to be temporarily impaired due to market or credit conditions, then there is considerable flexibility in accounting for that security. If, on the other hand, the impairment is deemed to be other-than-temporary, then the Financial Accounting Standards Board has provided amended guidelines (ASC Codification Topic 325: *Investments—Other*) for the valuation of these securities. – CH13

out-of-sample validation: In the selection and validation of a forecasting model, this process tests the forecast using data that were not used to develop it. – CH14

outsourcing: Utilizing a third party to perform all or part of a core function. – CH1

over-the-counter (OTC) market: A type of market that is more decentralized than a formal securities exchange. OTC markets also rely upon electronic communication to conduct trading activity in an auction-style market between participating brokers and dealers. Government, municipal, and corporate debt, and some equity issuances that are not traded on exchanges, are sometimes traded in the OTC markets. – CH2

overdraft: A situation that occurs when items are presented against a demand deposit account in excess of the balance in that account. – CH3

par value: An arbitrary amount (usually stated in the corporate charter) that indicates the minimum amount stockholders have put up (or must put up) in the event of bankruptcy. – CH2

payable through draft (PTD): A payment instrument resembling a check that is drawn against the payor rather than the bank. It is handled like a check through the clearing process, but the responsibility for paying the draft lies with the payor, referred to as the *drawee* in the case of drafts. – CH4

payables conversion period: See *days' payables.* – CH10

payback period: The number of years required to recover the initial investment in an asset or project. – CH9

payee: In a payment system, the one receiving the payment. – CH4

payee positive pay: A positive pay service that matches against the payee field, in addition to the serial number and amount of a check, in an effort to detect an altered payee. – CH12

paying bank: In a payment clearing process, the bank or financial institution where the payor's account resides. The paying bank processes the value transfer on the payor's behalf. – CH4

Payment Card Industry Data Security Standard (PCI DSS): A worldwide information security standard defined by the Payment Card Industry Security Standards Council. The standard was created to help organizations that process card payments prevent payment card fraud through increased controls around the data they hold and exchange. The standard applies to all organizations that store, process, or transmit cardholder information from any card branded with the logo of one of the major card brands. – CH4

payment float: The period of time between the day that a bill or invoice is sent/received (depending on the perspective of the seller or buyer) and the day that payment is actually credited to the biller's bank account. – CH10

payment system: A series of processes and technologies (a payment instrument, a clearing channel, and a settlement mechanism) that transfer monetary value from one party to another. – CH4

payor: In a payment system, the one making the payment. – CH4

payroll card (pay card): A prefunded stored-value card used to replace payroll checks or direct deposit of payroll. – CH4

pension fund: A fund that invests contributions from employers and/or employees for the future retirement needs of the employees. – CH2

pension plan: A type of retirement plan, usually tax-exempt, wherein an employer makes contributions toward a pool of funds set aside for an employee's future benefit. The pool of funds is then invested on the employee's behalf, allowing the employee to receive benefits upon retirement. – CH2

per-occurrence basis: A method for determining the deductible on an insurance policy claim, where the deductible applies for each occurrence during the policy period. – CH16

percentage-of-sales method: A medium-term cash forecasting technique that involves projecting financial statements based on the historical relationship between sales and liquid balance sheet accounts that tend to change in value along with sales. Cash, accounts receivable, inventory, and accounts payable are the more important accounts. Account size (e.g., cash or inventory) is expressed as a percentage of sales. This percentage is then used in conjunction with forecasted sales to produce a forecast of account size. – CH14

performance guarantee: A type of guarantee requested by a lender for a loan to a subsidiary of another organization. In some cases, the lender may ask for specific performance guarantees relative to the assets being financed. Under a full guarantee, the parent fully guarantees performance by the subsidiary. Under a best-efforts guarantee, the parent agrees to use its best efforts to persuade the subsidiary to perform, but it does not guarantee subsidiary performance. – CH6

performance measurement: The ongoing monitoring and evaluating of the performance of an investment, portfolio, individual, department, or organization. – CH7

performance ratio: A type of ratio that measures profit relative to the amount of revenue or the level of financing. – CH9

permanent capital: Capital that is made up of common stock. This type of capital is called *permanent* because (unlike loan capital) it is meant never to be paid back. – CH20

personal guarantee: A type of guarantee in which a lender may require a personal pledge on the part of the owner or other principals in a business before granting a loan to the business. This is more common for smaller, privately held companies. – CH6

Phoenix-Hecht's *The Blue Book of Bank Prices*: An annually published comparison of key bank service charges. – CH7

physical and electronic security risk: Risk related to unauthorized physical or electronic access to premises or information. Many organizations require physical security for their premises and employees to help prevent physical or electronic access to critical information (e.g., identity theft), as well as to ensure employees' safety. Security measures also may include biometric systems, using such technologies as fingerprint, face, or iris (eye) recognition to control physical access to facilities or key equipment. Physical security is especially important for financial institutions, utilities, and defense contractors. – CH16

physical pooling: A type of pooling that requires the use of a single currency because balances are physically transferred out of subaccounts and into a main account on a daily basis. This type of pooling can be used in cross-border structures. – CH12

pledge: Collateral pledged or promised by a borrower to a lender (usually in return for a loan). The lender has the right to seize the collateral if the borrower defaults on the obligation. – CH6

Point-of-Purchase (POP) Check Conversion: A type of check conversion that occurs when customers' checks are scanned at the cash register (point of purchase, or POP), capturing the account information from the magnetic ink character recognition (MICR) line on the check. The MICR line data are converted into an automated clearinghouse (ACH) debit, and the check is voided and returned to the customer, who then signs a debit authorization in the form of a register receipt. Also, a US ACH format for the same process. *POP* is the standard entry class (SEC) code for this format. – CH12

political risk: A term applied to a variety of actions that a government may take that negatively impact a company's operations and/or value. It includes the risk that a company's operations in a foreign country may be nationalized or expropriated by the government of that country. – CH6

pooling: A typical method of cash concentration in countries where banks can pay interest on excess demand deposit balances and charge interest on deficit balances. – CH12

positive pay: A disbursement service used to combat payment (primarily check, but increasingly ACH) fraud, wherein a company transmits a file of payment information to the disbursement bank either at or before the time of the physical distribution of checks or anticipated ACH debits. The bank matches check serial numbers and dollar amounts of checks presented for payment against the issue database and pays only those checks or ACH transactions that match all relevant criteria. Any exceptions are conveyed to the company for its decision whether to pay or return the item. – CH12

prearranged bankruptcy: A type of bankruptcy in which management arranges a tentative deal with some of the creditors or parties, but not with all of them. Generally, these deals are done on an informal basis and are not legally binding. – CH2

Prearranged Payment and Deposit (PPD): A US automated clearinghouse (ACH) format that acts as the payment application by which consumers authorize a company or a financial institution to credit or debit an account for normally recurring payments in fixed amounts. *PPD* is the standard entry class (SEC) code for this format. – CH12

pre-authorized draft: A payment instrument that authorizes the payee to draw/draft against the payor's account. Also known as a *remotely created check (RCC)*. – CH4

predictable cash flow: In the cash flow forecasting process, this is a cash flow component that can be predicted with reasonable accuracy. – CH14

predictive forecast: A type of forecast that attempts to predict or project what will happen in the future. – CH14

preemptive right: A shareholder right that provides existing shareholders the first right to purchase shares of any new stock issue on a pro rata basis and based on the proportion of shares owned. – CH20

preferred stock: An investment security that is a type of equity, but is different from common stock in terms of its stockholder rights and dividend payment streams. In terms of cash flows, it is more like debt than equity because of the fixed dividend payments. Unlike with debt, however, a company does not risk bankruptcy by missing a preferred stock dividend. Another difference is that dividend payments on preferred stock do not have the tax deductibility feature that interest payments on debt do; therefore, the cost is generally much higher than that of a similar debt issue. – CH6

prepackaged (prepac) bankruptcy: A type of bankruptcy in which management files with the US Securities and Exchange Commission a formal plan that all classes of creditors have voted on and accepted. Essentially, the firm goes to court with all of the details worked out and with everyone agreeing to the plan. – CH2

present value (PV): The value at the present time of anticipated future cash flows or payments. – CH9

primary market: A financial market that offers newly issued debt and equity securities to investors when firms or government units sell securities to raise funds. – CH6

principle preservation: See *capital preservation*. – CH1

private equity: An investment of either common or preferred stock in an operating company that is not publicly traded on an exchange. This investment sometimes involves the acquisition of an entire company. – CH2

private-label financing: A type of financing in which a third party operates the credit function in the seller's name rather than the seller administering a credit program in-house. – CH10

private market: A financial market for private, or direct, placement, in which securities are offered and sold to a limited number of investors and not offered to the general public. The investment banking firm, acting as a broker to bring the issuer and investors together, meets with prospective buyers and confirms the details of the offering. – CH6

private placement: The practice of the direct sale of long-term loans to institutional investors, such as insurance companies and hedge funds. – CH3

process risk: A type of internal operational risk related to an organization's processes. Many organizations experience substantial exposure to losses related to the processes employed in day-to-day business operations. Process risk can arise from any functional area of a business, including procurement, manufacturing, sales, or fulfillment. The risk usually comes from a lack of proper controls or the failure of employees to follow procedures. – CH16

processing float: The time interval or delay between the time the payee or the payee's processing site receives the payment and the time the payment (typically a check) is deposited into the payee's account. – CH10

procure-to-pay timeline: The time from the purchase of raw materials, retail goods, or services until payment is received and collected. – CH10

profitability index (PI): A cost/benefit measurement that is similar to net present value, PI is a ratio of the present value gained to the cost required to obtain that value. It shows value gained per dollar of investment. PI is calculated as present value of cash inflows divided by present value of cash outflows. – CH9

project financing: A type of financing that applies to large projects, often in the energy area (e.g., energy exploration, refineries, and utility power plants). Project financing is also used for private infrastructure (e.g., stadiums, shopping centers, toll roads, and commercial or residential developments). The typical project financing arrangement is complex, involving several companies or sponsors forming a separate legal entity to operate the project. Lenders are paid from the project's cash flows and generally do not have recourse to the project's individual sponsors or owners. – CH6

projected closing cash position: A forecast of the day's ending cash position that is determined by taking the day's opening available bank balance(s), adding any expected settlements in the collection (lockbox, wire, and automated clearinghouse) and concentration accounts (depository banks), and deducting any projected disbursement totals. A projected closing cash position statement is also known as a *daily cash forecast* or merely a *cash report*. – CH14

promissory note: The legal portion of a debt contract; an unconditional promise to pay a specified amount plus interest at a defined rate either on demand or on a certain date. – CH6

proof of deposit (POD): An availability assignment method used in banking in which availability is assigned to each check as it is processed. – CH4

property insurance: A type of insurance that provides for reimbursement in the event of a loss of or damage to some type of asset (e.g., buildings, equipment, or inventory). Policies often cover the replacement value of the items in question, paying the costs of completely replacing those assets at their current market prices rather than at their historical or book value. – CH16

proxy: An instrument by which a shareholder can assign his/her right to vote at the annual meeting to another individual. – CH20

public-key infrastructure (PKI): A data encryption methodology designed to provide security over traditionally unsecure networks, such as the Internet. PKI involves the use of dual keys: a public key and a private key. – CH15

purchase price: The price that an investor pays for a security. This price is important as it is the main component in calculating the returns achieved by the investor. – CH13

purchasing card: A payment card, typically a credit card, used by a business for the purchase of supplies, inventory, equipment, and service contracts. Also known as a *procurement card* or *p-card*. – CH4

put option: A type of option contract that gives the contract owner the right, but not the obligation, to sell (put) the underlying asset to the contract writer at a fixed price through the delivery date. – CH17

put provision: A condition that allows a bondholder to resell a bond back to the issuer at a price, which is generally par, on certain stipulated dates prior to maturity. The put provision is an added degree of security for the bondholder, since it establishes a floor price for the bond. – CH6

qualified institutional buyer (QIB): In US law, this is an investor that is specifically recognized as being financially sophisticated and needing less protection than typical consumers. QIBs are primarily institutional investors that manage at least $100 million in securities, and can be financial institutions, pension funds, corporations, insurance companies, investment companies, or employee benefit plans, or an entity owned entirely by qualified investors. Known outside the United States as a *qualified institutional investor (QII)*. – CH6

qualified institutional investor (QII): An investor that is specifically recognized as being financially sophisticated and needing less protection than typical consumers. QIIs are primarily institutional investors that manage at least $100 million in securities, and can be financial institutions, pension funds, corporations, insurance companies, investment companies, or employee benefit plans, or an entity owned entirely by qualified investors. Known in the United States as a *qualified institutional buyer (QIB)*. – CH6

quantitative credit analysis: A type of credit analysis that begins with an analysis of the applicant's financial statements, usually using ratio analysis. Liquidity and working capital ratios, debt management and coverage ratios, and profability measures are most often included. – CH10

quick ratio (acid test ratio): A liquidity ratio that is calculated as cash plus short-term investments and accounts receivable, divided by total current liabilities. It is also known as the *acid test ratio* because it is a more stringent measure of liquidity than the current ratio. – CH11

RAROC: See *risk-adjusted return on capital.* – CH9

rating agency/credit rating agency: A company that assigns credit ratings which rate a debtor's (1) ability to pay back debt by making timely interest payments and (2) likelihood of default. – CH6

real risk-free rate of interest: The rate demanded by savers (or investors) to compensate for delaying their use of the money today, in the absence of any risk or inflation, for a one-year maturity. – CH13

real-time gross settlement (RTGS) system: A type of payment system in which each transaction results in a separate value transfer between the payor and payee, and the payment to the payee is final and irrevocable at the time the receiving bank's account is credited or at the time the receiving bank is notified of the payment, whichever is earlier. A common example of an RTGS system is a wire transfer system. – CH4

receipts and disbursements forecast: A short-term cash forecasting model, this forecast begins by creating separate schedules of cash receipts and disbursements, and then combining them. The schedules are prepared on a cash basis, rather than on an accrual basis, due to the need to forecast cash rather than earnings. The model tends to forecast cash accurately in the short term and near medium term, especially when accounts receivable and accounts payable data are incorporated. – CH14

receipts schedule: A component of the receipts and disbursements forecast process, this is a projection of collections from customers (e.g., cash sales or payments on accounts receivable) and other cash inflows (e.g., interest or dividends received from investments). It also should include expected, nonrecurring cash inflows, such as the proceeds from asset sales and external financing activities. – CH14

receivables conversion period: See *days' receivables.* – CH10

receiver: The payee or beneficiary of an ACH payment whose account is credited (increased) for the value of the transaction. – CH4

receiving bank: In a payment clearing process, this is the bank or financial institution where the payee's account resides. It processes the transaction on behalf of the payee. – CH4

receiving depository financial institution (RDFI): In an automated clearinghouse transaction, this is the financial institution that acts as an intermediary between the originator and the receiver, on the receiver's side of the transaction. – CH4

recourse: A term related to using a factoring arrangement. In this case, the seller is liable for any bad debts the factor cannot collect. – CH6

Red Flags Rule: US regulation requiring FIs and creditors to develop and implement written identity theft prevention programs that provide for the identification of, detection of, and response to patterns, practices, or specific activities (i.e., red flags) that could indicate identity theft. – CH2

refinancing: The replacement of an existing debt with a new obligation before the maturity of the original debt, typically with different terms. Refinancing of bonds is often done following periods of high interest rates. During high interest rate periods, many entities that must issue bonds attach call provisions that allow the bonds to be redeemed prior to maturity. – CH6

regression analysis: A statistical cash forecasting method that can be used to assess the impact that multiple variables (or causes) have on a value or an outcome. It is a sophisticated method that requires large amounts of data. – CH14

regulatory compliance risk: A type of operational risk that relates to compliance with regulatory requirements. Part of overall operational risk stems from the requirement to comply with many regulations of federal, state, local, and industry-specific regulatory agencies, as well as compliance with accounting rules and guidelines for financial transactions and money laundering. This also can include tax risk (related to uncertainty about future tax liabilities), especially for multinational organizations that deal with a wide variety of sometimes conflicting tax codes and regulations. There is also an operational risk component to tax risk, given the penalties often assessed with missed filings or the underpayment of taxes. – CH16

reinvestment risk: The risk associated with the potential of lower interest rates when investing proceeds from maturing investments. – CH5

re-invoicing: An intracompany method of centralizing the responsibility for monitoring and collecting international accounts receivable to more effectively manage related foreign exchange exposures. – CH10

reject item: A check that is rejected by a bank's automated check-processing equipment. Most reject items arise either because of physical defects in the MICR line or because the MICR line does not meet banking industry specifications. – CH4

relationship review: A periodic assessment of service levels and responsiveness, both quantitatively and qualitatively, of a financial service provider. Scorecards are tools that are useful in conducting this type of review. – CH7

relaxed current asset investment strategy: A current asset management strategy in which a company maintains high levels of current assets relative to sales. A large investment in current assets is likely to lower investment returns, but the firm operates with less risk because of its larger liquid asset balances. – CH10

remitting bank: In a documentary collection process, this is the bank of the seller/exporter. It receives the collection documents from the seller. – CH12

remote deposit capture (RDC): In an over-the-counter field deposit system, this is a process that allows an organization to scan and image checks, then transmit those images to its depository bank for posting and clearing, instead of having to deposit physical checks. In the United States, the bank then transmits the images to the Federal Reserve or another image exchange network for clearing. – CH4

remotely created check (RCC): See *pre-authorized draft.* – CH4

repatriation of capital: The transfer of funds from foreign subsidiaries back to the parent company in the home country. – CH20

repetitive wire: A type of wire transfer used when a company makes frequent transfers to the same credit parties. Only the date and the dollar amount may be changed on a repetitive wire. – CH12

representations: Along with warranties, these are the existing conditions at the time when a loan agreement is executed, as attested to by the borrower. – CH6

Re-Presented Check Entry (RCK): A US automated clearinghouse (ACH) format used to transmit ACH debit entries in place of a paper check that has been returned for insufficient or uncollected funds. The general requirements are that the item be less than $2,500 and be drawn on a consumer account. RCK originators must provide advance notice to the check writer (e.g., in a customer statement or at the point of sale) that any check returned for insufficient or uncollected funds may be collected electronically. *RCK* is the standard entry class (SEC) code for this format. – CH12

repurchase agreement (repo): An agreement in which a bank or securities dealer sells government securities it owns to an investor and agrees to repurchase them at a later date and at a slightly higher price. In most cases, this type of agreement is referred to as a *repo agreement* from the perspective of the entity selling the securities and agreeing to repurchase them at a later date. From the perspective of the entity that buys the securities with a promise to sell them back at a later date, it is generally known as a *reverse repo.* – CH5

reputation risk: The risk that customers, suppliers, investors, and/or regulators may decide that a company has a bad reputation and decide not to do business with that company. For financial institutions, this type of risk is especially important and is covered under Basel guidelines. Reputation risk also relates to how companies react to unexpected events that can impact their reputations and ultimately their futures. – CH16

request for information (RFI): A document requesting information about a vendor's interest in, and ability to, provide services. The requesting company provides a formal description of its needs and asks selected vendors to provide general information as to how they could meet the company's needs. – CH7

request for proposal (RFP): A formal document prepared by a sourcing company that outlines objectives, needs, and service requirements and may be used to obtain bids for anything ranging from one specific service to a company's entire relationship. – CH7

request for quotation/quote (RFQ): A document whose purpose is to invite suppliers into a bidding process on specific products or services. It is best suited to products and services that are essentially standardized and/or commoditized, which makes each supplier's quote easily comparable to others. – CH7

required majority ownership: A type of political risk in which a government requires that companies must be owned by resident nationals. – CH7

reserve requirement: A central bank requirement that establishes the minimum percentage of customer deposits that financial institutions must hold as reserves and not lend out to other customers. The reserve requirement is an important part of managing monetary policy. In the United States, the reserve requirement is also a factor in the computation of earnings credit computation, since it represents a US financial institution's compensation for the level of balances it is required to maintain with the Federal Reserve. As of the date of publication, the reserve requirement was 10% of collected balances. – CH2

residual value: (1) The amount of value remaining after all allowable depreciation charges have been subtracted from a depreciable asset. (2) The estimated value of an asset at the end of a lease. – CH20

restrictive current asset investment strategy: A current asset management strategy in which a company maintains low levels of current assets relative to sales. This strategy is typically the most profitable as long as unexpected events do not drive down liquidity to the point that it causes severe problems. – CH10

retail lockbox: A lockbox system used primarily to process high-volume, small-dollar consumer remittances (consumer-to-business) that frequently involve recurring, monthly installment payments. – CH12

retained earnings: A balance sheet account that represents the accumulated net earnings of a corporation since its inception, less dividends paid to shareholders. It also represents the changes in shareholders' equity arising from the retention of profits and losses of the company, less any dividends paid out to shareholders. – CH8

retrospectively (retro) rated insurance program: A type of insurance program in which the insured's cost of coverage for a policy period varies with the insured's losses during that period. Such programs are used often for workers' compensation and product liability insurance plans. The insured pays a standard, or deposit, premium at the beginning of the coverage period. At the end of the period, the insurer computes a final premium based on an agreed-upon formula that varies with the insured's actual costs or losses (subject to limits) for the policy period. – CH16

return item: A check that is returned to the bank of first deposit. – CH4

return on assets (ROA): A performance ratio that measures net income in relation to the investment in assets. A greater value for this ratio implies a larger net income per dollar invested in assets. It is computed as net income divided by total assets. – CH9

return on common equity (ROE): A performance ratio that measures the amount of earnings available to common shareholders relative to the level of their investment in the company. It is computed as earnings available to common shareholders divided by common equity. – CH9

return on investment (ROI): A performance measurement ratio that calculates profit per dollar of invested capital. It is computed by dividing net income by invested capital (or long-term debt and equity). – CH9

reverse positive pay: A process whereby a company's bank transmits a file of the checks presented for payment to the company on a daily or intraday basis. Within a specified time deadline, the company matches this file to a list of checks issued and notifies the bank of any items to be returned. – CH12

revolver: See *revolving credit agreement*. – CH10

revolving credit: A form of credit extension whereby a company grants credit without requiring specific transaction approval, as long as the account remains current. – CH10

revolving credit agreement: A committed line of credit established for a specified period of time, often on a multiyear basis. Revolving credits are formal, contractual commitments with loan agreements, including covenants. Also known as a *revolver*. – CH10

risk-adjusted discount rate (RADR): A type of cost/benefit analysis that essentially requires high-risk endeavors to earn a higher rate of return in order to justify the investment. When properly applied, RADR allows a firm to more closely match its capital needs to available sources and to better manage its overall levels of risk and return. – CH9

risk-adjusted return on capital (RAROC): A method of determining the economic value of a transaction or activity based upon the anticipated risk-adjusted performance of the activity. – CH9

risk and control self-assessment (RCSA): A risk profile analysis process that identifies the risks, classifies each risk into clearly defined categories, and quantifies the risks with respect to the probability of occurrence and the impact on value and/or cash flows. The analysis can be used to evaluate the effectiveness of the risk reduction measures that are employed. In some organizations, this process is known as a *risk self-assessment*. – CH16

risk financing: The process of identifying and/or raising the funds needed to recover from a loss. Risk-financing techniques involve resources that an organization may draw upon to finance recovery from losses and liabilities for which it is held responsible. Risk financing competes with other uses of corporate funds. Sound financial management requires integrating the organization's risk-financing needs with other more traditionally productive uses. – CH16

risk-free asset: A type of asset that has a certain future return. US Treasuries (especially Treasury bills) are considered to be risk-free because they are backed by the US government. – CH19

risk profile: An assessment of how a company's overall value changes as the price of financial variables changes. The basic risk profile for a public company shows how the firm's earnings per share, common stock price, or overall value respond to changes in interest rates, foreign exchange rates, or commodity prices. – CH16

risk retention: A risk-financing approach that involves the use of an organization's internal financial resources (including credit, if appropriate) to provide funds to finance a recovery from losses. In other words, the organization retains some or all of the loss, rather than transferring it by paying someone else (e.g., an insurance organization) to take it. – CH16

risk retention group: A special type of group captive formed under the terms of a US federal law that is designed to enable business firms to work together to jointly finance product liability claims. It is often used in industries with a high potential for catastrophic losses, such as the airline industry and certain professional occupations (e.g., physicians in high-risk practice areas, accountants, or lawyers). To the extent that risks are shared, this is considered insurance. – CH16

risk/return trade-off: The principle that potential return rises with an increase in risk. Low levels of uncertainty or risk are associated with low potential returns, whereas high levels of uncertainty or risk are associated with high potential returns. According to the risk/return trade-off, invested money can render higher profits only if the investor is willing to accept the possibility of losses. – CH18

risk transfer: The shifting of responsibility for a risk from one party to another, often through insurance. The essence of any risk transfer is a contract between a transferring organization (the transferor) and another entity (the transferee), under which the transferee agrees to pay designated types of the transferor's losses within contractual limits. The transferor may have to pay the transferee a fee (e.g., an insurance premium) for this promise of indemnity, or the transferor may have the bargaining power to secure this promise as a condition for agreeing to do business with the transferee. – CH16

rolling forecast: A type of forecast in which the period of the forecast assumptions are reviewed and the forecast is updated or "rolled" forward at the end of each period. Typically, the number of periods in the forecast (days, weeks, months, etc.) remains constant, but old periods are dropped and new periods are added as the forecast progresses. – CH14

Rule 2a-7: A regulation instituted by the US Securities and Exchange Commission (SEC) that restricts investments in money market funds by quality, maturity, and diversity. The 2010 version of this rule imposes minimum liquidity requirements, implements daily and weekly liquidity requirements, and restricts the ability of funds to purchase illiquid and lower-quality securities. New rules implemented in 2016 include a floating net asset value (NAV), redemption fees if a fund's weekly liquid assets fall below a threshold, and the ability to suspend redemptions (using restrictions known as *redemption gates*) for a period of up to 10 business days. – CH5

sales tax: A type of tax that is charged at the point of purchase for certain goods and services. The tax amount is typically calculated by applying a percentage rate to the taxable price of a sale. – CH2

Sarbanes-Oxley Act of 2002 (SOX): US legislation that requires companies to evaluate and disclose their internal financial controls as they relate to financial reporting, and requires auditors to attest to, or confirm, the effectiveness of these controls. It further requires that chief executive officers and chief financial officers certify financial statements, and specifies fines and jail sentences for knowingly and willfully misstating information therein. The act also requires companies with publicly traded securities to maintain independent audit committees (of the board of directors) that can interact with the external auditor in an unfettered way. – CH2

Sarbanes-Oxley Act (SOX) Section 404: A section of SOX that requires managers to state their responsibility for establishing and maintaining adequate internal controls for financial reporting. – CH18

savings account: A type of interest-bearing depository account owned mainly by individuals and not-for-profit institutions. Historically, many of these accounts were known as *passbook savings accounts*. – CH3

scenario analysis: A method for assessing investment risk, this type of what-if analysis assesses possible outcomes under a range of circumstances. It is used frequently to establish the lower bound (i.e., worst case) and upper bound (i.e., best case) of outcomes. Scenario analysis is similar to sensitivity analysis, but more than one variable is altered at a time. Scenario analysis usually starts with a base case—an expected value for each input variable affecting the final value. – CH9

scorecard: A management tool used to measure a service provider's performance in both a qualitative and quantitative method. The primary purpose of a scorecard is to provide a quantitative measure of the service provided and the benefit received, but it also provides feedback for the service provider to better understand how the customer perceives the value, quality, and cost of the service(s) provided. – CH7

scrap/obsolete items: A category of inventory that includes items from the production process that are left over (i.e., scrap) or no longer useful (i.e., obsolete items). In some industries, such as steel and aluminum manufacturing, scrap from production can be reused in later batches or sold to recyclers. A portion of a company's inventories may become obsolete or damaged, especially in environments where there are rapid changes in existing products or introductions of new products. – CH10

seasonal dating: A term of sale whereby the seller agrees to accept payment at the end of the buyer's selling season. – CH10

seasoned equity offering (SEO): A type of stock offering in which new stock shares are sold by a company that has shares already trading on an exchange or in the over-the-counter market. The market price of existing shares guides the price for new shares. – CH6

secondary market: A financial market that trades previously issued securities. Existing debt and equity issues are traded by retail and institutional investors in secondary markets through established exchanges or through over-the-counter markets. Since the securities are bought and sold among investors, the issuing firm neither experiences a cash flow nor a change in the number of securities outstanding. – CH6

Securities and Exchange Commission (SEC): A US federal agency designed to maintain a fair and orderly market for investors by regulating and supervising securities sales. – CH2

securities exchange: An organized stock exchange that facilitates the buying and selling of debt and equity securities. – CH6

securities trader: Within an investment bank or brokerage firms, this is a market participant who helps to maintain active, orderly, secondary markets for all equity and debt instruments. – CH6

securitization: The practice of pooling various debt contracts, such as consumer loans, credit card debt, and mortgages, and using them as a basis for issuing securities. Many types of debt instruments are securitized to increase liquidity, thus lowering the cost of capital to borrowers. The primary corporate applications of securitization are accounts receivable and inventory. These are bundled together to collateralize securities, making them more liquid and attractive to investors. – CH6

security device: In electronic payment security, this is a key or token used to guard against misuse or fraud. – CH15

segregation of duties: The concept of having more than one person required to complete a specific activity, such as making a vendor payment or collecting and posting revenue from customers. Segregation, or separation, of duties is a key internal control issue that is important in managing risk and reducing fraud. At an operational level, responsibilities such as approval, authorization, and verification functions, including expense approval, check-signing authority, and account reconciliation, should be separated. – CH12

seigniorage: Government revenue from the issuance of coin and currency, which is based on the difference between the value of the money and the cost to produce it. Historically, it arose from the manufacture of coins, which were worth more than the metal used to mint the coins. – CH2

self-insurance: An approach used by some organizations as an alternative to purchasing insurance, this practice is not technically a form of insurance because it does not involve a transfer of risk to an insurer or another separate entity; instead, the organization will cover its own losses. It is often used by large organizations to manage their employee health care expenses. The term *self-insurance* can describe any risk retention program, even quite informal, unfunded arrangements. Self-insured retention (SIR) is the component of loss covered by the insured in a policy. – CH16

semi-repetitive wire: A type of wire transfer where the debit and credit parties remain the same (as in a repetitive wire transfer), but the description (e.g., a customer or an invoice number) may be changed, along with the date and the dollar amount. – CH12

sensitivity analysis: A method of assessing investment risk, this type of analysis determines how a final outcome, such as net present value, is influenced by changes in the value of a particular variable (e.g., sales, or an operating or financing cost) and how vulnerable the expected outcome is to changes in a specific assumption. Note that with sensitivity analysis only one variable at a time is changed, rather than a set of variables as in scenario analysis. – CH9

service agreement: A legal document (contract) that describes the requirements and expectations of both the purchaser and provider of a specific service or services. – CH7

service charge: An explicit fee or price charged for service(s) provided by a financial institution. Service charges are either expressed as a flat monthly fee or as a per-item or per-unit price. In the case of the latter, the unit price is multiplied by the volume to arrive at the analysis period total (in the account analysis process). – CH3

service industry ratios: Ratios used in ratio analysis of firms in the service sector. Service companies typically have small investments in buildings and land, and rely more on human talent than physical assets. – CH9

service lease: See *operating lease*. – CH20

service level agreement (SLA): An agreement (which may be a separate document or part of a service agreement) that specifies the level of service expected from a financial service provider, along with a description of any penalties for failure to comply with the requirements of the agreement. – CH7

settlement: In a payment system, this is the actual movement of funds from the payor's account to the payee's account. – CH4

settlement mechanism: In a payment system, this is the mechanism or operation used to complete the transfer of value from the payor to the payee. – CH4

settlement risk: A form of counterparty credit risk that is related to the probability that a party funding a particular transaction will default on the actual payment or settlement obligation. In a foreign exchange (FX) transaction, settlement risk is the risk that one party to the transaction provides the currency it agreed to sell but does not receive the currency it agreed to buy. Thus, the transaction is not settled. – CH4

shared services center (SSC): A department or operation within a multiunit organization tasked with supplying multiple business units and their respective divisions and departments with specialized services, such as information technology (IT), human resources (HR), or accounts payable (A/P) services. In some companies this includes day-to-day treasury operations (cash management) and other treasury functions, which may be operated as SSCs. – CH1

short-term financial investment: An investment using short-term instruments with a maturity of less than one year. – CH5

short-term financing: A financing strategy used to meet temporary cash needs for periods of one year or less. – CH10

short-term forecasting: A type of cash forecasting in which the forecasts typically range from one to thirty days in length and predict cash receipts and disbursements, as well as the resulting balances, on a daily, weekly, or monthly basis. – CH14

sight draft: A draft that is payable upon presentment, provided all of the terms of the draft have been met. Sight drafts are often presented in combination with other documents, such as titles or bills of lading. If all the documentation is in order, then the draft is payable upon presentment (i.e., at sight). – CH4

signature card: A document businesses furnish to banks to show the signatures of authorized signers (or specimens of both facsimile and computerized signatures) for all accounts. – CH7

simple moving average: A statistical cash forecasting methodology (and type of time series forecasting) that bases the forecast on a rolling average of past values for a series. – CH14

simulation: A method of assessing investment risk, this method combines scenario and sensitivity analyses, allowing certain assumptions in a decision model to fluctuate simultaneously. – CH9

Single Euro Payments Area (SEPA): The name of the European Union (EU) payments integration initiative. SEPA focuses on the technical, legal, and commercial barriers to paying and/or receiving euros cross-border within SEPA boundaries. SEPA establishes minimum standards and common pricing for payments processing within the EU. – CH2

single-parent captive: An approach to risk retention in which a subsidiary is owned for the purpose of insuring the risk of a parent company or its affiliates. The captive provides guaranteed access to insurance, may be used to provide unique types of insurance coverage or favorable rates, and often generates tax advantages for the parent company. A major loss could result in insolvency for the captive, but the parent company would survive. – CH16

single payment note: A type of note that is usually granted for a short period of time and specific purpose, with both the principal and interest amounts paid at maturity. Because of the limited duration and precise maturity of a single payment note, a specific cash flow event is frequently identified as the repayment source at the time the funds are advanced. – CH13

single sign-on (SSO): A software technique that allows an individual to enter one user name and password in order to access multiple applications on the same network or at the same host. – CH15

single-use card: A disposable credit card number that looks like a regular credit card number, but includes an embedded expiration date and security code, and will only work for a single use. – CH4

sinking fund: A fund that is the result of a provision that may be attached to a bond issue. It generally requires the issuer to set aside this pool of funds, which can be used to repay the bond's principal at maturity. – CH6

small-value transfer system: An electronic network for the exchange of smaller payment instructions among financial institutions, typically on behalf of consumers. Examples include ACH in the US, Bacs in the United Kingdom, and ECG in Hong Kong. – CH4

smart card: A typical payment card with the addition of a computer chip with related circuitry that can be used to store information for security or transaction processing. Transactions made with a smart card can update the card's memory and be stored for future processing. Smart cards are used with special card readers that can read and write to the card. Also known as a *chip card*. – CH4

smart card authentication: See *token*. – CH15

smart safe: An alternative to having armored cars collect deposits from a firm's retail outlets is a product referred to as a *smart safe* (also known as a *virtual vault*). The armored carrier, working in conjunction with the firm's depository bank, provides a special safe (i.e., smart safe) to the retail outlet that records deposits into the safe and reports them to the armored carrier and the bank. The bank provides provisional credit at the time of the deposit into the safe, and the armored carrier picks up the contents of the safe on a reduced schedule, perhaps weekly instead of daily. – CH12

Society for Worldwide Interbank Financial Telecommunication (SWIFT): A financial industry-owned, cooperative, interbank telecommunication network that enables banks and corporations to send authenticated electronic messages in standard formats. – CH4

sovereign bond: A bond issued by a national government and typically denominated in the currency of the issuing government. Also referred to as *sovereign debt*. – CH6

sovereign fund: A government-owned investment fund composed of a wide variety of financial assets, sometimes known as a *sovereign wealth fund (SWF)*. – CH2

sovereign risk: The risk that a central bank could alter its monetary policy significantly or impose foreign exchange (FX) regulations that would reduce or negate the value of FX contracts or currency trades. – CH7

special dividend: A dividend that is paid on a one-time basis, rather than as a regular quarterly dividend. – CH20

special drawing right (SDR): An artificial currency created by the International Monetary Fund whose asset value is based on a basket of currencies consisting of the euro, Japanese yen, British pound sterling, and US dollar. – CH6

specific-project guarantee: A type of loan guarantee in which the guarantee party guarantees only loans relating to specific projects of the subsidiary rather than all loans. – CH6

speculation: A practice that involves taking a position on the direction of the market in order to make a profit, which is not usually a treasury objective. In some organizations, however, speculation in certain markets may be a treasury objective, as determined by the board of directors. – CH17

Spot foreign exchange (FX) rate: A rate quoted for the delivery (or settlement) of currency one or two business days following the date of the trade. – CH17

spot market: The market for immediate trading of currency or commodities. – CH17

spread: The difference between the bid and ask price of a particular security or asset. – CH5

standard operating procedure (SOP): The normal or usual way of completing a specific task or duty. SOPs are often documented so that they can be performed on a routine basis and executed in a consistent manner. – CH18

standby letter of credit (L/C): A variation of a commercial L/C that is issued primarily by US banks. Once issued, a standby L/C serves as a vehicle to ensure the financial performance of a bank's customer to a third-party beneficiary. Standby L/Cs are the equivalent of guarantees issued by non-US banks. – CH2

standing wire: A type of wire transfer where a company establishes repetitive transfer instructions to move funds between two specified accounts automatically when previously determined criteria are met. – CH12

statement of beneficial interest: A document that specifies who has control over funds or accounts. This may be separate from who has signature authority or legal title. – CH7

statement of cash flows: A financial statement that provides a detailed picture of the sources of a company's cash flows and how these sources are used. Also known as a *cash flow statement*. – CH8

Statement on Standards for Attestation Engagements (SSAE) 16: An auditing standard for service organizations, superseding Statement on Auditing Standards No. 70, or SAS 70. – CH7

state-owned enterprise (SOE): A company that is created by a national government in order to participate in or help support various commercial activities on the government's behalf. These organizations are generally formed for a specific purpose and are designed to support a certain economic sector. SOEs are also known as *crown corporations* (in Canada and the United Kingdom, for example) or *government-sponsored enterprises*, or *GSEs* (in the United States). – CH6

static forecast: A type of forecast in which the period being forecasted, such as a calendar year, does not change as the forecast is updated. – CH14

stock dividend: A dividend that pays shareholders additional shares of stock rather than cash dividends. – CH20

stock repurchase: A practice where a company uses some of its profits to purchase existing shares of its stock, either on the open market or directly from shareholders. This usually tends to increase the price of the stock. – CH20

stock split: A process in which a company replaces one existing share of stock with multiple shares of new stock. It is often done when a company's stock price is determined to be too high. The basic idea is to get the price of the stock down to a better trading range. – CH20

stored-value card (SVC): A type of debit card that may be offered by financial institutions, retailers, and other service providers, and can be a branded, open-loop card (e.g., Visa or MasterCard), or a private-label, closed-loop card (e.g., Starbucks or other merchant gift card). Generally, an open-loop card can be used almost anywhere while a closed-loop card can only be used at one selected merchant or group of merchants. Gift cards are one of the most commonly used types of SVC. – CH4

stores and supplies: A category of inventories that are not used directly in a production process; rather, they support the production process. They are also known as *indirect purchases*. – CH10

straight-through processing (STP): An initiative used by companies in the financial industry to optimize the speed at which transactions are processed. STP refers to eliminating all manual intervention so that a particular process is totally electronic from beginning to end. – CH7

strategic risk: The risk of major investments for which there is a significant uncertainty about success or profitability. Examples in this area would include entering into new markets, trying to spot and take advantage of trends, and investing in new technology. – CH16

street name: The registered name for securities in a brokerage account in which the customer's securities and assets are held under the name of the brokerage firm, rather than in the name of the individual who purchased the securities or assets. – CH5

stress test: An analytical exercise that assumes an adverse change in one or more of the firm's funding sources, or a major shock to the company's core business due to a competitor's action, litigation crisis, product recall, production plant disaster, financial crisis, or other source of business trauma. The proposed change in funds availability may involve the loss of one or more of the firm's borrowing facilities, a sudden and large increase in borrowing costs, or both. Such changes may reduce the firm's credit rating, violate loan covenants, or cause a technical default on a credit facility. – CH2

sub-sovereign bond: A type of bond issued by a level of government below the national or central government, which includes regions, provinces, states, municipalities, etc. Sub-sovereign bonds are subject to a wide variety of national and regional provisions in their country of origin and may have tax implications. – CH6

sub-sovereign entity: A government entity that is smaller than and subordinate to a national government. Examples of sub-sovereign entities include states, provinces, counties, and territories. – CH6

supplier-managed replenishment program: An inventory management process whereby the supplier maintains and tracks the inventory of materials it provides to a customer. Title to the product is transferred at the shipping dock. – CH10

supplier risk: Risk related to an organization's suppliers and outsourcing arrangements. Supplier risk is a specific type of counterparty risk that also entails significant operational risks. The more critical the supplier or commodity is in the production process, the more risk an organization faces if the supplier either fails to deliver according to plan or provides substandard products and services that result in customer dissatisfaction. – CH16

supply chain management: The integration of business processes with the entire chain of trading partners, which can include suppliers, intermediaries, third-party service providers, and customers. – CH10

swap: An agreement between two parties to exchange (or swap) a set of cash flows at a future point in time. The most common type of swap is an interest rate swap. – CH17

sweep account: An account used by an organization that has its depository institution sweep any excess, end-of-day funds into an investment account. Though sweep accounts are not actually a separate category of short-term investment, they are used widely and are diverse, offering investment in repos or other money market instruments, managed accounts, and mutual funds. Some sweeps offer tax-exempt, offshore investments. – CH12

systemic risk: The risk of collapse of an entire financial system or entire market, as opposed to risk associated with any one individual organization, group, or component of a system. It is a risk imposed by linkages and interdependencies in a market or an economy that lead to a potential cascading failure that could bring down an entire banking system or market. – CH2

target capital structure: The specific capital structure that a company has set as its desired structure. This is typically the mix of debt and equity the company will use in raising new capital. – CH20

target cash balance: The ideal amount of cash that a company wishes to hold in reserve at any given point in time. This figure hopes to strike a balance between the investment opportunity costs of holding too much cash and the balance sheet costs of holding too little. – CH14

tax anticipation note (TAN): A short-term debt security issued in anticipation of future tax collections. TANs are generally issued by state and municipal governments to provide immediate funding for a capital expenditure, such as highway construction. – CH5

tax increment financing (TIF) bond: A type of bond used primarily for local financing in which a municipality may use all or a portion of new property taxes within a designated district to assist in the project's financing. – CH6

technology risk: The risk an organization faces as a result of its use of technology. As the treasury area of an organization relies increasingly on technology, the operational risk associated with the use of technology increases. Technology risk includes risks associated with (1) security breaches, (2) use of computer-based spreadsheets, and (3) the choice of a particular technology platform or vendor. – CH16

Telephone-Initiated Entry (TEL): A US automated clearinghouse (ACH) format used for payments that are not pre-authorized, but are approved by consumers over the phone. *TEL* is the standard entry class (SEC) code for this format. – CH12

tender option bond: A type of bond (also known as a *put bond*) that allows the holder to redeem the bond (i.e., sell it back to the issuer) either once during its life or on specified dates. Redemption is usually at par value. – CH6

term loan: A type of loan with a fixed maturity, usually greater than one year, which can be repaid either in installments or in a single payment. – CH6

term note: A medium-term debt instrument, typically with terms from two to ten years, issued by an organization. In most cases, these notes pay interest at periodic intervals. – CH6

terrorism risk: Risk related to terrorist attacks or other terrorist activities. Terrorism has become a significant threat to the operations of many organizations. Many disaster recovery plans specifically include recovery from terrorist events, in addition to natural disasters. Most organizations try to manage exposure to terrorist activities by increasing the level of security for both their premises and employees. – CH16

thinly capitalized: A description of a company that has a very small amount of capital or initial investment in relation to the amount of business the company conducts. The term is often used by taxing authorities in referring to subsidiary companies run by foreign corporations with minimal initial investment. Also known as *thin cap*. – CH20

time deposit account (TDA): A depository account that must be maintained at an FI for a contractually specified period of time. – CH3

time draft: A draft that is payable at some future date, provided all of the terms of the draft have been met. As with sight drafts, time drafts are often presented in combination with other documents, such as titles or bills of lading. If all the documentation is in order, then the draft is payable at the specified future date. – CH4

time series forecasting: A medium- or long-term statistical cash forecasting process where a serial chain of values (known as a *time series*) for some variable (e.g., sales) is identified. Every time series contains a trend, seasonal pattern, cyclical pattern, and random movement. A trend is the general direction that the values are moving. A seasonal pattern repeats with regard to time of year. A cyclical pattern repeats without regard to time of year. Random movement is a change in the series not identifiable as a trend, or a seasonal or cyclical influence. – CH14

time value of money: A fundamental finance principle that establishes the relationship between cash flows received at different times. For example, a dollar received today is worth more than a dollar received tomorrow because today's dollar can be invested to earn a return. Conversely, a dollar received tomorrow is worth less than a dollar received today because the opportunity to earn interest is lost. – CH9

times interest earned (TIE) ratio: A coverage ratio that measures a firm's ability to service its debt through interest payments. It is computed as operating income (i.e., earnings before interest and taxes, or EBIT) divided by interest expense. – CH9

token: A security device that the owner uses to authorize access to a network or online service. Tokens are electronic devices that contain circuitry that encodes assigned user-specific information or personal information to help ensure password protection. – CH15

total asset turnover ratio: An efficiency/asset management ratio that measures how many times a firm's asset base was used (i.e., turned over) in generating the flow of revenue during the period. It is computed as revenues divided by total assets. – CH9

total liabilities to total assets ratio: A type of debt management ratio that measures the percentage of all liabilities to total investments or total assets. It is computed as total liabilities divided by total assets. – CH9

tracking stock: A special type of stock that is a separate stock created by a parent company to track the financial progress of a particular piece of business. Despite being part of a publicly traded entity, tracking stocks trade under unique ticker symbols. These stocks are meant to create opportunities for investors to buy into a fast-growing unit without investing in the whole company. – CH6

trade acceptance: A financial instrument that is similar to a banker's acceptance (BA) except it is drawn on, and accepted by, a buyer (importer). – CH12

trade credit: A form of credit that arises when a buyer receives goods but payment is not made to the supplier until some later date. Trade credit is the primary source of short-term financing used by many businesses. – CH10

trading companies: A trade payment method whereby an exporter (seller) sells products at a discount to an export trading company, which then resells the products internationally. – CH12

transaction risk exposure: A type of exposure that arises when a company creates future receivables and/or payables that are denominated in a currency other than its home, or functional, currency. – CH17

Transaction Workflow Innovation Standards Team (TWIST) bank services billing (BSB) format: A format that was developed as a standard intended for use by banks and their wholesale transaction service users to facilitate a monthly electronic communication of banking fees to the banks' corporate customers and others incurring those fees. – CH7

Trans-European Automated Real-time Gross settlement Express Transfer 2 (TARGET2) system: A system that provides real-time settlement for cross-border electronic payments in euros. – CH4

transfer pricing: The setting of the price that subsidiaries of a large corporation charge one another for components sold among them. – CH20

transit check: A check deposited with a financial institution that is drawn on another financial institution. – CH4

translation risk exposure: A type of exposure that is created when a foreign subsidiary's financial statements are converted (translated) into a parent company's home currency as part of the process of consolidating a company's financial statements. The exposure occurs because the value of the foreign assets and liabilities may change from one accounting period to the next as the underlying foreign exchange rates change. – CH17

travel card: A credit card used by a business for employee travel purposes. Also known as a *travel and entertainment (T&E) card.* – CH4

traveler's check: A prepaid instrument, similar to a money order, where two signatures usually are required by the purchaser: one at issuance and one at the time the check is used to pay for goods or services. – CH4

Treasury bill (T-bill): A short-term debt obligation backed by the US government with a maturity of less than one year. T-bills are sold in denominations of $1,000 up to a maximum purchase of $5 million and commonly have maturities of 4, 13, 26, and 52 weeks. – CH5

Treasury bond (T-bond): A marketable, fixed-interest US government debt security with a maturity of more than 10 years. T-bonds make interest payments semiannually and the income that holders receive is only taxed at the federal level. – CH13

treasury management dashboard: A type of financial dashboard intended to provide management immediate feedback on the overall status of treasury operations, while also publishing key financial information useful in running the business. – CH15

treasury management system (TMS): A computer system, typically a stand-alone personal computer- (PC-), client/server-, or cloud-based system, which has software that gathers information from both internal and external sources for use by the treasury area of an organization. – CH15

Treasury note (T-note): A marketable US government debt security with a fixed interest rate and a maturity between one and ten years. T-notes can be bought either directly from the US government or through a bank. – CH17

treasury policies and procedures: Policies (i.e., statements to guide activities in a particular area or function of an organization) and procedures (i.e., specified series of actions or operations) that provide a framework for the design of treasury workflow processes, systems, and controls that support a company's objectives. – CH18

treasury stock: Stock issued by a company and later reacquired. It may be held in the company's treasury indefinitely, reissued to the public, or retired. Treasury stock receives no dividends and does not carry voting power while held by the company. It is considered issued, but not outstanding; therefore, it is deducted from any capital calculations. – CH6

Treasury/Reserve Automated Debt Entry System (TRADES): An entity of the US Federal Reserve that provides for the processing and clearing of most money market investments in the United States. Also known as the Commercial Book-Entry System (CBES). – CH5

triple-net lease: A lease agreement in which the lessee pays all expenses of the underlying property, in addition to any rent payments to the property owner (lessor). These expenses usually include taxes, insurance, and maintenance costs, hence the term *triple*. – CH20

Truth in Lending Act of 1968 (TILA): A US legislative act that requires lenders to disclose the effective annual interest rate, termed the *annual percentage rate*, and the total dollar cost on loans. – CH2

turnover tax: A type of tax that is essentially a sales tax on goods and services. – CH2

tying: The act of requiring a purchaser to buy one product or service in order to be allowed to buy a second, typically unrelated, product or service. – CH2

unanimous consent procedure: A type of procedure for formulating a reorganization plan in a US Chapter 11 bankruptcy filing. Under this procedure, all classes of creditors and equity holders must consent to the reorganization plan, with a two-thirds vote of all members in each class required for consent. – CH2

underwriting: An investment bank function, this is the act of purchasing all or a part of a block of securities issued by a company and thereby becoming responsible for their ultimate distribution. The underwriter normally assumes all the risk or liability for the sale of the securities. – CH3

Uniform Bank Performance Report (UBPR): An analytical tool, published by the Federal Financial Institutions Examination Council (FFIEC), created for bank supervisory, examination, and management purposes. In a concise format, it shows the impact of management decisions and economic conditions on a bank's performance and balance sheet composition. The performance and composition data contained in the report can be used to help evaluate the adequacy of earnings, liquidity, capital, asset and liability management, and growth management. – CH7

Uniform Commercial Code (UCC): A uniform set of laws governing commercial transactions in the United States. It defines the rights and duties of all parties in a commercial transaction and provides a statutory definition of commonly accepted business practices. This code provides guidelines for paper-based contracts, business transactions, and payment instruments. – CH2

Uniform Customs and Practice for Documentary Credits (UCP) 600: A set of rules established by the International Chamber of Commerce (ICC) which govern the operation of commercial letters of credit, and are known as *UCP*. The current rules are outlined under UCP 600, and these rules affect almost every credit issued under the ICC's UCP. – CH12

United Nations/Electronic Data Interchange for Administration, Commerce and Transport (UN/EDIFACT) standards: A set of internationally agreed-upon standards, directories, and guidelines for electronic commerce. – CH15

use tax: A type of tax that is imposed directly on the consumer of goods that were purchased without paying sales tax (generally items purchased from a vendor in another state or over the Internet and delivered to the purchaser by mail or common carrier). – CH2

value-added tax (VAT): A type of sales tax that involves charging a separate tax at each discrete stage of production and/or distribution based on the increased value (i.e., value added) occurring at that stage. – CH2

value at risk (VaR): A risk management measurement that is used to determine how changing financial variables will affect a company's value. It is designed specifically to incorporate a wide range of risk factors and summarize their impact in a single measure. The VaR approach uses the probability and monetary impacts of specified adverse events over a period of time to assess risk. – CH16

value-dated automated clearinghouse (ACH) transactions: ACH transactions where the payment instructions include settlement dates. – CH4

value dating: A process whereby a bank sets a forward value date on which the value of funds credited to an account is determined and establishes a back value date on which the value of funds debited from or credited to an account is determined. – CH7

variable costs: Costs in a business whose total amount changes in direct proportion to the level of business activity. In cost accounting, variable costs are contrasted with fixed costs, which do not change based on volume or activity levels. – CH9

variable-rate demand obligation (VRDO): A type of security issued as a long-term bond that carries a short-term liquidity feature, or put. Generally, this put option, which is an investor's option to sell (or put) the instrument back to the issuer at par, allows for liquidation either weekly or monthly and is typically supported by a credit facility, such as a bank letter of credit. While interest from VRDOs is often tax-exempt, VRDOs exist as both taxable and nontaxable instruments. – CH5

virtual currencies: A type of unregulated, digital money that is issued and usually controlled by its developers, and is used and accepted among the members of a specific virtual community. Bitcoin is an example of this emerging type of payment. – CH4

virtual vault services: In an over-the-counter field deposit system, this type of vault service may be offered by banks or through third-party, nonbank companies, such as armored car services. The basic approach is to utilize armored car and courier services to replace or enhance physical bank branch locations. In addition, many of these services offer immediate availability of any funds processed through their vaults. These services typically include a smart safe that verifies deposits to the safe. – CH12

warranties: Along with representations, these are the existing conditions at the time when a loan agreement is executed, as attested to by the borrower. – CH6

weighted average cost of capital (WACC): Used in determining the overall cost of capital, this cost is computed as a weighted average of the effective cost of debt and the cost of equity. – CH9

wholesale lockbox: A lockbox system that is used primarily to process low-volume, large-dollar business-to-business payments that, unlike consumer payments, must often be matched to specific invoices (i.e., several invoices are paid with one check). – CH12

withholding tax: A type of tax that may be charged on funds being moved from one country to another. Companies may be required to pay such taxes when moving funds outside a foreign country. The amount can vary from 1% to almost 35% of the repatriated flow. – CH2

without recourse (no recourse): A term related to using a factoring arrangement. In this case, the factor must absorb the loss if a customer fails to pay. – CH10

work in progress (WIP): A type of inventory that represents items or materials that are in the process of being manufactured. – CH10

workflow management system: Technology that enables a company to use software to implement, monitor, and enforce the specific processes and procedures (i.e., the workflow) that it wants used throughout the company. – CH15

working capital: The sum of a company's current asset accounts (primarily cash, accounts receivable, and inventory) less the sum of its current liability accounts (primarily payables and accrual accounts). Also known as *net working capital*. – CH1

working capital gap: The time gap between a cash outflow and a cash inflow. – CH1

Yankee CD: A certificate of deposit that is denominated in US dollars and issued in the United States by a branch of a non-US bank. – CH5

year basis: The number of days in a year, when calculating the yield on an investment. Money market yield is traditionally based on a 360-day year, while bond equivalent yield is based on a 365-day year. – CH13

yield: The income return on an investment. This refers to the interest or dividends received from a security and is usually expressed annually as a percentage based on the investment's cost, its current market value, or its face value. – CH5

yield curve: A plot of the yields to maturity on the same investment instrument or class of instruments, but with varying maturities, as of a specific date. For example, a yield curve for US Treasury instruments is a plot of yields to maturity for US Treasury bond issues with varying periods to maturity as of the close of business on a particular date. – CH13

yield to call (YTC): The yield a bond would provide if the issuer calls it prior to maturity. Since callable bonds usually are called only if interest rates have fallen, the YTC is typically lower than the yield to maturity. If all possible YTC values have been determined for a certain bond, the lowest value is considered the *yield to worst (YTW)*. – CH19

yield to maturity (YTM): The rate of return anticipated on a bond if it is held until the maturity date. YTM is considered a long-term bond yield expressed as an annual rate. The calculation of YTM takes into account the current market price, par value, coupon interest rate, and time to maturity. It is also assumed that all coupons are reinvested at the same rate. Sometimes, this is simply referred to as *yield*. – CH19

zero balance account (ZBA): A type of bank account (typically used for disbursements via check or electronic funds transfer) where the end-of-day balance in the account is maintained at zero. Transfers are made from a master account to fund this account, typically at the end of the day. A ZBA can also be set up as a depository account from which funds are debited and transferred to a master account at the end of each day. – CH12

zero-coupon bond: A debt security that does not pay interest (a coupon) but is traded at a deep discount, rendering a profit at maturity when the bond is redeemed for its full face value. – CH6

INDEX

NOTE: Appendix is indicated by *A* following the page number. Footnotes are indicated by *n* and the note number (e.g., 234*n*12).

NOTE: Appendix is indicated by *A* following the page number. Footnotes are indicated by *n* and the note number (e.g., 234*n*12).

NOTE: Appendix is indicated by *A* following the page number. Footnotes are indicated by *n* and the note number (e.g., 234*n*12).

NOTE: Appendix is indicated by *A* following the page number. Footnotes are indicated by *n* and the note number (e.g., 234*n*12).

NOTE: Appendix is indicated by *A* following the page number. Footnotes are indicated by *n* and the note number (e.g., 234*n*12).

NOTE: Appendix is indicated by *A* following the page number. Footnotes are indicated by *n* and the note number (e.g., 234*n*12).

NOTE: Appendix is indicated by *A* following the page number. Footnotes are indicated by *n* and the note number (e.g., 234*n*12).

NOTE: Appendix is indicated by *A* following the page number. Footnotes are indicated by *n* and the note number (e.g., 234*n*12).

NOTE: Appendix is indicated by *A* following the page number. Footnotes are indicated by *n* and the note number (e.g., 234*n*12).

NOTE: Appendix is indicated by *A* following the page number. Footnotes are indicated by *n* and the note number (e.g., 234*n*12).

NOTE: Appendix is indicated by *A* following the page number. Footnotes are indicated by *n* and the note number (e.g., 234*n*12).

NOTE: Appendix is indicated by *A* following the page number. Footnotes are indicated by *n* and the note number (e.g., 234*n*12).

NOTE: Appendix is indicated by *A* following the page number. Footnotes are indicated by *n* and the note number (e.g., 234*n*12).

NOTE: Appendix is indicated by *A* following the page number. Footnotes are indicated by *n* and the note number (e.g., 234*n*12).

NOTE: Appendix is indicated by *A* following the page number. Footnotes are indicated by *n* and the note number (e.g., 234*n*12).

NOTE: Appendix is indicated by *A* following the page number. Footnotes are indicated by *n* and the note number (e.g., 234*n*12).

NOTE: Appendix is indicated by *A* following the page number. Footnotes are indicated by *n* and the note number (e.g., 234n12).

NOTE: Appendix is indicated by *A* following the page number. Footnotes are indicated by *n* and the note number (e.g., 234n12).

NOTE: Appendix is indicated by *A* following the page number. Footnotes are indicated by *n* and the note number (e.g., 234*n*12).

NOTE: Appendix is indicated by *A* following the page number. Footnotes are indicated by *n* and the note number (e.g., 234*n*12).

NOTE: Appendix is indicated by *A* following the page number. Footnotes are indicated by *n* and the note number (e.g., 234*n*12).

cyberrisk, 434, 435

D

daily cash position, 372, 373

dashboards (information technology), 396–397

data breach/compromise, 434, 435

data identification and organization, 374

daylight overdrafts, 83, 350, 350n16

days' inventory, 253, 287–288

days' payables, 253, 288

days' receivables, 253, 288

days' sales outstanding, 293

DBRS (Dominion Bond Rating Service), 110

debentures (unsecured bonds), 131

debit cards (EFTPOS), 94, 95–96

debt

    capacity, 535

    defeasance of, 137

    priority of claims, 130, 144n5

debt financing, 129–140, 356–363. *See also* capital structure

    base rates, 360

    bond ratings, 139

    collateral and, 138

    contract provisions, 135–138

    costs of, 358, 533, 539–540

    credit enhancements, 138

    credit ratings, 139

    debt capital, 134–135, 533–545

    debt contract provisions, 135–138

    efficiency of debt markets, 533, 533n2

    equity financing. *See* equity financing and management

    guarantees, 138–139

    interest rate components, 357–358

    interest rate levels and forecasts, 139

    international bond market, 131

NOTE: Appendix is indicated by *A* following the page number. Footnotes are indicated by *n* and the note number (e.g., 234n12).

NOTE: Appendix is indicated by *A* following the page number. Footnotes are indicated by *n* and the note number (e.g., 234*n*12).

NOTE: Appendix is indicated by *A* following the page number. Footnotes are indicated by *n* and the note number (e.g., 234*n*12).

NOTE: Appendix is indicated by *A* following the page number. Footnotes are indicated by *n* and the note number (e.g., 234*n*12).

NOTE: Appendix is indicated by *A* following the page number. Footnotes are indicated by *n* and the note number (e.g., 234*n*12).

NOTE: Appendix is indicated by *A* following the page number. Footnotes are indicated by *n* and the note number (e.g., 234*n*12).

NOTE: Appendix is indicated by *A* following the page number. Footnotes are indicated by *n* and the note number (e.g., 234*n*12).

NOTE: Appendix is indicated by *A* following the page number. Footnotes are indicated by *n* and the note number (e.g., 234*n*12).

NOTE: Appendix is indicated by *A* following the page number. Footnotes are indicated by *n* and the note number (e.g., 234*n*12).

NOTE: Appendix is indicated by *A* following the page number. Footnotes are indicated by *n* and the note number (e.g., 234*n*12).

NOTE: Appendix is indicated by *A* following the page number. Footnotes are indicated by *n* and the note number (e.g., 234*n*12).

NOTE: Appendix is indicated by *A* following the page number. Footnotes are indicated by *n* and the note number (e.g., 234*n*12).

NOTE: Appendix is indicated by *A* following the page number. Footnotes are indicated by *n* and the note number (e.g., 234*n*12).

NOTE: Appendix is indicated by *A* following the page number. Footnotes are indicated by *n* and the note number (e.g., 234*n*12).

NOTE: Appendix is indicated by *A* following the page number. Footnotes are indicated by *n* and the note number (e.g., 234*n*12).

NOTE: Appendix is indicated by *A* following the page number. Footnotes are indicated by *n* and the note number (e.g., 234*n*12).

NOTE: Appendix is indicated by *A* following the page number. Footnotes are indicated by *n* and the note number (e.g., 234*n*12).

NOTE: Appendix is indicated by *A* following the page number. Footnotes are indicated by *n* and the note number (e.g., 234*n*12).

NOTE: Appendix is indicated by *A* following the page number. Footnotes are indicated by *n* and the note number (e.g., 234*n*12).

NOTE: Appendix is indicated by *A* following the page number. Footnotes are indicated by *n* and the note number (e.g., 234*n*12).

NOTE: Appendix is indicated by *A* following the page number. Footnotes are indicated by *n* and the note number (e.g., 234*n*12).

NOTE: Appendix is indicated by *A* following the page number. Footnotes are indicated by *n* and the note number (e.g., 234*n*12).

NOTE: Appendix is indicated by *A* following the page number. Footnotes are indicated by *n* and the note number (e.g., 234*n*12).

NOTE: Appendix is indicated by *A* following the page number. Footnotes are indicated by *n* and the note number (e.g., 234*n*12).

NOTE: Appendix is indicated by *A* following the page number. Footnotes are indicated by *n* and the note number (e.g., 234*n*12).

NOTE: Appendix is indicated by *A* following the page number. Footnotes are indicated by *n* and the note number (e.g., 234*n*12).

NOTE: Appendix is indicated by *A* following the page number. Footnotes are indicated by *n* and the note number (e.g., 234*n*12).

NOTE: Appendix is indicated by *A* following the page number. Footnotes are indicated by *n* and the note number (e.g., 234*n*12).

NOTE: Appendix is indicated by *A* following the page number. Footnotes are indicated by *n* and the note number (e.g., 234*n*12).

©2016 ASSOCIATION FOR FINANCIAL PROFESSIONALS. ALL RIGHTS RESERVED.

689

NOTE: Appendix is indicated by *A* following the page number. Footnotes are indicated by *n* and the note number (e.g., 234*n*12).

NOTE: Appendix is indicated by *A* following the page number. Footnotes are indicated by *n* and the note number (e.g., 234*n*12).

NOTE: Appendix is indicated by *A* following the page number. Footnotes are indicated by *n* and the note number (e.g., 234*n*12).

NOTE: Appendix is indicated by *A* following the page number. Footnotes are indicated by *n* and the note number (e.g., 234*n*12).

NOTE: Appendix is indicated by *A* following the page number. Footnotes are indicated by *n* and the note number (e.g., 234*n*12).

NOTE: Appendix is indicated by *A* following the page number. Footnotes are indicated by *n* and the note number (e.g., 234*n*12).

over-the-counter/field deposit systems, 325

over-the-counter (OTC) market

    European regulation of, 35

    organized security exchanges vs., 550

    US regulation of, 38, 42

overdrafts

    accounting for, 63, 84

    daylight, 83, 350, 350*n*16

    handling of, US vs. foreign accounts, 63

    intraday cash forecasts reducing, 371

P

paid-on-production process, 272

par value

    balance sheet exhibits, 190, 235

    common stock, 140

    discount rate in short-term investments, 345

    FX quotes, 467

    at maturity, 114, 516

    preferred stock, 54, 142, 517–518

payable through draft (PTD), 84

payback period, 214

paying bank, 80

Payment Card Industry Data Security Standard (PCI DSS), 96, 311

Payment Card Industry Security Standards Council, 96

payment date (dividends), 555

payment discrepancies, 264

payment factories, 305

payment float, 251

payment systems, 73–103. *See also* card-based payment systems; check-based payment systems

    about, 73–77

    automated clearinghouse (ACH), 75, 88–90

    basic payments and participants, 73–74

    cash payments, 76, 77

    China, 103

NOTE: Appendix is indicated by *A* following the page number. Footnotes are indicated by *n* and the note number (e.g., 234*n*12).

NOTE: Appendix is indicated by *A* following the page number. Footnotes are indicated by *n* and the note number (e.g., 234*n*12).

NOTE: Appendix is indicated by *A* following the page number. Footnotes are indicated by *n* and the note number (e.g., 234*n*12).

NOTE: Appendix is indicated by *A* following the page number. Footnotes are indicated by *n* and the note number (e.g., 234*n*12).

NOTE: Appendix is indicated by *A* following the page number. Footnotes are indicated by *n* and the note number (e.g., 234*n*12).

NOTE: Appendix is indicated by *A* following the page number. Footnotes are indicated by *n* and the note number (e.g., 234*n*12).

NOTE: Appendix is indicated by *A* following the page number. Footnotes are indicated by *n* and the note number (e.g., 234*n*12).

NOTE: Appendix is indicated by *A* following the page number. Footnotes are indicated by *n* and the note number (e.g., 234*n*12).

NOTE: Appendix is indicated by *A* following the page number. Footnotes are indicated by *n* and the note number (e.g., 234*n*12).

NOTE: Appendix is indicated by *A* following the page number. Footnotes are indicated by *n* and the note number (e.g., 234*n*12).

NOTE: Appendix is indicated by *A* following the page number. Footnotes are indicated by *n* and the note number (e.g., 234*n*12).

top 10 worldwide, 145*A*

stocks. *See also* equity securities; preferred stock

    beta of, 525–528

    classes of, 551

    as dividends, 556

    private equity, 537–538

    purchase warrants, 143–144

    repurchases, 115, 351

    splits, 556

stored-value debit cards (SVCs), 95–96

straight-through processing, 405

strategic objectives

    cash forecasting and, 370

    corporate governance, 19

    enterprise risk management and, 425

strategic planning, budgets and, 219

strategic risk, 430

strike price (options), 460

sub-sovereign bonds, 132

sub-sovereign entities, 126

supplier risk, 433

supply chain management

    inventory financing, 272

    payment float, 251, 251*n*2

    as short-term finance alternative, 347–348

swaps (derivatives), 459–460

    credit default swaps, 524, 524*n*8

    currency swaps, 473–474

    interest rate swaps, 478–479

sweeping. *See* cash concentration and pooling systems

SWIFT (Society for Worldwide Interbank Financial Telecommunication), 64, 87, 315, 407

T

T-bills (Treasury bills). *See* Treasury securities

NOTE: Appendix is indicated by *A* following the page number. Footnotes are indicated by *n* and the note number (e.g., 234*n*12).

NOTE: Appendix is indicated by *A* following the page number. Footnotes are indicated by *n* and the note number (e.g., 234*n*12).

NOTE: Appendix is indicated by *A* following the page number. Footnotes are indicated by *n* and the note number (e.g., 234*n*12).

NOTE: Appendix is indicated by *A* following the page number. Footnotes are indicated by *n* and the note number (e.g., 234*n*12).

NOTE: Appendix is indicated by *A* following the page number. Footnotes are indicated by *n* and the note number (e.g., 234*n*12).

NOTE: Appendix is indicated by *A* following the page number. Footnotes are indicated by *n* and the note number (e.g., 234*n*12).

NOTE: Appendix is indicated by *A* following the page number. Footnotes are indicated by *n* and the note number (e.g., 234*n*12).

NOTE: Appendix is indicated by *A* following the page number. Footnotes are indicated by *n* and the note number (e.g., 234*n*12).

NOTE: Appendix is indicated by *A* following the page number. Footnotes are indicated by *n* and the note number (e.g., 234*n*12).

NOTE: Appendix is indicated by *A* following the page number. Footnotes are indicated by *n* and the note number (e.g., 234*n*12).